Joe Pinto
May 19-1937.

Volume I

STORIES *of the* GREAT

OPERAS

~~~~~

RICHARD WAGNER

STORIES
OF THE
GREAT OPERAS
And Their Composers

BY ERNEST NEWMAN

GARDEN CITY PUBLISHING CO., INC.
Garden City, New York

CONTENTS
Volume I

INTRODUCTORY NOTE · vii

~~~~~

TANNHÄUSER · 3

THE MASTERSINGERS OF NUREMBERG · 41

LOHENGRIN · 63

TRISTAN AND ISOLDE · 96

PARSIFAL · 124

THE RHINEGOLD · 158

THE VALKYRIE · 187

SIEGFRIED · 222

THE TWILIGHT OF THE GODS · 253

THE FLYING DUTCHMAN · 286

~~~~~

RICHARD WAGNER — A SHORT BIOGRAPHY · 319

CONTENTS
Volume II

By *WOLFGANG AMADEUS MOZART* (1756–1791) · 3
THE MARRIAGE OF FIGARO
DON GIOVANNI
THE MAGIC FLUTE

By *LUDWIG VON BEETHOVEN* (1770–1827) · 122
FIDELIO

By *GIOACCHINO ROSSINI* (1792–1868) · 200
THE BARBER OF SEVILLE
WILLIAM TELL

By *CARL MARIA VON WEBER* (1786–1826) · 260
DER FREISCHÜTZ

By *AMBROISE THOMAS* (1811–1896) · 306
MIGNON

CONTENTS
Volume III

GIUSEPPE VERDI (1813–1901) · 3

RIGOLETTO

LA TRAVIATA

IL TROVATORE

AIDA

OTELLO

CHARLES FRANÇOIS GOUNOD (1818–1893) · 158

FAUST

GEORGES BIZET (1838–1875) · 196

CARMEN

JACQUES OFFENBACH (1819–1880) · 236

THE TALES OF HOFFMANN

ENGELBERT HUMPERDINCK (1854–1921) · 258

HÄNSEL AND GRETEL

GIACOMO PUCCINI (1858–1924) · 291

LA BOHÈME

TOSCA

MADAM BUTTERFLY

INTRODUCTORY NOTE

THIS work has a double object. Every great opera has a two-fold character; the two component parts are supreme music and supreme romance. The aim of this work, therefore, is to tell the story of the *Mastersingers, Tannhäuser, Lohengrin,* and so on, accompanied by a descriptive analysis of the music. The two things, the narrative of the story, or legend, and a full descriptive analysis of the music of the opera (accompanied by illustrative musical quotations) go hand in hand, linked together in each chapter.

The point of view assumed is that of the ordinary music lover who, though an ardent follower of opera, has neither time, nor opportunity, nor aptitude, to study scores and musical history and biography for himself. The main object has been to give such a person all the information he requires for a thorough understanding of what is going on in front of him on the stage, and, further, to help him to grasp many an intention on the composer's part that, for one reason or another, may not always come out clearly in the performance.

TANNHÄUSER

A S was the case with all his later operas, Wagner derived the
material for the drama of *Tannhäuser* from a variety of
sources. During his stay as a young man in Paris (from September
1839 to April 1842) he had become acquainted with a poem on the
subject by Tieck, and also with a story by E. T. A. Hoffmann that
describes a contest of song on the Wartburg. Tieck's treatment of
the subject he found rather too sugary and prettified.

In a quasi-biography entitled *A Communication to my Friends,*
which he published in December 1851, Wagner tells us that during these Paris days " the German Folk-book of Tannhäuser " fell
into his hands. What this " Folk-book " may have been it is now
impossible to say, as the scholars have not been able to trace any
volume corresponding to that description. All we can be sure of is
that from some source or other Wagner obtained more first-hand
information about the figures of the Tannhäuser story than he had
been able to do from either Tieck or Hoffmann. He now probably
had an intuition that an excellent subject for an opera lay awaiting
him in these legends, so he began to study the Middle-High German poem of the *Sängerkrieg* (the Contest of Song).[1] In this
poem, by the way, he also found the nucleus of his future libretto
of *Lohengrin.*

With his mind already working at white heat upon the Tannhäuser subject he left Paris for Dresden, and, as luck would have it,
passed through the Thuringian valley above which the famous hill

---

[1] " Middle-High German " is a term denoting a particular epoch of German literature, the centre-point of which was the thirteenth century.

of the Wartburg rises. To one of the ridges in the hill his fancy at once gave the name of Hörselberg, the legendary scene of the association between Tannhäuser and Venus. In his autobiography he tells us that as he drove through the valley he saw in imagination the setting for the third act of his opera; and his memory retained all the external details so vividly that long afterwards he could give the Parisian artist who was painting the scenery for the first production the most exact indications.

He took this chance meeting with the Wartburg as a good omen for his as yet unwritten opera. On this occasion he did not actually ascend the hill. This he did for the first time seven years later, when he was fleeing from Germany owing to his complicity in the Dresden rising of 1849. Finding himself at Weimar for a few days in his course from Dresden to Switzerland, he took advantage of his momentary freedom from arrest to make an excursion to Eisenach, and to ascend the battlements of the Wartburg. In 1861, on a journey from Paris to Weimar, he once more crossed Thuringia and passed the Wartburg, which, as he says, "whether I visited it or merely saw it in the distance, seemed so peculiarly connected with my departures from Germany or my return to it."

Fact and fiction are almost inextricably blended in the story of Tannhäuser as we now have it. We know that early in the thirteenth century the Landgrave Hermann of Thuringia organised what are sometimes called "contests of song" on the Wartburg. It is practically certain, however, that in these contests music played no part; they were competitions not of musicians but of poets.

There has come down to us a quaint old picture of one of these contests, from a German manuscript of the fourteenth century; the contestants have no musical instruments, nor is there even any suggestion of their being engaged in singing. Two figures in the upper part of the picture represent the Landgrave Hermann and his wife; the seven figures in the lower half are celebrated poets of the time, whose names are written above them; we can distinguish those of Walther von der Vogelweide, Wolfram von Eschenbach, Klingsor (Wagner afterwards made out of this personage the

magician in *Parsifal*), and Heinrich von Ofterdingen. Wagner
compounded his figure of Tannhäuser out of the last-named singer
and another, largely mythical, who bore the actual name of Tannhäuser, and was the hero of legends similar to that set forth for us
in the opera.

The historical Tannhäuser seems to have been, judging from his
poems, fond of the good things of this life, especially wine, good
cheer, and love. Apparently his sensuousness did not wholly commend itself to his contemporaries, and the legend grew that for
having spent a year with Venus the Pope condemned him for his
sin to hell fire, from which sentence, however, he did not, as in
Wagner's opera, achieve redemption through repentance and
Elisabeth.

Wagner finished his libretto in May 1843 at Dresden. The music
of the first act was written between July 1843 and January 1844,
the second act in the summer and autumn of the latter year, and
the third act before the end of 1844. The instrumentation was
finished by April 1845. The original title of the opera was *Der
Venusberg* (*The Hill of Venus*). He was induced to discard this
title by the publisher of the score, Meser, of Dresden, who, Wagner
tells us in his autobiography, " maintained that, as I did not mix
with the public, I had no idea what horrible jokes were made about
this title; these jokes, he thought, must come from the professors
and students of the Medical School in Dresden, as they had a special talent for that kind of obscene joke. The mere suggestion of
such objectionable trivialities was enough to induce me to consent
to the change." The title under which the opera was published,
and by which it was henceforth to be known, was *Tannhäuser and
the Contest of Song on the Wartburg.*

In the summer of 1844 the King of Saxony returned to his own
territory after a visit to England, and Wagner, who was then one
of the conductors of the Dresden Opera, seized the opportunity
to pay his homage to him at his country seat at Pillnitz. Wagner
took with him the Opera-house orchestra and the members of the
Dresden Glee Club, of which latter he was the conductor. Exhila-
rated by the occasion and by a pleasant drive through the country

in delightful summer weather, there occurred to him a vigorous theme that first made its entry into the world in connection with this act of homage to the King of Saxony, but which Wagner afterwards developed into the highly popular march in the second act of *Tannhäuser*.

Wagner having become a person of considerable importance in Dresden by this time, the new opera was soon put into rehearsal. So confident in advance were the theatre authorities of the success of the work that they went to the unusual expense of having the scenery painted by the artists of the Paris Opera, which was at that time the leading opera-house of the world. New and beautiful costumes were also ordered.

The only point upon which Wagner came into collision with the Intendant of the Dresden Opera, Lüttichau, was in connection with the scenery for the Hall of Song. Lüttichau, no doubt thinking that the new opera was already costing quite enough, wanted to use the setting for the grand hall of the Emperor Charlemagne that had been recently ordered for a production of Wagner's *Oberon,* and Wagner found it almost impossible to convince him that this would not be the right thing at all for *Tannhäuser*.

Finally, in face of Wagner's strongly expressed irritation, Lüttichau gave way and commissioned a proper setting from Paris. This did not arrive in time for the first production, and Wagner perforce had to use the *Oberon* scene after all. The dissappointment of the audience when the curtain rose upon this familiar setting was one of the causes of the lukewarm reception of the opera at its first performance.

We are so familiar with *Tannhäuser* to-day, and even inclined to regard it, in comparison with Wagner's later operas, as a little old-fashioned, that it is somewhat difficult to realise that in its own day it was an effort on the composer's part to do several things that had hardly been attempted in opera before. In the first place, the dramatic motive was every whit as important in his eyes as the music; in the second place, the old distinction between song and recitative had been completely swept away. Both these innovations caused him infinite trouble with his artists. It was with the utmost difficulty that he could get them to refrain from delivering the more declamatory portions of the music in the dry and somewhat unrhythmic way in which they were accustomed to deliver the ordinary recitative. It was in vain that he insisted that in *Tannhäuser* song was declamation and declamation was song; it was not, indeed, until many years later, and after a good deal of exhausting exposition on his part, both in the theatre and in the Press, that he managed to bring the ordinary opera-singer round to his point of view.

In the matter of the dramatic conception of the various parts he had even more trouble, especially with the tenor, Tichatschek. This gentleman was a typical operatic " star " tenor. He was an excellent fellow, if not particularly intelligent, had a fine presence and a big and brilliant voice, and was the idol of the Dresden public. He had already made a great success in *Rienzi*. But first and foremost he was a singer, in a much less degree an actor, and very little at all of a thinker; his main idea was to have brilliant arias to sing and to sing them brilliantly, and to prance about in magnificent costumes.

Tichatschek had the greatest admiration for the young Wagner, and would willingly have done anything for him that was in his power; the sole trouble was that he had not brains enough to understand Wagner's new dramatic ideals. For one thing, his voice, while of an extraordinarily stirring quality in brilliant and joyous music, had little capacity for expressing suffering or the darker emotions generally. He made a tremendous effect in the closing moments of the first act of *Tannhäuser,* and the audience was so enthusiastic that the success of the opera appeared assured. In the second act, however — the act that is crucial for the drama — he failed Wagner completely.

From the dramatic point of view, the culminating point of the second act is Tannhäuser's phrase in the great finale, " To lead the sinner to salvation, the heaven-sent messenger drew near." Wagner tells us that Tichatschek had not intelligence enough to perceive the importance of this phrase and to impress the meaning of

it upon the audience. The first result of his deficiency of understanding was that the second act fell flat. The second and even
more serious result was that Wagner felt compelled, in view of
Tichatschek's fiasco, to omit this passage from the second performance; and as his motives in doing so were not generally understood,
it was taken for granted that this was just an ordinary " cut," and
it became the practice everywhere to omit the passage from future
performances.

How little Tichatschek understood of the dramatic significance
of his part may be estimated from the fact that in the Contest
scene in the Hall of Song, when, forgetting his present highly respectable surroundings, his mind reverts to the Hörselberg and he
bursts out with a passionate invocation to Venus and sensual love,
he actually moved towards Elisabeth and poured his unholy raptures into *her* chaste ears! The good fellow's mental processes were
very simple. Was he not the leading tenor, and was not Elisabeth
the leading lady? To whom, then, if not to the leading lady, should
the tenor address himself in his big moment?

The Venus was Wilhelmine Schroeder-Devrient, the greatest
German dramatic singer of her epoch, but at this period rather
past her best, both vocally and physically. She had been quick to
distinguish the exceptional genius of Wagner some years before,
and had willingly done all she could to help him forward. She was
conscious that Venus was hardly a part for her, and she seems to
have undertaken it, in some measure, only for a sense of its importance to the dramatic scheme and a consequent desire to help
Wagner all she could at a critical point in his career.

Wagner himself was conscious that the part of Venus had not
been developed in the opera at sufficient length, a defect which he
rectified in the 1861 production of *Tannhäuser* in Paris. The part
could only have been made thoroughly effective in the first days
by a singer who was wholly absorbed in it, and this, for various reasons, chiefly connected with her physical appearance, Schroeder-
Devrient found it impossible to be. " The only thing," says Wagner in his autobiography, " that might have helped to achieve the
effect I had desired in the part of Venus would have been the ac-

tress's confidence in her own youthful beauty, and in the purely sensuous appreciation of beauty of this kind by the audience. The conviction that these means of effect were no longer at her disposal paralysed this great artist, who was already becoming matronly in form. She necessarily felt somewhat embarrassed, and so was unable to employ her usual means for making her effects. On one occasion, with a despairing smile, she declared herself incapable of playing Venus, for the very simple reason that she could not wear a costume appropriate to that goddess. ' What in heaven's name am I to wear as Venus? ' she said. ' After all, I cannot go on in just a girdle! I should look like something at a fancy ball! ' " Her fears and Wagner's proved only too well founded; the inability of Schroeder-Devrient to carry through the part of Venus had a good deal to do with the comparative coolness of the audience at the first performance.

The Elisabeth was Wagner's niece Johanna Wagner, who was physically well adapted for the part, with her youthful appearance and her tall and slender figure; she also, at that time, had an exceedingly good voice. She had been well coached by the composer, and succeeded so well in the part that it may be said to have laid the foundation of her future great reputation. Even with her, however, he had something of the same difficulty as with Tichatschek. She could not render the prayer in the third act as he wished it to be done, with the result that in future performances he had to make a considerable cut in it.

The Wolfram was Mitterwurzer, an intelligent young baritone with a good voice. He was thoroughly willing to carry out Wagner's intentions, and the composer was surprised to find that even a man of his gifts had some difficulty in grasping the true nature of his part. At the rehearsals he sang Wolfram's song in the Contest scene so dryly and mechanically that it was evident to Wagner that he regarded it merely as a piece of the old conventional recitative. When Wagner pointed out his error to him, Mitterwurzer begged to be allowed to work the thing out quietly in his own way; and this he did with such success that it was through his impersonation of Wolfram that the Dresden public gradually came to understand the dramatic significance of the new work, so far as they could understand it at all.

The first performance, on the 19th October, 1845 (under Wagner himself, of course), was only moderately successful, and Wagner was greatly depressed after it. He was ready enough to perceive that most of his singers were, in this degree or that, answerable for the comparative failure, but he was less willing to acknowledge that his own incurable long-windedness may also have had something to do with it. He saw, however, the necessity of making considerable cuts for the second performance, though he complained that they deprived the dramatic action of a good deal of its meaning. One reason for the partial non-success of the new opera was that it was in a style different from what the town had come to expect from the composer of *Rienzi* and *The Flying Dutchman*. Another reason was that religious controversy was in the air in Germany at that time, and the story became current that just as Meyerbeer in *The Huguenots* had glorified Protestantism, so, in *Tannhäuser*, Wagner's intention had been to glorify Catholicism. He was even accused in some quarters of having been bribed by the Catholic party!

The second performance took place a week after the first, Tichatschek having in the interval been too hoarse to sing again for some days. The new scenery for the Hall of Song had now arrived, and Wagner was very pleased with it; but unfortunately at the second performance the house was nearly empty. But somehow or other word must have gone round the town that the unfavourable opinion of the audience at the first production needed modifying, and the third performance was given before a full house. From that time its success was virtually assured, though in his inmost heart Wagner felt that the public approval was mostly for the music, instead of for the drama, which he himself regarded as of even greater importance.

For many years he had a hard fight of it to get the average German opera-singer to see that before the question of the singing of the music came the question of understanding the dramatic psychology of the character. In 1852 he wrote an exhaustive treatise on *The Performing of Tannhäuser*, in which he gave singers and stage directors the minutest instructions as to the proper conception of the work. He had two hundred copies of the booklet printed, and sent a copy to every opera-house in Germany. Some years after, being without a copy himself and wanting one for a special purpose, he asked the Vienna Opera to send him theirs. When he received it, it was still uncut.

In the first version of the opera, in the scene of Tannhäuser's frenzy in the third act, Venus did not appear in person, but her malign influence upon Tannhäuser was suggested by a rosy glow on the distant Hörselberg. Nor was the death of Elisabeth positively announced; it was merely conveyed to the audience by the sound of funeral bells in the distance, along with the faint light of torches on the Wartburg. It was apparently as the result of a suggestion from Mitterwurzer that he altered this latter scene to allow of the body of Elisabeth being brought in; while his desire for greater visual definiteness in the stage action — a desire that was always strong in him — led him to bring Venus on in person in the scene immediately preceding this.

The overture to *Tannhäuser*, like the overtures of Wagner's predecessor and model Weber, employs the main themes of the opera to summarise the dramatic action; but Wagner raises this form of overture to a height of which Weber probably never dreamed.

The overture opens with the theme of Salvation by Grace:

The theme has a decidedly religious character, that comes not merely from its melody and harmony but from the peculiar colour given to it by its being set for wind instruments alone — clarinets, bassoons, and horns. It is succeeded by the motive of Repentance: [2]

Wagner discourses upon these two themes with his usual deliberation, the Salvation motive being given out fortissimo by practically the whole orchestra (the trumpets not being used, however; he is reserving these for the final climax), and the violins playing round the melody with an excited figure of broken triplets that is meant to symbolize the Pulse of Life:

The passion gradually dies away, and we hear once more, in quiet tones, the opening theme (No. 1) in the same church-like colouring as before. This time its development is abruptly interrupted

[2] The reader must always bear in mind that the titles affixed to the motives in Wagner's operas are for the most part not his own but those of his commentators. The general sense of a particular motive is unmistakable, but it occasionally happens that different commentators call it by different names.

by the first of the themes associated with the Bacchanalian revels
in the kingdom of Venus:

This motive makes its feverish way upwards in the violas. It is
succeeded almost immediately by a second Bacchanal theme:

and this by a third, given out at first in the soft tones of the flutes,
oboes, and clarinets.

This last is more particularly associated with the Sirens, and it is
completed by another hectic theme:

No. 5 may be regarded as the Sirens' call to pleasure. After repetitions of No. 4, now expanded by the addition of a new figure:

we hear yet another Bacchanal motive

which leads into the theme of the Glorification of Venus; it is to this latter melody that Tannhäuser, in the first act, sings of his passion for the goddess:

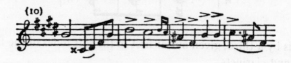

Further development of the various Bacchanal themes brings us to a fresh motive, given out with insidious quietness by the clarinet, under soft, seductive tremolandi in the violins:

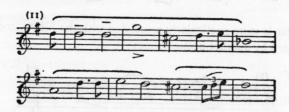

This motive symbolises the Charm of Venus; it is to this strain that the goddess, finding Tannhäuser likely to escape from his prison, tries once more to cast her full spell over him.

Again the Bacchanal themes are resumed, and culminate, as before, in the song of Tannhäuser to Venus (No. 10).

In the original version of the overture this led in time to a resumption of No. 1 in the full orchestra, with No. 3 playing about it as before, the poetic idea being the final triumph of spiritual over fleshly love. For the Paris performance of the opera in 1861, however, Wagner revised and expanded the overture from the point we have now reached.

At the Paris Opera in those days a ballet in the second act was *de rigueur;* it had to be in the second act so that late diners who were not intellectually interested in the first act of an opera could arrive in time for the ballet. Wagner, incredible as it may seem to us to-day, was asked by the management to comply with this absurd rule. He flatly refused, of course, as the dramatic evolution of Tannhäuser gives no opportunity for a conventional ballet in the second act; but as a partial concession to the public, and also, we may take it, because he liked the Bacchanal music and felt he could now do rather more with it than he had done at first, he consented to expand the musical development at this point, so that it could be associated, if not with the ordinary ballet, at any rate with seductive stage pictures and posings that would at once placate the French lovers of ballet and serve to make the voluptuous attractions of the Court of Venus more convincing.

It is hardly necessary to say that the average Parisian patrons of opera were *not* placated; indeed, Wagner's blunt refusal to fall in with their wishes had a good deal to do with the blackguardly opposition to his opera that was gradually worked up in certain quarters. The added portion is now usually known as the New Venusberg Music — sometimes also as the Bacchanal. We will now describe the course taken by the new overture from the point at which we have left the old.

After playing for a while with motives Nos. 4 and 8, Wagner proceeds to develop the already familiar Bacchanal themes with a freedom and passion of which he was incapable in 1845, and two new themes are added to them:

The latter has a touch of *Tristan* about it; and indeed the whole of the New Venusberg Music suggests *Tristan* rather than the *Tannhäuser* of sixteen years earlier.

The music rises to a height of voluptuousness that has probably never been surpassed in any other work of any composer, then dies down gradually and merges into the Call of the Sirens:

In the theatre this is sung (to the words " Come to these bowers ") by an invisible chorus of female voices; in the concert arrangement it is given to the strings alone.

The most exquisite melodies and harmonies are developed out of this and the material already familiar, and the passion of the music gradually dies away into a sort of quietly ecstatic contentment.

In the Paris version of the opera, which is now the one generally played in the larger theatres, the curtain rises at the point where the old overture merges into the New Venusberg Music. The stage represents the interior of the Venusberg — a wide grotto that curves away in the background until it seems to be lost in the distance. A waterfall plunges through an opening in the rocks and forms a lake in which Naiads are seen bathing, while Sirens recline on the banks. In front of the grotto Venus is seen reclining on a rich couch, bathed in a soft, rosy half-light; Tannhäuser half kneels before her with his head in her lap, his harp by his side. The Three Graces group themselves round the couch. Sleeping Cupids are huddled at the side of and behind the couch " like children who, tired after play, have fallen asleep " — to quote

Wagner's own description. While the orchestra pours out its
delirious music, Satyrs, Fauns, Nymphs, and pursuing Youths
fill the stage with movement.

At the point where the chorus of Sirens is heard (No. 14), the
mist in the background dissolves, showing a cloud-picture of the
Rape of Europa by the white bull, escorted by Tritons and
Nereids. During the second song of the Sirens, Leda is seen in the
soft light of the moon reclining on the banks of a woodland lake,
with the swan laying his head on her bosom. As this picture
gradually fades away, the mist itself completely disappears, showing the grotto empty except for Tannhäuser, Venus, and the
Three Graces; the latter make a smiling obeisance to the goddess
and slowly depart.

As we have said, Wagner elaborated considerably the opening
scene of the opera for the Paris production of 1861; his object
was to develop psychologically the part of Venus, to emphasize
her power over the more sensual side of Tannhäuser's nature, and
so to give more interest to his struggle to free himself from her
chains.

When the last traces of the Bacchanal have faded away, the
knight raises his head suddenly from the lap of Venus, as if
wakening from a dream; she draws him back caressingly, to the
strain (in the orchestra) of the Sirens' song (No. 14). He passes
his hand across his eyes, as if trying to recall and fix the dream.
To her question, " Beloved, say, where strays thy thought? " he
replies convulsively, " No more, no more! " and then, more slowly
and softly, cries, " Oh that I now might waken." [3]

Venus as yet has no suspicion that her hold upon him is weakening. Still caressing him she asks him to tell her what is in his
thoughts. He answers that in his dream he has heard again in
imagination what has long been strange to his ears — the joyous
sound of bells. (A suggestion of faintly tinkling bells is given
by the flute and oboe reiterating a sort of chime over a sequence

[3] In one of the older English versions this was mistranslated " Oh that I
ne'er might waken " — an unfortunate perversion of Tannhäuser's real
sentiments.

of descending harmonies in the strings.) " How long is it," he asks, " since I heard their tones? " Venus tries to soothe him by passing her hand gently over his brow. He continues wistfully: " I know not how to measure the time I've dwelt here with thee. Of days and months I have lost count, for no longer do I see the sun, nor the friendly stars above; no longer do I see the tender grass, with its promise of summer; no longer do I hear the nightingale telling me that spring is nigh. Shall I never see and hear these again? "

Venus, still serenely sure of herself and of her empire over him, reminds him, in a tone of quiet astonishment, of how she had brought balm to his sufferings, and bids him take his harp and sing once more the praises of love, as in the days when by his singing he made the Goddess of Love herself his own. Tannhäuser, moved by a sudden resolution, takes the harp from her and sings, to the melody of No. 10, of all her bounties to him. But soon the old sadness, the old nostalgia, creeps across his soul again. He longs to return to the world of men; it is not alone the pleasures of the Venusberg that he desires, he says, but the pains and sorrows of humanity, and he implores his enchantress to set him free. Venus herself now begins to waken to a sense of the reality of the situation. She reproaches him gently: in what has her love been lacking that he should grieve her thus?

Once more Tannhäuser breaks into song in praise of her love and of the delights of her kingdom, and once more he ends with a cry of yearning for the ordinary world of men, for the flowers, the meadows fresh with dew, the sound of bells, the song of birds; and again he begs her to set him free. At this, Venus springs from her couch and upbraids him passionately for his ingratitude and inconsistency: he " praises love, and yet from love would flee? " Is he sated with the joys she has showered on him? He tries to justify himself: it is from her too powerful charm that he would fly; never has he loved her more truly than now, when he must leave her for ever.

At this point in the original version of the score, Venus directs on him at once the full battery of her seductiveness. In the Paris version, the dramatist and the musician in Wagner, both ripened by the years, take better care that the most is made of this crucial moment. Venus buries her face in her hands and turns away from him with a cry of dismay. There is a long silence, both on the stage and in the orchestra: Wagner always knew the value of silence in the theatre in moments of tragic intensity. Then the orchestra launches out into a soft and sweetly seductive strain that might have come out of *Tristan*. While this music is unfolding itself, Venus attracts Tannhäuser's glance to her again, and turns suddenly to him with a ravishing smile. She makes a sign and a magic grotto appears, filled with rosy perfumed vapours. (In the original version she merely speaks of the grotto as being visible to Tannhäuser.) She points to it and invites him to enter it with her. The music here is in essence the same as in the Dresden version. The vocal melody is the one already heard in the overture (No. 11); the orchestral accompaniment, however, is now much richer and more elaborate.

As she draws nearer to him, an invisible chorus of Sirens sings " Come to these bowers " to the melody of No. 14; but the phrase is now sung only once, instead of twice, as in the first version of the opera. In place of the old repetition, Venus herself takes up the Sirens' strain, and, to the accompaniment of some of the music that appears for the first time in the 1861 Bacchanal, bids him come where he shall " drink draughts divine, drink deep of love's own wine," from her lips and her eyes. The music becomes more and more languorously seductive as it proceeds, and at last dies away almost to inaudibility as Venus whispers, " Say, dearest friend, tell me, beloved, wilt thou fly from me? "

Wagner's instinct in making this long interpolation was a sound one: it came from a keener sense of dramatic effect than he had when he drafted his poem in 1843. In the version of that year Tannhäuser succumbs again too quickly. He has already sung his song in praise of love twice; there is a touch of the ineffective in making him sing it a third time almost immediately after the second.

By prolonging the intermediate scene, Wagner in the first place postpones the third stanza of the song till we have had time to forget the second, and so, on the third recurrence of the melody, it comes to us again with most of its original force; and in the second place, by interposing this long and passionate appeal of Venus the dramatist makes us realise how serious is the contest in Tannhäuser's soul between desire for the goddess and the longing to be free of her. Like him, we find her appeal irresistible, and so we are not surprised when once more, " completely carried away," as the stage directions put it, he seizes his harp and breaks again into a song of adoration of Venus that is even more passionate than its predecessors. Yet, in spite of all his protestations that while life is in him he will be her " true and fearless champion," the old longing for the cool sweetness of earth masters him once more; freedom he must have, strife and battle in the world of men, even though death be the end of it all.

The remainder of the scene follows, in the Paris version, the general lines of the earlier one, but the dramatic motive, as before, is extended, and the music made much richer. In the original, Venus in anger bids him go back to the cold and loveless world of men, where disappointment will soon drive him back to her

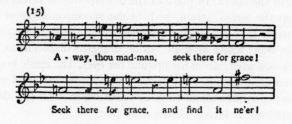

(15)

A - way, thou mad-man,   seek there for grace !

Seek there for grace,   and find   it   ne'er !

arms. In the later version, Wagner, in some pages that once more remind us of *Tristan*, enlarges upon this idea. He has scorned men, she reminds him, flouted them by coming to her; what reception will they give him when he returns? Their hatred and derision will send him back to her; in faint, dull tones she sings for him, in anticipation, the words, expressive of utter weariness and humiliation, in which he will then plead with her to grant him her favour again. He will lie upon her threshold, and beg now not for love but for pity, and she will spurn him like a beggar: " not to slaves, only to heroes, open I my door! "

But cajoleries and threats are now equally vain. " No," replies Tannhäuser; " my pride that last distress shall spare thee, to see me kneeling in dishonour; for he who now leaves thee, oh goddess, will never more return." Here is the opportunity, which Wagner at once seizes, for a further elaboration of the psychology of the situation. Womanlike, Venus at once undergoes a revulsion of feeling. From the scorner she becomes the suppliant. His threat to leave her for ever breaks down her pride; and to some of the loveliest, most insinuating music in the whole scene she reminds him of their happiness together, and pleads with him not to inflict on her the last pain of all — to hear him, in the other life, lamenting, and not be able to bring him solace as of old. But instantly upon this comes another change of mood. If he does not return, she cries despairingly, her curse will be on him and on the world: " the earth shall be a desert when the goddess smiles on it no more."

Tannhäuser answers that he well knows that he who flies from her leaves all grace behind him, but tells her once again that it is combat, not the soft joys of the Venusberg, for which his soul now longs, and that he understands that it is towards death that his new desire is imperiously driving him. " When even death flies from thee," she pleads, " and the grave itself is closed to thee, then return to me! " " But it is here in my heart," says Tannhäuser, " that I bear death and the grave! Through repentance and penance alone shall I find rest "; and then, to the goddess's last frenzied appeal to return to her if he would be saved, he cries, " Goddess of all delights! No, not with thee shall my soul find peace! My hope is in Mary alone! " In the original version the stage directions are that " Venus shrinks away with a cry, and vanishes." In the Paris version she simply disappears, and the scene at once changes.

Tannhäuser has not altered his position, but we now see him in a beautiful valley, with a blue sky and bright sunshine. In the

background, to the right, the Wartburg is visible; through an
opening in the valley on the left the Hörselberg can be seen. To
the right a mountain path runs down from the Wartburg, turning
aside in the foreground, where, on a slight eminence, there stands
a shrine to the Virgin. From the heights on the left, sheep-bells
are heard; on a cliff sits a young shepherd with his pipe, which
he is now playing upon as the curtain rises:

(16) Clar.

He sings a simple little melody in praise of Holda, the old German
goddess of goodness, kindness, and grace, whose yearly coming
brought prosperity to the land.

Wagner's intentions here are almost too subtle for ordinary
theatrical comprehension. Holda, he tells us in his treatise on the
poem of *Tannhäuser,* was, like other of the heathen gods, banished into the interior of the earth at the coming of Christianity,
and from a beneficent deity she came to be regarded as an evil
one. She now figured as a symbol of rather wild pleasure, and in
fact became identified in time with Venus, the source of all the evils
of the senses, and was supposed to have her habitation in the
Hörselberg. Wagner, therefore, by making the unsophisticated
shepherd sing of Holda and the coming of May, seems to be im-
pressing on us that what was Venus to Tannhäuser in the days
when he was enslaved by his senses in the Hörselberg is the sweet
and beneficent Holda now that he has come to himself again in
the pure air of the valley.

In his autobiography Wagner tells us that while he was sketch-
ing out the plan of the opera at Töplitz, in the summer of 1842,
he one day climbed the Wostrai (the highest peak in the neighbourhood), where, on turning the corner of a valley, he heard a
merry dance-tune whistled by a goatherd perched on a crag.
Wagner seemed to see himself at once among the Pilgrims of
his opera, filing past the goatherd in the valley below. He made

a mental note of the situation, but not of the tune, so that when he came to compose the opera he had, as he humourously says, "to help myself out of the matter in the usual way":

In the Dresden version the shepherd's song was continuous. In the Paris version he inserts in the middle of it another little strain on the pipe:

(which reminds us slightly of more than one motive in the *Ring*). When the song is over, the final words being "Now on my pipe I merrily play, For May is here, the lovely May!" the boy indulges in a lively final flourish on his instrument:

Almost simultaneously there is heard the song of the elder Pilgrims as they come down the mountain path from the Wartburg; and between each of the lines of their song the shepherd boy continues for a time to develop his merry fantasia, which is always in a faster tempo than that of the choral song.

The Pilgrims' chorus is in four parts (two tenors and two basses), and commences thus:

After the fourth line the shepherd ceases his piping and listens reverently to the hymn, in which the Pilgrims speak of their journey to Rome, there to implore pardon for their sins. The second part of their strain, to which they sing the words:

> " My heart is sad, by sins oppressed,
> No longer can it bear its burden;
> My weary feet shall take no rest
> Until the Lord shall grant me pardon,"

to a melody that has already been heard in the overture (No. 2), though now, like the rest of the hymn, it is in common instead of three-four time.

As the Pilgrims reach the height opposite to that on which he is sitting, the shepherd waves his cap and calls out to them, " Good speed! Good speed to Rome! There for my soul, oh! ask a blessing! " Tannhäuser, all this while, has remained in the centre of the stage as if rooted there. Now at last his emotion finds voice; deeply moved, he sinks on his knees and utters a great cry: " Almighty God be praised! Great are the marvels of His mercy! " It is one of the electrifying moments of the score; even at this early stage of his development Wagner had an infallible sense of where to place his climaxes, and how to get them with the simplest possible means.

The Pilgrims turn up the path that runs by the shrine, and slowly pass off the stage, still singing their hymn, which, formerly unaccompanied, now has a running accompaniment in the plucked violas and cellos, while the shepherd again pipes his little tune, which also gradually recedes into the distance. Where the last of the Pilgrims has disappeared from the stage, Tannhäuser, on his knees, sunk in prayer, takes up the second strain of the hymn (No. 2) to the same words as theirs. Then tears choke his voice, and he is unable to finish the phrase, which is taken up for the last time by the Pilgrims, now very far away. Tannhäuser bows his head low and appears to weep bitterly; and from the background, as it were from Eisenach, comes the distant chiming of bells. The last phrase of the Pilgrims' hymn:

deserves to rank as a separate motive; it symbolises the Steadfastness of Faith, and is sung each time to the words, " Oh, blest is he whose faith is sure."

Just before the hymn finally dies away, a solitary note on a hunting-horn is heard in the distance; this develops into a joyous fanfare for the horns (behind the scenes, and still in the distance):

This develops and draws nearer, until at last the Landgrave of Thuringia and his Minstrels, in hunting array, come one by one along a path from the eminence on the left. Half-way down the height the Landgrave perceives the kneeling Tannhäuser. All wonder who he can be — a penitent they assume, but, from his appearance, obviously a knight. Wolfram, Tannhäuser's closest friend of old, is the first to hasten towards him and to recognise him with a cry of " 'Tis Henry! " The cry is taken up by them all. Tannhäuser rises in astonishment, quickly collects himself, and bows to the Landgrave without speaking, after having thrown a swift glance on the Minstrels; he is apparently not sure of the kind of reception he will have, for he has left their company, as the libretto tells us, " in haughty pride." The Landgrave and the others ask him if he has really returned to them at last,

and what the return portends; the grim Biterolf demands bluntly
whether he is friendly or " dreams of further strife "; Walther
von der Vogelweide also asks, " Com'st thou as friend or
foe? " The gentle Wolfram protests against their harshness:
is Tannhäuser's demeanor, he asks, that of pride? He approaches the knight with a friendly air and extends a welcome to
him; too long, he says, has Tannhäuser been absent from their
midst:

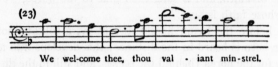

(23)

We wel-come thee, thou val - iant min-strel.

Wolfram's friendliness finds an immediate echo in the others,
and at last the Landgrave himself bids Tannhäuser welcome, but
would know where he has stayed so long. Tannhäuser, in a sort of
dream, replies, " I've wandered in a distant, distant land, where
never could I rest nor solace find. Ask not! To strive with
you I came not here; let it be reconciliation between us,
and then let me go my way." To their combined appeal to
him to stay he answers again that he can nowhere find rest;
he is doomed to wander on for ever; he dare not look behind
him.

But all their urgency is of no avail: the more insistent their
appeal, the harder becomes his resolution, until out of the ensemble there comes a clear cry from Wolfram, standing in front
of Tannhäuser, " Stay for Elisabeth! " The name sets all the old
memories stirring in Tannhäuser; deeply and yet joyfully agitated, he stands as if spellbound, repeating in ecstacy the word
" Elisabeth! " that seems to him to have reached him from
heaven. With the permission of the Landgrave, Wolfram thereupon tells him how, when he dwelt among them and contended
with them for the prizes of song, his singing won for him the
greatest prize of all — the love of Elisabeth. The heartfelt second
strain of the song is typical of Wagner's melody of this period

at its best, and is a full revelation of the character, sincere, affectionate, and earnest, of Wolfram:

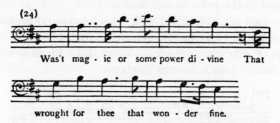

(24)

Was't mag - ic or some power di - vine   That

wrought for   thee   that won - der   fine.

Since Tannhäuser has left them, says Wolfram, Elisabeth has pined away, and has been seen no more at the Contests of Song. Wolfram urges him to return among them and take part again in their friendly rivalries, and his strain is taken up and developed by the rest of the Minstrels in a sonorous piece of choral writing. Tannhäuser's pride can resist no longer; profoundly moved, he throws himself into Wolfram's arms, greets each of the Minstrels in turn, and bows to the Landgrave in deep gratitude. " To her! To her! " he cries — " oh, lead me to her! " and the Minstrels break out into a joyous chorus, in which Tannhäuser joins with a jubilant melody that will be heard again in a later scene:

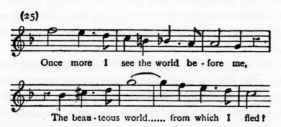

(25)

Once more I see the world be - fore me,

The beau - teous world...... from which I   fled !

By this time the whole of the hunting retinue of the Landgrave has come upon the scene, and the hunters add merry horn fanfares to the voice parts. The Landgrave sounds his horn, he and the Minstrels mount the horses that have been brought them from the Wartburg, and the curtain falls. (That, at least, is how Wagner desired the scene to close; his intentions cannot always be realised to the letter in our theatres.)

The second act commences with a long orchestral prelude of a type that Wagner may be said to have originated in the theatre. It is a sort of miniature symphonic poem. First of all a vigorous, leaping theme, with a dancing pendant

describes the felicity of Elisabeth. It is succeeded by the " Jubilation " motive, which, quoted as No. 25, we have already heard from Tannhäuser's lips in the preceding scene. The development of these sunny motives is interrupted for a moment when, in the dark tones of the wood-wind, the " Warning " motive casts a shadow over the music. This is the motive shown as No. 15; it is to this that Venus has sung her admonition to Tannhäuser in the first scene. But the shadow soon passes, and No. 25 is heard again in all its brilliance as the curtain rises, showing the Hall of Song in the Wartburg; in the background is a view of the courtyard and the valley.

Elisabeth enters joyfully, with springing steps, and sings her greeting to the Hall of Song. Tannhäuser has returned, once more his songs will echo through the Hall, and joy is in her heart again. The aria pulsates with a vitality that must have acted like a tonic, even an intoxicant, on the audiences that heard it for the first time eighty years or so ago: there was nothing else in contemporary music to set beside it for vigour and brilliance. When it is over, Tannhäuser conducted by Wolfram, descends the stairs and appears in the background. He throws himself at Elisabeth's feet, while the tactful Wolfram remains discreetly remote from

them, leaning against the wall. Elisabeth is at first all modest
confusion. She bids Tannhäuser rise from his knees; her melody
is typical of Wagner at this period, especially in its use of the
" turn ":

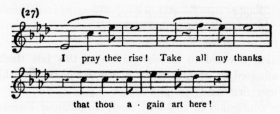

(27)

I   pray thee rise! Take   all my thanks

that thou a · gain art here!

" But where," she asks him, " hast thou wandered so long? "
Tannhäuser rises, and in veiled tones, as if trying in vain to recall
a dream, tells her he has been " far from her, in distant, distant
regions; a dark oblivious cloud 'twixt to-day and yesterday has
rolled." Memory of it all has vanished; one thing only can he
recall, that he had lost all hope that he should ever see her again.
It is some " wonder " that has brought him back, " a mighty
and mysterious wonder." " I praise this wonder," Elisabeth rejoins, " from the depth of my heart."

With delicate art Wagner paints for us the conflict of emotions
in her breast — her innocent joy in Tannhäuser's return, her
sadness at his departure and long absence, her maidenly inability
to comprehend all the varied emotions she is now feeling; at the
finish the cry is wrung from her, " Henry, Henry! What hast thou
done to me? " It is the god of love, declares Tannhäuser, that has
brought him back; and the pair break out into a joyous duet,
commencing thus:

(28)

Oh, bless · ed   hour............. of meet-ing.

and continuing with a strain in which we see once more Wagner's
use of his beloved " turn ":

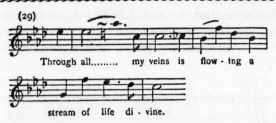

(29)

Through all......... my veins is flow-ing a

stream of life di-vine.

The section devoted to an elaboration of this last theme was greatly admired by Mendelssohn; it was one of the few things in *Tannhäuser* that really pleased him.

At the conclusion of this long duet, Tannhäuser leaves Elisabeth, rushes to Wolfram and embraces him warmly, and the two disappear by the staircase, Elisabeth gazing after them from the balcony. From a side-passage the Landgrave now enters; Elisabeth hastens to him and buries her face in his breast. The grave and benevolent Landgrave has read his niece's secret, but he refrains from urging her to speak of it.

Trumpets sound a fanfare far away in the castle yard, summoning the Minstrels and the rest of the company to the Contest of Song:

(30)

The Landgrave and Elisabeth ascend the balcony and receive the guests — Knights and Ladies — each pair being announced by four noble Pages, the orchestra the while developing No. 30 into an imposing Processional March, with the following as its main theme:

(31)

(Note again the "turn.") At the climax, when most of the guests have been received, trumpets on the stage peal out once more with No. 30, and the Knights and Nobles sing, to the strain of No. 31, a greeting to the noble Hall in which they find themselves, and to their beloved ruler, patron of the arts, the good Landgrave Hermann of Thuringia. The Ladies take up the second strain:

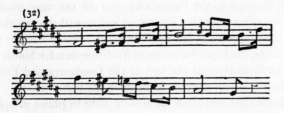

the male voices answer them, and finally the whole of the forces unite in the song of praise.

The Minstrels now step forward, bow to the assembly with great dignity, and take their seats, which are arranged in a narrow semicircle in the centre of the Hall. Tannhäuser is in the middle, to the right: Wolfram at the end, to the left. The orchestra gives out, in quiet tones, a kind of ceremonial music, commencing thus:

and when this has been concluded, the Landgrave rises and addresses the assembly. He reminds them of their services to the land in war, and their no less worthy services to it in the arts of peace, especially that of song. The return of Tannhäuser shall be celebrated in another friendly contest as of old. The secret of his going and returning has not yet been disclosed; perhaps it will be revealed in song. To this end he proposes, as the theme of their contest, the nature of Love; the Minstrel who can most truly show this forth will be allowed to claim his own reward from the hands of Elisabeth.

The four noble Pages come forward and take from each Minstrel a small roll of paper bearing his name: these they place in a golden bowl, which they present to Elisabeth; she draws a roll out and hands it to the Pages, who read out the name on it. This ceremony is accompanied by the orchestra with the music based on the theme quoted as No. 33. The Pages advance into the middle of the stage, read out the name of Wolfram von Eschinbach, and then seat themselves at the feet of the Landgrave and Elisabeth. Tannhäuser, lost in dreams, leans upon his harp.

Wolfram rises and sings an austere song in praise of spiritual, undeclared, unselfish love: it is clear that from afar he worships Elisabeth. The assembly approves the song. Tannhäuser seems to awake from his dream: his expression changes from one of gloomy pride to one of ecstasy. He stares into vacancy, and a convulsive shudder passes through him: he has become oblivious of his surroundings, even of Elisabeth.

Wagner revised the scene at this point in the later version. In the original opera, Tannhäuser breaks into a preliminary song in praise of love — or rather desire, as he conceives it. Walther von der Vogelweide rises and reproves him for confusing love with unhallowed passion, and Tannhäuser taunts him with never having tasted love. In the new version Walther's song is omitted, and Tannhäuser's two outbursts are compressed into one — a rapturous eulogy of sensual delights. There is general consternation. Elisabeth is astonished and perplexed; the grim, uncompromising Biterolf starts to his feet, angrily denounces Tannhäuser, and defies him to mortal combat for his blasphemy. The protest only serves to raise Tannhäuser's temperature. He defies and insults Biterolf, who draws his sword. The Landgrave bids Biterolf contain himself, and the gentle Wolfram sings again in praise of ideal love:

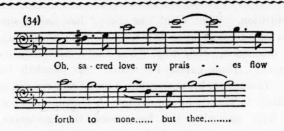

(34)

Oh, sa · cred love my prais · · es flow

forth   to   none...... but thee.........

But by this time Tannhäuser's mind is back again in the courts of Venus. To the strains of No. 13 he lauds her as the source of all light and joy, and finally tells the Knights that if they would know what love is, let them " swift to the hill of Venus fly." The assembly breaks up in horror; the Ladies leave the Hall in dismay — all except Elisabeth, who, deadly pale, masters herself by a great effort, supporting herself against one of the wooden pillars of the canopy of the throne. The Landgrave and the Knights form into a group; Tannhäuser remains alone at the extreme left, still sunk in his ecstatic dream. The Knights, in an agitated chorus, cry out for vengeance on the sinner who has dwelt with Venus, and are advancing upon Tannhäuser with drawn swords, when Elisabeth places herself between them. Shielding Tannhäuser with her own body, she asks them what wound they could inflict upon her, even unto death itself, that could compare with the wound that he has dealt her heart.

From this point the Act is one steadily rising climax. Elisabeth pleads with them to give the sinner a chance to repent and atone for his sin:

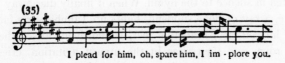

(35)

I plead for him, oh, spare him, I im · plore you.

for was it not for such as he that the Redeemer died? The unholy fire has all this time been gradually dying out in Tannhäuser, and now, at these words of Elisabeth, he sinks down, overwhelmed

with contrition. "Woe! Woe!" he cries; "how have I sinned!"
A softer mood comes upon the Knights. "An angel hath from
heaven descended," they sing, "and God's most holy message
brought. . . . Thou gavest her death. She pleadeth for thy
pardon." Tannhäuser breaks out into a cry of remorse and appeals
passionately to heaven for forgiveness. A magnificent choral climax is built up; when this has passed, the Landgrave steps
solemnly into the centre of the stage, casts the sinner from
among them, and tells him that one path alone is now open to
him: a band of Pilgrims is on its way to Rome, and he must join
them, and prostrate himself in penance at the feet of God. The
Knights take up the exhortation:

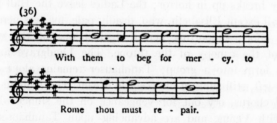

otherwise they will slay him at once. Through the turmoil are
heard the voices of Tannhäuser, in an agony of remorse, and of
Elisabeth, still interceding for him. This was the scene — the most
vital one in the whole opera — in which Tichatschek failed so
lamentably.

At the height of the tumult the Pilgrims' hymn is heard far
away in the valley. All on the stage are involuntarily calmed,
and listen in silence to the hymn. When it finally dies away in the
distance, a ray of hope suddenly lights up Tannhäuser's face: he
throws himself at Elisabeth's feet, convulsively kisses the hem
of her robe, and then rises in the utmost agitation, cries out,
"To Rome!" and rushes from the stage. They all call out "To
Rome!" after him, and the curtain falls, the orchestra thundering
out the motive of Atonement (No. 36).

The third act opens with a long orchestral introduction that
bears the title, in the score of "Tannhäuser's Pilgrimage." This

opens with the theme of Penitence, taken from the Pilgrims'
hymn (No. 14), which is answered by the motive of intercession,
sung by Elisabeth during the final scene of the second Act (No.
35). The two dialogue for a while, and then we hear, in the
violas, followed by the violins, what may be most conveniently
referred to as the Brokenness motive, for it symbolises the mortal
and physical collapse of Tannhäuser under the weight of his sin
and his sufferings:

These three motives are skilfully woven together into one co-
herent tissue. Then comes the theme of Repentance (No. 2), and
later other phrases from the Pilgrims' hymn (No. 37), also making itself heard from time to time. The strings give out the motive
of the " Pulse of Life " (No. 3), which is interrupted twice by a
new theme, that of Heavenly Grace:

given out with the full power of the brass. Later it is heard in
greatly softened tones high up in the muted violins, and by
slow steps it melts into a gently flowing single line in the 'cellos,
to the accompaniment of which the curtain rises.

The scene is the valley in front of the Wartburg, as at the end
of the first Act, except that now everything is in the colours of
autumn. Evening is descending. On the slight eminence to the
right Elisabeth is seen prostrate, praying before the shrine of the

Virgin. From the wooded heights on the left comes Wolfram; halfway down the descent he sees Elizabeth, and pauses. In deeply-felt accents he muses upon the sadness of her lot: always, when he wanders down from the heights of the valley, he is sure to find her here, deep in prayer for Tannhäuser, and daily expecting the return of the Pilgrims, who were to be home again when the leaves were sere. Will Tannhäuser be among them? " Oh, grant her prayer, ye saints in heaven! But if it may not be, if her wound may never heal, oh, grant her some solace."

Just as he is about to descend farther into the valley he pauses: he has heard, far off but gradually approaching, the Pilgrims singing the song of Salvation by Grace (No. 1), to words in which, with gladsome hearts, they greet the familiar and beloved scenes again. Their penance is complete, pardon has been won, and henceforth their pilgrims' staves can rest. The strain has reached Elisabeth's ear also: she raises herself and listens, and stammers out, between the phrases of the hymn, her hope that the saints will strengthen her for what she now has to do.

The Pilgrims, drawing nearer, continue with the motive of Repentance (No. 2), and at last come upon the stage from the right: still singing their gratitude to heaven, they pass slowly by the little eminence and down to the valley in the background, where they gradually disappear. It is the tradition among operatic sopranos that Elisabeth shall move along the line of the Pilgrims, scrutinising each face in turn in the hope of finding Tannhäuser's; but judging from the stage directions, Wagner intended her to remain where she has been from the first, merely scanning the ranks of the Pilgrims as they pass her. When the last of them has gone by she cries, in simple accents that, for all their resignation, are of a heart-rending intensity, " He will return no more! " Wagner always rose to an occasion of this kind: when the whole tragedy of a situation had to be summed up in two or three bars he invariably found the inevitable musical phrase for it.

The last phrase of the Pilgrims is lost in the distance as Elisabeth, in solemn exaltation, falls on her knees and pours out an impassioned and yet spiritually elevated appeal to the Virgin to take her into her own pure kingdom: the expressiveness of her music, with its broad melody and rich harmonies, is heightened by an obligato phrase that keeps recurring in the bass clarinet. She ends with a prayer that her pleadings may win Tannhäuser salvation for his sin.

For a long time she remains in devout rapture: when she rises from her knees she perceives Wolfram, who is approaching as if to speak to her. With a gesture she entreats him to be silent; but the Knight begs to be allowed to conduct her homeward. Still unable to trust herself to speak, she thanks him with a gesture for his love and faithfulness, and indicates that her path is towards heaven, where she has a high duty to fulfill; and she must go alone. Slowly she ascends the height and disappears along the path leading to the Wartburg, while the orchestra softly intones the theme of Wolfram's unselfish, renunciatory love (No. 34), from his song in the second Act. The orchestral tones mount higher and higher, and become of a more and more spiritual fineness in the wood-wind; while Wolfram, after following Elisabeth with his eyes until she is out of sight, seats himself on the rising ground to the left, and begins to preludise upon his harp.

Then, by one of those effects in which Wagner excelled, in which things seen and things heard are blended into one impression, we are made aware that night has fallen by means of deep trombone colour that is like a dark mantle falling over the clear colours that have hitherto prevailed in association with Elisabeth. Wolfram sees in the coming of the night a symbol of death casting its dark shadow over the earth, terrifying the soul that would fain leave the valley for the heights. But in the sky is the evening star, against whose pure radiance the night cannot prevail, and that " points the way through the vale." Accompanying himself on his harp, he sings the well-known song to the " Star of Eve " that has so often lightened his heart of its load of care; he conjures it to greet the sorrowful maiden when she leaves " this sad vale of earth " and " soars aloft to peace unending." His eyes raised to heaven, he continues to play on his harp after his song is over, the 'cellos of the orchestra singing the familiar strain once more.

It is now quite dark. A sombre motive is heard in the horns and bassoons, with a surging figure against it in the strings: it is the motive of the Curse:

Tannhäuser enters, in a tattered pilgrim's robe; his face is pale and contorted, and he walks with difficulty, leaning heavily on his staff. His ear has caught the melancholy tones of the harp. Wolfram accosts the stranger, asking him who he is and whither he is wandering. But Tannhäuser has recognised him, and addresses him scornfully: " Who am I? *Thy* name I know right well! Wolfram art thou, the skilful minstrel! " Wolfram starts forward eagerly with a cry of " Henry! " and asks why, unabsolved, he has returned to his old haunts. Tannhäuser, his heart still full of suspicion and enmity, bids him have no care, for he seeks neither him nor any of his worthy companions. A note of unnatural craving comes into his voice: there is only *one* whom he seeks, one who can show him that path that once of old he found with wondrous ease — the path to the hill of Venus. Wolfram, in horror, conjures him to tell him everything. Has he then not been to Rome after all? Has he not sued for pardon?

Tannhäuser, as if recalling to memory by an effort something far distant, bitterly and wrathfully replies, " Yes, I have been to Rome! " But soon he realises, to his surprise, that Wolfram is not his enemy, and, seating himself exhaustedly at the foot of the rock, he is about to tell his story, when Wolfram makes to sit beside him. Tannhäuser bids him keep apart from one who is accursed, and Wolfram remains a short distance from him. Then

Tannhäuser tells him the story of his pilgrimage in full: how he
went with the other pilgrims to Rome, denying himself on the
way such comforts as they permitted themselves, always thinking
of the angel who had raised her voice in intercession for him, and
resolved that his penitence should wipe out all the tears he had
wrung from her; through the narrative we hear incessantly, in the
orchestra, the tortured theme of " Brokenness " (No. 37). At
last, he says, he reached Rome: the day had broken, the bells
were pealing from every steeple, and every heart was full of joy
and hope. Kneeling before " him who holds the keys to heaven,"
he saw thousands pardoned and go on their way rejoicing; in the
orchestra we hear the theme of Grace (No. 38). But when he
begged to be shriven, he was repulsed with the terrible words,
" If thou hast dwelt in Venus's hill thou art eternally accursed!
As on the dead staff in my hand never again a leaf shall grow, so
thou shalt never find salvation from the consuming fires of hell! "
He fell to earth, confounded, and when he awoke night had fallen
and he was alone, though in the distance he could hear the happy
songs of the pardoned returning home. Then he turned and fled,
with only one longing in his heart — to be received by Venus
once more. His reason deserts him as he calls on her in frenzy
to take him into her kingdom again.

The night deepens; light vapours gradually envelop the stage,
and Wolfram feels an unholy influence in the air. In terror he tries
to draw Tannhäuser to him; but just then the vapours begin to
glow with a rosy light, and behind the scenes is heard the music
of the Sirens(Nos. 5, 6, 7, etc.). As the enchantment draws nearer,
and a whirl of dancing forms is visible, Tannhäuser becomes more
wildly excited. At length Venus appears reclining on her couch
in a clear roseate light. In seductive tones she bids him come to
her, reminding him how she had foretold that men would reject
him and he would return to her; she promises him raptures
exceeding those of old. Ciying out that his soul is lost, Tannhäuser struggles with Wolfram to get to her. Just as he shakes
himself free, Wolfram utters the name of Elisabeth; Tannhäuser
repeats the name and stands as if rooted to the spot. Behind the

scenes are heard the voices of the Knights praying for the soul
of Elisabeth, that has just left its body. Wolfram cries, " Thine
angel prays for thee at God's high throne: her prayer is heard:
Henry, thou art redeemed! " Venus cries out despairingly, " Woe's
me! I have lost him! "

The vapours darken for a time, showing the gleam of torches
through them; then they pass away entirely. Morning dawns, and
from the Wartburg descends a torch-lit procession — first the
elder Pilgrims, then the Minstrels bearing on an open bier the body
of Elisabeth, finally the Landgrave, Knights, and Nobles. The
men about the bier sing " Blessed be the pure one, who now
appears with the saints round the throne of the Lord," and
Tannhäuser, who has been led to the bier by Wolfram, bends
over Elisabeth's body and sinks lifeless to the earth, crying with
his last breath, " Holy Saint Elisabeth, pray for me! " All invert
their torches, so extinguishing them; the stage is now illumined
only by the red light of dawn. And now the younger Pilgrims
enter, bearing in their midst a staff covered with green leaves,
and singing, to the following melody:

of the miracle that symbolises the redemption of Tannhäuser's
soul. Finally, everyone joins in a majestic intonation of the motive of Salvation by Grace (No. 1), round which the pulsating violin figures (No. 3) play as in the overture.

THE MASTERSINGERS OF
NUREMBERG

T HOSE who know the scale on which the *Mastersingers* is
planned will be amused to hear that Wagner originally
intended it, in contrast to the impracticable *Ring,* as a thoroughly
practicable little opera that should be well within the scope of
any European theatre. He first conceived the idea of it in the
summer of 1845, soon after he had finished *Tannhäuser.* Just as
a merry satyr-play used to follow the tragedy in the Athenian
theatre, so would he have a comedy as a pendant to the tragedy of
Tannhäuser.

The real hero of the *Mastersingers* was to be the " Folk," whom
Wagner was very much given to idealising at that time; this Folk
was to be typified in Hans Sachs, the old Mastersinger of the
sixteenth century. The French troubadours, and after them the
German Minnesingers, were in the main aristocratic. The Mastersingers, who followed the Minnesingers, were a more democratic development; they were the ordinary working townspeople
of the mediæval guilds, very much as Wagner has shown them
in his opera. He derived his information about them from various
old books, in which he found details not only of their contests
of song but of their quaint rules of art. Almost everything in connection with their poems and their music was systematised, and
it was only by complying with the rules that anyone could earn
the title of " Master." This could be won only at an open contest
before the guild, and it was the business of the official " Marker "
to decide whether the candidate had or had not committed enough
breaches of the rules to disqualify him.

Wagner was always guided by his subconscious rather than his conscious self in the creation of his works, and his instinct soon decided that it was not yet time for him to proceed with the *Mastersingers*. His view of life was still predominantly serious, and he worked out this mood in *Lohengrin* and the first sketch for the *Ring*. In 1857, for practical reasons, he suspended work upon the *Ring* and took up *Tristan*. It was not till after the *Tannhäuser* catastrophe in Paris in 1861 and the difficulties in connection with the production of *Tristan* in Vienna that he turned seriously to the *Mastersingers*; and it is curious that it was only during the period of his worst troubles that he should find the humour and the serenity of soul to create his comedy.

During the last few years there have been published the whole of the preliminary sketches of the libretto. The first dates from 1845, the second and third from the winter of 1861. In the latter year Wagner had met once again in Vienna the famous critic Hanslick, and come to the conclusion that he did not like him. In the third prose sketch, which was written about that time, the name of the Marker is not Beckmesser, as it ultimately became, but Hanslick (*sic*); Wagner's intention to satirise and caricature his hated critic is therefore beyond dispute. As Wagner used to be always reading his poems and sketches to his friends, there cannot be the slightest doubt that Hanslick knew that Beckmesser was intended to be a malicious portrait of himself; and this knowledge must have played some part in his later attacks upon Wagner.

The final libretto was written in Paris in November 1861 and January 1862, but it was not until 1867 that the music was finished. The first performance was given in Munich on the 21st June, 1868, under Hans von Bülow; the overture, however, had been performed six years earlier at a concert in Leipzig.

The subject of the opera is a simple one. A young Franconian knight, Walther von Stolzing, has made the acquaintance in Nuremberg of a rich goldsmith, Veit Pogner, and his daughter Eva, and has of course fallen in love with the latter. Pogner has been distressed by discovering in what low estimation the burghers are held on account of their absorption in business; so on Midsummer Day he offers his daughter, with all his money, to whoever shall win the prize in a contest of song.

The middle-aged Beckmesser, the town clerk, has pretensions to Eva's hand, but Pogner insists on his taking his chance with the others in the contest. Before Walther can compete as a " Master " he must undergo a preliminary trial; from this, how-ever, he emerges discomfited, the Marker having unfortunately been Beckmesser himself, who not only disapproves of the im-pulsive young man's many departures from the rules, but has an intuition that Walther will prove a dangerous rival. In the end, after Beckmesser has tried and failed, and covered himself with the ridicule of the crowd, Walther, though not officially a Master, sings so much to the satisfaction of everyone that he wins Eva.

The overture is one of Wagner's most elaborate works in this genre; it passes in review most of the main themes of the coming opera.

The opening strain is that of the Mastersingers idealised — large-handed, full-bodied, generous:

This is followed by a hint of the expressive theme associated with the wooing of Walther:

and this by the magnificent Mastersingers' Fanfare, which is a genuine old Mastersinger tune:

Then comes a superb expansion of a theme that is heard in the final chorus of the work, in which the Nuremberg population sing the praises of German art:

According to Wagner, this represents the fundamentally sound art of the Folk as against the rather peddling pedantry of the official Masters.

After a magnificent climax there comes an intermediate section devoted to various aspects of Walther's love. Three chief themes may be distinguished. The first typifies his youthful passion in general:

The second is a quotation from the Prize Song:

The third is the Call of Spring, which is first heard in his Trial Song, in the first act, and that haunts the memory of Hans Sachs in a later scene:

Once more the music works up to a climax, but Wagner suddenly brake off in order to introduce the pattering theme of the Apprentices, which, it will be seen, is a sort of miniature, perky version of the Mastersingers motive (No. 1):

It is given out staccato by the wood-wind. A little later the continuation of this merry theme, still in the chattering wood-wind, is combined with another theme in the 'cellos:

This latter is the phrase to which the populace jeer at Beckmesser in the third act when he is making himself ridiculous in the rôle of wooer.

The music now gradually gathers up its whole strength and settles down into a marvellous contrapuntal combination of three of the themes we have already heard, that of the Prize Song (No. 6), the Fanfare (No. 2), and the theme of the Mastersingers (No. 1); and the grand flood of the music sweeps on to a broad estuary, as it were, not coming to a formal close but debouching in the opening scene of the opera.

This represents an oblique section of St. Catherine's Church in Nuremberg; on the left are the last few rows of pews; in the foreground is the open space before the choir; and in the last row of seats Eva and Magdalena, her maid, are sitting. Leaning against a pillar close by, and looking fixedly at Eva, who every now and then turns her face to him, stands Walther von Stolzing.

The chorus (mostly at the back of the stage), accompanied by the organ, give out a splendid chorale — perhaps the only first-rate German chorale written since the seventeenth century. During the pauses between the lines of the chorale, while Eva and Walther are corresponding by means of looks and gestures, the orchestra breaks out into a series of expressive phrases based on Walther's love theme (No. 2). The congregation rises from its knees to leave the church, the while the organ pours out a majestic voluntary, which also is based on No. 2. Eva manages to delay her entry to the last, and as she approaches Walther, and the latter begs to be allowed to say a single word to her, she sends Magdalena back to find her handkerchief, which, with great forethought, she has left in her pew.

This little comedy is repeated a couple of times more: when Magdalena returns with the handkerchief and interrupts the conversation between the lovers she is sent back for a missing pin; and having returned with this, she discovers that she has forgotten her own hymn-book. On her last return, before Walther can get from Eva a reply to his question whether she is betrothed or not, Magdalena thanks him for his kindness in attending to her mistress, and informs him that while it is quite true that Eva will shortly be a bride, nobody yet knows who the bridegroom will be; the matter will be settled at the trial of song on the next day.

Walther is astonished at this method of bestowing a young lady's hand; but he is a little reassured when Eva impulsively tells him that whomever the Masters may select, she will choose him or no one. This bold declaration is a little too much for Magdalena, who attempts to hurry her mistress home, reminding her that it was only yesterday that she saw the young knight for the first time. Eva's reply to this is that he is the living image of David — not David the Prentice, who is in love with Magdalena, nor David the harpist, who is shown on the shield of the Masters' guild, but the glorious young Goliath-slaying David painted by Albrecht Dürer, with sword at his side, sling in his hand, and his golden locks shining in the sun.

They are interrupted by David, Hans Sachs's apprentice, who enters with a rule and a large piece of white chalk and proceeds to plan out the stage for the coming meeting of the Masters. He explains that they are about to hold a trial of song with the object of elevating a Prentice to the guild. Magdalena takes Eva off, first of all asking David to do all he can for the young knight, especially as regards putting him in the way to become a Master. The lovers bid farewell to each other, promising to meet again in secret that evening.

During the following scene the Prentices, with a good deal of rough hilarity, set the stage for the coming meeting of the guild, while David, full of simple, boyish self-importance, pours into the

stunned ears of Walther a full account of the complicated rules
of the guild. He drives Walther almost distracted with the long
list of " modes " and the regulations of the " tablature " — i.e.
the rules for the arrangement of the words in stanzas, the treatment
of the melodies, the management of the breath, the necessity for
clearness of diction, and so on. David's oration is really a summarised description of the rules of the historical Mastersingers.
Throughout this scene there runs the merry little theme of David:

and when the lad speaks feelingly of his own troubles in mastering
the tablature under the guidance and correction of his master,
the cobbler Hans Sachs, we hear a motive that is always associated
in the opera with Sachs himself in his cobbling capacity:

David of course warns Walther what he has to expect from the
Marker, whose somewhat cantankerous motive runs thus:

In the later scenes of the opera this motive is of course appropriated
to Beckmesser.

At the conclusion of David's address, Walther decides that he

must become a Master, for which purpose he will sing the guild a
song of his own invention. Meanwhile the Prentices, who have
been devoting themselves to play rather than to work, have managed to set the scene all wrong. David makes them do it all over
again under his direction, and the Prentices join hands and dance
round the Marker's box, singing a joyously ironic greeting to the
young knight, whom they evidently regard as fatally over-
ambitious. Two of their typical phrases may be quoted:

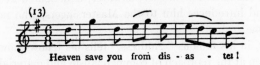

(13)

Heaven save you from dis - as - ter!

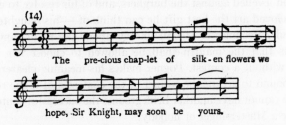

(14)

The   pre-cious chap-let of   silk - en flowers we

hope, Sir Knight, may soon be   yours.

The Prentices scatter in alarm as the vestry door opens and Pogner enters with Beckmesser. They are discussing the forthcoming
contest for the hand of Eva; the elderly Beckmesser, who is town
clerk of Nuremberg, has so high an opinion of his own art that he
does not doubt his ability to be victor in the contest of song the
next day, but he is uneasy about the clause in the regulations that
gives Eva the right to reject even the successful suitor if he is not
otherwise agreeable to her. During their colloquy Wagner makes
plentiful use of a little figure:

(15)

that always typifies the guild.

Pogner refuses to alter the rule he has laid down, and Beckmesser walks aside with a peevish gesture. Walther now comes forward and courteously accosts Pogner. He assures the latter that his object in coming to Nuremberg was to perfect himself in the arts of verse and tone, and that nothing would give him greater pleasure than to become a Mastersinger. He receives a little setback when he is told that he can only become a Master, and so qualify for the contest for the hand of Eva, by passing through the usual examination. Pogner, however, is delighted at his resolution, and introduces him to the Mastersingers, who now enter one by one.

Pogner, in his famous " Address," tells his fellows how grieved he has been at the reproach of commercialism and materialism that has been levelled against the burghers, and of his resolve to give to their beloved art the best gift he can think of — his daughter and his goods. Beckmesser is still uneasy about the affair, and now suggests that the maiden shall be allowed to choose her bridegroom without a contest. Pogner makes his meaning clearer: Eva is not bound to accept the winner of the contest, but if she refuses him she cannot have another bridegroom; the successful contestant must be a Mastersinger or nobody.

Sachs suggests what he thinks is a better way — to leave the decision to the Folk and the maiden in conjunction; such a combination of unspoiled natures, he thinks, cannot possibly go wrong. The suggestion is flouted by the Mastersingers, who have a wholesome contempt for the common people. Beckmesser taunts Sachs with composing doggerel for the mob, and also hints, satirically, that Sachs himself might become a wooer; the cobbler humorously puts the suggestion aside with the remark that the favoured one must be younger than either himself or Beckmesser — a reflection upon his age which Beckmesser does not appreciate.

Pogner now introduces Walther to the guild to undergo his trial, and the young knight steps forward with easy, well-bred dignity to the following strain:

His replies to the Mastersingers' questions show that he has learnt his art from nature and from the long-dead Master Walther von der Vogelweide rather than from the guild. Beckmesser does not deny that Walther von der Vogelweide was a Master, but as he has long been dead it is impossible that the guild should have learned any rules from him!

Some of the Masters are for deciding the matter there and then, but Sachs prevails upon them to let the trial run its usual course. Kothmer, the baker, reads out the rules of the tabulature, informing the candidate of the scheme upon which a master-song must be constructed — it must be in three parts, consisting of two stanzas followed by an after-song, with the same melody for the first two stanzas but a different one for the after-song; and so on. Walther bursts into an ardent song of love and spring, and we soon hear, behind the curtains of the Marker's box, the grating pencil of Beckmesser, who has with great glee undertaken the office of Marker. Walther commits practically every fault that is possible, and puts the final touch to the horror of the guild by rising from the chair; for it was a rule of the contest that the singer must remain seated.

Beckmesser and the other Masters are for declaring Walther to be " outsung," i.e. rejected; but Hans Sachs begs them not to be so hasty. He is wiser and more humane than his colleagues. It is true, he says, that the song is new and not according to the rules, but for all that there is something masterly about it. If it did not obey the rules of the guild, may it not have obeyed equally good rules of its own, and ought they not therefore to try to find out what those rules are?

At this point we hear, for the first time, a noble motive that is afterwards always associated with the melancholy of Sachs, his sense of his difference from his fellows, and his feeling that happiness is to be found only in renunciation:

(17)

His plea, of course, merely horrifies the already outraged pedants, and Walther is unanimously declared " outsung." Finally, unable to make himself heard through the uproar, the young man, with a proud, contemptuous gesture, leaves the chair and walks off the stage, followed by the others. At last only Sachs remains. He gazes thoughtfully at the empty chair; as the Prentices take hold of this, the wise old cobbler turns away with a gesture half humorous, half despairing, and the curtain falls.

The second act shows a street in Nuremberg, which is crossed by an alley running from the front of the stage to the back, where it turns crookedly. On the right of this alley is a large house — Pogner's; on the left, opposite to it, is the humbler house of Hans Sachs. To the right of the stage, by Pogner's house, is a large lime tree, with a stone bench in front of it. By Sachs's house is an elder tree, the branches of which hang over the door. His house is entered by a door from the main street; i.e. the door faces the audience on the left of the stage. The house has two windows facing the alley; one of these belongs to the cobbler's workshop, the other to a room farther back.

It is a beautiful summer evening, and David is closing the shutters of the windows of Sachs's house. The other Apprentices are engaged in the same work on their respective masters' houses, and they sing a short snatch of song in anticipation of the coming delights of Midsummer Day. Magdalena comes out of Pogner's house with a basket on her arm. After some chaff of the pair by the other Prentices, Magdalena manages to get a word with David. The basket is full of good things for him to eat, but first of all she must know how the knight fared at the contest. David has to tell her of his defeat. Horrified at the news, which she knows will bring grief to her mistress, Magdalena snatches the basket away and leaves him. This gives the boys a better chance than ever to tease David, and they are enjoying themselves to the full, when, just as David's temper is at breaking-point, Sachs enters and disperses them.

Sachs and David enter the former's house as Pogner and Eva come up the alley, as if returning from a walk, the daughter hanging on her father's arm. David comes out of the room with a light, places it on the work-bench that is by the window, and sets to work. Both Eva and Pogner are thinking over the scene in the church. Pogner is a little worried at the course events have taken, and is beginning to doubt the wisdom of his promise, which involves the happiness of his child. During the colloquy we hear the theme that always typifies fine old Nuremberg:

Eva, on her part, is burning to know how Walther fared at the contest. Neither of them, however, is in the mood to disclose his mind to the other. Finally Pogner enters his house, leaving Eva outside. Magdalena enters at that moment, and Eva learns the distressing news of the rejection of Walther. The poor girl wants to know more, and her thoughts instinctively turn to Sachs; she will go to him, she says, and ask him to tell her everything, for she knows how he loves her. Magdalena tries to dissuade her, but just then Sachs, in indoor dress, comes from the inner room into the workshop and bids David place the table at the door, where the air is fresh and cool, and then get to bed.

Left to himself, Sachs arranges his work, makes as if to begin upon it, then lays it down and leans back, lost in thought. The beauty of the evening and the scent of the elder tree have worked upon his poetic soul, and he muses upon the lovely song of spring that Walther had sung. It haunts him; he cannot completely grasp it, and yet, do what he will, he cannot escape its magic. He comes to the conclusion that these are not thoughts appropriate to his age and station, so he will get on with his cobbling, " and let all this poetry be." And yet, and yet — the melody will not leave his mind; the Masters, he says, may deny this young man the title of Master, but one hearer his song certainly pleased — Hans Sachs.

Just as he has thought himself into a more cheerful frame of mind, and is settling down to his work, Eva enters. A long and beautiful fluent musical dialogue occurs between the two. Each at first fences with the other; Sachs divines the reason for her coming to him, while Eva expects him to spare her modesty the task of disclosing her real purpose. The elderly widower has always loved her, and we gather that had Walther not come upon the scene, the old cobbler's love would have been sufficient for Eva. At last the knight's name is mentioned, and some apparently unsympathetic remarks by Sachs betray Eva into a revelation of what is in her mind. She turns petulantly upon the supposed enemy of her lover, and crosses the street with Magdalena with the intention of entering her house, but pauses in great agitation at the door. Sachs follows her with his eyes, his heart full of understanding, love, and pity.

He now closes the upper half of his door so that only a glimmer of light comes through it, with the result that he himself is hardly visible. Eva bids Magdalena go inside and say that her mistress has gone to bed. But Magdalena has a message for her from Beckmesser; Eva is to be at the window that night, when Beckmesser will sing her a serenade — a rehearsal of the song with which he hopes to secure the prize the next day. This, in Eva's present angry mood, is the last straw. Walther now comes to the rendezvous, and the lovers, after a passionate scene, resolve to elope. Walther's heart is black within him at the memory of his reception by the Masters, but he sees a beautiful world before him in which he is Master by right. A night-watchman sounds his cow horn and frightens the lovers for a moment; when he has passed by, Eva goes into the house to change into Magdalena's clothes, while Walther waits for her under the linden tree.

Eva returns, and the pair are about to make their way up the alley in the darkness, when Sachs, who has heard the dialogue, and feels that he must find a better way out of the difficulty than this, suddenly opens his shutter so that a bright light strikes across the street; Eva and Walther, suddenly made visible, withdraw hastily into the shade. For a moment the pair debate the best way of escaping. Eva tells Walther that it is Sachs who is sitting there. Walther is delighted; is not Hans Sachs his friend? Eva, remembering her recent conversation with Sachs, assures him that the cobbler is as great an enemy of his as any of them. Walther, in a rage, says that in that case out shall go the cobbler's light at once; but before he can make a move, Beckmesser appears; he has crept up behind the night-watchman. He looks up at the windows of Pogner's house, then sits on a stone seat that is between the two windows of Sachs's house in the alley, and begins to tune his lute.

As soon as Walther realizes who it is, he thinks the opportunity has come to pay off an old score; but once more the lovers' plans are frustrated by Sachs, to whom an idea has occurred. Without being perceived, he has now placed his work-bench right in the doorway, where he makes preparations to commence his work. Eva counsels delay; Beckmesser, she says, will sing his song and go, and then they will be able to escape without fear of detection by her father. But just as Beckmesser, after strumming on his lute, prepares to sing, Sachs lets his light fall full on the street once more, hits his last a heavy blow with the hammer and bursts out into a robust and racy cobbling song:

the words of which, dealing with the adventures of Adam and Eve
in Paradise, and the pity of the Lord for the sorry condition of the
barefoot couple, refer obliquely to Eva and Walther. When Sachs
comes to the final verse of his song, a counterpoint to the melody
comes out loudly in the wood-wind and horns:

This phrase, which is an outpouring of the sadness that is so
often at the bottom of the gentle old man's heart, is generally known
as the Renunciation motive; it afterwards becomes the chief theme
of the Introduction to the third act of the opera.[1]

Beckmesser, who is greatly annoyed at this interruption, begs
to be allowed to proceed with his serenade; but Sachs points out
that unless he gets on with his work he cannot possibly finish the
shoes he has promised for the Marker; has not the latter already
reproached him for thinking too much about poetry and music
and neglecting his cobbling? They arrive at a compromise: Beckmesser is to go on with his serenade and Sachs is to continue with
his work, but only in the capacity of a sort of cobbler-marker: he
will hammer a nail only when Beckmesser commits a fault. The
faults, however, happen to be so numerous that the shoes are completed before the serenade.

Beckmesser, worked up into a temper, then throws prudence
to the winds. The noise he and Sachs have made between them has
roused the neighbours from their sleep, and heads in nightcaps
begin to appear at the windows. David enters and discovers, as he

---

[1] No. 17 is also called a Renunciation motive by some commentators. The
themes were not labelled by Wagner himself.

thinks, Beckmesser serenading Magdalena, who is at Eva's window in her mistress's clothes. He begins to belabour the minstrel; the Apprentices, the Townspeople, and finally the dignified Masters themselves are all dragged into the fray.

When the confusion is at its height, Sachs seizes his opportunity; he takes possession of Walther and draws him into his shop, while Pogner discovers what he takes to be Magdalena and hurries her into the house. Once more the night-watchman's horn is heard approaching, and the crowd breaks up. The street-doors close and all the window lights go out, and when the watchman arrives all is quiet. Wagner, like the great poetic artist he was, would not let the curtain ring down, as most other composers would have done, upon the scene of the riot. He puts a lovely old tune into the mouth of the night-watchman, who blows a final discordant blast on his horn; then, as he walks slowly down the alley, the full moon shines out, and the orchestra fills the theatre with the magic of an exquisite summer night. Even when, in the final bars, the bassoon plays a last broken reminiscence of the grotesque serenade of Beckmesser, this too is turned to poetry and beauty.

The third act commences with the famous orchestral prelude that describes Sachs's attempt to reach spiritual happiness through renunciation. The 'cellos begin with the Renunciation motive which has already been quoted as example No. 20. It is taken up by one instrument and another, worked out very expressively, and succeeded by a solemn passage for the horns, which is an anticipation of the magnificent chorus with which the populace greets Hans Sachs in a later scene:

Reminiscences of the cobbler's song from the second act appear; the music floats aloft and seems to lose itself in the spaces of the sky, then descends, and a last noble meditation upon the Renunciation theme brings the prelude to a close.

When the curtain rises we see the inside of Sachs's workshop. In the background is a door leading to the street; on the right, a staircase leading to another room; on the left, the window that overlooks the alley, with flowers before it. Sachs sits in a large armchair at this window, reading a large folio. The morning sun streams through the window.

David comes in from the street-door with a basket upon his arm, which he places by the work-bench behind the door. He produces flowers and ribbons from the basket, which he lays on the table, and finally a sausage and a cake, which he is about to eat when Sachs, who has not seen him, or at all events taken any notice of him, noisily turns over a leaf of the huge book and startles him; David hastily conceals the food and turns round. He is not at all at his ease on account of the events of the night before. He assumes that his master is in a temper with him and humbly implores forgiveness. " Can a Prentice," he says plaintively, " always behave? " If Sachs only knew Magdalena as well as he (David) does, he would forgive the escapade, for she is always so kind to him; she feeds him when he is hungry, and consoles him when he has been thrashed. He admits having given Beckmesser a drubbing, but Magdalena has now explained the whole affair, and has sent him flowers and ribbons to wear on Midsummer Day.

He goes on babbling in this vein for a long time before Sachs notices him, so absorbed is the latter in his book. Sachs is in one of his kindly philosophical moods. He pardons his apprentice, makes him repeat his " verse " for the day, and then tells him to go and dress himself up for the coming festivity in the meadows. There is a droll musical touch while David is singing his song. The words describe John the Baptist, on the banks of the Jordan, baptising a little boy by the name of Johannes, who, when his parents took him back to Germany, found that in Nuremberg Johannes had become Hans. Hans? Hans? Why that is Sachs's own name, and this is his name-day! David's mind is so full of the events of the night before that when he commences his song he unconsciously sings the first line of it not to the proper melody, but to the tune of Beckmesser's absurd serenade.

Left alone, the old cobbler-poet broods upon the world and its problems — the illusions of mankind, the hatred of man for man, the madness that seems to hover over all human endeavour. He thinks of his beloved Nuremberg, usually so serene, disturbed by such an episode as that of the preceding night. And yet — there was the elder's scent to beautify Midsummer's Eve, and now has come Midsummer Day, the day on which he, Hans Sachs, will bring good out of all this hatred and folly, both to Nuremberg and to the lovers. This is the famous monologue " Wahn! wahn! " (" Mad, mad, all the world mad! "). When Sachs speaks of Nuremberg we hear the typical Nuremberg theme that has already appeared in the second act (No. 18).

The monologue over, Walther enters from the room on the right. He has had a lovely dream, and Sachs assures him that it is in dreams that insight into the inner meaning of things is given to man. He persuades him to tell his dream in poetic form, and Walther, in response, sings the future Prize Song — all of it but the conclusion, which he is not in the mood for then. Sachs wisely refrains from pressing him, assuring him that it will come in the right place and at the right time; then he escorts Walther to the inner chamber and bids him dress richly for the festival.

When they have left, Beckmesser enters furtively; he is aching all over from the thrashing he has had from David, and the orchestra, by its reminiscences of themes from the second act, lets us see that his mind is still running frantically on the awful scene of the night before. Finding himself near the table, the sheet of paper on which Sachs has taken down Walther's dream-song attracts his attention. Beckmesser, after reading the glowing words, naturally assumes that Sachs himself intends to enter the lists for the hand of Eva, and that this is the song he means to sing. Partly with the desire to frustrate a rival, partly in the knowledge that this is a better effort than anything he himself is capable of, he slips the manuscript into his pocket just as Sachs enters, and then upbraids his supposed rival for what he takes to have been his deception.

It is a little while before Sachs can understand, but a glance at the table, from which the manuscript is missing, enlightens him. Greatly amused, he assures Beckmesser that he has no intention of competing, and that he feels so friendly towards the town clerk that he will even present him with the song. Beckmesser is now in the seventh heaven of delight; he cannot find words to express his admiration for Sachs, and finally dances out in a very ecstasy of joy. One thing only he insists upon — that Sachs will not disclose the secret of the authorship of the verses.

When Beckmesser has danced himself out, Eva enters. She makes the excuse that her foot is pinched by the new pair of shoes that Sachs has made for her, but the wise old man understands very well why she has come. While he is pretending to put the shoe to rights, Walther, in gorgeous knightly raiment, appears on the stairs leading from the inner room. The sight of Eva releases a spring in him, and he sings, spellbound, the rapturous final stanza of his dream. Eva breaks down, and pours out her gratitude to Sachs in words that let us see clearly enough how deeply she has been in love with him. When he humorously contends that he is too old for her, and that he would not, by marrying her, willingly bring upon himself the fate of King Marke, the orchestra points the moral with a quotation from *Tristan*.

A new song, he tells them, has been created, and must now be baptised. Magdalena and David must act as witnesses, but as no Prentice can be a witness, Sachs confers Mastership upon David with a box upon the ear; it was the formula by which a Prentice was elevated to the rank of journeyman. The five characters thus being conveniently got upon the stage together, Wagner sets them singing the magnificent quintet, and the curtain goes down as the characters leave the house, David closing the shop-door.

A brief orchestral interlude leads the way into the final scene, which shows us an open meadow outside Nuremberg, with the River Pegnitz winding across it. Joyous crowds arrive by boats, and there is much merrymaking among the Apprentices and the crowd. A mediæval trade procession starts, the shoemakers marching across in grand style to the accompaniment of general cheers,

followed by the tailors, and these by the bakers. Girls arrive and
dance with the Prentices; the waltz (it is perhaps hypercritical to
point out that the waltz was not invented at that time) is of delightfully rustic quality:

Finally the Mastersingers enter in great pomp, Pogner leading
Eva. They all mount the platform on the left of the stage, and the
crowd breaks out into a song of loving welcome of its idol, Hans
Sachs. The melody is that shown as No. 21; the words, which are
a greeting to Luther and the German Reformation, are from a
poem by the historical Hans Sachs. Sachs, in reply, tells the company of the offer made by Pogner, and the contest begins.

Beckmesser, perspiring profusely, mounts a little grassy mound
that has been made in the centre of the stage, and attempts, with
many furtive consultations of the manuscript, to sing the song he
stole, though he can neither understand nor even remember it.
His grotesque efforts bring upon him the derision of the crowd,
and at last he rushes away in rage and disgust, accusing Sachs of
having led him into this trap.

Sachs explains to the company that it is quite true he gave Beckmesser a song, but it was not such nonsense as the town clerk has
made of it. The fault was in the singing; if the words and the
tune are blended in the right way the song is a fine one, and he is
prepared to call a witness to prove it. At a signal from him Walther
comes forward, salutes the Masters and the people with high-bred
courtesy, and takes his place upon the mound. He sings the Prize
Song in its complete form, the crowd, towards the end, joining in
with comments of satisfaction. When he has finished he is led to the
steps of the platform, where he kneels to Eva, who places on his

brow a wreath of laurel and myrtle and leads him to her father, before whom both of them kneel while Pogner gives them his benediction. But when Pogner would give Walther also the gold chain of the guild, the young man pushes it angrily away, so bitter is his memory of his reception by the Masters the day before.

Once more Sachs comes to the rescue. He takes Walther by the hand and exhorts him not to disdain the Masters like that, but to honour their art; they have done their best for it according to their lights. Then he turns to the company with a note of warning. An evil day, he says, may dawn, when a disunited Germany shall be under foreign rulers, when " foreign mists before us rise to dupe and blind our German eyes." When that happens, it will be the death of all that is good and true if the German race betrays its German art. So let them honour their German Masters — let them but take these to their hearts and no harm shall come to German art, though holy Rome itself go down into dust.

Eva takes the wreath from Walther's brow and places it upon that of Hans Sachs, who in turn takes the chain from Pogner and hangs it round Walther's neck. The scene ends with an apotheosis of Sachs, Walther and Eva standing one on each side of him, with Pogner before him on one knee, as if in homage, and the remaining Mastersingers pointing to him as their chief, while the whole assembly repeats the final words of the old cobbler.

The Mastersingers is, and will probably long remain, the greatest of all comedies in music, if indeed " comedy " is the correct word to apply to an opera that, in addition to its humorous episodes, contains so much that is the quintessence of serious beauty, of profound philosophy, and of mellow wisdom. That such a work should be written during the period of Wagner's worst luck and deepest depression is a striking proof of how independent the artist's inner nature is of the circumstances of his outer life. *The Mastersingers* has had only one real successor in music — Strauss's masterpiece *The Rose-Cavalier*.

LOHENGRIN

WAGNER had first conceived the idea of an opera on the subject of Lohengrin during his stay in Paris (1839-42), but the autumn of 1842 and the years 1843 and 1844 were mostly occupied with the production of *Rienzi* and *The Flying Dutchman*, his work as conductor at the Dresden Opera, and the composition of *Tannhäuser*. This last was completely finished by the middle of April 1845.

In July of that year Wagner went to spend his holiday at Marienbad in Bohemia. He was in a state of great nervous excitement over the coming production of *Tannhäuser* and other matters, and his doctor had ordered him complete quietness, baths, and a water cure. But Wagner found it impossible to rest. In his autobiography he attributes his excitable condition partly to the hot summer, partly to the " volcanic " soil of Bohemia, which always had a curiously exhilarating effect on him. One of his books he had taken with him to read on his holiday was the old anonymous German epic of *Lohengrin*. With this under his arm he used to wander into the neighbouring woods, and there, stretched out on the bank of a brook, he would re-create in his mind's eye the world of the old legends.

" The result," he says, " was an ever-increasing and distressing state of excitement. *Lohengrin*, the first conception of which dates from the end of my sojourn in Paris, suddenly stood fully formed before me, down to the smallest detail of the dramatic construction. The legend of the swan, which forms such an important feature of all the versions of this body of myths that my studies had made me acquainted with, had in particular an enormous fascination for my imagination." He remembered his doctor's advice to keep as quiet as possible, and tried to drive *Lohengrin* out of his mind by taking up another and less nervously exciting subject.

He had recently become interested in Hans Sachs and the Mastersingers, and, the subject taking possession of him, in a very little while he had drafted out the first sketch for his subsequent comic opera. " As it was a particularly cheerful subject," he says, " and one much less exciting than the other, I saw no harm in putting it on paper in spite of my doctor's orders. I did so, and I hoped it would free me from my preoccupation with *Lohengrin*. But I was mistaken; for no sooner had I got into my noontide bath than I felt so strong a desire to write out *Lohengrin* that, unable to remain in the bath for the prescribed hour, I jumped out impatiently after a few minutes, and, barely giving myself time to dress, ran like a madman to my lodging to put on paper what was crying out for expression within me. The same thing occurred for several days, until *Lohengrin* was sketched out complete." The doctor, of course, gave him up as a hopeless case. Wagner's excitement went on increasing every day, and he could work off his superfluous energy only by long, fatiguing walks.

It was not until the September of 1846 that he could settle down in good earnest to the composition of the music to *Lohengrin*. Between that month and March 1847 he wrote the third act of the opera. The first was written in May and June 1847, and the second act, with the Prelude, between June and August. The orchestration was finished by March 1848.

It will be remembered that in May 1849 Wagner had to flee from Dresden to escape arrest for his complicity in the revolutionary disturbances of that month. In January 1850 he went from Switzerland to Paris, hoping to get an opera produced there. It was about this time that he became involved in the affair with Madame Jessie Laussot that almost ended in his flight to the East with her. The hectic affair came to a sudden close in April, and Wagner, cut to the heart, turned for consolation to music again.

He looked over the score of *Lohengrin* and sent it to Liszt, who was at that time in authority in Weimar. He implored Liszt to produce the opera, declaring that to no one else would he entrust its destiny. Liszt put the new work in hand at once, and it was produced at Weimar under him on the 26th August, 1850.

As usual, Wagner insisted on the opera, long as it was, being performed without cuts; the only excision he would consent to was one of fifty-six bars in Lohengrin's Narration in the third act; and, again as usual, the great length of the opera was at least as much responsible as the novelty of its style for the relative coldness of its reception by some hearers.

Wagner could never be got to see that he induced sheer physical fatigue in many of his admirers by the mere length of time he kept their attention on the strain in the theatre. In the years immediately following, his anger with conductors who insisted on the necessity or the advisability of cuts did a great deal to delay the progress of the opera. However, in spite of everything, it made its way to such an extent that Wagner, towards the close of his long exile from Germany, could say with humorous bitterness that he was the only German who had not heard *Lohengrin*. He first heard the opera in Vienna on the 15th May, 1861, when he received from the whole house such an ovation as had never yet fallen to his lot.

In the spring of 1860 he gave some concerts in Brussels, and one day he went to Antwerp, being interested in the town not so much because of its works of art and antiquities as because of its association with *Lohengrin*. But, he says, " I was very much put out of humour by my disappointment over the position of the famous citadel. For the benefit of the first act of my *Lohengrin* I had assumed that this citadel, which I had imagined as the ancient fortress of Antwerp, would be a rather prominent object from the opposite side of the Scheldt; instead of which, nothing whatever was to be seen but an undiversified plain, with fortifications sunk into the earth. Whenever I saw *Lohengrin* again after this, I could not help smiling at the scene-painter's castle on its stately hill in the background."

The story of Lohengrin, even as we now have it in the earliest form in which it was reduced to writing, is probably a fusion of several mediæval legends; while Wagner, in his turn, has subjected the story to drastic condensation and manipulation for his own purposes. He sets the scene in Brabant, in the plain of the Scheldt.

Henry I of Germany (" The Fowler ") has come to enlist a force to help him to fight the Hungarians, who are about to invade his own country. He finds the land in a distracted state. The late ruler of Brabant has left two children, a daughter, Elsa, and a younger brother, Gottfried, the latter being the actual heir to the throne. The guardian of the orphans has been Count Frederick of Telramund, who fell in love with Elsa and asked her hand in marriage. Being refused, he married Ortrud, the daughter of Radbod, Prince of Friesland. Ortrud's ambition has long been to seize the throne of Brabant.

To this political motive is now added that of hatred of her rival, Elsa; and she manages to inspire her husband with something not only of her own resentment against Elsa but of her political ambition. Under the influence of Ortrud, Frederick charges Elsa with having a lover whom she desires to elevate to the throne, with which end in view, he declares, she has spirited away young Gottfried. The truth is that Ortrud has decoyed Gottfried into a forest, and, by her enchantments, changed him into a swan; she has then told her credulous husband that she has seen Elsa drown her brother in a pool.

Summoned before King Henry to answer this charge, Elsa makes no defence; and judgment is about to be given against her when Lohengrin, the Knight of the Swan, appears and vanquishes Telramund in combat. Lohengrin, before championing the cause of Elsa, has laid down the condition that she shall never ask his name nor whence he comes; and it is from her inability to keep this promise that the subsequent tragedy comes.

The Grail is the cup in which the Saviour's blood had been poured at His crucifixion. Lost to sinful men for a time, it had finally been entrusted by the angels to the custody of an order of knights having their home on Mount Monsalvat. Of one of these, Parzival, Lohengrin is the son.

The central motive of the Lohengrin story is probably much older than the Middle Ages. We have a somewhat similar idea in the Greek story of Zeus and Semele; in this, the god loves a mortal woman, who at length, unable to conquer her curiosity, asks that he shall show himself to her as he is. Out of love for her, Zeus grants her wish; but at the revelation of his godlike glory Semele falls dead. In the Lohengrin story the catastrophe comes from Elsa demanding to know Lohengrin's name.

It is not improbable that the remote root of this form of the legend is to be found in the primitive belief that a man's name is part of his own being, and that if a savage discloses his name to a stranger and possible enemy he gives the latter power over his life.

The Prelude to *Lohengrin* is one of Wagner's most perfect conceptions, both in idea and in execution. The spiritual atmosphere of Monsalvat is first established by a few chords in the divided violins, playing high up in their register (reinforced by the flutes); at the fourth bar we hear in the violins the theme representative of the Grail:

The two notes marked (*a*) are specially appropriated later in the opera to the Swan.

This Grail motive is worked out in stately, deliberate fashion, the music slowly descending in the scale, while oboes and clarinets are added to give a slightly deeper colour when the theme is repeated in the key of E, with a syncopated accompaniment above it in the violins. The music flows on placidly into a passage derived from Elsa's prayer (see No. 8 below); it ends with a quotation

from Lohengrin's words to Elsa in the third act, when he asks her
if she will give him all her trust:

No. 1 is now resumed in warmer colours than at first, and
gradually works up to a great climax:

the highest emotional peak of the whole Prelude being reached at
the commencement of the last bar of our quotation, when the
whole resources of the orchestra are for a moment brought into
play. From this point the music makes a gradual descent by way of
the theme of the Farewell of the Angels:

which will be heard later (in the third act), at the close of Lohengrin's Narration; and the Prelude ends, as it began, with a suggestion of the spiritual atmosphere that envelops the Grail.

Wagner's own poetic interpretation of the Prelude is interesting; it may be summarised thus:

" Out of the clear blue ether of the sky there seems to condense a wonderful yet at first hardly perceptible vision; and out of this there gradually emerges, ever more and more clearly, an angel-host bearing in its midst the sacred Grail. As it approaches earth, it pours out exquisite odours, like streams of gold, ravishing the senses of the beholder. The glory of the vision grows and grows until it seems as if the rapture must be shattered and dispersed by the very vehemence of its own expansion.

" The vision draws nearer, and the climax is reached when at last the Grail is revealed in all its glorious reality, radiating fiery beams and shaking the soul with emotion. The beholder sinks on his knees in adoring self-annihilation. The Grail pours out its light on him like a benediction, and consecrates him to its service; then the flames gradually die away, and the angel-host soars up again to the ethereal heights in tender joy, having made pure once more the hearts of men by the sacred blessing of the Grail."

Interesting also is Liszt's description:

" It begins with a broad, reposeful surface of melody, a vaporous ether gradually unfolding itself, so that the sacred picture may be delineated before our secular eyes. This effect is confided entirely to the violins (divided into eight different desks), which, after some bars of harmony, continue in the highest notes of their register. The motive is afterwards taken up by the softest wind instruments; horns and bassoons are then added, and the way prepared for the entry of the trumpets and trombones, which repeat the melody for the fourth time, with a dazzling brightness of colour, as if in this unique moment the holy edifice had flashed up before our blinded eyes in all its luminous and radiant magnificence.

" But the flood light, that has gradually achieved this solar intensity, now dies rapidly away, like a celestial gleam. The transparent vapour of the clouds retracts, the vision disappears little by little, in the same variegated fragrance from the midst of which it appeared, and the piece ends with a repetition of the first six bars, now become more ethereal still. Its character of ideal mysticism is especially suggested by the long *pianissimo* of the orchestra only broken for a moment by the passage in which the brass throw out the marvellous lines of the single motive of the Prelude."

The second act of *Lohengrin*, which was the last of the three to be written, was finished on the 2nd August, 1847. The Prelude was written on the 28th August. This noble piece of music was the last to be written by Wagner for over six years; it was not until October 1853 that he commenced work upon the score of the *Rhinegold*.

When the curtain rises we see a meadow on the banks of the Scheldt near Antwerp. Under the judgment oak sits King Henry; by his side are the Counts and Nobles of his Saxon forces; while opposite them stand the Counts and Nobles of Brabant, with Frederick of Telramund at their head; by his side is Ortrud. A Herald steps out from among the king's retinue into the middle of the stage; he gives a sign, whereupon four of the royal trumpeters blow a summons:

The Herald, in broad diatonic tones, hails the nobles and freemen of Brabant, and tells them that Henry, the German King, has come to speak with them on affairs of state; do they greet him in peace and will they follow his behest? Clashing their arms, the Brabantines signify their acceptance of the terms, and the trumpets ring out once more with their fanfare (No. 5).

The King rises majestically, gives the Brabantines his blessing, and explains what has brought him among them. Again and again, he says, the wild Eastern tribes have invaded Germany and brought woe upon it; from the farthest borders there goes up a prayer from women and children, " Almighty God, protect us from the Hungarians' rage! " As the head of the State, it is now for him to put an end to this reign of terror. By weight of arms he had been able to impose a nine years' truce upon the enemy, which time he has spent in strengthening the defences of the kingdom. The nine years have expired; he has refused to pay tribute, and the wild tribes are threatening Germany once more. Now is the time for all loyal men to unite and put an end to this oppression. The Saxons, clashing their weapons together, echo his appeal.

The King resumes his seat, and from his throne tells the people of Brabant that he had come to bid them to Mainz with him, but to his grief he finds them without a ruler and torn by dissension. "You, Frederick of Telramund," he says, "I know of as a knight of famed virtue; speak now, and tell me the cause of all this trouble."

Frederick, first declaring that falsehood is strange to him, tells his story — how the late Duke of Brabant, when dying, made him guardian of his children, Elsa and Gottfried; how tenderly and truly he had fulfilled his duty towards Gottfried, who was the very jewel of his honour; of his grief when he was robbed of his jewel, for Elsa, taking the boy one day to the woods, had returned without him, alleging that, having chanced to wander a little way from him, she had been unable to find trace of him again. They had looked for him everywhere in vain; but when Elsa had been questioned with threats, her pallor and her agitation had betrayed her guilt to all. "Then," he says, "I was filled with horror of the maiden. The right to her hand, that had been conferred on me by her father, I willingly renounced, and took a wife more truly to my mind — Ortrud, daughter of Radbod, Prince of Friesland."

Now he charges Elsa of Brabant with the murder of her brother; and he claims the rulership of the land by right, for he is next of kin to the late Duke, while his wife also is of the race that once gave its princes to the land. His charge against Elsa is accompanied in the orchestra by the Accusation motive:

The men comment on his words in grave, awestruck tones, and the King asks how it is possible that there should be such great guilt in Elsa. Frederick, in growing excitement, tells him that she is given up to dreams, and that her reason for refusing his hand in pride was a secret passion for another. His exasperation still growing, he claims that the reason for her crime was her desire to set her lover on the throne. The King checks his excitement with a grave gesture and bids the accused maiden appear and meet the charge.

The Herald once more comes forward into the middle of the stage, and the fanfare quoted as No. 5 is heard again in the trumpets. The King solemnly hangs his shield on the oak tree, signifying that a court is to be held and that he will not don the shield again till he has given judgment in strictness and in mercy. All the men draw their swords; the Saxons thrust theirs into the earth before them, while the Brabantines lay theirs flat upon the ground; all vow that the swords shall never again be sheathed until the truth has been learned and justice done. In ringing tones, accompanied by softly sounding chords in the brass and wood-wind, the Herald calls upon Elsa to appear.

As in *Tannhäuser,* so in *Lohengrin,* Wagner chooses a particular orchestral colouring for particular people or circumstances. We have seen the violins, in their most tenuous tones, used to convey the atmosphere of the Grail; now the purity of Elsa is suggested in the wood-wind colouring of the phrase to which she makes her appearance accompanied by her Ladies:

(7)

She remains a little while at the back of the stage, then advances very slowly and timidly to the centre of the foreground; her Ladies do not follow her, but remain at the back, on the outer edge of the judgment circle.

The motive of Elsa's entry (No. 7) runs on into that of her Prayer for Help:

This theme, it will be remembered, has been already hinted at in the Prelude.

The men are prepossessed in her favour; they could not believe in the possibility of any crime being done by one so obviously pure. The King accosts her: " Art thou Elsa of Brabant? " Elsa, without replying, bows her head affirmatively. " Dost thou accept me as thy judge? " asks the King. Elsa turns her head towards him, looks him in the eye, and again, with a trustful gesture, signifies her assent. Is she conscious of the grave charge that has been brought against her? he continues. Elsa throws a glance at Frederick and Ortrud, shudders, droops her head sadly, and again signifies the affirmative. Then what answer has she? asks the King. Still silent, Elsa, by a gesture, answers " Nothing! " Does she then admit her guilt? Elsa gazes for a time sadly before her, and for only answer cries softly to herself, " My hapless brother! "

The King is deeply moved, and asks her if she will not confide in him. There is an expectant silence; then Elsa, gazing tranquilly before her, tells how, when she was praying to heaven in her sorrow, she cried loudly for help, heard the cry echoing in the distance, and then fell into a gentle sleep.

Her rapt self-absorption somewhat awes the men, who ask themselves, in whispers, if she is distraught. The King tries to rouse her from her dream, and bids her defend herself before the court. But Elsa's expression now changes from one of dreamy self-absorption to a sort of spiritual illumination.

Before she can speak, the violins of the orchestra, giving out the theme of the Holy Grail (No. 1), reveal to us what is in her mind: in a vision she has seen a Knight in shining armour, with a golden horn at his girdle and a sword at his side; his aspect is pure beyond anything she has ever seen. Out of the clouds he came to her, and by signs consoled her: he alone, she says, shall be her champion. As she speaks of this Knight we hear in the orchestra the theme of Lohengrin as the Knight of the Grail:

while the theme of Elsa's Prayer for Help (No. 8) receives a lovely completion:

(Wagner tells us that the wandering modulations of this passage confused some quite good musicians in his own time.)

The King appeals to Frederick to reconsider his charge against Elsa; but Frederick, who all through this scene is the victim of a morbid excitement which we have to attribute to the influence of Ortrud upon him, declares that although he has witnesses of the guilt of Elsa, he scorns to make use of them, preferring to put his accusation to the arbitrament of the sword. He reminds the King of his faithful service to him against the Danes, and the King, assuring him that he has no need of the reminder, consents that the matter shall be decided by combat. He draws his own sword and thrusts it in the earth before him. The trumpets and trombones give out a bold phrase:

that may perhaps be described as the motive of Ordeal by Combat (by some writers, the motive of Judgment). It is rather curious that the first part of it (the first two bars of our quotation) should so strongly resemble the Sword motive in the *Ring,* while the latter part of the phrase is very like the Treaty motive in that work.

" Now," says Frederick, after the King has asked Elsa if she will trust her cause to the judgment of heaven, and if so, who is to be her defender — " now we shall know the name of her lover! " Elsa has not moved, and her face has preserved its expression of rapt self-absorption. To the strains of No. 8 and No. 10 she declares that her only champion shall be the Knight who appeared to her in a vision and consoled her; to him she will give not only her father's lands and crown but her own hand.

The Herald steps forward with the four trumpeters, whom he orders to stand at the four cardinal points on the outer edge of the judgment ring and blow the challenge. The phrase given out by the trumpets is that of the first part of No. 11. " He who would fight under the judgment of God for Elsa of Brabant, let him appear! " cries the Herald.

Elsa, whose tranquil air has hitherto not been disturbed, now shows uneasy expectation. She approaches the King and implores him to let the summons be sounded once again; her Knight, she says in all innocence, " dwells so far away that perhaps he has not heard it." At the bidding of the King the four trumpeters again take up their positions and blow their fanfare, after which the Herald repeats his summons, this time in a higher key than before. For a moment there is an impressive silence, and the men, in hushed tones, declare the failure of the champion to appear to be the judgment of heaven.

In the orchestra is heard a theme in the clarinets that curiously suggests the theme in the oboe that accompanies Brynhilde's appeal to Wotan at the commencement of the last scene of the *Valkyrie*. Elsa falls on her knees in ardent prayer, while the women, anxious for their lady, come nearer the front of the stage. Elsa passionately implores the Almighty to send to her aid the Knight who appeared to her in her vision. The motive of the Knight of the Grail (No. 9) is heard shimmering in the orchestra, and at once the chorus betray signs of excitement.

Those standing nearest the river bank have caught sight of a boat in the distance, drawn by a swan. The excitement spreads until the whole of the men have made for the background to see the advancing boat, leaving in the foreground only the King, Elsa, Frederick, Ortrud, and the women. The excitement is worked up in magnificent style in both chorus and orchestra; finally all the men rush to the foreground, crying out, " See, he comes! A marvel, a miracle never before seen or heard! "

The King, from his raised place, has seen everything; Frederick and Ortrud are struck motionless with astonishment and terror. Elsa, who has listened to the cries of the men with increasing transport, still remains motionless in the centre of the stage, as if not daring even to look around her. The women fall on their knees and give thanks to heaven. All eyes are turned expectantly towards the background, where at last the boat, drawn by the swan, has reached the bank. Within it stands Lohengrin in shining silver armour, helmet on his head, shield on his breast, and a little golden horn at his side; he is leaning upon his sword. Frederick looks at him in speechless astonishment; while Ortrud, who all through the preceding scenes has preserved her cold, proud demeanour, is struck with mortal terror at the sight of the swan. All uncover their heads and are deeply moved. Elsa at last turns round and utters a loud cry at the sight of Lohengrin. The chorus, men and women, greet the Knight in rousing tones.

The rich colours of the orchestra fade away into softly sustained chords in the violins and flutes as at the beginning of the Prelude, and we hear once more the tenuous motive of the Grail (No. 1). As Lohengrin makes his first movement as if to quit the boat, silence falls upon all. Lohengrin, with one foot still in the boat, inclines himself towards the swan; he thanks it for bringing him thither, and bids it take back the boat to the happy land from which they had come. The swan slowly turns the boat round and swims away up the stream, Lohengrin gazing sadly after it for a while. His final farewell is sung to the representative Swan motive:

The chorus express their awe in a brief but highly expressive ensemble, and Lohengrin, leaving the bank, advances slowly and solemnly towards the foreground. He makes his obeisance to the King, hails him, and wishes victory to his sword. He has come, he says, as champion of a maid against whom a grievous accusation has been brought. Then, turning more towards Elsa, he asks her whether, if he fights for her, she will trust entirely in his protection.

Elsa, who, since she first perceived Lohengrin, has remained motionless, as if spellbound, now throws herself at his feet as if overwhelmed with rapture. She hails him as her hero, and gives herself entirely to him. If heaven grants him the victory, he asks, will she become his wife? This too she promises at his feet. Further, he asks, if he becomes her husband, will she promise that she will never either ask him certain questions, or even harbour them in her mind — whence he has come, or what his name and nature may be? This he does to the motive of Warning, which becomes of great importance in the later stages of the opera:

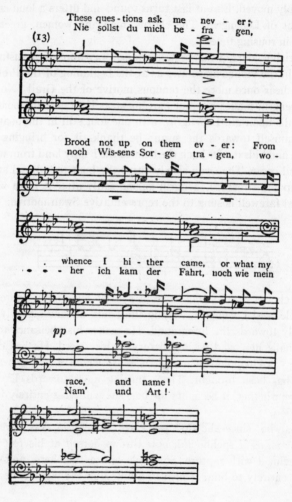

Half-unconsciously Elsa gives this promise also, but Lohengrin is not yet fully satisfied. In heightened and more earnest tones he repeats the question and Elsa, gazing up at him fervently, declares herself willing to give herself completely into his hands and obey his every wish. He clasps her to his breast for a moment, then leads her to the King, into whose care he gives her. Then he steps solemnly into the centre of the circle, proclaims his belief in Elsa's innocence, and gives the lie to Frederick.

The men urge Frederick to forbear to fight with this emissary from heaven, but he declares violently that he would rather die than yield. He does not fear, he says, this stranger, bold of speech and bearing as he is, and brought thither as he seems to have been by sorcery. He himself has spoken nothing but the truth, and he accepts the challenge.

At the bidding of the King, three Saxon Nobles advance for Lohengrin, and three Brabantines for Frederick; they measure out the field of combat, and having made a complete circle thrust their spears into the ground. The Herald advances into the centre of the space, and, to the Judgment motive (No. 11), orders that none shall interfere in the fight; whoever does so shall, if he be a freeman, forfeit a hand, and if a serf, lose his life.

The King, with great solemnity, advances to the centre, and while all bare their heads he prays to heaven to look down upon the fight and declare itself in favour of the truth. The prayer, which commences thus:

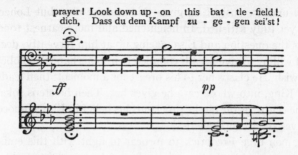

prayer! Look down up - on   this   bat - tle - field!
dich,   Dass du dem Kampf zu - ge - gen sei'st!

is a noble piece of quasi-religious writing; it is taken up by the
whole of the chorus and by the other principals, and developed at
some length. (The reader may notice that this is the first of our
quotations in 3/4 time. It is a singular fact that the whole of *Lohengrin*, with the exception of this passage, is written in duple
metre; and it is remarkable what variety of expression Wagner has
managed to draw from this metre alone.)

In deep and solemn emotion all return to their places, the six
witnesses remaining by the ring with their spears, the remainder of
the men grouping themselves around. Elsa and her Ladies are in the
foreground under the oak with the King. At a sign from the Herald
the trumpeters blow the call to battle (No. 5); the fight is conducted to the accompaniment of the motive of Judgment (No. 11).
Lohengrin, with a mighty stroke, fells Frederick, who, after an
attempt to recover himself, staggers back a few paces and falls
to the ground. Lohengrin spares his life, and bids him depart and
repent of his crime. The warriors resume their swords and sheath
them; the witnesses withdraw the spears from the earth, and the
King takes down his shield from the oak. All rush joyfully to the
battleground, while Elsa, hastening to Lohengrin, breaks out into a
song of joy and gratitude:

(15)

O   songs... of   joy I'd raise thee,
O   fänd'... ich Ju - bel - wei-sen,

wor - thy   of   thy   fame.
dei - nem Ruh - me   gleich.

which is developed into a brilliant ensemble. Some of the young men raise Lohengrin upon his own shield and Elsa upon the King's, and they are carried off with shouts of jubilation.

When the curtain rises for the second act we find ourselves in the citadel of Antwerp. At the back is the Pallas (the Knights' quarters); in the left of the foreground the women's quarters (the Kemenate); on the right is the cathedral. It is night. Ortrud and Frederick, both in sombre and wretched clothes — for they have lost their rank — are seen sitting on the cathedral steps: Frederick is sunk in gloomy brooding; Ortrud keeps her eyes fixed on the brightly-lit windows of the Pallas.

After a couple of bars of *tremolando* in the kettledrums we hear in the 'cellos the sinister theme of Ortrud's Witchcraft:

(16)

In the character of Ortrud Wagner intended, in the first place, to set over against the spiritual world of Lohengrin and the more earthly purity of Elsa a symbol of pagan evil, and in the second place to depict a woman who is immune from the ordinary weaknesses of her sex.

He has analysed her in a letter to Liszt, in which he says: " Ortrud is a woman who does not know love. . . . . Politics are her essence. The political *man* is repulsive; the political *woman* is horrible, and it is this horror I have to represent. There is a kind of love in this woman, the love of the past, of dead generations, the terribly insane love of an ancestral pride, which finds its expression in the hatred of everything living, actually existing." The less strong-minded Frederick is simply a tool in her hands.

After No. 16 has gone its writhing way, we hear in the wind instruments the Warning motive (No. 13), and after that, again in the 'cellos, the motive of Doubt:

(17)

symbolizing the doubt of Lohengrin that Ortrud means to sow in the heart of Elsa. The development of these motives is broken for a moment by festal music heard from within the Pallas; then Frederick rises hurriedly and bids the "companion of my shame" arouse herself that they may leave before the dawn discloses them to all.

A violent quarrel ensues between the pair. Frederick is not yet lost to all sense of honour; he sees that it is Ortrud's wiles that have brought his misfortunes on him, and he pours out a passionate lament over his lost honour. He regrets that, his sword having been taken from him, he cannot slay her. Ortrud, who never loses her sinister composure, asks him with quiet scorn why he has lost his faith in her. Frederick, in reply, runs over the tale of her lies and schemings. She denies nothing, but reproaches him with cowardice in his combat with Lohengrin, and derides his excuse that heaven was on the side of his opponent.

Gradually she establishes her ascendancy over him once more. Nobody, she says, knows who this Knight is who has come among them guided by a swan; his power resides in the mystery that surrounds him; for him to have to declare his name and station would be the ending of the spell. No one but Elsa has the power to draw his secret from him; it is she, then, who must be wrought upon to ask the fatal questions. To awaken her suspicions, Lohengrin must

be charged with sorcery. Through her black art Ortrud knows that
Lohengrin is not invulnerable, and that if the smallest wound be
made in his body all his might will ebb away.

Frederick's anger rises again at the thought that it was only
through magic that he was brought to shame before the court; he
will do anything to wipe out his degradation, but woe to Ortrud if
she is deceiving him once more! Ortrud contemptuously calms him,
and the pair, seated side by side, break out into a sinister appeal to
the powers of darkness and a warning to the happy ones within the
citadel to beware of the ruin that is lying in wait for them.

As the strains of their duet die away, a door on the balcony of the
Kemenate opens, and Elsa appears in a white robe; she advances
to the balustrade and leans her head on her hand; Frederick and
Ortrud, unseen by her, remain sitting on the cathedral steps.

By means of one of those magical changes of orchestral colour
in which Wagner was so skilled he substitutes in a moment the
serenely pure atmosphere of Elsa for the murk that envelops the
minds of Ortrud and her husband. Elsa has come to pour out to
the night air the fullness of her happiness. The clarinet gives out
the placid motive of Elsa's Bliss:

after which she herself takes up the strain:

Ortrud sees her opportunity. In a whisper she sends Frederick away, telling him to leave Elsa with her, the Knight being for him. Frederick withdraws and disappears in the background.

Ortrud breaks in upon Elsa's ecstasy with a loud wail of " Elsa! " Having attracted Elsa's attention, she appeals to her sympathy; how, she asks, has she ever harmed the maiden? Frederick indeed has wronged her in his madness, but now he is broken with remorse. She contrasts her own misery with the happiness of Elsa, and so works upon the latter's sympathy that she leaves the balcony to descend and open the door to Ortrud. The moment she has disappeared, Ortrud leaps up from the steps in a frenzy, and sends out a wild appeal to the pagan gods to help her: " Odin! On thee, strong one, I call! Freia! Hear me, exalted one! Hallow my feigning and my lies; grant me sweet vengeance! "

Her manner changes when Elsa comes upon the scene from the lower door; Ortrud throws herself at her feet in hypocritical humility, and Elsa is shocked at the wretched appearance of her rival. When her noble Knight leads her to the altar, she says, she will intercede with the King for the hapless pair. Gradually, to the accompaniment of the motives of Doubt and Warning, Ortrud insinuates the question, " What if he should some day leave thee, magically departing as he magically came? " Elsa, after a momentary show of indignation, turns sorrowfully and compassionately to Ortrud, and tells her that one like her can never know the bliss of perfect faith. She invites her into the Kemenate, and the two voices blend in a lovely duet, in which, while Elsa sings of her own happiness and trust, Ortrud, in an aside, tells us of a plan by which she will drag Elsa's pride in the dust. With hypocritical reluctance she accompanies Elsa through the little door into the Kemenate.

Frederick now advances from the background, and after the ominous remark, " Thus evil enters yonder house! " he pours out his hatred of Elsa and Lohengrin. Day gradually dawning, he hides himself behind a buttress of the cathedral. Two watchmen on the terrace blow the reveille, which is answered from a distant tower:

The brazen fanfare and their echoes continue for some time, while the watchmen descend and open the gate. and servants and retainers enter and go quietly about their daily duties. The doors of the Pallas open, and the four trumpeters of the King advance and blow their call (No. 5), after which they re-enter the Pallas.

The servants have by now quitted the stage, which gradually fills with the Nobles and other inhabitants of the fortress, entering from all quarters. After an eight-part chorus of the men, in joyful anticipation of a day of rejoicing, and praise of the mysterious Knight who has wrought such a wonder, the Herald, stepping out on to the elevation before the gate of the Pallas, proclaims the King's decree of disgrace and banishment against Frederick and all who help or harbour him. The men express their approval of the decree, and the Herald continues with the announcement that the god-sent stranger who has won the hand of Elsa, since he declines the title of Duke, shall henceforth be known as the Guardian of Brabant. Again the chorus express their joy, after which the Herald, in solemn tones, gives them a message from Lohengrin: this day he will hold his wedding-feast with them, but on the morrow he will lead them, with the King, to battle. There is another joyous outburst from the chorus, followed by an episode that is generally omitted in performance, though it is vital to the understanding of the subsequent course of the drama.

While the people are moving about in happy excitement, four Nobles, former adherents of Frederick, draw together and in furtive tones cast doubts on the advisability of the expedition. Frederick comes forward and stands before them, uncovers his head, and tells them of his intention to challenge Lohengrin's power and accuse him of sorcery. The Nobles hurry him away from the

sight of the populace as four Pages enter from the door of the
Kemenate on to the balcony, run briskly down the stairs, and
station themselves on the terrace in front of the Pallas. They bid
the crowd make way for Elsa of Brabant, who is about to proceed
to the cathedral.

Soon a long procession of women splendidly attired advances
slowly from the door of the Kemenate on the balcony, and makes
its way towards the cathedral to a solemn strain in the orchestra:

(21)

to which is added the motive of Elsa's Bliss (No. 18). When Elsa
herself appears, the Nobles bare their heads in reverence. A superb
ensemble, at once majestic and grave, is built up in chorus and
orchestra.

As Elsa is about to ascend the steps of the cathedral, Ortrud, who
has hitherto been in the background among the Ladies, rushes forward and confronts her. She now throws off the mask; never, she
declares, will she, whose right it is to lead, follow Elsa as a menial;
it is Elsa who should bow before her. She avers her faith in her
husband, who has been falsely judged; but can Elsa show a similar
faith in *her* hero, whose name even she does not know? In face of

the protests of all she presses home this point, insisting that no one knows the race to which Lohengrin belongs, or even if he is of noble birth; whence did the river bear him, whither will it take him back again some day? Elsa passionately declares her faith in her deliverer, and the chorus support her; but Ortrud repeats her taunts more venomously than before.

At last the door of the Pallas opens, and the four trumpeters of the King advance and sound their instruments, bidding the crowd make way for the King, who enters accompanied by Lohengrin and the Saxon Counts and Nobles. Elsa, greatly agitated, throws herself on Lohengrin's breast; perceiving Ortrud, he understands the cause of her trouble. He sternly orders Ortrud to leave them, and taking Elsa under his protection he turns with her and the King to lead the procession to the cathedral.

All are about to follow, when Frederick suddenly appears on the cathedral steps; the Ladies and Pages start back in horror at the sight of him. Frederick makes a last appeal to the King to be heard, and, like Ortrud, charges Lohengrin with sorcery; but at a word of command from the King he is seized by the men. In the wildest excitement he urges them to demand from Lohengrin his name and station. For a moment the faith of the crowd is shaken; even the King is not without a certain sympathy for Frederick.

Lohengrin proudly refuses to answer him, declaring that not even at the bidding of the King would he reveal himself; to one alone he is answerable — Elsa. When he turns to her, however, he is dismayed to find that she too is perturbed. All the conflicting emotions of the situation are summed up in a fine ensemble, during which we are made to feel that Elsa, though still trusting Lohengrin, cannot quite repress the doubts that have been sown in her by Ortrud.

While the King and the men are expressing their faith in Lohengrin, Frederick creeps up to Elsa and softly tells her how she can put Lohengrin to the test; let Frederick wound him ever so slightly, even to the cutting off of the tip of his finger, and all that the Knight is concealing shall be revealed; then, giving her all his confidence, he will never leave her. He, Frederick, will be near her that night; let her call him, and what has to be done will be done quickly.

Elsa, though visibly shaken, refuses, and Lohengrin, coming forward, in a terrible voice bids Ortrud and Frederick depart from her and never let his eyes light upon them again.

Once more he appeals to Elsa to have faith in him, and once more, in shame and confusion, she promises him her fealty. Then, conducted by the King, Lohengrin and Elsa slowly advance to the cathedral to the solemn strains of No. 21. On the highest step, Elsa turns, deeply moved, to Lohengrin, who takes her in his arms. Modestly starting from his embrace, she turns round and catches sight of Ortrud, who raises her arm against her as if in triumph. Elsa, terrified, averts her face, the Warning motive rings out in the brass, and as the King, Elsa, and Lohengrin enter the cathedral the curtain falls.

The brilliant orchestral introduction to the third act is descriptive of the wedding festivities. The first section of it is based on two chief themes, one of which is dashed into by the orchestra at once:

while the second:

is given out in heavy colours by the 'cellos, bassoons, and horns underneath hammering triplet chords in the violins. There follows a middle section, devoted to a quieter strain:

which, from its predominantly wood-wind colour, and knowing Wagner as we do, we may perhaps associate more particularly with the feminine element of the wedding. Nos. 22 and 23 are then resumed; the music rises to a climax, then dies away, and merges gradually into the Wedding Chorus.

The scene is the bridal chamber. On the right is an open window in a recess. From behind the scenes comes the sound of music; the chorus are giving their blessing to the newly-married pair:

The strains draw nearer, and midway through the chorus the doors on each side at the back are opened and the Ladies enter conducting Elsa, while the King, with the men, escorts Lohengrin. The two processions meet in the centre of the stage. Elsa is led to Lohengrin: the pair embrace, and are relieved by pages of their heavy upper garments. The King embraces and blesses Lohengrin and Elsa; the pages give the signal for departure, and the two processions re-form and pass out. When they have completely disappeared, with the tones of the Wedding Chorus dying away in the distance, Elsa, filled with happy emotion, falls upon Lohengrin's breast. He seats himself on a couch by the window and draws her tenderly to him.

Then commences the long and beautiful duet that is the finest piece of writing of its kind that Wagner has given us in this, his first main period. As Lohengrin speaks of the outer world being shut out from them like a dream we hear a tender, intimate phrase in the oboe:

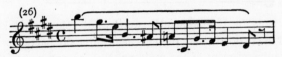

while Elsa expresses the depth of her bliss in a graciously flowing melody:

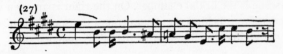

which is afterwards taken up by Lohengrin and made the occasion of a brief blending of the two voices.

But soon Ortrud's poison begins to work. How sweet, says Elsa, her name sounds in Lohengrin's mouth! Perhaps some day she shall learn his — some time when they are alone together and the ears of the world are closed. Lohengrin, without answering her directly, embraces her gently and points through the open window to the flower garden, and compares the charm of the flowers to that which binds his heart to hers:

He reminds her that when he came to her rescue he knew her not nor asked to know her; he had seen her, and his heart had understood everything. Elsa, at his gentle chiding, hides her confusion on his breast. But against her own will the fateful question keeps forcing itself to her lips: she is faithful to him, she says; will he not reveal to her in secret whence he came?

Again he implores her to have trust in him, and breaks out into a new strain of tenderness:

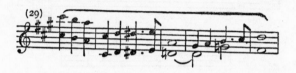

To him, he assures her, her love and confidence are reward sufficient for all he has done; will she not return him these? " I come not out of the night and sorrow, but from a land of light and joy." We hear the Doubt motive in the orchestra (No. 17) as Elsa seizes upon his words to press her question home again; if he has come from so glorious a home, what power can one so humble as she have to hold him?

In vain he begs her not to torment herself and him; but she cannot banish from her mind this new thought of his possible departure. Gazing wildly before her, in a kind of trance, she fancies she sees once more the swan approaching up the river to take her lover away. Finally, losing command of herself completely, she conjures him to say who he is and what is his name. Before he can reply she sees, through an open door at the back, Frederick and his four companions advancing with drawn swords. With a shriek she warns Lohengrin and hurriedly reaches him his sword, which is resting against the couch. As Frederick is aiming a blow at him, Lohengrin strikes him dead; the terrified Nobles let their swords fall, and sink on their knees before him. Elsa throws herself upon Lohengrin's breast, and then sinks to the ground in a swoon.

There is another of those long silences with which Wagner knows so well how to create an effect of emotional tension; then Lohengrin, deeply moved, sums up the whole tragedy in one expressive sentence:

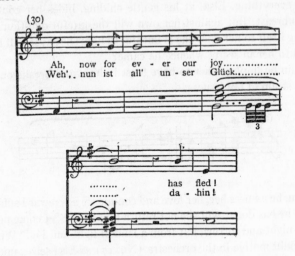

As he bends over Elsa, raises her gently, and places her on the couch, we hear in the soft tones of the orchestra a sorrowful reminiscence of a theme from the love-duet (No. 27).

At a sign from Lohengrin the four Nobles rise and bear away the body of Frederick, the orchestra giving out once more the theme of Judgment (No. 11). Lohengrin strikes a bell: two women enter, whom he orders to dress and adorn Elsa and lead her before the King; there he will tell her all she has desired to know. Slowly and sadly he goes out, while the women lead off Elsa, who is still incapable of speech; and in the orchestra we hear the terrible Warning motive (No. 13) as the curtain descends for a moment.

Trumpet fanfares are heard behind the scenes, as if from the courtyard, and when the curtain rises again we see once more the meadow on the banks of the Scheldt as in Act I. Day is dawning. To stirring martial music the Nobles and their troops enter and take up their positions under their respective banners; finally the King arrives with his Saxons. He congratulates them on their loyalty and offers to lead them against his enemy. But where, he asks, is the Knight whom heaven has sent to be the glory of Brabant?

Before an answer can be given to his quest the crowd is thrown into commotion by the entry of the four Nobles with the body of Frederick on a bier. " It is the will of the Guardian of Brabant," they say; " soon we shall know more." Elsa, accompanied by her Ladies, now enters and comes forward with slow, vacillating steps; the King meets her and conducts her to a seat opposite to the oak. She is incapable of speech; she can only look up to him pathetically, while in the orchestra we hear the theme of her Prayer for Help (No. 8), to which, however, a melancholy turn is now given by its being phrased in the minor.

There is a great stir in the background, and Lohengrin, armed exactly as in the first act, enters, and strides gravely and solemnly to the front. The King and the warriors think he has come to lead them to battle; but he has, he tells them, sad tidings for them. He cannot accompany them to the war; he has come, in the first place, to be declared justified in slaying Frederick, whose corpse, to the general horror, he uncovers. All absolve him.

But, he goes on, he has another complaint to make in the ears of all the world; the wife whom heaven has given him has allowed herself to be led into betraying him; lending ear to evil counsel, she has broken her oath. No longer shall the truth be concealed; " Hear," he says, " whether my nobility is not equal to yours." Then, accompanied by the Grail motive (No. 1), he tells them of the castle on Monsalvat in which a company of sinless men have custody of the Grail, and how the sacred vessel arms its chosen servants with supernatural power, so that magic cannot prevail against them. They are protected in their fight for the virtuous and oppressed so long as they remain unknown; for so pure and rare is the blessing conferred by the Grail that none of its Knights can remain among men when once he becomes known.

He himself is one of these Knights — his father is Parzival, he himself is Lohengrin. His final words are enriched by the theme of Lohengrin as the Knight of the Grail (No. 9).

All are deeply moved, and their emotion finds expression in a brief chorus on the descending motive of Farewell (No. 4). The distracted Elsa gives full voice to her remorse and despair, and it is in vain that Lohengrin tries to comfort her. Remorse is of no avail now, nor, he tells the King and the warriors, can he share the coming combat with them; he gives them, however, the assurance that no Eastern hordes shall ever again oppress the German lands.

There is again wild excitement among the men nearest the bank, and Elsa, awaking from her swoon, sees, with them, the swan approaching again, drawing the empty boat. Lohengrin bends sorrowfully over the swan. In the orchestra we hear the Swan motive (No. 12), as Lohengrin sings his last sad greeting to it. This will be their last journey together, he says; soon its year of service would have been ended, and then, set free by the might of the Grail, it would have been transformed. With a heart-breaking cry he turns to Elsa, and explains that had she but trusted him for a year the Grail would have restored to her her brother, Gottfried, whom she has thought dead.

All are astonished at the news. Handing Elsa his horn, sword, and ring, he bids her give them to Gottfried if ever he should return — the horn to help him in the hour of danger, the sword to win him victory in battle, the ring to remind him of one who served both him and Elsa in their hour of need:

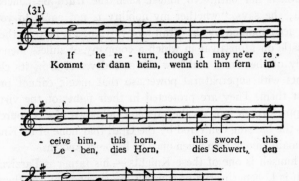

(31)

If he re - turn, though I may ne'er re - ceive him, this horn, this sword, this ring, to - kens I leave him.

Kommt er dann heim, wenn ich ihm fern im Le - ben, dies Horn, dies Schwert, den Ring sollst du ihm ge - ben.

Repeatedly kissing Elsa, who is incapable of movement, he bids her a passionate farewell, and goes quickly up the bank; but before he can step into the boat Ortrud advances, and in triumph tells him that by the chain round the swan's neck she recognises it as the young Gottfried who had been transformed by her sorceries; thanks to Elsa's betrayal it is this very swan that shall now take her Knight away from her again.

Lohengrin sinks on his knees in silent prayer; and in the orchestra we hear the Grail theme (No. 1) as the white dove of the Grail hovers over the boat. Lohengrin, perceiving it, with a look of gratitude springs up and unfastens the chain, whereupon the swan immediately sinks, while in its place Lohengrin raises to the bank a beautiful youth in gleaming silver garments. " Behold," says Lohengrin, " the Duke of Brabant, your leader! "

At the sight of Gottfried, Ortrud has sunk down with a shriek. Lohengrin springs quickly into the boat, which the dove, seizing the chain, draws down the stream. Gottfried comes forward and makes obeisance to the King, and the warriors bow before him in homage. Then he hastens to Elsa's arms; after a moment of rapture she looks wistfully towards the shore, but Lohengrin is no longer visible.

As she gives a last despairing cry of " My husband! My husband! " Lohengrin reappears once more for a moment in the distance, standing in the boat with drooping head, leaning on his shield. Elsa falls lifeless into Gottfried's arms as Lohengrin slowly recedes in the distance.

T HE first idea of an opera on the Tristan subject came to
Wagner in 1854, but he did not begin to work seriously at the
theme until the summer of 1857. Recognising that the *Ring* was
not only going to occupy him for some years yet, but that, when
ready, it would be almost impossible to produce it under then
existing conditions, he planned *Tristan and Isolde* as a more practicable work for the ordinary German theatre. The score was
finished in August 1859; but it had to wait until the 10th June,
1865, for its first performance (in Munich, under Hans von
Bülow).

Of all Wagner's operas, *Tristan and Isolde* is the most difficult
to understand; even after years of acquaintance with it one cannot
be quite sure that Wagner's intention has been grasped at every
point. There is a good deal in the poem that is obscure; if the motives of his characters were invariably clear to the composer, as
we are bound to assume was the case, he has occasionally failed
to make them perfectly clear to the spectator, or even to the careful
student of the text. While there are few operas more popular, there
is probably not one that is the subject of so much misconception
on the part of its admirers.

As usual with Wagner, the drama is a synthesis of legends from
various sources. The Tristan story is an old one, and apparently
Celtic in origin. In its main outlines it runs thus in the most
ancient versions we possess, that date from the thirteenth century.

Tristan is the son of a King of Parmenia named Rivalin, who
makes his way to the court of King Marke in Cornwall and marries

the King's sister, Blanchefleur. Rivalin is killed in battle, and Blanchefleur's sorrow is so great that she dies, in the fortress of Kanoël overseas, in giving birth to Tristan, whose name is thus descriptive of the unhappy circumstances in which he first saw the light. Tristan is brought up by his tutor Kurvenal.

In the course of his adventures he reaches King Marke's court at Tintagel, where he is recognised as the King's nephew and treated with great honour. After his return from a war in Parmenia he finds that Cornwall has been conquered by the Irish King Gurmun, and that the latter's brother-in-law, Morold, has come to collect the tribute agreed upon. Tristan challenges Morold to single combat, slays him, and sends his head to Ireland in scorn and defiance.

But Morold's sword has dealt Tristan a poisoned wound, for the healing of which he has to go to Ireland, there to be treated by the magic art of Isot, wife of Gurmun. He visits Ireland disguised as a merchant (or a minstrel) named Tantris, is healed and made tutor of the Queen's daughter, Isot the Fair, and at length returns to Cornwall, where he finds himself caught up in political complications. A party among the nobles is bent on deposing the childless old King Marke. Tristan, as the latter's nephew, is the heir to the throne; but out of fear for his own safety he persuades King Marke, against his will, to marry, proposing Isot the Fair as bride. Once more he goes to Ireland.

He wins the country's gratitude by slaying a dragon that is ravaging the land, but is afterward recognised by the two Isots as Tantris: moreover, in his sword they find a notch that corresponds with a splinter that had been left in the head of Morold, whose slayer Tristan is now seen to have been. Isot the Fair goes to slay him in his bath with his own sword, but he manages to buy his life with the promise to find her a rich husband.

The Queen, before the pair set out on the voyage to Cornwall, prepares and gives to Isot's maid Brangaene a love-philtre which is to be secretly given to King Marke and Isot on their wedding-day. On the ship Isot does not conceal her hatred of Tristan, but one day, when the pair are thirsty, they accidentally drink the philtre and fall violently in love with each other. When they reach Cornwall, Brangaene, who is in the secret, takes Isot's place in the King's bed. The lovers deceive the old King in various ways, till at length Tristan has to leave the court.

He flies to Sussex, where he falls in love with and marries the reigning Duke's daughter, Isot of the White Hand. After various other adventures Tristan is wounded in battle. No one can heal him but Isot of Ireland; she is sent for, and it is arranged that the messenger who has gone on the quest is to hoist a blue-and-white sail if she returns in the ship with him, a black sail if he has failed. The blue-and-white sail is hoisted, but the jealous Isot of the White Hand tells the sick man that the sail is black. He dies, and Isot the Fair after him, holding him in her embrace. Isot of the White Hand malignantly buries them on opposite sides of the church, so that even in death they should not be united; but from each grave there springs a mighty oak, and the branches of the two meet over the roof of the church.

All this is very crude, in the mediæval way, and Wagner had to simplify and spiritualise it all to make it a worthy subject for modern musical treatment. He reduces the two Isots to one, and for the raw mediæval motive of a hulking thickhead of a warrior and an amorous woman playing their common tricks on an old husband he substituted the motive of a love that is not, and by its nature never can be, satisfied.

It is not clear from Wagner's text whether Isolde really marries King Marke at all, but the indications are that she does not; and so far are Tristan and Isolde from being the conventional lovers of operatic romance, gratifying a guilty passion and singing melodiously about it for our benefit, that their whole pathos and their whole tragedy are that a union between them is for ever impossible: Tristan's honour stands in the way of that.

To save that honour he is at all times ready to die; it is to the last convulsive effort to preserve it that he owes his death. There could be no more grievous misunderstanding of the opera than to suppose it to be a magnificent musical glorification of illicit love.

Wagner makes the slain Morold the betrothed of Isolde, and

the very centre of the drama is an incident that does not occur in it, but is only mentioned. When Isolde raised the sword to slay Tristan, having recognised him, through his disguise, as the slayer of Morold, the sick and helpless knight turned on her a look that made her pause, and then caused the sword to fall from her hands. This " Look " has been variously interpreted. Some writers hold that Isolde has read in Tristan's eyes an unconfessed love for her, others that she loves him also, but as yet is unaware of it herself. The point is, indeed, an obscure one; all we can be certain about is that it is from the " Look " that the drama as we see it on the stage takes its origin.

It is generally supposed that the inspirer of *Tristan and Isolde* was Mathilde Wesendonck, the young wife of the Swiss silk merchant Otto Wesendonck, in whose beautiful home overlooking the lake of Zürich Wagner found refuge from April 1857 to August 1858; but we may take it as certain that the opera would have been written had he never met the lady.

It is less probable, indeed, that he wrote *Tristan and Isolde* because he was in love with Mathilde than that he was in love with Mathilde because he was writing *Tristan and Isolde*. But that she was closely associated in his mind with the opera is beyond question. A selection from his letters to her has been published that throws considerable light on his intentions and his ideals in writing the work. In the winter of 1857–8 Frau Wesendonck wrote five poems which Wagner set to music, drawing largely for his material on the themes of the opera; one of them the *Träume (Dreams)*, is virtually a whole section from the duet in the second act.

The Prelude to *Tristan and Isolde* does not, like that to the *Mastersingers*, set forth the coming drama in detail, but, like the Prelude to *Lohengrin*, gives us the spiritual essence of the drama in a highly concentrated form. Wagner's instinct in these matters was unerring. In the *Mastersingers* the action is incessantly changing, and the Prelude could fitly take up the themes representing the chief characters and incidents and weave them all into one big tapestry. But in *Tristan and Isolde* hardly anything " happens," in the ordinary theatrical sense of the word. The tragedy comes about not because of what happens to the fated pair, but because of what they are; *Tristan and Isolde* is a drama of spiritual states, not of outward actions. The Prelude is a slow, inexorable working out of one sad mood in all its sweet and bitter implications.

It commences with an unharmonised line high up in the 'cellos, that is completed by harmonies in the oboes, clarinets, English horn and bassoons:

The reader who knows this passage only from a pianoforte arrangement of the Prelude must be careful not to imagine that the melodic line is one throughout, running from the opening A in the bass clef to the final B in the treble. In the orchestral score, and in performance, the seemingly single motive becomes two.

The 'cello motive is A, F, E, D sharp (which is here written in the treble clef only for the convenience of the pianist); on the D sharp the English horn strikes in and carries the motive to its conclusion on the D natural.

The other motive — a most important one in the opera — is made up of G sharp, A, A sharp and B in the oboes. It is unfortunate that Wagner did not label his themes himself; as it is, different commentators give different names to many of them, according to the later passages in the score with which they more particularly identify them, or the meaning they read into these passages.

No. 1A will be referred to in the following analysis as the Grief or Sorrow motive, though it must be understood that its expression is too complex to be tied down to one descriptive word: it has in it something of pain, something of resignation, something of hopelessness, and much more. No. 1B is called by some writers the Desire motive, by others the motive of Isolde's Magic; we shall adopt the latter description of it.

Wagner himself has given us a sort of clue to the signification of this motive, in a letter to Mathilde Wesendonck of 1860. He is in Paris, in the thick of the exhausting preparations for the production of *Tannhäuser*. He speaks of his unhappiness, his sense of homelessness, his wistful looking " towards the land of Nirvana." But Nirvana is identified in his mind with Tristan, and the character himself, he says, with the Buddhist theory of creation — how a veil of mist covers the heavens, then condenses into solidity and becomes the world; and he writes out the theme of No. 1B. It is to be hoped that all this was clearer to Frau Wesendonck than it is to us; but it seems evident that in Wagner's mind the theme was associated with love and longing.

In the opera it is associated with various words: at one point it accompanies a reference to " Frau Minne " (the Goddess of Love) as healing the world by her magic (see musical example No. 19); at another point it is linked with the more specific healing " magic " of Isolde and her mother. The only conclusion we can come to is that Wagner's themes were very often associated in his mind with generalised moods rather than with one definite conception that can be fixed in a single word.

When we are listening to the opera we do not need to worry about the precise verbal significance of this, that, or the other theme; the difficulty exists only for the analyst who has to show forth the musical structure of the work, and for purposes of reference has to settle upon some one term or other as a convenient label for a motive. No. 1B may symbolise either Isolde's own magic or her mother's, or the broader magic of love, or the unhappiness that love brings, or the desire that is part of love, or many other things; indeed, it means each of these things at this point or other of the drama. But purely for convenience' sake we will agree to call it the motive of Magic, only warning the reader that he must not interpret " magic " in any crude sense.

After this digression, which has been made necessary by the peculiar " portmanteau " quality, so to speak, of many of Wagner's themes, let us resume our analysis of the Prelude.

Two new motives soon make their appearance:

The first, which is given to the violins, is that of the hero Tristan; the second, given to the 'cellos, and commencing in the second half of the second bar of our quotation, is the Look motive. Whenever this occurs, it forces itself on the attention by reason of the strongly-marked physiognomy given it by the falling seventh.

The next theme to be noted is that of the Love Potion:

Here again the fall of a seventh is a conspicuous feature, due, perhaps, to the association of love with death in Wagner's mind.

Blended with this motive of the Love Potion is that of Death. This latter is of great importance, but most listeners and students of the piano score alone miss it. It is made up of the B, C, and low D sharp in the last two bars of our quotation, and is thrown out in a strongly-coloured line by the bassoons, basses and bass clarinet.

The difficulty of finding the correct literary labels for Wagner's themes is shown again by the various names given to the next motive of the Prelude:

that passes several times from one instrument or group of instru-ments to another. One commentator calls it the motive of the Magic Coffer (from which Brangaene later takes the fateful po-tion). Wagner, however, in a letter to Frau Wesendonck, identifies it with the ivy and vine branches that, according to legend, grew up in an embrace over the graves of Tristan and Isolde. The theme is obviously related to the Look motive.

Next comes the motive of Longing for (or Deliverance by) Death:

The music swells to a superb climax, in which the Magic motive, the Look motive, and the motive of Tristan's Sorrow are com-bined; then it subsides into the opening strain of the Prelude (No. 1), and short passage for 'cellos and basses in octaves brings the marvellous tone-poem to an end. It is the concentration into a few pages of the passion, the pain, the unsatisfied longing that rack Tristan and Isolde throughout the opera.

When the curtain rises we see a tent-like space on the fore-deck of a ship; at the back it is closed off by curtains. Isolde is reclining on a couch, her face buried in the cushions; Brangaene, holding a side curtain back, is looking over the side of the ship. From above, as if from the mast, comes the voice of a young sailor, singing a little song about an " Irish maid " :

West-warts schweift der Blick, ost-wärts streicht das
West-wards sweeps the eye, east-ward   on we

Schiff. Frisch weht der Wind der Hei-mat zu: mein
fly.   The   wind so wild blows homeward now: my

i-risch Kind, wo wei-lest du?
I-rish child, where tarriest thou?

that Isolde takes to apply to herself. The phrase marked A is henceforth associated, all through the act, with the sea.

Wagner's method in *Tristan and Isolde* is more " symphonic " than in any other of his works; he develops, sometimes at great length, his chief themes in the orchestra very much as if they were the substance of a symphony — a fact that makes detailed analysis impossible within ordinary limits of space. It is over an orchestral development of this kind that the voices of Isolde and Brangaene play in the scene that ensues; our following quotation:

is typical of the modifications the theme undergoes.

Isolde starts up, half in anger, half in bewilderment, like one rudely roused from a dream; she has been brooding upon what has happened in Ireland, and the fate that is now leading her to Cornwall, there to be the bride of King Marke. " Where are we? " she asks Brangaene. " By evening," says the maid, " we shall make Cornwall." " Never! " cries Isolde; " neither today nor to-morrow." She bewails the degeneracy of her race: where now is the might that used to command sea and storm? The magic of the sorceress has been tamed: now it can brew only healing draughts. In the orchestra we hear the theme of Magic:

In rage and anguish she calls on the winds and waves to destroy the ship and all who are in it.

Brangaene laments over the desolation that has settled on Isolde since she set foot on the ship, and offers such consolation as she can. Isolde cries wildly, " Air! Air! " and Brangaene draws aside the curtains in the background, thus revealing the stern of the ship. Round the mast the sailors are busy with ropes; on the deck above them are a number of knights and squires, near whom stands Tristan, his arms folded, looking thoughtfully out to sea. At his feet lies his trusty old servant Kurvenal.

Again the song of the young sailor floats down from the unseen height of the mast. Isolde fixes her eyes on Tristan and says gloomily to herself, " Chosen for me, lost to me, strong and good, brave and coward, Death-devoted head, Death-devoted heart! " The latter words are sung to a phrase with some striking modula-tions in it:

Tod - ge-weih-tes Herz!
Death-de-vo - ted heart!

She speaks scornfully to Brangaene of Tristan, who is " bringing a bride as corpse to his lord," and orders the maid to take a peremptory message to the hero to attend upon her. Isolde seats herself on the couch, keeping her eyes fixed on the stern of the ship throughout what follows. Kurvenal wakes Tristan from his trance by a pluck at his robe, and draws his attention to the coming of Brangaene.

The knight, with quiet courtesy, evades the challenge implied in Isolde's message: if he deserts the helm, he asks, how can he pilot the ship safely to Cornwall and King Marke? Brangaene becoming more insistent, Kurvenal, like the rough old war-dog he is, leaps to his feet and gives her a defiant and insulting answer in which Isolde is reminded of the thraldom of Ireland to Cornwall after the defeat and death of Morold, and of the sending of the latter's head to Ireland by way of grimly ironic " tribute." Kurvenal's speech commences thus:

(10)

Wer Korn-walls Kron'   und Eng-lands
Who Corn-wall's crown   and Eng-land's

Erb   an Ir-lands Maid ver-macht,
realm   to E-rin's maid be-queaths,

and breaks out at the end into a mocking refrain:

(11)

Herr Mo-rold zog zu   Mee-re her, in
A - cross the sea our   tax to gain, to

Korn-wall Zins zu ha - ben,
Corn-wall Mo-rold hur-ried;

ending with a shout of contemptuous defiance:

Hei! unser Held Tris-tan, wie der Zins zah-len kann!
Hei! Tris-tan our lord tribute pays with his sword!

that is taken up by the sailors as the baffled Brangaene beats a
retreat.

She closes the curtains again and throws herself with a cry of
distress at Isolde's feet. Isolde's gestures show that she is on the
verge of a terrific outburst; but checking herself by a great effort
she bids Brangaene tell the whole story of the interview with
Tristan. Not that there was any need for this, as she had heard
all; but it is as if she feels a bitter pleasure in being assured by
another of her own humiliation.

Then she tells Brangaene — and us — the whole course of
events in the past; how a sick and almost dying man had come
to Ireland to be healed of his wound by her magic arts; how, from
the evidence of the notch in his sword blade, she learned that this
" Tantris " was the Tristan who had slain Morold; how, in anger at
this discovery, she had stood over him with the sword, meaning
to wreak vengeance for Morold, when from his sick-bed the man
had looked up, " not on the sword, not on my hand, but into my
eyes, and his anguish wrung my heart, so that I let my sword fall " ;
how she tended and cured the slayer of Morold, so that he might
return home whole and sound again, no more to trouble her with
his Look; how he had sworn a thousand oaths of eternal gratitude
and honour.

" Hear now how a hero keeps his oath! " she cries in scorn; and
the feverish tale goes on over its impassioned orchestral accompaniment — how Tristan had boldly come back in his own guise
to win Ireland's heiress for the weary old King of Cornwall, his
uncle Marke — an insult no one would have dared to offer had

Morold been living, for Cornwall had been Ireland's tribute-paying vassal; how Tristan had told them in Cornwall what she had kept deeply secret, her sparing of his life; how he had praised her beauty to the King, and offered to take sail and bring her to him. " Curses on thee, traitor! " she cries in her frenzy. " Curses on thy head! Vengeance! Death! Death for us both! " Through her monologue runs the moving theme of Tristan's sickness:

Isolde rejects Brangaene's tender attempts to console her by turning her thoughts to the happy life that awaits her as the bride of the powerful Marke, and, staring fixedly before her, broods upon Tristan and herself.

Her real trouble reveals itself in her next words — " Unbeloved, ever to see the noblest of men near me! How could I endure that torment? " Brangaene, who does not penetrate her meaning, reminds her of the Love Potion that her mother has compounded in order to ensure her love in her marriage. Brangaene shows her the phial; but Isolde takes another from the casket, and says, " 'Tis *this* draught that I need." " The draught of Death," cries Brangaene, recoiling with horror. We learn that Isolde had put a mark of her own upon the phial to identify it; and it is thus made evident to us that even before leaving Ireland she had resolved on death.

Cries are heard from the sailors, and Kurvenal comes boisterously through the curtains to tell them to prepare for the landing and the presentation to King Marke. Isolde, with quiet dignity, orders him to take a message to Tristan; before she leaves the ship he must come to her and make atonement for a wrong he has done her that is as yet unforgiven.

When Kurvenal has gone, Isolde orders the shrinking and protesting Brangaene to prepare "the cup of Peace," meaning the draught of Death; then she composes herself to meet Tristan, who comes forward, with great dignity, to the accompaniment of the tremendous motive of Tristan as Hero, with the motive of Morold trailing at its heels:

He fences with her for a time, pleading that his avoidance of her during the voyage has been out of respect and in accordance with custom. She reminds him of another custom — of making atonement with foes ere they can become friends. She reminds him of the blood-feud between them, which, he rejoins, was ended by truce in the open field after the defeat of Morold.

But it was not there, she goes on to say, that she had once held "Tantris" hidden when Tristan was in her power, and had pledged herself to silence. She would have him and us believe that when sparing Tantris she had secretly sworn to have vengeance for Morold; she would nurse the knight back to health only that some man appointed by her might in due time strike him down. But who is to do this now, seeing that Tristan is everywhere triumphant and honoured?

Tristan gloomily hands her his sword, bidding her deal the fatal blow herself. But she rejects this weapon, asking him what King Marke would think of her if she slew the very pearl of his knighthood. Their difference is not to be settled thus: there is one way only — they must drink atonement together; and she beckons to the agitated Brangaene to do what is required of her. The psychological motives of this scene are not always as clear as could be wished. Is Isolde really incensed against Tristan for killing

Morold, and anxious to avenge him, or is she merely feigning this resentment to get an excuse for persuading him to share the draught with her? A great deal of ink has been spilt over this problem.

The cries of the sailors taking in sail are heard without. " Where are we? " asks Tristan, starting from his gloomy brooding. " Near the goal! " replies Isolde, with an obviously double meaning; " wilt thou make atonement? " His answer is, " The Queen of Silence bids me be silent; if I grasp what she concealed, I conceal what she grasps not." She reminds him that they are very near the land: would it not be well if, when he is presenting her to King Marke, he can tell the monarch that the cup of atonement has been drunk between them?

Giving a hasty order to the sailors, he takes the cup from her, speaks of his honour, his truth, his anguish, his heart's deception, his foreboding, and drinks " oblivion's good drink, sole balm for endless mourning." With a cry of " Traitor! I drink the half of it to thee! " Isolde snatches the cup from him and drains it. Then follows the scene that on the stage makes such demands on the actors' powers and on the sympathetic credulity of the audience.

For a time only the orchestra speaks, giving out motives 1 and 2; Tristan and Isolde, expecting death, find love instead stealing over them, for Brangaene, either by accident or design, has substituted the Love Potion for the Draught of Death. But it is wrong to assume, as the casual spectator is apt to do, that it is to the physical effect of the potion that their love is due; the real point is that they have secretly loved each other all along, though Tristan's honour has prevented him from acknowledging it, and that the imminence of death, as they believe, has made it unnecessary for them to disguise their feelings any longer. But it must be admitted that Wagner has not succeeded in making his profound psychological intentions unmistakably clear to the ordinary theatre audience.

The lovers awake from their long dream of honour and shame to the realisation that each is all in all for the other, and they pour out their hearts in the most rapturous music that the world till then had ever known. The curtain being drawn aside, the shore is seen, with a castle crowning the heights. The lovers are still in a trance; Brangaene breaks in between them and throws the royal robe over the unconscious Isolde. Kurvenal tries to rouse the dream-bound Tristan to a sense of reality, and Brangaene tells Isolde that the draught she has drunk was that of Love. The Eternal Night and Oblivion for which the pair have longed are denied them; they must still live on in the cruel light of Day. The curtain falls as preparations are being made for the landing, the orchestra ringing out with a vigorous, joyous version of the Sea motive (No. 6A) that seems a mockery of the lovers' pain.

It is with the longing for an escape into Eternal Night that the second act is concerned, not, as is too generally supposed, with the sensual ecstasies of two lovers, one of whom is another man's wife. It is doubtful even whether Isolde has been married to King Marke; nor are we given the slightest clue to the time that elapses between the first act and the second.

The passionate, almost feverish, orchestral introduction is based mainly on four motives, that of the garish Day (in the mystical rather than the material sense of the words) that the lovers hate:

that of Isolde's Impatience:

that of Isolde's Ardour:

and one to which it is impossible to give a name that will meet
with universal agreement, but that may be called the motive of
Ecstasy, that term, like so many others that we have to use here,
being interpreted in a spiritual rather than a physical sense:

Hunting horns are heard as the curtain rises, showing us the
garden in front of Isolde's chamber. It is a summer night, and
the King is out hunting. At the side of the open door of the castle
a torch is burning. Isolde, who is waiting for Tristan, comes out
to Brangaene in great agitation; deceived, as her maid tells her,
by desire, she no longer hears the sound of the horns; she hears only
the murmuring of the fountain, telling her that one is waiting
for her in the silence of the night.

Brangaene warns her to beware of Tristan's enemy, Melot, who
has watched them ever since they left the ship; this night hunt,
she tells the incredulous Isolde, has been arranged by him to bring
down a nobler prey than any beast of the field. Reiterating her
belief in Melot, whom she regards as Tristan's trustiest friend,
Isolde bids Brangaene give the signal by extinguishing the torch,
as a symbol of the Night that is to enfold the lovers. Brangaene
reproaches herself with having brought woe upon them all by her
substitution of the Love Potion for the Draught of Death, but
Isolde reassures her; the change in Tristan and herself was
not Brangaene's work, but the all-powerful magic of Frau Minne,
the Goddess of Love; and we hear in the orchestra an expansion of
the Magic motive (No. 1B, No. 8):

"Life and Death are in thrall to her; she weaves them from joy and grief, changing hate to love. Daringly I took in hand the work of Death; Frau Minne wrested it from me. The Death-devoted she took in pledge; she did the work in her own way." Isolde's praise of Frau Minne is accompanied by a new motive, which we may call, for simplicity's sake, that of Love:

Her mystical ecstasy increasing, Isolde takes down the torch that symbolises the hateful Day, the orchestra, with a slower version of No. 18, rising to its first great climax in this act. She sends Brangaene up into the watch-tower, and as she extinguishes the torch the Death-devoted Head motive (No. 9) is given out *fortissimo* by the trumpets — an important psychological point that is liable to be missed by the student of the piano score alone.

An intensive working-up of No. 16 in the orchestra symbolises Isolde's impatience. She waves her veil as a signal to Tristan; in the following quotation this summons is shown combined with No. 16:

A famous Wagnerian singer, Rosa Sucher, began, with Wagner's approval, the practice of waving the veil up and down to the rhythm of the motive: the effect is, as a rule, so mechanical as to be woefully disillusioning.

At the climax of the orchestral excitement:

Tristan rushes in, and the pair fall into each other's arms with rapturous, almost incoherent ejaculations: their opening words — "Art thou mine?" "Do I hold thee again?" etc. — are taken by some commentators to imply that they have not seen each other since they set foot on land. The point, like so many in *Tristan and Isolde,* is obscure.

There now follows what is usually called the love duet — a convenient but somewhat misleading term. It is impossible to make its real meaning quite clear without quoting virtually the whole of the text, which must be read not only in full but in the original, for it is impossible to convey in any other language the many mystical, metaphysical double meanings of Wagner's words. The essential thing to remember is that the lovers escape from the cruel, blinding, detested Day into a Night in which their souls can become one; the Day is illusion and error, Night is a Truth and an Illumination beyond all the wisdom of earth.

They go over the past, making clear their motives to each other. Tristan, living in the world of Day and Illusion, had been a traitor to Isolde; to save him and her from the consequences of treachery and error she had sought to unite herself to him in death, but the gates of death had opened only to let love in. The Night, beneficent, consoling Night, is typified in a new motive:

which is made the basis of some of the most exquisite music in the whole scene. (It is the substance also of the song *Träume.*) New motives spring up in the course of the duet. When Tristan speaks of the "longing for holy Night" that fills him who is tired of the falsehoods of the Day, the "Death-devoted Head" motive takes a new form:

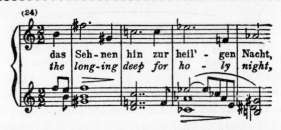

Later there comes a motive expressive of the lovers' yearning for release in Death:

(This seems to be a variant of No. 5.) Death may seize upon their bodies, but their Love would still endure in a mystic world beyond life:

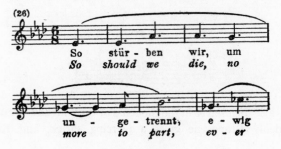

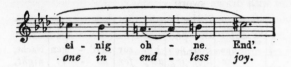

ei - nig   oh - ne.   End'.
·one   in   end - less   joy.

Twice the voice of Brangaene floats down from the tower, warning them that Day lies in wait for them, but the lovers pay no heed to her. The climax of their ecstasy is reached in a resumption of No. 26, to which is now added a theme that becomes of great importance in the closing scene of the opera:

When the pair speak of the Darkness in which there will be no more need for them to shun each other, the motives of Tristan as hero and Isolde's Magic are joined together and developed in the most natural manner:

oh - ne Mei - den,   oh - ne Schei-den,
no more shun-ning,   no more part-ing,

Finally, No. 18 is expanded into the last and supremest cry of rapture:

as they lose themselves in the thoughts of the " highest joy of love."

Suddenly Brangaene gives a piercing shriek, and Kurvenal

rushes in with drawn sword, crying, " Save thyself, Tristan! " To
the accompaniment of the hunting horns King Marke, Melot, and
the courtiers enter and pause in horror as they see the lovers.
Brangaene runs down from the tower and hastens towards Isolde.
The latter, seized with involuntary shame, leans on a bank of
flowers with averted face, and Tristan stretches out his mantle to
hide her from the men.

A lingering echo of No. 26 and No. 27 is heard in the orchestra,
followed by the theme of Day (No. 15) as Tristan says sadly, " The
barren Day, for the last time! " Melot, in triumph, asks King
Marke if his words were not true; but the good old King cannot
agree that his honour and his name have been saved as Melot says.
His one thought is sorrow at what he takes to be the failure of Tristan in honour. Two principal motives run through his long and
mournful monologue. The first:

is expressive of Marke's sorrow. The second:

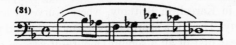

is more symbolical of him as he is in himself — noble and good, but
as yet unable to understand the higher mystical world into which
the love of Tristan and Isolde has raised them.

Both motives are entrusted in the first place to the bass clarinet,
the dark tones of which give a distinctive colouring to the whole
of the scene. Marke's long speech is regarded by some people as a
bit of an anti-climax; but for those who understand the inner

motives as distinct from the outer action of the drama, it is not a line too long.

Marke gently reproaches Tristan, whom he had thought the paragon of honour, for having brought this shame upon him. It is at this point we gather, from certain words of Marke's, that the marriage with Isolde has not yet taken place. He asks who can explain to him " the undiscovered, deep, mysterious cause " of all this woe.

Tristan is sorry for him, but feels the impossibility of making the mystical matter clear to him by explanation. He turns to Isolde and asks if she will follow him to " the dark land of Night," from which he awoke when his mother brought him in sorrow into the world. She replies that as she once followed him " to a foreign land, so now will she go with him to his own real land, his heritage." As he bends over her slowly and kisses her gently on the forehead, the oboe gives out, in heart-rending tones, a new and most exquisite form of No. 18.

Melot draws his sword to attack Tristan, who exposes his false friend's treachery to the King: it was Melot who had urged him to bring Isolde to Cornwall, and being in love with her himself, it is jealousy that has now moved him to the betrayal of his friend. Tristan attacks Melot, but, for the second time seeking death, and relying on Isolde's promise to follow him, lets his guard fall and sinks wounded into Kurvenal's arms. Melot would follow him up, but King Marke holds him back as the curtain falls.

The third act takes place in the garden of the ramparts of Tristan's castle in Karéol, in Brittany, where Kurvenal has brought him for safety. There is a short but poignant orchestral prelude, in which we hear first of all a sombre, mournful version of the Day motive:

(32)

followed by a slowly-ascending passage in the violins, that gives
an effect of great sea-space; then a sad theme in the horns and
'cellos:

After various repetitions of these themes the curtain rises, showing
the sick Tristan lying on a couch; in the distance we catch sight of
the sea. An English horn behind the scenes gives out a melancholy
melody:

that is supposed to be played by a shepherd whom Kurvenal has
stationed on a watch-tower to look for the coming of Isolde's ship;
the strange sadness of the tune is heightened by the frequent
intrusion of a G flat into it, as in the following:

and again:

It is Kurvenal who has sent to Cornwall for Isolde to heal his
master. Tristan, awakened by the shepherd's pipe, faintly asks
Kurvenal where he is, and the faithful old servant tells him how he

brought him home to Karéol to be healed: accompanying his speech
is the typical Karéol motive:

It is with difficulty that Tristan seizes the reality of the things
about him; his soul is still sunk in the Night of Forgetfulness into
which he had hoped to plunge for ever. One thought alone possesses him: Isolde still lives " in the kingdom of the Sun," and he
must seek and find her, that he may lose his being for ever in hers.
His tired and confused brain sees the light in the castle, and hears
Isolde calling to him out of the night. Kurvenal tells him that he
has sent for Isolde. The rough old warrior knows nothing of the
nature of Tristan's suffering: he has only argued, in his simple way,
that as Isolde's leechcraft healed his master of the wound dealt by
the sword of Morold, it can surely heal also the wound dealt by
Melot's.

Tristan raises himself at this news, and, seizing Kurvenal, pours
into his ears an impassioned song in praise of friendship — such
friendship as this there never was on earth, for those he hates,
Kurvenal hates too, and those he loves, Kurvenal also loves; Kurvenal had been King Marke's true man, but when Tristan betrayed
his King, Kurvenal too betrayed him. He is willing to suffer
with his lord: " but what I suffer, that canst thou never suffer!
This terrible yearning that consumes me; this ravaging fire
that eats me away; could I but name it, couldst thou but know
it, thou wouldst no longer tarry here, but hasten to the tower,
there to scan the seas for her sail! " In imagination he sees the
ship.

His frenzy at last breaks under its own terrific weight, and as he
sinks back exhausted, and Kurvenal sadly tells him no ship is in

sight, the shepherd's melody threads itself in the most expressive
way through Tristan's next despairing monologue. This was the
strain he had heard when, as a child, he learned of his father's
death; it was the same strain that rang in his mother's ears when
she died in giving him birth. And now, what fate does it foretell
for him? " To yearn! To die! Oh, ah no! Yearning, yearning! In
dying still to yearn, to yearn but not to die! "

In mystical terms he recalls his association with Isolde, and
grows frenzied again at the thought of the draught and the madden-
ing, burning pain that has come from it; " the terrible draught that
brought this anguish, 'tis I myself by whom it was made! From
father's need and mother's woe, from lovers' tears in every age,
from laughter and weeping, from rapture and sorrow, I distilled
the poisons of the draught! " This mad thought is summed up
musically in an agonised motive that keeps tearing its way through
the tissue:

Once more he falls back exhausted, to the despair of Kurvenal,
who thinks him dead; then, recovering consciousness, he describes
his vision of Isolde crossing the sea to him; the lovely music culminates in a long cry of " Ah, Isolde! Isolde! How fair art thou! "
that has not its equal in all music for expressiveness. While Kurvenal is trying to calm him once more, the shepherd blows a mer-
rier tune:

Kurvenal rushes to the tower, and calls out " The ship! From northward she comes." He describes its pennon to Tristan, then the danger from the breakers, the skill of the steersman, the safe passing of the rocks, and at last Isolde's signal and her stepping to shore. Tristan sends him away to help her.

Left alone, his frenzy seizes upon him again; at its height he springs from his couch and staggers forward, Wagner cunningly suggesting the disorder of his brain by a use of the irregular metre of five-four:

He tears off his bandage and staggers to the middle of the stage. Outside Isolde's voice is heard in a cry of " Tristan! Beloved! " " What, do I hear the light? " cries the frenzied man. " The torch! Ah! The torch is quenched! To her! To her! " As Isolde enters he rushes, half fainting, to meet her; she receives him in her arms, and he sinks slowly to the ground, the orchestra giving out slowly the opening strains of the Prelude (No. 1). He ejaculates the one word " Isolde! " to the accompaniment of the Look motive (No. 2B), and dies in her arms.

At first she cannot believe that he is dead: " Not of the wound, ah, not of the wound must thou die: let the light of life go out with us twain united! " She at last sinks unconscious on his body just as the shepherd comes forward to tell Kurvenal that a second ship is in sight. The steersman rushes in, and the three hastily barricade the gate against what Kurvenal thinks to be the attack of King Marke, come to avenge himself on Tristan. Brangaene's voice is heard without, then that of Melot; as the latter forces his way in, Kurvenal strikes him dead.

King Marke appears in the gateway and tries to bring Kurvenal to reason, but the maddened old man-at-arms attacks the incomers; he is wounded, drags himself with his last strength to Tristan, and dies heroically and pathetically at his feet. Marke, in deepest grief, tells them all how, having learned of Tristan's freedom from dishonour, he had come over the sea to unite him to Isolde, and now all are dead! Brangaene tries to arouse Isolde, who is unconscious of everything but the body of the man who at last has preceded her into the realm of Night, where she must follow him. Over the body she sings the *Liebestod* — the two souls are now made one with each other and with the breath of the universe. At the very last there surges through the orchestral tissue, in the sad, piercing tones of the oboe:

the theme of Isolde's magic and Isolde's longing.

PARSIFAL

W AGNER was fond of laying stress on the distinction between Heart and Head, and stressing the superior virtue of the former. Certainly in his own practice, while his head might occasionally lead him astray, his heart — or, to give it another term, his instinct — was almost invariably right. We may call it his subconscious self or what we will, but the fact remains that an inner voice always counselled him wisely in his art; something within him invariably warned him when he was not intellectually or musically ripe for some subject or other that had attracted his attention.

Between the conclusion of *Lohengrin* in January 1848 and his commencement upon the *Rhinegold* in October 1853, a period of nearly six years, he wrote no music at all. The explanation of this curious phenomenon is that, while his head was full of dramatic schemes of an absolutely new kind, he knew instinctively that as a musician he was not yet ripe for them.

Upon this point we shall touch later when we come to deal with the *Ring*. Meanwhile we have to note a similar phenomenon in the case of *Parsifal*. Something corresponding in essence to the Parsifal subject had hovered vaguely at the back of his consciousness for some twenty years before he embarked upon the opera as we now know it, but he had to wait, as usual, till what was dimly trying to realise itself in the lower strata of his subconsciousness forced its way, by virtue of its own inner growth, into his upper consciousness.

After his flight from Dresden in 1849 he passed some years in a painful intellectual and emotional ferment. He was thoroughly

unhappy in himself, because with his own life everything seemed
to have gone wrong; he was equally unhappy about the state of the
world in general, for he had seen the high hopes of the revolution-
aries and reformers of 1848 scattered into dust. He thought that
both in the theatre and in political and social matters a new world
was struggling towards the light; but how to bring it to birth he
did not know.

This is, in part, the explanation of his devoting so much of his
time during these years to the writing of prose works, in which he
tried not only to set the world to rights, but to clarify his own ideas.
In the meantime he was struggling desperately to come to a clear
understanding with himself as a dramatist. The truth is that his
faculties at this time were in unstable equilibrium. He was growing
mentally at a tremendous rate, but the different parts of his mind
were not all growing at the same speed.

Although he himself hardly knew it, the *Ring, Tristan,* and
Parsifal were all vaguely stirring within him. But before he could
work out these vast schemes in the right way he had to bring about
a stable equilibrium among his various energies; and the years
immediately following 1848 were unconsciously devoted to this
task.

First of all he projected a drama on the subject of the Emperor
Frederick Barbarossa, and then drafted a sketch for a play on the
theme of Jesus of Nazareth. He soon realised that both schemes
were unfit for musical treatment in his peculiar way; indeed, from
the fact that *Jesus of Nazareth* was planned for five acts, and
from other indications, it is practically certain that he never intended to write music — except, perhaps, a little incidental music
— to this subject. His mind was obsessed at this time with thoughts
of Love, Renunciation, and Salvation, and the *Jesus of Nazareth*
was only one of the various attempts he was making to find the
proper musical and dramatic form for these ideas.

" I was burning," he tells us, " to write something that should
take the message of my tortured brain, and speak in a fashion to be
understood by present life. Just as with my Siegfried, the force of
my desire had borne me to the fount of the Eternal Human: so

now, when I found this desire cut off by modern life from all appeasement, and saw afresh that the sole redemption lay in flight from out this life, casting off its claims on me by self-destruction, did I come to the fount of every modern rendering of such a situation — Jesus of Nazareth, the Man."

There is already something of *Parsifal* in this, just as there is already something of the later Tristan in a passage he wrote in 1851: "What, in fine, could this love yearning, the noblest thing my heart could feel — what other could it be than a longing for relief from the present, for absorption into an element of endless love, a love denied to earth and reachable through the gates of death alone?" This, as the reader of our *Tristan* analysis will know, is virtually the theme of that opera.

In 1856, while he was working at the *Ring*, and a year or more before he had commenced *Tristan*, he wrote a sketch for a drama called *Die Sieger* (The Victors), which was not published until after his death. This was a Buddhistic play, the central motive of which is that Prakriti can only be united to Amanda if she shares the latter's vow of chastity. In this there is already a touch of *Parsifal*. And that Wagner's subconscious mind was running upon the Parsifal subject is shown by the intention he had at one time of introducing Parsifal into the third act of *Tristan*. In the process of the years his intuitions gradually sorted themselves out and the vital parts of them coalesced.

In Parsifal himself, as the reader will recognise, there is something both of Jesus and of the Buddha. But although Wagner had the Parsifal theme more or less in his mind since 1845, when he became acquainted with the Parsifal poem of Wolfram von Eschenbach, the Minnesinger, it was not until 1865, when more than half of the *Ring*, the whole of *Tristan*, and part of the *Mastersingers* had been written, that he at last saw his way clear through the jungle of the Parsifal subject.

In August of that year he made his first sketch of the libretto, but it was not until considerably later that the text assumed its final form, in 1877. In December of that year he published the poem. He had begun work upon the music a little while before that, and the actual composition was completed in the spring of 1879, though the orchestration was not finished till January 1882. The first performance took place at Bayreuth on the 26th July, 1882, under Levi. The Prelude had been written in December 1878, and on Christmas Day of that year, in celebration of his wife's birthday, it was played for the first time in Wagner's house, Wahnfried, by the Meiningen Orchestra, Wagner himself conducting.

During the Bayreuth Festival of 1882 *Parsifal* was given sixteen times. At the last of these performances, on the 19th August, Levi being taken ill during the first act, Wagner himself, unknown to anyone in the theatre, took charge of the performance from the Transformation Scene to the end of the first act.

The story of *Parsifal* is one of those associated with the old legend of the Holy Grail. The Castle of the Grail is Monsalvat, standing on a mountain in Spain, where are gathered together a company of holy Knights who guard two precious objects — the Spear with which Christ's side was pierced on the Cross, and the Cup from which He drank at the Last Supper, and that received His blood while on the Cross. Only the perfectly pure in heart can be of this chosen company, whose mission it is to do good in the world of men through the miraculous powers conferred upon them by the Grail.

The crisis from which the opera takes its starting-point has occurred some time before our story opens. A Knight named Klingsor, whose ambition to be one of the Knights of the Grail had been frustrated by the incurable sinfulness of his heart, in his rage against the Brotherhood adopted the ways of magic; he created a beautiful garden and peopled it with lovely women, through whom he snared the souls of some of the weaker of the Knights. Amfortas, the son of the old Titurel who had built Monsalvat, one day took the sacred Spear with him to exorcise the magic of the garden, but he too succumbed — to the wiles of Kundry, who was in the service of Klingsor. The latter had thus been able to take possession of the Spear, with which he had dealt Amfortas a wound in the side for which no remedy has yet availed.

For a performance of the Prelude for the King of Bavaria at Munich in 1880 Wagner drafted an explanatory note, which, in Mr. Ellis's translation, runs thus:

" Love — Faith: — Hope? "

First theme: " Love."

" Take ye My body, take My blood, in token of our love! "
(Repeated in faint whispers by angel-voices.)
" Take ye My blood, My body take, in memory of Me! "

(Again repeated in whispers.)

Second theme: " Faith."

" Promise of redemption through faith. Firmly and stoutly faith declares itself, exalted, willing even in suffering. To the promise renewed Faith answers from the dimmest heights — as on the pinions of the snow-white dove — hovering downwards — usurping more and more the hearts of men, filling the world, the whole world of Nature, with the mightiest force, then glancing up again to heaven's vault as if appeased.

" But once more, from out the awe of solitude, throbs forth the cry of loving pity; the agony, the holy sweat of Olivet, the divine death-throes of Golgotha — the body pales, the blood flows forth, and glows now in the chalice with the heavenly glow of blessing, shedding on all that lives and languishes the grace of ransom won by Love. For him who — fearful rue for sin at heart — must quail before the godlike vision of the Grail, for Amfortas, sinful keeper of the halidom, we are made ready: will redemption heal the gnawing torments of his soul? Once more we hear the promise, and — we hope! "

The Prelude opens with the Love Feast motive in the strings and wood-wind:

The quotation here given, which constitutes the first six bars of
the Prelude, really contains three distinct themes — that of the
Love Feast proper, that of Suffering (which we have marked A),
and that of the Spear (marked B). Further repetitions of No. 1,
interspersed with broad chords and arpeggios, are followed by the
theme of the Holy Grail, which the reader will recognise as the
Dresden Amen:

Then comes the theme of Faith, given out in ringing tones by the
trumpets:

This and the Grail theme are repeated, and No. 3 is developed at
some length and in various colours.

Just when we are beginning to fear that the repetitions are becoming excessive Wagner introduces a skilful touch; he changes
the time from 6/4 to 9/4, and by the prolongation of certain chords
creates a totally different system of rhythm and accent. The contrast thus afforded makes it safer for him then to introduce the
theme once more in the original 6/4 metre. The remainder of the
Prelude is devoted to metamorphoses of No. 1, the most agonising
expression being drawn from the motive of Suffering and from
that of the Spear. In its own way the Prelude to *Parsifal* is the
most expressive piece of music that had ever been written until
that time.

It is sometimes said in the analytical programme books that
Wagner described the Prelude as symbolising " Love — Faith —
Hope." If the reader, however, will glance again at the note that

Wagner himself wrote for King Ludwig, he will see that the Hope is followed by a note of interrogation. Wagner does not mean to imply that the Prelude fulfils the hope, but only that it suggests the possibility of it — a possibility to be resolved in the coming drama. And on referring to the score of the Prelude as it occurs in the opera, not in the arrangements for concert purposes, the reader will see that it too ends, as it were, with a question mark; in the eighth bar before the end, just as we are expecting that the music will settle down upon the tonic A flat chord, the melody soars upwards and upwards over a harmony that is left in doubt until the very end, the Prelude coming to a finish with the chord of the dominant seventh still unresolved.

When the curtain rises we see a forest — solemn and shady but not gloomy — in the domain of the Grail. On the left is a road ascending to the Castle. At the back the ground sinks down to a lake. Asleep under a tree are Gurnemanz — an elderly but vigorous man — and two young Esquires. From the left, as though from the Castle, comes a solemn morning reveille in the trombones; the theme is that of the Love Feast (No. 1). Gurnemanz wakes and rouses the Esquires; as they spring to their feet we hear the Dresden Amen in the rich tones of the trumpets and trombones behind the scenes. Gurnemanz and the Esquires kneel and silently offer up the morning prayer, the orchestra giving out very softly the motive of Faith (No. 3), which is succeeded once more by the theme of the Grail (No. 2).

The King (Amfortas) is expected, and Gurnemanz bids the Esquires prepare the bath; at the mention of the King we hear the typical Amfortas motive:

Two Knights enter to announce the coming of the litter with the King. Gurnemanz accosts them; he hopes that the herb that the Knight Gawain has obtained with difficulty has brought the King some solace. The Knights tell him that the hoped-for remedy has had no effect, and that Amfortas is in more grievous pain than ever; " sleepless from pain past bearing, he bade us quick prepare the bath." Gurnemanz sinks his head sadly, and over the motive of the Pure Fool in the orchestra:

(5)

declares that they are fools thus to look for material remedies when only one thing and one man can heal Amfortas. The others ask who is this mysterious one, but Gurnemanz turns aside and evasively orders them to see to the bath.

The two Esquires have gone to the background; looking to the right they announce that the " wild rider " is coming. Rushing figures and a rhythm as of galloping:

(6)

are heard in the orchestra as the Esquires excitedly describe the fury of the ride of Kundry on the " Devil's mare," and as they speak of the wild woman flinging herself off her steed the orchestra gives out a wild, uncanny motive associated with Kundry and her mad laughter:

She rushes in almost reeling. Around her looped-up robe is a girdle of snake-skin with long ends. Her black hair hangs down in loose locks; her complexion is a deep reddish-brown; her black and piercing eyes sometimes flash wildly, but more often remain fixed and staring like the eyes of the dead.

This Kundry is a character so enigmatical that it is difficult to explain her in words. There is something in her of Herodias, something of Gundryggia, the messenger who serves the heroes in some of the northern sagas, something also of the Prakriti of *The Victors*. More or less unconsciously she is half good, half evil. She is devoted to the service of the Grail, yet Klingsor can use her for his own evil ends. Both the conception and the musical treatment of such a character would have been impossible to any genius less stupendous than that of Wagner.

Kundry staggers up to Gurnemanz and forces a small crystal vial into his hand, ejaculating, " Here! Take it! Balsam. . . ." She has brought it " from farther hence than thy thought can fly " ; and should this fail, Arabia holds nothing more for the healing of Amfortas. " Ask no further; I am weary," she moans, and throws herself on the ground. Gurnemanz turns from her to greet a train of Esquires and Knights that now enters with the litter on which Amfortas lies. While the train is coming upon the stage Gurnemanz breaks out into a cry of grief over " the proudest flower of manhood faded, the master of the conquering race

to his own sickness bound a slave! " And we hear in the orchestra
the broad motive of the Knights of the Grail:

which will be recognised as a variant of the theme of Faith (No. 3).

The litter having been set down, Amfortas raises himself slightly,
and, over the grievous Amfortas motive, speaks of the beauty and
solace of the morning light after his night of pain; while in the
orchestra we hear the exquisite theme associated with the Wood:

He calls for Gawain, and is told that the Knight, finding that the
herb he brought had only deceived their hopes, has set out again
upon his quest. Amfortas fears that he may fall into the snares of
Klingsor, and then expresses his own faith in the Deliverer that has
been promised — the one who has been " made wise by pity, the
Blameless Fool." Gurnemanz hands him Kundry's vial and begs
him to try the balsam. Whence came it? asks Amfortas, and before
Gurnemanz can answer, the orchestra gives the answer with the
motive that typifies Kundry's passion for service:

At Gurnemanz's suggestion Amfortas takes the vial that Kundry
has brought; he thanks her, but, still prostrated on the ground,

she almost sullenly rejects his thanks and bids him go to the bath. The litter moves away, and the stage clears, except for Gurnemanz, Kundry, and four Esquires. The young men look with an unfavourable eye on Kundry; to them she is merely a sort of wild beast with a touch of the witch about it; they fear that she will work some evil upon the King.

Gurnemanz defends her; he tells them of all her services to the Brotherhood — how she acts as messenger between Monsalvat and the Knights who are fighting in distant lands, how she is always ready to serve, and never asks for even a word of thanks. The Esquires are not convinced; to them she is simply a heathen and a sorceress. Gurnemanz explains that perhaps she lies under a curse; she may be expiating the sins committed in a former life. At any rate, she is now doing her best to make atonement by service among the Knights. He has to admit, however, that often misfortune has come upon the Brotherhood while she has been away, and the motive of Klingsor's Magic in the orchestra:

(11) Lento.

tells us that on these absences she is helping him to carry out his evil plans. Titurel, when he built the Castle, had found her lying benumbed under a thicket; and it was thus that Gurnemanz himself lately found her about the time that the misfortune of the loss of the Spear and the wounding of Amfortas had come upon them. Turning to Kundry, he asks her where she was then, and why she withheld her help; but she only mutters, " I never help! "

The Esquires suggest that if Kundry is so devoted to the Brotherhood, she might be sent to find the missing Spear; but Gurnemanz replies that that is beyond her; no one knows the way. While the orchestra plays again and again upon the poignant motives of Suffering and the Spear (No. 1A and No. 1B), Gurnemanz pours out a lament over the loss of the Spear, which was torn from Amfortas's hand while he was lost in the embrace of a beautiful woman. At the King's cry Gurnemanz had rushed forward, only to see Klingsor flying with the Spear, mocking the King with his laughter. In the King's side was a burning wound that since that day has never closed.

All are now seated under a great tree, the Esquires being grouped round Gurnemanz, who, at their request, tells what he knows of Klingsor. First comes the story of how the messengers from heaven long ago descended, bearing with them the Grail and the Spear, which they gave into the keeping of Titurel. An important new theme:

is heard at this point in the orchestra. It is a little difficult to find a title for it, and various commentators refer to it under different names. Here we will think of it as the Miracle motive, meaning by that the miraculous bringing of the Grail and the Spear to Monsalvat. In the final pages of the score the theme is more particularly associated with the recovery of the Spear through Parsifal.

Titurel, Gurnemanz continues, had built a sanctuary for the precious relics, and founded the Order of Knights to which only the pure of heart could be admitted. To one who would have joined it, however, admission had been denied — Klingsor. This Knight, unable to tame his lusts, had in desperation mutilated his

body, thinking thereby to qualify for admission to the Order.
It was not so, however, and Titurel drove him scornfully from
Monsalvat.

Then Klingsor's heart was filled with rage; he learned that the
deed he had wrought upon himself had endowed him with command
over the powers of magic, and these powers he now used to compass the destruction of the Order. He turned the desert into a
beautiful garden, in which he placed the fairest women to lure the
Knights from virtue. Many Knights had thus been lost; and when
Titurel, finding age advancing upon him, surrendered his office
to his son Amfortas, the latter burned with zeal to crush this
plague. The sad outcome of his effort they know — Amfortas
himself fell, the Spear was ravished from him, and as the Spear
gives Klingsor power over the Brotherhood, he hopes by means
of it to seize the Grail also. Two important new motives make
their appearance during this narrative — that of Klingsor:

and that of the Flower Maidens (No. 19 below). When Gurnemanz
speaks of the fall of Amfortas, the orchestra, by the use of the
Kundry motive (No. 7), hints to us who was the woman who
accomplished his downfall.

During the telling of this story Kundry has frequently turned
round in passionate disquiet. She is dimly aware, and is tortured
by the knowledge, of her own dual nature, and of her servitude to
Klingsor when he has put his enchantment on her.

Gurnemanz continues with his story. The repentant Amfortas
had bent in agony before the sanctuary and asked for a sign of

redemption; a holy radiance had poured from the Grail, and one who appeared in a vision had spoken these words:

> " Made wise through pity,
> The Blameless Fool,
> Wait for him;
> My chosen is he."

Gurnemanz sings this message to the motive of the Pure Fool (No. 5), and the strain is taken up and given out with exquisite effect in four-part harmony by the Esquires.

Cries are heard from the direction of the lake, and Gurnemanz and the four Esquires start to their feet and look round in alarm. A wounded wild swan, followed by Knights and others, flies brokenly across from the lake and sinks heavily to the ground. One of the Knights draws an arrow from its breast. Amfortas, it seems, had caught sight of it crossing the lake, and had hailed it as a good omen; then there came an arrow, and the swan had sunk mortally wounded. Among the crowd is a young man very simply clothed, and carrying a bow and arrows. He is dragged forward, and all point to him as the slayer of the swan. The young man, to the typical motive of Parsifal as Hero:

does not deny the charge.

Gurnemanz reads him a moving lecture on the sin of slaying the gentle, trusting creatures of the forest, and as he points to the bleeding and stiffening body and the glazing eye of the swan, the young man is so affected that he breaks his bow and throws the arrows away. He does not *know* how or why what he has done is wrong, but he *feels* that it is wrong; pity has come upon him, and we hear in the orchestra for the first time the Pity motive:

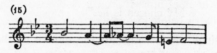

that will be put to such touching uses later. It will be seen to be derived from the final part of the Love Feast motive (No. 1).

(Wagner was at all times a great lover of animals, and in his later years he was a passionate protester against vivisection. Gurnemanz's moving oration over the dead swan is in part an expression of Wagner's lifelong feeling about animals, in part a reminiscence of an incident in the life of the Buddha, where the wounding of a swan stirs the Buddha to teach compassion to the world.)

Not only does not the young stranger know that he has done wrong, but it appears, from his answers to Gurnemanz's questions, that he does not know whence he has come, who is his father, or what his own name is. Turning wearily and contemptuously from this dullard, Gurnemanz orders the Esquires to take the dead swan away. Only Gurnemanz and Parsifal remain, with Kundry still prostrate at one side of the stage. The old man once more tries to find out if Parsifal knows anything. He replies that he knows that he has a mother, whose name is Heart of Sorrow (Herzeleide), and the orchestra gives out the moving Herzeleide theme:

He can tell Gurnemanz nothing more than that he and his mother once had their home in the wild woods, and that he himself made his bow and arrows.

Kundry, however, who has been stirring restlessly all this time, breaks in hoarsely upon the conversation. She knows more about Parsifal than he does himself. His father was Gamuret, who had been slain in battle before his son was born. His mother had brought the boy up in the desert, a stranger to arms, dreading a violent death for him also. But her care was in vain; Parsifal made primitive arms for himself, and one day, catching sight in the woods of what he describes as " glittering riders on beautiful animals " (presumably the Knights of the Grail) he had followed them, and, having lost them, had searched for them day and night through the wilderness, his bow and arrows defending him when wild beasts or giants or robbers had threatened him. This narration is accompanied by the Gallop motive (No. 6) and the Parsifal motive (No. 14).

Kundry breaks in upon the simple boy's enthusiasm with the announcement that his mother is dead: " As I rode by I saw her dying; and, Fool, she sent thee, by me, her greeting." Half in sorrow, half in rage, Parsifal springs at Kundry and seizes her by the throat. Gurnemanz restrains him, and reproaches him for what, following the needless killing of the swan, seems to be the brutal violence of his nature. Parsifal is seized with a violent trembling, and falls fainting into the arms of Gurnemanz.

Kundry hastens away to a spring in the wood, whence she returns with water in a horn; she sprinkles Parsifal and hands him the water to drink. Gurnemanz thanks Kundry, but she only mutters, " Good do I never: only rest I long for: I am weary. To sleep! Oh that no one e'er might wake me! No! Not to sleep! Horrors seize upon me! " While Gurnemanz is attending to Parsifal she drags herself to a thicket in the wood, and the orchestra, by giving out the themes of Klingsor's Magic Power (No. 11) and of Klingsor himself (No. 13), tells us of the malign influence that is now overcoming her. She staggers behind the thicket, and for the remainder of the scene remains unnoticed.

Gurnemanz has gently placed Parsifal's arm round his own neck and his own arm round Parsifal's body, and he leads the boy along with slow steps as the orchestra gives out the motive of the Bells of Monsalvat:

The old man has been struck by the artlessness of the boy, and there seems to be an idea at the back of his mind that this stranger, in virtue of his innocence, may prove to be the Deliverer promised in the vision.

The pair are now supposed to walk through the wood to the Hall of the Grail. This illusion Wagner intended to be conveyed by means of moving scenery, though not all theatres have the apparatus for this; the wood gradually disappears and rock is seen; in the rock a gate opens through which the pair pass and become lost to sight for a time, later becoming visible again ascending a path. All the while the orchestra pours out the magnificent Transformation Music, that for a while has a march-like quality given to it by No. 17, but that later swells to a poignant climax as the heartrending theme of the Penitence of Amfortas is given out three times in succession, the last time with the utmost richness of colour of which the orchestra is capable:

As Gurnemanz and Parsifal come nearer to the Hall, the sound
of bells ceases, while six trombones behind the scenes give out
fortissimo the theme of the Love Feast (No. 1). At last the pair
come to a vast hall, surmounted by a great vaulted cupola, through
which alone the light enters.

Gurnemanz now means to put Parsifal to the test. " Give good
heed," he says, " and let me see, if thou art a Fool and pure, what
knowledge may be given to thee." Gurnemanz leaves Parsifal at
the side of the stage, and then, to music of the utmost splendour,
the Knights of the Grail enter for the solemn Feast. Two long
covered tables are so arranged that, running in parallel lines from
back to front, the centre of the stage is left open. On the tables
there are only cups. The Knights, entering from the background
through a great door, come forward in two files in solemn procession, followed by the Esquires. At last the Knights place themselves at the tables. Amfortas is borne in on a couch, preceded
by four Esquires carrying a shrine wrapped in a purple-red cover,
and is placed on a raised couch under a canopy in the centre background, while a chorus of youths' voices floats down from the mid-
height of the dome with the heartrending theme of Amfortas's
Penitence (No. 18).

In front of Amfortas's couch is an antique oblong marble table,
like an altar, upon which the Esquires place the covered shrine.
From the extreme height of the dome steals an exquisite four-part
harmony of soprano and boys' voices singing the theme of Faith
(No. 3), and after a momentary pause (all the Knights having
taken their seats at the tables) from the extreme background comes
the voice of old Titurel, as if from a tomb. Titurel asks if he must
die before the coming of the Deliverer. Amfortas, half raising
himself on his couch, breaks into passionate self-accusation; he
implores his father to serve the office, and to live and let him die.

"In the grave I lie," Titurel replies, "by the Saviour's grace; too feeble am I to serve Him. Serve thou, and so thy guilt atone. Uncover the Grail!"

Amfortas tries to prevent the Esquires from removing the cover, and once more he breaks out into a grievous lament, the music of which is of heartbreaking poignancy. "Have mercy!" he cries at last. "Have mercy! Thou God of pity, oh have mercy! Take back my birthright, so Thou but heal me, that holy I may die now, pure for Thy presence!" He sinks back as though unconscious, and from the middle height comes floating softly down, in four-part harmony in the boys' and youths' voices, the enigmatic theme of the Pure Fool.

Once more the voice of Titurel is heard bidding them unveil the Grail. Amfortas raises himself slowly and with difficulty on his couch, and the Esquires, having unveiled the shrine, take from it the Grail (an antique crystal cup); this also they uncover and place before Amfortas. He bows devoutly before the cup in silent prayer.

The Hall grows darker and darker, and from the mysterious heights come the voices of the invisible choir exhorting the Knights, to the motive of the Love Feast (No. 1), to take the Body and drink the Blood in love's remembrance. Suddenly a dazzling ray of light from above strikes upon the chalice, which glows with a deepening purple, shedding a soft radiance on them all. Amfortas, his expression transfigured, raises the Grail on high and waves it gently to every side, consecrating the bread and wine. He sets the Grail down again, and as the semi-darkness that has filled the Hall disperses, the glow of the chalice slowly fades away. The Esquires enclose it in its shrine and veil it as before. Gradually daylight fills the Hall once more. Then follows the solemn ceremony of the partaking of the bread and wine, which are served by the Esquires, while the clear youthful voices in the dome sing the story of the Last Supper.

Gurnemanz has seated himself with the other Knights for the communion, keeping a place empty beside him. He makes a sign to Parsifal to come and sit with him, but the boy remains as he has

been from the commencement of the scene, motionless at the side
of the stage, as if completely entranced. The Knights exhort each
other to virtue and brotherhood in the name of the Bread and Wine,
and after the voices have floated up to the heights to the strain of
the Grail motive, the Knights rise, pace forward from both sides,
and solemnly embrace each other.

The brief ecstasy of Amfortas has died away. He bows his head
and presses his hand to his wound, and the movements of the
Esquires show that the wound has broken out afresh. They tend
him lovingly and help him to his litter, which they bear out of the
Hall, accompanied by the shrine. The Knights follow in solemn
procession as at the commencement of the scene, the orchestra
pouring out the while an exquisite tissue of sound, made up of
the Faith motive, the Processional motive (No. 17), the Lament
of Amfortas (No. 18), and other themes.

When the whole company have left the Hall, Gurnemanz turns
to Parsifal, who is still standing on the same spot, the only movement he has made being a convulsive pressure of his heart during
Amfortas's cry of agony and remorse. He stands motionless, as if
petrified. Gurnemanz goes up to him in ill-humour and asks him if
he understood what he had seen. Parsifal, without speaking, again
clutches his heart and shakes his head. Gurnemanz, disappointed
and greatly irritated, reproaches him with being after all no more
than a fool, opens a narrow side door, and bids him go on his way.
Pushing Parsifal out and angrily closing the door after him, he
himself follows the Knights out by the other door. A single alto
voice from the heights sings the theme of the Pure Fool; other
voices from above float down with the theme of the Grail; the bells
peal out once more, and the curtain falls. The whole scene is in
many respects the most moving ever put upon the stage, while the
music is of a heartrending pathos and beauty.

The second act opens with an impetuous orchestral introduction,
woven chiefly out of the two Klingsor motives and that of Kundry's
Laughter; the piano arrangement gives no idea of the power and
the colour of the music as it foams out from the orchestra in the
theatre.

The curtain having risen, we see the inner keep of Klingsor's magic tower, with steps at the side leading to the edge of the battlements. All around are magical implements and necromantic apparatus; on the projecting wall, before a metal mirror, Klingsor is seated. " The time is come! " he ejaculates. His magic power has lured to his Castle the Fool, who is now drawing near in childish delight. Klingsor comes down towards the centre of the stage, and at the back a bluish vapour arises. He again seats himself before his magical apparatus, and with mysterious gestures calls into the gulf below, " Arise! To me! Thy master calls thee, nameless woman! First of witches! Rose of Hades! Herodias wert thou, and what more? Gundryggia there, Kundry here! To me! Come hither, Kundry! Thy master calls: appear! "

The rigid form of Kundry, who seems asleep, rises up in the bluish light. A convulsive movement passes through her as if she were awakening, and as the orchestra throws out *fortissimo* the descending line of her motive (No. 7) she gives a frightful cry, followed by a loud wail that gradually subsides into a low, terrified moaning. Klingsor reproaches her with having been again among the Brotherhood, where she is regarded merely as a brute beast. He gloats over the power he exercises over the Knights through her, and tells her that today the one he fears most must be met — " one strong as fools are strong."

Kundry struggles against this subjection of her other nature to the magician, but in vain; he reminds her of the secret of his power over her — the mutilation that has made him, unlike the others, insensible to her witchery. He pours out his venom upon her, the Knights, and even himself. One desire alone possesses him now — the subjugation of the proud ones who have cast him out in scorn. He has brought the King down, and soon the Grail will be his own. Kundry bewails the weakness of men and her own part in the destruction of them, and longs for release from her doom; but Klingsor bids her make ready for the temptation of the boy who is now approaching.

He mounts to the wall of the tower, and, leaning out, blows a horn that summons his knights and warders. For Kundry's benefit

he describes the fight below, how the fearless boy has wrested
Ferris's sword from him, and with it struck fiercely into the swarm
of defenders, and of the execution he does there. Kundry, unable
to resist the will of Klingsor, gives a shriek and disappears. The
blue light is now extinguished.

Klingsor, still watching the fight, gloats over Parsifal's mal-
treatment of the degenerate Knights whom, having ruined, he
hates as he does everything. The victorious Parsifal, we hear, now
stands laughing on the ramparts, looking down like an amazed
child into the garden. Klingsor turns to call Kundry, but not perceiving her, congratulates her on already having got to work; then
with a last sinister look towards Parsifal, whose coming doom
he prophesies, he sinks rapidly with the whole tower, in place of
which a magic garden instantly rises.

The garden, which is of tropical luxuriance, occupies the whole
of the stage. Upon the ramparts at the back, Parsifal is seen gazing
down in astonishment. Lovely maidens rush in from all sides,
from the palace as well as from the garden, at first singly, then in
numbers; they are clothed in light, soft-coloured veils, that appear
to have been thrown over them hastily as if they had been startled
out of sleep. In the orchestra we hear the motive of Parsifal as
Hero (No. 14). Then the excitement is worked up in both orchestra and chorus.

The maidens are at first alarmed at this new-comer who has so
grievously maltreated their lovers, but finding that Parsifal, who
has come a little farther into the garden, means them no harm,
and is, indeed, more astonished than they, they take courage again.
Gradually their mood changes from wonder to gaiety; they break
out into merry laughter, and as Parsifal approaches them they
begin to exercise their charms upon him. Some, who have left the
stage for the moment, come back completely dressed in flowers,
and looking like flowers themselves. While these maidens press
round the boy, the remainder leave the stage to adorn themselves
in the same fashion.

Dancing and playing round Parsifal, the Flower Maidens sing
an enticing strain:

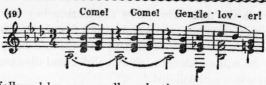

that is followed by one equally seductive:

Out of these elements a chorus of ravishing beauty is built up.

Parsifal, too innocent to understand the meaning of their seductions, and half amused and half angry at their importunities, is about to flee when from a neighbouring hedge of flowers the voice of Kundry strikes in with a long-drawn-out cry of " Parsifal! " The effect in the theatre of this entry of the solo voice after the long chorus is indescribable. The name sets Parsifal's memory stirring; he remembers that once his mother called him so. He pauses in perplexity.

Kundry comes forward gradually, dismisses the Flower Maidens, whom she bids go and attend to the wounded, and when Parsifal once more looks timidly round to the hedge from which the voice came he sees a young and beautiful woman reclining on a couch of flowers, in a light, gauzy, fantastic garment of Arabian style. She has waited long for him, the son of Gamuret, she says; and then, in a long monologue of exquisite beauty, largely based upon the Herzeleide motive (No. 16), she tells him of the mother's loving care for her babe and of her death in sorrow when he left her in search of adventure.

Parsifal, who has listened intently and earnestly, is overwhelmed; crushed with grief, he sinks at Kundry's feet and breaks out into a torrent of self-reproach. Kundry promises him solace from his grief, and, still reclining, she bends over Parsifal's head, gently touches his brow, and winds her arm about his neck. She

invites him to learn the rapture of love that Gamuret once learned
when he burned for Herzeleide. His mother, she says, sends him
her blessing, and " greets thee with this first kiss of love." Bending
her head over him completely, she joins her lips to his in a long
kiss, and during the silence that ensues the orchestra gives out very
softly the theme of Klingsor's Magic.

Suddenly Parsifal starts up with a gesture of utter terror. His
demeanour shows that some fearful change has taken place in him.
He presses his hands hard against his heart as if to quiet an unbearable pain; then he cries loudly, " Amfortas! The Spear wound! "
At last he understands. Illumination has come to him, and he knows
the meaning of the tragedy and of the anguish of Amfortas. In
himself he feels the wound of Amfortas burning; he knows now
the meaning of sin, the despair of the Brotherhood, the longing
for the unspotted Deliverer. Throwing himself despairingly on
his knees he cries loudly, " Redeemer! Saviour! Lord of Grace!
How for my sin can I atone? "

Kundry returns to the assault, but with each exercise of her
wiles the now illuminated Parsifal recognises the arts by which
Amfortas was ensnared: " Aye, thus she called him! This was the
voice, and this was the glance; truly I know it now, what torment
its smiling menace brought him! The lips too, aye, so thrilled they
him; so bent this neck above him, so boldly rose her head, so
fluttered her looks as in laughter; so twined she this arm round
his neck; so fawningly smiled she on him. . . . His soul's salvation
for that one kiss he lost! " Springing to his feet, he pushes Kundry
violently from him.

She appeals now to his pity: " If e'er thy heart can feel another's
sorrow, then let it suffer for mine now! " The latter words are sung
to a phrase:

(21)

that hardly constitutes a motive, and to which no satisfactory name
can be given, though we shall meet with it again in the third act.
For endless ages, she tells Parsifal, she has waited for him — the

redeemer who has come so late, the redeemer whom once she re-
viled. In bitter self-torment she recalls her mocking of the Saviour
and the " one look " he had directed upon her, that tore her heart
in twain. From world to world she seeks him now in penitence and
the hope of redemption; and then, and then — " a sinner sinks
upon my bosom," and the old unearthly laughter breaks from her
once more. " Let me," she cries, " be with thee united, and though
by God and man cast forth, in thee be cleansed of sin and redeemed! "

" Eternally wouldst thou be damned with me," Parsifal replies,
" if but for one hour, unmindful of my mission, into thine arms
I gave me! " It is true that he has been sent for her salvation, but
she can be saved only by repenting of her old desire. The only
fountain that can wash her clean is that which he has seen rising in
the pure hearts of the Brotherhood. In wild exultation Kundry
reminds him that it was through her kiss that the secret of the
world's heart became revealed to him; in her arms he has become
a god. Love she shall have, redemption she shall have, he replies,
if she will show him the way to Amfortas. At this she breaks out
furiously; never shall he find the King; let the fallen one go down
to ruin, him whom she tempted and derided; " he fell by his own
Spear! "

Once more she beseeches Parsifal's pity and love if only for an
hour; then she would show him the way to Amfortas. She tries to
embrace him, but he repulses her violently. Recovering herself
with a furious cry, she calls towards the background, telling them
to bar every passage and seize upon this miscreant; " for fleddest
thou from here, and foundest all the ways of the world, the one
that thou seekest, that path thy foot shall never find; each track,
each pathway that leads thee from Kundry, thus I curse beneath
thy feet! " " Thou whom I know," she shouts to Klingsor, " take
him for thine own! "

Klingsor appears on the castle walls and brandishes a Spear at
Parsifal. " To fitting weapon shalt thou fall! " he cries; " the Fool
I win me now with his master's Spear! " He hurls the Spear,
which remains suspended over Parsifal's head. Parsifal seizes it,

and holding it above his head cries, " With this sign thy magic is
routed. As the wound shall be closed by the Spear that dealt it, in
rack and in ruin thy lying pomp shall it lay! " He seizes the Spear,
makes the sign of the Cross, and the castle collapses as if by an
earthquake. The garden at once withers to a desert; the ground
is strewn with faded flowers. Kundry sinks down with a cry. As
Parsifal is hastening away he pauses, turns to Kundry from the
top of the ruined wall, and says gravely, " Thou knowest where
thou mayest find me when thou wilt! " As he disappears, Kundry
raises herself a little and gazes after him as the curtain falls.

The wonderfully expressive slow orchestral introduction to the
third act describes by anticipation what will be more fully disclosed
to us later — the weariness and despair that have settled upon
the community of Knights, which is symbolised in a motive which
we may call that of Desolation:

which is followed by the Straying motive:

The " Straying " must be taken in a double sense; it signifies not only Parsifal's physical wanderings in search of Amfortas, but the confusion that has reigned in his soul. Later in the Introduction we hear a new and more poignant version of the Pure Fool theme.

The curtain having risen, we see a pleasant landscape in the domain of the Grail; it is springtime. In the background are gentle slopes covered with flowers. The foreground represents the forest; at one side is a spring; opposite this is a modest hermit's hut, built against a mass of rock. The time is early morning.

Gurnemanz, now a very old man, and dressed as a hermit with the tunic of a Knight of the Grail, comes out of the hut and listens. The sound of groaning has caught his ear; and the motive of Klingsor's Magic in the orchestra apprises us that the groaning is associated with Kundry. Gurnemanz finds the strange creature in a thorn thicket at the side of the stage. He draws her out, stiff and lifeless, and bears her to a grassy mound close by. He cries to her to " waken to the Spring "; but she is so stiff and cold that he fears that this time she is dead. But gradually the numbed body comes back to life, and as she awakens and opens her eyes she utters a piercing cry. She is now in the rough garb of a penitent, as in the first act, but her face is paler; all the wildness has gone out of her look and her demeanour.

After a long look at Gurnemanz she rises, arranges her clothing and hair, and at once humbly betakes herself to service like a maid. Her one cry at her awakening is the only sound Kundry makes throughout the whole of the act, apart from two hoarse ejaculations of " Service, service! " when Gurnemanz hints at his deserving thanks for having awakened her from her deathly sleep.

Her toil will be light now, he tells her, for the Brotherhood is almost broken up; no messages now are sent and so no messenger is required; each Knight seeks his own simple food in the herbs and roots of the forest. Kundry, going to the spring with a pitcher, points out to Gurnemanz that someone is approaching. We hear in the orchestra the motive of Parsifal as Hero (No. 14), and soon

Parsifal himself appears. Kundry, having filled the pitcher, goes into the hut. Parsifal is clothed in black armour. With closed helmet and lowered spear he comes forward slowly, hesitatingly and dreamily, his head bowed as if in utter weariness, and seats himself on the little mound.

Gurnemanz, unable to draw speech from him, finally tells him that, though his vow may impose silence on him, none the less it is his duty on this holy day, Good Friday morn, to lay aside his armour and his weapons. Thereupon Parsifal raises himself in silence, thrusts the Spear into the ground, lays shield and sword beneath it, removes his helmet and places it by his weapons, then kneels before the Spear in prayer. To Kundry, who has again emerged from the hut, Gurnemanz softly says, " Dost thou recognise him? It is he who dealt our swan its death." With a slight inclination of her head Kundry signifies that she too knows him again. Gurnemanz has recognised the Spear also, and, deeply moved, he hails the holy day that has dawned.

After his prayer Parsifal rises slowly, looks around him tranquilly, recognises Gurnemanz, and gently holds out his hand to him in greeting. He tells the old man of his long wandering through terror and suffering and illusion in search of Amfortas, " him whose grievous lament I once heard in foolish wonder, and for whose healing I now deem myself appointed." Parsifal has wandered wide and endured woes innumerable, and often he has been filled with despair; many wounds have been inflicted upon him in battle, for there he would not use the Spear, which he has always carried unprofaned at his side.

Gurnemanz breaks out into a transport of gratitude for this grace, and tells Parsifal that if indeed a curse has been lying upon him until now it is removed, for he is at last in the Grail's domain — he whom they have so long expected. He tells Parsifal of the misery that has come upon them all: how Amfortas, in despair, refused to fulfil the holy office, longing only for death; how, deprived of their divine food, the Knights' strength had ebbed away and they were no longer able to do the service on earth to which they had been appointed; and how Gurnemanz himself came to dwell in silence in the forest, himself awaiting death now that his aged lord Titurel has died. This recital is accompanied in part by No. 22, in part by a second motive of Desolation:

(24)

Parsifal breaks out into passionate self-reproach that all these evils should have fallen upon the Brotherhood through his own foolishness and blindness. He seems about to faint; Gurnemanz supports him and lowers him into a sitting position on the mound. Kundry runs for water, but when she offers it to Parsifal she is gently repulsed by Gurnemanz, who declares that " the holy spring itself must refresh our pilgrim." At this point we hear in the orchestra a new theme — the motive of Benediction (called by some writers the Baptism motive):

(25)

They lead Parsifal gently to the spring, where they divest him of the remainder of his armour.

They must now go to the Castle, says Gurnemanz, to attend the solemn death-rites of Titurel; in the orchestra we hear the impressive theme of the Burial of Titurel:

(26)

This day, says Gurnemanz, the long-neglected office shall once more be served. Kundry bathes the feet of Parsival, while Gurnemanz, taking some water in his hands, sprinkles Parsifal's head. Kundry draws a golden vial from her bosom, part of the contents of which she pours over Parsifal's feet, which she dries with her hair. The remainder of the contents of the vial Gurnemanz pours over Parsifal's head, and gives him a blessing. Parsifal takes some water from the fragrant spring, bends over the kneeling Kundry, sprinkles her head, and says, " Baptised be thou, and trust in the Redeemer! " Kundry bows her head to the earth and seems to weep passionately.

Turning away, Parsifal gazes in tranquil ecstasy at the forest and the fields that are now glowing in the morning light, and over lulling harmonies the oboe gives out the exquisite theme of Nature Redeemed:

(27)
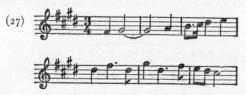

This marks the commencement of the inexpressibly lovely episode that is known in the concert-room as the Good Friday Magic music. Parsifal speaks of the supreme beauty of the fields and flowers and the benediction that appears to rest upon them, and Gurnemanz assures him that this is the magic of Good Friday, the day on which all creation rejoices in the Saviour's sacrifice and love. Kundry looks up into Parsifal's eyes in mute entreaty; he bends over her and kisses her gently on the forehead.

Bells are heard in the distance, gradually increasing in tone, and blended with them is the motive of Titurel's Burial. Gurnemanz, who has brought his Grail Knight's mantle from the hut, helps Kundry to invest Parsifal with it; the latter solemnly takes up the Spear, and, with Kundry, follows Gurnemanz out slowly.

The grief-laden theme of the Burial of Titurel is now worked up by the orchestra into a magnificent slow march, during which another Transformation is effected, as in the first act, but this time in the reverse direction. The wood slowly vanishes and rocks appear. The bells become louder and louder, and at last the rock walls open, showing the Hall of the Grail as in Act 1, but without the tables. The Hall is faintly lighted. From one side comes a procession of Knights bearing Titurel's coffin, from the other side another procession carrying Amfortas in the litter, preceded by the covered shrine containing the Grail.

The Knights sing a moving lament over their old King, and then, turning to Amfortas, who has been placed on the couch behind the altar of the Grail, before which the coffin has been set down, they urgently implore him once more to perform his office; but raising himself wearily on his couch, he cries out again for death. The coffin is opened, and at the sight of Titurel's body all break into a cry of woe. To a strain of the utmost solemnity in the orchestra:

(28)

(29)

Amfortas cries in anguish to his dead father, imploring him to intercede for him with the Saviour in heaven. His music is of almost unbearable beauty. Pressing round him, the Knights still more urgently insist upon his uncovering the Grail. At last he springs up in despair, rushes among the Knights, who recoil in terror from him, tears open his garments and shows the bleeding wound, and cries to them to end his sufferings with their swords; then, he says, when the sinner is no more, the Grail will shine on them again.

By this time Parsifal, accompanied by Gurnemanz and Kundry, has entered unobserved. He advances and touches Amfortas's wound with the point of the Spear, saying, "One weapon only avails — only the Spear that dealt the wound can close it." Amfortas's face glows with rapture; he staggers, as if overcome with emotion, and Gurnemanz supports him. "Be whole, purified and absolved!" says Parsifal, "for now I hold thy office. Blessed be thy suffering, for it has taught pity's highest might and wisdom's purest power to the timid Fool."

He steps towards the centre and raises the Spear high before him; all gaze in rapture on it. Ascending the altar steps, he takes the Grail from its shrine and kneels before it in silent prayer; the chalice begins to glow with a soft light, while the stage becomes darker and a stronger light comes from above. The Knights and the voices in the dome join in a song of praise and gratitude: "O highest holy marvel! Salvation to the Saviour!" A ray of light falls upon the Grail, which now glows at its brightest. A white dove descends from the dome and hovers over Parsifal's head. Kundry, gazing upwards at Parsifal, slowly sinks lifeless to the ground before him. Amfortas and Gurnemanz kneel in homage before Parsifal, who waves the Grail in blessing over the Brotherhood, and the curtain falls to the mystical strains of the theme of Faith

(No. 3), the Grail motive (No. 2), and finally the Love Feast motive (No. 1).

It was Wagner's wish that *Parsifal* should never be given elsewhere but in Bayreuth; owing to the solemnity of the subject, he felt that it required a special stage, a special occasion, a special atmosphere, and a special audience. "Never," he wrote to King Ludwig in 1882, "shall *Parsifal* be produced in any other theatre for the amusement of the public."

To the great impresario, Angelo Neumann, who was the first to popularise *The Ring* by taking it on tour throughout Europe, and to whom Wagner was under very great obligations, he wrote in 1881: "*Parsifal* is not to be performed anywhere but in Bayreuth, and this for interesting reasons, which (to give you an example) appeared so obvious to my illustrious benefactor the King of Bavaria, that he quite gave up the idea of a repetition of the Bayreuth performance in the Munich Theatre. How could I, in view of this fact, dispose of *Parsifal* in accordance with your proposal? [Neumann wanted to take this work also on tour.] Never can or may I allow it to be performed in other theatres."

Nevertheless, if we are to believe Neumann himself (and there seems no reason to doubt his story), Wagner did actually at one time as good as grant him permission to produce *Parsifal* elsewhere. In his *Reminiscences of Richard Wagner* Neumann tells us that when he was in Bayreuth in August 1882, arranging a fresh contract in connection with *The Ring,* Wagner, who at that time was a little out of tune with his Bayreuth surroundings, gave him a verbal promise that at their next meeting he would give him a contract for *Parsifal* also.

A day or two later Neumann called at Wahnfried, and after *The Ring* contract had been completed they turned to the *Parsifal* agreement, which stipulated that if Wagner should decide to allow the work to be given anywhere but at Bayreuth, the exclusive rights for all countries should be given to Neumann. Wagner sat down at the writing-desk with the pen in his hand; he remained for a while lost in thought, then turned round slowly to Neumann and said in a low voice, "Neumann, I have given you my promise, and if you hold me to it I will sign the agreement; but you would give me great pleasure if you would not press the point today. You have my word that the rights of producing *Parsifal* shall go to no one but you."

Neumann answered, " Master, when you tell me that I should be giving you a great pleasure it goes without saying that I am content with your word." " Then," he continues, " Wagner said with emphasis, ' Neumann, I thank you! ' and a strong pressure of the hand and a kiss closed one of the most difficult moments of my life. In the avenue leading to the house my son was waiting for me. I told him what had happened in this notable hour, and added, ' Carl, today, by renouncing *Parsifal*, I have given up millions.' ' Father,' my seventeen-year-old son replied, ' that Richard Wagner should thank you as he did is worth more to me than millions.' "

As early as 1901 Wagner's widow addressed to the German Reichstag a memorial praying that in the case of *Parsifal* the ordinary rule of the expiry of copyright thirty years after the author's death should not be operative. When the thirty years were nearly run out another appeal was made for the extension of the period, but without success. The copyright expired at the end of 1913, and in the first days of January 1914 *Parsifal* was performed in a number of European opera houses. Some time before then, however, the work had been performed at the Metropolitan Opera House, New York, in spite of Cosima Wagner's protest, the producers being protected by a legal technicality.

TWENTY-SIX years elapsed between the first conception of *The Ring of the Nibelung* and the completion of the gigantic work. During his Dresden period Wagner had become deeply interested in the Scandinavian, German, and Icelandic sagas. As usual with him, he dealt with the traditional material in a way of his own, selecting, dovetailing, piecing. His first attempt to reduce the colossal mass of material to a manageable dramatic form was a poem entitled *Siegfried's Death,* which he wrote in November 1848.

The Ring is often reproached with being longwinded and repetitive. There is some truth in the latter charge, and the reason for it is that Wagner wrote the poem of *The Ring* backwards, so to speak. *Siegfried's Death* virtually corresponds with the poem that we now know as *The Twilight of the Gods,* the last of the four evenings of *The Ring.* As it represents the culmination of the long action, the earlier incidents of the story have to be told to the audience through the mouths of the characters on the stage.

As the years went on, Wagner felt that not only was the subject too big for a single opera, but the work he had already written required to be led up to by another; so to *Siegfried's Death* he prefixed, in the summer of 1851, a second drama which he called at that time *Young Siegfried;* this corresponds to the present *Siegfried,* the third evening of *The Ring.* In the following year he renamed the two dramas already completed, and placed in front of them yet another, *The Valkyrie.* He still felt, however, that the action as presented on the stage was not as clear as it might be;

so in front of *The Valkyrie* he placed *The Rhinegold,* which he describes as a " Fore-Evening " to the three evenings proper of *The Ring.* A few copies of the complete poem were printed for private distribution in 1853.

The music was composed in the proper order of the dramas. *The Rhinegold* was written between 1853 and 1854, *The Valkyrie* between the summer of 1854 and the spring of 1856. In the autumn of the latter year he began work at the music of *Siegfried,* and by July 1857 had finished the first act and part of the second.

By this time it had become perfectly clear to Wagner that the ordinary German opera house was quite incapable of producing so difficult a work, and the old desire for a theatre of his own once more arose within him. Meanwhile, in order to keep himself before the public, he wrote what he thought were the more practicable operas of *Tristan* and *The Mastersingers,* and it was not until July 1865 that he cast his eyes upon *Siegfried* again. Once more he was interrupted, however, and the real resumption of work upon the second act dates from February 1869. *Siegfried* was finished by the autumn and work commenced upon *The Twilight of the Gods,* which, so far as the actual composition was concerned, was finished in February 1872, though the orchestration was not completed until November 1874.

Meanwhile, despairing of ever seeing the titanic work on the stage, Wagner had issued the poem to the general public in 1863, with a preface in which he expressed the hope that a German prince might some day be found who would be at once powerful enough and enlightened enough to realise this dream of the poet-musician.

A year after that, in May 1864, Wagner found his deliverer in the young King Ludwig of Bavaria. The association with the King, however, was not without its annoyances for Wagner. Ludwig's impatience to hear each of Wagner's new works was so great that he could not wait until the gigantic scheme of *The Ring* was completed and a special theatre had been built for the work; and, very much against Wagner's will, *The Rhinegold* was performed at Munich on the 22nd September, 1869, and *The Valkyrie* on the 26th June, 1870. The other two operas of *The Ring* did not see the light until August 1876, when the whole work was performed for the first time at Bayreuth under Hans Richter.

It is impossible, in the space at our disposal here, to go into details with regard to the various sources from which Wagner derived his material, or to show how he altered and condensed the various sagas; but the reader who wishes to pursue the subject further may profitably read *The Fall of the Nibelung*, done into English by Margaret Armour, *The Volsunga Saga*, translated by William Morris and E. Magnusson, and William Morris's epic poem *Sigurd the Volsung*.

The central motive of the drama as Wagner has conceived it is Wotan's love for power. To consolidate his power he has had a great castle, Valhalla, built for him by the giants. For the ultimate payment of the giants' wage he has trusted more or less to luck. When the time arrives for payment it comes about, in ways that will be described in the following analysis, that he has to satisfy them with gold stolen from the Rhinemaidens by Alberich, upon which, when it was taken from him in turn by Wotan, Alberich has laid a curse. From the gold Alberich has had made for himself a ring that confers on its possessor power over the world; and this ring passes into the possession of one of the giants, Fafner.

Wotan's problem, during the three later evenings of *The Ring*, is to ensure that the ring will come into the possession of someone who will not use it, as Alberich would were he to regain possession of it, for the destruction of the gods. The devious ways by which this is brought about are best told by a straightforward account of *The Ring* as it is set upon the stage in four consecutive evenings.

The Prelude to *The Rhinegold* is of an originality that must have staggered people who heard it for the first time in 1869. It consists of nothing else but a persistent sounding, for 136 bars, of the tonality of E flat. It is meant to suggest the Rhine; and the idea is first of all of a sort of ground-swell, then of heavy waves, then of lighter and still lighter waves. First the double basses give out a deep-down and long-held E flat, over which, later, the bassoons impose a B flat. Later still the horns give out softly over this open fifth the following theme:

The movement of the waters seems to become gradually more rapid, and No. 1 becomes metamorphosed into what, in the later scenes of the work, does duty as the typical Rhine motive:

The sense of irresistible motion goes on increasing as the theme is still further altered rhythmically and taken up into higher and higher registers of the orchestras.

At about the 130th bar the curtain rises, showing us the bottom of the Rhine. In the upper part of the scene the river seems to be flowing restlessly, while towards the bottom, for a space about the height of a man above the stage, its waters resolve themselves into a mist. Craggy rocks jut up everywhere. A greenish twilight, lighter above than below, reigns in the water. When the curtain rises a Rhinemaiden, Woglinde, is seen swimming gracefully round a rock in the centre of the stage, the pointed summit of which is visible in the lighter part of the river. When she begins to sing, the music modulates for the first time; and the sudden change to the key of A flat after 136 bars of E flat is electrifying:

Woglinde is joined by her sister Wellgunde, and to the pair of them comes a little later the third of their number, Flosshilde. The three tease and chase each other in sport, darting like fish from rock to rock, laughing merrily, though they are conscious of a little naughtiness in not attending more closely to their appointed task — that of guarding the gold.

Meanwhile, from a dark chasm below, Alberich, a hairy and uncouth gnome, has emerged. He clambers up to a rock, pauses, and, still hardly visible to the audience, watches with great delight the play of the Rhinemaidens, whom he accosts in accents as uncouth as his appearance and his movements. When the Rhinemaidens see him they are horrified at his ugliness, and think it wise to guard the gold against a possible foe. Recovering a little from their first fears, however, they coquettishly invite him to come higher, which he does by clambering, though with frequent fallings back and much spluttering, to the top of the rock.

He tries to embrace one or other of the maidens, but all elude him gracefully and mock him. Changing their tone, they lure him on further by means of pretended cajolements, and then, when he believes that his happiness is on the point of being completed by one of them, they break away from him again with mocking laugh-

ter. It is in vain that he pursues them; in spite of his uncanny agility he is no match for these nimble swimmers. At last, losing his
temper, he pauses breathless, foaming with rage, and shakes his
clenched fist up at the maidens.

But just then a curious spectacle arrests his attention. Upon
the waters there comes an ever-increasing glow, which gradually
concentrates on the peak of the central rock till it becomes a blinding golden gleam, that in turn sheds a golden radiance over the sur-
rounding waters. It is the gold waking from its sleep; and the Gold
motive is given out by the horns:

The maidens greet the lovely sight in rapture:

Rhine-gold!   Leuch-ten-de Lust,   Wie
Dazz-ling de-light,   Thou

lachst du so hell und hehr!
laugh-est so bright and brave!

Their trio ended, the maidens swim round the rock in delight, and
in reply to Alberich's questions they tell him of this marvellous
eye "that wakes and sleeps in the depths, and fills the waves with
its light." To the amorous gnome the gold, of the properties of
which he knows nothing, seems a poor thing in comparison with
the love of the maidens; but they explain to him that "the world's
wealth would be won by the master who from the Rhinegold fashioned the Ring that measureless might would confer"—and the
wood-wind of the orchestra give out softly the typical Ring motive:

The maidens' father, it seems, has ordered them to guard the gold carefully, so that no robber should ravish it from them. One alone, they continue, can shape the gold to a ring — one who has forsworn love:

The gold is safe then, says Wellgunde, " for all that liveth loveth; no one will forfeit love's rapture." " And least of all," adds Woglinde, " this languishing imp, with love's desire ravaged and racked! "

But the sight of the gold and the talk of the maidens have wrought a change in Alberich. Since his love is scorned, and with the gold he can win the mastery of the world, he will forswear love and choose power. Springing furiously over the rocks he clambers up to the central one, the maidens scattering in terror before him. With a final spring he attains the summit of the rock, stretches his hand out towards the gold, and cries, " Your light, lo, I put out; I wrench from the rock the gold, forge me the Ring of revenge; for hear me, ye floods; Love now curse I for ever! " With terrible force he tears the gold from the rock and plunges with it into the depths, where he disappears.

With the passing of the gold, thick darkness suddenly descends on the scene. The distracted maidens dive below after the robber, and the waters seem to fall with them into the depths below. From the lowest depths Alberich's shrill and mocking laughter is heard.

The rocks disappear in the darkness, and the whole stage appears to fill with billowing black water. Gradually the waves change into clouds, which in turn disperse in a fine mist as an increasingly strong light seems to pierce them from behind.

The orchestra makes play with various themes, especially the characteristic cry of the Rhinemaidens (the first bar of No. 5), the motive of Renunciation of Love (No. 7), and the motive of the Ring; and when the mist has entirely lifted away we see an open space on a mountain height.

At one side, on a flowery bank, lies the supreme god Wotan, with his wife Fricka by him; both are asleep. The light of the dawning day increases, and on the top of a cliff in the background there appears a magnificent castle with glittering battlements. Between this and the foreground is a deep valley, through which the Rhine is supposed to flow.

For a time neither of the sleeping figures stirs, while from the brass of the orchestra there wells up the noble motive of Valhalla:

At last Fricka awakes; her eyes fall on the castle, and with a startled movement she calls upon Wotan to awaken also. Wotan, still dreaming, muses upon the security of his mighty castle, and of the " measureless might " that is now to be his. When fully awake he raises himself slightly and hails the castle, " the everlasting work " that is at last ended, the " stately fortress, peerless and proud."

Fricka, however, cannot share his satisfaction; what delights him fills her with dread. The fort, it is true, is his, thanks to the labour of the giants; but what of Freia, the goddess of youth and beauty who has been given to the giants in pledge of payment for their work? The mention of the agreement between Wotan and the giants is accompanied in the lower strings of the orchestra by the Treaty motive:

Wotan carelessly brushes Fricka's fears aside; the work has been done, and as for the price, let her have no fear about that. Woman-like, she breaks out into reproaches of him for having, behind her back, pledged her radiant sister Freia for the payment, but Wotan tranquilly asks her whether the castle was not as much her wish as his. True, rejoins Fricka; but she makes clear her own motive for having desired the castle. Distressed at her husband's many wanderings from home, she had thought to keep him by her side by means of this magnificent toy. She finds, however, that his own idea in building the castle had merely been to win security while he could work out his plans for overlordship of the world.

The dialogue between the pair runs very much on the lines that, judging by his letters, the conversations between Wagner and his wife Minna must frequently have done. Wotan smilingly claims his right to go " ranging and changing " through the earth, while Fricka reproaches him with scorning " love and a woman's worth " in order to satisfy his lust for power. Wotan pleads that so far from despising women, rather does he honour them more than Fricka likes; and he reminds her how, when he was wooing her, he left an eye in forfeit — an incident that accounts for Wotan always appearing on the stage with a lock of hair covering one of his eyes. He assures Fricka that he has no intention of letting Freia be lost to them; and just at that moment Freia herself enters, as if in hasty flight, crying, " Help me, sister! Shelter me, brother! "

The giants, Fasolt and Fafner, it seems, are coming over the mountains to claim her. Wotan calmly brushes their threat aside; his faith is in Loge. Fricka reproaches him passionately for putting his trust in that trickster (Loge is the elusive god of fire); but Wotan tells her that, while he can rely upon his own strength where strength alone is needed, Loge's arts are useful to him where craft and deceit are necessary. It was under Loge's advice that

Wotan promised Freia to the giants; and he still has faith that when the crisis comes Loge will help him out of his difficulty.

Freia, to the accompaniment of the motive that was heard in the orchestra when she entered:

cries urgently to her absent brothers to help her — to Donner, the god of thunder, and his brother Froh. Despairingly Fricka tells her that all have abandoned her, and a lumpish, plodding theme in the orchestra, the rhythm of which is strongly marked by the kettledrums, announces the coming of the giants:

They are men of gigantic stature, clothed in rough animal skins, and carrying strong staves.

Pointing to the castle, Fasolt, who is the more amiable of the two, reminds Wotan that the fortress has been completed, and demands the promised wage. Wotan affects to be ignorant of the terms of the compact, but the Treaty motive in the orchestra reminds us of the solemnity of his pledged word. Fasolt recalls to him that the price was Freia, whose beauty and eternal youth have touched a tender spot in the heart of the susceptible giant. Wotan quickly and roughly tells them they must be mad to dream of such a thing: let them ask some other payment; Freia he will not grant.

For a moment the giants cannot believe their ears; can it be that the great god Wotan thinks so little as this of his pledged word, that the runes of solemn compact graven upon the shaft of his spear are, so to speak, only a scrap of paper? Very earnestly, and with a good deal of dignity, Fasolt reminds the god that what he is he is only by treaties; " in form set forth, well defined is thy might." He is as wise as they, the lumbering giants, are foolish; but a curse will be upon all his wisdom, and peace will be no more on earth, if Wotan does not honour the bond he has made.

Once more Wotan pretends that the thought of giving Freia to louts such as they never seriously entered his mind; and once more Fasolt earnestly reproaches him for this breach of his word.

Fasolt is of a somewhat softer type than his brother, who now breaks in roughly. For Freia herself he cares little; but it were well, he thinks, to take the maid away, because, deprived of the golden apples that grow in her garden, which she alone can tend — the apples that confer on her kindred youth everlasting — the gods will be under a blight; sick and old and weak, they will waste away. As Fafner speaks, the lovely theme of Freia as the Giver of Youth is intoned by the horns:

The atmosphere now grows tense. Muttering anxiously, " Loge tarries long! " Wotan asks the giants to accept another reward, but they refuse, and make as if to seize upon Freia. Donner and Froh enter at this moment; Froh clasps Freia in his arms, while Donner, the god of thunder, placing himself in front of the giants, threatens them with his huge hammer.

The Treaty motive is heard once more in the orchestra as Wotan, stretching out his spear between the disputants, reminds them that what is written upon it is written; force, therefore, cannot avail. Freia gives a despairing cry of " Woe's me! Woe's me! Wotan forsakes me! " Wotan, who has turned away in perplexity, sees Loge coming, and in the orchestra we hear the elusive, flickering themes associated with that god:

The last of these is the motive always associated with Loge's Fire Magic. Loge now climbs up from the valley at the back; he is in flame-coloured garb, and both his hair and his ceaseless gestures suggest the flickering of flames. He tells them how, after the building of the castle, while others were dreaming of the joys of house and hearth, he, true to his nature, went wandering over the earth.

Wotan puts a check on his garrulity; he reminds him that he is disliked by the gods, and that Wotan is his only friend, for the others do not trust him. Now he must have counsel from Loge. When the giants, before they built the fortress, demanded Freia as quittance, Wotan would never have given his promise had not Loge pledged his word that when the time came he would extricate him from his difficulty. That he promised to look for some means by which Freia could be redeemed, Loge admits; but how could he ever have promised definitely to find " some sure way out where no way lies? "

Fricka turns on him fiercely. " See," she says to Wotan, " the traitorous rogue thou didst trust! " " Loge art thou named, but liar [Lüge] I call thee! " says Froh; while the irate Donner, always inclined to settle differences by physical force, raises his hammer and threatens to quench Loge's fire. But Wotan steps between them and orders peace. They do not know, he says, Loge's wiles; the charier he is with his counsel, the craftier this always is.

The giants again becoming urgent, Wotan turns sharply to

Loge and asks him where he has been wandering so long. The elusive one, commiserating with himself on the ingratitude that is always his lot, tells them that, like the faithful fellow he is, he has been wandering unceasingly to all the ends of the earth, searching for a ransom for Freia that would be acceptable to the giants. It was all in vain, however; "in the whole wide world nought is so rich that man will value it more than woman's wondrous delight." All show astonishment and perplexity, while Loge, over a symphonic treatment in the orchestra of a new version of the Freia motive:

(16)

tells them how, wherever life ebbs and flows in the world, in water, earth, or air, he had asked of all men what they would prize above woman's love, and had everywhere received the same answer.

One alone had he met with who had forsworn love for gold. From the heart-broken Rhinemaidens he had learned how Alberich the Nibelung, having tried in vain to win their love, in revenge had robbed them of the gold, which now he values more than all the grace of woman. To Wotan the Rhinemaidens have sent a message by him — an appeal to punish the thief and return the gold to the waters. "This to tell thee I promised the maidens," says Loge: "his trust has Loge now fulfilled."

Angry and perplexed, Wotan turns to him with a petulant question — "Myself seest thou in need; what help for others have I?" But Loge's words have sunk deep into Fasolt and Fafner. Alberich has always been the enemy of the giants, and now that the possession of the gold confers such power upon him he will surely bring some new mischief upon them. What is it, Fafner asks Loge, that makes the gold so precious in the Nibelung's eyes? Loge explains that so long as the gold remained sleeping in the waters it was a mere toy for laughing children; but that if it be fashioned to a round ring it will confer measureless might on its possessor, and win him the mastery of the world.

It is not only the giants who have been stirred by Loge's recital. The evil latent in the gold, now that it has been wrested from its primal innocence, begins to act upon the others, each according to his nature. Wotan reflects upon the power and wealth that may come from this gold, of which he has already heard rumours. Fricka thinks that the glittering metal might serve for the adornment of woman's beauty; and Loge assures her that with it a wife could secure the fidelity of her husband.

Fricka turns cajolingly to Wotan and softly insinuates her own desire for the gold; while Wotan, wrapped up in his own dreams, feels the impulse to win him the Ring. By what art, he asks Loge, is this Ring to be wrought? Only by a certain magic rune, replies Loge; no one knows it, and it can be learned only by him who forswears love. At this Wotan turns away in ill-humour, to the sardonic amusement of Loge, who knows the great god's weaknesses. " That does not suit thee! " he says. In any case Wotan is now too late. Alberich did not delay; he forswore love, made himself master of the spell, and has wrought himself the Ring.

All now recognise the danger that threatens the gods, who will become slaves to the dwarf if the Ring be not wrested from him; though Wotan's motive is even stronger — he wants not merely to protect the gods but to make himself omnipotent. But how to get the Ring from Alberich? " By theft! " says Loge curtly and harshly. " What a thief stole, steal thou from the thief: could aught be more simply acquired? " But Alberich is strong and crafty, and the utmost guile will be necessary against him before the Ring can be taken from him and restored to the Rhinemaidens. This suggestion once more brings out the secret weakness at the heart of them all; Wotan is not disposed to enter upon the undertaking for the sake of others, while Fricka, as the protectress of virtue, has a grudge against the Rhinemaidens, who have wickedly lured many men to their lair.

A great struggle is going on in Wotan's breast. While he ponders his problems in silence, and the other gods keep their eyes on him in mute expectation, Fafner takes Fasolt aside and urges him to demand the gold rather than Freia. Fasolt's gestures indicate that he has finally been persuaded, though against his will, and the giants once more advance towards Wotan. Fafner announces their decision; they will leave Freia in freedom on condition that Wotan procures for them the Nibelung's gold.

Wotan protests that he is powerless to give them what is not his, and a quarrel breaks out, which is ended by the giants taking Freia away. They will hold her, they say, as a pledge until nightfall; then they will return; but if the ransom is not ready, no longer will they parley; Freia is forfeit and shall dwell with them for ever. The shrieking Freia is dragged away by the giants, and gloom settles upon the gods.

Soon a pale mist, that gradually grows denser, steals over the stage; it gives the gods an increasingly wan and aged appearance. Loge taunts them with the change that has come over them: " How sick and wan and withered ye seem! All the bloom has fled your faces, and dimmed is the light of your eyes! Courage, Froh, 'tis yet but dawn! From thy hand, Donner, now droppest the hammer? What grief hath Fricka? Is she afflicted for Wotan, gloomy and grey, grown an old man in a trice? "

To moving music the gods bewail their weakness, the explanation of which is given them by Loge: Freia has left them; of her fruit they have not eaten that day — the golden apples from her garden that each day renew their youth. On Loge the deprivation has no effect; Freia has always been sparing of the fruit to him, while by nature he is only half a god. But for the others, he tells them, the loss of the goddess is critical; deprived of the apples, and growing old and haggard, they will become the scorn of the world, and the race of the gods will cease.

At a reproachful wail from Fricka, Wotan starts up with a sudden resolution. He bids Loge come with him to Nibelheim, the abode of the Nibelungs, where he means to win the gold. After a moment's ironic pretence that he believes it is Wotan's desire to restore the gold to the Rhinemaidens, Loge asks, " Shall we descend through the Rhine? " " No! " replies Wotan. " Then swing ourselves through the sulphur cleft," says Loge; " slip down it yonder with me! " He goes to the side of the stage and disappears

in a cleft, from which a sulphurous vapour at once arises. Telling
the others to wait there till the evening, when their departed youth
shall be ransomed with the gold, Wotan descends after Loge into
the cleft. The sulphurous vapour rapidly spreads over the entire
stage, filling it with clouds, and rendering those on the stage
invisible.

In many theatres the opera is divided into two acts at this point.
Wagner, however, intended the *Rhinegold* to be played from
start to finish without a break, the change of scene here being
effected under cover of the thick black clouds into which the vapour
thickens. This cloud gradually changes into a solid rocky chasm
which moves continually upwards, so that the stage appears to be
sinking deeper and deeper into the earth. The music accompanying
this transformation is made up of a variety of motives, including
those associated with Loge, the Renunciation motive (No. 7) in a
new form:

themes associated with Alberich in the opening scene of the opera,
and the Gold motive (No. 4), all woven into a continuous symphonic tissue.

After a while a dark red glow shines from several quarters in the
distance, and an increasing noise as of smithying is heard on all
sides. At this point a pronounced rhythm:

begins to dominate the orchestra; this, in the later stages of
The Ring, and especially in *Siegfried,* is always associated with
the idea of smithying. It is hammered out now by eighteen anvils
behind the scene, while in the orchestra it takes the following
more definite melodic shape:

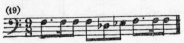

The music rises to an almost deafening clamour, then subsides
somewhat as the clang of the anvils dies away. We now see a subterranean cavern that stretches farther than the eye can reach, and
appears to open on every side into narrow shafts.

By the power of the gold Alberich has made all the other
Nibelungs subservient to him; they are now working to extract
treasure from the earth and cast it into forms for Alberich's pleasure
and profit. He is seen dragging one of the tiniest of the Nibelungs,
his brother, Mime, a poor little shrinking dwarf, out of a cleft at
the side of the stage. Mime had been set to do a special piece of
work, and Alberich, with considerable rough usage, is demanding
it from him. The shrinking Mime protests that all has been done
as he has been told, and he implores Alberich not to nip his ears
with his nails so fiercely. Releasing him, Alberich demands to be
shown the work.

Mime asks for a little more time, in case something may be
lacking in the work; but the suspicious Alberich making to catch
him by the ear again, Mime in terror lets fall a piece of metal work
which he had been convulsively clutching in his hand. Alberich
picks it up and examines it closely. In the orchestra we hear, in the
muted horns, one of the most curiously expressive motives in the
whole of *The Ring*:

This is the motive of the Tarnhelm, a metal network that, worn on the head, confers invisibility on its wearer. When we first hear the theme, which is at the moment Mime drops the object and Alberich picks it up, it appears in a fragmentary form only; our quotation shows it in its full form as it appears shortly afterwards and in the later stages of *The Ring*.

The motive is one of the most remarkable of Wagner's inventions; the hollowness of the harmonies, the slight strangeness in the modulations, and the mysterious colouring all combine to give it an extraordinary suggestiveness.

When Alberich examines the work he finds that everything is as he ordered, and he turns roughly on Mime, who, as he guesses, has been trying to keep the magic headdress for himself. Alberich puts the Tarnhelm on his head and at once disappears, only a column of vapour being visible where he had been standing; and the orchestra now gives out, for the first time, the Tarnhelm motive in full.

From the middle of the vapour comes Alberich's voice asking Mime if he can see him now. Mime looks round him in astonishment and says, " Where art thou? I see thee no more." " Then feel me, thou idle rogue! Take that for thy thievish thoughts! " says the invisible Alberich, and we see Mime writhing under the blows he receives from a scourge, the strokes of which are audible, though the scourge itself cannot be seen.

Mime howls with pain, and Alberich laughs loudly and harshly. Then, in a vehement tirade, he gloats over the race of the Nibelungs, who will now have to bow the knee to him, for everywhere he can secretly spy on them: " Rest and peace he will refuse you; still must ye serve him, though he be unseen; where ye least shall perceive him, trembling expect him! Thralls to him are ye for

ever! Hoho! Hoho! Hear him, he nears: the Nibelungs' lord! "
The servitude of the Nibelungs is symbolised by a descending
figure:

that is used in different forms throughout the work; it has already
been associated with Alberich in various ways, and the basis of it
will be seen in the motive of the Renunciation of Love.

The column of vapour now disappears towards the back of the
stage, carrying with it, we are to understand, Alberich, whose
roaring and scolding are heard receding into the distance. Evidently he is driving with blows the Nibelungs before him, and
their howls and shrieks are also heard dying away until they
become inaudible. Mime, left alone upon the stage, has cowered
down in pain. In the distance we hear the Smithying motive —
suggesting that the enslaved Nibelungs are at work again — combined with the motive of Servitude (No. 21).

Wotan and Loge now descend from a cleft. " This is Nibelheim,"
says Loge. Mime soon attracts their attention by a succession of
pitiful howls, and Loge, who knows him, asks the dwarf what it is
that " pricks and pinches him so." Mime bewails his hard lot,
while the orchestra gives out a curious theme known as the Reflection motive:

This is always used in the later stages of the work when Mime is
pondering upon or speaking about his difficult problems, and we
are probably intended to understand here that he is already
thinking how he can free himself of his servitude to Alberich.
Sometimes the motive is suggested by the use of merely two of
the chords. He has a cruel brother, he tells the gods, who has made
him his bondsman; from the ravished Rhinegold Alberich has

forged a Ring, by the power of which he has made himself master of the rest of his race.

To the rhythm of the Smithying motive, poor Mime, in a quite charming lyrical passage, tells the gods how happy the Nibelungs once were, working in their freedom, making gay little trinkets for the adornment of their women, and laughing lightly at their toil; but now Alberich compels them to creep into caverns and to work without ceasing for him alone. By the help of the Ring he can descry treasure concealed in the clefts; and then the others have to dig it out and melt it and fashion it into bars for Alberich to heap upon his hoard. Lately he had given Mime instructions to make him a helm.

Mime's mother-wit had perceived the power that lay in the work, and he had tried to keep the helm for himself, hoping thus to escape from Alberich's domination — even, perhaps, to overthrow the tyrant, to take from him the Ring, and make himself master. But alas, he goes on to tell Loge, though he could make the helm, he could not find the magic formula that gave it its power! Alberich alone knew this, and having taken possession of the helm and murmured the spell, he had vanished, and, invisible, laid his scourge upon poor Mime's back. Howling and sobbing he cries, " Such thanks for my toil, poor fool, I won! " He rubs his back ruefully, and the gods laugh. Perplexed by this, Mime observes them more attentively, and asks who they are. " Friends of thine," says Loge, " who will free the Nibelung folk from their need."

The Smithying motive reappears in the orchestra, combined with the theme of Servitude, and Mime, hearing Alberich approaching, shrinks back in terror. Wotan quietly seats himself on a stone, saying, " We'll wait for him here! " and Loge leans by his side. A crowd of Nibelungs rushes in from the cave below, driven by Alberich, who has removed the Tarnhelm from his head and hung it on his girdle.

The dwarfs are laden with gold and silver work, which, under the incessant goading of Alberich, they pile up in a hoard. He is still cursing and threatening them when he suddenly perceives Wotan and Loge. His suspicions aroused, he drives Mime away with his whip into the crowd of Nibelungs, and bids them all, if they would escape a flogging, delve into the new-made shaft and bring him the gold. Drawing the Ring from his fingers he kisses it and stretches it out threateningly: " Tremble in terror, downtrodden hosts! Quick, obey the Ring's great lord! " Howling and shrieking, the Nibelungs, with Mime among them, separate and run in all directions down into the shafts.

Alberich now turns a long and suspicious glance on Wotan and Loge, and asks them what they are doing there. In tranquil tones Wotan tells him that strange tidings have reached his ears of the wonders worked by Alberich in Nibelheim; and he and his companion have come down into the earth in the hope of seeing some of these wonders with their own eyes.

The gnome sneers at this pretence, but Loge reproachfully asks him if he does not know him; who is it, when he cowered in sunless caves, who gave him light and comfort in fire? What use would all his forging have been did Loge not light his forge fire?

But Alberich is not to be cajoled. He does not trust the shifty Loge, and, strong in the possession of the Ring, he defies the newcomers. Enormous treasures, he tells them, he has already amassed, and every day shall bring an increase of it. With this treasure he will win the world; even the gods, lapped in zephyrs there aloft, who spend their lives in laughter and love, shall one day bow to his will. He himself has forsworn love, and all who live shall be made to forswear it. The gods, on their radiant heights, despise the black elves who live in the bowels of the earth; but let them beware, for this gold shall be their undoing! " First ye men shall bow to my might, then your winsome women, who my wooing despised, shall sate the lust of the dwarf, though love they deny! " Laughing venomously, he warns the gods of the coming day when the hosts of night shall rise from the depths and destroy them.

Wotan turns on him in anger and disgust, but the crafty Loge, stepping between them, adopts his oiliest diplomatic tone. Who could fail to admire, he asks, the wonderful work of Alberich? If he can do all he says he can, he will indeed be the mightiest of all or

earth. When he holds aloft his Ring, it seems, the Nibelung hosts
must cower before him. But what of when he is alseep? Suppose
someone were then to steal the Ring from his hand?

Alberich falls into the trap; his vanity is aroused at this doubt of
his cunning. He tells them of the magic properties of the Tarnhelm,
under whose protection, made invisible, he can sleep in safety.
Loge professes to be lost in admiration of his wisdom, but artfully
insinuates another trifling doubt; how can they be sure that the
Tarnhelm is all that Alberich claims it to be, unless he proves it?
The raging Alberich demands a test; into what shape shall he turn
himself? " Into any shape thou wilt," replies Loge, " so that thou
make me dumb with amazement."

The mysterious Tarnhelm motive is given out by the orchestra;
Alberich puts on the Tarnhelm, murmurs the spell, instantly
disappears, and in his place a huge serpent is seen writhing on the
ground and stretching out its open jaws towards Wotan and Loge.
The Dragon theme, that is of importance later, is given to the
tubas:

(23)

Wotan gives a deep-chested laugh, while Loge pretends to be
seized with terror.

The serpent vanishes, and in its place Alberich reappears in his
proper form. Do the wise ones believe him now? he asks. Loge,
putting on a quaking voice, declares that his trembling sufficiently
attests the truth of the demonstration. Alberich has certainly
managed to transform himself into a big serpent; but can he also

turn himself into something correspondingly small, for surely, if danger should threaten, it would be an advantage to be small enough to creep anywhere into hiding?

The vainglorious Alberich laughs at Loge's incredulity. How small would Loge like him to make himself? " That the smallest crevice might hold thee where hides a toad in its fright," replies Loge. " Pah! Nothing simpler! " says Alberich, and once more donning the Tarnhelm and murmuring the spell he disappears, and the gods perceive a toad on the rocks, crawling towards them. " Quick! Seize it! " cries Loge. Wotan places his foot on the toad, while Loge takes it by the head and seizes the Tarnhelm. In a moment Alberich becomes visible in his own form, writhing under the foot of Wotan. Loge binds him hand and foot with a rope, and in spite of his violent struggles the gods drag him to the shaft by which they came down. There they disappear; the scene changes as before, but in the reverse direction. There is an orchestral interlude, made up of motives with which we are by now familiar, and after a time we see Wotan and Loge come up out of the shaft, dragging Alberich with them bound.

The next scene takes place on the mountain height, as in Scene II, though at present a pale mist hangs over the stage. Loge, bidding Alberich seat himself, dances round him, snaps his fingers at him, and asks him ironically which corner of all the world that belongs to him he will graciously grant to Loge for his stall. Alberich bursts out into bitter revilings of the gods and self-reproaches for his own credulous blindness; but their only reply is that they will set him free when ransom has been paid in the form of the hoard.

Alberich curses them once more, but mutters to himself that if only he can retain the Ring he will soon be able to gain as much wealth for himself as before, and the lesson will have been well worth what he has lost. He consents to give up the hoard, and Loge unties the rope from his right hand. Alberich puts the Ring to his lips, murmurs a secret command, and from the cleft the Nibelungs ascend, laden with treasure, which they pile up in a heap. Raging at the disgrace of thus appearing bound before his vassals, Alberich storms at them in the old way, and when their work has been done dismisses them with an imperious gesture. He kisses the Ring and stretches it out commandingly, and as the Nibelungs disperse in terror the orchestra lets loose a tornado of tone that is more eloquent of Alberich's fury than any mere speech could be.

Now, he presumes, he can depart, and take his helm with him. Loge, however, throws the Tarnhelm also on the hoard, claiming it as part of the ransom. Once more Alberich reflects that he who made the first Tarnhelm for him can make him another and again he asks if he may now depart. But Wotan claims also the Ring on his finger. In vain the horrified gnome pleads that this shall be left to him; Wotan, adopting a high moral tone, reviles him for the theft by which he came into possession of the Rhinegold, and in spite of the protests of the frenzied Nibelung he seizes him and violently tears the Ring from his finger. Alberich gives a horrible shriek. Wotan, after contemplating the Ring, puts it on his own finger and says, " 'Tis mine now, the spell of might, that makes me lord of the world! " Loge, having untied the remainder of Alberich's bonds, orders him to " slip away home."

Alberich, insane with fury, raises himself and laughs wildly, while the orchestra gives out the syncopated theme that is henceforth to be associated with his resolve to bring about the Annihilation of the Gods:

Then comes the most significant moment of the drama as it **has** so far shaped itself. Alberich lays his curse upon the Ring:

Wie durch Fluch er mir ge-riet, ver-
As by curse came it to me, ac-

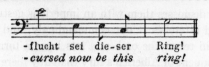

-flucht sei die-ser   Ring!
-cursed now be this   ring!

" As it gave me measureless might, let each who holds it die, slain
by its spell! To none on earth joy shall it give, in its radiant lustre
shall none delight! Care shall consume its wretched possessor, and
envy gnaw him who owneth it not! Each shall lust after its delights, yet none shall know pleasure who winneth it! To its lord
no gain shall it bring, yet shall murder follow it close! His doom
ever knowing, racked shall his soul be with fear: while life shall
last, daily wasting away, the Ring's great lord to the Ring shall
be a slave, till once more to my hand the ravished treasure re-
turneth. So, moved by the direst need, the Nibelung blesseth his
Ring! " He vanishes quickly in the cleft, while the orchestra
thunders out the threatening Servitude motive (No. 21).

The thick vapour in the foreground gradually clears away,
and from now onwards the stage slowly becomes lighter. Loge
makes an ironical comment on the fury of the departed Alberich;
Wotan, lost in contemplation of the Ring on his finger, dreaming
of the power it is to confer on him, makes no reply. In the clearer
foreground light the aspect of the gods regains its former freshness. In the background, however, the veil of mist still lingers, so
that the castle in the distance remains for the present invisible.

Donner, Froh, and Fricka enter, followed a little later by Fasolt
and Fafner, leading Freia between them. Fricka runs joyfully to
her sister and hails her with loving words, but Fasolt wards her off.
A victim to the charm of Freia, he has been reluctant to bring her
back; but the word of the giants had been given, and now they
have come to claim the price of Freia. Wotan points to the hoard
that is to be Freia's ransom. Fasolt, still grieving over the loss of
Freia, stipulates that if he is to forget her beauty the treasure must
be heaped so high that it will hide her loveliness completely from
his sight.

Wotan consents to this, and Freia is placed by the giants in the
middle of the stage. They thrust their staves into the ground on

each side of her, thus measuring her height and breadth, and Loge and Froh heap up the treasure between the poles. The covetous Fafner, peering closely into the mass, finds various crevices which he insists on being stopped. Wotan and Fricka are filled with shame at the spectacle, while Donner, as usual, would resort to violence; Wotan, however, restrains him. Fafner, surveying the hoard closely once more, protests that he is dazzled by the gleam of Freia's hair, and insists on the Tarnhelm being thrown on the heap. At a word from Wotan, Loge lets the Tarnhelm go, and asks the giants if now they are contented.

But the lovelorn Fasolt, taking a last look at the fair one, catches a radiant glance from her eye, and declares that he cannot part from her. This last crevice too has to be filled up, and Fafner, catching sight of the Ring on Wotan's finger, insists on that being used for the purpose. After a wild protest, Wotan refuses, and the angry Fasolt pulls Freia out from behind the pile and is about to hurry away with her, but is restrained by Fafner.

Wotan, sore and angry, has turned aside, and the stage has again become dark. Now, from a rocky crevice at the side, a bluish light breaks forth, in which Erda, the goddess of the earth and wisdom, suddenly becomes visible, rising from the ground to half her height, and in the orchestra we hear the solemn Erda motive:

(26)   Lento

In grave accents Erda warns Wotan to give up the Ring and avoid the curse: " All that exists endeth! A day of gloom dawns for the gods; I charge thee, give up the Ring! " She sings down slowly and disappears, and the bluish light dies out. The troubled Wotan, anxious for further knowledge, tries to follow her into the cleft, but he is held back by Froh and Fricka.

Wotan now comes to a sudden resolution. Turning to the giants, and brandishing his spear in token of a bold decision, he throws the Ring on the hoard. The giants release Freia, who hastens joyfully to the gods, who caress her each in turn with the greatest joy. Fafner meanwhile has spread out an enormous sack, into which he prepares to pack the hoard. Fasolt interrupts him, claiming measure for measure, but is roughly repulsed by Fafner, who reminds him that it was more on Freia than on the gold that his doting eyes were set, so that it is only right that Fafner should retain the greater part of the treasure for himself.

A violent quarrel breaks out between the clumsy pair, from which Wotan turns away in contempt and disgust. Loge whispers to Fasolt the advice to let his brother have what he will, but to make sure of the Ring. A struggle for the Ring ensues; Fasolt wrests it for a moment from Fafner, but his brother fells him to the ground with one blow and wrenches the Ring from the dying man's hand: " Now glut thee with Freia's glance," he says, " for the Ring see'st thou no more! " Fafner puts the Ring in the sack and callously goes on finishing his packing of the hoard, while the horror-struck gods watch him in silence. From the orchestra, in the loudest tones of the trombones, there rings out the Curse motive, and we realise that the malediction that Alberich has laid upon the Ring has already begun its work.

The shattered Wotan would descend to the earth to take counsel of Erda, but Fricka, caressing him, tries to turn his thoughts into more cheerful channels by pointing out to him the fort that awaits his occupation. The mists in the background lie like a load on Donner's brow. He ascends a high rock, swings his hammer, and the clouds gather round him more quickly; in time he disappears completely within them:

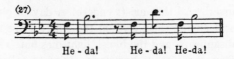

(27)

He - da!   He - da! He-da!

This marks the commencement of the episode often given in the concert room under the title of " The Entry of the Gods into Valhalla." After a time Donner's hammer-stroke is heard on the rock; a vivid flash of lightning shoots out of the cloud, followed by a tremendous clap of thunder; then the clouds suddenly disperse, Donner and Froh become visible once more, and from their feet there stretches, across the valley to the castle, a rainbow bridge of blinding radiance; the castle itself gleams nobly in the rays of the setting sun. Meanwhile Fafner has left the stage, dragging after him the sack and Fasolt's body.

The gods are lost in admiration of the glorious spectacle now afforded by the rainbow bridge and the castle, and Wotan hails the fort in a magnificent apostrophe, giving it the name of Valhalla. As he speaks of the security that the fort will afford him a new motive, that of the Sword, peals out in the trumpet:

This motive, especially in connection with Siegmund and Siegfried, becomes of great importance in the later stages of *The Ring*. But as yet, of course, there has been no mention, and indeed no thought, of either the Sword or any of the persons to be associated with it, or of the means by which, through the Sword, the deliverance of the gods is ultimately to be worked. These considerations seem to have occurred to Wagner; and during one of *The Rhinegold* rehearsals at Bayreuth in 1876 he laid it down that a sword from the treasure-heap should be left on the stage by Fafner, and that Wotan should pick this up and point it solemnly towards the castle.

Fricka asks the meaning of the title of Valhalla given to the castle, and Wotan gives her the somewhat enigmatic answer, "What strength against my fears my spirit has found, when victory is mine, will make the meaning clear." Taking Fricka by the hand he walks slowly towards the bridge, followed by Froh, Freia, and Donner; Loge remains in the foreground and gazes after them, saying ominously, "They are hastening to their end, though they deem themselves strong and enduring." For his part, he will transform himself once more into flickering fire and go wandering over the earth, "rather than blindly end with the blind, even were they of gods the most godlike!" He carelessly saunters after the gods, while from below, invisible in the depths of the valley, the three Rhinemaidens, in a ravishing trio:

(29)

Rhine - gold!   Rei - - nes
Rhine - gold!   *Guile - - less*

Gold!   wie   lau - ter und hell
gold!   *How   pure and how bright*

leuch - te - test   hold   du   uns!
once fell thy   beams   on   us!

lament the loss of the gold.

Loge gives them a derisive answer, and as the gods laugh and cross the rainbow bridge the trio breaks forth afresh: " Rhinegold! Guileless gold! Oh would that again in the waters thy gleam might shine! Tender and true it is only in the waters: false and base are those who revel above! " From the orchestra surges up the noble Valhalla theme (No. 8), followed by one that has been associated with the rainbow; and while the gods are still crossing the bridge to the castle, the curtain falls.

It need hardly be said that this crossing of the valley by means of the rainbow bridge presents difficulties of staging that few theatres can overcome.

Wagner regarded *The Ring* as a musical drama not in four parts but in three, *The Rhinegold* being described by him as a " Fore-Evening." It resembles, indeed, in some ways the first or " exposition " section of a great symphony: the main motives, psychological and musical, are here set forth, to be worked out in detail in the later movements, blended, contrasted, and at last brought triumphantly to their logical conclusion.

THE VALKYRIE

A T the end of our analysis of *The Rhinegold* we saw the gods entering into Valhalla, greatly troubled. The Ring has passed out of the hands of Wotan into those of Fafner. The giant himself is too stupid to realise the terrible uses to which the Ring might be put; all his dull brain has been capable of, indeed, is to make him change himself, by means of the Tarnhelm, into a dragon, and in this form to retire into a cave where he slumbers upon his gold.

But the wily Alberich is always scheming and lying in wait, and Wotan knows that if the Ring falls again into his hands he will use it to destroy the gods. The problem for Wotan, then, is to get the Ring into his possession once more. But he sees now that he must do this neither by craft nor by violence, for he is the god of those treaties and that truth without which the world cannot hold together.

The present trouble has come upon the gods through his forgetfulness of the runes engraved upon his own spear, and his breach of faith with the giants, followed by his rape of the Ring, the gold, and the Tarnhelm from Alberich. If the Ring, then, is to be his once more, and so made harmless to the gods and the world, it must be by some means morally above reproach, and without any direct intervention on his part.

The plan he has thought out, in the interval between the *Rhinegold* and the *Valkyrie*, is to raise up a hero who shall be free of him, and yet, unconsciously, do his will.

Since *The Rhinegold* closed, Wotan has had by Erda — the earth goddess of ancient wisdom, whose warning restrained him

from violent action at the end of the first evening of *The Ring* —
nine daughters, the Valkyries whose function it is to bring to
Valhalla the bodies of slain heroes, who, reanimated, will be a
guard for the threatened gods. The chief of the Valkyries, and
Wotan's favourite among them, is Brynhilde.

Moreover, " ranging and changing " as is his wont, as he tells
Fricka and us in *The Rhinegold*, he has had an alliance with a
mortal woman, from which has sprung the race of the Wälsungs
(Volsungs). One of these children, Siegmund, Wotan hopes will
prove to be the deliverer of the gods. With Siegmund and his sister
Sieglinde he has lived in the woods as their father Wolfe. Some
time before *The Valkyrie* opens the home has been raided by an
enemy tribe, and Sieglinde carried off to be the wife of Hunding.
Wolfe disappears, and Siegmund remains alone in the world, with
seemingly everyone's hand against him. *The Valkyrie* opens at
the point at which Siegmund, exhausted, is fleeing from the latest
enemies who have assailed him. Chance has brought him to the
hut of Hunding.

There is no formal overture, but only a short orchestral prelude
depicting a storm. Against a continually reiterated D in the violins
and violas the 'cellos and basses give out a motive:

(1)

suggestive of the steady pelting of heavy rain. The gloomy atmosphere is broken here and there by flashes of lightning (sharp,
discordant chords in the wood-wind), while later the tuba thunders
out the theme that, in *The Rhinegold*, we have seen to be associated with Donner as the god of the weather in general, and of
bad weather and thunder in particular:

(2)

When the curtain rises we see a room that is built round the stem
of a great ash tree which forms its centre. In the background is
a wide entrance door. In the foreground, on the right, is
the hearth, behind which is a store-room; on the left, towards the
back, there are steps leading to an inner chamber. Also on the
left, but more in the foreground, is a table, behind which is a
broad bench, set into the wall; in front of this are some wooden
stools.

After the curtain has risen, the stage remains empty for a few
moments, and we hear the storm dying down outside. Then the
door is opened from without, and Siegmund enters, evidently utterly exhausted; finding the room empty, he closes the door behind
him, and with a last effort staggers towards the hearth, where
he throws himself down on a bearskin rug, saying, " Whose hearth
this may be, here must I rest me! " While this has been happening,
the Storm motive has merged imperceptibly into one typical of
Siegmund:

Sieglinde enters from the inner room on the left. Having heard
the door open, she has thought it was her husband returning; her
look changes to one of surprise when she sees a stranger stretched
out on the hearth. He seems to be in a swoon. She comes nearer
and contemplates him, and bends down to see if he is still breathing.
Siegmund, suddenly raising his head, cries out for a draught of
water, which Sieglinde brings him in a drinking-horn, the Siegmund motive being put through some exquisitely tender modulations as she does so. Mingled with the development of this motive
is that of Sieglinde's Pity:

As Siegmund, having drunk, hands the horn back to Sieglinde, his gaze becomes fixed with growing interest on her face, and the orchestra, in an eloquent and moving theme given out by the 'cellos:

(5)

suggests that love has already forged its mysterious link in the heart of the pair. Siegmund asks who it is that has first assuaged his thirst and then gladdened his weary eyes, and Sieglinde tells him that she is the wife of one Hunding, in whose house he now is. He is their guest, she says, and must take his ease there till the master returns.

A weaponless and wounded man, Siegmund answers, should be safe; and he tells her how he has been hunted by his foemen and bruised by the tempest. To the gentle strains of the Pity motive in the strings Sieglinde goes to the store-room, whence she emerges with a horn filled with mead, which she offers to Siegmund. He begs her first to touch it with her lips, which she does; then he takes a long draught from it, his gaze all the time resting upon her with increasing ardour, while the orchestra discourses softly but warmly on the Love motive.

Now that he is refreshed, he tells her, he must fly, for wherever he goes, ill fate follows. She impulsively calls him back just as his hand has raised the latch: " Abide thou here," she says; " no ill fate canst thou bring there, where ill fate has made its home "; and the 'cellos intone the expressive motive of the Wälsung's Woe:

(6)

Looking searchingly into her eyes, which she lowers in sad confusion, he returns to the hearth. " ' Wehwalt ' [which we may render as ' Woeful '] named I myself; Hunding here will I await."

He stands by the hearth again, and the pair search out each other's souls with their eyes during a long silence, which is suddenly broken by a sound that makes Sieglinde start; it is Hunding outside, leading his horse to the stable. She runs to the door and opens it, and Hunding, a huge, sombre, sinister figure, armed with shield and spear, stalks in to the accompaniment of his representative motive — given out in dark and threatening tones by the tubas:

This motive is one of Wagner's greatest triumphs of characterization; in two or three bars the whole gloomy, loveless, overbearing nature of the man is painted.

Hunding turns to Sieglinde with a look of hard enquiry, and she explains how she found this exhausted man lying by the hearth, gave him cooling drinks, and treated him as a guest. The surly Hunding takes off his armour and gives it to Sieglinde, roughly bidding her prepare the evening meal. She hangs the arms on branches of the ash tree, and then, bringing food and drink from the store-room, prepares the table for supper. While she is doing this she cannot help her gaze straying to Siegmund, and

Hunding, who has been scanning the latter's features keenly, is struck by their resemblance to those of his wife.

Here the orchestra gives out the Treaty motive (associated with Wotan):

that we have already heard in *The Rhinegold*.

Hunding conceals his surprise, however, and turning to Siegmund with assumed unconcern asks him how he came thither. Siegmund cannot tell him; he has been driven by the storm and his enemies through field and forest, but he knows neither the way he came nor where he is now. He is in Hunding's house, the black giant tells him, and demands his guest's name. Sieglinde is now sitting next to Hunding and opposite to Siegmund, and during the latter's recital the eyes of the pair are almost constantly on each other, while Hunding observes them both critically.

Siegmund tells Hunding that he is neither " Friedmund " (Peaceful) nor " Frohwalt " (Joyful), but " Wehwalt " (Woeful). His father was Wolfe, and with him there came into the world a twin-born sister, whom he has scarcely known. As a boy he went hunting and warring with his father, and one day when they returned from the hunt they found the wolf's nest laid waste; the stately hall was burnt to ashes, the mother lay dead, and not a trace of the sister was left; this was the work of the evil Neidings. Then for years he roamed the woods with his father, the twain for ever fighting.

One day the Neidings made a furious onslaught on them; Wolfe and the son scattered the foe like chaff, but the boy became separated from his father, whom he never saw again; all that remained of him was a wolf skin that Siegmund found in the forest. From the orchestra, that gives out in the softest tones the Valhalla motive that has already appeared in *The Rhinegold:*

we learn that this father was Wotan. In pathetic tones Siegmund goes on to tell of the loneliness of his life from that time and of his failure to find love or friendship anywhere; " whate'er I did, where'er I fared, if friend I sought or woman wooed, still was I held in suspicion. Ill fate lay on me. Whate'er to me seemed right, others reckoned it ill; what I held to be foul, others counted as fair. In feuds I fell where'er I dwelt, wrath ever against me I roused; sought I for gladness, found I but grief; so must I ' Woeful ' call me, for woe still walks in my wake."

In response to a question from Sieglinde he goes on to tell of his last affray — he had fought in defence of a maiden whom her kinsmen were trying to force into loveless wedlock; in the end he had been forced by numbers to fly, wounded and weaponless. As he ends his melancholy tale, turning on Sieglinde a look full of sorrowful ardour, the orchestra tells us who he is by giving out the long and expressive theme of the Wälsung race:

(10)

Hunding, rising gloomily, speaks darkly of a turbulent race that he knows, that is at deadly feud with his own; he had come too late to levy toll for his kinsmen's blood, but returning he finds his flying foeman in his own house. For that night Siegmund will have the immunity of a guest, but in the morning he must defend himself: " no longer life I allow; for murder toll will I take." Sieglinde steps anxiously between the two men, but Hunding harshly orders her away to prepare his night draught and then wait for him within.

For a considerable time after this not a word is spoken by any of the three actors. Sieglinde, after a moment's hesitation and reflection, turns slowly towards the store-room, where she again pauses, seemingly lost in thought. Then, with quiet resolution, she opens the cupboard, fills a drinking-horn and shakes some spices into it from a box. She turns again to Siegmund, whose eyes have never left her; but perceiving that Hunding is watching them, she moves towards the bed-chamber. On the steps she once more turns round, bends upon Siegmund a look full of longing, and with her eyes indicates, explicitly and urgently, a particular spot in the great ash tree that occupies the centre of the hall. Hunding, his anger rising at this significant interchange of glances, starts up and dismisses her with a violent gesture; and with a last look at Siegmund she goes into the inner room.

While she has been looking at the tree, the bass trumpet has given out softly a theme:

(11)

which we recognise as the Sword motive that has already beer heard in the final scene of *The Rhinegold*. The harsh, threatening Hunding theme (No. 7) is heard again as Hunding, taking his weapons down from the tree, takes leave of Siegmund with a final threat for the morrow. He goes into the inner chamber, and from within the bolt is heard to shoot.

Siegmund is left alone. It has become quite dark by now, the room being lit only by a faint gleam from the hearth. Siegmund sinks on to the couch by the fire and broods in sad silence, with the Hunding motive pounding threateningly through his tortured brain; sometimes it is heard as a sinister rhythm alone, in the kettledrums, sometimes clothed in the gloomy colours of the horns and brass.

Once more the bass trumpet gives out softly the Sword motive, as Siegmund bitterly and despairingly recalls how his father once promised him that in his direst need he should find a sword. Here, surely, is the need; he is in a foeman's house, weaponless, held as a hostage awaiting vengeance! He has seen a woman, winsome and pure, whose soft enchantment has kindled a flame within him; but she is held in thrall by the very man who now mocks his weaponless foe. "Wälse!" he cries in anguish to his father, "Wälse! Where is thy sword — the trusty sword that in strife shall serve me, when there shall burst from my breast the rage that consumes my soul?" As he speaks, the expiring fire falls together, and from the glow that arises from it a light suddenly strikes on the spot of the tree stem that Sieglinde had indicated by her glance, and in which the hilt of a buried sword is now visible. The Sword motive keeps flashing out in the orchestra.

For the moment Siegmund does not grasp the significance of what he has seen. His thoughts are still running on Sieglinde, and he wonders if this lingering radiance that he sees can be the parting look the lovely woman gave him, that has remained clinging to the tree. The fire on the hearth dies down once more as he muses, and at last it is extinguished entirely; in the complete darkness the door at the side opens softly, and Sieglinde, in a white garment, comes out, moving lightly but rapidly to the hearth. "Sleepst thou, guest?" she asks softly, and Siegmund springs up in joyful surprise.

Hurriedly and with an air of secrecy she tells him that she has mixed a drug with Hunding's night draught, so that the guest may escape. She will show him a weapon, if he can make it his own; then would she indeed name him the noblest of heroes, for by the strongest alone can the weapon be won; and the orchestra gives us a hint of a Cry of Victory that will become of importance later:

(12)

Sieglinde proceeds to tell him the story of the weapon. At the wedding with Hunding into which she was forced, his kinsmen were all feasting in this very hall, and she was sitting alone in sadness while they were drinking, when a stranger strode in — an old man garbed in grey, with his hat so low on his brow that one of his eyes was hidden, though the flash of the other struck fear into all who saw it. She alone, of all there, felt something sweet and solacing, sad and yearning, in that glance.

In the old man's hand was a sword; this he swung and then struck deep into the stem of the ash tree, burying the blade up to the haft. (The Valhalla motive in the orchestra tells us who the visitor was, while the Sword motive rings out in the trumpet as Sieglinde describes the burying of the weapon in the tree.) The sword should be his who had strength to draw it forth. But none could do this, labour as mightily as they would; there, in silence, still bides the inviolate sword. Once more the Valhalla theme is softly intoned by the orchestra as Sieglinde says that then she knew who he was who had greeted her in her grief, and now she knows, too, who is he for whom the weapon waits.

The tempo quickens, the Sword motive peals out once more in the trumpet, and over the Victory theme (No. 12) Sieglinde pours out the passionate story of her trouble and of her longing for the coming of the one who should deliver her. Embracing her ardently, Siegmund tells her that he who now holds her is the friend who shall win both weapon and wife. For he, like her, has suffered shame and sorrow, spite and dishonour; and now for him as for her is to come the joy of vengeance.

As the passion of the music soars to its climax the great door in the background, opening upon the forest, suddenly flies open. Sieglinde starts back in alarm and tears herself away from Siegmund with a cry of " Ha! Who passed? Who entered here? " The door remains open. It is a glorious spring night, and the full moon, shining in, enables the pair to see each other now with the utmost clearness. In gentle ecstasy Siegmund answers her, "No one passed, but one has come: see now how Spring smiles in the hall! "

Into the music, as into the room, has come the gentle radiance of the moon and the soft pulsation of spring. Siegmund, with tender force, draws Sieglinde towards him on the couch, where she sits beside him; then he breaks into a song of Love and Spring:

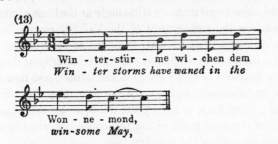

(13)

Win - ter-stür - me wi - chen dem
Win - ter storms have waned in   the

Won - ne - mond,
win-some May,

in which he describes Spring wandering through wood and meadow, gladdening everything with his laughing eye, rousing everything to life with his breath. The seasonal miracle of nature is symbolical of what has happened to them; and the Love motive (No. 5) comes into its splendid own as Siegmund describes to Sieglinde how the brother has been led here to free his sister and bride, now made one with him by Love and Spring.

It is to the strain of the Love motive again that Sieglinde cries in reply, " Thou art the Spring, that long I have sighed for through winter's ice-bound days. My heart greeted thee with the holiest fear when thy look at first on me lightened. All things seemed strange to me, friendless all was around me; like things I never had known, all that ever came near. But thy soul lay bare at once to me; when my eyes fell on thee, knew I mine own one: what lay hid in my heart, what I am, clear as the day dawned on my sight, in resonant tones rang in my ear, when in winter's dreary desert there came first my friend to me." She hangs in ecstasy on his neck and gazes closely into his face. The orchestra sweeps up in a great wave, that at its crest breaks into a new motive — that of Felicity:

(14)

O sü - sses-te Won - ne!
O sweet-est en-chant-ment!

Se - lig-stes Weib!
wo-man most blest!

An old, submerged memory stirs dimly at the back of Sieglinde's mind, and by the employment of the Valhalla motive in the orchestra Wagner lets us see what is hidden as yet from her — that what first drew her to Siegmund was the community of their blood. Sieglinde has seen her own image in the stream, and now she sees it again in Siegmund; in his voice she recognises the echo of her own voice given back to her by the wood; in his eye she sees the gleam that the grey guest of old turned on her when he soothed her sorrowing soul at the wedding feast.

No longer, she says, shall he be "Woeful"; "Joyful" she will call him now. Was Wolfe indeed his father? she asks him. A wolf indeed he was to fearful foxes, Siegmund replies gaily, but his name was Wälse. Beside herself with ecstasy, Sieglinde names this Wälsung, for whom their father Wälse struck the sword in the stem, "Siegmund!" Joyously accepting the name, Siegmund springs towards the ash tree, seizes the hilt of the sword, and, to a strain that has already appeared in *The Rhinegold,* where he knew it as the Renunciation motive:

(15)

cries "Holiest Love's most mighty need, passionate longing's feverish need, brightly burns in my breast, drives to deeds and death!" "Nothung!" (Needful) he now names the sword:

16)

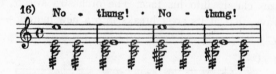

"Needful! Needful! So name I thee, sword: Needful, masterful steel! Show me thy sharpness, bare me thy teeth; leap forth from thy scabbard to me!" With a mighty effort he plucks the sword from the tree and shows it to the wondering and enraptured

Sieglinde; it is the bride-gift of Siegmund the Wälsung to the bride with whom he flies from the foeman's house, " forth to the laughing house of Spring."

Sieglinde, whom he has taken in his arms, tears herself away from him in mad intoxication, and cries, " Art thou Siegmund standing before me? Sieglinde am I, who for thee longed: thine own true sister thou winnest at once with the sword! " She falls on his breast with a cry, and the curtain falls to the accompaniment of a tumultuous outburst of passion in the orchestra, in which the Sword motive is prominent.

It was a curious habit with Wagner, once he had symbolised something or other in a leading motive, to use that motive again to represent something that had no more than a merely verbal connection with the thing originally symbolised.

In *Parsifal*, for example, when the wounded swan comes upon the scene, Wagner uses the Swan theme from *Lohengrin*. There can be no suggestion, of course, that the two swans were the same bird; the explanation is that having settled in 1846 upon a theme to represent a particular swan, Wagner, more than thirty years later, utilised it as descriptive, more or less, of swans in general.

We have another instance of the same curious habit of mind in the orchestral prelude to the second act of *The Valkyrie*. This is a magnificently fiery piece of music, mainly descriptive of the flight of Siegmund and Sieglinde from the house of Hunding. In the first couple of bars we have a harmonically modified version of the Sword theme; this recurs again and again in the course of the prelude.

If the reader will now turn back to our analysis of *The Rhinegold*, and look at quotation No. 14 (the motive of Freia), he will see, in the second and third bars, a phrase that, in the earlier opera, is always associated with Freia's flight, or attempts at flight, from the giants. In this prelude to the second act of *The Valkyrie*, Wagner, having once more a flight to describe, reverts to this figure, which he works out symphonically. People who have become used to associating the theme with Freia in *The Rhinegold* are inclined to wonder what it is doing here, for of course Freia has nothing to do with *The Valkyrie*. The explanation is that curiously literal bent of Wagner's mind to which reference has just been made.

Towards the end of the prelude a new and striking theme tears its way upward in the bass trumpet and trombone:

This is the theme of the wild Valkyries.

The curtain having risen, we see a wild, rocky pass. In the background is a gorge running from below to a high ridge of rocks, from which the ground falls gradually again to the foreground. We see Wotan in warlike array, grasping his spear; before him stands Byrnhilde, in the garb of a Valkyrie, also fully armed. Hunding is naturally in pursuit of Siegmund and Sieglinde, and in the impending fight Wotan intends to take Siegmund's side. He has summoned Byrnhilde to dispatch her for this purpose to the scene of the fight. Springing from rock to rock on the heights, Byrnhilde utters the half-savage cry that is characteristic of the Valkyries:

Brynhilde is in a merry mood. Looking down from a high peak into the gorge at the back she has seen Fricka approaching in her ram-drawn chariot. Fricka is evidently in a temper, and Brynhilde knows that this bodes a storm for Wotan. So Brynhilde will leave him, she says; in the fights of heroes she revels, but from strife like this she holds herself aloof; and reiterating her savage Valkyrie cry she disappears behind the mountain at the side just as Fricka comes upon the scene. The latter dismounts and advances impetuously towards Wotan, while the orchestra gives out for the first time the vigorous and pointed theme of Fricka's Wrath:

(19)

The scene of recrimination that ensues between Wotan and Fricka is probably a faint reflection of similar scenes between Wagner and Minna after the love had died out from their union.

In a long letter of the 26th January, 1854, to his friend August Roeckel, in which he expounds the whole philosophy of *The Ring*, Wagner explains the situation as between Wotan and Fricka in terms that could be applied without alteration of a single word to the situation between Minna and himself: " The necessity of prolonging beyond the point of change the subjection to the tie that binds them — a tie resulting from an involuntary illusion of love — the duty of maintaining at all costs the relations into which they have entered, and so placing themselves in hopeless opposition to the universal law of change and renewal, which governs the world of phenomena, these are the conditions which bring the pair of them to a state of torment and mutual lovelessness."

People have come to regard Fricka as merely a rather tiresome termagant, who inflicts a long curtain lecture on her husband in the hearing of the audience. That is a complete misconception of her; and it may safely be said that wherever the spectator receives that impression the fault lies with the interpreter. When the part is played by an actress of intelligence who can rise to the full height of it, Fricka becomes a dignified and worthy figure, who commands our sympathies at least as much as Wotan himself.

Wagner was far too great an artist to make the elementary mistake of photographing slavishly from the life; and however much of Minna he may originally have intended to put into Fricka, when his incomparable dramatic imagination began to work upon the latter character he lifted it to an intellectual height to which poor Minna could never have attained.

Standing with quiet dignity before Wotan, Fricka tells him her reasons for seeking him out, in spite of his efforts to avoid her; Hunding has appealed to her, as the protectress of the marriage bond, for justice to be done upon the " infamous pair " who have wronged him. Wotan tries to evade the point: what wrong, he asks mildly, has been done by this pair, " whom Spring in love did unite? " For his part he deems that oath unholy " that binds lives without love."

Fricka roughly brushes this familiar sophistry aside; he knows well, she says, that not only have Siegmund and Sieglinde betrayed Hunding, but they are brother and sister. A suggestion from Wotan that in spite of everything she should bless the union of the pair rouses her full indignation. She pours out a torrent of biting reproach upon him. Since he begat the Wälsungs he has neglected his own noble kindred, and especially his wife; moreover he is always flying to the fray with the savage Valkyrie maidens whom he has begotten. Lately he has been wandering wolflike through the woods as Wälse; and now, crowning disgrace and insult of all, he would throw his very wife at the foot of these wolf-whelps! As she pours out her passionate indictment the Wrath motive also works itself up into a fury in the orchestra.

Wotan, who so far has preserved a certain tranquillity, tries to reason with her. She goes too much by custom, he tells her; she will not admit even the necessity of finding a new rule to meet a new case. He lays before her the situation of himself and the gods in general. For their salvation they need a man who, not being sheltered by the gods, is not bound by the law of the gods; only such a man is meet for the deed which, though the need of the gods demands that it shall be done, a god himself may not work. To Fricka this seems merely sophistical; what deed could a hero do that could not be done by the gods to whose grace alone the hero would owe his power?

Fricka knows her husband, and sees in this sophistry only one of his usual attempts to gain his end by guile. Of one thing she is certain — that this Wälsung who has betrayed Hunding and wedded his own sister shall not escape her. In vain Wotan pleads with her that Siegmund owes nothing to him — that he won the sword himself in his need. " And who but thou," counters Fricka, " made him the need and gave him the sword? "

Was it not for him, and for him alone, that the god had struck the sword in the tree stem? Was it not by Wotan's roundabout craft that Siegmund was lured to the hall where it would be found? Wotan becomes more and more dejected as Fricka proceeds with her indictment, and recognising his embarrassment she presses her point still more urgently; with Wotan, the god, she might wage war, but this Siegmund, she says with superb contempt, she will punish merely as a slave.

An impulse of revolt surges up in Wotan, but recognising his moral impotence, he asks her gloomily what is her will with him. She exacts from him a promise that he will not shield Siegmund in the fight with the avenger; then, quickly reading what is obviously at the back of his mind, she insists also that the Wälsung shall not be helped by Brynhilde. Writhing helplessly in her coils, the unhappy Wotan mutters that the Valkyrie shall be free to act as she chooses. But Fricka will have none of this; Brynhilde has no will but that of her father Wotan, and Fricka demands that he shall forbid her to act for Siegmund. " I cannot forsake him," cries Wotan in his grief; " he found my sword! " " Then withdraw its magic," replies Fricka; " let the blade break, and send him to fight without a guard."

Just then Brynhilde's cry is heard again from the heights, and Wotan has to admit that he had sent her to prepare to ride to Siegmund. She appears with her horse on the rocky path to the right, but catching sight of Fricka she suddenly breaks off her Valkyrie cry, and slowly and silently leads her horse down the rocky path and leaves it in a cave. In the few moments that Brynhilde is away, Fricka addresses a last dignified appeal to Wotan to do, and to order Brynhilde to do, what is demanded by the honour of the gods if the moral rule of the gods is to continue in the world. For Fricka's honour Siegmund must fall: does Wotan confirm that by oath?

Throwing himself on to a rocky seat in the profoundest dejection, Wotan mutters brokenly, " Take my oath! " Then comes a moment that, in the hands of two actresses of the requisite calibre, is one of the most dramatic and breath-catching in the whole of *The Ring*. Striding towards the back, Fricka meets Brynhilde, and the two unfriendly women pause and regard each other for a moment in fateful silence. Then, in quiet, dignified tones, Fricka says to Brynhilde, " Wotan doth wait for thee: let him inform thee how the lot is to fall." She drives quickly away. Brynhilde, surprised, runs anxiously to Wotan, who is lost in gloomy brooding, and from the trombones we hear, quietly but suggestively, the motive of the Curse, which is followed by the significant motive of Wotan's Dejection:

(20)

This motive plays a great part in the scene that follows.

Byrnhilde anxiously asks what is amiss with her father. Wotan breaks into a terrible cry of grief and rage: this is the end of the gods, he says, and he himself is the saddest of all living things. Throwing from her her shield, spear, and helmet, Brynhilde sinks at his feet, and laying her head and hand confidingly on his knee and breast, she implores him to tell his beloved child the cause of his grief. He can confide in her, she says, for what is she but his own will incarnate?

Wotan has been sunk in deep thought: coming to himself out of this, and saying, very softly, " What secret I hold from all others still will remain unspoken for ever; myself I speak to, speaking to thee," he proceeds to tell her all the events of the story with which she is unfamiliar, but which have mostly been made known to us through *The Rhinegold* — how, when love had died out within him, he thirsted for power, and, lured craftily on by Loge, used fraud and deceit to consolidate that power; how Alberich, by

forswearing love, won the gold and wrought the Ring; how Wotan
in turn wrested the gold from him, meaning to pay the giants
with it for the building of Valhalla; how Erda warned him of the
ill fate that lay in wait for him if he kept the Ring; how, tortured
by the desire to know more of this misfortune that threatened him
and the gods, he went into the womb of earth, subdued Erda to his
love, mastered her wisdom and pride and so at last won speech
from her, and how she bore him " the world's wisest of women,"
Brynhilde, together with eight sisters; how, unceasingly oppressed
by the thought that the gods might come to a shameful end,
wrought by those whom they had kept in bondage by craft and
deception, he had made his Valkyrie daughters fill Valhalla with
a host of guardian heroes; how there never dies out from his mind
the fear that Alberich will regain the Ring and use its power to
destroy the gods; and how, though the Ring could easily be torn
from the dull-brained Fafner, Wotan may not attack him, for the
honour of his treaty forbids. He, the god of treaties, he cries
bitterly, to his own treaty is now a slave!

Only in one way and by one man can the gods be saved — by
one who will do what Wotan himself may not do, a hero unhelped
by him, who shall do Wotan's will unknowing, wholly through his
own need. In the orchestra the 'cellos give out softly the motive
of the Need of the Gods:

(21)

But where, the distracted god cries in his anguish, is this deliverer
to be found?

" But the Wälsung, Siegmund," Brynhilde interjects, " does not
he work for himself? " Sadly Wotan has to admit that he has
always been behind Siegmund, and that Fricka has fathomed the
fraud. And now he must abandon Siegmund, betray his trusted
one and let him go down to his death!

In the madness of his grief he invokes ruin upon the godhead;
for one thing only does he now long — the end, the end! And for

the destruction of the gods Alberich is always working and scheming; did not Erda warn Wotan that when Alberich, the dark foe of love, should get him a son, the end of the gods would be near? He has heard of late that by means of gold Alberich has won the love of a mortal woman, and that " grim envy's son now stirs in her womb." Truly Alberich is more fortunate than he: " this wonder befell to him, the loveless; yet of my love so boundless the free one was born not to me! " Wotan, in bitter wrath, gives Alberich his blessing, and with it the whole garish pomp of the gods with which to sate his envy.

What would he of Brynhilde? she asks him. Wotan tells her that she must fight for Fricka, the offended guardian of the marriage vow. Brynhilde, knowing how he loves Siegmund, impetuously declares that never will she fight against him, even at her father's bidding; but the god turns on her in towering anger and crushes her presumption. With a final cry of " Take heed my bidding to do! Siegmund dieth! This be the Valkyrie's work! " he strides away and disappears among the rocks.

The music of this long scene has been mainly made up of the most magical compounding and interplay of the various motives with which the reader is already familiar.

Left alone, Brynhilde stands for a while bewildered and terrified. Then, bending down sadly, she takes up her weapons and dons them again, but finds them heavier than before. Her heart is full of sorrow at the thought of having to abandon Siegmund, whom she loves almost as much as Wotan does. But the god's will must be obeyed, and slowly and mournfully she leaves the stage for the scene of the coming combat. When she arrives at the summit of the mountain she looks down into the gorge, and the Flight motive in the orchestra makes us aware that she sees Siegmund and Sieglinde approaching. After watching them for a moment she goes into the cave, disappearing from the view of the audience.

The Flight motive rises to greater and greater urgency in the orchestra, and at last Siegmund and Sieglinde, the latter sorely agitated and distressed, appear on the summit of the mountain.

Siegmund would have her rest awhile; but the terrified Sieglinde at first will hardly listen to him. Lovingly and gently he pleads with her; she is fleeing now not from Hunding only but from Siegmund himself, for though she loves him, her conscience has risen to accuse her, and she regards herself as unholy and accursed. He has brought her imperceptibly to the stone seat on which Wotan formerly sat. She throws her arms round his neck and remains thus for a moment, then starts up again in sudden terror and, heaping reproaches on herself, implores him to leave her in her shame. For whatever shame she has known, Siegmund replies, the miscreant to whom she had been bound against her will shall pay. Let her wait here; Siegmund will seek out Hunding, and " when Needful at his heart shall gnaw, vengeance then wilt thou have won! "

He is interrupted by a hoarse horn-call, afar off, punctuated by the typical Hunding rhythm (No. 7), and Sieglinde starts up again and listens in terror; it is Hunding hot on the hunt after them with his kinsmen and hounds. She stares before her as if demented with fear, and a succession of crashing discords in the trumpets and horns hints to us that her mind is cracking under the strain. Suddenly she melts in weakness and throws herself sobbing on Siegmund's breast, then starts up again in horror as she hears the savage baying of the hounds and the grim summons of Hunding's horn; in imagination she sees the hounds flinging themselves upon Siegmund and tearing him asunder, while his sword is broken into splinters and the ash tree is split and crashes to the ground. She collapses faintly into the arms of Siegmund, who lets her sink down with him, so that when he frees himself her head is resting on his lap. In this position he remains through the whole of the scene that immediately follows.

There is a long silence, during which Siegmund bends over her tenderly and presses a long kiss upon her brow, while the orchestra gives out a soft and infinitely sweet reminiscence of the Love theme (No. 5). Brynhilde, leading her horse by the bridle, comes out of the cave and advances slowly and solemnly. She pauses to contemplate the couple from a distance, then, again advancing

and again pausing, at last stands near to Siegmund and gazes long
and earnestly at him, one hand resting on the neck of her horse,
the other carrying her shield and spear. The brass give out the
solemn theme of the Annunciation of Death:

the kettledrum figure in which is presumably a reminiscence of a
figure in the Valhalla theme. To this motive succeeds, in the
trumpet and trombones, one of the most moving of all Wagner's
thematic inventions, the Death motive:

Upon this there follows a soft intonation of the Valhalla motive,
which at the end unexpectedly shifts over to the minor, leading to a
magical effect when Brynhilde strikes in with the solemn admonition, " Siegmund! Look on me! I come to call thee hence! "

This whole scene is one of the most searching expressions of
Wagner's genius, both musical and dramatic.

Siegmund asks who is this beauteous and fair visitor and what
she has to say to him. Gravely she tells him that it is only to men
fated to die that she appears; who once has seen her face must
go forth from the light of life, and him whom she greets she
chooses for her own — most of this to the accompaniment of the
Valhalla motive, indicating where the soul of the slain warrior is
to be taken.

And when the hero is hers, Siegmund asks, whither does she lead
him? To Wotan and Valhalla, she replies; there, as well as Wotan,
he will find a host of fallen heroes, who will give him greetings
of love; there too he will find his father Wälse. And will a woman
give him fond greeting there? Siegmund asks. Wish-maidens will

wait on him there, is Brynhilde's answer, and Wotan's daughter
herself will hand him the draught. For Wotan's child Siegmund now
recognises this grave and holy messenger, and one thing more
he would ask of her: will the bride and sister attend the brother
to Valhalla? Shall Siegmund there hold Sieglinde in his arms?
Gravely and sorrowfully Brynhilde tells him that his bride must
remain on earth awhile yet; Siegmund will not see Sieglinde there!

Siegmund at once bends over Sieglinde, and, to the strain of the
Love theme (No. 5) in the orchestra, kisses her softly on the
brow; then, turning tranquilly to Brynhilde, he bids her greet
for him Valhalla and Wotan and Wälse and all the heroes and the
gracious wish-maidens; but as for him, he will follow her not!
In the orchestra, by means of a quiet reiteration of the Annunciation motive (No. 22), we realise the inexorability of his fate; and
to the strain of the Death motive Brynhilde reminds him that
having looked upon the Valkyrie's face, with her he must now
fare. He is strong and brave, she knows, and while life is in him
he dreads nothing; " but death, thou vain one, prevails, and death
to foretell thee came I here."

" By the hand of what hero shall I fall? " he asks. Being told that
it is Hunding, he pours scorn on the idea. Sadly shaking her head,
Brynhilde tells him that all is in vain. Siegmund, showing her the
sword, given him by one who has care of him, makes light of her
threat; but, a note of rigid insistence coming into her voice, she
informs him that he who gave the sword now withdraws its virtue,
and himself sends Siegmund to death.

Upon this, Siegmund breaks out into a passionate lamentation
over his betrayal. If he must be parted from Sieglinde, he cries,
he cares nothing for the glories of Valhalla; rather would he go to
dwell with Hella! Brynhilde is touched by the completeness of this
love, and, disregarding his reproaches and insults, she implores
him to leave Sieglinde in her charge, for the sake of the child she
is to bear. But Siegmund will not listen to her. Raising the sword
he makes to slay Sieglinde, crying, " This sword, that a traitor
to true man did give, this sword, that now before the foe plays me
false; served it not then against the foe, it truly shall serve against

a friend! Two lives now laugh to thee here: take them, Needful, envious steel! Take them with one sure stroke! "

This decides Brynhilde. In an uncontrollable outburst of sympathy she cries to him that Sieglinde shall live and not be parted from Siegmund, for the Valkyrie will shield him in the fight. The sinister horn-calls are heard again in the distance, and she bids him hasten to the battlefield. She herself rushes away with her horse, and Siegmund looks after her with joy and relief.

The stage has gradually been growing darker; heavy thunderclouds have descended upon the background, and these gradually envelop the rocks, the gorge, and the mountains. Siegmund bends over the sleeping Sieglinde and speaks softly and lovingly to her; then, laying her gently on the rocks, he kisses her brow in farewell, and hearing Hunding's horn-call once more, starts up resolutely, draws his sword, and hastens to the mountain-top, where he disappears in the thunderclouds, that are broken for a moment by a flash of lightning.

When he has gone, Sieglinde begins to move restlessly in her dreams; she believes herself to be back again in her childhood's home, with her father and her brother roaming in the woods; cruel strangers descend upon the house, that goes up in flames. She gives a cry of " Siegmund! Siegmund! " and breaks out into her old terror as Hunding's horn-call is heard again, this time quite close. From the mountain pass at the back, Hunding's voice is heard hoarsely calling upon Woeful to face him in the fight, and Siegmund's voice, from farther away in the gorge, hurling back defiance.

For a moment a flash of lightning illumines the pass, and Sieglinde sees Hunding and Siegmund in combat. She rushes towards the pass, but is dazzled by another flash of lightning, and reels to one side as if blinded. In the glare of the light, Brynhilde is seen soaring over Siegmund and defending him with her shield. But just as Siegmund aims a deadly blow at Hunding, a red light breaks through the clouds from the left, and Wotan is seen standing over Hunding and holding out his spear in front of Siegmund. He orders Siegmund to stand back from his spear, upon which the

Wälsung's sword splinters, whereupon Hunding thrusts his spear into the breast of the unarmed man. Siegmund falls to the ground dead, and Sieglinde, who has heard his death-sigh, sinks down with a cry.

The fierce light has now died out from the mountain-top, and through the semi-darkness Brynhilde is dimly seen running to Sieglinde; she lifts her quickly on to her horse, and immediately disappears with her. The clouds above dividing, Hunding becomes visible, withdrawing his spear from the breast of the prostrate Siegmund; behind him, on a rock, leaning sombrely on his spear and surrounded by clouds, stands Wotan. In cold, devastatingly disdainful tones the god addresses Hunding: " Get hence, slave! Kneel before Fricka: tell her that Wotan's spear avenged what wrought her shame. . . . Go! . . . Go! " A contemptuous wave from the god's hand, and Hunding clatters dead to the ground. Then wrath against the disobedient Brynhilde surges up in Wotan's breast. " Woe to the guilty one! " he cries; " harshly will I punish her crime, if my steed be swift as her flight! " He disappears among thunder and lightning, and the curtain falls to a fortissimo enunciation, in the trombones, of the theme of the Need of the Gods (No. 21).

The third act opens with the magnificent scene descriptive of the Ride of the Valkyries. There is a short orchestral prelude before the curtain rises, based on the Ride motive (No. 17), accompanied by realistic spurts in the violins and whinnyings in the wood-wind.

The scene is the summit of a rocky mountain, with a pine wood on the right, and on the left the entrance to a cave, above which the rock rises to its highest point. The rocks at the back form the verge of a precipice. Storm-clouds fly swiftly past the mountain-peak. Four of the Valkyries, Gerhilde, Ortlinde, Waltraute, and Schwertleite, all in full armour, are assembled on the rocky point above the cave. The other Valkyries are as yet not in sight, though they are within hailing distance of the four on the rock. A flash of lightning pierces the clouds, and a Valkyrie on horseback becomes visible, a slain warrior hanging across her saddle. Other Valkyries, carrying a similar grim burden, appear from time to time, and the wild maidens keep calling excitedly to each other, those in the distance using speaking-trumpets in the first place.

In time the four other Valkyries — Helmwige, Siegrune, Grimgerde, and Rossweisse — arrive, and all now await Brynhilde, who, they know, has been sent by their father to Siegmund the Wälsung. At last they perceive Brynhilde in the distance, pounding towards them in furious haste, and, to their astonishment, leaving her winded and staggering horse, Grane, in the wood. Something hangs from the saddle, but it is not a man.

From the excited ejaculations of the Valkyries we learn that Brynhilde takes no notice of their greeting; Grane has sunk to the earth exhausted, and Brynhilde, leaping from the saddle, has lifted the woman she has been carrying there.

At length Brynhilde enters, supporting and leading Sieglinde. Breathlessly she explains to her sisters that for the first time she is not pursuing but pursued: " War-father [Wotan] hunts me close! " All give an exclamation of terror, while Brynhilde anxiously begs them to look northward from the mountain height, to see if War-father be nearing. They see a thunderstorm approaching from the north, that portends the coming of Wotan.

Hurriedly Brynhilde explains to her sisters that the woman with her is Sieglinde, and that Wotan's fury is aroused against not only the Wälsung but against Brynhilde herself for disobeying his commands. She implores them to lend her their swiftest steed that she may bear the woman away from Wotan's wrath; but the others are unwilling to bring their father's anger down upon themselves. Sieglinde breaks in upon the excited conversation with a quiet appeal to Brynhilde to have no further thought of her: it would have been better had she died with Siegmund, but there is still a way out; if Brynhilde would not have her curse her, let her strike her own sword through Sieglinde's heart. But Brynhilde begs her still to live " for love's fulfilment: rescue the pledge he has left of his love; a Wälsung bearest thou to him! "

Sieglinde starts violently, then her face lights up suddenly with an exalted joy, and she implores Brynhilde and the others to rescue her and her babe.

The thunderclouds at the back become darker, and the thunder draws nearer. The other Valkyries dare not help; but in response to another appeal from Sieglinde, Brynhilde bids her fly swiftly into the forest, while she will remain and await Wotan's vengeance. Which of the sisters, asks Brynhilde, came from the east? Siegrune replies that eastward is a wood, and there, in a cavern, Fafner, changed into a dragon, guards Alberich's ring. Mention of the dragon is accompanied by the slow-moving Dragon motive in the deeper and darker colours of the orchestra:

No place is that wood, Grimgerde thinks, for a helpless woman; but Brynhilde answers that Sieglinde will be safer there than anywhere, for Wotan dreads and shuns the place. Hurriedly and excitedly Brynhilde urges Sieglinde to fly eastward, and to be brave through all suffering and want, for in her womb she bears " the world's most wonderful hero " — upon which we hear in the orchestra the theme that henceforth will characterise Siegfried:

Producing the pieces of Siegmund's sword from under her armour, she hands them to Sieglinde, bidding her preserve them, for from them the sword shall some day be re-wrought: as for the child's name, it shall be " Siegfried," and he shall rejoice in victory (*erfreu' sich des Sieg's*).

Then comes one of those tremendous emotional climaxes that Wagner always knew how to hold back to the very last and then launch with overwhelming effect. The orchestra gives out fortissimo a theme — that of Redemption by Love:

(26)
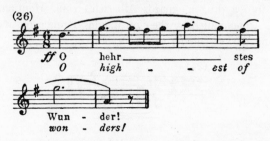

that will play an important part in the later stages of the *Ring*, and over it Sieglinde's voice soars in an ecstasy of joy: " Oh, highest of wonders! Noblest of maids! Thou, true one, holiest comfort dost give! For him whom we loved I save the beloved one: may my heart's deep thanks win for thee joy! " Then she hastens away.

A storm now rages up from the back; the mountains are enveloped in black thunderclouds, while from the right a fiery glow appears. Wotan's voice is heard booming through a speaking-trumpet, imperiously bidding Brynhilde remain and face him. The Valkyries, trembling at the thought of the coming vengeance, conceal Brynhilde among them, and look anxiously towards the wood, that is now lit up by a bright glare.

At last Wotan, blazing with wrath, enters from the wood and strides impetuously towards the group of Valkyries on the height, searching for Brynhilde. The others, in a moving ensemble, plead with him to have compassion on her, but the angry god upbraids them bitterly for their womanish weakness: " I bred you to fare with joy to the fight, stony and ruthless your hearts I made, and ye wild ones now weep and whine when my wrath doth a traitor chastise! "

Again and again the orchestra gives out, in a fierce fortissimo, the theme of Wotan's Dejection (No. 20) as he asks them if they realise the crime that Brynhilde has committed. She was his loved one, his trusted one; no one but she knew the innermost depths of his thought; no one but she saw to the springs of his spirit; what he but wished, she shaped into deeds; and now she has broken the holy bond between them, defied his will, openly scorned his imperious commands, and turned against him the weapon that his will alone made hers! " Hear'st thou, Brynhilde? " he cries to the shrinking and still hidden Valkyrie; " thou, on whom byrnie, helm and spear, glory and grace, honour and fame I bestowed? Hear'st thou of what I accuse thee, and hid'st from thy accuser, in hope to escape his scourge? "

The tempest dies out of the music as Brynhilde emerges from the midst of the Valkyries, steps down from the rock humbly but still firmly, and approaches to within a little distance from Wotan. " Here am I, father," she says in quiet tones; " pronounce thou my sentence! " Wotan storms at her again: it is not he who sentences her, it is she herself who has shaped her own sentence. His will alone it was that woke her to life, yet against his will she has worked; her work was to fulfil his command, yet against him she has commanded; she was his wish-maiden, yet against his will she has wished; she was his shield-maid, yet against him she has raised her shield; she was his lot-chooser, yet against him she has chosen the lot; her task was to stir up heroes, yet against him has she stirred them up. What she once was he now has told her; what she now is, let her say to herself. She will be his wish-maiden no more; a Valkyrie once she was, henceforth she shall remain what she now is.

Brynhilde breaks into a wail at this denunciation of her, but the pitiless god goes on: no more shall she be sent forth from Valhalla to bring heroes to fill his hall; no more shall she fill his drinking-horn at the feasts of the gods; no more will he kiss her like a child; she is cast out from the race of the gods; broken is the bond between them, and she is for ever banned from his sight. " Thou takest away, then, all thou hast given? " asks Brynhilde.

" No," replies the god, " one shall come who will take it all away " ; for the god means to lay her in sleep here upon the rock, defenceless against any man who shall find her and wake her.

The Valkyries make a passionate appeal for mercy, and the raging god now turns the full blast of his anger on them. Have they not heard his decree? The traitorous sister is banished from among them; no more shall she ride through the cloud-rack to the combat with them; her maidenhood's flower shall fade away, and a husband shall win him her womanly grace; she shall obey a masterful lord and sit by the hearth and spin, a sport and a shame to all mockers!

Brynhilde sinks to the ground with a cry, and the horror-struck Valkyries recoil from her. Does her fate affright them? Wotan asks. If so, let them leave her, and henceforth bide far from her; for if one of them should disobey his commands and give Brynhilde help, she shall share Brynhilde's fate. " Hence with you now; come to this rock no more! Swiftly hence on your coursers, lest my curse light on you here! " The Valkyries separate with wild cries and fly into the wood, crying " Woe! Woe! "

A mad clamour is heard in the wood, and by a vivid lightning flash that rends the clouds we see the Valkyries with loose bridles, crowded together and rushing madly away. Gradually the storm dies down and the scene becomes more tranquil as the evening twilight falls. Wotan and Brynhilde are left alone, she lying prostrate upon the ground. There is a long and solemn silence, during which we hear in turns an expressive version of the Death motive (in the bass clarinet), and then, in the same instrument, a new motive, that of the Wälsungs' Love:

which, as will be seen, shades off into the motive of Wotan's Dejection. The theme of the Wälsungs' Love, changed into the major:

(28)

becomes of great significance later.

For a time the positions of Wotan and Brynhilde do not alter; then at length she raises her head slowly, and at first timidly, then more firmly, asks Wotan if what she did was so shameful that her offence must so shamefully be scourged; was it so base that she herself must go down into such deep debasement; was it so full of dishonour that her own honour must be lost for ever? Gradually raising herself to a kneeling position she begs her father to look into her eyes, to master his wrath, and to reveal to her the hidden guilt that has made him set his face like a stone against her.

Anger has by now died out of Wotan, leaving behind it only a trail of bitterness and sadness. Brynhilde would have him see that in disobeying his commands she was really carrying out his secret wish, for he loved the Wälsung, and needed him for his own purpose. She had read Wotan, and seen what his sorrow hid from him. And when she had faced Siegmund, and looked into his eyes, and heard his defiance of life and death, she realised the hero's distress, and was moved to pity and love. And in doing this she has been more truly Wotan than Wotan himself, for he who had breathed this love into her breast — here we hear, in the orchestra, in soft tones, the major version of the Wälsungs' Love motive (No. 28) — was he whose will had bound Siegmund's lot with hers; and reading the god's thought, she had defied the god's command.

Wotan has to admit that in doing so she did what he himself would fain have done but might not do. He goes once more over the story of his problems, his difficulties, and his misery, and in the end dryly and sadly casts her off from him again; no more can he take whispered counsel with her, no more can they work together as comrades.

Brynhilde recognises the justice of her punishment, though her offence, as it seems to her, was simply that she loved what she knew he loved. But for his own sake, she continues, let him not bring her to a shame that would stain him as well, for she is the half of his own being. If indeed she is to be banished from Valhalla, and to have a man for her master, let Wotan at least not deliver her up to any craven. The gloomy god repeats that from War-father she has turned, and War-father may not choose for her now. Then, softly and intimately, she touches him on what she knows is a weak point. The bravest of heroes, she tells him, will spring from the Wälsungs' line, and Sieglinde guards the fragments of the sword that Wotan shaped for Siegmund.

But Wotan, though sad at heart, still will not let himself be moved. He must fulfil her chastisement; she is to lie fast bound in sleep, and the man who finds the weaponless maid shall wake her and win her for his wife. His words are accompanied softly by the expressive modulations of the theme of the Magic Ban:

(29)

Falling on her knees before him, Brynhilde implores him to grant her one thing — at least to surround the rock with appalling horrors, so that only the freest and bravest of heroes may find her; if not, let Wotan destroy her with his spear, but not condemn her to woeful shame.

Her appeal is accompanied in the orchestra by a new motive that at first appears in the minor, but afterwards changes to the major form in which it is most generally known:

(30)

This is the Slumber motive. The crackling of Loge's fire-music is heard as she begs Wotan to surround the rock with fire, to lick with its tongue, to rend with its teeth, any craven who shall rashly dare to draw near to the dangerous height.

A wave of love and tenderness at last sweeps over Wotan; deeply moved, he turns quickly to Brynhilde, raises her to her feet, and gazes with profound emotion into her eyes. He bids his beloved child farewell. Never again may he give her loving greeting; never again shall she ride forth with him, or bring him the mead-cup at the gods' banquets; but around her couch he will kindle such a fire as never yet burned for a bride. At least no coward shall come to the rock, " for one alone winneth the bride, one freer than I, the god! " Who that free one shall be we are told by the orchestra, that gives out the Siegfried motive (No. 25).

Radiant and exalted, Brynhilde falls on Wotan's breast; he holds her silently in a long embrace, while the orchestra pours out a passionate interlude commencing with the Wälsungs' Love motive (No. 27), that gradually merges into the Slumber motive (No. 30). Over a long symphonic development of this last in the orchestra, Wotan takes farewell of the eyes and lips of his loved one: on him, the care-ridden god, those eyes must now close for ever:

Zum letz-ten Mal letz' es mich heut, mit des
Their gleam once more gladdens me now, as my

Le - be-woh-les letz - tem Kuss!
lips meet thine in love's last kiss!

(the " Parting Kiss " motive), but they may yet beam on one more fortunate; now he must turn from her and " kiss her godhood away."

The mysterious modulations of the Magic Ban motive are heard, followed by a further treatment of the Slumber motive in combination with the melody of Wotan's last address to her, as he imprints a long kiss on her lips. Unconsciousness gently steals over her, and she sinks back in his arms with closed eyes. Underneath a broad-branched fir tree is a mossy bank, to which he leads her tenderly and on which he lays her down. He closes her helmet, contemplates the sleeping figure for a moment, and then completely covers it with the great steel Valkyrie shield.

With one more sorrowful look at her, he steps with solemn resolution into the centre of the stage, and turning his spear-point towards a large rock he loudly summons Loge to appear.

There is a quivering in the lower strings:

then a first dull flickering of fire in the orchestra as Wotan strikes the rock three times with his spear. Finally a stream of fire gushes from the rock:

It grows brighter and brighter, the Loge motive (see *Rhinegold,* No. 15), scored for glockenspiel, piccolo, harp, etc.:

now taking complete possession of the orchestra.

The vivid flames dart around Wotan, who, with his spear, commandingly directs them to form a sea of fire that engirdles the rock. " He who my spear-point's sharpness feareth," he cries, " ne'er breaks through this fierce-flaming fire " ; and Wagner, by making him sing the words to the Siegfried motive, once more plays the part of prophet to us. With a last sorrowful look at Brynhilde the god departs slowly through the fire, the orchestra discoursing all the while upon the lulling Slumber motive.

This second opera of the *Ring,* by reason of its rich emotions, may be regarded as akin to the slow movement of a symphony. *Siegfried* is something of a scherzo, and the *Twilight of the Gods* the finale.

SOME years elapsed between the close of the *Valkyrie* and the commencement of *Siegfried*.

Sieglinde, whom we have seen sent by Brynhilde into the wood to escape the vengeance of Wotan, came to Nibelheim, the abode of the Nibelungs, where she was cared for by the tiny folk. She died in giving birth to a son, the Siegfried whom Brynhilde had foretold and named. Mime fancies he sees in this boy, who is healthy and fearless, a means by which to make himself possessor of the Ring and the Tarnhelm.

After Fafner (in the *Rhinegold*) had slain his brother Fasolt, he retired with his booty into a cave, Neidhöhle (the Cave of Envy), where, the better to guard his treasure, he transformed himself, by means of the Tarnhelm, into a dragon. He is too dull-witted to realise the illimitable possibilities that lie in the Ring; his sole instinct is to guard what he has already won by stretching out his monstrous bulk upon it. The slaying of the dragon would be a feat beyond the powers of the puny Mime, but the scheming dwarf thinks he may train up the young Siegfried to do the deed.

The Prelude gives us a tone-picture of Mime thinking out his problem. First of all, over a continuous rumble in the kettle-drums, we hear in the bassoons the motive of Reflection:

that we have already seen associated with Mime's thinking processes in the *Rhinegold*. A little later there comes out in the tuba the heavy theme that symbolises the Hoard:

(2)

This is followed by the hammering motive of the Nibelungs (see *Rhinegold* analysis, example No. 19), and this by the motive of Servitude (*Rhinegold*, No. 21). These last three motives are worked up to a climax, and then we hear the motive of the Ring (*Rhinegold*, No. 6) — another hint of what is passing through Mime's mind. We have yet a further light upon his thoughts when the bass trumpet suddenly gives out softly the theme of the Sword.

When the curtain rises we see a rocky cavern, with a large entrance in the background opening into the wood. On the left, against the wall, is a large smith's forge, built out of the natural rock. A rough chimney, also natural, goes up through the roof of the cave. The enormous bellows are of course artificial. Not far from the forge stands an anvil, and near it are implements pertaining to the craft of the smith. Little Mime, looking more shrunken and bleached than ever, and evidently with a load on his rudimentary mind, sits at the anvil, talking to himself as he hammers away at a sword.

We learn that Mime's swords are as a rule considered good enough for anyone; but the " malapert boy " with whom Mime has the misfortune to be associated has a way of smashing them with a single blow as if they were mere children's toys. Dejectedly and pettishly Mime throws the sword on the anvil, puts his arms akimbo, and stares reflectively at the ground. There is *one* sword he knows the boy could never shatter — Nothung; but the welding of the fragments of that weapon is beyond his skill. Sinking back, Mime makes a desperate effort to think the worrying problem out.

Deep down in the orchestra we hear the Dragon motive (*Valkyrie* analysis, No. 24), as Mime tells us how Fafner broods in the darkness of the cave, guarding the Hoard under his enormous body. Siegfried, boy though he is, would soon destroy Fafner and win the Ring for Mime if only he had Nothung in his hands; but this Nothung, Mime wails, he cannot weld! He takes up his hammer again, but without much heart for his work, for he knows that this latest effort of his will share the fate of its predecessors as soon as Siegfried gets hold of it.

At this point Siegfried bursts in from the wood — a young man of perfect health and the most boisterous spirits, wearing a rough forester's dress, with a silver horn slung from a chain. He has bridled a great bear with a rope, and he amuses himself by driving the animal at the terrified Mime. His entry is signalised by the horn-call that will henceforth be associated with him:

Mime drops the sword in terror and takes refuge behind the forge; Siegfried, pursuing him and pretending to set the bear on him, tells the animal to ask the dwarf for the promised sword. When Mime tells him that the weapon is there, all finished, Siegfried gives the bear a stroke on the back with the rope and drives him into the forest, whereupon Mime, trembling all over, emerges from his shelter behind the forge.

He peevishly asks why the boy treats him so badly, and Siegfried, having recovered from his laughter, explains that he has been out in the woods looking for a better friend than Mime, and the bear having appeared in response to the horn, he liked the animal better than his foster-father and brought him in with him to ask for the sword. Snatching the weapon from Mime, Siegfried soon smashes it in pieces on the anvil, and then vents his rage upon the shrinking dwarf to a theme:

that typifies the boy's Joy in Life.

Having given his opinion of Mime's craftsmanship in the most insulting terms, he throws himself raging on a stone seat. Mime, who has prudently kept out of his way, reproaches him for his ingratitude; then, cautiously approaching the sulking boy, he tries to tempt him with some broth and meat he has prepared for him, but Siegfried, whose back remains turned to him, knocks the bowl out of his hand. Mime sends up a querulous squeak of self-pity: this is how his devotion is rewarded! And he tells Siegfried how he brought him up from a whimpering babe:

Als zullendes Kind   zog ich dich auf.
A whimpering babe brought I thee up.

fed him and clothed him and made toys and a horn for him, smoothed his bed for him, quickened his wits, and now stays at home toiling and moiling for him while he is wandering through the woods at his pleasure; and for all this love and service his only wage is torment and hatred! Thoroughly sorry for himself, he bursts into sobs, but meeting Siegfried's gaze he timidly lowers his own eyes.

Scornfully Siegfried tells him that much indeed Mime has taught him, but one thing he has never been able to teach him — how to endure his sight! The more Mime does for him, he says, the less he likes him; and when he stands before him shuffling and scraping and blinking he feels an almost uncontrollable impulse to take him by the neck and make an end of him. *That* is how he has learned to love Mime! Why, he asks, does he ever return to him? Everything he meets in the forests, the trees, the birds, the fish in the brook, all these he loves far more; what is it, then, that brings him back to Mime again? If the dwarf is as wise as he pretends to be, let him find the answer to that puzzle.

Mime, recovering confidence a little, but still thinking it prudent to keep some way off, explains, to a motive in the orchestra that is associated in *Siegfried* with Love:

that it is because deep down in his heart the dwarf is really dear to him. Accompanied by the tender No. 6, he explains that always the young one yearns for the parent nest, even as he, Siegfried, longs for and loves his Mime.

But Siegfried is not convinced. While the orchestra weaves the loveliest strains out of No. 6, the boy puts another poser to the dwarf. He is not ignorant of what love is, for he has seen the birds singing for happiness together in the spring, husband and wife building them a nest and bringing up the tiny fledglings; he has seen also the deer and even the foxes and wolves in pairs, the father bringing the food, the mother suckling the young; where now is Mime's wife, that he may call her mother? The whimpering babe Mime indeed brought up, but how came the whelp to him?

Mime, in great embarrassment, tries to persuade him that he himself is " father and mother in one " to Siegfried. The angry boy tells him he is lying, for he can see for himself that the young ones are like the elders; he has seen his own image in the brook, and he is as unlike Mime as a toad is to a glittering fish, and surely no fish ever had a toad for father? Seizing Mime by the throat he threatens to tear him to pieces unless he tells him who are his father and mother. When Mime has been released and has recovered his breath, he reproaches Siegfried once more for his ingratitude and hatred, and promises to give him the truth at last.

(From this point onwards to the end of the *Ring* it becomes almost impossible to keep referring in detail to the various musical motives as they recur. In *Siegfried* and the *Twilight of the Gods* the majority of the motives employed are those we have already heard in the *Rhinegold* and the *Valkyrie*. The orchestral tissue is almost entirely made up of repetitions or variations of these motives; and the reader may take it for granted that wherever mention is made of any character that has already appeared in the earlier operas, or anything that has happened there, the corresponding motive will be drawn upon. Thus in the narrative of

Mime with which we are now about to deal, we start with the theme of the Wälsungs' Woe (*Valkyrie*, No. 6), pass from that to the Wälsungs' Love (*Valkyrie*, No. 5), thence to the Sword motive, and so on).

Mime's story is of how he once found a woman weeping in the wood, how he helped her to his cave, sheltered her, and tended her as best he could, and how she died in giving birth to a son; it was the dying mother herself who had given him his name, so that as " Siegfried " he should be fair and strong. The dwarf keeps interlarding his story with whining testimonials to his own kindness to the child, but Siegfried keeps pressing him for more vital details.

Mime can tell him that his mother's name was Sieglinde, but of his father he only knows that he was killed in combat. Siegfried is sceptical, and demands evidence of the truth of all this. Reflecting for a moment, Mime produces the two fragments of the broken sword — the only " paltry pay," he pathetically interjects, he has received for all he has done for Siegfried; these fragments the dying mother gave him, saying that the child's father had borne the sword in the last of his fights.

Exuberantly Siegfried cries that this is his own rightful sword, and that Mime must forge it for him, and that this very day; then, when his father's sword is his, he will fare forth into the world, never more to return; he will be free, as the birds, the animals, and the fishes are free:

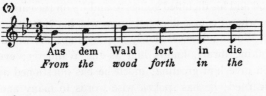

He rushes impetuously into the forest, leaving Mime in the utmost terror. Here is a new problem for the dwarf to think out. If this young hero leaves him, how can he hope to deal with Fafner? On the other hand, though Siegfried may slay Fafner with Nothung, how, with *his* limitations as a smith, is Mime to weld these formidable fragments together again?

While he is thinking distressfully about all this, Wotan comes in from the forest by the door at the back of the scene. Wotan is now the Wanderer; he wears a long mantle of dark blue, and carries his spear as a staff; on his head is a large hat with a broad round brim, that comes low down over the eye that is lacking. Two motives, or rather two complementary sections of the same motive:

are always used henceforth to characterise the majesty of the disguised god and his dignified goings to and fro on the earth.

Mime, who of course does not know who his visitor is, starts up in terror. Wotan advances slowly step by step: the world, he tells the shrinking dwarf, knows him as the Wanderer; everywhere good men give him greeting; much he has questioned and much he has learned; he has spoken wise words to many and warded from them woe and sorrow. He keeps advancing slowly till he has come right down to the hearth.

Mime, who has become more uneasy, asks him to take his leave, for he has wits enough of his own, and has no need of the newcomer's boasted wisdom. If he is so proud of his wits, the Wanderer good-humouredly rejoins, let them put each other to the test; his own head shall be Mime's should he be unable to answer anything the dwarf may ask him. Pulling himself together, Mime agrees to ask the Wanderer three questions.

After a great intellectual effort, he shoots out the first of these. The Wanderer, by his own account, has gone over all the world: what then is the race that dwells in the deepest caverns? The Wanderer gives the answer in full — it is the Nibelungs, who dwell in Nibelheim; Alberich was once their master, having tamed them by the might of a Ring. Mime's second question, put after still more profound meditation, is: " What is the race that dwells on the broad back of the earth? " The Wanderer replies that it is the giants: the chief of them were Fasolt and Fafner, who made the Hoard their own, and with it the Ring, but the Ring bred strife between the brothers, and Fafner slew Fasolt, and now guards the Hoard as a fearful dragon.

Mime, quite overcome by the wisdom of his visitor, reflects still more deeply and produces his third question: " What is the race that dwells on the cloud-covered heights? " The Wanderer, to the soft accompaniment of the Valhalla motive, tells him that on the cloud-covered heights dwell the gods, with Valhalla for their hall. Wotan is their head; from a branch of the world's ash tree he made a shaft, and then ruled the world, with the point of the spear on which were engraved the runes of treaties (here the deep brass of the orchestra gives out an important new motive, that of the Might of the Gods):

before him bow both the Nibelungs and the giants — before him, the spear's mighty lord! As if by accident the spear touches the ground, and a slight rumble of thunder is heard, which terrifies

Mime. Has he answered the questions? asks the Wanderer placidly; does his head remain his own?

Baffled and perplexed, Mime has to admit that the visitor has won the right to retain his head, and once more he begs him to go on his way. But the Wanderer has not finished with him yet. Mime, it seems, did not greet the guest with due courtesy; and having tried to capture his visitor's head, his own now, by rule, is forfeit unless he too can answer three questions.

Terrified but submissive, the dwarf braces himself for the ordeal; his mother-wit, he admits, is moidered, but he will do his best. Seating himself comfortably, the Wanderer poses the first question: " What is the name of the race that Wotan wreaked his wrath on, and yet loves more than his life? " Plucking up courage, Mime replies that they are the Wälsungs; from two of them, Siegmund and Sieglinde, sprang Siegfried.

Good-humouredly complimenting him on his cleverness, the Wanderer puts the second question: " Siegfried is being brought up by a wise Nibelung who means to send him to fight Fafner, so that the dwarf may win him the Ring and the Hoard; now, what sword is it with which Siegfried shall slay Fafner? " Mime is sure of himself now. Rubbing his hands together gleefully, and quite forgetting his fears in the bright prospect of the future, he replies that the sword is Nothung; it was struck in an ash tree by Wotan, and only a mighty hero could draw it forth; Siegmund was that hero, and he bore the sword in fight till it was shattered on Wotan's spear; the pieces are being treasured by a cunning smith, for he knows that with them the Dragon will be slain by Siegfried.

With a deep-chested laugh, the Wanderer compliments Mime on his cleverness; never was there so wise a smith on earth! But now for the third question: " By whose hand shall the fragments of Nothung be welded again? " This is too much for Mime. Starting up in the wildest terror he screams out that he does not know; would he had never seen the accursed steel, for it is so hard that he hammers at it in vain! What with the old vexations and the new terror his jarred nerves give way, and he throws his tools about as if demented.

Rising quietly from the hearth, the Wanderer tells him that though Mime, over-confident in his own wisdom, has forfeited his head, he will give it him back along with a valuable piece of information: only he who has never known what fear is shall forge Nothung afresh. Let Mime look well to his wise old head; it shall be forfeit to him who has never known fear.

When the Wanderer has left, Mime's nerve goes completely; he stares wildly before him and begins to tremble violently. In a marvellous piece of orchestral tone-painting Wagner shows us the whole of nature apparently conspiring to drive the poor little Nibelung mad: the forest is alive with flickering flames; the wind howls and the earth roars, and from the maw of the Dragon in his distant cave comes a fearsome bellowing. With a loud shriek Mime collapses behind the anvil just as Siegfried bursts in from the forest to demand the expected sword.

For a time he cannot find Mime; when at last he discovers him, the mammering imp manages bit by bit to tell him that he has learned that Nothung can be forged only by one who has never known fear. It has already occurred to his little brain that Siegfried may be such a one, in which case he may perhaps still be able to use him for his own ends. The first thing is to find out whether Siegfried has even known fear. He describes such a scene in the forest as that which he himself has recently witnessed, and asks if Siegfried has ever been terrified when the forces of nature have hurled themselves at him like that. Siegfried assures him that the feeling is strange to him, but he would like to experience it were it possible. Can Mime teach him what this fear is?

Mime will do his best if only Siegfried will follow his instructions faithfully. He knows of a horrible dragon who slays and swallows men; let Siegfried follow him to Fafner's lair, and he shall learn what fear is. Siegfried is delighted at the prospect; let Mime forge him his father's sword, take him to Fafner's cave, and then — out into the world and freedom! Once more Mime assures him that the forging of the sword is beyond his poor powers. Belike one who has never known fear might accomplish it, he suggests; and the impatient boy, striding to the hearth, vows that he will forge his father's sword himself.

A new motive, symbolising Siegfried's joy in his own strength (it is obviously derived from Siegfried's horn-call, No. 3):

takes possession of the orchestra as Siegfried sets impetuously to work. He makes a great heap of charcoal on the hearth, blows up the fire, places the fragments of the Sword in the vice, and files them, Mime all the while watching him from a little distance. Mime offers technical advice from time to time, but the impatient youth prefers his own unconventional methods, and Mime has to admit that they promise to be successful; " the fool is favoured by folly alone," he says.

While Siegfried is filing away at the fragments, Mime speculates anxiously on the future. Siegfried will forge the sword, that is clear, and then will he not use it against Mime himself, unless he first learns fear from Fafner? On the other hand, if Siegfried does learn fear, how then will he slay the Dragon and win the Ring for Mime? Or again, by what means can *he* master the fearless boy?

Siegfried, still busy at his work, demands the name of the sword, and learning that it is Nothung, he addresses it in a motive formed out of the descending octave we have already seen associated with the Sword:

This is the Forging Song — a masterpiece of musical characterisation, in which we have not only the whole expression of all Siegfried's vigour and joy in life, but the most extraordinary realism in the orchestra, that seems to be belching out the heat of the forge and sending up tongues of flame.

As the song goes on, Mime, having collected his wits, works out a plan. After the fight with Fafner, Siegfried will be faint; Mime will bring him a refreshing draught, in which he will put spices that will send him into a sound sleep; then, with the selfsame weapon that Siegfried forged, he will put him out of his way, and the Ring and the Hoard will be his. He rubs his hands in delight, and asks the absent Wanderer gleefully if *now* he thinks Mime dull.

By this time the contents of the crucible are glowing; Siegfried pours them into a mould and plunges the mould into the water-trough, which steams and hisses as the mould cools. Then he thrusts the steel into the fire and pulls vigorously at the bellows for a time, after which he takes the mould from the fire, breaks it, and lays the glowing steel on the anvil in the centre of the stage, where he proceeds to hammer it into shape. Meanwhile Mime, who has sprung up in delight, shakes spices and herbs into a cooking-pot, which he places on the hearth. Flatteringly and with many a snigger he explains to Siegfried that the old smith has been brought to shame, and now is reduced to cooking for the boy turned master. Siegfried, exulting in his strength and skill, keeps hammering away at the Sword, that once laughed cold, he tells it, but now is flushed with fire as it yields up its inward strength to him who has tamed its pride. Two fresh motives, both associated with the forging:

play prominent parts in the music to this episode.

The hammering finished, Siegfried brandishes the Sword and plunges it into the water-trough, laughing lustily at the hissing sound it makes. Then he fashions the blade into a handle, Mime all the while painting for himself a rosy future in which he will win the Ring and make Alberich and the other Nibelungs his slaves; the poor dwarf they despised shall be master of them all; even the gods and the heroes shall bow to his might, and the whole world fall prostrate at his command.

By now the Sword is completely finished. Siegfried brandishes it aloft and hails it with a great exulting cry, an extraordinary effect of consummation and triumph being attained at the climax by the apparently simple means of swinging the previous minor tonality of the Forging Song over to the major. With one great blow he splits the anvil from top to bottom. He holds the Sword aloft exultantly, while Mime, who has jumped on to a stool in his ecstasy, falls terrified to the ground as the curtain falls.

The second act opens with an orchestral prelude that, in Wagner's usual way, elucidates the drama by the juxtaposition of various motives. First of all we hear the theme of Fafner as the Dragon:

(14)

This will be seen to be derived from the motive of the Giants (*Rhinegold*, No. 11), the deepening of the interval of a perfect fourth into an augmented fourth being curiously suggestive of the descent of Fafner into the kingdom of the brute. This kettledrum figure plays a large part in the Prelude. We also hear, among other motives, those of the Ring, the Curse, and Annihilation (*Rhinegold*, No. 24).

The curtain having risen, we see a deep forest; at the back of the stage is the entrance to a cave; towards the middle of the stage the ground rises and forms a little knoll. To the left, through the trees, can be seen a fissured cliff. It is a dark night, and at first the spectator's eye can distinguish nothing. To the accompaniment of the Annihilation motive we hear the voice of Alberich, who is lying by the rocky cliff, brooding darkly; it is only gradually that his form can be picked out in the obscurity.

Alberich is at his accustomed task of waiting and watching
by the cave, and longing for the day to dawn that shall decide his
own fate and that of the others. From the forest on the right comes
a storm of wind, accompanied by a bluish light, which latter attracts Alberich's eye. The glow comes nearer for a moment; then
the wind dies down and the light fades away as the Wanderer,
emerging from the forest, pauses opposite Alberich. The latter
challenges the intruder; then, recognising him by a ray of moonlight that suddenly breaks through the clouds, the angry Nibelung
bids his old enemy go on his way and leave him in peace; but the
Wanderer calmly assures him that he comes now only as witness,
not as worker.

Alberich bittery reproaches Wotan for his treachery and taunts
him with his fatal weakness — in virtue of the runes of treaty
upon his spear he cannot repeat his former exploit and rob Fafner
of the Ring, for were he to try to do so the spear would crumble
to dust. He knows the care that oppresses the god, the fear that
the Ring will again fall into Alberich's hands. Were it to do so,
he says, he would not use it like the dull-witted Fafner, but by its
might would bring Valhalla's towers crashing down and make himself master of the world.

Quietly the Wanderer tells him that he knows all this well, and
it troubles him not; the might of the Ring shall go to him who
can win it for himself. Alberich knows Wotan's plan to rear a
youth who shall do the gods' will without help or urging from the
gods, and he scornfully throws this knowledge at the Wanderer.
Tranquilly the god advises him to spare his wrangling for his
brother Mime, who is bringing to him a boy who shall slay Fafner
for him. The boy is ignorant of the gods and their will, ignorant
even of the Ring, and Wotan will give him no help; he is his own
lord, and will stand or fall by his own power.

At this point we hear a motive:

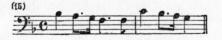

typical of Siegfried's Freedom. The Wanderer makes everything clear to Alberich: a hero is coming to rescue the Hoard; Fafner will die, and the gold shall be his who shall seize it. If he would know more, let him speak to Fafner; perhaps if Alberich warns the Dragon of his coming death he will give up the Hoard peaceably. The Wanderer himself will waken Fafner for him.

Standing on the knoll in front of the cave he calls loudly to the Dragon within: " Here stands a friend to warn thee of danger; thy life he will leave thee, wilt thou but grant him the treasure thou guardest! " From within the cave, through a speaking-trumpet, comes the heavy voice of the aroused Fafner. Alberich tells him that a hero is coming to measure his strength with his. " My hunger's keen! " is the laconic reply. It is the Ring alone that the hero wants, continues Alberich; let Fafner give that to the Nibelung and he will stay the fight; the Hoard shall be Fafner's, and long and undisturbed he can sleep upon it. Fafner's famous reply is regarded by the commentators as typical of the brutish possessor of wealth who merely loves gold for its own sake: " I lie and possess; let me slumber! " He gives a cavernous yawn and relapses into silence.

The Wanderer laughs aloud and then turns again to Alberich with a parting piece of advice; to the accompaniment of a motive that has already figured in the *Ring* in one shape or another, notably in connection with Erda:

(46)

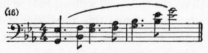

he tells him that " all things go as e'en they must, and no whit may they be altered." Now he will leave him to himself and his brother Mime — but soon he shall know what now he does not know.

The god disappears rapidly into the forest, accompanied by a rising wind and a bright gleam. Sending a curse after him, Alberich settles down again to his watch. He slips into the cleft at the side, and the stage remains empty for a moment.

Morning dawns as Siegfried and Mime enter, the former wearing the Sword in a girdle of bast-rope. Mime, after a cautious look round, tells Siegfried that this is the place. Seating himself under a great lime tree, Siegfried asks if it is here that fear shall be taught him. A long way has he journeyed hither with Mime, he says, and now the dwarf must leave him; for if he does not learn what fear may be he will go forth into the world alone. " Trust me, dear one," says Mime, " if today and here thou learnst it not, truly no other place, no other time will teach thee fear "; and he shows him the gloomy cavern in which lies the grim dragon who will swallow him up with just one snap of his vast and horrible jaws. From his mouth the Dragon pours a poisonous slaver, one drop of which, should it light on him, will rot Siegfried's bones and body; and he swings a monstrous tail, which, if it should clasp him, will break his bones like glass.

Siegfried tranquilly assures him that he will guard against all this, and asks if the monster has a heart, and if it lies where it usually is in beasts and men; if so, he will strike Nothung straight through his heart. Is this babble all that the old bungler has to say to him? he asks impatiently. But Mime bids him wait; when once he sees and hears the dragon, and his sight grows faint and the forest spins around him, and his heart begins to beat wildly in his breast, he will think then of the great love of old Mime who brought him hither.

The impatient boy drives the " slinking and blinking " dwarf away, and Mime goes off to lie by a spring close by, telling Siegfried to look for his foe when the sun is at its height, for then Fafner may crawl from the cavern to drink at the fountain. Mime makes a last attempt to offer counsel and help, but Siegfried rises and with furious gestures drives him away.

Then begins the scene that is known in the concert room as the Forest Murmurs. A gentle rustling:

(17)

is heard as Siegfried stretches himself out comfortably under the lime tree and gazes after the departing Mime. " No father of mine, this! " he says, and he gives himself up to the soft delights of the woodland, that is all the sweeter to his young senses now that the ugly old dwarf no longer grieves his eyes.

He falls into a reverie and wonders what his father was like in life — " full sure like myself! " What his mother was like, alas! he can never learn; but he is sure that her eyes were clear and tender, and gentle like those of the roe-deer, but much more beautiful. Why did she die through him? he asks softly; must all human mothers perish in giving life to their sons? Sad were that were it true! " Ah! " he cries as the lovely No. 5 wells up in the violas and 'cellos, " might these eyes by my mother be gladdened! "

Sighing gently, he leans still farther back, and a deep silence settles upon the scene, broken only by the vague murmurs of the forest. Siegfried gradually becomes conscious of the song of a bird in the branches above him, whose call takes at various times the following forms:

The dreaming boy longs to be able to understand the bird's message, for surely it would tell him something of his mother? Mime has told him that the song of birds has a meaning, if man could only discover it. But how is this to be done?

After a moment's reflection he resolves to try to follow the bird's singing with notes of his own, on a reed; thus singing the bird's language himself, it may be that the meaning of the song will become clear to him. Running to a stream that flows near by, he cuts a reed with his sword and hurriedly fashions a rude rustic pipe out of it. He makes three or four attempts to play upon this rough instrument (the tones are made for him by an English horn behind the scenes, playing harshly and out of tune). Siegfried is angry for a moment at his failure, then gives it up with a smile. But the bird's singing will not let him rest; on the stupid reed, he says, he cannot make an intelligible sound, but how if he were to give the bird a strain of his own on his horn? Taking the silver horn that hangs at his waist he blows on it, loudly and lustily, a fantasia upon his typical call (No. 3), every now and then sustaining a note for a long time and looking up expectantly at the bird.

At last there is a movement in the background. Fafner has been disturbed in his cave; the Dragon's theme in the tuba is heard in combination with Siegfried's horn-call as Fafner breaks through the underwood and drags his huge bulk up to the higher ground until the fore part of his body rests on this; then he utters a cavernous yawn. Siegfried turns round and looks at him in astonishment; Fafner, who has at the same time caught sight of Siegfried, pauses on the knoll.

The situation strikes Siegfried as humorous; he has been making music to draw some living thing of loveliness to him out of the forest, and this ugly monster is what his lay has brought him! " What is there? " Fafner bellows at him. (The player of the part sings through a speaking-trumpet that passes up into the Dragon's jaws.) Siegfried accosts him cheerily. He would fain know what fear is; perhaps this new-found companion can teach him? If not, he shall perish by Siegfried's sword. Fafner laughs heavily at this arrogance: " Drink I came for," he says, " and now I find food! " whereupon he opens his jaws and shows his teeth.

The irreverent boy compliments him on these, but thinks he has opened his gullet far too wide, and says it will have to be closed. Badinage and repartee are not the Dragon's strong points: resenting Siegfried's crude humour, he threatens him with his tail, and at last, losing his temper, roars to the boastful boy to come on.

Siegfried draws his sword, springs towards Fafner, and puts himself in an attitude of defiance. Fafner drags himself farther up the knoll and spits fire from his nostrils at Siegfried, who avoids the venom, springs nearer, and stands at one side. Fafner lashes at him with his tail, and has nearly caught him, when the boy leaps over him at one bound and wounds him in the tail. With a roar of pain and rage Fafner draws his tail back quickly and rears up the front part of his body to hurl it on Siegfried; his breast is thus exposed, and Siegfried, quickly perceiving the place of the heart, plunges his sword in it up to the hilt. Fafner raises himself still higher in his pain, then sinks down on the wound as Siegfried lets go the sword and leaps to one side.

The dying monster, in a weaker voice, asks the stripling who it was that goaded his childish spirit to this murderous deed. The boy cannot tell him, nor even who he is; it seems to him that he had been stirred to the fight only by his own heart. Fafner, in pity for the boy, enlightens him as to certain things. Of the two mighty brothers, he says, Fasolt and Fafner, both are now dead; Fafner slew Fasolt for the gold, and now he himself falls by the hand of a boy. Let the young hero heed himself well, for he who drove him so blindly to this murderous deed is plotting his death also.

Fafner raises himself with a sigh and expires, and in doing so rolls to the side. Siegfried, in drawing the sword out of his breast, gets some of the Dragon's blood on his hands. He involuntarily puts his fingers into his mouth to suck the blood from them, and thereby makes himself able now to understand the song of the forest bird, which, from the branches of the lime tree above him, sings, to the melodies of Nos. 20 and 21, " Hei! Siegfried has won him the Nibelungs' Hoard! Hid in the cavern he will find it! If he finds the Tarnhelm it will serve him for wonderful deeds, but could he discover the Ring it would make him the master of the world! " Siegfried has listened enraptured: softly and earnestly he thanks the bird for its counsel, then turns towards the back and disappears for a while into the cave.

When the stage is empty Mime slinks on, looking round timidly and cautiously to make sure that Fafner is dead; at the same moment Alberich comes out of the cleft on the other side. He looks hard at Mime, who, not being able to find Siegfried, is making towards the cave at the back, when Alberich rushes at him and bars his way. There ensues a scene, that is most amusing for the spectator, of hectic recrimination between the pair of precious rogues. Each claims the gold for his own, and bids the other keep his greedy eyes and hands off it. " It is mine by right," claims Alberich, " for who was it robbed the Rhine of its gold and wrought the spell of the Ring? " " And who," counters Mime, " made the Tarnhelm for you? "

So the rapid and petulant dialogue goes on, each upbraiding and taunting the other. Alberich's greater vehemence at last beats Mime down. Scratching his tousled and bewildered head, the dwarf suggests a compromise: Alberich can have the Ring if he will let Mime keep the Tarnhelm; that is surely fair to both. He rubs his hands insinuatingly, but Alberich rejects the suggestion with a scornful laugh: would he ever be safe in his sleep if Mime had the Tarnhelm? Beside himself with rage, Mime shrieks, " Not the Tarnhelm? Naught then do I get? " The ruthless Alberich declares that he will not even give him a nail. Then, in a towering temper, Mime shouts that neither the Ring nor the Tarnhelm shall Alberich have, for he will call Siegfried, who will avenge him with his sword on this dear brother of his.

Just then Siegfried appears in the background. They notice, as he comes forward slowly and thoughtfully, that he has passed over the treasure as a whole, taking only what have no doubt seemed to him charming childish toys — the Tarnhelm and the Ring. Laughing maliciously, Mime tells his brother to ask Siegfried to give him the Ring: then he slips back into the forest. Alberich at the same time disappears into his cleft, saying as he goes, " And yet to its lord shall it again belong! "

The unsophisticated boy muses upon his booty. He has brought away these two baubles not because he understands the value of them, but because the bird had counselled him to do so, and because they will serve as witnesses that he has vanquished Fafner in fight: of fear, however, he has still learned nothing. He thrusts the Tarnhelm into his girdle and puts the Ring on his finger.

Once more there is a deep silence except for the forest murmurs (No. 17); then the voice of the bird is heard once more, telling Siegfried not to trust in the treacherous Mime, and to listen alert to the lies of the hypocritical knave, for having tasted the blood of the Dragon Siegfried will now be able to pierce through the dwarf's words to the secret meaning of his heart.

By a gesture Siegfried signifies that he understands. Seeing Mime slinking towards him he remains motionless, leaning on his sword, observant and self-contained, during the whole of the scene that follows. Mime now sets himself to cajole the boy, whom he believes to be as unsophisticated as ever. Coming nearer to Siegfried, bowing and scraping and making wheedling gestures, he greets him, in music that is a masterpiece of oily hypocrisy, as the hero who has slain the Dragon.

When Siegfried speaks, we realise that a change has taken place in him. In quiet, grave tones he tells the dwarf that, grim and furious as the Dragon was, his death grieves him when he sees that far eviller rascals go through the world unpunished: " He who egged me on to the fight, I hate him more than the Dragon! "

What follows calls for a little sympathetic imagination on the part of the spectator. Mime imagines himself to be saying cajoling and deceiving things to Siegfried, but the latter hears through them the secret murderous thought of the cunning dwarf, and it is these words, of course, that *we* hear. Soon, he says, he will close Siegfried's eyes in eternal slumber, for he has done the deed that Mime desired, and now Mime will rob him of all he has won: at this point we hear a new motive in the orchestra, that of the Booty:

(22)

He has always hated Siegfried and all his kind, he continues, and longed to get the gold from the Dragon, and now, unless Siegfried gives him all, the boy in turn shall lose his life.

It puzzles and annoys Mime that Siegfried answers him not according to what he is saying but according to what he is thinking. The boy must be tired after his fight, the dwarf continues; will he not take a draught of the cordial that his loving Mime has brewed for him? " So then," says Siegfried, " of my weapon and what it has won me, ring and booty, you would rob me? " Mime makes a last desperate attempt to make the booby understand: let the boy just take one draught, and his darkened senses will make him an easy prey to Mime; but as the dwarf would nowhere be safe should Siegfried awake, he will take the sword and hack his head off; then shall Mime have both rest and the Ring — and he gives a childish chuckle at the thought.

He pours the liquor into the drinking horn and offers it to Siegfried, assuring him that this is the last draught he will ever drain. Siegfried, unable to endure the loathsome scene any longer, raises his sword, and, his whole being expressive of violent loathing, aims a swift blow at Mime, who immediately falls dead; from the cleft Alberich's mocking laughter rings out, while the orchestra gives out an echo of Mime's Reflection motive (No. 1), as if ironically drawing attention to what the dwarf's elaborate scheming has brought him to.

Siegfried quietly puts back his sword again, gazes at the fallen body, and says, " Nothung pays envy's wage: therefore truly did I forge it " ; but from the orchestra there wells up a sinister reminder of the motive of the Curse. Siegfried picks up Mime's body, carries it to the knoll, and throws it into the cave, bidding it there lie on the Hoard that the dwarf has so long desired, and that can now be his for ever; and by way of a guardian against thieves he pushes the body of the Dragon before the entrance to the cave, thus stopping up the latter completely.

It is now midday. Siegfried, after gazing thoughtfully for a while into the cave, turns away and passes his hand over his brow. He is hot and somewhat agitated: he lies down in the shade of the lime tree and again looks up into its branches. The stabbing thought comes that he is alone in the world: he has neither brother nor sister; his mother died, his father fell, and neither saw their son; the only comrade he has ever had was a loathsome old dwarf who never loved him, but plotted only to entrap him, until in the end he was forced to slay him.

To the accompaniment of a new motive symbolical of the Joy of Love:

(23)

that is followed by a lovely version of the expressive No. 5, he implores the bird to give him his counsel again and find for him a faithful friend. The bird replies that Siegfried has slain the evil dwarf, and now a glorious bride awaits him; she sleeps on a rocky height, but is surrounded by fierce flickering fire; he who shall break through the flames and waken the bride shall win Brynhilde for wife.

Siegfried starts up joyously, a new life throbbing in his veins. The bird has told him that Brynhilde shall be wakened by one alone — one who has never felt fear. Laughing with delight, Siegfried declares that this is he, and bids the bird show him the way to the rock. The bird flutters forth, circles over Siegfried for a moment, and after teasingly leading him hither and thither for a little while takes a definite course to the background, Siegfried following it.

The orchestral Prelude to the third act is another of those symphonic pieces in which Wagner, by the play of one leading motive against another, partly recapitulates the preceding action, partly forecasts the future course of the drama. The Prelude is mostly made up of reiterations of the theme of the Need of the Gods (*Valkyrie*, No. 21), the Treaty motive (*Valkyrie*, No. 8), the motive that is associated at times with Erda, at times with the Norns (*Rhinegold*, No. 26), and a motive typical henceforth of the Twilight of the Gods:

These motives are woven into a tissue of magnificent energy.

The curtain having risen, we see a wild spot at the foot of a rocky mountain, which rises steeply at the left towards the back. It is night: a storm is raging, with violent thunder and lightning; the former ceases after a while, but the lightning continues to flash through the clouds. We hear the Magic Ban motive (*Valkyrie*, No. 29), and that of the Annunciation of Fate (*Valkyrie*, No. 22), as the Wanderer enters and strides resolutely to a cavernous opening in a rock in the foreground; there, leaning on his spear, he calls towards the mouth of the cave a summons to Erda to awake from her timeless sleep.

The cavern begins to glow with a bluish light, and Erda rises slowly from the depths: she appears to be covered with hoarfrost, and her hair and garments give out a shimmering light. In deep, impressive tones she asks who it is that breaks her dream.

The Wanderer opens out his troubled heart to her. He has been through the world, searching for knowledge and wisdom; to Erda, the wisest of women, is known everything that the deeps hide and that air and water, hill and dale enclose; she alone can see to the secret heart of the world; it is to win him her wisdom that he has wakened her from sleep. She bids him go to the Norns, who wake while she is sleeping; it is they who wind the rope of fate, and sit and spin what Erda knows.

Urgently Wotan tells her that the Norns have no power either to make or to mar; they are merely the obedient weavers of fate. It is of Erda's wisdom he would now ask a question — how to hold back a rolling wheel? To Wotan, Erda replies tranquilly, she once bore a wish-maiden, who is both brave and wise; why does he not go and ask counsel of Erda's and Wotan's child? The Wanderer answers that Brynhilde disobeyed him and he laid her to sleep upon the fire-girt rock: what counsel can come from her? Erda seems for a while sunk in dreams, then, after a long silence, she says in deep tones, " Dazed am I since I awoke: wild and strange seems the world! The Valkyrie suffers penance of sleep while her all-knowing mother slept? Doth then pride's teacher punish pride? Is the deed-enkindler wroth with the deed? He who wardeth right, he the truth's upholder, tramples on right, reigns by untruth? Let the dreamer descend again! Let sleep again seal my wisdom! "

But Wotan will not be put off. He will not let the all-wise one go until she, who once planted a bitter barb in his heart and filled him with fear of ruin and shame and anguish, now tells him how the god may conquer his care; her wisdom is great, but his will is greater, and she must answer him.

After a long silence he resumes: " Thou unwise one, hear thou my words, that care-free ever thou mayst sleep! " No more is he grieved, he says, by the thought of the downfall of the gods, since he himself has willed it so: what once he resolved when his mind was torn with anguish he now wills gaily and gladly. Once, in his anger and loathing, he flung the world to the Nibelung Alberich; now he wills his heritage to the young Wälsung — one who, though chosen by him, knows him not — the bravest of boys, free of Wotan's counsel, has won for himself the Ring, and being full of the joy of love and knowing no envy, Alberich's curse has no power over him; and as he knows no fear, it is he who shall waken Brynhilde, who shall do a deed that shall redeem the world. So let Erda slumber on, and in her dreams behold his downfall: whatever may betide now, the god in rapture yields to the ever-young. As he speaks of willing his heritage to another we hear in the orchestra the World-Inheritance motive:

(25)

He dismisses Erda, who, her eyes closed, begins to descend gradually and at last disappears, the light dying away with her. The storm has ceased, and the scene is faintly lit by the moon. Advancing close to the cavern, the Wanderer leans with his back against it, his face turned towards the stage, awaiting the coming of Siegfried, whom he has seen in the distance.

The forest bird now flutters across the scene, and then, as if alarmed, disappears hastily at the back. (It has caught sight of Wotan, " the lord of the ravens," and fears for its life.) Siegfried enters in the foreground. The bird, he says, has led him well so far, but now it has flown away, and he must make his way alone to the rock. He is going towards the back when the Wanderer, who is still in the same position at the cave, accosts him, asking him what is the way of which he speaks. Siegfried turns round to him, and coming closer, tells him that he is seeking a rock, surrounded by flaming fire, where sleeps a woman who must waken to him.

Quietly the Wanderer interrogates him, and Siegfried tells him how he slew the Dragon, by the taste of its blood learned to understand the song of the birds, and then followed one of them hither. The Wanderer's questions take him further and further back in his story: he tells first of all of how he followed Mime, who had undertaken to teach him fear, then how he forged his own sword. Siegfried becomes a little impatient when the Wanderer asks him who made the mighty splinters from which the sword was forged He replies that he does not know; he knows only that the fragments would not have availed him had not the sword been shaped anew.

The Wanderer breaks into a good-humoured, approving laugh, and says, " That can I well believe! " The puzzled boy, becoming still more impatient, asks the old man to plague him no more with his questions, but if he knows the way to the rock, to show it to him, and if not, to talk no more.

Placidly the Wanderer advises him to be patient: " If I am old," he says, " that is a reason why thou shouldst honour me." Siegfried breaks out in scorn at this: all his life long his path has been barred by one old fellow whom lately he swept away; if the Wanderer holds him much longer with his chatter, let him have a care lest he share Mime's fate. Then going closer to the Wanderer he asks why he looks so strange — why he wears that great hat, and why it hangs so low over his face.

Still immovable, the Wanderer replies, " That is the wont of Wanderer when against the wind he goes." Inspecting him more closely, Siegfried finds that one eye is lacking, and hints that it may have been struck out by someone whose way the garrulous old man had barred; let him now take himself off, or soon he may find himself short of the other. The tranquil Wanderer answers him in words that the boy cannot understand: " With the one eye that for long I have lost, thou lookest thyself on the other that still is left me for sight."

The seeming foolishness of this reply moves Siegfried to loud laughter; then, once more becoming impatient, he orders the Wanderer to cease his chatter and show him the way. Softly and tenderly the Wanderer tells him not to scoff at and threaten one who loved his race of old, though once he scourged it in his wrath: " Thou whom I love so, all too fair one, wake not wrath in me now, to the ruin of thee and me! " The raging boy bids him move out of his path, for that way, he now knows, leads to the slumbering Brynhilde.

It has now become quite dark again. Wrathfully and commandingly the Wanderer bids Siegfried stand back, for he shall not find the way pointed out to him by the bird; it is his might that has bound the maid in slumber in the midst of the fire, and he who wakes her and wins her will make the Wanderer mightless for ever. The fire motive flames out in the orchestra as he points out to Siegfried the light on the rocky heights in the distance; this fire shall seize and consume the foolhardy boy if he persists in his quest.

Siegfried advancing farther, the Wanderer bars his way with his spear: " Hast thou no fear of the fire," he says, " at least shall my spear bar the path. Still holdeth my hand the haft of power; the sword thou dost bear was shattered once on this shaft; now once again be it broken on the everlasting spear! " Siegfried draws his sword: he has found then, he cries, his father's foe! Glorious vengeance is in his grasp; thus he shatters the spear with his sword! With one blow he hews the Wanderer's spear in two; there is a flash of lightning and a rumble of thunder, that quickly dies away. The fragments of the spear have fallen at the Wanderer's feet; quietly picking them up and falling back he says, " Advance! I no more can stop thee! " and disappears in complete darkness.

Siegfried's attention is attracted by the increasing brightness of the fire-clouds. " Through fire will I fare to the bride! " he cries; " now at last shall I win me a dear comrade! " Placing his horn to his lips and sounding his call he plunged into the sea of fire, which has now swept down from the height of the foreground, and soon he becomes invisible.

While the scene is being changed the orchestra pours out a molten flood of tone, in which the themes of the Fire and of Siegfried's the Magic Ban and the Slumber motive (*Valkyrie,* No. 30), followed by that of Siegfried (*Valkyrie,* No. 25).

The setting of the final scene is precisely the same as that at the end of *The Valkyrie,* with Brynhilde lying asleep in her armour. Siegfried, coming from the back, appears on the summit of the cliff. He looks around him for some time in astonishment while the orchestra plays softly with the Sleep and other motives, the music giving a curious impression of clear air on a great height.

Looking into the wood at the side Siegfried sees a horse standing in deep sleep. Then his eye catches the glint of the bright sunlight on Brynhilde's armour, and coming forward and raising her shield he sees what he takes to be the figure of a warrior, Brynhilde's face being still mostly concealed by the helmet. He carefully loosens and removes this, and a mass of hair falls down; but he still believes that the sleeper is simply a man of great beauty. Unable to loosen the breastplate he cuts with his sword through the rings of mail on both sides, raises the breastplate and the greaves, and starts back in amazement and alarm with a cry of " That is no man! "

A new emotion flames through him; greatly distressed at this apparition of something that has never yet come within his experience, he cries, " On whom shall I call that he may help me? Mother! Mother! Remember me! " and then sinks, as if fainting, on Brynhilde's bosom. After a long silence he rises with a sigh, and, to the accompaniment of the ardent No. 23, he resolves to venture to waken the maiden, even though her eyes should blind him. " Can this be fear? " he asks as he listens to the unaccustomed beating of his heart. From a sleeping woman he has at last learned fear, and to conquer it he must waken her.

More and more enchanted with her beauty he gives a despairing cry of " Awaken! Awaken! Holiest maid! " Then, as she seemingly does not hear him, he sinks, as if dying, on the sleeping figure, and with closed eyes presses his lips to hers.

The kiss awakens Brynhilde. Slowly rising to a sitting position, she raises her arms and gives a solemn greeting to the sky and earth that she sees once more:

Then, to music that seems to be quivering with light and warm with the pulsing of a long-restrained energy, she hails the glorious sun. Who is the hero who has wakened her? she asks; and when she learns that it is Siegfried who has fought his way through the fire she pours out a new song of thankfulness to the gods.

A long duet follows between the pair, in which she tells him how he had been her care before he was born, for she divined the secret of Wotan that the god himself dared neither speak nor shape to thought, and how what possessed her then was love for the unborn Siegfried. Various new motives make their appearance from time to time, among the most important of which are that of Love's Greeting:

and that of Love's Rapture:

Sadness comes over Brynhilde as she gazes on her horse and her shield and helmet, and realises that she has lost her godhood and is now only a sorrowful woman awakened by a mortal man.

When Siegfried in his ardour tries to embrace her she springs up, repulses him with the strength of terror, and flies to the other side: " No god's touch have I known! " she cries. " Before the maiden low bent the heroes; holy came she from Valhalla. Woe's me! Woe for the shame, the pain, and the disgrace! For he who wakes me deals me this wound! He has broken byrnie and helm; Brynhilde am I no more! " At the mention of Valhalla the orchestra softly intones a phrase:

that, in *The Rhinegold*, figured at the end of the representative Valhalla motive, but that later will have a significance of its own.

Gradually, with loving words, Siegfried soothes her, and at last her expression shows that a sweet vision has arisen in her mind. As she turns a gentle gaze on him the strings give out very softly a new motive, that of Peace:

Another new motive appears immediately afterwards as Brynhilde hails Siegfried as the Treasure of the World, the Life of the Earth:

She implores him to leave her as untroubled as the reflection of his own face in the crystal brook — to love himself and leave her in peace, not strike his own one into the dust. But in the end his passion fires her too, and laughing wildly in her joy she cries that she loves him and if need be will go laughing down to death with him.

The horns give out a new motive, that of Love's Resolution:

(32)

as the voices blend in a rapturous final duet, in which Brynhilde bids farewell to the glitter of Valhalla, that may now crumble to dust along with the glory and pomp of the gods, for henceforth over her head shines Siegfried's star. Siegfried hails the day that has brought him Brynhilde, laughter, and love, and at the end their voices unite in a cry of " Light of loving, laughing death! " Brynhilde throws herself into Siegfried's arms while the orchestra thunders out the theme of Love's Rapture (No. 28), followed by that of Siegfried in the trombones.

AS the first act alone of *The Twilight of the Gods* lasts two hours, and the whole opera runs to close on five hours of actual performance without reckoning the intervals, it is obviously necessary for cuts to be made on most occasions. Generally the opening scene is sacrificed, greatly to the damage of the inner dramatic idea.

Fate broods over the whole of this last evening of *The Ring*, and it is the weaving of the fates of gods and men that we witness in the opening scene. The weavers of Fate in the Scandinavian mythology are the Norns, who pass to each other the cord of Fate, which is made fast to a fir tree.

A brief orchestral prelude presents us first of all with the short motive to which Brynhilde, when awakened on her rock at the end of *Siegfried*, had greeted the world:

This is followed by a motive typical of the Norns, that is merely a slightly altered rhythmical version of the now familiar theme of Erda. The solemn motive of the Annunciation of Fate is next heard in the brass, to be succeeded by a new motive, that of the Weaving of Fate:

The scene is once more Brynhilde's rock, as at the close of *The Valkyrie* and *Siegfried,* but as the stage is almost completely dark we do not recognise any of the familiar objects. From the valley at the back comes the gleam of the fire.

We dimly descry the three Norns — tall women in long, veil-like, sombre draperies. The first, who is the oldest, lies in the foreground on the right, under a wide-spreading fir tree; the second, who is younger, is stretched out on a rock in front of the cave; while the third, who is the youngest, sits in the centre of the background on a rock at the edge of the peak.

During the conversation of the Norns a golden rope is passed at intervals from one to the other, and fastened in turn to the fir tree and the rock.

The first Norn tells how she once wove at the world ash tree, when a dauntless god came to drink at the spring near by, and left an eye in payment for a draught from the waters of wisdom; how Wotan then broke a great branch from the world ash tree and made a spear-shaft out of it; how, as time went on, the wound cankered the tree, that languished and died, while the water dried up in the spring. (Here we hear a new motive, that of the Twilight of the Gods):

The second Norn takes up the tale, telling how Wotan engraved runes of treaties on the shaft of the spear, and with it ruled the world; how a hero shattered the spear, and how Wotan then bade Valhalla's heroes cut in pieces the withered trunk and branches of the world ash tree.

From the third Norn we learn how Wotan now sits in state in Valhalla with the gods and the heroes: round the mighty castle is heaped up a great wall of the riven boughs of the world ash tree; and when fire shall seize upon the wood and ravage the glittering hall, then the doom of the gods is nigh, and they shall all go down into the dusk.

The tale goes on that Wotan, by the magic of his spear, found the wandering Loge and fixed him as a fire about the rock. " Knowest thou what now shalt be? " asks the second Norn, and the third Norn replies prophetically, " The broken spear-shaft's piercing splinters Wotan strikes to the depths of the burning one's breast: furious fire flares from the glow; this Wotan hurls at the world ash tree's wall of boughs about Valhalla."

The Norns would fain know when this shall come about, but the night wanes, and they can no more see or feel the strands of the rope. A terrible sight mocks and maddens them; the Rhinegold, that was once robbed by Alberich — what came from that? The second Norn cries out that the jagged edge of the rock is cutting through the rope: " the web wavers and tears; from grief and greed rises the Nibelung's Ring; a vengeful curse gnaws at the sundering strands." Further in the Book of Fate the Norns cannot read, for the rope breaks. Starting up in terror they take hold of the broken pieces, and, going to the centre of the stage, bind their bodies together with them, crying, " The end this of our wisdom! The world hears us wise ones no more! Descend to Erda! "

They vanish, to the accompaniment of a last reminiscence of the theme of the Annunciation of Fate in the orchestra. Day dawns, and as the red glow increases the fire in the valley at the back grows fainter. Softly the horns give out the theme of Siegfried as hero:

followed by the Brynhilde motive in the clarinet:

This last is developed and carried up higher and higher in the orchestral registers, till at last it bursts forth in glory as full daylight comes upon the scene.

Immediately afterwards the Siegfried theme thunders out in all the power of the brass, followed by that of the Valkyries (*Valkyrie*, No. 17), as Siegfried, fully armed, enters from the cave, accompanied by Brynhilde, who is leading her horse Grane by the bridle. She is about to send her hero forth to deeds of glory, after having endowed him with all the wisdom the gods had taught her. He is now her master, having overcome the Valkyrie she once was and wakened her as a woman; she is weak in wisdom, she says, but strong in will and rich in love.

The motive of Heroic Love:

which appears at this point, is heard again when Siegfried assures her that if he has learned no other wisdom he has at least laid to heart eternal love for, and remembrance of, Brynhilde. The theme of Love's Greeting, to which, in the duet at the end of the preceding opera, Siegfried and Brynhilde poured out their ecstasy:

reappears as she speaks of the hero who wakened her and became the lord of her life; and various other motives with which we are already familiar are heard again as she exhorts him never to forget her and the pledges of love they have exchanged.

If Siegfried must now leave her, he says, in the ward of the watchful fire, he will give her, in return for all her runes of wisdom, a Ring, which he now draws from his finger and places on hers. In this Ring lies the whole virtue of the deeds of valour he has wrought from the time when he dealt out death to the Dragon; now it shall be the token of his love, and its strength be Brynhilde's guard.

In exchange she gives him Grane, who, like her, has lost his former supernatural quality, and can no longer ride over the clouds through thunder and lightning, but will carry him anywhere on earth, even through fire itself. To the accompaniment of the Freedom motive:

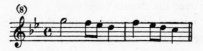

he vows that with Brynhilde's horse and Brynhilde's shield he is no longer Siegfried, but Brynhilde's arm; endowed with her spirit, he is Siegfried and Brynhilde in one. To a last rapturous outpouring of No. 8 the pair hail each other in a final ecstasy, after which Siegfried quickly leads the horse down the rocks, Brynhilde following him.

A long orchestral interlude follows, to allow of a change of scene; this is the excerpt known in the concert-room as " Siegfried's Rhine Journey." Siegfried, of course, is from this point onwards invisible to the spectator, but from the gestures and the expression of Brynhilde, who stands on the slope following him down the valley with her eyes, we can trace his course in our imagination. After various soundings of his horn-call, which she answers with a joyous smile, we hear the motive of Love's Resolution:

given out in the full strength of the orchestra. At this point the curtain falls, but the music continues. The horn-call is combined with a variant of the Loge motive: then comes the great upward-surging theme of the Rhine (*Rhinegold*, No. 1), followed in turn by the Song of the Rhinemaidens and the motive of the Ring, to which succeed the motives of Renunciation, the Rhinegold, and Servitude.

Towards the end the music, by a transition so gradual as to be almost imperceptible, has lost in pace, slackened in vitality, and darkened in colour; the youthful joyousness and morning freshness of the preceding scene have died out of it, and Fate seems to be brooding over the drama once more.

By the most natural means imaginable the music at last merges into a fresh motive, that of Hagen:

as the curtain rises, showing us the hall of the Gibichungs on the Rhine. The hall is entirely open at the back, where we see an open shore extending to the river.

(The Gibichungs are the children of Gibich; their king is Gunther, who has a sister, Gutrune, and a half-brother, Hagen, the last-named being the product of a loveless union between Alberich and Grimhilde, the mother of Gunther and Gutrune. Hagen, in keeping with his Nibelung origin, is dark-complexioned, gloomy, and sinister.)

When we first catch sight of the three new characters, they are seated at a table with drinking utensils on it. A new motive, that of the Gibichungs:

is heard as Gunther asks his half-brother how it stands with the fame of Gibich on the Rhine. He puts aside Hagen's assurance that all are filled with envy at the king's fame and fortune. Not at all is he to be envied, he says; rather should he envy Hagen, for though Gunther was the first-born, Hagen is the possessor of wisdom.

Hagen, being importuned again, tells him the truth: Gunther's fame is not so glorious as it might be, for there are great things he has not yet won him: he is still without a wife, and Gutrune without a husband. For the increase of his fame he should win a woman of whom Hagen knows, the noblest in the world, whose home is on a rock surrounded by fire. But Gunther may not fight through that fire; that deed has been reserved for a stronger man, Siegfried the Wälsung, whom Hagen would like to see wedded to Gutrune. Hagen tells the others of the great deeds of Siegfried — how he slew the Dragon and made himself possessor of the Hoard, and with it the lordship of the world; only he can win through the fire to Brynhilde.

Gunther rises angrily at this, and striding agitatedly about the hall asks Hagen why he thus spurs him to vain desire. Without moving from his seat, Hagen stops Gunther with a mysterious sign: and we hear the Tarnhelm motive in the orchestra as he asks, " But if Siegfried bring home the bride to thee, *then* were not Brynhilde thine? " He unfolds his plan to the still restless and fretted Gunther: Siegfried would win Brynhilde for Gunther were he himself in love with Gutrune, and that could be brought about by means of a magic potion that would make the hero forget that he had seen any woman before her. Gunther praises Grimhilde for having given him such a brother, while the gentle Gutrune murmurs, " Would that Siegfried I might see! "

Gunther is just asking how the hero may be found when a horn is heard from the background; a little later this develops into the characteristic horn-call of Siegfried (*Siegfried*, No. 3), and Hagen, who has gone to the shore and is looking down the stream, calls back that he sees a vessel approaching carrying a man and a horse; and none but Siegfried, the vanquisher of the Dragon, could with so easy a stroke drive the boat against the stream. Hagen hails the hero through his hollowed hands, and soon Siegfried appears in the boat. He fastens it to the shore and springs on land with his horse, where he is greeted by Gunther and Hagen, Gutrune, from her seat at the table, gazing on him in wonder and admiration. As Siegfried sets foot on the land the trombones give out, with the maximum of their power, the terrific theme of the Curse.

Siegfried, standing calmly by the boat, leaning on his horse, greets Gunther courteously, says he has heard his praises sung beyond the Rhine, and bids him fight him or be his friend. Gunther, to the accompaniment of the Friendship theme:

gives him a fair welcome, and Hagen leads Grane away to the back of the hall, Siegfried gazing thoughtfully after them. At a gesture from Hagen, Gutrune retires, unobserved by Siegfried, through a door on the left into her chamber; Gunther then brings Siegfried forward into the hall, where, in the ancient fashion, he places himself and all he has at the service of his guest. For himself, says Siegfried, he has neither field nor folk nor father's house to offer in return; his whole birthright is his body; but he has a sword, shaped by himself, and that shall be the witness to his oath of friendship.

Hearing Siegfried's disclaimer of wealth, Hagen, who has now returned and is standing behind Siegfried, remarks that rumour names him as the lord of the Nibelung's Hoard. The unsophisti-

cated hero, it seems, has forgotten this; so little does he prize
the booty that he has left it, he says, in the cavern with the body
of the Dragon who once watched over it. One thing alone he took
away with him — here he points to the woven metal work that
is hanging at his belt — and of that he does not know the worth.
Hagen, however, declares this to be the Tarnhelm, that will disguise its wearer as he wills, or take him in the twinkling of an
eye wherever he may wish to be.

Was there anything else Siegfried took from the Hoard? " A
Ring," Siegfried replies, " and that is now worn by a woman.''
" Brynhilde! '' ejaculates Hagen aside. He opens Gutrune's door,
and the maiden enters to the gentle motive that is so descriptive
of her tender, yielding, love-desiring nature:

She bears a filled drinking-horn, which she offers to Siegfried, welcoming him as guest in Gibich's house.

He takes it from her courteously, and, with his thoughts evidently turned inwards, pledges Brynhilde in undying love and remembrance. But the draught has had mixed with it the subtle
essences of which Hagen spoke; the Magic Deceit that lies in it is
symbolised in one of Wagner's most subtly expressive motives:

Some transformations of the Gutrune motive, growing in ardour
from bar to bar, give us a hint of the working of the potion on
Siegfried; he returns the horn to Gutrune, who, shamed and confused, lowers her eyes before him. His blood already fired with
love for her, he asks Gunther, in a trembling voice, the name of

his sister, seizes her hands impetuously, and asks her if she like her proud brother, would disdain the offer of himself were he to make it. Gutrune encounters Hagen's look; she humbly bows her head, then, with a gesture indicating her feeling of her own unworthiness, leaves the hall with unsteady steps, Siegfried, closely watched by Hagen and Gunther, following her with his eyes as if bewitched.

Has Gunther a wife? he asks. "Not yet," replies the Gibichung: he has set his heart on one whom he can never make his own; her home is on a towering rock, surrounded by fire; and only he who breaks through the wall of flame shall win Brynhilde for wife. Siegfried, in astonishment, repeats each of Gunther's sentences after him, as if trying, by an intense effort, to recapture something that should be familiar to him; but at the mention of Brynhilde's name he shows by a final gesture that the memory quite evades him.

Coming to himself out of his dreamlike state he turns gaily to Gunther and declares that he, who does not fear the fire, will win the bride for the King if he himself may have Gutrune; he will gain access to the rock by means of the Tarnhelm, changing his form into that of Gunther.

The theme of the Curse has already been heard in the horns during the scene in which Siegfried followed Gutrune with his eyes, and now it is heard again in the tuba as the two men prepare to take the oath of Blood-brotherhood. Hagen having filled a drinking-horn with fresh wine, he holds it out to Siegfried and Gunther, each of whom cuts his arm with his sword and lets the blood fall into the mouth of the horn. Then each lays two fingers on the horn, which is still held by Hagen between them, and swears Blood-brotherhood to the other:

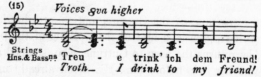

There follows upon this a solemn passage:

Gunther

Bricht ein Bru - der den Bund,
Breaks a bro - ther the bond,

Siegfried

Trügt den Treu - en der Freund,
False if friend be to friend,

in which each speaks of the Atonement that shall be due if either
fails to keep the oath: " Breaks a brother the bond, false if friend
be to friend, what in drops today we two have drunken, in streams
unceasing shall flow; so shall the traitor atone! "

Gunther and Siegfried drink from the horn in turns, the orchestra giving out the motive of the Oath of Fidelity, which is best
quoted here in the expanded form it assumes later:

Its salient characteristics are the fall of an octave and the clinching
effect of the second note of each bar.

Siegfried having drunk, he holds out the horn to Hagen, who
smites it into pieces with his sword as Gunther and Siegfried clasp
hands. Siegfried demands why Hagen has not shared in the oath,
and the sinister one explains that his blood, being stubborn and
cold and not as noble as theirs, would only poison their drink.
Gunther bids Siegfried take no heed of the gloomy creature, and
the hero, turning to Gunther again, unfolds his plans. They two
will go down the Rhine together in the boat, and in this, when
they reach the mountain, Gunther will hide while Siegfried conquers Brynhilde and brings her to him.

They place their weapons in the boat, and just as Siegfried
pushes off into the middle of the stream Gutrune appears at the
door of her chamber and, learning from Hagen the destination of

the pair, sighs out the desire of her heart that Siegfried may be hers, and returns within in great agitation.

The boat is soon lost to view. Hagen, who has taken up his spear and shield, sits down with his back against a post at the entrance to the hall, and there, quite motionless, sings that he will watch and ward the hall while the others, unknown to themselves, go to perform his secret will and bring him, perhaps, the Ring. " Ye sons of freedom," he cries, " lusty companions, laugh as ye sail on your way! Base though ye deem him, ye both shall serve the Nibelung's son! "

The curtain falls, and during the change of scene the orchestra reviews a number of the motives with which we are already acquainted, including the Ring, Siegfried's horn-call, the typical Siegfried motive, the Servitude motive, and various motives associated with Brynhilde and Siegfried. Wagner's musical and dramatic genius was at this time at its height, and we find him now hitting off his characters with the minimum of notes — sometimes in a single stroke — as well as giving the subtlest new meanings to the old motives by slight changes in the harmony, and combining themes in such a way that of themselves they tell a story or paint a scene.

For example, in the early part of this orchestral interlude, we have the following:

The upper melody is the motive of the Ring; the syncopated rhythm in the lower stave is that of the Annihilation motive associated with Alberich (*Rhinegold*, No. 24); while in the first two notes in the lower stave we have the sinister motive of Hagen given out by the double basses and tuba.

When the curtain rises again we see Brynhilde's rock once more; Brynhilde is sitting at the entrance to the cave, thoughtfully contemplating Siegfried's ring, which, as if lost in blissful memories, she covers with kisses.

While she is absorbed in her happiness, thunder is heard, accompanied by a lightning flash, and a dark thunder-cloud is seen approaching the rock; Brynhilde recognises the old familiar sound of a steed sweeping like a storm through the air. Outside is heard Waltraute's voice calling her from a distance, and soon Waltraute enters, with anxiety written on her face. Brynhilde, in delight, asks her for news of Valhalla: does Wotan's heart turn to his child again? With no thought for anything but her own happiness she runs over the story of her wakening by Siegfried, and only gradually does she become aware of Waltraute's gloom and agitation.

In a long and magnificent monologue known as Waltraute's Narration the Valkyrie tells her sister what it is that has brought her hither. Since Brynhilde was lost to Wotan, she says, Wotan has sent the Valkyries out no more to the battlefield to bring him heroes. He journeyed through the world as Wanderer, and one day returned home holding in his hand the broken fragments of his spear, shattered by a hero's sword.

With a silent sign he sent the warriors out to hew the world ash tree in pieces, which he bade them build into a great rampart about Valhalla. Then he assembled the gods and heroes, and there he now sits, mute and grave, the spear's fragments in his grasp, while the gods gaze at him awestruck and spellbound. Round his knees the trembling Valkyries entwine themselves (here we hear in the orchestra a motive expressive of the Calamity that is to fall upon the gods):

(19)

Then, to music of the most soul-searching beauty, Waltraute describes how Wotan's looks grew soft as he remembered Brynhilde, and sighing in his dream he whispered, " If ever the river-maidens win back the Ring from Brynhilde again, from the Curse's load released were gods and world! "

The words sank deep into Waltraute, who stole forth alone, mounted her horse, and flew to Brynhilde, to implore her to take pity upon them all and end the grief of the gods by returning the Ring to the Rhinemaidens again. The outraged Brynhilde, when at last she understands, refuses to part with the Ring, the seal of Siegfried's love for her; it is more to her than Valhalla's rapture, more than the fame of the eternal gods, for out of the gleam of the gold there sings perpetually to her the ecstatic refrain, " Siegfried loves me! Siegfried loves me! "

She dismisses Waltraute with a message to the council of the gods: " While life doth last will I love, from love they never will win me: fall first in ruins Valhalla's splendour and pride! " Waltraute, after trying to shake her resolution, gives a terrible cry of despair and rushes away, storm-clouds and tempest rising from the wood as she departs.

Evening has fallen, and the light of the fire below the rock gradually becomes brighter. At first Brynhilde is happy in the thought of its guardianship; then she becomes aware that the flames are leaping and seething more madly than usual. Through the swirling mass of the fire music a horn behind the scenes gives out the theme of Siegfried (*Valkyrie*, No. 25), followed by Siegfried's horn-call, and Brynhilde starts up in delight to welcome the returning hero.

The flames flare up and then immediately draw back, henceforth being visible only in the depths below. Siegfried has come through the fire, but as he steps upon the rock he wears the form of Gunther; on his head is the Tarnhelm, which conceals the upper part of his face, leaving only the eyes free. Verbal description can convey no sense of the horror of the moment in the theatre; it is the most blood-curdling scene in the whole range of opera.

The dazed Brynhilde asks who it is that has thus forced a way through the fire. To the accompaniment first of all of the motive of Magic Deceit (No. 14), then of the Gibichungs (No. 11), then of the Tarnhelm, Siegfried, in a feigned voice that is deeper than his own, tells her that a wooer has come whom the fire could not affright; he has won her for wife, and she must follow him where he leads. He is a Gibichung, he says, in answer to her questions, and his name is Gunther. The trapped woman gives a despairing cry of " Wotan! Thou vengeful, pitiless god! Now my sentence its meaning shows: all shame and sorrow thou sendest to me! "

The sombre motive of Hagen dominates the music as Siegfried, springing down from the rock and drawing nearer to Brynhilde, tells her that that night she must be wedded to him in her cave. She summons up her last strength to stretch out threateningly towards him the finger that bears the Ring, bidding him stand back from her, for this is her sure guard. It is Gunther's, as husband's right, replies Siegfried, and seizes her; she wrenches herself free, flies, is caught again, and after a violent struggle he grasps her by the hand and tears the Ring from her finger. With a violent shriek she collapses into his arms as if broken, and her unconscious look meets Siegfried's eyes. He lets her fainting body sink down on to the stone bench at the entrance to the cave, and orders her, as Gunther's bride, to point him the way.

With an imperious gesture he drives the exhausted woman before him, and as she totters into the cave he draws his sword and, in his natural voice, cries, " Now, Nothung, witness thou that pure my wooing was! That troth I may keep with my brother, bar thou me from Gunther's bride! " He follows Brynhilde into the cave, and the curtain falls.

In the last page or two of the long act Wagner's genius for concentration is seen at its finest. There is an especially tremendous passage at the point where Siegfried draws the sword that is to separate him in honour from the bride of Gunther: first we hear the incisive motive of the Oath of Fidelity (No. 17); then comes this:

in which we have in the trumpet a changed version of the Sword motive, in the upper part of the lower stave the Treaty motive in the horns and trombones, and in the bass the threatening two-notes theme of Hagen.

Throughout the brief orchestral introduction to the second act and the whole of the first scene there runs the syncopated rhythm characteristic of the Annihilation motive; in the introduction we hear also from time to time the gloomy motive of Hagen.

When the curtain rises we see the hall of the Gibichungs from another angle. The open entrance is now on the right; on the left is the bank of the Rhine, with rocky heights in the distance. It is night; Hagen, his arm round his spear and his shield by his side, sits asleep, leaning against a post of the hall. A sudden flood of moonlight reveals to us not only Hagen but the head and shoulders of Alberich, who is crouching before his son with his arms on the latter's knees.

In the dialogue that ensues, Hagen speaks softly and always without moving, so that although his eyes are open he appears all the while to be sleeping. The Nibelung appeals feverishly to his son to work for him against their enemies; the power of the gods is broken, he says; soon they will sink to ruin, and then the world shall be Alberich's. The Ring has passed into the possession of the

Wälsung boy, over whom the Curse has no power, for he does not know the worth of the Ring, and so makes no use of it for his own ends; he lives only for love. Hagen must get the Ring, for if, at Brynhilde's advice, Siegfried should restore it to the Rhine-maidens, the gold and the power which it can confer will be for ever lost to the Nibelungs. It is to achieve this vengeance that Alberich has bred Hagen and instilled hatred in him.

Hagen's reply is that from his mother he indeed got his stout heart, yet may he not thank her that she was caught by Alberich's craft, for being the Nibelung's son he is old too soon, pale and wan, ever joyless, hating the happy. But he bids his father remain in peace, for he will win him the Ring; and Alberich disappears slowly in a gradually deepening shadow, reiterating anxiously, "Be true, Hagen, my son! Trusty hero! Be true! Be true!"

Like the great dramatist he is, Wagner lets us see the two char-acters not as they appear to us — not as the villains of the piece, that is to say — but as they appear to themselves. Alberich is wholly justified in his own eyes, especially after the injury that Wotan did him; and his hunger for the Ring is as vital an expres-sion of his own being as Siegfried's longing for love is of his. In the course of the dialogue a new motive has made its appearance, that of Murder:

We shall meet with it again later, when the tragedy is working up to the climactic point of Siegfried's death.

Day dawns, and Hagen gives a slight start, as if awakening. Siegfried enters suddenly from behind a bush on the shore; he is in his own form again, but the Tarnhelm is still on his head; he takes it off and hangs it at his belt as he comes forward. The others, he tells Hagen, are following in the boat. He asks if Gutrune is awake, and Hagen calls her from the hall. From this point onward the Gutrune motive undergoes several modifications, one of the most typical of which may be quoted here:

although it does not appear till later in the scene.

Siegfried and Gutrune give each other gracious greeting, and he tells her how he has mastered Brynhilde for her brother, and so won Gutrune for himself. He assures her that though Brynhilde submitted to her lord till the morn, " Siegfried was here by Gutrune! " for though Brynhilde lay beside him, " between east and west is north," he says, pointing to his sword; " so near was Brynhilde, and so far." In the morning he had taken her through the dying fire to the valley below, where, by the magic of the Tarnhelm, Gunther was wafted to them and swift as thought stood there in Siegfried's stead.

Far away down the river Hagen sees a sail, and Gutrune tells him to call the vassals together to the hall for the wedding. With the wedding is associated a new variation upon the Gutrune motive:

Siegfried gives Gutrune his hand and goes with her into the hall, while Hagen, ascending a rock in the background, blows lustily on his discordant cow-horn and hoarsely summons the vassals.

His sinister joviality is expressed in a theme that first of all appears in the bassoons:

First singly, then in pairs, the armed vassals come hurrying along the various paths across the rocks and gather on the shore in front of the hall. Then, for the first and only time in *The Ring*, we have a chorus, and however much it may savour, as is sometimes com-

plained, of " opera " rather than of " musical drama," it is undeniably welcome not only as a relief from the constant succession
of single voices, but for itself, for it is a superb expression of bar-
baric gaiety. Orchestrally it has (if the adjectives may be permitted) a peculiarly rough, hoarse colouring that is thoroughly
appropriate to the scene and the singers.

The first thought of the vassals is that they have been summoned to guard the hall against a foe, but Hagen explains to them
that they have been brought there to welcome the king and his
bride. They are to slaughter steers on Wotan's altar, a boar for
Froh, a goat for Donner, and sheep for Fricka, that she may smile
on the marriage. Then from their women they are to take the
drinking-horns filled with mead and wine, and carouse till they
fall like logs — all to win the favour of the gods for the marriage.
The savage vassals burst into ringing laughter, and, to the strain
of No. 24, sing the praises of " Hagen, the grim one," who has now
become a bridal herald!

Becoming serious again, Hagen sends the vassals to greet the
arriving pair, and tells them to serve their lady royally; " if she be
wronged, swift be your vengeance! " Gunther and Brynhilde arrive
amid great excitement and step ashore from the boat, the vassals
arranging themselves respectfully to greet them. Gunther leads
Brynhilde ceremoniously by the hand and presents her to the
vassals, who shout and clash their weapons together; she is very
pale and her eyes are lowered.

As Gunther and Brynhilde near the hall, from which Siegfried and Gutrune have come forth accompanied by women, we
hear in the bassoons a new motive, that of the Covenant of
Vengeance:

(25)

which will become of great significance later. The Gutrune motive
takes on another and still more exquisite form:

as Gunther greets the other pair: " two happy bridals bless we together," he says, " Brynhilde and Gunther, Gutrune and Siegfried! "

At the last of these names Brynhilde raises her eyes and perceives Siegfried; her gaze remains fixed on him in stunned amazement. All, including Gunther, from whom Brynhilde has torn her violently trembling hand, look at her in blank perplexity, and the vassals softly ask themselves what the meaning of this can be.

Siegfried, who, we have to remember, has had the memory of his own association with Brynhilde taken from him by Hagen's potion, calmly advances a few steps towards her and presents to her Gutrune, " Gunther's gentle sister, won by me, as thou by him! " " I? Gunther? " cries Brynhilde vehemently; " thou liest! " She staggers and seems about to fall, and is supported by Siegfried, who is next to her. She looks up to him feebly, unable to understand why he does not know her. Siegfried calls Gunther to tend his wife, and just then Brynhilde, seeing the Ring on his outstretched finger, gives a terrible cry. Hagen, knowing that the crisis is at hand, comes from the background and tells the vassals to listen intently to this woman's words.

Trying to master her agitation, Brynhilde, pointing to the Ring, tells Siegfried that it should be worn of rights by Gunther, and bids the latter take it from Siegfried. Gunther does not understand this, nor Brynhilde's later question, " Where hidest thou the Ring that from my hand thou torest? " Greatly perplexed, he takes refuge in silence, and Brynhilde, breaking out into a violent rage, proclaims the truth to all: it was Siegfried, the treacherous thief, who wrenched the Ring from her! All look at Siegfried, who, as if bemused, is contemplating the Ring, which he says no woman gave him, for he won it with his own sword in combat at Neidhöhle.

Stepping between them, Hagen asks her if she knows the Ring in truth, for if it is the one that Gunther wrested from her then it is his, and Siegfried must have won it by craft, and the traitor must now atone.

The bewildered and maddened Brynhilde cries out shame and deceit and betrayal upon Siegfried, and bitterly asks the gods if this sorrow that has come upon her was part of their punishing decree. She cries out to them to grant her a vengeance greater than any the world has yet known. Gunther implores her to calm herself, but the angry woman waves him aside, declaring that he as well as she has been betrayed. " Hearken to me all," she cries, " not his, but this man's wife " — pointing to Siegfried — " am I! "

Siegfried still does not understand. The memory of his union with Brynhilde having vanished, he takes her charge of betrayal to refer only to the night he spent with her in the cave in the guise of Gunther; and of that he is guiltless, he says, for had he not sworn Blood-brotherhood with the king? Did not his sword lie between him and Brynhilde then?

The episode immediately following has been the subject of a good deal of misunderstanding, that cannot be said to have been cleared up quite satisfactorily. Brynhilde gives Siegfried the lie: well she knows the sword, she says, and well she knows the sheath also, and in its sheath on the wall the sword rested when its master conquered her love. One's first assumption on hearing this is that she is deliberately lying in order to arouse the others' vengeance against Siegfried, and one cannot help experiencing a slight alienation of sympathy from her.

The explanation seems to be, however, that she is referring to her *first* meeting with Siegfried, for she does not associate him with the second one, in which he bore the semblance of Gunther. The men, of course, take her words in their literal sense, both they and Gunther believing that Siegfried has played the king false. Even Gutrune for a moment doubts her hero, and calls upon him to bear witness that Brynhilde is speaking falsely. Siegfried declares himself willing to answer on oath.

The vassals form a ring round Siegfried and Hagen; the latter holds out his spear, upon the point of which Siegfried lays two fingers of his right hand as he offers up his life to the spear if Brynhilde's words be true and he betrayed his brother:

He has no sooner finished than Brynhilde, striding furiously into the midst of them, wrenches Siegfried's hand from the spear and seizes the point with her own hand. Siegfried's oath is false, she swears, and may the spear point deal him death!

Siegfried, unable to stand her frenzy, puts it down to the working of some demon within her, and advises Gunther to give her time to rest and compose herself. The Tarnhelm, he thinks, may have hidden only half of his face; but anyhow he has won her for Gunther, and her woman's spite will soon be at an end. Turning again to the vassals and the women he urges them to give themselves up to the joys of the wedding. Throwing his arm gaily round Gutrune he draws her away with him to the hall, and the women and the vassals follow him, slaves to his charm and infected by his gaiety.

On the stage only Brynhilde, Gunther, and Hagen remain. Gunther, in deep shame and dejection, sits on one side and covers his face; Brynhilde, standing in the foreground, looks sadly for some time after Siegfried and Gutrune, and then lets her head droop.

The long silence of the characters, that is filled expressively by the orchestra, is broken at last by Brynhilde, who, as if to herself, asks what evil power it can be that has woven this misfortune about them; then, her rage mastering her again, she cries wildly, " Who will bring me now the sword wherewith I may sever my bond? " Hagen comes close to her and tells her that *he* will wreak vengeance for her on Siegfried. She turns on him with a bitter laugh: one flash from the hero's eyes, she says, one glance such as gleamed through the helm, shedding its glory on her, and fear would strike through Hagen's heart; his spear will be impotent unless he can back it by something stronger than its own strength.

Well he knows Siegfried's unconquerable might, replies Hagen; but cannot she, out of her wisdom, whisper to him how he may overcome him? Alas! she replies, in her love for him she wove her magic so closely about him that nothing can wound him — in battle, that is to say, for knowing that he would never turn his back upon a foe, she has set no spell there. " And there," says Hagen in triumph, " there striketh my spear! "

He turns quickly to Gunther and exhorts him to master himself, but the king, starting up passionately, cries shame and woe upon himself as the most wretched of all living. Brynhilde taunts the weakling with hiding cravenly behind the hero, and the maddened king cries to Hagen to help him save his honour. " No help from brain, no help from hand," answers Hagen; " there helps but — Siegfried's death! "

Gunther recoils with horror at the words, and the solemn No. 15 is heard in the orchestra as he cries in his anguish, " Blood-brotherhood I swore with him! " The bond, urges Hagen, has been broken by Siegfried, and only his blood can atone. Brynhilde cries out in her intolerable pain that while Siegfried betrayed only Gunther, she has been betrayed by them all. All the blood of the world could not wash out their guilt to her, but as to her vengeance, one man's death alone can glut that: Siegfried must die!

Insidiously Hagen reminds his brother that Siegfried's death will bring him the Ring, that coveted Ring that was once the Nibelung's; and Gunther, sighing deeply, consents to the deed, though he is sorry for the gentle Gutrune, who so truly loves

Siegfried; "What were we worth in her eyes," he asks, "with her husband's blood on our hands?"

The mention of Gutrune's name converts Brynhilde into a fury again; it is for Gutrune and her magic that Siegfried has betrayed her! Once more Hagen has a plan; if her hero's death will grieve Gutrune, let her not know how it came about; on the morrow they will go hunting, and a boar's tusk can let out Siegfried's life. So shall it be, the others decide, Brynhilde thinking only of her vengeance upon Siegfried and Gutrune, Gunther welcoming the opportunity to wipe out his shame, Hagen gloating over the prospect of gaining possession of the Ring and the Hoard.

Once more we hear the Gutrune motive in the orchestra as Gunther and Brynhilde, turning towards the hall, are met by the outcoming bridal procession. Siegfried is carried by the men on a shield, Gutrune on a chair; boys and maidens, strewing flowers, run in front of them, while in the background the vassals and the women bring sacrificial beasts and instruments to the altar. The women invite Brynhilde to accompany them; Gutrune also beckons to her with a friendly smile, but Brynhilde only stares blankly at her. Hagen urges her on to Gunther, who takes her hand. The king himself is lifted by the men on to a shield, and as the procession moves towards the heights the curtain falls, the orchestra giving out in the final bars the darkly suggestive Hagen theme once more, followed by the motive of the Covenant of Vengeance.

The opening scene of the last act of the great drama is set in a wild, wooded valley on the Rhine, which is seen flowing in the background past a steep cliff. Siegfried is out hunting with Gunther and Hagen and the others, and apparently the Rhinemaidens are awaiting his coming. Before the curtain rises we hear, behind the scenes, Siegfried's horn-call, followed by the sound of other horns, some in the far distance, some nearer. Interspersed with these hunting sounds are the theme of the Rhine (*Rhinegold*, No. 2), and hints of the melody of the Rhinemaidens that will be heard a little later from the maidens themselves.

When the curtain rises, Woglinde, Wellgunde, and Flosshilde are swimming in the water, circling as if in a dance. Wagner gives them an enchanting new melody to sing:

as they greet the sunlight and once more lament the loss of the shining, innocent gold. Horns and their echoes are heard again in the distance, and the Rhinemaidens, splashing about joyously in the water, call upon the sunlight to send them soon the hero who shall restore the gold to them.

Once more Siegfried's horn is heard, and the three Rhinemaidens dive swiftly to take counsel together. While they are away, Siegfried appears on the cliff, fully armed: he has lost both his quarry and his way. The Rhinemaidens rise to the surface again, and, resuming their dance, accost him teasingly. He looks at them with a smile: perhaps it was they, he asks, who lured away from him the shaggy brute he was hunting; if he is their lover, he leaves him to them.

The maidens, laughing merrily, ask what he will give them if they should restore his quarry. His hands are empty today, he answers, but let them say what they would have of him. They demand the Ring that gleams on his finger, but this he refuses them: to win it he slew a mighty Dragon, and shall he now part with it for a paltry bearskin? They call him mean; he should be freer with his gifts to maidens! Were he to part with his goods in this way, he says smilingly, his wife would scold him; whereupon the Rhinemaidens laugh immoderately at this hero who is so afraid of his

wife: perhaps she beats him, they suggest. With a parting sarcasm
at his miserliness they dive beneath the waters again.

Siegfried has apparently been a little nettled by their gibes.
Coming lower down he calls on them to return, saying that he will
give them the Ring, which he has drawn from his finger and now
holds aloft. When the Rhinemaidens come to the surface again
they are grave and solemn. They bid him keep the Ring and ward
it well till he learns the ill fate that lies in it; then will he fain be
saved by them from the curse that lies upon it.

Quietly replacing the Ring on his finger, he asks them to tell
him all they know. In gravely warning tones:

they tell him that the Ring is made from gold ravished from the
Rhine, and that he who shaped it by cunning and lost it in shame
laid a curse upon it, so that everyone who possesses it is doomed
to death; as Siegfried slew the Dragon so shall he himself be slain,
and that this very day, unless he returns the Ring to them, to be
hidden in the depths of the Rhine, whose waters alone can wash
out the curse.

The blind young hero replies that as he was not deceived by their
fawning he will not be moved by their threats. Still more urgently,
the harmonies shown in the first two bars of No. 29 taking on a yet
more anxious tinge, as it were, they exhort him to reflect while it is
yet time; but he only answers that he had already been warned
of the curse by the Dragon, and still could not learn what fear is;
through the magic of the Ring, he has been told, he could win him

the inheritance of the world, but that he despises; he would barter it for the grace of love, but never under a threat, for life and limb he counts of no more worth than this — picking up a clod of earth, holding it over his head, and throwing it behind him.

The Rhinemaidens can do no more with the infatuated young man; they call upon each other to leave to his doom this madman who thinks himself so valiant and wise and strong and yet is so bound and blind. He does not even know that he has been false — that a glorious gift was once in his hands and that he spurned it. But this very day a woman shall inherit the Ring — one who will work their will better than he.

They resume their dance, and, singing once more their liquid song, swim away to the background and are lost to sight. Looking after them, in smiling thoughtfulness, Siegfried muses upon the ways of women: they fawn upon a man, and when he is deaf to them, they try to frighten him with threats; then, when he smiles at these, they give him the edge of their tongue! And yet, he says, had not Gutrune his troth, he would have won for himself one of these delightful maidens.

When the last echo of the Rhinemaidens' song has died away in the orchestra, the trombones give out softly a fateful reminder of the Curse motive; then horns are heard from the background again, and the voices of Hagen and the vassals hailing Siegfried. These, accompanied by Gunther, soon appear, and descend the height to rest and prepare a meal on the level ground, where the game is piled up in a heap. All lie down; wine-skins and drinking-horns are produced, and Hagen calls upon Siegfried to tell them of the wonders of his hunting.

Siegfried laughingly declares that he has had no success; he went out after wild beast and found only wildfowl! — three young water-birds who, from the Rhine, sang a warning to him that he should be slain that day. At this, Gunther starts violently and looks darkly at Hagen.

Lying down between Hagen and Gunther, Siegfried, who is thirsty, asks for wine, and Hagen hands him a drinking-horn.

Siegfried drinks and offers the horn to Gunther, who, looking sadly and thoughtfully into it, mutters in choked tones, " The draught is dull and blanched: thy blood alone is there! " " Then thine with mine will I mingle," says Siegfried with a laugh, and he pours the contents of Gunther's horn into his own. The wine overflows, and Siegfried draws Gunther's attention to their blended blood flowing over and sinking into the earth — an unconscious forecast of what is to happen later.

Hagen now remarks that he has heard that Siegfried understands the song of birds. The hero answers lightly that since he has heard the sweet singing of women he cares no more for the birds, but if it will ease the heart of the gloomy Gunther he will sing them the story of his boyhood and its wonders. All lie down around him, he remaining upright.

To the accompaniment of motives all of which are by now very familiar to us he tells them how Mime brought him up to work the dwarf's will upon a fierce Dragon that brooded like a brute over a hoard; how he forged his father's sword and slew Fafner; how after tasting the Dragon's blood he was able to understand the song of the wood-bird; how he took from the cavern the Ring and the Tarnhelm, and, on the advice of the bird, swept the treacherous Mime away.

Hagen breaks out into hoarse laughter: " The sword he could forge not," he says, " yet did Mime feel it! " He has had another horn filled, into which he drops the juice of an herb; he hands the draught to Siegfried, who drains it slowly while the motive of Magic Deceit (No. 14) is heard again in the orchestra.

Siegfried's memory is restored by the potion, and he proceeds to tell how, guided by the bird, he found the rock, fought his way through the flames, and won Brynhilde for his wife. His ecstasy grows with the remembrance: " Sleeping I found the fairest of maids," he says; " the helm I loosed from the glittering maid; my kiss awoke her to life; to her burning breast was I folded, fast in Brynhilde's arms! "

Gunther, who has been listening intently and in amazement, now springs up in the utmost horror. Two ravens fly up out of the

bush, circle over Siegfried, and then take their course towards the
Rhine. " Can you read me," Hagen asks Siegfried, " the runes
of those ravens also? " Siegfried, starting to his feet and gazing
after the ravens, turns his back to Hagen, who at once thrusts
his spear into the hero's back. Gunther strikes Hagen on the
arm, but it is too late; Siegfried swings his shield on high with
both hands and tries to crush Hagen, but his strength fails
him, the shield drops behind him, and he himself falls on it with
a crash.

The horrified vassals ask Hagen what deed is this that he has
done; pointing to the prostrate body he merely answers, " Death
for a broken oath! " turns quietly away and slowly strides out of
sight over the heights, in the twilight that has begun to fall at the
appearance of the ravens.

The solemn rhythm shown in the next quotation is heard in the
orchestra, followed by the motive of the Annunciation of Fate.
Gunther, grieved and stricken, bends down at Siegfried's side;
the vassals, also filled with sympathy, stand round the dying man,
who, supported by two of them in a sitting position, opens his eyes,
and, to the music to which Brynhilde greeted the world on her
awakening on the rock, gives a last greeting to Brynhilde. Then he
sinks back and dies.

Night has now fallen. At a signal from Gunther the vassals raise
Siegfried's body and carry it in a solemn procession over the rocky
heights, Gunther following, while the orchestra pours out the
solemn Death March:

To us who have followed the course of the drama, the March
is a musical epitome of the story of the Wälsungs and of Siegfried.
We hear, in succession, the motives of the Wälsungs, Sieglinde's

Pity, the Love of Sieglinde, the Sword, Siegfried, Siegfried as Hero (in a magnificently glorified form):

and Brynhilde.

During the playing of the March, mists are supposed to come up from the Rhine and gradually envelop the stage, making the funeral train invisible. In practice, however, the curtain is dropped shortly after the March commences, and when it rises again we see the hall of the Gibichungs, as in the first act. It is night, and the Rhine is bathed in moonlight. Gutrune comes from her chamber into the hall; she has been unable to sleep for evil dreams, and she fancies she has heard the sound of Siegfried's horn and the neigh of his horse. She has heard Brynhilde's laughter, and seen a woman steal silently towards the Rhine; and looking into Bryn-hilde's room she finds it empty. In the distance is heard Hagen's hoarse voice calling " Hoiho Hoiho! Awake! Awake! Torches! Fine booty home do we bring! " and Gutrune stands motionless, paralysed by terror.

The glow of torches is seen outside, and Hagen enters, grimly bidding Gutrune come forward and greet her Siegfried, for " the mighty hero comes home again! " The procession enters with Siegfried's body, Gunther accompanying it, while men and women with lights enter in great confusion. The body is set down in the middle of the hall, and Hagen tells the horrified Gutrune that Siegfried's bloodless mouth will blow his horn no more; no more will he hunt or fight or woo winsome women to love him; a wild boar has slain him, and Siegfried, Gutrune's husband, is dead. She falls on the body with a shriek and is gently tended by Gunther, whom she pushes back violently, accusing him of treachery and murder.

" Reproach not me," he says; " keep thy curses for Hagen; he was the accursed boar that dealt the hero his death! " Then the agonised king breaks forth into a passionate reproach of Hagen, who, stepping forward and throwing off the mask, admits that he slew Siegfried, and glories in the deed. And now, he cries, the Ring is mine! Gunther claims it, and Hagen throws himself upon him; the vassals try to come between them, but Gunther falls dead from a stroke from Hagen's sword. Hagen grasps at Siegfried's hand, which raises itself threateningly, so that the women shriek with horror and all stand motionless, frozen with fear.

At this point Brynhilde comes forward from the background slowly and solemnly, and bids them make an end of their wailing; the woman they all have betrayed has come for vengeance: their cries are like those of children crying to their mother because sweet milk has been spilled, but no knell has she heard befitting so great a hero as Siegfried.

In deep pity she puts aside Gutrune and her lamenting, and Gutrune, realising that she, like Brynhilde, has been betrayed by Hagen, turns away from Siegfried in shame, and, dissolved in grief, bends over Gunther's body, remaining in that attitude to the end of the scene. Hagen leans defiantly on his spear and shield, sunk in gloomy brooding. Brynhilde, alone in the centre of the stage, gazes for a long time at the body of Siegfried, at first deeply agitated, then overwhelmed with grief; finally she turns to the men, and in tones of solemn exaltation bids them erect a great funeral pyre by the river-side and kindle a fire to consume the body of the greatest of heroes. His horse they are to bring to her, that he and she may follow their lord.

Her commands are carried out. For a time Brynhilde is lost in contemplation of the face of the dead Siegfried; then her expression becomes transfigured, and she sings a long and noble elegy upon him. She knows the whole truth now; no one was truer than Siegfried, yet, the victim and the dupe of fate, he broke his troth. She and he have been the instruments for the working out of Wotan's plans, and both have been broken by them.

Signing to the vassals to lift the body on to the pyre, she takes the Ring from Siegfried's finger and gazes at it thoughtfully. Once more the fatal symbol has come into her possession, and now it shall go back to the Rhine, and the fire that burns her with Siegfried shall cleanse the Ring from its curse, while the maidens shall keep the gold for ever innocent and pure in the depths of the waters.

Putting the Ring on her own finger, she turns to the pile of logs on which Siegfried's body lies stretched, and taking a firebrand from one of the men she swings it and points to the background. " Fly home, ye ravens! " she cries; " tell this tale to Wotan, that here on the Rhine ye have heard! Wend your way to Brynhilde's rock, and bid Loge hasten to Valhalla, for the gods' twilight comes at last! So cast I the brand on Valhalla's glittering towers! " She throws the brand upon the pyre, which instantly breaks into flame; two ravens fly up from the rock by the shore and disappear in the background. The men bring forward her horse; she goes to it, unbridles it, speaks loving, confidential words to it, and gives herself up to the rapture of the thought of a fiery death for both of them with their hero.

Mounting the horse, she urges him towards the pyre, into which he leaps with her. The pyre blazes up, filling the stage in front of the hall, and appearing to seize on this also. The men and women, in horror, press towards the extreme foreground.

A cloud of smoke floats towards the background; at the same time the Rhine swells mightily and pours its flood over the fire. On its waves the three Rhinedaughters are seen swimming forward. At the sight of them, Hagen, who has been watching Brynhilde with increasing anxiety, hastily rids himself of shield, spear, and helmet, and plunges madly into the flood. Two of the Rhinemaidens throw their arms about his neck and draw him down into the depths with them, while Flosshilde exultantly holds the recovered Ring on high.

Through the cloudbank on the horizon there comes a bright red glow, in which the three Rhinemaidens are seen swimming in circles and sporting with the Ring in the calmer waves of the river, which has gradually subsided into its bed. The hall crashes in ruins, and in the fiery glow in the distance we see the interior of Valhalla, in which the gods and heroes sit assembled, as de-

scribed by Waltraute to Brynhilde in the first act. Flames seize
upon the hall as the curtain falls.

The orchestra all this while has been pouring out a mighty
flood of tone, and the gloom and the power of it and the extremity
of the catastrophe become oppressive. But for the final bars of all
Wagner reserves an exquisite stroke: the last strain to greet our
ears is a new version of the motive of Redemption by Love:

given out in soft consolatory tones by the strings.

THE LEGEND of the Flying Dutchman is an old one. It tells of a certain sea-captain who, finding himself prevented by contrary winds from rounding the Cape, swore he would get past though Hell itself should prevail.

The bold resolution apparently gave great offence to Satan, who punished the audacious mariner by condemning him to sail the seas for ever, the only mitigation of the sentence being that he might land once in every seven years in the hope of finding a woman who would love him and be faithful to him; the Devil seems to have been cynically confident that the original sentence would begin to run again after each break between the periods of seven years.

The subject must have been treated in dramatic or novel form on many occasions, and two stories based on it — one by the German novelist Wilhelm Hauff, the other by our own Captain Marryat in *The Phantom Ship* — are fairly well known. It is extremely unlikely that Wagner ever heard of Marryat, though he may possibly have read Hauff's story.

Wagner seems to have first become seriously interested in the story during his Riga period (1837–1839), where he came across it in Heine's *Memoirs of Herr von Schnabelewopski*. Heine there gives an account of a play on the subject which he alleges he saw at Amsterdam. It has been said that he probably had in mind a play on the Flying Dutchman theme by the English dramatist Fitzball, which was staged at the Adelphi Theatre during Heine's visit to London in 1827; but some learned men have thrown doubt upon this theory, which, in any case, is hardly of the first importance.

Heine characteristically treats the saving clause, as we may perhaps call it, of the Dutchman's sentence as a joke; he assumes that the Devil, knowing women as well as he did, had no objection to the harried mariner wasting his time looking for a faithful one, while the Dutchman, according to Heine, after each brief experience of married life was glad to escape to the sea again. Heine drew a double moral from the story — for women, not to marry Flying Dutchmen; for men, to beware of women.

As usual with Wagner, the legend, having once thrust its roots into him, had to be left to work its way upwards to the light in virtue of the laws of its own unconscious growth. Wagner was always very sorry for himself, regarding himself as a man particularly ill-used by fate; and in these early days of his he was mainly possessed by two great longings — for rest and comfort and for an ideal woman's love.

The story of the Flying Dutchman seemed to him to describe his own case exactly. In *A Communication to my Friends,* an account of his spiritual and artistic development which he published at the end of 1851 as preface to three of his libretti, he describes the legend of the Flying Dutchman as a blend of that of Ulysses and that of the Wandering Jew.

Wagner does not regard the Devil of the story as being merely the somewhat crude Satan of theology, but a symbolisation of the unresting element of Flood and Storm. Like Ahasuerus, he says, the mariner yearned for death to end his sufferings. The redemption that is denied to the Wandering Jew, however, he is given the chance of finding at the hands of " a woman who of very love, shall sacrifice herself for him." " The yearning for death thus drives him on to seek this woman; but she is no longer the housewifely Penelope of Ulysses, as courted of old, but the quintessence of womankind; and yet the still unrevealed, the longed-for, the dreamed-of, the infinitely womanly woman — let me say it in one word: *the Woman of the Future*."

Partly because his creditors were pressing him hard, partly

because he thought *Rienzi* would bring him fame and fortune in Paris, Wagner, in July 1839, resolved to go to the French capital. He somehow or other managed to smuggle himself across the Russo-Prussian frontier, and, making his way to the port of Pillau, sailed thence for London in a small sailing-vessel named the *Thetis*, accompanied by his wife Minna and a huge Newfoundland dog named Robber.

The voyage, which usually took about eight days, lasted on this occasion some three and a half weeks. The most violent storms were encountered; more than once the ship was in danger of running aground; Wagner and Minna, who were the sole passengers, suffered incredible hardships; and to make matters worse, the superstitious sailors regarded them as the cause of the exceptionally bad weather. The sea brought up before him the legend of the Flying Dutchman again, and no doubt during the voyage he began to cast the story into some sort of dramatic shape.

The ship put in for safety in one of the Norwegian fjords, at a little fishing-village called Sandwike. Here he was struck by the call of the crew as they cast anchor and furled the sails; this call, which fascinated Wagner by the way it echoed from the cliffs of the fjord, gave him the germ of the theme of the Sailors' Song (see musical example No. 8).

Wagner arrived in London early in August, spent a week or so there, then sailed to Boulogne, where he stayed a month, and finally arrived in Paris on the 18th September. He remained there for two and a half years, he and Minna suffering incredible hardships and privations.

He soon found that there was very little chance of an unknown young German composer having a work of his produced at the Paris Opera. He drafted the scenario of *The Flying Dutchman*, which came to the notice of Léon Pillet, the manager of the Opera. Pillet took a fancy to it and asked Wagner to sell him the plot, as he was under contract to supply various composers with operatic libretti. Wagner pointed out to him that it had been his idea to set the subject to music himself, but Pillet assured him that there was not a ghost of a chance of his having anything accepted at the

Paris Opera for at least seven years, as the already existing con-
tracts extended that far.

Wagner took the advice of friends on the matter and was advised to sell the draft, as there was nothing to prevent another
librettist setting to work on the same subject, and, in fact, the
brother-in-law of Victor Hugo had already thought of doing so.
At a further interview with Pillet, Wagner was offered five hundred
francs for his draft, and, five hundred francs being five hundred
francs, he very wisely took them. A libretto based on Wagner's
scenario was prepared and set to music by Dietsch, one of the
conductors at the Opera. The work was actually performed in 1842,
but apparently has not been heard of since. It would be very
interesting to see the score of it now.

Meanwhile, with five hundred francs to relieve his more immediate necessities, Wagner set to work at his own *Flying Dutchman*.
To get fresh air and freedom from the noise and the feverish haste
of Paris he had taken rooms at Meudon, then a little country
place near the capital. He hired a piano, a thing he had not
possessed for months, and found, to his relief, that, as he said, he
was still a composer. The poem of *The Flying Dutchman* was
written between the 18th and the 28th May, 1841.

On the 29th June came the good news that *Rienzi* had been
accepted at Dresden and would be produced there in the course
of the following winter. The news both put new heart into him
and awakened the desire to see his native country again. The music
to *The Flying Dutchman* was composed in July and August, in
the short space of seven weeks; the orchestration was completed
during the winter in Paris, whither he had returned at the end of
October.

Wagner promptly offered *The Flying Dutchman* to Munich and
Leipzig, but each of these towns declined it; the answer given in
one of the cases was that the opera was " not suitable for Germany " ; " and I, poor fool," he wrote some time afterwards,
" had thought that it was suitable *only* for Germany, since there
was something in it that could strike responsive chords only from
German hearts."

The opera was accepted by Berlin, but apparently only out of complaisance for Meyerbeer; there was a change of directorship about this time, and the new director, Küstner, who had declined the opera when he was at Munich, was not particularly pleased about carrying out an arrangement made by his predecessor. For the time being, however, Wagner believed that the opera would be produced in Berlin; and with the certain prospect of the production of *Rienzi* at Dresden he left Paris for his native land in the April of 1842.

Rienzi was produced with great success at Dresden on the 20th October, and the first performance of *The Flying Dutchman* took place in the same theatre on the 2nd January, 1843. It was not given in Berlin till a year and five days later.

After the enthusiasm that *Rienzi* had created in Dresden, Wagner was astonished at the comparatively cool reception of its successor. Apart from the quality of the music, *Rienzi* had pleased because, with its stirring theme and its brilliant ballets, it made a lively and fascinating entertainment. The setting of *The Flying Dutchman* must have looked drab in comparison; the subject seemed a gloomy one to the good Dresdeners, nor did they realise all at once that what they were expected to be interested in was not a stage spectacle but a problem in psychology.

The staging seems to have offered more difficulties than the Dresden machinists could cope with, and the third act missed a good deal of its effect because the sea and the ship both remained almost unmoved in spite of the terrible wind that howled through the orchestra. The singer of the Dutchman's part, Michael Wächter, had a face, a figure, and a manner, to say nothing of an intelligence, that even at the rehearsals, made Wagner realise that the part had been miscast; he was excessively fat, and never knew what to do with his stumpy arms and legs. The Senta was the great Schroeder-Devrient. Her also Wächter drove to despair at the rehearsals; when, in the climactic moment of the second act, she had to proclaim herself as the Dutchman's heaven-sent angel and bring him the message of salvation, she broke off and whispered despairingly to Wagner, "How can I say it when I look into those beady eyes? Good God, Wagner, what a mess you have made!"

Schroeder-Devrient, who from the first was conscious of Wagner's exceptional genius, seems to have put her own heart into the work, and, in spite of the fact that she was physically no longer a romantic young figure, she seems to have been satisfactory even to the exacting Wagner. She was at the time in the thick of one of the many crises in her love-affairs; she was secretly conscious that her new lover was a bad substitute for his immediate predecessor and that her friends disapproved of her incomprehensible infatuation, and she was living at the time in a stage of perpetual nerves, hardly eating or sleeping. But curiously enough, as Wagner noted to his satisfaction, her emotional upset gave her Senta a quality it might not otherwise have had.

Wagner was probably right when, some thirty years later, he said, "So far as my knowledge goes, I can find in the life of no artist so striking a transformation, in so short a time, as is evident between *Rienzi* and *The Flying Dutchman*, the first of which was hardly finished when the second also was almost ready."

As he himself put it, in *Rienzi* his sole aim had been to write an "opera"; in *The Flying Dutchman* he made his first tentative step towards the musical drama. In the older opera the music was the first consideration, the libretto being constructed in such a way as to provide the composer with the conventional opportunities for aria, duet, trio, ensemble, and so on. In the musical drama as Wagner came to conceive it the drama is the first consideration, and it is from the drama that the music must take its expression, its colour, and its form.

It is true, as Wagner himself admitted, that to all intents and purposes the old divisions of aria, duet, etc., still exist in *The Flying Dutchman*, but they are not there for their own sakes, merely as so many "numbers"; they are not imposed arbitrarily upon the dramatic subject, but grow naturally out of it. In *Tannhäuser* he got further away than in *The Flying Dutchman* from the opera of "numbers," and in *Lohengrin* further still; while in the works of his prime all traces of the old arbitrary divisions for their own sakes disappear.

In planning *The Flying Dutchman* he did not begin, as was customary before that time, from the circumference, as it were, and work towards the centre, but from the centre itself. He tells us that the opera evolved spontaneously from a single dramatic germ — the ballad of Senta in the second act. This was the " number " he actually wrote first; dramatically the whole conception of the opera is contained in essence in this cry of sympathy of Senta for the unhappy sailor whom she has never seen, while musically, as he said later, the dramatic germ of the ballad spread itself in all directions over the remaining tissue of the opera.

Next after the Senta ballad he appears to have written the song of the Norwegian sailors and the " Phantom Song " of the crew of the Dutchman's ship. These sections were written when he was still hoping to have the future opera produced in Paris; he had the German words, indeed, translated into French, for a sort of trial demonstration before the Opera authorities, which, however, never took place. When, after the arrival of the piano at Meudon, he set to work upon the text again, wondering half doubtingly whether he was still a composer, the first things he wrote were the Helmsman's Song and the Spinning Chorus; and he was so pleased with these when he tried them on the piano that he plunged forthwith into the body of the work, and, as we have seen, completed the music within seven weeks.

The overture, which was written last, is the finest piece of work in its genre that the world had known since the great overtures of Beethoven; it is a worthy forerunner of the overtures to *Tannhäuser* and *The Mastersingers*.

Wagner himself has left us an explanatory analysis of the overture, from which we see that he intended it as a summary of the action of the opera. Through a harmony of bare fifths and octaves we hear in the horns and bassoons the striking motive typical of the Dutchman:

It has recently been claimed that this motive is identical with a phrase in one of the folksongs of the Hebrides, but too much importance need not be attached to the resemblance; the notes composing the theme are the leading ones of the natural scale — the octave, the fourth, and the fifth — and many a primitive melody or call must have been based upon them.

After this curt statement of it the Dutchman's theme is thundered out by the trombones and tuba and runs into a tearing discord, at the end of which a new motive appears in the wood-wind:

To this motive (seen in bars two and three of the above quotation), it is difficult to give a precise name; it may be regarded as part of the curse laid on the Dutchman.

From Wagner's analysis it is clear that at the commencement of the overture we are to imagine the Flying Dutchman's ship scudding before the storm; it puts to land, where the captain has so often been promised rest and redemption. The motive of the Dutchman grows fainter and fainter in the orchestra, till finally nothing is left of it but repetitions of the basic A in the kettle-drums; then, after a pause, the motive of Redemption comes out in the wind alone, the English horn having the melody:

This part of the melody is at once repeated an octave higher, the oboe taking the tune, and it is followed by the second strain, the melody reverting to the English horn again:

This is instantly followed by a motive to which again it is difficult to attach a name, for in the opera it is used in connection with both the Dutchman and the Norwegian sailors; the melody plays upon two notes only, while the harmonic basis keeps slipping down chromatically:

Once more we hear the Dutchman's theme in the horns, and then a fresh motive, suggestive of the Dutchman's weary wanderings on the sea:

that has already been hinted at a little earlier, is taken up and handled at rather greater length, in conjunction with the motive of the Dutchman's Longing for Death:

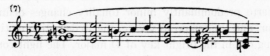

and the main Dutchman motive (No. 1).

From Wagner's explanation we see that what he had in his mind was the Dutchman, even after he is safe on land, running over in imagination the endless sufferings brought upon him by the Curse.

Suddenly we hear in the wood-wind a song that does not appear in the opera until the second act, when it is sung by the crew of the Norwegian ship:

From Wagner's analysis we gather that we are here to picture to ourselves a stately ship sweeping past the anchoring-place of the Dutchman; he hears the sailors on the ship singing in glad anticipation of home. The joyous sound fills the Dutchman with rage; he sets sail again and rides madly through the storm, frightening and silencing the happy singers. All this is represented to us in the overture by further handlings of the motives already quoted.

Gradually the motive of Redemption takes possession of the orchestra; the Dutchman, as he crashes through the tempest, has now one thought only in his mind — that of the woman whose love is to bring him salvation and peace.

Suddenly, says Wagner, a ray of light pierces the gloom of the night like a lightning flash; no doubt this is the point at which the hitherto predominantly minor tonality changes definitely to the major, and the tempo to vivace, the Redemption motive (No. 3) coming out in the bright key of D major. The light comes and goes; the mariner drives steadfastly towards it; " it is a woman's look, which, full of sublime sorrow and godlike sympathy, thrusts towards him. A heart has opened its fathomless depths to the monstrous sorrows of the damned; this heart must sacrifice itself for him, break with sympathy for him, and in destroying his sorrows destroy also itself.

" At this divine sight the unhappy man breaks down as his ship also is shattered to atoms; but from the waves he rises hallowed and whole, led by the victorious redeemer's rescuing hand to the day-dawn of sublimest love." This final section of the overture is, for the most part, a joyous rhapsody upon the theme of Redemption, towards the finish of which the Dutchman's theme thunders out triumphantly in the heavy brass.

Wagner subjected *The Flying Dutchman* to a slight revision in later years, when both his spiritual and musical development dictated to him a change for the better both in the ending of the opera and in the ending of the overture. In the original score, published in 1844, both the opera and the overture end with a transformed statement of the Redemption motive:

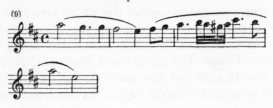

followed by the theme of the Dutchman in the brass. It was in later years that he added the ten bars that give its magical quality to the present ending both of the overture and of the opera.

Just as we think the overture is about to end in the now firmly established key of D major, Wagner suddenly switches into G major, tones the orchestra down in a moment from *ff* to *p*, and lets the wood-wind, accompanied by the harp, give out softly and gently the Redemption motive in its original form (No. 3). In another half-dozen bars the key of D major is re-established, and the overture, instead of finishing *fortissimo,* as it had done in the first version, ends softly and slowly in a sort of spiritualised transfiguration. More will be said on this point when we come to consider the final page of the opera itself.

It will be seen how strictly Wagner has kept to the central dramatic purpose of the opera in his overture. Had he been writing a mere *potpourri* of the melodies of the opera, in the style of so many of his predecessors and contemporaries, we should certainly have had some reference to the other main characters of the opera — Erik and Daland — and it is safe to say that no other composer of the time would have neglected the easy opportunity to ingratiate himself with the audience by including the charming Spinning Chorus in his overture. Wagner keeps strictly to the Curse on the Dutchman and his redemption from it by Senta; the only apparently extraneous musical matter introduced is the Sailors' Song, and this, as we have shown, is really justified in terms of Wagner's programme for the overture.

The setting of the first scene shows us a sea-coast with steep, rocky cliffs. The greater part of the stage is occupied by the sea, which stretches far back; the rocks in the foreground form gorges on each side, that give back the many echoes heard during the scene. On the sea a violent storm is raging, but it is calmer between the rocks. The ship of a Norwegian captain, Daland, has just cast anchor near the shore, and the sailors are busily furling the sails, throwing ropes, and so on. Daland himself has gone on shore; he has climbed a cliff and is looking landwards, trying to recognise the locality.

In 1852 Wagner wrote an article intended for the German theatres, giving minute instructions as to the proper way of producing *The Flying Dutchman*. He insisted that the orchestra and the stage should be in perfect accord — that when there was an audible storm in the orchestra, for instance, there should be a visible storm on the stage. We are, as it were, to be put in tune with the Dutchman's psychology before he actually appears; we are to be shown such a storm that we shall be in anticipatory sympathy with him.

The sea, said Wagner, should be shown as boisterous as possible, while the treatment of the ship cannot be too realistic; for instance, when, between the two stanzas of the Steersman's Song that comes later, there is a wild upward surge in the orchestra, we should have it made quite clear to us that here the ship has been violently shaken by an unusually large wave.

The sailors, at their work, give cries of " Hoyohe! Halloho! " and so on, to fragments of the motives always associated with the sailors — in this case the first three notes of No. 8 and the figure of two notes characteristic of No. 5. Their cries are echoed from the gorges.

Daland, descending from the cliff, announces that the storm has blown them seven miles out of their way just when they were nearing home. He knows the bay; it is Sandwike — the bay in which, it will be remembered, the *Thetis* put it on the voyage from Pillau. He has actually seen the shore on which stands his own house. He had thought that soon he would have his daughter Senta in his arms; then all the winds of hell blew, and drove them where they are now. But the storm is at last abating; and going on board he tells the crew they can now sleep, as the danger is over. The sailors go below; Daland also goes into his cabin, telling the Steersman to take the watch for him that night, but to be careful not to sleep.

The Steersman alone remains on deck. The storm has died away, except for an occasional roughness out on the open sea. The horns and bassoons give out softly a theme:

associated with the jollification of the sailors. The Steersman yawns, pulls himself together, and, by way of fighting against sleep, bursts into a little song to his love:

> Mit Ge-wit-ter und Sturm aus fer-nem Meer, mein Mä-del bin dir nah!
> *Thro' the thun-der and storm, from dis-tant seas, My maid-en, come I near!*

He exhorts the soft south wind to fill their sails and blow them home:

> Mein Mä-del, wenn nicht Süd-wind wär', ich nim-mer wohl käm' zu dir:
> *My maid-en, if the south wind fails, no more can I come to thee;*

and finishes up with a vigorous "Hoyoho!":

> Ho-ho - jo! Hal-lo-ho - -ho! hol-lo ho ho ho!

At this point the ship is shaken by a great wave; the Steersman starts up and looks round him apprehensively; then, convinced that everything is right, he sits down again and sings a second stanza of his song, but, overcome with weariness, falls asleep before he can finish it.

The storm increases and the stage grows darker. In the distance appears the Flying Dutchman's ship, with black masts and blood-red sails; it rapidly approaches the shore, on the opposite side to the Norwegian ship. The storm-music of the overture breaks out again, the Dutchman's theme (No. 1) is heard first of all in the horns, then in the trumpets and trombones, and at the height of the orchestral turmoil the Dutchman's ship casts anchor with a tremendous crash.

The Steersman starts at the noise; the Sailors' Dance (No. 10) comes out softly in the bassoons, and the Steersman, after a hasty glance at the helm, is reassured and makes yet another effort to complete his song; after only a couple of bars of it, however, he falls asleep again. To the strain of No. 5, heavily phrased and darkly coloured, the spectral crew of the Dutchman's ship furl the sails in dead silence. The Dutchman's theme is given out low down in the trumpets, then again in the horn, as he steps ashore, dressed in black Spanish costume.

Wagner tells us that the slowness of his gait should be in marked contrast with the supernatural swiftness of the incoming of the ship. A stumbling sort of figure:

(14)

comes out in the violas and 'cellos, and we have Wagner's own authority for regarding this as descriptive of the rolling walk characteristic of the sailor when he first steps on land after a long voyage.

During the recitative and aria that follow, the actor, according to Wagner, is not to indulge in exaggerated stridings to and fro; outwardly he is to preserve a certain " terrible repose " even in the most passionate expression of his anguish and despair. " The term is past," he says, " and once again behind me lie seven long years; the weary sea throws me once more on land."

Half wearily, half defiantly, he apostrophises the " haughty ocean," that is for ever changing, while his pain is eternal. Never, he knows, will he find on land the salvation he seeks there; to the ocean he will be true until its last billow shall have rolled and itself be swallowed up. To the accompaniment of the swaying figure that already, in the overture, has symbolised his endless wanderings, he tells us how he has often sought death on the sea, but always in vain:

(15) Allegro molto agitato

Wie oft in Mee - res tief-sten Schlund
How oft in o - cean's seeth-ing deep

stürzt' ich voll Sehn-sucht mich hin - ab, —
Death have I sought, e - ter-nal sleep:

He has flung himself on pirates and offered his ship, filled as it is with treasure, as rare booty; he has driven the ship straight on to the cliffs; but nowhere and nohow can he find the death he desires, for his curse is eternal.

Turning his gaze towards heaven he sends up a poignant prayer to " the heaven-appointed angel " to say whether the promise given to him was not simply a ghastly mockery:

(16) Maestoso

Dich fra - ge ich, ge-pries-ner En - gel
Tell me, I pray. O an - gel sent from

Got - tes, der mei - nes Heils Be -
hea - ven, Bear-ing me hope of

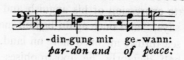

-din-gung mir   ge-wann:
par-don and   of peace:

Then, with a cry of " Vain hope! " he gives full vent to his fury
and despair: " Cursed am I for aye! For love and faith unchanging
in vain I pray! " The passion of the orchestra dies down to an
exhausted quivering in the basses and kettle-drums as he falls to
the ground as if undone; then he permits himself one last hope:

(17)

Molto passionato

Nur ei - ne Hoff - nung soll   mir
One hope   a - lone   my heart   sus-

blei - ben,   nur ei - ne un - er -
-tain - eth,   One ray   a - lone   doth

- schüt - tert steh'n:
light   my   gloom:

that some day the earth itself will crash to ruin and he, perishing
with it, at last find peace. With the last remains of his energy he
cries a mad curse upon the world; then he leans gloomily, with
folded arms, against a cliff in the foreground, while from the hold
of the ship there comes from the invisible crew a sombre echo of
his last words, " Endless destruction on us fall! "

As the Dutchman's motive comes out in the dark colour of the
horns, Daland steps on deck to see the direction of the wind, and
perceives, to his astonishment, a strange vessel. He wakens the
Steersman, who makes another attempt to get on with his ditty,
and the Steersman hails the Dutch ship through a speaking-
trumpet. His " Ahoys! " are echoed by the cliffs, but no answering
sound comes from the other ship.

At last Daland, noticing the Dutchman on shore, hails him and
asks him his name and his country. There is a long silence, and

then the violas and 'cellos, with the trombones and tuba coming in on the final chord, give out a motive that we may call that of Brokenness:

it is expressive of the exhaustion and despair of the Dutchman, and is a curious anticipation of the motive of Wotan's Dejection in *The Ring*.

Daland goes on shore and engages in conversation with the stranger. He learns that the newcomer is Dutch, that his ship has been unharmed by the storm, that for years he has wandered on the face of the waters, and that his heart longs for haven and home. Hearing that Daland's cottage is within a few miles of their anchorage, the Dutchman asks the Norwegian to make him for a while his guest, for which he will pay him with the treasures that are piled up in his ship. To prove the truth of his words he makes a sign to the watch, and some of the sailors bring on shore a chest; opening this, the Dutchman shows the astonished Daland pearls and jewels and riches of all kinds; all these he will give Daland for a single night's shelter, for what is wealth to him, who has neither wife nor child, and seeks his native land in vain? Has Daland a daughter? he asks. " I have a loving child," answers Daland, whereupon the Dutchman cries, " May she be my wife! "

The simple Daland is delighted with the proposition:

Wie! Hör' ich recht? Mei-ne Tochter sein Weib? Er
What? Is't a dream? Make my daughter his bride? For

selbst spricht aus dem Ge - dan - ken!
her all this wealth doth he prof - fer!

The bargain is soon concluded; Daland is rejoiced at the prospect of so rich a son-in-law, while the Dutchman believes that one who is so faithful a daughter as Daland describes his Senta to be will be an equally faithful wife. " Will she my angel be? " asks the Dutchman aside; and once again the old hope of salvation revives in him.

During the duet between the two men the wind has changed and the weather cleared up. The Norwegian Steersman and the sailors jointly greet the south wind, and to the strain of No. 10 Daland points out to the Dutchman how good the omens are. While the mariners hoist the sails, the Dutchman bids Daland put out to sea first; he must rest his own crew awhile, he says, but he will follow soon, and as his ship is swift it will soon overtake the other. Daland pipes the crew and the ship is cast loose, the sailors joining in the Steersman's Song (No. 11, etc.). The Norwegian ship sails away; the Dutchman goes on board his own ship, and the curtain falls.

The part of Daland is one that it is difficult for the actor to make credible to us today. Wagner seems to have realised this, and he earnestly beseeches the player of the part not to drag it down to the obviously comic. Daland, he says, is just a rough, everyday sort of sailor, who is used to braving storms and dangers for the sake of gain, and to whom there can be nothing disgraceful in the apparent sale of his daughter to a rich man; " he thinks and acts, like a hundred thousand others, without the least suspicion that he is doing anything wrong."

Wagner originally planned *The Flying Dutchman* in one act, partly because of the desire for concentration in the action and the psychological motives, partly because he thought that in this form it would stand a better chance of acceptance as a curtain-raiser before a ballet at the Paris Opera. It was divided into three acts later to suit the convenience of the theatres and the public.

When the opera is given in three acts, as is done practically everywhere but at Bayreuth, the second act commences with an orchestral Introduction in which we hear first of all the Steersman's Song, then the Sailors' Dance, then other motives associated with the sea, such as the first bar of No. 2 and No. 5.

When the curtain rises we see the interior of Daland's house —

a large room on the walls of which are sea-pictures, charts, and so on. Prominent on the wall at the back is the portrait of a pale man with a dark beard, in a black Spanish costume. Senta, Daland's daughter, is leaning back in a large chair, her arms crossed, her eyes fixed dreamily on the portrait. Senta's nurse, Mary, and a number of maidens are sitting round the fireplace spinning. A humming that has already been heard in the strings before the curtain rose now becomes fully definite, and over it the orchestra hints for a few bars at the melody of the Spinning Chorus, which is then sung by the maidens in harmony:

(20)

Summ' und brumm', du gu-tes Räd -
Hum, hum, hum, good wheel, go whirl -

- chen, mun-ter, mun-ter dreh'
ing; Gai - ly, gai - ly turn

dich um!
thee round!

The lovers of all the maidens are on the seas, and the maidens, while they spin, pray for a favourable wind to send the men home to them.

Mary interrupts the chorus for a moment, and after it has been resumed and concluded she turns to Senta, who is neither spinning nor singing with the others: if she does not spin, she reminds Senta, she will get no gift from her lover. The other maidens laughingly remark that Senta has no need to work at spinning like them, for her lover does not sail the sea; he is a hunter, and brings her game instead of gold.

Too much absorbed in her own thoughts to notice their badinage, Senta, without moving, softly sings to herself a verse of the ballad that will follow later; the melody, which is here given out only by the orchestra, is that shown as No. 3. Why, Mary asks her, will she lose her young years dreaming before that picture? Senta, still motionless, sighs deeply, and asks why Mary ever filled her with sadness by telling her the fate of that hapless man. The others again indulge their wit at her expense; they hope no blood may be shed, for " Erik is a fiery lad " and may shoot the rival who is hanging on the wall.

Aroused at last by their laughter, Senta starts up passionately and bids them cease their jesting. The maidens turn their spinning-wheels rapidly and noisily, as if to drown Senta's scoldings, and sing their Spinning Chorus more loudly than before. At last Senta asks for a respite from this eternal humming. Will no one sing a better song? Will not Mary sing the old ballad? Mary holds up her hands in horror at the suggestion; better leave this terrible Flying Dutchman in peace! Thereupon Senta, in spite of Mary's protests, declares that she will sing the ballad herself, and awaken their pity for the unfortunate victim of fate.

The maidens stop their wheels to listen, but Mary peevishly declares that she will go on with her spinning. This she continues to do, staying by the fire, while the others put their spinning-wheels aside and gather round Senta.

Then follows the ballad that Wagner declared to be the central psychological and musical point of the opera. The Dutchman motive thunders out in the lower strings, bassoons, and tuba; Senta, still sitting in the armchair, repeats it to the words " Yohoho! Hohoho! " then plunges into the melody of the ballad itself:

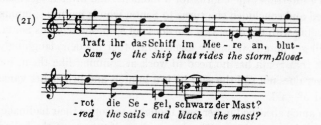

(21)

Traft ihr das Schiff im Mee - re an, blut-
Saw ye the ship that rides the storm, Blood-

-rot die Se - gel, schwarz der Mast?
-red the sails and black the mast?

The words are a description of the Dutchman's ship, with black masts and blood-red sails, riding the storm, with the pale captain

striding up and down the deck unrestingly. In only one way can
he find salvation, says Senta to the melody of No. 3 — by a wife
who will be faithful to him unto death; may Heaven soon grant
the unfortunate man this boon! At the end of the ballad Senta leaps
up from the chair in exaltation, and, to the melody of No. 9,
prays that she may be the one appointed to save him: " O, may
God's angel hither speed thee; my love to grace again shall lead
thee! "

During the singing of the ballad Senta's auditors have become
more and more interested, even Mary ceasing her spinning to
listen; but at this last wild cry of Senta's the maidens start to their
feet in terror. At the climax of the excitement the door opens and
Erik, Senta's lover, is seen standing in the doorway. He has heard
Senta's cry. The maidens appeal to him to help them, for Senta
is out of her senses; while Mary vows that the horrible picture
that is the cause of all this trouble shall be burnt as soon as the
father returns.

Erik gloomily announces that Daland's ship is already in sight,
and Senta, who has so far seemed oblivious to her surroundings,
starts up joyfully. The delighted maidens are for hurrying on at
once to the shore, but Mary insists on their staying to prepare
wine and food for the sailors. She drives the excited girls out of the
room; Senta would go with them, but Erik holds her back. He
implores her to set him free from his torment: her father will soon
be here, and before he sails again will no doubt accomplish his
purpose to marry her to another.

In a smoothly running aria of a somewhat Italian type:

(22)

Mein Herz, voll Treu - e____
A lov - ing heart a____

bis ___ zum Ster - ben, mein dürf - tig'
lone___ I bring thee; No goods nor

Gut, mein   Jä - ger - glück:
gold,   a   hunt - er's   lot!

Erik pleads with Senta to accept him as her husband, although he is only a humble hunter and cannot bring her such wealth as seamen can.

He grows more desperate as Senta tries to break away from him to go to greet her father. He knows, he says, where her heart is set — on the portrait; the ballad she has just sung is only another proof of her infatuation. Senta confesses that one thought alone possesses her — that of redeeming the Dutchman from his endless pain; and Erik, to some wild discords in the orchestra:

cries out despairingly that she has been caught in Satan's toils.

She falls exhausted into a chair, and Erik, in a subdued voice, tells her of a vision he has had in a dream; Senta appears to fall into a " magnetic sleep " and to dream the episode herself as Erik, leaning over the side of the chair, tells it to her. In his dream, says Erik he saw, from the cliffs, a strange ship put in to shore; from it came two men, one of whom he knew to be her father, while the other, clothed in black, pale and ghostly, was the Dutchman of the portrait; Senta flew to give her father greeting, but suddenly turned to the stranger, fell at his feet, and clasped his knees; the seaman raised her up, she fell on his breast and kissed him, and then both sailed away.

The story kindles Senta's enthusiasm afresh; waking from her hypnotic sleep she cries, " He seeks for me! His fate I go with him to share! " Erik, with a cry of " She is lost to me! My dream was true! " rushes off in horror and dismay. But Senta's exaltation dies away as quickly as it had come. Sinking into a brooding silence again, she remains motionless, her gaze riveted on the portrait; then, very softly but with deep feeling, she sings the concluding words of the ballad, praying once more that Heaven may grant the stricken one redemption from his curse by the discovery of the woman who will be faithful to him.

Almost before the phrase has finished, the door opens, and the Dutchman and Daland appear. The latter remains for a while in the doorway, as if waiting for Senta to welcome him; the Dutchman enters at once, and, with his eyes fixed on Senta, moves slowly to the foreground. Senta's eyes shift from the picture to him; she gives a startled cry and then stands as if spellbound.

For a while there is one of those stage silences — the most famous of them is that in the first act of *Tristan and Isolde* — in which Wagner so delighted; and he makes the silence more tense by very much the same methods as in his later works; the kettle-drums throb fatefully, while the strings softly give out a phrase:

that has some curious affinities with the music heard in the orchestra when Brynhilde opens her eyes at the coming of Siegfried.

Daland, after a word of reproach to Senta for not greeting him more warmly, approaches her and draws her to him. "Who is this stranger?" she asks. The orchestra breaks out into a joyous melody of the somewhat Italian type that obsessed Wagner at this stage of his career:

and the bluff Daland smilingly tells her he has brought with him a seaman like himself, who has long wandered over the restless waters, has brought back great wealth with him, and would now be their guest:

(26)

Mögst du, mein Kind den frem-den
Wilt thou, my child ac - cord this

Mann will-kom-men hei - ssen?
stran - ger friend-ly greet - ing?

Senta nods assent, and, turning to the Dutchman, Daland asks triumphantly if his praise of his daughter's beauty was justified. The Dutchman makes a gesture of agreement, and Daland, turning again to his daughter, suggests that on the morrow she shall give the stranger her hand. He produces some jewels and pearls, which, he assures her, are a mere trifle to what shall afterwards be hers.

Senta and the Dutchman all this while keep their eyes fixed on each other without paying any attention to Daland, who, at last noticing their absorption in each other, thinks it well to leave them alone. He goes out slowly, a trifle perplexed, wondering to the last why neither of them makes any attempt to approach the other.

There is another fateful silence, and then, after we have heard No. 1 in the orchestra once more, followed by Wagner's favourite kettle-drum effect, the Dutchman, deeply moved, muses upon this apparition that seems to be the realisation at last of his eternal dream. The duet proper commences with an expressive melody:

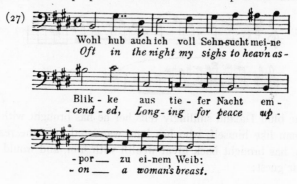

(27)

Wohl hub auch ich voll Sehn-sucht mei-ne
Oft in the night my sighs to heavn as-

Blik - ke aus tie - fer Nacht em -
- cend - ed, Long - ing for peace up -

- por __ zu ei-nem Weib:
- on __ a woman's breast.

to which the Dutchman tells of his eternal longing for release through a woman's love: would that it might be through such an angel as this! Taking up the strain, Senta, in the same subdued voice, asks herself if this is all a dream:

(28)

Ver-sank ich jetzt in wun-der-ba - res
Was all a dream, a vis-ion fair and

Träu-men? Was ich er -blik - ke,
fleet-ing? Can sight and hear-ing

ist's ein Wahn?
thus be - tray?

Then her melody takes a great upward movement:

(29)

Er steht vor mir mit lei-den-vol-len
See, there he stands, with sor-row wan and

Zü - gen, es spricht sein un-er-hör -ter
wea-ry, His grief he pours in-to my

Gram zu mir:
will - ing ear:

She will bring him love and peace, she says, while the Dutchman's voice blends with hers in a passionate cry for rest and release.

The music goes into the minor key as the Dutchman, drawing nearer to Senta, asks her if she is willing to give herself to him for ever in love and faith; then the key of E major establishes itself again as Senta enthusiastically declares that whoever he may be and whatever may be the curse upon him, whatever horrors fate may have in store for her through him, she will obey her father's will. He warns her of the doom that will fall upon her if she should break her troth, for her word, once given, will be without recall; but she bids him have no fear, for well she knows her woman's sacred duty, and to him whom she chooses she will be faithful unto death:

Their voices blend in ecstasy, and a new melody is launched by Senta:

and taken up by the Dutchman after her.

While Senta is appealing fervently to Heaven for help in her trial, and the Dutchman is seconding the prayer, a more earthly strain makes its appearance in the orchestra:

and Daland, entering hurriedly, tells them that the seamen and their mates are hastening to celebrate the end of the voyage. Can he announce to them that Senta and the Dutchman are plighted? Senta, with solemn determination, gives the Dutchman her hand, vowing to be true unto death, and the act ends with a joyous trio.

The third act commences with a vigorous orchestral introduction in which we hear first of all the motive of Senta's Ecstasy (No. 31), then a phrase from the ballad (No. 4); this is followed by the theme of the Sailors' Jollity (No. 10), and this in turn by No. 5. Finally the music settles down into the Sailors' Song (No. 8), to the rollicking strains of which the curtain rises.

We see a creek with a rocky strand; in the foreground, to the side, stands Daland's house; in the background, fairly close to each other, the ships of the Dutchman and Daland are seen at anchor. It is a clear, bright night; the Norwegian ship is lit up, and on the deck the sailors are merrymaking; but the Dutchman's ship is enveloped in an unnatural gloom and a deathlike silence.

The Norwegian sailors begin with the now familiar melody of No. 8, which is soon followed by another merry tune:

(33)

Furch-ten we-der Wind noch bö - sen Strand,
Fear-ing nei-ther wind nor rock - y strand,
wol-len heu-te 'mal recht lust - ig sein!
We will all the day right mer - ry be!

They dance on the deck to the strain of No. 10, stamping their feet heavily at the commencement of each down beat of the music. The maidens come out of the house, carrying baskets of food and drink, with which they go up to the Dutch ship: " A nice sort of dance *there*," they say; " the fellows do not seem to have need of maidens! "

The Norwegian sailors hail them, and are told that the maidens are taking part of the wine to their neighbours, who need it as much as they. " Full sure! " replies the Steersman; " they are tired and dumb with thirst "; and he and his mates comment on the darkness and the ghostly silence of the other ship. The maidens stop as they are on the point of going on the Dutchman's ship; they can still see and hear no one, nor are there any lights to guide them. Going close to the water they call to the crew of the ship, but no reply breaks the sinister silence. " They must be dead," say the sailors mockingly, with affected sadness; " no need have they of wine or bread! "

In a sequence of rousing choruses the maidens and Norwegian sailors keep calling upon the Dutchmen to rouse themselves and come and dance with them on the strand. " They're old and grey, their hearts are lead," say the sailors, " and all their sweethearts long time dead! " More and more urgently they call on the Dutchmen, but without effect; there is another long silence, followed by gloomy, nervous runs in the 'cellos.

The terrified and perplexed maidens cannot be pacified by the rough jokes of the Norwegians; and at last they run away in terror from the Dutch ship and hand their baskets to the sailors on board the Norwegian vessel. Then they go away, promising to return at dawn, but exhorting the Norwegians meanwhile to let their weary neighbours rest.

The Norwegians open the baskets, treat themselves freely to the wine, and burst out in more boisterous merriment than before. As they break out into No. 8 again, signs of life begin to be noticeable on the Dutch ship, the sea around which gradually begins to move, though the waters elsewhere are perfectly calm. On the ship appears a blue flame — a watch fire; a violent wind whistles through the rigging; the crew seems to have been called into life by the flame. They are still invisible, but their " Yohoho! " to the melody of No. 1, comes booming hoarsely through speaking-trumpets. The storm-music of the overture breaks out again, No. 2 being particularly prominent.

The Dutch sailors' song is divided between savage defiances of the storm wind — for their sails are stout, Satan having blessed them ages ago — and ironic appeals to their gloomy captain to go on land again to seek for the faithful maiden's hand, for seven more weary years have gone by. During this chorus the wind howls about the Dutch ship and the sea is in commotion round it, although elsewhere sea and air are calm as before. The Norwegian sailors, who have listened to the Dutchmen's chorus first in astonishment, then in horror, try to keep up their courage by singing their own song again, but this is ultimately swept aside by the Dutchmen's chorus, which ends in an outburst of uncanny laughter.

The Norwegian sailors, awed to silence by the supernatural storm and the unearthly shouting of the crew of the other ship, leave the deck in terror, making the sign of the Cross; it is this action of theirs that provokes the harsh laughter of the Dutchmen. There is a *fortissimo* crash in the orchestra; then the former death-like silence and darkness settle on the Dutch ship again, and sea and air become everywhere calm, as at the commencement of the scene; the horns give out softly the Dutchman's theme (No. 1), which is answered by the motive of Redemption, and after a long kettle-drum roll a sombre chord in the bassoons and horns prolongs itself for a time and then dies into silence.

After a brief pause an agitated figure appears in the orchestra, terminating in a phrase that will be associated afterwards with Erik's denunciation of Senta:

Senta comes hurriedly out of the house, followed by Erik, who is in a state of wild excitement. Is what she has just told him true, he asks her, or is he dreaming? To the accompaniment of a figure expressive of her agitation:

Senta, painfully moved, turns away, saying, " Oh, ask me not! " Upon a restless orchestral basis compounded of Nos. 34 and 35 Erik breaks out in despair: what evil power, he asks, is it that has led her astray, what spell is it that blinds her? Scarcely had the stranger crossed the threshold, he says, when she gave him her hand. She implores him to leave her, swearing that she is driven onward by powers within her stronger than herself: but the self-pitying Erik will not be denied. He reminds her of something she has apparently forgotten — she had once plighted her troth to himself and promised him eternal love.

Wagner lays it down that Erik must not be made " a sentimental whiner," but " stormy, impulsive, and sombre, like every man who lives alone, particularly in the highlands of the North " ; his cavatina in the third act should not be sung in a " sugary " style, but ought rather to express " the very depths of affliction and melancholy."

It is perhaps a little difficult for the actor to carry out these instructions to the full, for the cavatina:

(36)

Willst je-nes Tags du nicht dich mehr ent-
Is that sweet day so soon by thee for-

-sin-nen, als du zu dir mich rie-fest in das
-got-ten, When thou didst call me to yon val-ley

Tal?
fair?

in which Erik reminds Senta of their days of simple happiness together, melodious as it is, has, for our modern ears, a touch of Italian softness in it.

During the course of the cavatina the Dutchman has appeared. Overhearing Erik's final words asking if, when Senta laid her hand in his, she did not promise to be true to him, he rushes forward with a terrible cry of " All is lost! My hope has fled for ever! " Erik recoils horror-struck; Senta places herself before the Dutchman, who frenziedly reproaches her with having broken her troth and bids her farewell; he will to sea again, but she shall not perish with him. He pipes shrilly on his whistle to his crew, bidding them hoist the sails. The voices unite in a trio based on Nos. 34 and 35, the Dutchman upbraiding Senta with her faithlessness and mockery of him, Senta protesting that she is still faithful, and Erik asking himself in horror if he is dreaming.

Moving apart from them, the Dutchman tells Senta that there lies upon him a grievous curse, from which he can be ransomed only by the love of a woman faithful unto death itself; though she gave him her promise, she did not swear it before God; this has saved her, for the fate of those who break their troth to him is eternal damnation; the curse has already claimed victims unnumbered, but Senta at least shall escape it.

Bidding her farewell he turns to go, but Senta holds him back. Well does she know him, she says, and well she knows his doom: the end of all his woes has come, for her love and faithfulness shall take his curse away. Erik gives a despairing cry for help, and Daland, Mary, and the maidens come out hurriedly from the house, and the sailors from the ship. She knows him not, replies the Dutchman to Senta; and pointing to his ship, the blood-red sails of which are now spread, he cries that he is the Flying Dutchman, whose ship is known to all who sail the sea. He rushes on board the ship, which immediately leaves the shore for the open sea, the Dutch crew singing No. 1 in wild chorus.

Senta attempts to follow the Dutchman, but is held back by Daland, Erik, and Mary. She tears herself free and, rushing to a rock that overhangs the water, cries after the departing Dutchman, with all her strength, the last assurance of her love and faithfulness:

(37)

Preis' dei - nen En - gel   und sein Ge -
Praise thou thine an`- gel   with thy last

- bot!___   Hier steh' ich,   treu
breath!__   Here stand I,   faith-

dir   bis   zum Tod!
- ful,   yea,   to   death!

Then she leaps into the sea. The Dutchman's ship instantly sinks with all the crew and quickly disappears; the sea throws up a huge wave and then falls back in a whirlpool. The orchestra, as at the end of the overture, breaks into the two motives of Redemption (No. 3 and No. 9), which are followed by a thundering response of the Dutchman's motive in the heavy brass. The stage directions in the original score at this point run thus: " In the glow of the setting sun the glorified forms of the Dutchman and Senta are seen rising above the wreck, clasped in each other's arms, soaring upwards."

As we have already said, the opera, like the overture, originally ended in a strain of high exultation. At some later date Wagner conceived the happy idea of ending both of them with the soft effect, as of transfiguration, to which we have drawn attention in our analysis of the overture. It was presumably when he made this magical change in the ending of the opera that he added some final stage directions that appear in only one of the many editions of the *Flying Dutchman*: " A dazzling glory illumines the group in the background; Senta raises the Dutchman, presses him to her breast, and points him towards heaven with hand and glance."

Rienzi was too much of a " grand opera " to be pure Wagner; but *The Flying Dutchman* was a work that no one but himself could have written at that time.

RICHARD WAGNER

RICHARD WAGNER was born at Leipzig on the 22nd May, 1813. He was ostensibly the son of Karl Friedrich Wagner, a police-court clerk in the town, and his wife (*née* Johanna Bertz), but there is reason to suppose that his true father was a friend of the family, the gifted actor, painter, and dramatist, Ludwig Geyer. Karl Friedrich Wagner died on the 22nd November of the same year, and on the 28th August, 1814, Geyer married the widow and undertook the charge of her seven children, the eldest of whom was fourteen and a half. The new household removed at the same time to Dresden, returning to Leipzig thirteen years later. Geyer meanwhile had died in 1821.

Wagner's musical studies were casual; the only systematised instruction he had was from a Leipzig teacher, Weinlig, and even this lasted only some six months (in 1831). In all essentials Wagner may be regarded as a self-taught musician, like Hugo Wolf and Elgar.

The family had extensive theatrical connections, owing to Geyer, and more than one member of it adopted the stage as a profession. At the age of twenty Wagner took up, at Würzburg, the first of a number of engagements as conductor and trainer with small operatic companies; the others were at Magdeburg (July 1834), Königsberg (August 1836), and Riga (August 1837). In these wretched surroundings he learned his theatrical and musical technique at first hand. At Königsberg, on the 24th November, 1836, he married Minna Planer, an actress connected with the troupe.

His earliest operas were *The Fairies* (1833) and *The Ban upon Love*, founded on Shakespeare's *Measure for Measure* (1834–6). *Rienzi* was written between 1838 and 1840. In the hope of getting this produced in Paris he went there, *via* London, in September 1839. After two years and a half of bitter disappointments and cruel privations he returned to Germany in April 1842, *Rienzi* having been accepted by Dresden, where it was performed on the 20th October. In February 1843 he became one of the conductors at the Dresden Opera. *The Flying Dutchman* was produced there on the 2nd January, 1843, and *Tannhäuser* on the 19th October, 1845. He finished *Lohengrin* in March 1848, but this opera was not produced till the 26th August, 1850, when Liszt gave it at Weimar.

Meanwhile, owing to his having become mixed up with the political agitations of 1848 and 1849, Wagner had had to flee the country in May of the latter year, a warrant having been issued for his arrest. His exile lasted till 1860, when he was given permission to return to any part of Germany but Saxony; this last restriction also was removed in 1862. During all these years his chief headquarters were Switzerland. His time was mainly occupied in thinking out his new theories of the musical drama, working at the *Ring, Tristan,* and the *Mastersingers,* and trying to get his operas given in Paris and elsewhere. In Paris, in 1861, he produced *Tannhäuser* in a revised version.

He was practically ruined financially when, in 1864, the eighteen-year-old King Ludwig II, who had just succeeded to the throne of Bavaria, took him under his protection and invited him to Munich, where *Tristan* was first produced on the 10th June, 1865, followed by the *Mastersingers* on the 21st June, 1868, the *Rhinegold* on the 22nd September, 1869, and the *Valkyrie* on the 26th June, 1870. It was not long before he was virtually driven out of Munich. Various political parties and persons tried to make him their cat's-paw, his influence with the King being enormous; and his refusal to mix himself up with politics only brought on his head the enmity of all the intriguers. There were other reasons for his unpopularity — his notorious association with Cosima von Bülow (the daughter of Liszt), the jealousy aroused in professional circles in the town by his bringing in protégés of his own, such as Bülow and Peter Cornelius, and, above all, the expense he was proving to the State, owing to the King's infatuation for him. A great scheme drawn up by him for a model Music School in Munich came to nothing. A project for a splendid Wagner theatre in the town, the architectural plans for which were actually drawn up, met with the same fate.

In December 1865 the feeling in the Bavarian capital was so strong against him that the King had to request him to leave it for a time, though the royal favour was not withdrawn, and an annuity was settled on him. After a little wandering in Switzerland, Wagner settled in the spring of 1866 in a villa at Triebschen, near Lucerne, which remained his home for some years, though he occasionally visited Munich.

His first marriage had never been happy. Minna died in Dresden on the 25th January, 1866; and on the 25th August, 1870, Wagner married Cosima; their son, Siegfried, had been born on the 6th June, 1869.

The last years of Wagner's life were mainly occupied with the completion of the *Ring* and the founding of his own theatre at Bayreuth. This, after the overcoming of incredible difficulties of all kinds, was opened in August 1876 with the first complete performance of the *Ring,* under Hans Richter.

The years immediately following 1876 were largely devoted to efforts to raise funds for the Bayreuth theatre. Friends and admirers came to his help, and he himself set out to raise money by giving concerts. In May 1877 he conducted six concerts in the Albert Hall; Queen Victoria, being unable to attend the concerts in person, invited Wagner to Windsor. The six concerts were so great a success that a further two had to be given.

The *Ring* was popularised by an enterprising German impresario, Angelo Neumann, of Leipzig, who, while most of the other theatres were hesitating before its difficulties, took the work on tour through several countries in 1881, London being among the towns visited.

Parsifal, which had been written between January 1877 and April 1879, was given at Bayreuth on the 26th July, 1882, under Hermann Levi. Wagner died suddenly in Venice, of heart disease, on the 13th February, 1883; five days later he was buried in the garden of his stately house — Wahnfried — at Bayreuth.

*

Volume II

STORIES *of the* GREAT

OPERAS

〰〰〰

MOZART (*1756–1791*) TO THOMAS (*1811–1896*)

THE composer whom we know to-day as Wolfgang Amadeus Mozart was baptised under the name of Johannes Chrysostomus Wolfgangus Theophilus. In the home circle he was always called by the name of Wolfgang, or one of its diminutives. In later years the composer retranslated the Gottlieb (the German equivalent, favoured by his father, of Theophilus) into the Latin Amadeus; and his usual signature to his letters was Wolfgang Amade. Occasionally, in his youthful letters, he would add to his signature his confirmation name, Sigismundus.

Mozart came of a line of respectable small-business people and mechanics in Augsburg. In October 1708 one Johann Georg Mozart, a bookbinder (1679–1736) took as his second wife Anna Maria Sulzer (1696–1766?); their eldest son, Johann Georg Leopold, born 14th November, 1719, became the father of the great composer.

Leopold was apparently destined first of all for the Church (he sang as a boy in the choir), then for the law, his education being seen to by the Benedictines of the Convent of St. Ulrich in his native town. This convent was affiliated to the University of Salzburg, and it was no doubt with a recommendation and a certain amount of assistance from the Benedictines of St. Ulrich that Leopold entered upon his legal studies at Salzburg in his eighteenth year (1737). He had already had some musical education, however, and music soon declared itself as his master passion.

In 1740 he joined the household of Count Johann von Thurn as a combination of musical and house servant. This mode of service was common in Germany during the eighteenth century; almost every rich man's household had a number of servants who could also, when required, make music. In an age when public concerts were few, and when a composer could make little by the sale of his music, there were, roughly speaking, only three ways by which musicians could live, apart from teaching — by incessantly turning out commissioned operas, by occupying some public post (such as that of church or town organist), or by taking service at a Court or in the house of some rich patron of music. Haydn spent more than forty years of his life in the service of the Esterhazy family.

An interesting picture of the conditions under which these domestic musicians lived is given in the autobiography of Mozart's contemporary and rival, Dittersdorf. If the musician resided in the great man's house, as Haydn and Dittersdorf did, he wore his master's livery. Technically he was one of the house servants, and might have to take his meals with the others; but conditions in this as in other respects varied with the artistic standing of the musician and the courtesy, intelligence, and good feeling of the master.

The system seems to us now a degrading one, but it was not so regarded in the eighteenth century. In most cases the composers were better off under it than if they had had to throw themselves into the rough-and-tumble of the world. Their position was secure, the duties were not heavy, and, as some of the domestic orchestras were quite large ones for that time, men of talent had exceptional opportunities for mastering every detail of their art.

The Esterhazys, who were great Hungarian landowners, maintained an excellent orchestra in their country mansion, for which Haydn wrote a large number of symphonies, quartets, and other works.

Three years later (1743) Leopold's gifts as instrumentalist and composer obtained for him the post of fourth violinist in the Kapelle (i.e. the musical establishment) of the then ruler of Salzburg, the Archbishop Sigismund, Count von Schrattenbach. By 1758 he had risen to be second violinist, and in 1763 he became Vice-Kapellmeister. This was the highest rank he ever reached in

Salzburg, though he received also (in 1757) the title, and fulfilled the duties of, Court composer. He ended his days in 1787 in the service of the Court, and though during those forty-three years the post of head Kapellmeister became vacant four times, it was never given to Leopold. Among his other duties he had to teach the violin and the clavier,[1] and he was allowed to take private pupils.

Salzburg was a small provincial town with a rather low standard of culture; the inhabitants were notorious for their rough humour, and the official music was of poor quality.

In 1756, the year of his son's birth, Leopold wrote an excellent *Violin School*, which went through many editions during his lifetime and was still being reprinted in the early nineteenth century. He composed industriously, especially during his early manhood, but none of his music has now any except a historical interest.

On the 21st November, 1747, he married Maria Anna Pertl (or Bertel), a sensible, level-headed, humorous woman of twenty-seven, whose portrait shows that it was from her that Wolfgang inherited his inordinately large nose. There were seven children of the marriage, but five died; the survivors were Maria Anna (known in the family circle by the diminutive " Nannerl "), born 30th July, 1751, and Wolfgang, who was born on the 27th January, 1756; his birth almost cost his mother her life.

Nannerl became an excellent clavier player, and not only accompanied Wolfgang on his first tours as an infant prodigy but afterwards, by her teaching, helped to maintain the household. After two abortive love-affairs she married on the 23rd August, 1784, a Baron von Berchtold, of Sonnenberg, a man of forty-eight who had essayed matrimony twice already. Left a widow in 1801, she returned to Salzburg and supplemented by teaching the modest annuity her husband had left her. She died on the 29th October, 1829, nearly forty years after her brother; during the last

---

[1] This is a convenient general term for the keyboard instruments of that time other than the organ. It covers both the harpsichord and the pianoforte. In the second half of the eighteenth century the former instrument was gradually being superseded by the latter.

three years of her life she was quite blind. In character she is said to have taken after the father rather than the mother.

Leopold has been somewhat harshly dealt with by the majority of Mozart's biographers. He is accused of having exploited his gifted children for commercial purposes, and of having ruined Wolfgang's constitution by dragging him all over Europe as an infant prodigy, therefore depriving him of any chance of getting proper physical exercise — indeed, of anything that could be called a real childhood. The probability is, however, that Leopold honestly believed he was doing the best for his children.

His nature was narrow, but solid; he was rather bigotedly religious, and methodical in all his ways. In some ways he was a man decidedly superior to his surroundings. He had considerable native intelligence and a certain amount of culture, and it is evident from his letters that he was incessantly galled by the disagreeableness of his position as a Court musician in so unmusical a town as Salzburg.

He was the servant of people to whom he felt himself to be intellectually superior. Some of his associates in the Kapelle were coarse, illiterate, hard-drinking people, with whom he could not feel that he had anything in common. It was his sense of the unpleasantness and precariousness of his own position that made him anxious to secure a well-paid post for his son; and the only way in which this could be done was by letting the gifted child display his talents, both as executant and composer, in the larger European cities.

Leopold was of the nervous, hypochondriac type that, in face of continuous misfortune, runs easily to a fretful pessimism; his portrait shows us the face of a highly strung, worried, disappointed man. His view of his fellow-creatures generally was a disparaging one; he was always ready to attribute the worst motives to them, and was irrationally suspicious of, and unfair to, everybody who stood, or seemed to him to stand, in Wolfgang's path. " Men," he wrote to his son in 1777, " are all bad. The older you get, the more experience you have of them, the more you will realise this sad truth. Think of all the promises, all the fine talk, and all the events that have come our way, and you will see for yourself how little human help is to be relied upon."

It soon became evident to Leopold that his little son had a most remarkable gift for music. He quickly learned to play the clavier and the violin, and while still a child began composing little pieces that had all the instinctive shapeliness that was so characteristic of his music in his maturity. Whether it was from choice or necessity it is difficult to say, but he took practically no part in the ordinary games and recreations of childhood. His absorbing passion from the first was music.

The Court trumpeter at Salzburg, Andreas Schachtner, who was an intimate friend of Wolfgang's father, furnished Nannerl, a year or so after the composer's death, with some interesting reminiscences of him as a child; they were perhaps slightly idealised here and there by the lapse of time, but must be substantially true. The child had an abnormally fine ear; Schachtner tells us that at the age of seven he declared, quite accurately, that there was a difference of one eighth of a tone between the tuning of his own violin and that of one he had heard a day or two before. From the first he was completely wrapped up in his father; the child's favourite saying was " After God comes papa."

He was barely six years old when his father took him and Nannerl on the first of their tours. This was to Munich, where they stayed three weeks (from the 12th January, 1762, to early in February), the children playing before the Elector. The second tour lasted from the 19th September, 1762, to January 1763; the main objective was Vienna, but calls were made at Passau, Linz, and Pressburg. The mother was of the party. The third tour of the family lasted three and a half years — from the 9th June, 1763, to the end of November 1766; the first part of it included, among other places, Munich, Augsburg, Stuttgart, Ludwigsburg, Schwetzingen, Heidelberg, Mainz, Frankfort, Coblenz, Bonn, Cologne, Aix-la-Chapelle, Brussels, and Paris.

They arrived in the French capital on the 18th November, 1763, and remained there until the 10th April, 1764, when they left for London by way of Calais, arriving in London on the 23rd

April. There they stayed until the 24th July, 1765, living first in Cecil Court, St. Martin's Lane, then in Chelsea, then in Five Fields (now Lower Ebury Street), then in what is now Frith Street, Soho. They were back in Calais on the 1st August, and made their way by slow stages through Lille, Ghent, the Hague, Amsterdam, Mechlin, and other places to Paris once more, where they arrived on the 10th May, 1766.

Two months later, on the 9th July, they left the capital again and made their way home *via* Dijon, Lyons, Geneva, Lausanne, Berne, Zürich, Donaueschingen, Biebrach, Ulm, and Munich (8th November), arriving in Salzburg towards the end of the same month.

Everywhere the children, and especially the precocious little Wolfgang, won the greatest admiration by their talents. Most of the performances were given before Courts or at great houses, but occasionally a public concert was ventured upon. Leopold, of course, was furnished with letters of introduction to influential people in most of the towns they visited.

Wolfgang showed himself to be a natural and very lovable child, behaving towards the great ones of the earth, from the Emperor of Austria downwards, with delightful unconcern. In addition to playing pieces from his studied repertory he improvised whenever requested to do so, and played or accompanied at sight. The Emperor having humorously suggested that he could not play the harpsichord with a cloth covering the keys, the boy did so without hesitation and without fault. Wherever he went he heard as much as he could of the music of other composers, and then and later showed the most surprising facility for entering into the spirit of the various national and personal styles, each of which left its mark for a time upon his own compositions; until his last years he was extraordinarily susceptible to influences, and did not disdain to learn from anyone who had anything to teach him.

Physically it was hardly the best life imaginable for a growing child, and when we take into consideration not only his exclusion from exercise and games and from the society of children of his own age but the hardships and discomforts of travel in those days, it is no wonder that he occasionally had a serious illness. In Vienna, for instance, during his second tour, he was laid up for a fortnight with scarlet fever.

Leopold had been censured for compelling, or at any rate permitting, him to give a concert the day after his recovery; but it was probably a matter of sheer necessity for the children to earn money to cover the heavy travelling and lodging expenses of the family. Frequently, instead of receiving money from the master of the house at which they had played, the children would be rewarded with a watch, a piece of jewellery, or some similar present — beautiful in itself, no doubt, and very gratifying, but not of much use for the immediate payment of bills.

Leopold's advertisement in a Frankfort paper of 30th August, 1763, will give an idea of the nature of the tours as a whole:

" The general amazement aroused in all hearers by the cleverness, never before seen or heard to such a degree, of the two children of the Salzburg Court Kapellmeister, Herr Leopold Mozart, has led to the threefold repetition of what was at first meant to be only a solitary concert. It is owing to this general amazement and at the desire of various great connoisseurs and amateurs that another concert — positively the last — will be given this evening, the 30th August, in the Scharf Hall on the Liebfrauenberg, at 6 o'clock; not only will the little girl, who is twelve years of age, and the boy, who is in his seventh year [he was really in his eighth], play concertos on the harpsichord or the piano, and the most difficult pieces of the greatest masters, but the boy will also play a concerto on the violin, accompany on the clavier in symphonies, and, with the keys covered by a cloth, will play as well as if he had the keyboard under his eyes. Further, from a distance he will name exactly any note that may be sounded either separately or in chords on the clavier or on any other instrument, or on bells, glasses, clocks, etc. Finally he will improvise as long as he is desired to not only on the clavier but on the organ, and in any key, even the most difficult, that may be stipulated, in order to show that he understands also the

art of organ playing, which is quite different from the art of playing the clavier. Admission one small thaler per person. Tickets
may be had at the Golden Lion."

During this Frankfort visit, by the way, Goethe, then a boy of
fourteen, heard the youthful Mozart. Thirty-seven years later
Goethe had a distinct recollection of the smartly dressed little
fellow.

In each town, as we have said, Wolfgang eagerly studied the
leading composers of the time and place, and in London he was
particularly influenced by Handel and by Johann Christian Bach,
one of the sons of the great Sebastian. We have an interesting
contemporary account of him from the pen of the Hon. Daines
Barrington, which appeared in the sixtieth volume of *The Philosophical Transactions of the Royal Society* (1770); it relates to
the exhibition performances of Wolfgang in London in 1765:

"ACCOUNT OF A VERY REMARKABLE YOUNG MUSICIAN

" In a Letter to Mathew Maty, M.D., Sec. R.S.

" SIR, .

" If I was to send you a well-attested account of a boy who
measured seven feet in height, when he was not more than eight
years of age, it might be considered as not undeserving the notice
of the Royal Society.

" The instance which I now desire you will communicate to
that learned body, of as early an exertion of most extraordinary
musical talents, seems perhaps equally to claim their attention.

" Joannes Chrysostomus Wolfgangus Theophilus Mozart was
born at Saltzbourg, in Bavaria, on the 17th of January, 1756.

" I have been informed, by a most able musician and composer,
that he frequently saw the boy at Vienna, when he was little
more than four years old.

" By this time he not only was capable of executing lessons on
his favourite instrument the Harpsichord, but composed some in

an easy stile and taste, which were much approved of. His extraordinary musical talents soon reached the ears of the present empress dowager, who used to place him upon her knees whilst he played on the harpsichord. This notice taken of him by so great a personage, together with certain consciousnesss of his most singular abilities, had much emboldened the little musician. Being therefore the next year at one of the German courts, where the elector encouraged him, by saying, that he had nothing to fear from his august presence; little Mozart immediately sat down with great confidence to his harpsichord, informing his highness, that he had played before the empress.

" At seven years of age his father carried him to Paris, where he so distinguished himself by his compositions that an engraving was made of him. . . .

" Upon leaving Paris, he came over to England, where he continued more than a year. As during this time I was witness of his most extraordinary abilities as a musician, both at some public concerts, and likewise by having been alone with him for a considerable time at his father's house; I send you the following account, amazing and incredible as it may appear.

" I carried to him a manuscript duet, which was composed by an English gentleman to some favourite words in Metastasio's opera of Demofoonte. The whole score was in five parts, viz. accompanyments for a first and second violin, the two vocal parts, and a base. I shall here likewise mention, that the parts for the first and second voice were written in the counter tenor cleff; the reason for taking notice of which particular will appear hereafter.

" My intention in carrying with me this manuscript composition, was to have an irrefragable proof of his abilities as a player at sight, it being absolutely impossible that he could have ever seen the music before.

" The score was no sooner put upon his desk, than he began to play the symphony [2] in a most masterly manner, as well as in the time and stile which corresponded with the intention of the

[2] I.e., the instrumental introduction.

composer. I mention this circumstance, because the greatest masters often fail in these particulars on the first trial. The symphony ended, he took the upper part, leaving the under one to his father.

" His voice, in the tone of it, was thin and infantine, but nothing could exceed the masterly manner in which he sung.

" His father, who performed the under part in this duet, was once or twice out, though the passages were not more difficult than those in the upper one; on which occasions the son looked back with some anger, pointing out to him some mistakes, and setting him right.

" He not only however did complete justice to the duet, by fingering his own part in the truest taste, and with the greatest precision; he also threw in the accompanyments of the two violins, wherever they were most necessary, and produced the best effects. It is well known that none but the most capital musicians are capable of accompanying in this superior stile. . . .

" When he had finished the duet, he expressed himself highly in its approbation, asking, with some eagerness, whether I had brought any more such music.

" Having been informed, however, that he was often visited with musical ideas, to which, even in the midst of the night, he would give utterance on his harpsichord; I told his father that I should be glad to hear some of his extemporary flights.

" The father shook his head at this, saying, that it depended entirely upon his being as it were musically inspired, but that I might ask him whether he was in humour for such a composition.

" Happening to know that little Mozart was much taken notice of by Manzoli, the famous singer, who came over to England in 1764, I said to the boy, that I should be glad to hear an extemporary *Love Song*, such as his friend Manzoli might choose in an opera.

" The boy on this (who continued to sit at his harpsichord) looked back with much archness, and immediately began five or six lines of a jargon recitative proper to introduce a love song.

" He then played a symphony [instrumental piece] which might correspond with an air composed to the single word, *Affeto*.

" It had a first and a second part, which, together with the symphonies, was of the length that opera songs generally last; if this extemporary composition was not amazingly capital, yet it was really above mediocrity, and showed most extraordinary readiness of invention.

" Finding that he was in humour, and as it were inspired, I then desired him to compose a *Song of Rage,* such as might be proper for the opera stage.

" The boy again looked back with much archness, and began five or six lines of a jargon recitative proper to precede a *Song of Anger.* This lasted also about the same time with the *Song of Love;* and in the middle of it he had worked himself up to such a pitch, that he beat his harpsichord like a person possessed, rising sometimes in his chair. The word he pitched upon for this second extemporary composition was, *Perfido.*"

" After this he played a difficult lesson, which he had finished a day or two before; his execution was amazing, considering that his little fingers could scarcely reach a sixth on the harpsichord.

" His astonishing readiness, however, did not arise merely from great practice; he had a thorough knowledge of the fundamental principles of composition, as, upon producing a treble, he immediately wrote a base under it, which, when tried, had a very good effect.

" He was also a great master of modulation, and his transitions from one key to another were excessively natural and judicious; he practised in this manner for a considerable time with an handkerchief over the keys of the harpsichord.

" The facts which I have been mentioning I was myself an eyewitness of; to which I must add, that I have been informed by two or three able musicians, when Bach the celebrated composer [3] had begun a fugue and left off abruptly, that little Mozart hath immediately taken it up, and worked it after a most masterly manner.

" Witness as I was myself of most of these extraordinary facts, I must own that I could not help suspecting his father imposed

[3] I.e. Johann Christian — the " London Bach."

with regard to the real age of the boy, though he had not only a most childish appearance, but likewise had all the actions of that stage of life.

"For example, whilst he was playing to me, a favourite cat came in, upon which he immediately left his harpsichord, nor could we bring him back for a considerable time.

"He would also sometimes run about the room with a stick between his legs by way of horse. . . ."

"*Jan.* 21, 1780.

"On this republication of what appeared in the LXth volume of *The Philosophical Transactions*, it may be right to add, that Mozart (though a German) hath been honoured by the pope with an order of merit called the Golden Spur, and hath composed operas in several parts of Italy. I have also been favoured by Dr. Burney with the following account of one of his latest compositions.

"' Mozart being at Paris, in 1778, composed for Tenducci a scene in 14 parts, chiefly obligati; viz. two violins, two tenors, one chromatic horn, one oboe, two clarinets, a Piano forte, a Soprano voice part, with two horns, and a base di rinforza.

"' It is a very elaborate and masterly composition, discovering a great practice and facility of writing in many parts. The modulation is likewise learned and recherchée; however, though it is a composition which none but a great master of harmony, and possessed of a consummate knowledge of the genius of different instruments, could produce; yet neither the melody of the voice part, nor any one of the instruments, discovers much invention, though the effects of the whole, if well executed, would, doubtless, be masterly and pleasing.' "

On the whole the financial results of the first three tours were gratifying; Leopold found himself with a net profit of about 7,000 gulden, in addition to numerous watches, rings, snuff-boxes, and so on. The majority of these presents were sold in the later years of the family's need, but a few of them were retained and have

survived to our own day: a ring that was given to Wolfgang by the
Empress Maria Theresa and another presented to him in Augsburg by the Prince Archbishop are now in the Mozart Museum
in Salzburg.

With such a capital in hand, Leopold was willing, indeed anxious, to embark upon another tour as soon as opportunity arose.
He thought he saw his chance in the summer of 1767, when he
heard of the marriage, to be celebrated in Vienna towards the
end of the year, of the Archduchess Maria Josepha and King
Ferdinand of Naples.

The Mozart family left Salzburg on the 11th September, and
arrived in Vienna on the 15th. Leopold's plans, however, were
defeated by the death of the Archduchess, who fell a victim to
smallpox on the 15th October. Leopold fled with his children to
Olmütz to escape the dread disease, but both the boy and the
girl were attacked by it, and Wolfgang was blind for eight or
nine days.

It was not until the 10th January, 1768, that the family reached
Vienna again. There they stayed for the remainder of the year,
but the results of the sojourn did not come up to Leopold's expectation. The Viennese were more interested in pleasure and
sensation than in music, and Wolfgang, being now of the age of
twelve, was no longer a youthful prodigy and not yet a mature
and established artist. Still he was of sufficient importance to be
the object of anxious suspicion on the part of some of the professional musicians at Court and at the opera-house, and though
we must never swallow whole everything that Leopold says about
his son's colleagues and rivals, it is not improbable that intrigues
were set on foot to keep the boy out.

At the desire of the Emperor, Wolfgang wrote an opera buffa,
La Finta Semplice; but the impresario, Affligio, managed to postpone production week after week, and the work did not come to
performance. A German comic opera, *Bastien and Bastienne,*
had better luck; it was performed with great success in the
private theatre of a Dr. Mesmer. Wolfgang met many musicians
during this Vienna visit and heard a great deal of music, and was

particularly impressed by Gluck's *Alceste* and Piccini's *La Buona Figliuola*.

The family was back in Salzburg at the end of December, and on the 1st May, 1769, *La Finta Semplice* was performed by permission of the Archbishop in the theatre of the palace. The Archbishop also gave the boy the status of Konzertmeister, but without salary. The year was mostly spent by Wolfgang in study and composition.

The father's eyes now turned towards Italy, which was then held to be the land of music *par excellence;* a success there would launch the boy in Germany. Leaving the mother and Nannerl at home, Leopold and Wolfgang set out at the end of December 1769 upon the first of their three Italian journeys.

They visited, among other towns, Verona, Mantua, Milan, Lodi, Parma, Bologna, Florence, Rome, Turin, Venice, and Padua, returning to Salzburg on the 28th March, 1771. Wolfgang repeated his triumphs of the Paris and London visits; he played in public and in private, improvised, wrote music, was painted by the artists, was elected member of the renowned Accademia Filarmonica of Bologna, and received from the Pope the order of the Golden Spur, which entitled him to call himself " Cavaliere."

In Milan he had the powerful support of Count Firmian, the Austrian Governor-General (this part of Italy was at that time under the dominion of Austria). Thanks largely, no doubt, to Count Firmian's patronage, the boy received a commission to write an opera for the next season. The libretto chosen was Metastasio's *Mitridate Rè di Ponto* (*Mithridates, King of Pontus*). The opera was produced on the 26th December, 1771, with gratifying success, and was repeated some twenty times. On the strength of this triumph he received a new commission for an opera for the Milan Carnival of 1773, while the Empress Maria Theresa also commissioned from him a serenata for the marriage of her son the Archduke and the Princess Beatrice of Modena, which was to take place in October in Milan.

Father and son started on their second Italian tour on the 13th August, 1771, arriving in Milan eight days later. The libretto of the serenata, *Ascanio in Alba,* was not ready until the end of August, so that Mozart had to compose the music in a fortnight. The wedding took place on the 15th October, and the serenata was performed on the 17th with great success.

Hasse, one of the most admired opera composers of the day, had had an opera performed on the 16th; the old man (he was seventy-two at that time) showed Wolfgang great friendliness during his stay in the town, and prophesied that " this boy will cause us all to be forgotten." Wolfgang and his father returned to Salzburg on the 16th December.

On the same day the Archbishop Sigismund died, to be succeeded on the 24th March, 1772, by the Archbishop Hieronymus, who rejoiced in the further name and title of Count von Colloredo-Wallsee-Mels; he was a man of about forty years of age. The disparaging portrait of him painted in the ordinary Mozart biography is not to be relied upon. He and the Mozarts came into violent collision during the succeeding years, and the sentimental tendency of the nineteenth century was to assume that Hieronymus was an ignorant and malignant tyrant who did all he could to make the life of Wolfgang a misery to him.

Modern German historians who are not the victims of musical prepossessions assure us, on the contrary, that he was a man of culture and character, who did indeed earn the dislike of his subjects, but only because of the energy with which he set himself to effect some much-needed reforms in the town.

The musical historians have taken their cue regarding him from Leopold's and Wolfgang's letters; but, as we have already hinted, Leopold's judgments upon men who did not serve his and his son's ends as he would have liked are not to be taken as gospel. The Archbishop soon made an enemy of him by placing first Fischietti and then Lolli above him as Kapellmeisters. Leopold thought his age and the length of his service entitled him to the chief post; but it seems probable that what stood in his way was his well-known misanthropic discontent with everything and everybody, and his complete inability to make himself agreeable to his colleagues, or to his superiors unless they were doing him favours.

Moreover, he was continually away on leave or asking for leave, and it must have been evident to the Archbishop and everyone else that his heart was not in his Salzburg work — that the one thing he lived for was the advancement of his son.

For the moment, however, matters seemed to go fairly well, and Wolfgang was commissioned to write an opera for the Allegiance Festival of the Archbishop. This work, *Il Sogno di Scipione* (*Scipio's Dream*), shows every sign of having been written to order. It was performed at the end of April 1772. On the 9th August Wolfgang, as Konzertmeister to the Archbishop, was granted the small salary of 150 gulden a year.

He and his father set out on their third Italian tour on the 24th October, 1772. They arrived at Milan on the 4th November, and on the 26th December his new opera, *Lucio Silla*, was produced. Leopold, in his letters home, speaks of the enormous success of the work; it was always his habit to paint Wolfgang's successes in glowing colours in order to impress the Salzburg Court and the local musicians. But the plain fact seems to have been that it was not to the Italian taste; certain it is that Mozart never again received a commission to write an opera for any Italian theatre.

The father and son returned to Salzburg on the 13th March, 1773, and apart from two absences, one for ten weeks, the other for three months. Wolfgang remained in his native town until 1777, producing an enormous amount of music in all *genres*. Leopold had heard that Gassmann, the Court Kapellmeister at Vienna, was seriously ill, and with an eye on the post for his son he took him to Vienna on the 17th July, 1773, remaining there till the 30th September. Gassmann died in the January following, but the vacant post was given to a Viennese musician, Joseph Bonno.

Once more Wolfgang seems to have fallen into a hotbed of intrigue. Vienna at that time was teeming with musicians, German and Italian, those who had good positions holding on strenuously to them, those whose positions were less good doing all they could to oust the possessors of the better ones. Dr. Burney visited Vienna in 1772, and his journal of his tour through Germany gives us an interesting picture of the town, that was then swarming with composers, poets, librettists, singers, players, actors, and their hangers-on. Except that Wolfgang heard a great amount of new music, instrumental and operatic, the visit was of no practical use to him.

In the winter of 1774 he received from the Elector of Bavaria, Maximilian III, a commission for a comic opera for the Munich Carnival of 1775. Father and son left Salzburg on the 6th December, 1774, arriving at Munich the next day. The opera, *La Finta Giardiniera* (*The Feigned Gardener*), was produced on the 13th January with the greatest success. Leopold and Wolfgang were back in Salzburg in March. In April 1775 the Austrian Archduke Maximilian was being entertained in Salzburg, and on the 23rd Wolfgang's cantata *Il Rè Pastore* was performed as part of the festivities.

Between September and the end of the year Wolfgang wrote only three Masses — a very small output for a composer of his fertility. It is conjectured that his health was bad at this time; the so-called Bologna portrait of him, in which he is painted wearing the decoration of the Golden Spur, is very suggestive of illness. It may have been some spiritual as well as physical crisis through which he was passing that caused him to concentrate, in the latter part of 1776, on religious works.

At the beginning of 1777 Leopold seems to have felt more strongly than ever the necessity for establishing his now twenty-one-year-old son in some safe post or other. He applied to the Archbishop for long leave of absence, but this was refused him; it was no doubt felt that he had sufficiently neglected his Court duties during the last fifteen years.

The tour Leopold now had in mind for his son was a long one, and as the boy seems always to have been singularly incapable of taking care of himself, the father had to decide to let his mother accompany him. The pair left Salzburg on the 23rd September, 1777. It was with a heavy heart that Leopold said good-bye to them; it was the first time his son had been out of his keeping, and he had a foreboding of evil. As it happened, he was never to see his wife again.

This ninth of the Mozart tours is known as the Grand Tour. It lasted until January 1779, and was to prove rich both in experience and in disappointments for the young man. The route lay through Munich, Augsburg, and Mannheim to Paris, where they arrived on the 23rd March, 1778. There his mother died, after a short illness, on the 3rd July; Wolfgang considerately wrote to a friend in Salzburg asking him to prepare his father for the news that would reach him in a later letter. He left Paris on the 26th September, making his way home by way of Nancy, Strassburg, Mannheim, and Munich, arriving in Salzburg about the 8th January, 1779.

On his first passage through Augsburg he was greatly smitten by a young girl-cousin (known as the " Bäsle "), to whom he wrote some curious letters that have only recently been published in unexpurgated form.

In Mannheim, on his way to Paris, he stayed four months and a half. Mannheim at that time was a very small town, but it had the most remarkably efficient orchestra in Germany — which the boy had already heard in July 1763 — and it was the centre of a new school of instrumental composition.

Wolfgang learned a great deal from the Mannheimers, but was disappointed in his hopes for an official appointment in the town. It was here that he had his first real love-affair. Attached to the theatre in the dual capacity of bass singer and prompter was a certain Fridolin Weber, a man of forty-five years of age. He was living in exceedingly poor circumstances with a wife and four daughters — Josepha, Aloysia, Konstanze, and Sophie. (A brother of Fridolin, Frantz Anton, was the father of Karl Maria von Weber (1786–1826), the composer of *Der Freischütz*, who was thus the cousin of the Konstanze Weber who later became Mozart's wife.)

Aloysia in 1777 was seventeen years old, and already showing great promise as an operatic singer. Mozart fell in love with her, and it is to his passion for her that we owe one of the most remarkable of his detached arias, " Non so d'onde viene," the words of which are by Metastasio. From the correspondence between

Wolfgang and his father it is evident that the latter viewed the
new situation with considerable anxiety; Wolfgang was plainly losing valuable time on Aloysia's account, and even planning an artistic tour with her in Italy. The distracted father told him peremptorily to be off to Paris at once.

In Paris Wolfgang profited as usual by the new music he heard,
but materially had comparatively little success. He was no longer
an interesting prodigy, and so had not the same vogue in fashionable drawing-rooms as he had had ten years before. He was received politely enough in fashionable circles, but the politeness
rarely led to anything more substantial.

" It is true," he says in a letter to his father, " that people say
all kinds of civil things, but there it ends, as they appoint me to
come on such and such a day, when I play, and hear them exclaim,
' Oh! c'est un prodige, c'est inconcevable, c'est étonnant! ' and
then, *Adieu.* . . . Besides, Paris is much changed; the French
are far from being as polite as they were fifteen years ago; their
manners now border on rudeness, and they are odiously self-
sufficient."

He had some pupils, and no doubt could easily have had more;
but he found it rather expensive taking coaches about Paris, and
in any case he never had much liking for giving lessons to amateurs with no particular aptitude for music. He was offered an
organistship at Versailles, but declined it; Versailles was so far
away from Paris that he would have been out of the great
world there, and thus liable to miss a better chance if it should
come his way. He received no commission for an opera, and,
all in all, could hardly with reason expect one. He was completely unknown in Paris as an operatic composer; his little local
successes in Italy and Munich were unknown to the greater musical world of Europe. He wrote a little ballet *Les Petits Riens,*
which was produced on the 11th June; the great Vestris and La
Guimard danced in it.

For one of the Concerts Spirituels he composed his so-called
" Paris " symphony in D major. As usual with him in his early
years, he wrote in the taste of the town in which he happened to be

living, and on this occasion he hit off the French taste so well that the symphony was a great success.

A letter to his father describing the reception of the work shows us that the audiences of those days must have had the curious habit of applauding in the course of an orchestral work if a particular passage took their fancy. " Just in the middle of the *Allegro* a passage occurred which I felt sure must please, and there was a burst of applause; but as I knew at the time I wrote what effect it was sure to produce I brought it in once more at the close, and then rose shouts of ' *da capo!* ' The *Andante* was also liked, but the last *Allegro* still more. Having observed that all last as well as first *Allegros* here begin together with all the other instruments, and generally *unisono,* mine commenced with only two violins, *piano* for the first eight bars, followed instantly by a *forte.* The audience, as I expected, called out ' Hush ' at the soft beginning, and the instant the *forte* was heard began to clap their hands."

Durng his stay in Paris the town was torn in two by the quarrel between the partisans of Gluck and those of Piccinni. Mozart must have heard operas of each of these composers, and he profited in his own way by their example, without attaching himself slavishly to the school of either.

What Wolfgang's father wanted was to get his son back in Salzburg and fix him profitably there. But the one thing Wolfgang did not want was to return to Salzburg. He had hoped that the Elector of Mannheim would offer him a post; but no doubt the prudent Elector, though he knew Wolfgang's value as a composer, hesitated, as other rulers did, to place so young and physically insignificant a man in a position of responsibility. The Elector having become ruler of Munich, the Mannheim Court was transferred there, and with it, of course, the musical personnel. The presence of the Webers in Munich was another reason for Wolfgang's wishing to settle there.

In Salzburg, however, there had been changes during his absence. One of the Court musicians, Adlgasser, had died, and Leopold had managed to get the offer of a vacant post of Kapellmeister for Wolfgang. The latter hoped that the Archbishop would refuse;

but everything was arranged to the satisfaction of Leopold, who again and again pointed out in his letters to his son the solid advantages of the post. The united incomes of the family would enable them to live in comfort, while the central situation of Salzburg — within easy reach of Munich, Italy, and Vienna — made it an ideal centre of operations.

There was nothing for it but for Wolfgang to accept, and he made his way home in great discontent, taking, as we have seen, as long as possible over it. At Munich another disappointment awaited him. When he again met Aloysia, who by this time was laying the foundations of her great reputation as a singer, she plainly showed him that if ever she had had any real affection for him, nothing of it survived now. The Weber family was never noted for its refinement, and Aloysia especially wounded Mozart by laughing at his red coat, which was part of the Archbishop's livery.

He found a little consolation in a visit from his Augsburg " Bäsle," who accompanied him back to Salzburg. The future of this young lady may be told here. Born less than three years after Mozart, she survived him half a century, dying in 1841, at the age of eighty-three, in Bayreuth, in a household in which, apparently, she had been a servant of some kind. She had in 1793 an illegitimate daughter, named Marianne Victoria Mozart, who died in 1857. Descendants of the latter are said to be still living in Vienna.

Wolfgang arrived in Salzburg on the 17th January, 1779. He remained there until the autumn of 1780, producing a great number of works of all descriptions, including the choruses and entr'actes for a drama entitled *King Thamos*, and part of the music for a German opera, which was not performed, and to which the title of *Zaide* was given after his death.

He had received a commission for an opera for the Munich carnival of 1781, and to that town he repaired in November 1780. The opera, *Idomeneo*, was produced on the 29th January, 1781, with the usual success; it did much to establish his reputation as an opera composer in Germany, but had no enduring popularity. Mozart altered parts of it a few years later, apparently in view of a revival that did not eventuate. It was put upon the stage in Dresden in 1854, but again failed to establish itself. It is rather curious that Mozart should never have been able to make an enduring success of an opera that was serious throughout; his greatest music was written for works, such as the *Seraglio, Figaro, Don Giovanni,* and *The Magic Flute,* in which the expression is by turns serious and humorous.

Leopold and Nannerl had been able to attend the production of *Idomeneo* owing to the absence of the Archbishop in Vienna, whither, seemingly, he had been called on political business. From Vienna there came in March a summons to Mozart to take his place there in the Archbishop's Kapelle. The stage was now set for the decisive scene in the drama of Mozart's life; within the next couple of months he was to break away from his father's control, throw from him the livery of a Salzburg Court musician, and enter upon that last decade of his life that was to be so glorious to him as an artist, and so full of disappointments and miseries to him as a man.

The Archbishop has been painted in the blackest colours by the older Mozart biographers for his share in these events of the spring of 1781. It was apparently overlooked that the only account we have of the affair is that of Mozart himself, in his letters to his father; and neither Leopold nor Mozart can be accepted as perfectly unbiassed witnesses where Salzburg and the Archbishop are concerned.

The later Mozart biographers try to do the Archbishop justice. His musical sympathies, it is true, were mainly Italian, but there is evidence enough that he really appreciated Mozart as a composer. From the Court point of view, however, both Leopold and Wolfgang were unsatisfactory servants. Both were notoriously discontented with the town and with their service.

During Mozart's later tours the father and son adopted, for safety's sake, a cypher for such passages in their letters as related to the Archbishop and to Salzburg; but their opinions on both subjects must have been perfectly well known in the town. Ever since Wolfgang had been of the age of six the Court had been granting his father or himself leaves of absence, some of them of very long duration; and it was obvious to everybody that the object of these tours was to place Wolfgang advantageously in some other Court, both father and son using Salzburg only as a stop-gap.

During the *Idomeneo* period in Munich Wolfgang had once more overstayed his leave, and it seems likely also that the Archbishop had heard unfavourable reports of his conduct in the town, where he was enjoying himself as young men will who are just beginning to realise their manhood. The Archbishop and his officials would probably have put the matter in this way — that either Wolfgang should leave the Archbishop's employment, or, if he chose to remain in it, he should perform the duties of it in a proper way. Wolfgang, on his side, was conscious only of his expanding genius, of his cramped life in provincial Salzburg, of the social and financial attractions offered by larger cities such as Munich and Vienna, and of a vague desire for freedom that was not unnatural in a young man who had spent the first twenty-five years of his life in complete subjection to his father's will. The spirit or revolt was in him, and it needed very little to bring it to a head.

He arrived in Vienna on the 16th March, and took up his residence in the same house as the Archbishop. The latter's establishment consisted of his Chamberlain (Count Arco), a private secretary, a Comptroller, two valets, a Court Messenger, other household officials and servants, and a few of the Salzburg musicians.

The company dined at two tables, the place of the musicians being among the ordinary servants. At the top of this table sat the two valets; Mozart was at least placed above the cooks, but his pride was hurt at having to sit with the servants at all; it certainly must have been galling to a young man who had been fêted as he had been in great houses in so many cities.

He admits that he made no attempt to popularise himself; he took no part in the rough joking that went on at the table, spoke only when spoken to, and left the moment he had finished his meal. He saw opportunities of making money by playing at other houses in the town, and was angry at having to miss them owing to his enforced attendance on the Archbishop. His letters to his father show that he rather prided himself on making it perfectly clear to everybody around him, from the Archbishop and Count Arco downwards, that he thoroughly disliked them and performed unwillingly such duties as he could not escape. He was beginning to be very conscious of his musical powers, and was convinced that if only he could win the favour of the Emperor his fortune would soon be made.

Early in April the Chamberlain told Brunetti, one of the household musicians, who passed the information on to Mozart, that the musicians were to return to Salzburg, for which travelling expenses by the diligence would be allowed them; but that those who wished to remain might do so at their own expense.

That the proposition was not an unreasonable one is shown by Brunetti's delight at the prospect of remaining in Vienna on these terms. Another musician, Ceccarelli, was less happy about it, as he was not so much in demand in Vienna as either Mozart or Brunetti; he was not anxious to leave the town, but he would try, he said, to get a living allowance from the Archbishop.

Wolfgang had no desire at all to leave Vienna; he was popular there, and was asked out so frequently that his expenses in the matter of food would not be great were he to remain. He took a deliberately provocative line. He told Brunetti that he would ignore the communication made to the Kapelle until he received a similar one from Count Arco personally, and when that happened, " I will then let him know my intentions." " Not a bad hint? " he writes to his father. . . . " Oh! I certainly mean to play the Archbishop a nice little trick, to my great delight, and with the utmost politeness, for it seems he does not know me yet."

When a servant — and after all, that was what Wolfgang was in the Archbishop's household — goes looking for trouble like this, he can hardly complain if he finds it. From his own point of view Mozart was perfectly right in cursing a state of affairs in which he found himself tied to an ill-paid post while he saw opportunities of making more money slip by him. From the officials' point of

view he was an undesirable servant who would neither leave his
employment nor perform amiably the duties connected with it.

On the 28th April, writing to his father to announce his approaching return to Salzburg, he says, " I do entreat you, dearest
father, to allow me to return to Vienna next winter, towards the
end of carnival; this depends on you alone, and not on the Archbishop, for whether he thinks fit to grant me permission or not, I
shall certainly go; no fear of its doing me any injury — assuredly.
Oh! if he could only read this, it would be just what I should
like! "

Before the next letter could be sent home the crisis had come.
On the 9th May he writes to his father, " I am still filled with the
gall of bitterness; and I feel sure that you, my good kind father,
will sympathise with me. My patience has been so long tried that
it has at last given way. I have no longer the misfortune to be
in the Salzburg service, and to-day is a happy day for me."

Three times already, he goes on to say, the Archbishop had said
the most insulting and impertinent things to his face; " he called
me a knave and a dissolute fellow, and told me to take myself
off." It seems that Mozart had originally fixed his journey for that
very day, the 9th (Wednesday). In order to collect some money
due to him, however, he had postponed the journey till the following Saturday.

When he went to see the Archbishop on the 9th, the valet told
him that the Prince wanted him to take charge of a packet for
Salzburg. Wolfgang asked if it was pressing, and was told that it
was of great importance. " Then I regret that I cannot have the
honour of being of use to His Highness on this occasion," he said,
" for, owing to particular reasons (which I mentioned) I am not
to leave here till Saturday."

The Archbishop lost his temper. " Then came all in a breath
that I was the most dissipated fellow he knew, no man served
him so badly as I did, and he recommended me to set off the same
day, or else he would write home to stop my salary. It was impossible to get in a syllable, for his words blazed away like fire.
I heard it all with calmness; he actually told me to my face the

deliberate falsehood that I had a salary of five hundred florins, called me a ragamuffin, a scamp, a rogue. Oh! I really cannot write all he said. Then my blood began to boil and I said, ' Your Grace does not appear to be satisfied with me.' ' How! Do you dare to threaten me, you rascal? There is the door, and I tell you I will have nothing more to do with such a low fellow.' At last I said, ' Nor I with you.' ' Begone! ' said he; while I replied, as I left the room, ' The thing is settled, and you shall have it to-morrow in writing.' " The Archbishop naturally could not be expected to see in the young man before him the future composer of *Figaro, Don Giovanni,* and *The Magic Flute.* All he saw was a very unsatisfactory member of his household, who, as we have said, would neither leave his service nor perform with a good grace the duties he was paid to perform.

For a few weeks matters drifted on indecisively; apparently Mozart had not been formally dismissed, and, the fit of temper over, the Archbishop seems to have been willing to let bygones be bygones. Mozart, however, was determined to cut himself loose from Salzburg. There were plentiful signs now of his popularity in Vienna; he had received a commission to write an opera; he had several pupils, and could have had more had he wished to spend more of his time in teaching. The financial prospects were rosy. No one who reads his letters impartially can escape the conclusion that the young man was beginning to feel his strength, and was not too tactful in the way he let his detested employer see it.

His worried father again and again implored him to reconsider his decision, but in vain; Wolfgang was certain not only that he could maintain himself but that, if the Archbishop were to go to the improbable length of dismissing his father, he could maintain him also in Vienna. Leopold, with a wider knowledge of the world than his son, and knowing the latter's many weaknesses in the affairs of daily life, could not share this optimistic view.

Meanwhile Wolfgang missed no opportunity of making his intentions clear to the household. He prepared three memorials to the Archbishop, setting forth his desire to leave the service, but difficulties were put in the way of his presenting them; it seems

probable that Count Arco still thought that oil might be poured
on the troubled waters. When at last Wolfgang pressed him a little
too far, the Count, who, in his position as intermediary, had to
stand the fire of both parties, lost his temper; from the indignant
letter of Wolfgang to his father of 9th June, 1781, we learn that
he not only refused to give the young man access to the Archbishop but helped him through the door with a kick.

Wolfgang showed a commendable anger over the affair, and for
a few days kept threatening — to his father — that at the first
favourable opportunity he would return Count Arco's kick with
interest, even were it in the public street; but his rage, as usual
with him, soon died down.

The breach with the Archbishop was this time, of course, final.
Mozart would now have to face the world for himself, without
even his father at hand to advise him. He is at pains to rebut the
latter's suspicions that he is neglecting his work and pursuing a
round of pleasures in Vienna; it is true, he says, that for a time he
did surrender himself to the many distractions of the place, but
that was because he was depressed at the thought of returning to
Salzburg. He will now work hard, and everything will be for the
best in the best of all possible worlds.

Perhaps even at this time he had another reason, which he did
not disclose to his father, for wishing to leave the Archbishop's
service and settle on his own account in Vienna. Fridolin Weber
had died in October 1779, and the family had left Munich for
Vienna, where Aloysia had obtained a good engagement at the
National Theatre. The family was left poorly provided for, and in
spite of the assistance received from the Court the mother had
to let rooms.

Aloysia, in 1780, married Josef Lange, an actor and painter of
considerable all-round culture; Frau Weber, who was an excellent
business woman, made first-class terms of purchase with the husband. She was a vulgar, cunning, calculating, and not particularly
sober woman, always with an eye to the main chance; and her
next victim after Lange was Mozart.

From the 2nd May, 1781, Wolfgang had been living with the

Webers; he remained with them till September of that year, when his father insisted on his finding other lodgings. About the latter time he received a commission to write the *Seraglio;* his future seemed to be assured, he was one of the most talked-of young men in Vienna, he had an evident liking for the daughter Konstanze, and Frau Weber soon had the simple, easy-going young man in her toils.

The father got wind of the affair, and naturally thought it his duty to warn his son against possible complications; Leopold understood him better than any other human being did, and knew how unfitted he was to steer the ship of his life through difficult waters.

Wolfgang for a time keeps as many of the vital facts from his father as he can, but in December 1781 he makes a clean breast of the whole affair. He means, he says, to get married. His natural feelings are as strong as those of any other man, perhaps stronger than those of seemingly sturdier fellows than himself. He has remained ignorant of women so far because, in the first place, he has too great a sense of religion and too much honour to seduce any innocent girl, in the second place because, for prudential reasons, he has never resorted, as other young men did, to the women of the town. His inclination has always been towards domestic life; as his father knows, he is so little capable of looking after himself that from his youth upwards he has never been accustomed even to take charge of his own clothes or linen. He wants to marry not only from love but from a desire for domestic comfort.

" But now who is the object of my love? Do not be startled, I entreat. Not one of the Webers, surely? [Leopold never had a high opinion of the family.] Yes, one of the Webers — not Josepha, not Sophie, but the third daughter, Konstanze. I never met with such diversity of disposition in any family. The eldest is idle, coarse, and deceitful — crafty and cunning as a fox; Frau Lange [Aloysia] is false and unprincipled and a coquette; the youngest is still too childish to have her character defined — she is merely a good-humoured, frivolous girl; may God guard her from temptation! The third, however, namely, my good and beloved Konstanze, is the martyr of the family, and probably on this very account the kindest-hearted, the cleverest, and, in short, the best of them all; she takes charge of the whole house, and yet does nothing right in their eyes.

" She is not pretty — rather plain in fact, but has bright black eyes and a nice figure. She is not witty, but has plenty of sound sense. She is not extravagant; on the contrary, she has to dress very plainly, because when the mother has any money to spare she spends it on the two other girls. At the same time, though her clothes may be simple they are always neat and nice, and she is clever enough to make most of her things for herself. She dresses her own hair, understands housekeeping, and has the best heart in the world."

The news created consternation in the Salzburg household. Neither Leopold nor Nannerl was in favour of the marriage, and it is to be presumed that the father, in his letters, expressed himself in the most uncompromisingly unflattering terms about the Weber family, for no letters from him to his son after the 22nd January, 1781, have survived; Konstanze destroyed them all in later years. In deference to his father's wishes, however, Wolfgang left the Webers' house in the autumn of 1781 and took lodgings elsewhere.

Konstanze, of whom we shall have more to say later, was seven years younger than Wolfgang, having been born on the 6th January, 1763; she was thus in her nineteenth year at the time of the engagement. She survived her husband more than half a century, dying on the 6th March, 1842, having made a second marriage in 1809. The historians in general have treated her none too kindly. She seems to have been a simple, ordinary kind of young woman, reasonably intelligent and moderately musical; Mozart, who loved her greatly, dedicated a number of his works to her, though it is curious that he did not finish one of them.

The affairs of the Weber girls had been left in the hands of a guardian, who insisted on Wolfgang's binding himself by contract either to marry Konstanze in the course of three years, or, if he changed his mind, to pay her 300 florins a year for life. As soon as the guardian had left the room, Konstanze took the paper from her mother and tore it up, saying she required no written contract from Wolfgang.

One gathers that Konstanze, like others of her family, was a little given to flightiness. Before the marriage we find Wolfgang writing to her in gentle protest against the familiarities she had permitted herself with a young dandy at a party, and during the later years, when she was taking a " cure " in Baden, his letters show that he was a little anxious about the company she was keeping. She was evidently somewhat inclined to flirtation. The wedding took place on the 4th August, 1782; Leopold Mozart's consent arrived the day after, together with a message of good wishes from Nannerl. There was never any love lost, however, between the two women.

For the remaining years of Mozart's life Vienna was his home, though he still made an occasional tour. During these nine years he occupied one after the other no less than twelve lodgings.

The *Seraglio* was produced on the 16th July, 1782, and with this he made his first real operatic success — a success, that is to say, extending beyond the first few weeks of the production. The text was by Gottlieb Stephan (" Stephanie the Younger "), the Vienna Opera Inspector.

As was the pleasant habit in those days of unprotected copyright, he had taken his subject from a libretto, *Belmont and Konstanze, or the Seraglio Seduction*, by one Christoph Friedrich Bretzner, who himself, seemingly, had stolen it from certain predecessors. This gentleman was so annoyed that he inserted an advertisement in a Leipzig paper in 1782, to the effect that " a certain person named Mozart in Vienna has had the audacity to misuse my drama *Belmont and Konstanze* for an opera text. I hereby protest most solemnly." The good man could not be expected to know that the " misuse," and this alone, would preserve his name for all time.

There were the usual theatrical cabals against the *Seraglio,* but they were powerless against the public enthusiasm. The opera was given fourteen times in 1782, and remained in the bill till 1783, when the German opera venture (the *Seraglio* was written to a German text) came to an end in Vienna. It was highly popular in other towns also, and made a sensation in Prague that had the happiest results for Mozart, for it brought him later the commissions first for *Figaro*, then for *Don Giovanni*. Prague remained the town in which his genius was most fully appreciated, and he was never happier than when spending a few weeks there.

With his usual slackness in matters of business he would not put himself to the trouble of arranging a vocal score of the *Seraglio* for publication, though his father urged him to do so. It would certainly have been a commercial success. As it was, he let his opportunity go by, and one fine day in 1785 an unauthorised edition was brought out by an Augsburg publisher. The easy-going literary law of the time made piracy of this kind easy. Nor did a composer, except in Paris, receive royalties on his operas. The general rule was a lump sum down for the first performance, after which the work became the property of any theatre that bought a manuscript copy of the score for performance.

With the undoubted success of the *Seraglio* the ball seemed to be at Wolfgang's feet, and he looked forward to the future optimistically. In the late summer and autumn of 1783 he and his wife stayed some three months with Leopold in Salzburg, and the father visited them in Vienna in the spring of 1785; this was the last occasion on which he and Wolfgang saw each other. A child, Raimund Leopold, had been born on the 17th June, 1784, but it died on the 19th of the following August.

No further opera commission came to Wolfgang for more than three years after the production of the *Seraglio*. He was in great demand, however, in social and musical circles in Vienna, and in the absence of any work to do for the theatre he turned out a vast amount of music in various *genres* suitable to private or concert performance — concertos and chamber music of various kinds, including the six great quartets dedicated to Haydn (1785). In 1786 came a little play with music — *The Impresario*, the text of which was by Stephanie — and Mozart's best-known song, *The Violet*, set to words by Goethe.

In the autumn of 1784 he had become a Freemason, and for the funeral of a brother-mason he wrote, in the summer of 1785, his *Freemasons' Funeral Music.* His mind, which will probably ever remain, in its secret workings, a mystery to us, was running much on death at this time. Cheerful as he always seemed externally, he probably had a prevision of his own early death. A letter to his father of the 4th April, 1787 — the last he ever wrote to him, for the old man died on the 28th of the next month — shows us a Mozart we should hardly have suspected from his music.

" Since death," he says, " is, strictly speaking, the true end and aim of our life, I have during the last few years made myself so intimate with this true and best friend of man that his image not only no longer terrifies me but is something tranquillising and consoling for me. And I thank my God that He has granted me the happiness to recognise death as the key to this true felicity. I never lay myself down in my bed without reflecting that perhaps I, young as I am, shall not see another day; and no one who knows me can say that he ever saw me morose or melancholy." His later sufferings and disappointments were to break down, however, this serene philosophy of his.

The Austrian Emperor of the time, Joseph II, was an unusually enlightened man, but his taste in music, like that of the majority of the Viennese, was almost wholly Italian. His heart was not really in the growing movement towards a national opera, of which, with better luck, the *Seraglio* might have been the foundation-stone.

As we have seen, the short-lived official German opera in Vienna came to an end in 1783, and five years later the Italian opera that succeeded it also perished, owing mainly, no doubt, to political complications, war, and financial necessity. Mozart, though he would have preferred to write German operas, was not in a position to refuse the text of an Italian opera that was offered to him about July 1785.

The libretto was based on Beaumarchais's sparkling comedy *The Marriage of Figaro,* that had been first produced in Paris in April 1784, and had made such a sensation in Europe that no less than twelve German translations of it appeared in 1785, the year in which it was first printed.

Mozart's librettist was Lorenzo da Ponte, an Italian adventurer (of Jewish origin) who after various wanderings had drifted to Vienna and made some sort of success as an opera poet. After many more wanderings he died in poverty in New York in 1838, at the age of eighty-nine, leaving little behind him but his memoirs, in which he chatters far too much about Lorenzo da Ponte and tells us far too little about Mozart. The new opera was produced on the 1st May, 1786. It had eight more performances during that year, and then disappeared from the bill until August 1789. An interesting account of the production has been left by the Irishman Michael Kelly, who sang the part of the lawyer Curzio at the first production.

In 1777 Mozart had made the acquaintance of a young singer Josefa Duschek, who, though married, seems to have been generous in her favours to other men than her husband. In 1784 she had settled in Prague, where, as the consequence of the protection of a rich Bohemian nobleman, Count Christian Clam, she had been able to buy a charming little estate in the country near by.

The house — the Villa Bertramka — is for ever associated with the name of Mozart: it still stands in very much its original condition.

In January 1787 Wolfgang and his wife went to Prague to see the local production of *Figaro* by a troupe under the direction of the impresario Bondini; they stayed with Count Thurn, a music lover with whom Wolfgang was already intimate. He found the town *Figaro*-mad, and he received a great ovation when he was recognised in the theatre. Early in February he left with a commission for a new opera. In April he received the book of *Don Giovanni* from Da Ponte, and in September he was back in Prague, living in a state of ideal happiness, and working at his score in a little house in the garden of Bertramka. It was in this house that, according to the story, Frau Duschek locked him one day until he had carried out a long-standing promise to write a dramatic scena for her to sing.

The old legend that the overture to *Don Giovanni* was written on the eve of the performance, the orchestral parts arriving at the theatre only just in time, is now discredited. The incident that Konstanze described later, of her keeping her husband awake all night with punch and stories, must have occurred on the night but one before the performance, i.e. the night before the final rehearsal. Nor is Mozart's feat so remarkable as it looks at first sight. He was in the habit of composing whole works in his mind and retaining them in his marvellous memory till he could no longer delay writing them out; and there can be no doubt that everything in connexion with the *Don Giovanni* overture but the mere clerical labour had been done long before.

The first performance of the opera took place on the 29th October, 1787, with the usual success; and Mozart remained in his beloved Prague some weeks longer before returning to Vienna.

On the 15th November Gluck died in Vienna, and Mozart received the vacant appointment of " chamber musician and Court composer," but at a salary of 800 gulden in place of Gluck's 2,000. In the following May he received a visit from the seventeen-year-old Beethoven, who had come from his native Bonn to pursue his studies in Vienna, whence, however, he was recalled after a few weeks by the death of his mother. He received a few lessons from Mozart, and heard him play in public but not in private: his verdict was that Mozart " had a fine but rather broken touch — no *ligato*."

On the 7th May, 1788, *Don Giovanni* was given in Vienna, with sundry additions to the original score, made by Mozart out of complaisance for the singers; these additions are generally omitted in present-day performances. The opera was given fifteen times before the end of the year, then dropped out of the Vienna repertory; it was apparently too difficult for the easy-going Italianised taste of the Court and the town. It was revived by Schikaneder (the librettist of *The Magic Flute*) in November 1791 with a German translation; it is probably from these performances that we must date the deplorable tendency, that endured until comparatively recently, to stress the comic element of the opera at the expense of the serious.

Mozart continued to pour out other works besides operas in his usual profusion; the three great symphonies — the E flat, the G minor, and the C major (the " Jupiter ") belong to the summer of 1788, and a number of concertos and chamber-music works date from this time, as well as his additional accompaniments to *The Messiah* and other Handel works.

In April 1789 he accompanied the young Prince Karl Lichnowsky in the latter's carriage to Prague, Dresden, Leipzig, Potsdam, and Berlin, being greeted everywhere with the customary admiration and playing a great deal in public and private, but, as was the way with him, being too careless and having too little knowledge of men to make a financial success of his work, though he received handsome presents from the Saxon and the Prussian Courts. In Berlin the *Seraglio* was given twice in his honour. It used to be said that the King of Prussia offered him a Kapellmeistership at a salary of 3,000 thalers, and that Mozart, although moved and grateful, refused it out of loyalty to his own Emperor; but the story seems to be only one of the many legends associated with Mozart.

He was back in Vienna again on the 4th June, 1789, and now his epoch of greatest need and suffering began. With all his popularity, with all his colossal output, he found it difficult to make both ends meet. He always marketed his wares badly, and partly through the jealousy of the intriguing Italians at the Court, partly, we are compelled to believe, because in person he was insignificant and did not impress people as a man, he received no Court post sufficiently well paid to allow him to live on his salary.

Joseph II died on the 20th February, 1790. Mozart appealed to his successor, Leopold II, for the second Kapellmeistership and the post of music teacher to the young princesses, but in vain. His money troubles accumulated, and he was forced not only to pawn his valuables but to borrow from friends — his chief creditor was a certain Puchberg — and not only from friends but from usurers. Konstanze was away a great deal for reasons of health, and

Mozart, pinch as he would, found it impossible to provide for her " cure " and her pleasures in Baden and for his own modest necessities in Vienna.

Every now and then his native optimism reasserted itself — he would take more pupils, he wrote to Konstanze, or he would sell some more works, or he would write another opera, and all would be well with them again; but his health was now beginning to fail, and the net of evil fortune was drawn too tight round him for him ever to escape from it in his lifetime.

He went, on borrowed money, to Frankfort-on-the-Main in September 1790, knowing that the town would be full of important people for the coronation of the new Austrian Emperor in October, and hoping both for opportunities to make money by concerts and to advance his claims to a permanent post somewhere; but the material results were again slight, though *Don Giovanni* was staged as a compliment to him, and the musicians and the social celebrities of the town made the customary fuss over him. By the 10th November he was in Vienna again, no better off than before. In the same month he received an offer from Robert May O'Reilly, the director of the Italian Opera in London, to go there in December, stay six months, and contribute during that time at least two operas, serious or comic, at a fee of £300: we can account for his refusal of this offer only on the supposition of his ill health.

In the winter of 1789–90 he had received from Joseph II a commission for an Italian opera, and he had no choice but to accept the book of *Cosi fan tutte* from Da Ponte. The new work was given in Vienna on the 26th January, 1790, and though it ran to ten performances during the year it was more or less a failure. Contemporary criticism praised the music but was severe on the libretto, and time has confirmed this first judgment; *Cosi fan tutte* has never been able to keep the stage for very long, though whenever it is revived it gives the Mozart lover a special pleasure.

In March 1791 Emmanuel Schikaneder, a successful impresario who had shown that he thoroughly understood the popular taste, approached him with a suggestion for an opera on some " magic " subject: the idea pleased Mozart, especially as the text was to be in German, and he accepted the commission for *The Magic Flute*. The opera was mostly composed between May and July, though the overture was not written out till the 28th September; it had of course been complete in Mozart's head for long before that. The first performance took place on the 30th September, 1791.

Meanwhile, for the festivities in Prague in connection with the coronation of Leopold II as King of Bohemia he wrote another opera, *La Clemenza di Tito*. Konstanze joined him in the Villa Bertramka, and the opera was produced on the 6th September. The Empress called it a *porcheria tedesca* (a dirty German mess), but even Mozartian well-wishers who did not share her anti-German bias were constrained to admit that the new work was a failure. Mozart's heart was probably never in the greater part of the work; his favourite pupil Süssmayr, to save his harried and ailing master's time, wrote the recitatives and perhaps other portions of the score. Mozart left Prague in the middle of September, deeply hurt by his failure.

In the preceding July a mysterious visitor had called upon him — a tall, thin, cadaverous man, who refused to give his name, but asked him to write a Requiem Mass, for which he would be well paid; a proportion of the fee was given him in advance. The strange messenger called on various occasions later to see how the work was progressing. He was merely the servant of an eccentric Count Walsegg, who had a mania for commissioning musical compositions and having them performed as his own; the Mozart Requiem he proposed to give in honour of his recently deceased wife.

These facts only came out later; Mozart never knew of the Count's existence. Grievously ill and unhappy and despairing as he was at the time, he became obsessed with the idea that the mysterious messenger was one sent by the Fates to announce to him his own impending death. This morbid obsession of itself aggravated the decline of his health; he wrote with difficulty, and the Requiem, left unfinished at the time of his death, had to be completed by

Süssmayr, who not only had a thorough knowledge of his master's intentions but wrote a hand singularly like his own. Walsegg had the work performed at Wiener-Neustadt on the 14th December, 1793, Mozart's authorship of it being acknowledged.

The Magic Flute was given for the first time at Schikaneder's theatre on the 30th September, 1791; the composer conducted the first two performances. On the opening night the reception was doubtful, perhaps owing to the incomprehensibility of the story; but the opera soon established itself in public favour, and had a run of more than a hundred performances. It was Mozart's first indubitable popular success.

But success had been too long delayed; Mozart was already marked out for death. His constitution must already have been basically weakened by incessant mental labour from childhood onwards and by the many serious illnesses he had had, and now the combined strain and privations and money anxieties of the last few months were to carry him past the resistance point. He was visibly changing for the worse, both physically and mentally; he, who had always been so cheerful in company, now seemed to take less and less pleasure in the society of his friends. A spring had snapped in him; he became nervous, moody, and self-absorbed.

The thought of death was always with him. Konstanze tells us that one fine autumn afternoon, after his return from Prague, she was walking with him in the Prater and trying to distract him, when he began to speak of death and of his conviction that he was writing the Requiem for himself. Tears stood in his eyes; and when Konstanze tried to turn him from these gloomy thoughts he answered, "No, no, I feel it too surely. I shall not last much longer."

Ill as he obviously was, Konstanze had no scruple in leaving him once more while she took her "cure" and her pleasure in Baden. She was summoned thence about the middle of November; Mozart was now confined to his bed, from which he never rose again. His mind ran on *The Magic Flute,* which he longed to hear again, and on the still unfinished Requiem.

On the 2nd December, the day before his death, the score and sketches were laid on his bed, and he and three of his friends made an effort to sing the lovely " Lacrimosa ": Schack took the soprano part, Mozart himself the alto, his brother-in-law Hofer the tenor, and Gerl (the first Sarastro in *The Magic Flute*) the bass. After a few bars Mozart found himself too weak to proceed; and once more the thought that the Requiem was his own death Mass brought tears to his eyes. That evening his sister-in-law Sophie Weber came to see him. " It is good that you have come, dear Sophie," he said to her; " you must stay to-night and see me die." In vain she tried to turn his mind from these thoughts. " Already," he said, " I have the taste of death on my tongue; and who will then be here to sustain my dear Konstanze if you do not stay? " Sophie got his permission to go and tell her mother that she would not be home that night; on her return she found Süssmayr with Mozart; the dying man was giving his pupil instructions as to the finishing of the " Lacrimosa." He bade the two women keep his death a secret until Albrechtsberger, his successor in the Kapellmeister-ship he had held for some time in St. Stephen's Church, had been told of it.

The doctor was sent for; he was in the theatre, and said he would come at the conclusion of the performance. When he arrived he saw that all was practically over, but he ordered cold compresses on the burning head of the sick man. Mozart became unconscious, but his gestures and his expression indicated that he was still, in imagination, working at the Requiem. About midnight he suddenly sat up and looked around him with dull, non-seeing eyes; then he sank back, turned his face to the wall, and slept. He died fifty-five minutes after midnight on the morning of the 4th/5th December, 1791.

The news soon spread in the town. Süssmayr stayed with the dead man, and the proprietor of a gallery of wax figures came and took a cast, which is now lost, of the face. A rich Dutch amateur, Baron van Swieten, with whom Mozart had been very friendly and for whom he had fulfilled several commissions, among them the rescoring of *The Messiah,* called on Konstanze, recommended her to spend as little as possible on the funeral, and took his leave.

On the 6th December the plain coffin was carried through the streets on the shoulders of two men, followed by the faithful Süssmayr. At St. Stephen's Church a few others joined the procession, including, it is thought, Albrechtsberger, Lange, Schikaneder, Van Swieten, and Salieri; but the appalling weather — it was a day of storm and heavy snow — soon drove them all home.

The two bearers went on with the coffin to the cemetery that lay a quarter of an hour's walk outside the town; there they left it in the mortuary chapel. On the following day it was lowered into a common grave. It was not until 1808 that Konstanze visited the cemetery with the intention of erecting a cross over the grave; but by that time all hope of identifying the place of burial had long disappeared. It remains unknown to this day. The Mozart museum in Salzburg exhibits a skull, alleged to be that of Mozart, that was presented to it about 1842; but there is not the slightest reason to accept it as authentic.

Konstanze was granted by the Court a pension of $266\frac{2}{3}$ gulden — a third of Wolfgang's salary; and she seems to have maintained herself and her two children in fair comfort on this, by letting rooms, by concerts of her husband's works, and by the sale of his manuscripts. Only gradually, by all indications, did it dawn on her that she had been married for nine years to a great man; it needed the growing chorus of grief and admiration throughout Europe to convince her of this. In 1799 she sold the remaining Mozart manuscripts to the publisher André for 16,000 gulden.

Two years before that she had met Georg Nikolaus Nissen, the Secretary to the Danish Legation at Vienna: he was then a man about thirty-six years old. Apparently she lived with him for some time without being married, but their union was legitimised when he left in 1809 for Copenhagen, where the couple lived ten years. When he retired from the service he settled with Konstanze in Salzburg, about 1820, where he died in 1826.

The last few years of his life were spent in collecting the ma-

terials for the first real Life of Mozart: this was published in
1828. Konstanze had him buried in Leopold Mozart's grave and
over *this* husband she placed a fine monument, removing Leopold's tombstone for the purpose. Nannerl, who was now the
widowed Baroness Berchtold, was so angered at this that she
cancelled the clause in her will directing that she be buried in
her father's grave. Konstanze died at Salzburg on the 6th March,
1842, and the bones of Leopold, who could never endure her
when living, had to bear her forced companionship in the tomb
that was then Nissen's.

Two of Mozart's three children survived. The elder, Karl (17th
September, 1784–31st December, 1858) dabbled in music for a
time, but soon abandoned it for the career of an official. He lived
mostly in Italy, and died in Milan. The younger, Franz Xaver
Wolfgang (26th July, 1791–29th July, 1844) had a less happy
life. His mother insisted on his being a musician, and he became
a good piano player and a moderate composer. He was never able
to emerge from his father's shadow, and seems to have been a disappointed man during the last years of his life.

If it is asked, in wonder, why Mozart, whose genius was recognised wherever he went, remained all his life so poor, it can
only be suggested again that personally he was too unimpressive
for any Emperor or Prince or Grand Duke to feel that it would
be wise to appoint him to a post in which strength of character
and an ability to hold one's own with men were required.

He was small in stature, the head disproportionately developed,
and the nose excessively large. He had virtually no culture in the
broad sense of the term, and there are no traces of any real interest on his part in painting, sculpture, or literature. His whole
being was musical, and his brain must have been engaged almost
without intermission in the production of music. He was very fond
of company, and in congenial society was cheerful and lovable.
There must have been a dark side to his soul, for he had suffered
much; but he seems to have concealed it from everyone until near
the end.

Perhaps he did not care to face unpleasant realities; it was one of his father's complaints against him, and one of his explanations of his son's lack of worldly success, that he wanted to take everything lightly, becoming impatient when difficulties arose and turning his back on them as soon as possible instead of meeting and overcoming them.

Grimm, the experienced man of the world and shrewd judge of character, wrote from Paris to Leopold in 1778: "Wolfgang is too sincere, has too little energy, is all too easily deceived and too inexperienced in the ways that might lead to success. If he had half as much talent and twice as much adroitness I should not be anxious about him." Knowledge of men and of the world he never acquired. He was not the man to fight intriguers with their own weapons, and intrigue there certainly was in Vienna, though the amount of it has probably been exaggerated; even Mozart himself came to believe, in his last days, that he was being poisoned by his rival Salieri, who was the favourite composer of Joseph II.

He was very fond of dancing, ninepins, and billiards, of good cheer, and of the society of pretty women. The frail little body seemed to be in need of constant motion; observers noted that when he was talking his hands were always moving or playing with some object such as his watch, or a ring, or part of his clothing. His tongue, on occasion, could be sharp, and we gather that his frank criticisms of some of his contemporaries did not help to endear him to them; he could be very satirical when he liked. But the basis of his character was gentleness, cheerfulness, honesty, and the desire both to love and to be loved.

THE MARRIAGE OF FIGARO

[WOLFGANG AMADEUS MOZART]

TO understand fully Mozart's *Marriage of Figaro* it is necessary to have some acquaintance with the preceding drama, *The Barber of Seville*, which has been described in full in Part II of this work.

The action of *The Marriage of Figaro* takes place some years later at the Count's château of Aguas-Frescas, in the country near Seville. Figaro has been taken into the Count's service as valet and confidential man, and at the time the play opens is in love with the Countess's maid, Suzanna. The Count, however, is no longer as passionately in love with Rosina as he was; he has not given up his habits of gallantry, but he has turned his attentions to the girls of the neighbourhood. In virtue of his position as a feudal lord he possesses the mediæval right of the *droit du seigneur* — i.e. the right to possess a female vassal before she becomes the wife of another servant. Although he has relinquished this right, he would not be unwilling to exercise it in the case of the pretty Suzanna, who is shortly to be married to Figaro.

Political and social affairs in Paris at the time when Beaumarchais produced his two comedies were, though no one had yet realised it, already heading for a revolution. The Court was held in contempt even by the nobles, while the people disliked both impartially. The philosophers, headed by Voltaire and Rousseau, had done a great deal to undermine the old ideas on which the French State rested, and high society was largely liberal in opinion, if not exactly democratic. The extraordinary vogue of *Figaro* was due to the fact that it summed up, in one brilliant work, all that was in the minds of those who felt it was time a new régime replaced the old.

As a recent French author has put it: " There came a day when the whole of the feelings of every kind, moral, political, and social, that had been developed in men's hearts by the writings of the philosophers — the joy of life, thirst for enjoyment, intense intellectual excitement, hatred and scorn of the present with its abuses, its traditions, hope and need for *something else* — found vent in one unique explosion; this day of intellectual frenzy, when the society of the *ancien régime* applauded the ideas that were ultimately to bring it to ruin, was the day of the first performance of *The Marriage of Figaro* (27th April, 1784)." And *Figaro* was the sequel to *The Barber of Seville.*

The second play would have followed the first one earlier, but for three years the authorities refused permission to perform it, so dangerous did the King, the censor, and the police judge it to be. The news of the ban on the work only excited public curiosity the more; and when at last *Figaro* was given, its success was enormous. The witty insolence of Figaro to his aristocratic master was a symbol of the coming upheaval. *Figaro* was one of the most potent of the influences that led to the Revolution, as Napoleon recognised some years afterwards.

ACT I

When the curtain rises, Figaro is seen measuring the floor and walls of a partially furnished apartment, while Suzanna, before a mirror, tries on a hat. Figaro is trying to discover the best place for the bed that the Count has sent them as a wedding present. But Suzanna, who is quicker-witted than Figaro, has divined the intentions of their master. She will not have this room for their bedroom, in spite of Figaro's demonstration of its convenience as regards the fulfilment of their respective duties. The room lies between that of the Count and that of the Countess. Does the latter require Suzanna some night? All she has to do is to ring, and the maid is there in a moment. Does the Count require Figaro? Good; another bell tinkles, and the valet is there in a trice.

For a man of his experience, especially of the Count's love-affairs, Figaro is singularly obtuse. Suzanna enlightens him. Suppose some day the Count packs Figaro off miles away on some business or other. If, as Figaro has said, it is only three steps from their room to the Count's, does he not realise that it is also only three steps from the Count's room to theirs?

Figaro is at first incredulous, but in the end Suzanna leaves him in no doubt as to the Count's intentions, a hint of these having already been thrown out to her through the Count's intermediary, the same Basilio whom we have seen at work in *The Barber of Seville*. The Count, Suzanna tells Figaro, has indeed been generous to her in the matter of a dower, but hardly disinterested; he has his eye on the *droit du seigneur*. " But," says Figaro, " I thought he had renounced this feudal right." " True," replies Suzanna, " but Figaro's bride-to-be has caused him to repent of the renunciation."

The Countess's bell rings, and Suzanna flies to answer it. Figaro turns the matter over in his mind; now he sees the Count's object in taking him and his bride to London, where he has been appointed Spanish minister. Figaro has always regarded himself as the Count's superior in intelligence, and now he will prove it to him. This resolution he expresses in the aria " Se vuol ballare, signor contino " (" If you want to dance, my little Count, very well, I will play the guitar for you. Come to my school, and I will teach you how to caper. But I will be crafty until I have upset your little scheme ").

As he leaves the stage Dr. Bartolo enters, accompanied by his elderly housekeeper Marcellina. Bartolo has never forgiven Figaro for helping the Count to cheat him of Rosina. Now a chance for revenge has come. Marcellina is in love with Figaro, who owes her money; and she has a plan by which Suzanna is to be induced to reject the Count's attentions, whereupon, in his anger, he will favour Marcellina's scheme for marrying Figaro. In an aria that is masterly in its characterisation, Bartolo declares his resolve to use all his cunning to bring this about. When he has left the stage, there follows a duet between Marcellina and Suzanna, in which the former, already tasting victory in imagination, tries to score off her young rival, but is badly worsted in the duel of feminine malice.

As the discomfited old lady leaves in a huff, Cherubino enters. He is the Count's page — still hardly more than a child in years, but in his precocious passion for the other sex a worthy follower of his master. He is in trouble. The preceding night the Count had found him alone with Barbarina, the gardener's daughter, and dismissed him; for the Count is scrupulous enough where other people's morals are concerned. Cherubino's only hope is in the intercession of his godmother, the Countess. The charming young rascal appeals craftily to Suzanna, who has the ear of her mistress; if he is sent away, he says, he will never see his dear Suzanna again; but it soon becomes evident that he is in love also with the Countess herself.

Learning that the ribbon in Suzanna's hand belongs to her mistress's bed-cap, Cherubino snatches it from her, giving her in place of it the latest canzonetta he has composed. Not only the Countess and Suzanna and Barbarina but every woman in the world ought to hear it, he says; and he pours out his views on love in the charming aria " Non so più cosa son, cosa faccio." The music paints enchantingly the amorous flutterings of this youth, who is the prey of delightful emotions that he himself hardly understands. He feels a desire, he says, he cannot express. At the sight of a woman his heart palpitates; now he burns, now he freezes. Asleep or awake it is all the same; in both states his mind and his tongue are running upon love. He confides the troubles of his soul to the lakes, the mountains, the shades, the flowers, the fountains, the air, the winds, the echo; and if there is no one and nothing to listen to him, he will talk to himself of love. The exquisite music is a perfect expression of the vague emotions of a heart too young as yet to know itself in matters of sex.

The Count is heard approaching, and Cherubino, who, after the escapade of the night before, does not wish to be caught in intimate conversation with another pretty girl, hastily hides behind the big armchair. The Count, seating himself in the chair, asks the cause of Suzanna's obvious confusion. He has come to tell her his plans. Basilio, he supposes, has already hinted at his intentions; now he wants her to meet him in the garden that same evening. Before he has time to explain himself more clearly the voice of Basilio is heard. Like Cherubino, the Count feels that the situation may easily turn out an embarrassing one, so he in turn makes to hide behind the armchair; Cherubino, seeing this move, abandons his own place of refuge to the Count, and slips into the big chair, where Suzanna covers him with one of her mistress's dresses.

Basilio asks Suzanna if she has seen the Count, for whom Figaro is looking. " If that be so," says Suzanna pointedly, " Figaro is looking for one who, after yourself, hates him most." The Count is curious to see how Basilio will do his work as procurer. When Suzanna holds up her hands in horror at the suggestion that she should meet the Count's advances half-way, Basilio ventures on the sly surmise that he would have thought she would prefer such a lover, a rich and powerful gentleman, to a mere youngster like Cherubino. He maliciously hints that he has seen the page prowling round this very room to-day. And was that little song, he asks, intended for her or for the Countess? The young man really ought to be careful to control his eyes when they are all at table, for if the Count caught him looking at the Countess as he sometimes does there would be trouble; he is, he protests, only repeating what the whole neighbourhood is saying. This is too much for the Count, who now reveals himself.

The situation has thus worked up to one of those ensembles that moved Mozart to put forth the whole power of his genius. He defines psychologically each of the characters in an opening phrase, and then proceeds to evolve from this material a masterpiece of easy, flowing expression. The phrase of the Count, with its angry strides in the strings, shows us the outraged grandee determined to assert himself:

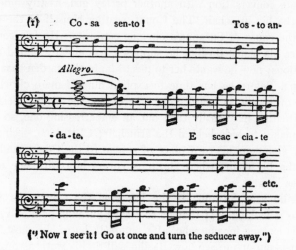

("Now I see it! Go at once and turn the seducer away.")

Basilio answers him in a deprecating phrase that suggests to perfection the oily cunning of the man:

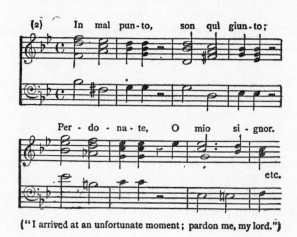

("I arrived at an unfortunate moment; pardon me, my lord.")

Suzanna's phrase is all agitation:

(3)

Che ru - i - na ! me me - schi - na ! Son op ▾

▾ - pres - sa dal ter - ror !

("What a disaster! Poor wretched me! I am overcome with terror!")

Suzanna is on the point of fainting. The two men attempt to place her in the armchair, but the mere suggestion is enough to cure her of her faintness.

The Count swears he will punish Cherubino, against whom he has now a double grievance — that little affair with Barbarina, and his daring to cast sheep's eyes at the Countess. The Count tells how he called at the gardener's house and found the door bolted; when Barbarina opened it his suspicions were aroused; he looked around the room, drew the cover from the table, and there, underneath, was the page! Suiting the action to the word, he lifts the dress from the chair, and of course exposes Cherubino, to his own astonishment, to the horror of Suzanna, and to the malicious delight of Basilio. It may be noted that when the Count describes his own cleverness in discovering the boy, he does so to phrases that are modelled upon the sly theme (quoted above) that was formerly given to Basilio.

All this, however, has in one way played into the Count's hands. Having, as he thinks, caught Suzanna out in an intrigue, he means to use his knowledge for his own purposes. He orders Basilio to bring the deceived Figaro to see for himself. Suzanna, however, begs to be allowed to explain. She tells how the page came to ask her to intercede for him with the Countess, and how, frightened at the Count's coming, he hid behind the chair, and from there slipped into the armchair. The explanation is not wholly agreeable to the Count, who now realises that his own advances to Suzanna must have been overheard; and he is not pacified by Cherubino's naïve assurance that he tried his very hardest *not* to hear anything.

Peasants enter, followed by Figaro with a bridal veil in his hand. The chorus sing the praises of their master, and Figaro asks him to place the veil upon the bride's brow in token of his gracious favour on this their wedding-day. Figaro's purpose is a subtle one; he wants to involve his master in a public admission that he has renounced the *droit du seigneur*. The Count graciously promises them his protection, and says he will give the bride the veil later, at a more imposing ceremony than this. The one person not partaking in the general jubilation is poor little Cherubino. The Count begins once more to express his disapproval of him, but a discreet little hint from the page as to his ability to keep his mouth shut makes the Count remember that to some extent he is in the boy's power. He ostentatiously pardons him; but he appoints him to an ensign's post that has just fallen vacant in his regiment, and the boy must join at once. Figaro, on behalf of the company, takes humorous leave of him in the aria " Non più andrai "; his days of love-making, he says, are over; now he will have to devote himself to the serious business of life among his warlike companions. The whole aria is couched in a delightfully mock-heroic vein.

ACT II

The first scene of the second act shows the Countess sitting in her room musing upon her happy romantic past and unhappy loveless present. Suzanna enters, followed by Figaro, and the three discuss the situation. Figaro has had a bright idea; without consulting anybody, he has sent to the Count an anonymous letter warning him of an assignation the Countess is alleged to have made with an admirer for that very night. The scheme rather frightens the Countess, who knows how jealous her husband is; but Figaro assures her that it is precisely his jealousy that will make him walk into the trap.

Suzanna is to give the Count a rendezvous in the garden, but her place will be taken by Cherubino dressed in girl's clothes.

The Countess will surprise her husband there, and reduce him to a condition in which he will be glad to promise anything she asks. The Count is at present out hunting, and meanwhile Cherubino must be rehearsed in his new rôle. Figaro goes to find him; before he leaves he sings an ironic fragment from that previous song of his in which he swore to make the Count dance to his tune.

When Cherubino enters, he is first of all prevailed upon by the Countess to sing his new canzonetta, the subject of which is, of course, love (" Voi che sapete "); the song is obliquely directed to the Countess, who, on her side, has a tender feeling for the boy.

First taking the precaution to lock the door, Suzanna proceeds to dress him in clothes of her own. He produces his ensign's commission, and the Countess notices that it has not yet been sealed. As Suzanna turns up his sleeves, the stolen ribbon is revealed. The Countess feels it her duty to chide him for his presumption, but is moved, in spite of herself, at this little incident, which gives her an insight into the page's feelings towards her. The atmosphere grows more and more tender, and Cherubino seems to be on the point of an avowal that may be rather awkward, when a knock is heard at the outer door.

It is the Count. The terrified Cherubino runs into the inner room, and the Countess opens the outer door. The Count's suspicions, that have already been aroused by the anonymous letter, are heightened by the evident confusion of his wife. To make matters worse, Cherubino overturns a chair, and the Count demands to be told who is in the other room. The flurried Countess replies that it is Suzanna, who, as a matter of fact, is hiding in an alcove. In an expressive little trio the Count calls upon Suzanna to answer him, the Countess bids the supposed Suzanna not to reply, while Suzanna herself comments quietly upon the situation and its possibilities of danger. The Count sees the wisdom of not making a scene before the household by calling the servants to break in the door, and goes out to get tools with which to do it himself, first of all locking each of the inner doors, and, by way of complete precaution, taking the Countess with him.

Suzanna now emerges from her hiding-place and calls upon Cherubino to unlock the door from the inside. The boy is thoroughly scared, and to avoid meeting the Count he jumps out of the window into the garden; Suzanna takes his place in the Countess's room. The Countess, of course, does not know what has happened during her absence, and when she returns with the Count she thinks it better to make a clean breast of the innocent affair. There is no need, she tells him, to break open the room, the only person in it being Cherubino, a mere boy, of whom it is absurd for him to be jealous.

In a sense the Count is relieved; but his temper is not improved by finding that once more he has been led into an absurd and embarrassing situation by the page. Swearing vengeance on Cherubino, he draws his sword and opens the door, only to be confronted by Suzanna. The Count is flabbergasted; the Countess is astonished but relieved; and Suzanna seizes the opportunity to twit her master over his mistake. The desperate man goes into the room to see if, after all, Cherubino is not concealed there; and Suzanna seizes the opportunity to whisper to the Countess that the boy has escaped.

The pair now hold the Count in the hollow of their hands. The Countess assumes the rôle of the falsely suspected wife, and is with seeming difficulty persuaded to take her reprobate husband back into favour. As the two women think they are mistresses of the situation, they do not mind telling the Count that the letter about which he now enquires was written by Figaro. For a moment he talks about revenging himself on his valet; but he is persuaded to forgive him, and everything seems set for an all-round reconciliation, with the repentant Count once more anxious to become the lover of his wife as in the old days.

With a dramatist less resourceful than Beaumarchais and a musician of less genius than Mozart, the scene, that has already been so rich in incident, would by now have attained its climax. Both Beaumarchais and Mozart, however, are really only just beginning. The dramatist gives several still more ingenious turns to the intrigue, while Mozart enters upon a finale that is unsurpassed, even among his own ensembles, for appositeness and variety of expression.

The new development begins when Figaro enters and asks the Count to come to the wedding festivities, where his vassals are waiting to greet him. The Count, still sore at his rebuff, and still with a lingering suspicion at the back of his mind, shows him the anonymous letter and asks him if he knows who wrote it. Figaro, who is of course ignorant of what has gone on during the preceding scene, denies all knowledge of it. For a moment the Countess and Suzanna save the situation once more; they give him a dexterous hint that they have already told the Count the truth, and advise him not to be so silly as to deny it. Again the Count feels himself to be worsted; his one desire now is to delay the marriage proceedings, and his only hope, he sees, is Marcellina.

Just then a new complication arises. The gardener Antonio enters, half tipsy, and holding a damaged pot of carnations in his hand. He is very angry; people are always annoying him, it seems, by throwing things out of the windows on to his flower-beds, but now the limit has been reached — they have thrown out a man. Again the Count dimly begins to suspect that there is more in all this than he has been told, while Suzanna and the Countess, scenting danger, surreptitiously exhort Figaro to be on the alert. As the gardener tells his story of the man who alighted on the flowers and then ran away, Suzanna manages to whisper to Figaro that it was the page.

When Antonio confesses to the Count that he cannot describe the appearance of the runaway, Figaro boldly asserts that it was he who jumped out of the window. Even Suzanna and the Countess are staggered by the fertility and the impudence of his invention. The Count has his doubts, however, and these are increased when Antonio naïvely asks Figaro how it is he has grown so tall since his jump, for the person he saw seemed to him more of a boy. The Count ejaculates " Cherubino! " " Oh," says Figaro, " as for Cherubino, no doubt he has returned on horseback from the town." The bucolic mind of Antonio takes this quite literally, and explains that he saw no horse when the man jumped from the balcony.

Through all this cross-talk and muddle the Count adheres to his resolve to have an explanation. He fastens upon Figaro and asks him why he jumped out of the window. " For fear of you," replies the valet; he was in the room, he says, with his Suzanna, when he heard the Count outside, and his conscience having smitten him in the matter of the anonymous letter, out he jumped, twisting his ankle in doing so; the Count can see for himself that he now limps. But there is yet another hurdle to be got over. Just as Figaro is pluming himself on having wriggled out of this little difficulty, Antonio produces a paper which he had picked up in the garden, and asks if this is his. The Count takes it before Figaro can get hold of it, and finds it to be the page's commission.

The cornered Figaro has to play for time; he rummages in his pockets and pretends to be trying to remember what papers should be there. But the Countess has recognised the paper, and she passes the word on to Suzanna, who in turn whispers it to Figaro. He remembers now that it is Cherubino's commission, which the boy had left with him. But once more he is thrown into confusion by the Count's asking him why. He manages to stammer out " It needed . . . ," and is very grateful for the whisper from Suzanna that it needed sealing. Again the Count has to admit that he has been checkmated. He tears up the paper in a rage. Marcellina, Bartolo, and Basilio enter and claim justice in the matter of Figaro's promise to marry the lady. The distracted Count again and again bids them all be silent: he will try the case in quiet and see that justice is done. The act ends with a septet in which each of the characters comments on the situation from his own point of view.

ACT III

In the third act the intrigue becomes so rapid and so involved that it can be carried on only by a liberal use of recitative, there being hardly time every now and then for music to spread its wings. The first scene shows a hall decorated for the wedding festivities. The Count is turning over in his mind the puzzling incidents of the second act; he feels that he has been duped, and yet can hardly believe it, for he is sure of the discretion of the Countess, while he can hardly conceive that any of his vassals would dare to take such liberties with so great a lord as he. Suzanna and the Countess enter in the background, and it is arranged between them that the latter will impersonate Suzanna at the rendezvous in the garden.

The Countess having retired, the Count accosts Suzanna; he is unable to rid himself of the suspicion that she has told his wife of his *droit du seigneur* designs; if she has, he will have his revenge by making Figaro marry Marcellina. The pair fence with each other; but in the end Suzanna promises to meet him in the garden that night, and they sing the exquisite duet " Crudel! perchè finora farmi languir così? "

Sure of victory now, Suzanna makes the mistake of saying softly to Figaro, when he enters, " You have won your case without a lawyer." The Count overhears her, and realises once more that he is being played with. He expresses his anger in a vigorous aria, " Vedrò, mentr'io sospiro." It is the business at this point of the actor who is playing Almaviva to lift the opera out of the light comedy vein in which the bulk of it has been played so far. This aria is the counterpoise to Figaro's " Se vuol ballare " in the first act. In that, the servant who knows himself to be intellectually the superior of his master looks forward half gleefully, half resentfully to a contest of wits between them; in this aria of the Count's the grandee's pride revolts at the thought that his servants should have dared to think so lightly of him as to try to play with him. He is now fully decided that Figaro shall marry old Marcellina.

The next scene shows the trial of Figaro's case before the Count, who, in virtue of his station, is the decider of causes upon his domain. Figaro has borrowed a thousand silver pieces from Marcellina; and the lawyer Curzio, who now enters with Marcellina, Figaro, and Bartolo, claims that he must either marry her or pay her. Figaro says he is of gentle birth, and therefore cannot marry without the consent of his parents. The Count, with humorous incredulity, asks who and where these noble parents are. Figaro replies that he has been looking for them for the last ten years. He was stolen as a child; does he not bear on his arm a mysterious hieroglyphic? Marcellina pricks up her ears at this. Is the mysterious sign, by any chance, a spatula on the right arm? It proves to be so, and Marcellina discovers that Figaro is the long-lost child of herself and Bartolo — their little Rafaello, who was stolen from them.

The family reconciliation is very affecting, but it does not appeal to Suzanna, who, entering with a purse (she has somehow raised the money with which to buy off Figaro), sees her bridegroom in the arms of Marcellina. She boxes his ears, and it takes a little time to convince her of the real state of affairs. The charming sextet in which this situation is developed was Mozart's favourite among the *Figaro* numbers.

The actors having left the scene, Cherubino enters with Barbarina. He has slipped back from Seville, and Barbarina invites him to her father's cottage, where he will find all the prettiest girls of the estate. So that the Count shall not recognize him, she will dress him up in clothes of her own. When they have left, the Countess enters. She is a little disturbed at the course the intrigue has now taken; she fears the jealousy and wounded pride of the Count, whom she still loves, and whose love for her she hopes to win back again. Her emotions are expressed in the exquisite air " Dove sono."

In a short recitative Antonio tells the Count that he is certain Cherubino has returned; and later Suzanna and the Countess, also in recitative, work out the details of the coming meeting in the garden. Suzanna, to the Countess's dictation, writes the crucial letter to the Count, confirming, in the guise of a song to the Zephyr, the assignation in the garden. This is the charming little " Letter Duet," that has a curious old-world simplicity and fragrance. The letter is sealed with a pin, and on the back is written, " Send back the seal."

Barbarina and other peasant girls enter, bringing roses for their mistress; among the girls is Cherubino in female clothes. His good looks attract the attention of the Countess; she asks for the flowers he is carrying, and he blushes as he hands them to her. Barbarina assures the Countess that the girl is her cousin, who has just arrived for the wedding. When the Count and Antonio enter, however, the latter pulls off Cherubino's headdress and substitutes for it his ensign's cap. Once more the Count is suspicious of his wife and angry with Cherubino; he threatens to punish him again, but Barbarina puts him to confusion by saying, " Your Excellency, you often used to say when you were embracing and kissing me, ' Barbarina, if you will only love me I will give you anything you ask for.' " She now asks to be allowed to marry Cherubino, but the Count is too confused to give the child a direct answer; all he can do is to mutter that the gods, the devil, and men seem to be conspiring to put him in the wrong.

When Figaro, who now enters, suggests that they should get on with the dancing, he is of course ignorant of the fact that the Count knows that it was Cherubino who jumped from the window and has now returned. Once more the Count tries to trap him with his questions, and once more Figaro escapes by his consummate assurance; if Cherubino says it was he who jumped on to the flower-bed, well, perhaps so, but if one man can jump out of a window, surely another can!

A bridal march is played, and the stage fills with people who have come to celebrate the wedding. A fandango is danced, and while Suzanna is kneeling before the Count to receive the bridal veil she quietly gives him the letter; when he secretly opens it he pricks his finger with the pin. Figaro, who is dancing, observes this, and remarks to Suzanna ironically that he presumes some lady has been sending a love-letter to the Count. The latter now breaks up the gathering, bidding them all depart to meet again at nightfall, when the nuptials shall be celebrated in proper style, with dancing, songs, feasting, and fireworks.

ACT IV

So far Figaro has been occupied in weaving a net round the Count; now he himself is to be caught in a net. The scene is the garden at night, with arbours at right and left. Barbarina enters with a lantern; she has lost the pin which the Count has given her for Suzanna along with a message as to the meeting. Figaro enters with Marcellina, and the little girl innocently lets out the secret. It is now Figaro's turn to be jealous and suspicious; he is convinced that Suzanna has been deceiving him. Now it is his turn to swear vengeance, not only for himself but for the whole race of injured husbands. Marcellina, who sees the trouble he is in, good-naturedly goes off to warn Suzanna.

In the eighteenth-century opera every chief character had to have an aria, and it is for this reason alone that Marcellina and Basilio are at this point given arias to sing that are of no great musical value, and so inessential to the dramatic action that they are usually omitted. The movement of the drama is resumed in a recitative and aria of Figaro, in which he pours out his complaint against Suzanna and against women in general. In Beaumarchais, Figaro's long monologue has a very bitter taste; Mozart, as was his wont, softens the expression considerably.

Figaro conceals himself as the Countess and Suzanna enter disguised in each other's clothes. Figaro knows, and Suzanna knows that he knows, that the assignation with the Count is among the pines. She loudly asks the Countess's permission to retire there a little while. Then she sings her exquisite aria "Deh vieni non tardar," in which she pours out all the love of her heart for Figaro, who, however, naturally assumes that the Count is the object of this ardent longing.

Cherubino enters in search of Barbarina. Seeing the Countess, whom he takes to be Suzanna, he thinks a little preliminary flirtation will be agreeable, one woman being very much the same as another to him. In the middle of his courtship, which greatly embarrasses the Countess, the Count enters just in time to intercept a kiss that Cherubino is trying to give the supposed Suzanna; he aims a box on the ear at Cherubino, but it is received by Figaro, who has drawn near to get a better understanding of what is going on.

From this point on the intrigue works itself out along the lines that might be expected. The Count makes love to the supposed Suzanna, giving her a ring as a pledge of his affection. The Countess goes into the pavilion on the right-hand side of the stage, where the Count means to join her. Figaro, prowling about, comes upon Suzanna, and, taking her to be the Countess, tells her how they can catch the Count with Suzanna in the pavilion. At first Suzanna disguises her voice, but when she forgets to do so for a moment Figaro realises who it is. He keeps his knowledge from her, meaning to pay her out for the trick she has practised upon him, while Suzanna's intention is to punish him for having doubted her. He pretends to make passionate love to the Countess, until Suzanna, unable to endure it any longer, bursts out in her natural voice and boxes his ears. He is delighted with this sign of her affection, and all is now well.

The pair act a comedy for the benefit of the Count, who has wandered back, having been unable to find the supposed Suzanna. Figaro falls at his bride's feet, and, after having staged a little love-scene, they make off towards the pavilion on the left side. The Count seizes Figaro, calls for his servants, and Basilio, Curzio, Antonio, and Bartolo come upon the scene. The Count goes to the pavilion on the left and brings out Cherubino and Barbarina (who have concealed themselves there for a little entertainment of their own), Marcellina and Suzanna; everybody of course takes the maid to be the Countess. She, still in the character of the Countess, implores the Count's forgiveness, but he is adamant. The situation is cleared up by the entry of the real Countess and the momentary humiliation of the Count; he pleads for pardon, which is granted him; and the opera ends with a joyous ensemble.

It may be added that in the delightful overture Mozart does not draw for his material on the themes of the opera itself, and makes no attempt, as later opera composers used to do, to tell the whole story in summarised form, but just writes a sprightly orchestral piece that is intended to tune the hearer in to the general mood of the coming comedy.

DON GIOVANNI

[Wolfgang Amadeus Mozart]

T HE world indirectly owes *Don Giovanni* to a young lady who was probably no better than she ought to have been — one Josefa Duschek.

Originally a Josefa Hambacher, she had been born in Prague in 1753, and consequently was about three years older than Mozart. She became the pupil of Franz Duschek, a Prague musician some seventeen years older than herself, who fell in love with her and married her in 1773. She seems to have been a good pianist and a fair all-round musician, but it was more particularly as a singer that she distinguished herself; she must have had a considerable coloratura technique, if we may judge from an aria that Mozart wrote specially for her.

In her career as an opera singer she seems to have used her charms freely to advance her material interests. She had the good fortune to win the affection of a rich Bohemian nobleman, Count Christian Clam, and it was presumably out of the money he lavished on her that she bought in April 1784 a charming little estate near Prague, with a fine house on it known as the Villa Bertramka.

The property came, in 1838, into the possession of a family that took pains to preserve it in memory of Mozart; and to-day the house, which, owing to the growth of Prague, is no longer in the country but in a suburb, is virtually as it was when Josefa owned it and Mozart visited her there. In the garden there is still the little summer-house in which he used to work, and in which *Don Giovanni* was completed. A German writer justly maintains that the Villa Bertramka has more title to be known as " the Mozart House " than either the place shown under that name at Salzburg, in which he was born, or that in Vienna, in which he lived.

Mozart first met Josefa in Salzburg in the summer of 1777, and the merry young people soon became very fond of each other. Later he met her again in Vienna. She was an enthusiastic admirer of his music, and did all she could to make it known in Prague; it was owing to her that the *Seraglio* was produced in that town soon after its first success in Vienna. In the capital, however, Mozart had never made much headway as an operatic composer.

The chief reason for this was probably the strong Italian proclivities of the reigning emperior, Joseph II, and of the Court generally. The theatre-going Viennese, too, were mostly a gay and somewhat superficial people, who preferred Italian music or the lighter productions of German composers to what they regarded as the almost too solid fare that Mozart gave them.

In 1786 there was an enterprising Italian impresario in Prague by the name of Pasquale Bondini, who ran a very capable opera company; he made a tremendous success with *Figaro,* which proved to be much more to the taste of the Prague public than it had been to that of Vienna. In December 1786, no doubt through the instrumentality of Josefa Duschek, Mozart was invited to Prague to see the production. He arrived there, with his wife Konstanze, on the 11th January, 1787, and found the town, as he wrote to his father and sister, *Figaro*-mad.

He went to see the opera on the 17th January, and was received with tumultuous applause when recognised by the audience. On the 20th he directed the performance himself. Mozart was as pleased with the Prague public as it was with him, and when he left for Vienna again in February it was with a commission from Bondini to write a new opera for his Prague troupe.

The librettist chosen for the new opera was Lorenzo da Ponte, a gifted but erratic Italian Jew who had settled in Vienna some years before and had made some success as a theatrical poet; the libretto of *Figaro* had been by him. The new text was in Mozart's hands by the beginning of April, and by the summer he had written a good deal of the score. At the beginning of September he went to Prague, and the remainder of the opera was finished, under the happiest circumstances, at the Villa Bertramka.

The first performance should have taken place on the 14th October, in connection with the festivities in honour of Prince Anton of Saxony and his young wife the Archduchess Maria Theresa, a sister of the Austrian Emperor. The rehearsals for the new opera not being sufficiently advanced, however, *Figaro* was substituted for it on the 14th October, and it was not until the 29th that *Don Giovanni* was produced.

The Don was Luigi Bassi, a young baritone of twenty-two years of age, and it is merely from the accident that the first representative of the part was so young a man that the tradition began of making Don Giovanni rather younger in appearance than is quite consistent with the length of his amorous record at the time the opera commences.

The Zerlina was Katerina Bondini, the wife of the impresario. The story goes that in the scene in which Don Giovanni takes Zerlina into a private room and makes impetuous advances to her, nothing would induce Katerina Bondini to shriek as loudly as the situation seemed to demand, until one day at rehearsal Mozart accompanied her off the stage, and at the critical moment pinched her so hard that she let out a shriek with which no fault whatever could be found on the score of realism.

The older versions of the story that used to pass from mouth to mouth were quite explicit as to where the pinch was administered; but as a modern German writer piously remarks, " Honi soit qui mal y pense! " There was the usual trouble with the singers, Bassi in particular complaining that he " had no big aria to sing "; and it is said that the duet " La ci darem " was worked over five times before he condescended to approve of it.

Even in Prague, where Mozart was so beloved, *Don Giovanni*, enthusiastically as it was received, did not make the enduring success that *Figaro* did; like Vienna, the taste of the town was too predominantly Italian. In Vienna the work was first performed on the 7th May, 1788, when, in order to satisfy the singers, Mozart had to make sundry alterations and write some new numbers.

As might have been expected, the work did not appeal to the Emperor and his Italianised subjects, and it disappeared from the bills after its fifteenth performance, on the 15th December. It was revived on the 5th November, 1791, after Mozart's death, this time in a German translation, and with a good deal of coarse exaggeration of the comic element. The opera spread gradually to other towns, but it was not until fairly well on into the nineteenth century that it can be said to have established itself firmly. It has to be remembered that *Don Giovanni* is both a difficult and an expensive opera to produce; it demands, for one thing, three women singers of the first quality.

The ultimate origin of the story of *Don Giovanni* is a moral play entitled *El Burlador de Sevilla, y Combidado de Pietra* (*The Mocker of Seville and the Stone Guest*), by a Spanish monk, Gabriel Tellez, who wrote under the pseudonym of Tirso de Molina. The play was printed in 1630. It is probable that the monkish author only blended for the first time in literary form certain old legends, on the one hand, of a young man of unbridled sensuality, and on the other, of a statue that interrupted a festivity.

Don Juan (to give him his Spanish name) is obviously, like Faust, the concentration of a universal type into a single personality. The theme, once reduced to writing, became immensely popular, and we find it being treated in one form or another by dramatists all over Europe. A drama on the subject, by one Giliberti, was acted in Naples in 1652, and another, about the same time, by Andrea Cigogni. Other Italian versions followed and various French dramatists took up the theme, including Molière, whose *Don Juan ou le Festin de Pierre* was acted in Paris in 1665. In England we have Thomas Shadwell's play *The Libertine* (1676). There are several other dramatic and operatic versions of the story, in Germany, Spain, and elsewhere; and Gluck made a ballet of it in Vienna in 1761. The Russian composer

Dargomijski left an unfinished opera on the subject (*The Stone Guest*).

The immediate predecessor of Mozart's work was an opera entitled *Il Convitato di Pietra* (*The Stone Guest*), the text by Bertati, the music by Gazzaniga, that was produced in Venice in 1787. This had a great popular success. That Da Ponte was familiar with it is shown by the numerous points of resemblance between his text and that of Bertati.

There is a romantic story told in all the Mozart biographies of how the overture was still unwritten on the day before the performance; how all that night Mozart's wife plied him with punch and kept him awake by telling him fairy-stories, while he wrote the overture; how the theatre copyist received the score at seven o'clock in the morning; and how the overture was played at sight in the evening.

Like so many other musical legends, however, this will not bear investigation. The evidence indicates that this incident took place not on the night before the performance but on the night before that — that is to say, on the night before the final rehearsal; Mozart's own dating of his score makes this a matter of certainty. Nor is the feat of writing the overture in a single night quite so remarkable as it sounds. Mozart had not only extraordinary facility in composition; he had a marvellous memory. " Composition," for him, meant developing a work in his head; he found the business of writing it out rather tiresome, and he would often postpone this as long as he could.

There can be little doubt that the overture to *Don Giovanni* had been worked out in his head long before the final rehearsal, and that all he had to do on that historic night was to put the notes on paper.

In the nineteenth century it became the fashion of writers upon music to read into the overture of *Don Giovanni* a number of programmatic intentions that were probably not in the mind of the composer. Mozart's usual practice was not to construct an overture out of themes taken from the opera, as was the way with the nineteenth-century opera composers, but to write an independent

orchestral piece that should be broadly suggestive of what was
to come.

In the case of *Don Giovanni,* however, the andante introduction
undoubtedly has a programmatic significance, for it is based on
the themes that, later on, accompany the supper to which the
Commandant has invited his murderer.

Death may be said to brood over this slow introduction. It commences with a loud chord of the tonic of D minor, followed by a
chord of the dominant; then come the solemn chords:

to which the Statue makes his terrifying entry in the supper scene.
This is followed by the syncopated melody, so admirably expressive of uncertainty, to which Don Giovanni greets his visitor:

and this, after a brief transitional passage, by the harmonies that express the agitation of Leporello at the sight of the Statue:

To this succeed the ghostly runs in the flutes and violins, with their sinister crescendi and diminuendi, that accompany the Statue's solemn warning to Don Giovanni:

With a modulation into D major the molto allegro begins. This may be taken, as has been said above, to represent in general terms the swirl of life that accompanies Don Giovanni wherever he goes, though there are passages here and there that tempt us to believe that Mozart had some idea of a programme in his mind. The main theme is that with which the D major section begins:

A later passage, based on an alternation of an impressive octave figure and a chattering one in the violins:

may or may not be intended to point the moral of the contrast between morality and the sternness of Fate, as represented by the Commandant, and the irreligion and levity of Don Giovanni. A fair proportion of the overture is devoted to this antithesis, and the striding figure shown in the first part of No. 6 plays so large a part in the development that we may be pardoned for believing it to have had some special dramatic association in Mozart's mind.

Though the overture is in D minor and D major, it ends, curiously enough, in C major, from which an easy transition is made into F major, in which key the opera begins.

ACT I

The setting of the story is in Seville. The first scene shows us the garden of the Commandant's house. A flight of steps leads up to the house; in the background is a small door leading into the street. It is getting on towards night.

Leporello, the servant of Don Giovanni, is seen striding up and down in front of the house, wrapped in a black cloak. To a melody that has become famous:

he tells us what he has to go through on account of his pleasure-seeking master; he has no rest day or night. He himself feels like playing the gentleman now and then, so he means to quit the service of Don Giovanni. It is all very well for his master, he says; *he* has a good time within doors, while Leporello has to hang about outside and play the sentinel. Hearing someone coming, he thinks it prudent to hide himself.

Out of the house comes Don Giovanni hurriedly, struggling with Donna Anna and trying to conceal his face from her. What has been going on inside we can only conjecture; but we realise that the lady is extremely agitated, and that she is as determined to discover the identity of the young man as he is to conceal it. She calls loudly on the servants for assistance against the betrayer; Don Giovanni bids her be quiet on pain of his anger, while the hidden Leporello joins in the trio half in amusement, half in fright.

Through the door in the background the Commandant, Donna Anna's father, enters, sword in hand; at the sight of him Donna Anna rushes back into the house. The Commandant bids the seducer prepare to fight him, but Don Giovanni brushes the proposal aside with scorn. His unwillingness to attack the older man is indicated in a short ejaculation of " Misero! " Then, brushing pity aside, he repeats the " Misero! " in louder tones, and bids his adversary approach if he wishes to die.

They fight, and the Commandant falls mortally wounded, crying out for assistance; Don Giovanni, *sotto voce*, lets us see that at the bottom of his heart he is sorry for the crime that has been forced upon him, for murder is not one of his amusements. The action is once more carried on by way of a trio, Leporello inserting his terrified comments. The Commandant dies to the accompaniment of a wailing phrase in the violins and oboe, and Don Giovanni in subdued tones (in recitative) calls for his servant.

The frightened Leporello, disclosing himself and coming forward, naïvely, asks his master whether it is he or the old man who has been killed. Don Giovanni reassures him on this point, and Leporello congratulates him ironically on his double achievement — to have seduced the daughter and killed the father is

quite a good evening's work. " It was his own will," says Don
Giovanni. " And Donna Anna," asks Leporello with sly malice,
" was it her will too? " Don Giovanni cuts his familiarity short
with a threat of a beating, and the two hasten away.

Donna Anna returns, accompanied by her betrothed, Don
Ottavio, and servants carrying weapons and lights. To the accompaniment of an anguished phrase in the orchestra Donna
Anna bends over the body of her father and, realizing that he is
dead, gives full vent to her grief. Ottavio tries to console her, and
the body having been removed by the servants, Donna Anna
breaks out again into a passionate lament over her father. Ottavio
again offers consolation, in a phrase that is like a caress:

She makes him swear to avenge the murder, and after a duet
on this theme they leave the stage.

The next scene shows us a street in the early morning. Don Giovanni and Leporello enter and carry on a conversation in recitative. Leporello, as usual, is disturbed about his master's little indiscretions. He asks if he may speak freely to him. Don Giovanni gives him permission, but Leporello first makes him promise that whatever he says he will not lose his temper with him. His master swears this on his honour, so long as the Commandant is not mentioned; Don Giovanni is already tired of that subject.

Taking precautions to see that nobody is within sight or hearing, and again anxiously reminding his master of his promise, Leporello says, " Well, my dear master, what I have to tell you is that the life you are living is that of a rascal." Don Giovanni's anger breaks out at this, and in spite of his promise he threatens Leporello with a thrashing if he does not behave himself better. He has, he tells his servant, some news for him. " Why do you think I am here? " he asks. Leporello does not know, but he has half an idea that it must be some new conquest; if that is so, will Don Giovanni kindly give him the lady's name, so that he may add it to the list?

Don Giovanni gaily and ironically compliments him on his business-like methods, and informs him that he is in love with a beautiful lady, who, he is certain, also loves him. He has seen her and spoken to her, and is to meet her that evening. " But softly," he says, in a phrase that has become famous; " I seem to catch the odour of femininity " (*Mi pare sentir odor di femmina*). " Good Lord! " exclaims the admiring Leporello; " that's what I call a perfect sense of smell! " " She seems handsome," continues Don Giovanni. " What eyesight also! " adds Leporello. " Let us take cover and observe," says Don Giovanni; and the pair hide themselves as Elvira enters.

She is a lady with whom Don Giovanni has had a hectic affair elsewhere, and she has come in search of the fickle one who has first captured her heart and then deserted her. The mistake is sometimes made of playing this part too tragically. *The* tragic female character of the opera is Donna Anna, whose mind is entirely filled with the thought of vengeance on her own seducer and

the murderer of her father. Elvira, for all her passion and her
capacity to feel resentment, represents a gentler, more affectionate,
and more yielding type.

She breaks out into an aria in which she expresses her desire to
find the lover who has left her; the orchestral accompaniment
paints the agitation of her heart:

At the moment she is full of rage against the man who has jilted
her; if she could find him, she assures us, she would tear out his
heart.

Don Giovanni, who has had so many little affairs of this kind
on his hands that he cannot reasonably be expected to remember
them all, for a little while does not recognise Elvira; he tells
Leporello she is probably some pretty girl who has been neglected
by her lover, and as Elvira continues with her denunciation of the
absent one he comments ironically, " Poor little girl! "

The opportunity for a new adventure seems to him too good to
be thrown away, so he proposes to go to her and offer consolation; to which Leporello slyly adds, " No doubt, in the way you
have consoled the other one thousand eight hundred." The orchestra comments slyly on their words:

try just to con - sole her,
- la - re il suo tor - men - to.

This phrase, that **is** like a quiet smile with a chuckle accompanying it, runs through the remainder of the scene.

Donna Elvira having brought her aria to an end, Don Giovanni steps forward, to the accompaniment of the ironical No. 10, with a polite " Signorina! " Leporello remains completely in the background, listening to all that is said, and occasionally giving us his own humorous comments on it.

Elvira and Don Giovanni recognise each other simultaneously. The latter is for a moment taken aback; the lady, being the first to find her tongue, overwhelms him with reproaches. It appears that he has made a conquest of her in Burgos and left her after three romantic days. She reels off the story of her wrongs with such fluency that Leporello is moved to remark, *sotto voce,* " She's just like a printed book! " Don Giovanni assures Elvira that there were important reasons why he had to leave her so suddenly, and he appeals to Leporello to confirm him in this. He leaves his servant to explain to the lady, and slips away quietly. Leporello is for the moment so flabbergasted that he can only stammer out some nonsense about a square not being round. The lady turns indignantly to Don Giovanni to upbraid him for putting this further insult on her, but finds that he has fled.

She breaks out into fresh lamentations, and Leporello feels that the time has come to administer consolation. This he does by asking her not to take her betrayal and desertion too much to heart, as she was not the first and will not be the last of his master's amorous episodes. He shows her a little volume which, he says, contains the names of the ladies he has loved, with the country, the town, and the village in each case; and he launches into his famous aria " Madamina! " In this he reels off in sprightly fashion the long list of Don Giovanni's lady-loves — in Italy, six hundred and forty; in Germany, two hundred and thirty-one; in France, a hundred; in Turkey, ninety-one; but in Spain here, he concludes, already a thousand and three, an almost astronomical figure which he repeats again and again, rolling it over his tongue with great gusto.

The list includes ladies of all social spheres — peasants, chambermaids, citizenesses, Countesses, Baronesses, Marchionesses, Princesses, in fact, every station, every age, and every shape. Then he describes the different kinds of technique adopted by his expert master; if the lady is a blonde, he praises her delicacy; if a brunette, her constancy, and so on. In winter he likes them plump, in summer rather on the slender side. The little débutante and the seasoned duenna both find a place on the list.

Having finished his aria, Leporello slips away, leaving Elvira to declaim indignantly against this lover of hers who first of all deserts her and then leaves her to his servant to be derided. Hell knowing no fury like a woman scorned, she swears she will track the wicked man down and have revenge.

The scene now changes to the country, where we see a village feast in progress. The local beauty, Zerlina, is about to be married to a sturdy swain of the village, Masetto. Led by Zerlina, the company join in a song in praise of the enjoyment of life. Don Giovanni, congratulating himself on his clever escape from Donna Elvira, comes upon the scene, accompanied by Leporello.

There are so many pretty girls there that Don Giovanni at once begins to take a kindly interest in the proceedings. He accosts the company condescendingly, and is told by Masetto and Zerlina, with all the respect due to his station, that they are respectively the bride and bridegroom of the day. Masetto is an honest bumpkin; Zerlina, who has ten times his brains, is a born coquette, and she and Don Giovanni very quickly come to a mutual understanding without anything definite being said on either side. Don

Giovanni bids Leporello invite the villagers to his palace, where they are to be provided with chocolate, coffee, and other refreshments. He is to do all he can to amuse them, show them the gardens, the gallery, the rooms, " in fact, do all you can to keep my friend Masetto contented; you understand me? " " I understand you," replies Leporello.

Zerlina, Don Giovanni has already intimated, will meanwhile remain under his own protection. Masetto jibs a little at this, but Leporello assures him that his master will be able to take quite as good care of Zerlina as he could do, and the minx assures her bridegroom that he need have no fear for her, for is she not in the hands of a cavalier? Masetto still grumbles a little, but Giovanni ends the dispute by touching his sword and giving Masetto a hint that if he does not mean to behave himself he will regret it. Masetto gives vent to his feelings in an aria in which he alternately reproaches Zerlina for having been his ruin, and declares himself to be ready, as a good vassal, to do what the master tells him.

Leporello having taken Masetto away, Don Giovanni proceeds to lay siege to Zerlina. He assures her that she is much too pretty to throw herself away on a peasant. Zerlina professes to be not quite sure of the honourableness of the intentions of the gentry as regards country maidens, but Giovanni assures her that the breed has been greatly calumniated. His intentions are so honourable, in fact, that he is willing to make her his wife there and then. He asks her to come with him into this little country house that belongs to him, and the pair break out into the enchanting duet " La ci darem la mano " (" There we will give each other our hands, there you will say ' Yes ' to me "). Zerlina is still a little coy, or pretends to be so; she would and yet she would not, she assures him. But at length her scruples are overcome, and the two are about to enter the house when Donna Elvira enters, calls Don Giovanni a scoundrel once more, and declares that Heaven has sent her to be the means of rescuing this poor innocent girl from his clutches.

Giovanni manages the pair of them very artfully; to Elvira he whispers that the affair with the village girl is just a little harmless diversion on his part, while he assures Zerlina that the great lady is crazy about him and, being the tender-hearted man he is, he has to humour her. Elvira warns Zerlina against him in an aria in the Handelian style that is often omitted in performance. At the end of it she goes away, taking Zerlina with her.

Don Giovanni is musing ruefully upon the scurvy way Fate has treated him when Donna Anna enters with Ottavio. The lovers are still discussing their plans of vengeance upon the murderer of the Commandant. Evidently what happened in the house in the first scene of the opera took place in the dark, for though Anna is acquainted with Don Giovanni, she does not as yet associate him with her misfortunes. She appeals to his friendship to assist her, and he gallantly protests that he is completely at her service. He is hypocritically asking the cause of her troubles when Elvira enters once more. Full of her own woes, as usual, she warns Anna against Giovanni, and the latter gets out of his difficulty for the moment by whispering to Anna and Ottavio that the poor girl is not quite in her right mind. Anna and Ottavio are not altogether convinced by him; and the expression of the varying thoughts of the four people is woven into a fine ensemble.

Elvira having left the stage, Don Giovanni follows her, professing to be anxious about her. When he has gone, Anna, almost collapsing, turns to Ottavio; she has recognised in this young man the murderer of her father; his voice and his manner have betrayed him. She tells her lover what happened on that fateful night; she was sitting alone in the darkness of her room when there entered a man in a mantle, whom for the moment she took for Ottavio; recognising, from the unaccustomed ardour of his embraces, that it was not her somewhat lymphatic lover, she struggled with the stranger, called on the servants, and followed the seducer into the street, where her father challenged him and was slain. Once more, in a long aria, she adjures Ottavio to take vengeance on the murderer. Then she goes out, leaving the stage free for Ottavio to sing his aria " Dalla sua pace," one of the interpolated numbers that is frequently omitted in performance.

He also having left the stage, Leporello enters, followed immediately by Don Giovanni. Leporello is once more resolved to leave this troublesome master of his. He tells the latter what has happened — how, as he had been told to do, he took the peasants away, gave them plenty of wine, and set them amusing themselves, but had a good deal of trouble with Masetto. Just when everything seemed to be going well, it seems, Zerlina had come in with Elvira, the latter, as usual, full of denunciations of Giovanni. Leporello had got out of the difficulty by escorting Elvira outside the house and then locking the door.

He is complimented on his presence of mind by Don Giovanni, who now thinks it time to return to the villagers. In what is known in Germany as the " Champagne Aria " he tells Leporello to invite all the villagers to his palace and set them enjoying themselves; while they are doing this he himself, with the co-operation of the prettiest of the girls, will have added by the morning, he hopes, another ten to the list. The aria, which commences thus:

(11)

is irresistible in its vivacity, its expression of the joy of life. It is marked presto, and the singer should take it as fast as he possibly can, and then a little faster.

The next scene is in the garden. While the other villagers are enjoying themselves, Masetto reproaches Zerlina for her incon-

stancy on the eve of their wedding. She protests her essential innocence; it was simply, she says, that for the moment she had
succumbed to the flattery of this very engaging young man. She
sets herself to the re-conquest of her rustic swain in the delicious
aria " Batti, batti ":

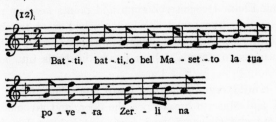

(12)

Bat - ti, bat - ti, o bel Ma - set - to la tua
po - ve - ra Zer - li - na

in which she protests her love for Masetto, and invites him to
beat her if he feels angry with her; she will take her thrashing
like a lamb! Her wiles and her charm are altogether too much
for simple, honest Masetto, who forgives her.

Just then Don Giovanni's voice is heard within. It revives
Masetto's suspicions. He will watch his lordship, he tells Zerlina;
and for this purpose he hides in an alcove as Giovanni enters with
some servants, whom he orders to do everything possible for the
entertainment of his guests. All gradually leave the stage except
Zerlina, to whom Giovanni once more makes love. The coquettish
Zerlina allows him to lead her towards the alcove, where Giovanni,
to his astonishment, sees Masetto. For the moment he is a trifle
confused, then, recovering himself, he tells Masetto that the
fair Zerlina was unhappy at being parted from her swain.
Masetto thanks him ironically, and the three go off to join the
others.

Ottavio, Anna, and Elvira now enter, masked; they are still
in search of Giovanni. In the distance a minuet is heard; Leporello
having drawn his master's attention to the masks below, Giovanni,
at the window, tells him to invite them in to the dance. Again
they recognise his voice. They accept the invitation, but before
entering indulge in a trio in which they solemnly appeal for the
protection of Heaven in their undertaking.

Once more the scene changes, this time to a ballroom, in which Don Giovanni and Leporello are making themselves agreeable to the peasants. Trouble, we feel, is brewing; Masetto is still watching both Don Giovanni and Zerlina suspiciously. The three masks enter and are courteously welcomed by Don Giovanni. Elvira recognises Zerlina and points her out to Anna and Ottavio as the brand she had plucked from the burning. Leporello forces Masetto to dance with him while Don Giovanni attends to Zerlina, whom finally he leads into an inner room.

Soon a wild cry for help is heard from her. Anna, Elvira, Ottavio, and Masetto break open the door, and are met by the ever-resourceful Giovanni, who comes out holding Leporello by the arm; he pretends to be angry with him, and makes as if to stab him with his sword. It is Leporello, Giovanni would have the company believe, who has been misbehaving himself with Zerlina. Anna, Elvira, and Ottavio unmask, and join with Zerlina and Masetto in a denunciation of Don Giovanni, who, they say, they now recognise for the villain he is. Don Giovanni's courage does not desert him; defying their wrath, he makes his escape sword in hand.

ACT II

The second acts opens with a scene in a street. Giovanni and Leporello are seen in lively conversation. Leporello has once more resolved to leave this master whose service is so full of embarrassments for him; but Giovanni overcomes his scruples with money. Leporello promises to stay with him on one condition — that Giovanni gives up the women. Giovanni can hardly believe his ears; " Give up the women? Never! They are more necessary to me than the bread I eat or the air I breathe! "

His infidelities, he assures Leporello, are really a superior fidelity to the sex; how can an affectionate heart like his be true to one without being untrue to all the others? He has a new adventure on hand. He has been smitten with the pretty serving-maid of Elvira, and intends that evening to try his fortune with her; but as the difference between their stations might cause a little trouble, he means to dress himself in Leporello's cloak. Leporello protests, but in vain. (In some modern productions of the opera it is made to appear that Zerlina has entered Elvira's service, and that it is she whom Giovanni is still pursuing. For this there is not the slightest warrant in the libretto.)

Evening comes on, and Elvira appears at her window, where she sings a sad little song; her heart has been broken by the traitor. Don Giovanni's present problem is how to get rid of her in order to make the way clear for him with the maid. To this end he hides behind Leporello (who, of course, now wears the appearance of his master), and protests his undying love for Elvira; and once more she is weak enough to believe him. The trio that constitutes this scene is full of the finest musical touches. Don Giovanni's artfulness and Leporello's amusement are suggested in a little figure that keeps winding in and out in the orchestra:

Don Giovanni's love-making, that is ostensibly addressed to Elvira, is really intended for the maid; one of his phrases:

seems to be an anticipation of the serenade he sings to the maid later.

This comedy having achieved its end, and Elvira having disappeared from the window, Don Giovanni hurriedly gives the protesting Leporello his instructions. When Elvira appears he is to make love to her in the guise of his master, and as soon as possible to get her out of the way. Don Giovanni stands aside and watches the burlesque that ensues; Elvira, when she appears in the street, pours out all her affection on the supposed Giovanni, and Leporello plays his new part of the gallant with great satisfaction to himself. Giovanni suddenly makes his appearance and pretends to attack them, and they make their escape, leaving him free to serenade the maid, which he does in the celebrated " Deh, vieni alla finestra," with its charming accompaniment of plucked strings and mandoline:

(15)

Deh vie - ni alla fi - nes - tra, o
From out thy case-ment glanc-ing, oh,

mio............ te - so - ro
smile............ up - on......... me

The resemblance between this and No. 14 is obvious. Mozart makes Giovanni address each of his victims in a style appropriate to her. The serenade of the serving-maid is in the popular vein she might be supposed to be familiar with and to appreciate; and as the melody of No. 14 is in the same vein, it is a fair assumption that Giovanni intends this to go over Elvira's head to the ears of her servant.

Just as Don Giovanni catches sight of the maid at the window, Masetto and several villagers enter armed with guns, pistols, and other weapons. Don Giovanni's genius at once rises to the occasion. Pretending to be Leporello, he accosts Masetto and runs down his master, of whose wickedness he professes himself to be weary; he is even willing to help them to find and punish him.

He describes Giovanni's dress, and sends the villagers out in various directions to look for him, keeping Masetto with himself.

When the two are left alone he pumps Masetto, and learns that the latter intends to kill the young nobleman if he finds him. By a ruse Giovanni gets the simple fellow's weapons from him, then beats him with the flat of his sword, and makes his escape. Masetto's cries bring Zerlina to him. She consoles him for his injuries in the aria " Vedrai carino," in which she tells him of the one sovereign remedy — love — for all hurts, whether of the body or the soul.

After she has taken the bruised swain away, still feeling very sorry for himself, Leporello, re-enters with Elvira. The scene is now a courtyard in front of the house of Donna Anna. While Elvira is indulging herself in the luxury of another little aria, Leporello is seeking a door by which he may escape. Meanwhile Ottavio and Anna enter in mourning, to the accompaniment of a solemn strain in the orchestra. Ottavio is at his eternal business of consolation.

As Leporello is trying to escape he is caught by Masetto and Zerlina, who enter at that moment. Elvira claims him as her husband, and Ottavio and the others recognise her. In spite of her appeals for him the others seize upon the supposed Giovanni and are about to deal with him as he deserves; but Leporello's whinings for mercy soon set them right as to his identity. All are for punishing him, partly for his own misdeeds, partly for those of his master; but by artfully rambling on and professing to be as much the victim of his master's wickedness as any of them, he manages to stay their avenging hands till an opportunity comes for him to slip away from them.

It has now become clear to all that the murderer of the Commandant was Don Giovanni. Commending Anna to the care of the others, Ottavio declares his intention of going to the authorities to invoke the law against Don Giovanni — a quite incredible proceeding on the part of a Spanish gentleman of the period, who would, of course, be expected to avenge a wrong of this kind by his own sword. Ottavio, however, is peculiarly ineffective all through the opera. Before leaving the stage he sings one of the star tenor arias, " Il mio tesoro intanto " — one of the loveliest of Mozart's creations.

In the score there follows at this point a scene of low comedy (an interpolation for the Vienna production) between Zerlina and Leporello, in which she first of all threatens him with a razor, then drags him about by the hair, and then, with the assistance of the peasants, ties him up in a chair. After volubly upbraiding him for his crimes, she and the peasants leave him, and he manages to make his escape. This scene is generally omitted in performance, while the magnificent aria of Donna Elvira that follows, " Mi tradì quell' alma ingrata " — also written for Vienna — is as a rule transferred to an earlier scene.

The next scene shows us a churchyard, with a newly erected equestrian statue of the Commandant. Don Giovanni enters, leaping over the wall. During the course of his nocturnal adventures he has met another pretty girl, who happens to have been a flame of Leporello's. After a little love-making on his part she had recognised Don Giovanni, taken fright, cried out, and brought a crowd about him, from which he escaped only by running away and leaping the churchyard wall. All this he tells to Leporello in a long recitative.

Giovanni's laughter over the amusing incident is abruptly broken in upon by a solemn warning from the Statue that before the dawn his laughter will be over. This short utterance of the Statue is accompanied only by oboes, clarinets, bassoons, bass strings, and three trombones, the latter instruments entering, with an effect of tremendous solemnity, for the first time in the opera:

(16)

Di   ri - der fi - nì - rai   prìa dell' au -
Your jest will turn to   woe   ere   it is

" Who spoke? " asks the startled Don Giovanni. Leporello replies, " Oh, some spirit from the other world, who knows you
through and through." Bidding him be silent, Giovanni puts his
hand to his sword and cries, " Who goes there? " The bass voice
of the Statue strikes in again with a warning to him to leave the
dead in peace.

Believing, or affecting to believe, that it is only someone on
the other side of the wall who is sporting with them, Giovanni
draws his companion's attention to the Statue of the Commandant.
He would like to know what that inscription on it says. Leporello
pretends not to be able to make it out by moonlight, but under
the imperious command of his master he at last reads out: " Here
I await vengeance upon the impious one who slew me." Leporello
is scared out of his wits at this; but the reckless Giovanni orders
him to tell the old man that his master invites him to sup with
him that evening. After a terrified protest Leporello does so, and
the Statue slowly inclines its head in assent. This is not enough
for Don Giovanni, who arrogantly orders the Statue to answer.
Will it or will it not come to supper with him? The Statue utters
the one word " Yes," and Don Giovanni drags Leporello away
with him to make the necessary preparations for the supper.

The scene changes to a room in a house in which Ottavio is
once more seen consoling Anna and assuring her that the murderer
of her father will soon be brought to justice. His suggestion of
marriage is turned aside by Anna, who cannot permit herself any
happiness till her father has been avenged. Ottavio having taken
this to mean that she no longer loves him, Anna, in the superb
aria " Non mi dir," seizes the opportunity to assure him that her
affection is unchanged.

The final scene shows us a brilliantly lit room in Don Giovanni's house, where he is entertaining a numerous and gay company to supper. In the gallery is a band of musicians who play snatches from some of the most popular operas of the time, including Martini's *La Cosa Rara,* and the melody of Figaro's aria " Non pitù andrai." Giovanni, as usual, is full of the hectic joy of life, while Leporello, whose appetites are more material, is indulging liberally in food and drink in the intervals of attending upon his master.

A last chance is offered Giovanni to save himself; Elvira rushes in, flings herself at his feet, and implores him, in the name of her love, to mend his ways and make his peace with God. His only reply is to deride her. Finding it impossible to penetrate his armour of egoism and sensuality, Elvira rushes away, but returns instantly, gives a great shriek, and makes another exit on the opposite side. Don Giovanni sends Leporello to discover the cause of her perturbation. Leporello has no sooner left the stage than he also gives a great cry; then he returns, shuts the door, and in accents of terror tells his master that outside is the Statue. While he is giving a graphic description of the apparition, a loud knocking is heard at the door. Giovanni orders Leporello to open, but this time the servant positively refuses.

Giovanni strides to the door himself, flings it open, and the Statue enters, to the solemn chords heard at the commencement of the overture. As already mentioned, the music to this part of the scene is virtually identical with that of the slow preamble to the overture. The Statue has come, it says, in fulfilment of its promise. Don Giovanni, whom, from the agitated orchestral accompaniment to his words (see No. 2), we may assume to be secretly perturbed, defiantly welcomes his guest and bids Leporello lay another cover for him. Leporello, who has hidden under the table, can only stammer out in his fright, " Ah, master, master! We are all lost! " The Statue waves aside the proffered hospitality with the intimation that those who have tasted of the celestial food have no need of mortal aliment:

(17)

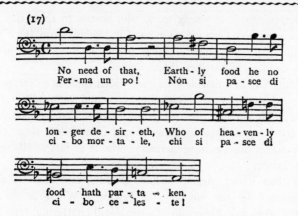

No need of that,   Earth - ly   food he no
Fer - ma un po!   Nón si   pa - sce di

lon - ger de - sir - eth,   Who of   hea - ven - ly
ci - bo mor - ta - le,   chi si   pa - sce di

food   hath par - ta ⌣ ken.
ci - bo   ce - les - te!

In spite of the bravado of Don Giovanni and the comic terrors of
Leporello under the table, the horror of the scene steadily accumu-
lates. The Commandant ends by returning Giovanni's invitation
to supper:

(18)

Then   an - - swer
Ri - spon - - di

me,   then an - - swer me,
- mi,   ri - spon - - di - mi,

and the vainglorious young man, who scorns to show any sign of fear, accepts. " Give me your hand in pledge," says the Statue. Giovanni places his hand in that of the Commandant, and at once a deadly chill strikes through him.

Holding him in a marble grip from which there is no escape, the Statue exhorts him to repent, but Giovanni heroically refuses. Releasing him at last, the Statue stalks out. Flames appear, the earth trembles, and an invisible chorus from below sings of the torments that are awaiting Giovanni, who is at last swallowed up in the flames.

Just then Elvira, Anna, Zerlina, Ottavio, and Masetto enter, accompanied by the ministers of justice. " Where is the miscreant? " they ask. Leporello, his teeth still chattering, tells them of the awful fate that has overtaken his master, and the opera ends in an ensemble that is a curious mixture of moods.

Ottavio begs Anna, now that her wrongs have been righted, to fulfil her vows to him, but she asks him to grant her a year's delay. Elvira announces her intention of going into a convent to end her days. Masetto and Zerlina, who are made of more ordinary clay, look forward happily to their speedy marriage. Leporello tells them all that he will look out for another and a better master. Finally all join in an ensemble in which they point the moral of the story.

THE MAGIC FLUTE

IT was apparently in 1779, when Mozart was twenty-three years
old, that he met in Salzburg the touring theatrical impresario
Emanuel Schikaneder, who was at that time performing in
Mozart's native town.

This Schikaneder, who was born in 1748 and died mad in 1812,
was a remarkable character in his way; he may, indeed, be regarded as an anticipation of certain theatrical managers and specu-
lators who are very much in the public eye at the present time.
He was a bit of everything, singer, actor, producer, poet, theatre
proprietor, and what not; and in most of these capacities he
seems to have done quite well.

Perhaps he was born before his due time; had he lived in the
America or the Germany or the England of the present day he
would probably have been a combination of P. T. Barnum, C. B.
Cochran, and Max Reinhardt, running anything from a rodeo to
a musical comedy or a miracle play, and making a commercial
success of them all. He was one of the first public entertainers to
know what the public really wants; and having discovered what
his public wanted he was always ready to supply it. Finding that
his compatriots had a great liking for spectacular shows, with
animals and plenty of clowning in them, he gave them these on
a large scale; at Graz, for example, he produced before some three
thousand spectators a spectacular soldier play in the realistic
surroundings of a military camp, the cavalry officers playing appropriate parts.

During his stay in Salzburg Schikaneder produced a play by

one Gebler, *Thamos, King of Egypt,* for which Mozart had written some instrumental music six years or so before; this he now revised and added to for the purpose of Schikaneder's production.

After that, Schikaneder, so far as we are concerned, disappears from the scene for about ten years. In the spring of 1789, after many wanderings, he settled in Vienna. There he found that his wife, with whom he had not been living for some years, was running the Theater auf der Wieden — which was a wooden erection in a courtyard in a big block of buildings outside the fortifications. Frau Schikaneder was doing none too well, mainly by reason of the competition of the theatre of a certain Marinelli, a busy producer of fairy-plays, comic operas, and so on, who had the light-hearted and light-headed Viennese public at his feet.

Schikaneder saw the possibilities of the situation, had himself made director of the Theater auf der Wieden, and then laid himself out to beat Marinelli at his own game. A favourite Viennese comic stage type, Kasperl, had been a roaring success in several of Marinelli's productions. Schikaneder invented, or found, an Anton as a counterpoise to Kasperl; and this Anton appeared with great success in no less than seven of Schikaneder's farces. In addition to these he produced a number of good serious plays and high-class operas, and in a very little while was a leading figure in the amusement life of Vienna.

Mozart, who was living in Vienna at the time, would in any case have had no difficulty in renewing his Salzburg acquaintance with Schikaneder, but matters were no doubt made easier for him by the fact that his sister-in-law Josefa Hofer, a brilliant coloratura singer, was a member of Schikaneder's theatrical company. In 1790 Schikaneder planned a magic opera, *Der Stein der Weisen,* the music for which was made up from various sources. Mozart is supposed to have contributed an aria, but his authorship of the piece printed under his name in the complete edition of his works is denied in some quarters.

Schikaneder's proposal to Mozart that he should write a German opera was received enthusiastically by the composer, for two reasons. In the first place, his financial affairs at this time were in so desperate a condition that he jumped at the prospect of making a little money by an opera. In the second place, it had long been his desire to write an opera to German words. His last work in this line had been the *Seraglio*, which was produced in 1782. But the tastes of the Emperor, the Court, and a great part of the public were immovably Italian, and the wave of national enthusiasm that cast up the *Seraglio* soon exhausted itself. Mozart's later operas, *Figaro, Don Giovanni,* and *Così fan tutte,* had all been written to Italian words.

Schikaneder probably did not very much care what the subject of the new opera was so long as it fulfilled two conditions; it must be in the prevailing taste of the moment, which was all for magic, spectacle, and the Oriental, and it must contain a good part for himself, for he was a comic actor of decided ability. He was a big person, and fond of the pleasures of the table; and after success came to him he lived freely.

There was a tradition in Vienna in the earlier part of the nineteenth century that during the last year or so of his life Mozart drank heavily. There is no direct evidence on the point, but it is by no means improbable that, miserable and ill and worried as he was, he found a good deal of pleasure in Schikaneder's gay parties, for Mozart always appreciated the simpler joys of life.

Schikaneder seems to have known his man. He had probably heard that along with Mozart's incredible facility for composing in his head there went a strange reluctance to put his music on paper until he was compelled to do so; he therefore took the wise precaution of lodging Mozart in a little summer-house in the courtyard in which the theatre stood, where, no doubt, he could see to it that some progress was made each day. This summer-house was fortunately preserved through the nineteenth century, and in 1877 it was removed to Salzburg, where it now stands.

Mozart would be all the more glad to have this residence for economic reasons. His wife Konstanze was away, as she so often was, in Baden, for however short of money her husband might be, and whatever difficulty he had in earning it, Konstanze seems to have seen no reason why she should give up her " cure " and the dancing and other amusements that accompanied it. Mozart, left alone — for Konstanze had with her the little Karl, then aged seven — and without a servant, would be glad to be comfortably housed in the immediate neighbourhood of Schikaneder and other laughter-loving theatrical friends.

The bulk of the music to *The Magic Flute* was written between May and July 1791. Konstanze returned to Vienna on the 11th July, and on the 26th a son, Franz Xaver Wolfgang, was born. In the late summer and early autumn Mozart orchestrated what he had written and completed the little that had been left over, the overture, as so often happened with him, being all ready in his head for some time, but not written down till the 28th September, two days before the performance.

The origins of the book of *The Magic Flute* are wrapped in mystery. For some reason or other the plan of the opera seems to have been altered shortly after practical work had been begun upon it — for apparently Mozart had not a complete libretto before him to begin with, but composed the music to this or that scene as it was handed him.

It is conjectured, probably with reason, that Schikaneder's original intention was simply to provide the Viennese public with another specimen of the sort of entertainment for which it had already shown so marked a liking — an Oriental tale of magic and mystery, with vice vanquished and virtue triumphant at the end, plenty of brilliant spectacle, live animals, and so on, and, above all, a prominent comic part for Schikaneder himself.

Schikaneder already had in rehearsal (it was produced on the 23rd July) an opera named *Oberon*, the music by Wranitzky, the plot being taken from a collection of pseudo-Oriental tales by Wieland and others. From one of these tales, *Lulu*, Schikaneder got the idea of *The Magic Flute*. The first conception seems to have been to work out the story along the conventional lines — a wicked magician has captured the daughter of the fairy queen, who sends a portrait of her daughter to the hero, who, by the help of a magic flute, rescues the maiden from captivity. Although *Oberon* was not publicly produced until the composition of *The*

Magic Flute was well advanced, Mozart must have made the acquaintance of it either at rehearsal or at Schikaneder's house, for the resemblances between Wranitzky's score and Mozart's are too many and too close to be explained by mere coincidence.

Why the plot was changed will probably never be known for certain. It has been said that it was because Marinelli, in June, brought out a comic opera at his own theatre founded on the same story, entitled *Kaspar der Fagottist, oder die Zauberzither* (*Kaspar the Bassoonist, or the Magic Zither*), the music of which was by Wendel Müller. Against this theory it has been urged that it was quite a common practice of that time for dramatists and librettists to treat the same subject. It is possible, however, that Schikaneder, like the smart impresario he was, suddenly saw that the immediate road to a big success lay in the direction of doing not what the public was already used to but something just a little different.

Accordingly the basis of the new opera was changed; it now dealt with the mysteries of Freemasonry, which were very much in the air at that time. The wicked magician was changed into a good one, and the fairy queen from a good fairy queen into a bad one, whose daughter had been taken from her by the magician for the girl's own benefit.

Without being a Freemason oneself, but with an elementary knowledge of the principles and the history of the order, it is easy to see, from a mere reading of the libretto, that a masonic intention and significance runs through the whole of the opera after the first scene or two.

During the eighteenth century Freemasonry had a political as well as a benevolent side. It attracted a great many men of high character whose ideal was the regeneration of humanity by moral means; but, rightly or wrongly, it was held by the Catholic Church and the political authorities to be dangerous both to religion and to the well-being of the State. At the same time it drew within its ranks, curiously enough, a fair number of highly placed politicians and ecclesiastics; and although some of these may have joined the lodges merely in the capacity of spies, the majority of them were no doubt sincere philanthropists and idealists.

The Emperor Franz I was a a member of a Viennese lodge, and in 1743 Vienna was treated to the piquant situation of the lodge's being raided by order of the Empress Maria Theresa, and her august husband's having to escape by the back stairs. Joseph II (1780–90) looked with a lenient eye on Freemasonry, and so, seemingly, did his successor Leopold II, though in the latter's reign the clergy did their best to get the lodges suppressed. Under Francis II, who came to the throne in 1792, an active campaign against Freemasonry was begun.

It has generally been held that the Queen of Night in *The Magic Flute* is the Masonic view of the Empress Maria Theresa, that the good Sarastro is Ignaz von Born, an eminent Austrian scientist and Freemason of Mozart's circle, the hero Tamino is the Emperor Joseph II, Pamina is the Austrian people, while the wicked Moor Monostatos represents the clerics in general and the Jesuits in particular.

The mystery in connection with the treatment of the subject of *The Magic Flute* extends also to its authorship. For more than half a century the libretto was supposed to be the work of Schikaneder, whose name appeared on the title-page. But in 1849 one Julius Cornet, who had begun his career as a tenor singer but afterwards became an opera director in Hamburg and Vienna, published a book in which he told how, in Vienna in 1818 (it was really in 1819), he met a venerable gentleman named Giesecke, who informed him and the other diners at the restaurant table that *he* was the real author of the libretto of *The Magic Flute,* Schikaneder having contributed only the figures of Papageno and Papagena.

This Giesecke, whose real name was Johann Georg Metzler, had a very extraordinary career. Born in 1761, he first studied law and then went on the stage. He became the friend of Goethe, Schiller, and other leading literary Germans of the day, translated *Hamlet,* studied mineralogy, dabbled in musical composition, and is said to have been the original of Goethe's *Wilhelm Meister*.

During the period of the putting together of *The Magic Flute* he was a member of Schikaneder's theatrical company in Vienna. Towards the end of the century he forsook the stage for science, particularly mineralogy. After he had lived for some time in Denmark and Sweden, King Christian VII sent him on a scientific mission to Greenland, where he remained over seven years. He returned to civilisation in 1813 by way of Hull, and in December of that year settled down in Dublin as occupant of the newly founded Chair of Mineralogy. He died in Dublin in 1833.

The only other evidence in favour of Giesecke's authorship of the libretto of *The Magic Flute* is that of the pianist and composer Sigismund Neukomm (1778–1858). Neukomm, who had known Giesecke in Vienna in 1798, assured Otto Jahn, the great biographer of Mozart, of Giesecke's authorship of the libretto, the information being presumably derived from Giesecke himself.

This is all we really know on the subject, and it is not much. It has been held that the more serious portions of the libretto could not have been written by Schikaneder, and must therefore have been written by Giesecke. The argument is hardly conclusive, especially when it is remembered that the greater part of the text of the opera is miserable hack work that would be within the powers of anyone who could handle a pen.

All that has been written on the subject, apart from the two statements of Cornet and Neukomm, is pure conjecture. There is not the slightest direct evidence as to what part Giesecke had in the libretto, or even that he had any considerable part at all; and it certainly seems odd that, if he were the true author of the book, he should have allowed it to come out with Schikaneder's name upon it. To this it has been replied that as Freemasonry was in ill odour with the Court and the Church just then, Giesecke may have thought it imprudent to avow publicly his connection with this Masonic opera; but that argument, one thinks, would apply equally to Schikaneder.

No doubt Giesecke, who, as we have seen, was a member of Schikaneder's troupe (he played the part of the First Slave in the opera), had something to do with the putting together of the book, along with Schikaneder and Mozart and, quite possibly, others; but the precise contribution of each of them it is now quite impossible to determine.

The ultimate source of the many plays, novels, and operas of the time that dealt with more or less imaginary Egyptian mysteries seems to have been the book of a certain French Abbé Terrasson (1670–1750) entitled *Sethos,* which the author pretended to be " translated from a Greek manuscript." The book may still be occasionally picked up in the sixpenny box on the bookstalls, and is worth reading by anyone who is interested in *The Magic Flute,* for whoever wrote the book of the latter certainly knew *Sethos,* two passages in the opera being taken almost word for word from the novel.

Terrasson's book was in great vogue among the Freemasons of the day, being regarded, indeed, as an authoritative exposition of the ancient mysteries; and it is not improbable that one element in the success of the opera may have been the Freemasons' approval of the general Masonic intention of the work.

While still engaged upon *The Magic Flute,* Mozart accepted that commission for a Requiem Mass that constitutes one of the strangest chapters in his life. A certain Count Walsegg, who had a mania for commissioning works from well-known composers and having them performed as his own, conceived in 1791 the idea of laying Mozart's genius under contribution. Keeping in the background himself, he ordered the Requiem anonymously through a servant of his, by all accounts a somewhat sinister-looking person. The peculiar appearance of this man and the mystery enveloping the commission so worked upon Mozart, who was already ill at the time, that he came to regard the strange emissary as one sent by Heaven to warn him of his own approaching death.

The Requiem, which was ultimately left unfinished, was interrupted in August and September by the composition of a new Italian opera *La Clemenza di Tito* (*The Clemency of Titus*), which Mozart wrote for the coronation of Leopold II at Prague.

The opera was a failure, and Mozart returned to Vienna, in the middle of September, more depressed than ever.

The first performance of *The Magic Flute* took place on the 30th of the same month; Mozart, from the piano, conducted the first two performances, his pupil Süssmayer (who completed the Requiem) turning over for him; Schikaneder, of course, was the Papageno, and Josefa Hofer the Queen of Night. After a doubtful reception on the first night the opera quickly became a tremendous success; it ran for more than a hundred consecutive nights in Vienna, was taken up by Prague in the following year and by Frankfurt-on-the-Main in 1793, and after that by many of the other German theatres. So popular was it, and so deep the impression made by it, that Goethe, in 1798, planned to write a second part to the opera.

Years of privation and overwork had undermined Mozart's constitution, and in November 1791 he had to take to his bed. There, watch in hand, he would follow in imagination the performance of *The Magic Flute* in the theatre. He died of malignant typhus fever at one o'clock in the morning of the 5th December, 1791.

The overture to *The Magic Flute* begins with an adagio preamble in which we hear first of all three solemn chords in the brass that are said to have a Masonic significance. The allegro begins with a theme in the second violins:

(1) Allegro

that is developed fugally, the first violins taking it up in the fifth bar of our quotation. When it is later given out in the orginal key

by the violas and 'cellos, an octave lower than at first, it is combined with a counter-theme:

These two main themes are worked out together for a while and
are succeeded by a fresh theme that commences in the oboe and
is echoed in the flute:

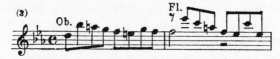

The accompaniment to this is a slightly modified version of the
main theme (No. 1). The form of the overture is a combination
of the fugue form and sonata form. The first section comes to a
pause on the dominant of the main key (B flat), and once more
we hear the three Masonic chords, this time, of course, in the
key of B flat, the dominant of E flat. Nos. 1, 2, and 3 are then
.leveloped, as before, in a fascinating blend of the sonata and
the fugue.

ACT I

One of the evidences of a change of plan in the book of *The
Magic Flute* is that in the stage directions for the opening scene
Tamino is described as wearing the costume of a Japanese prince.
This direction is of course disregarded in modern productions,
where Tamino is usually shown in a kind of Greek costume. There
are so many changes of scene in the opera that the method of production varies greatly from theatre to theatre; we shall therefore,
in the following analysis, deal with the settings only in the most
general way.

We are to understand that the action takes place in Egypt, in
the neighbourhood of a temple of Isis. The first scene is in the
open country. After an agitated orchestral introduction, in which
the hurry and breathlessness of Tamino are realistically sug-

gested, the hero enters, pursued by a great serpent; Tamino has a bow, but no arrows. He cries out in terror to the gods for protection, and falls exhausted upon a rock. Thereupon three veiled Ladies appear, each carrying a silver spear. They slay the serpent, congratulate themselves on their achievement, and then begin to sing the praises of the comeliness of the youth whom they have rescued from death. Were their hearts susceptible to love, they declare, it is to this fair youth that they would succumb. They will carry the news of his coming to their Queen; perhaps he will be able to bring back to her the peace that, it seems, has fled her.

Each suggests that the others shall be the bearer of the news, and each in turn politely but firmly declines to leave her susceptible sisters with so attractive a young man. Unable to agree on the matter, they at last decide to leave together, which they do after singing a charming trio, in which each of them looks forward to renewing the agreeable acquaintance as soon as possible.

When they have left the stage Tamino awakes, looks round him apprehensively and asks, " Where am I? " He is relieved to see the serpent dead at his feet, but cannot understand how the monster died. Hearing a man approaching the valley he hides himself. The merry strain of No. 5 is heard in the orchestra, interrupted occasionally by a flourish on the Pan-pipe:

at first in the distance, then drawing nearer; and at last Papageno comes upon the scene. He is in a costume mostly composed of feathers; on his back is a large bird-cage containing birds; he holds his Pan-pipe in both hands and now and then gives a flourish on it by way of accompaniment to his song, in which, for all the world as if he were presenting us with his business card, he tells us that he is a birdcatcher by profession, a man of mirth, known to old and young throughout the land; but there is an even finer trade than his, he continues — he would capture pretty girls if he could:

He is just going off with a final flourish when Tamino stops him, and a dialogue in prose ensues. Each asks the other who he is. When Tamino tells Papageno that he is of royal blood, the simple birdcatcher confesses that that is beyond him; whereupon Tamino explains that his father is a prince who rules over many lands and tribes. " Lands? Tribes? Prince? " asks the innocent Papageno; " are there then other lands and tribes beyond these mountains? " When he hears that there are many thousands of them, his first simple thought is of the glorious opportunities there must be to sell birds there.

He can give the stranger no useful information as to his own country. He does not know who rules over it, or how he himself came into it; he knows only that he has a little thatched cottage to shelter him from the cold and the rain, that he lives, like other people, by eating and drinking, and that he earns his food and drink by catching birds for the Queen of Night and her Ladies.

The Queen of Night! ejaculates Tamino aside; this must be the great person of whom he has already heard. Has Papageno seen her? No mortal has seen her, Papageno replies. " This then must be the Queen of Night of whom my father so often told me; but I cannot understand how I lost my way and came to these parts.

This man is evidently no ordinary person; perhaps he is one of her attendant spirits! "

Papageno, who is a timorous fellow at heart, does not like the way the stranger stares at him; and when Tamino says that he looks more like a bird than a man and tries to approach him, Papageno, his heart in his mouth, bids him stand back, for when he is roused he has the strength of a giant; adding under his breath, " If I don't manage to frighten him soon I shall cut and run! " If he has the strength of a giant, Tamino continues, no doubt it was he who killed the serpent and saved his life. Papageno starts in terror at the mention and the sight of the serpent, but finding that it is dead, and that the stranger is crediting him with the killing of it, he takes full credit for the deed, and boasts that he did it without weapons, by the mere strength of his arm.

He is interrupted by the re-entry of the Three Ladies, who greet him with a warning " Papageno! " He explains to Tamino that these are the Ladies who take his birds every day and give him wine, bread, and fruit in exchange for them. " They must be very beautiful," says the unsophisticated Tamino. If they were, Papageno replies, they would not veil their faces; but as another warning " Papageno! " comes from the Ladies he diplomatically adds that he never say anything so beautiful in all his life.

But the Ladies are not to be placated by this flattery. Papageno is to be punished by order of the Queen for his lies and boasting: no wine for him to-day — only cold water; no bread — only a stone; no sweet figs — but a golden padlock for his mendacious mouth; perhaps this will teach him not to tell lies to strangers. They ask him if *now* he sticks to it that he killed the serpent.

Papageno, to whose mouth one of the Ladies has fastened the padlock, can only shake his head and mumble. He does not even know who did kill the serpent; and the First Lady informs Tamino that it was she and her companions who saved him. She hands him a portrait sent him by the Queen of Night; it is that of her daughter; if the features do not find him indifferent, then happiness, honour, and fame await him. Assuring him that they shall meet again, they go off with a parting sarcasm or two for Papageno, who, greatly embarrassed, also makes his exit.

Tamino, who has been absorbed in contemplation of the portrait, sings an ardent aria in praise of the maiden's beauty:

Could he only find her, he cries, clasp her to his breast and make her his for ever!

The lovely aria over, the Three Ladies enter once more. Their royal mistress, it seems, has heard every word he said and has been favourably impressed by his appearance; if he has as much courage as tenderness he will be able to rescue the unhappy Pamina from the evil magician who one day seized her among her favourite cypress trees and carried her off.

Tamino is horrified at the information, and is drawing upon his imagination as to what may have happened to the girl when the Three Ladies reprovingly bid him not to be so doubtful of virtue; whatever miseries Pamina may have suffered, her virtue is still intact, for it is proof against both compulsion and flattery.

In some English versions the Ladies inform Tamino that the wicked magician is Sarastro, the High Priest of the Sun, but in the original libretto there is no mention of the name at this point or any hint that the captor of Pamina is the High Priest of the Sun. The malefactor so far is evidently the conventional evil magician of the popular stories; according to the Ladies, he has the power to assume any shape at will, and it was by disguising himself that he managed to decoy Pamina away.

The ardent Tamino is just imploring to be taken where he may rescue the maiden when there is a clap of thunder and the scene grows dark. These are the presages of the coming of the Queen of

Night, who now appears in the moonlight, standing in front of her throne among the stars. In a majestic recitative she exhorts the youth not to be afraid, for he is pious, gentle, and good — the sort of youth, indeed, fitted to bring consolation to a sorrowing mother's heart.

In a mournful aria:

(7) Larghetto

My days,— a - las, are spent in sor-row, for I have lost my daugh-ter dear,—
Zum Lei - den bin ich aus - er - ko-ren, denn mei-ne Toch - ter feh - let mir,—

the tells him how all happiness departed from her on the day when the miscreant carried off her daughter in spite of the anguished cries of the victim. Even the Queen's might was insufficient to rescue her; but the desired deed can be accomplished by the Prince, and when he returns victorious, she assures him in a brilliant piece of coloratura:

(8) Allegro moderato

Pamina shall be his.

There is another clap of thunder, and the Queen disappears, followed by her Ladies. It grows light again, and Tamino asks himself whether what he has seen and heard is reality or a dream. With a prayer to the gods to strengthen his arm and uphold his courage he is about to leave the stage when Papageno enters. He points sadly to the padlock as excuse for the mumbling of which alone he is now capable:

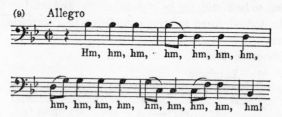

(9) Allegro

Hm, hm, hm, · hm, hm, hm, hm,

hm, hm, hm, hm, hm, hm, hm, hm, hm!

Tamino assures him that he is sorry for him but is unable to help him. The Three Ladies return, and after a few aphorisms on the wickedness of lying they remove the padlock from Papageno's mouth, leaving him free to join with them and Tamino in a quintet.

The First Lady gives Tamino a golden flute, a gift from the Queen, the magic of which, she assures him, will protect him in emergencies; it can master the passions of men, bring happiness to the sad, and even turn the bachelor's thoughts in the direction of love; it is a flute worth more than crowns and gold, for it can bring the whole world peace and contentment.

Papageno asks if he may now retire from the company, and is a little taken aback when the Ladies tell him that the Queen has appointed him to accompany the Prince on his rescue expedition. Papageno protests energetically: have not the Ladies themselves told him what a wild beast Sarastro is? The magician will have him plucked and roasted and thrown to his dogs! The Ladies try to persuade him that the Prince will protect him, but Papageno bluntly consigns the Prince to the devil; he knows what will happen — as soon as danger comes the Prince will slip away and leave him in the lurch! The Ladies give him a chime of bells which, they tell him, will protect him and the Prince. " How shall we find the way to the mountain? " asks Tamino; and in a charming trio the Ladies tell him that three Boys, young, beautiful, and wise, will direct and accompany them, giving them counsel when necessary; and bidding the pair farewell, the Ladies depart.

The scene changes to a room, splendidly furnished in the Egyptian style, in Sarastro's palace.

In the original libretto there is an opening scene that is now omitted in performance. In this, three slaves are seen bearing carpets, cushions, and a Turkish table. They are rejoicing over the latest piece of news; it seems that Monostatos, the wicked Moorish slave of Sarastro, had designs on the virtue of Pamina, but at the critical moment the maiden called on Sarastro; this scared the Moor, and while he was standing motionless with fright Pamina made her escape to the canal, jumped into a boat, and made for the palm woods. The slaves rejoiced to think of the punishment the hated Monostatos will receive from Sarastro, but just then the Moor's voice is heard behind the scenes, roughly ordering them to bring chains; and looking out they see, to their regret, that he has Pamina captive once more.

In performance the scene opens with Monostatos dragging Pamina in. At his orders the slaves fetter her, and she falls senseless on a couch. Monostatos sends the slaves away, after having rejected Pamina's appeal to give her death in preference to any other fate he may have in contemplation for her.

One of Mozart's charming little phrases now trips out in the violins, and Papageno appears in the doorway; it appears that he has strayed there by accident, and, having heard voices, thought he might as well enter. He is just addressing the beautiful maiden whom he sees before him when he and Monostatos catch sight of each other. Each is scared out of his wits, taking the other for the devil himself; and in an amusing passage each implores the other to spare him. Backing away from each other they run off in different directions.

Pamina awakes with a cry of " Mother! Mother! " and is again bewailing her fate when Papageno re-enters, calling himself a fool for having been so frightened: there are plenty of black birds in the world, so why should there not be black men? he asks. Is the maiden by any chance the daughter of the Queen of Night? If so, he has news for her. He introduces himself as Papageno, her Majesty's birdcatcher, of whom Pamina remembers that she has heard, though she has never seen him. Papageno, taking out the portrait that Tamino has given him and comparing it with Pamina, runs over the points of resemblance and difference: " Blue eyes (black) — really blue (black — red lips — really red — blond hair (brown) — everything seems correct except the hands and the feet. According to the picture you have neither hands nor feet; anyhow none are shown here." (We can imagine the guffaws that Schikaneder would draw from his audience in passages like these.)

This, indeed, is Papageno's scene throughout. With a great wealth of words, most of which are omitted in modern perform- ances, he tells Pamina of the events of the morning — how the Ladies gave the Prince her portrait, how he fell in love with the original at first sight, and how he has been appointed by her mother to rescue her.

Pamina is gratified by this intelligence, but cannot refrain from asking why, if the Prince is so madly in love with her, he is so long in coming to rescue her. Papageno has to explain that the three beautiful Boys whom the Ladies promised as guides having failed to appear, the Prince sent him on in advance to announce his coming. Pamina compliments him on his courage, but warns him that if Sarastro finds him there he will die a painful death. " In that case," says Papageno, " the sooner we go the better "; and Pamina agrees with him, for according to the position of the sun it must be near midday, and at midday Sarastro is in the habit of returning from the hunt.

Pamina for a moment has her doubts: what if Papageno were merely a decoy — another of Sarastro's wicked spirits? Papageno assures her that there is nothing wicked about him; he is as good a spirit as was ever on the earth; and, convinced by the evidence of the portrait that her mother has really a hand in the affair, she puts her fears aside again.

Papageno accepts her compliments on his good-heartedness, but confides to her his secret sorrow — Papageno has no Papagena, no little wife, not even a sweetheart, and there are times when he would be glad of a bit of pleasant company. Pamina exhorts him

to have patience, for heaven will surely send him a little friend
of his own sort one of these days; and this gives the cue for an
exquisite little duet on the universality of love and the depth of
its joys:

The man - ly heart that claims our
Bei Männ - ern, wel - che Lie - be

du - ty, must glow with feel - ings high and
füh-len, fehlt auch ein gu - tes Her - ze

brave.
nicht!

They go out singing, and the scene changes.

We see a grove, with three Temples. The centre one, which is
the largest, bears the inscription, " Temple of Wisdom." The right-
hand one is inscribed, " Temple of Reason," and that on the left,
" Temple of Nature." The Temples are joined by colonnades. The
three Boys (Genii), each with a silver palm-branch in his hand,
enter, leading Tamino, from whose neck hangs the magic flute.
From this point onward, in spite of an occasional touch of comedy, the opera is filled with a high seriousness. It is henceforth
dominated by Sarastro and the moral ideas of which he is the
embodiment.

In a solemn trio:

the Genii, having conducted Tamino to his goal, take leave of
him, exhorting him, through whatever dangers may beset him, to
be " steadfast, silent, and obedient."

Left alone, Tamino muses upon their words, which have graven
themselves deeply on his heart, and surveys the three Temples,
which, he thinks, must surely be the abode of the gods. Conscious
of the purity of his purpose and the nobility of his mission, he
goes to the right-hand entrance, but is sternly ordered to " Stand
back! " by a bass voice from within. He is similarly repulsed from
the left-hand entrance. Then he knocks at the central door. An
aged priest (the Orator) appears on the threshold, and a long
dialogue in recitative ensues.

Tamino learns that he has come to the Temple of Sarastro,
whom he forthwith reviles as the master of cruelty and lies; the
proof, he says, is a woman's tears that he has seen. The Priest
assures him he has been deceived: " A woman does little, but
chatters much; and it is like a boy to believe her." It is true that
Sarastro has taken Pamina from her mother, but in time he will
set forth his reasons for that act.

Eagerly Tamino asks where Pamina is, but the Priest only
replies, " Dear son, that I am not yet permitted to tell thee: my
tongue is bound by a solemn oath." " When will the bond of
silence be broken? " asks Tamino; and the Priest, to one of the
most solemn musical phrases in the whole opera:

(12)

replies, " When thou art led by friendship's hand to join our
Temple's sacred band." Voices from an invisible chorus bid
Tamino have courage and seek for the light, and assures him that
Pamina still lives.

Tamino takes up his flute, and to show his gratitude to the mighty ones he plays a melody upon it, which he then makes the main tune of the song that follows:

(13) Andante

Thy mag - ic tones shall speak for me and bear—— my mes - sage,

Wie stark ist nicht dein Zau - ber-ton! weil, hol - de Flö - te,

The aria is interspersed throughout with flute obbligati, of which the following is an example:

(14)

and in the original Vienna production wild animals came out to listen — evidence of the power of the magic flute to charm all created things.

At the end of this aria Tamino calls for Pamina. No reply comes from the maiden, but he is answered behind the scenes by Papageno's usual flourish (No. 4) on his Pan-pipe. Perhaps Papageno has found Pamina, he surmises; and he hastens away to find him in one direction just as Papageno and Pamina come on from the opposite side. They are in flight, and searching anxiously for Tamino. Papageno gives his usual whistle, which is answered from a distance by the flute, and the pair are just about to make off in quest of Tamino when they are intercepted by Monostatos and the slaves.

The latter are about to put fetters on Papageno and Pamina, and the situation begins to look desperate, when Papageno, as a last chance, plays a delightfully naïve melody on the magic bells given him by the Three Ladies. The effect is magical; just as Tamino's flute enchanted the animals, Papageno's Glockenspiel sets Monostatos and the slaves dancing and singing in the most absurd fashion. They finally dance themselves off the stage, and Papageno and Pamina sing a charming little duet in praise of the music of the bells; had everyone such a chime, they say, foes would be turned to friends, and everyone would live in the most beautiful harmony.

They are interrupted by the sound of voices behind the scenes, crying, " Long life to Sarastro! " The frightened Papageno wishes he were a mouse, that he might creep into a cranny and hide, but Pamina bravely swears that for her part she will face Sarastro and tell him the truth.

In the original, Sarastro was supposed to come in on a triumphal car drawn by lions; but modern theatres that lack a menagerie have to be content with a more modest production. Sarastro enters in great pomp, accompanied by Priests, men-at-arms, women, and slaves. He steps out of the car, and Pamina, throwing herself at his feet, confesses that she had tried to escape, but only to evade the unwelcome attentions of the Moor. In a grave and tender melody Sarastro comforts her with the assurance that he knows the secret of her heart, and that while he will never compel her to love, it is too soon as yet to set her free. She must put her mother from her thoughts, for restoration to her would be the end of all her happiness: " A man must guide your steps, for woman alone can never find the path that leads to wisdom."

Monostatos now runs in, dragging with him Tamino. Tamino and Pamina fall into each other's arms with ecstatic cries, but are parted by Monostatos, who, kneeling before Sarastro, tells how the audacious youth, aided by this other fellow who is half bird, half man, had tried to run off with the maiden. Modestly Monostatos claims the reward for his watchfulness and devotion, and gets it from the undeceived Sarastro — in the form of a sound bastinado.

The protesting Moor having been dragged off by the slaves,

Sarastro orders his followers to lead the two young strangers to the Temple of Probation, first veiling their heads. Tamino and Pamina are veiled by the Priests, and while Tamino and Papageno are led off to the right of the scene by two of the Priests, Sarastro, taking Pamina by the hand, goes with her to the middle door of the Temple, the chorus the while, to the accompaniment of the solemn trumpets and trombones, singing in praise of Sarastro, virtue, and justice.

ACT II

The second act is mainly concerned with the initiation of Tamino and Pamina into the mysteries. The opening setting is a palm grove. Sarastro and the Priests enter to the strain of a solemn march, at the conclusion of which Sarastro addresses the Priests in speech.

The Prince Tamino, he tells them, is waiting at the northern gate of the Temple, desirous to have the veil removed from him that he may see the sacred light. He assures the Priests, in reply to their questions, that Tamino is virtuous, that he can be silent, and that he is beneficent. The Priests blow their trumpets in sign of approval (the solemn brass chords with which the overture opens), and Sarastro, continuing, tells them that the gods have destined Pamina for this youth; it was for that reason that he removed her from the keeping of her mother, " that woman who, swollen with her power, thinks to dazzle the people with superstitions and destroy our Temple; but this she shall not accomplish." (Schikaneder's audience would no doubt take this as a fairly pointed reference to the anti-Masonic Empress Maria Theresa.)

Let Tamino, then, be initiated into the mysteries, continues Sarastro, and united with Pamina, and so ensure the safety of the Temple, the triumph of virtue, and the chastisement of evil-doers. Once more Sarastro and the Priests blow the usual chords three times on their trumpets. The first Priest (the Orator) asks whether Tamino will have strength to bear the ordeals that await him: " He is a Prince," he objects. " He is more," replies Sarastro; " he is a man." If, unable to endure to the end, he should perish in his youth, he will then be in the hands of Isis and Osiris, " and will know the joys of the gods sooner than we "; and again the three-fold chord is sounded.

Sarastro orders the Priests to conduct Tamino and his companion into the forecourt of the Temple, where the Orator will instruct them in their duty to the gods. Then Sarastro sings his majestic aria, the invocation to the gods, " O Isis and Osiris ":

(15) Adagio

O I - sis and O - si - ris,
O I - sis and O - si - ris,

lead ye in wis - dom's path this
schen-ket der Weis - heit Geist dem

faith - ful pair!
neu - en Paar!

to which the trombones lend their usual solemn colour.

The scene changes to the forecourt of the Temple. It is night, and distant thunder is heard as Tamino and Papageno are led in by the Orator and the second Priest, who remove the probationers' veils and then leave them. Papageno is horribly scared by the darkness and the thunder, but will not admit it; he pretends that if he feels shivers all down his back it is because a fever is coming on. " Be a man! " exhorts Tamino; and we can imagine the laugh Schikaneder would evoke with his reply, " I'd rather be a girl! "

Two Priests enter with lights, and the strangers are catechised. Tamino declares that it is friendship and love that have brought him within the Temple walls, and that for these he is ready to lay down his life if need be. He seeks wisdom and Pamina's love as his reward. Papageno, for his part, does not care a rap for wisdom; he is a simple child of nature, he says, wanting nothing more than food, drink, and sleep, and, if he could find it, a little wife into the bargain.

Hopes are held out to him of a wife, pretty, young, and feathered like himself, and bearing the name of Papagena. He prudently asks for a sight of the lady before he commits himself to matrimony, and is warned that though he may see her he must not speak to her till the appointed time. The same law of silence is imposed upon Tamino with regard to Pamina; this, indeed, is the first stage of his probation. The two Priests sing a duet warning Tamino and Papageno in particular, and the world in general, against the wiles of woman, and go out, taking the lights with them.

Tamino is just exhorting the frightened Papageno to be patient, for all this is the will of the gods, when the Three Ladies enter. They have been sent by the Queen of Night to warn Tamino against the trickery of the Priests, who will work his ruin, for whoever joins their band is doomed to everlasting perdition. Tamino sternly rejects their blandishments, while Papageno keeps interjecting naïvely comic remarks characteristic of his own Sancho Panza-like point of view. Disturbed by a chorus of the Priests behind the scenes, cursing these women who have profaned the sanctuary, the Three Ladies sink down into the earth, whereupon Papageno falls prostrate in terror. The Orator and the two Priests re-enter, congratulate Tamino on having been so steadfast, throw a veil over his head, and lead him away for further trials, Papageno following them in the company of the Priests.

The scene changes to a garden; Pamina is lying sleeping, and Monostatos is gazing longingly at her; from his opening speech we realise that even a good bastinadoing has not been able to damp the fire of this irrepressible amorist. He thinks he might venture just one kiss at any rate, and in a lively song:

(16) Allegro

All con-fess the ten-der pas-sion, bill and
Al - les fühlt der Lie-be Freu-den, schnäbelt

coo, and sigh for love,
tändelt herzt und küsst;

he asks why, seeing that love is universal, he should be barred
from it merely because he is black. A kiss he means to have, and
if the moon is likely to be shocked at the sight, let it close its eye!

He is interrupted in his fell purpose by the Queen of Night,
who enters from the back and dramatically bids him begone.
Pamina's ejaculation of " Mother! " apprises him that the new-
comer is the Queen, and he sneaks off into safety.

Pamina, who still believes in her mother, suggests that they
shall fly together, but the Queen confesses that she can no longer
shield her daughter; when Pamina's father died, it seems, he
handed over to Sarastro the sevenfold Shield of the Sun, and the
power that goes along with it. Only one chance remains; Pamina
is to take the dagger she now offers her, kill Sarastro, and bring
her mother the Shield of the Sun. The horrified Pamina protests,
but the Queen imperiously silences her and breaks out into the
celebrated coloratura aria.

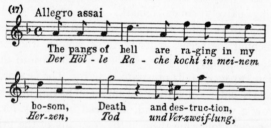

in which she casts all tender thoughts from her and calls for the
vengeance of hell upon Sarastro. For a soprano who has the F *in
altissimo* in her voice some of the coloratura passages present
magnificent opportunities for display:

After a last vigorous cry for vengeance the Queen of Night disappears, and Pamina, left with the dagger in her hand, is once more protesting that she cannot shed blood when Monostatos, rushing in and snatching the dagger from her, tells her that he now has both her and her mother in his power. There is only one way, continues the dusky blackmailer, by which Pamina can save herself — she must love *him*.

Pamina's tremulous ejaculation, " Ye gods! " seems amply justified under the circumstances. She falls on her knees and implores the Moor to spare her, but his only reply is to offer the stern alternative of love or death. Maddened at her refusal he is just about to stab her, when Sarastro comes between them and hurls him back. Monostatos drops on his knees and tries to justify himself by saying that Pamina intended to take Sarastro's life, but Sarastro, with the uncomplimentary remark that the Moor's soul is as black as his face, orders him away. But Monostatos, who in his way is as simple a child of nature as Papageno, manages to raise a last laugh from the audience by saying as he goes out, " If I can't have the daughter, I'll try my luck with the mother! "

Pamina begins to plead for her mother, but Sarastro gently interrupts her. He knows everything, he says; the Queen of Night plots vengeance against him in the subterranean chambers of the Temple, but if heaven grants Tamino courage and steadfastness in his trials Pamina shall be his, and her mother will retire baffled to her mountain. As for himself, he declares, in perhaps the noblest of all the noble melodies in *The Magic Flute:*

(19) Larghetto

With - in this hal - low'd dwell-ing re -
In die - sen heil'-gen Hal - len kennt

-venge and sor - row cease,
man die Ra - che nicht,

he knows no thought of vengeance, for the law of their community is friendship and love.

ACT III

The scene changes once more to a hall, into which Tamino and Papageno, unveiled, are led by the two Priests. They are told to remain there alone, and, as soon as they hear the trumpets sound, to proceed in the direction of these. The Priests leave them with a parting warning to them to remember their oath of silence, Papageno being further told that whoever breaks the silence in that sacred place is struck down by the gods with thunder and lightning.

But nothing in heaven or earth or the waters under the earth can keep Papageno's tongue quiet for long, and in spite of Tamino's attempts to hush him down he persists in chattering away. An ugly old woman enters with a cup of water which she offers to Papageno, and the birdcatcher welcomes the opportunity for a little sprightly conversation after his own heart. He learns, to his surprise, that the old woman is just eighteen years and two minutes old, and has a sweetheart just a little older than herself, by name Papageno. She is just about to tell him her own name when there is a crash of thunder and she hobbles away as fast as she can.

The three Genii now enter, carrying a table spread with food and drink, the magic flute, and Papageno's chime of bells. They greet the pair, they say, for the second time, now within Sarastro's own domain; he sends them the flute and the bells that have been taken from them, and food to refresh them; at their third meeting their virtue shall find its reward. They go out with a parting admonition to Tamino to be brave, for the goal is near, and to Papageno to be silent.

While Tamino is playing upon his flute and Papageno is devoting himself to the food and wine, Pamina enters and runs towards Tamino, who, however, mindful of his vow of silence, motions to her to depart. She naturally does not understand his silence, and, thinking he no longer loves her, bewails her vanished happiness in a mournful aria:

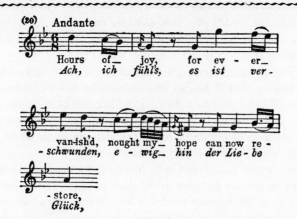

(20) Andante

Hours of— joy, for ev - er -
Ach, ich fühl's, es ist ver -

van-ish'd, nought my— hope can now re -
- schwunden, e - wig— hin der Lie - be

- store,
Glück,

Papageno, who has been feasting joyously, is just praising
Sarastro's cook and cellar-master when the trombones are heard
behind the scenes. Tamino motions to Papageno to go with him,
but the birdcatcher, according to the original libretto, refuses to
leave his excellent meal " even if Sarastro were to let loose his
six lions on him." Thereupon six fearsome lions enter and threaten
Papageno, who cries out in terror to the gods and Tamino. The
hero blows a strain on his flute, and the lions, their angry passions
calmed by music, go out again. This little episode is of course
omitted in modern performances.

The trombones ring out again, and Tamino drags his companion
out, Papageno protesting that there is no hurry, as they will get
there in quite time enough to be plucked and roasted.

In the next scene, which may be staged somewhere near the
Pyramids, Sarastro and the Priests (with torches) enter to the
strain of a solemn invocation to Isis and Osiris, to whose service
the noble youth is about to dedicate himself. At Sarastro's command Tamino, veiled, is brought in, followed by Pamina, also
veiled; she is told that Tamino is waiting to bid her a last farewell. Sarastro removes Tamino's veil, and Pamina runs towards
him, but he orders her back. There follows a short trio, Pamina
again mourning her incomprehensible fate, Tamino strengthening
himself for the coming ordeal, and Sarastro bidding both be brave,

for when the trial is over they shall see each other again. Sarastro takes Tamino by the hand and leads him away, the two Priests departing in the opposite direction with Pamina.

When the stage is empty Papageno enters, scared out of his wits and vowing that if he can find Tamino he will never leave him again. He goes first to a door on the left and then to one on the right, and from each he is ordered back by a voice behind the door. A flash of fire and a roll of thunder add to his terror. Thoroughly sorry for himself, he bursts into tears.

The Orator enters and tells him that he deserves to be sentenced to wander for ever in the dark passages of the earth, but the gods, it seems, have pardoned him, though he is too degraded ever to know the heavenly joys of the initiated. The greatest joy he can think of at the moment, says Papageno, is a glass of wine. The Orator leaves him, the stage grows dark for a moment, and a great cup filled with wine comes up out of the earth. Tossing the wine down, Papageno feels so happy that he bursts into a song in praise of love:

(21) Andante

A maid-en fair and slen-der is
Ein Mäd-chen o-der Weib-chen wünscht

what I fain would own,
Pa-pa-ge-no sich,

Ah, if only he had a little turtle-dove of his own, how happy he would be! (The melody is derived in part from the old German chorale, " Nun lob mein' Seel' den Herren.")

The Old Woman comes in again, dancing and supporting herself on a stick. She tells him that if he will swear to be true to her she will love him very tenderly, but when he asks for time to think it over she sternly warns him that if he delays giving her his hand he will be imprisoned and put on bread and water for the rest of his days. This is too much for Papageno: better an old wife, he says, than none at all! Giving her his hand, he promises to be true to her until, he adds under his breath, he meets with someone prettier. Instantly the Old Woman is transformed into a young one, covered with feathers. Papageno manages to stammer out "Pa-pa-papagena!" and is just about to embrace her when the Orator comes in and, declaring that he is not yet worthy of her, drags Papagena out, and, when poor Papageno attempts to follow, pushes him back. Papageno runs out after them, crying piteously, "Papagena! Papagena!"

The next scene shows us a palm garden. The Three Genii enter and sing a trio in greeting to the rising sun:

They are interrupted by the entry of Pamina, in a state of great distraction, and carrying the dagger she received from the Queen of Night. They are in time to prevent her from stabbing herself; they bid her not to despair, as Tamino still loves her, and offer to conduct her to him.

In the next scene we see two Men in Armour standing at each side of a door in a rock; on one side of the door, through a grating, there is visible fire, on the other water. After a solemn orchestral prelude, some of the material of which is used as accompaniment to the vocal melody that follows, Tamino is brought in by the Priests, and the two Men in Armour sing in octaves of the necessity of ordeal by fire and water for him who would overcome the fear of death. The broad, somewhat stiff melody is that of the old chorale, "Ach Gott vom Himmel sieh darein," with a slight modification of Mozart's own at the end.

Just as Tamino is swearing his readiness to bear any trial, the voice of Pamina is heard outside. She is brought in, and the lovers are now permitted to speak to each other. Lovingly and trustingly, hand in hand, they enter the doors and are seen passing through the fire, Tamino playing on his flute. They reappear on the stage, untouched by the flames, and pass through the next ordeal, that of water, whereupon they are welcomed at the now open gate of the Temple by Sarastro and the Priests and conducted inside.

The scene changes to a garden. We hear Papageno's Pan-pipe flourish, and the now doleful birdcatcher enters, carrying a rope with a noose; he has lost his Papagena, and means to hang himself. He prudently and hopefully takes as long as possible over the preliminaries, and delays so long that there is time for the Three Genii to enter and prevent him. At their command he performs on his magic bells:

(23) Allegro

Chim- ing sweet and   clear - ly,
Klin - get, Glöck-chen,   klin - get,

let   my maid - en   hear!
schafft mein Mäd-chen   her!

and the Genii, who have gone out for a moment, return with Papagena. There is a delicious duet between Papageno and Papagena, packed with the simple enchantment of which Mozart alone among musicians has ever had the secret; they will pair now, they say, and soon there will be a nest of little birds, first a little Papageno, then a little Papagena, then another Papageno, then another Papagena, and so, presumably, *ad infinitum:*

(24)

the pret - ty dar- ling Pa - pa -
wenn vie - le Pa - pa - pa - pa -

- ge- nas, Pa - pa - pa - pa - pa - pa -
- ge- na, Pa - pa - pa - pa - pa - pa -

- ge- nas, Pa - pa- pa- pa- pa- pa - ge - nas.
- ge- na, Pa - pa- pa- pa- pa- pa - ge - na.

The happy couple go out arm-in-arm, and the scene changes for the last time.

It is night, in a setting of rocky country. Monostatos enters, beckoning forward the Queen of Night and the Three Ladies, who have lighted torches in their hands. They are approaching the Temple to wreak vengeance on Sarastro and the good Priests, the promised reward for Monostatos's treachery being the hand of Pamina. There is a crash of thunder, and with a cry that their power is shattered the conspirators disappear. The Temple becomes visible, and in it Sarastro, Tamina, Pamina, the Genii, Priests, and others. The deeply impressive opera ends with a chorus of thanks to Isis and Osiris and congratulations to the young couple who by their courage, fidelity, and virtue have won through to beauty and wisdom:

(25) Andante

Hail,   ye true and   faith - ful,
Heil   sei euch Ge - weih - ten,

hail,   ye true and   faith - ful,
Heil   sei euch Ge - weih - ten!

T HE Beethoven family, on its male side, was of Belgian extraction. We find it first near Louvain in the seventeenth century, and later at Antwerp. The composer, by reason of his thick black hair and his swarthy complexion, was often referred to by his friends as " the Spaniard "; and when we take into consideration the Spanish occupation of the Netherlands in the seventeenth century it is not at all improbable that there was a certain amount of Spanish blood in him.

Beethoven's grandfather, Louis van Beethoven, was born at Antwerp on the 23rd December, 1712, left home at about the age of nineteen, and two years later was settled at Bonn, on the Rhine, as a bass singer in the service of the Elector of Cologne, of whose territories Bonn was part. He died there in 1773, after forty-two years' service at the Court. He married in 1734; the son who survived him, Johann, was born in Bonn at the end of 1739 or the beginning of 1740; he too — a tenor — was part of the Court and theatrical establishment of the little town, which at the end of the century had a population of about nine thousand. His mother had been addicted to drink, and Johann inherited this failing from her.

In 1767 he married Maria Magdalena Haym (née Kewerich) a young widow of less than nineteen years; her father was head cook at the palace of Ehrenbreitstein. Three children survived her — Ludwig, the composer (probably born 16th December, 1770 [1]), Caspar Anton Carl (baptised 8th April, 1774), and

---

[1] The exact date is not known for a certainty, as we have only the official record of the date of baptism. But as it was the custom of the country

Nikolaus Johann (baptised 2nd October, 1776). We shall hear more of both of these brothers in the sequel.

The mother was a serious woman, inclined to melancholia — a friend said she had never seen her laugh; the deaths of her father, her mother, and her first husband almost before she had reached the age of twenty may have predisposed her to gravity, and life with Johann, on an insufficient salary and with three boys to bring up, was not calculated to restore either her health or her spirits. Three other children did not survive infancy: one of them lived only six days, another only five, and the third two years and a half. Frau Beethoven died of consumption in 1787, at the age of forty.

The child Ludwig showed no such precocious gift for music as Mozart had done, and would perhaps not have been forced into the musical profession had his father not been in it himself; but it was necessary for the boy to help to increase the scanty income of the family as soon as possible, and the father gave him the rudiments of a musical education with an eye to a future post in the Elector's Kapelle. He received spasmodic instruction later from others, including Van den Eeden, the Court organist (then a very old man; he died in 1782), and from the latter's successor Neefe, a sound musician who gave the boy a good grounding in organ and piano playing and composition.

Ludwig was expert enough on the piano to perform in public when he was seven years old; and for a time he acted as assistant to Neefe at the organ as cembalist in the theatre orchestra, though without salary. It was not until the spring of 1784 that he was appointed assistant Court organist. Just about that time Elector Max Friedrich died; the theatrical company was dismissed with four weeks' wages, and the new Elector Maximilian Franz, wishing to economise at first, relied for some three years upon visiting companies for his theatrical fare. Beethoven thus had no duties

---

at that time to baptise a child within twenty-four hours of its birth, and the baptismal entry was made in the parish records on the 16th December, we are fairly safe in taking the 16th as the birthday.

except as organist, and consequently could call a large amount of time his own for study and other work.

In the spring of 1787 he spent a little while in Vienna — how he obtained the money is not known for certain — and took a few lessons from Mozart, who is said to have prophesied that " one day he will give the world something to talk about." The last illness of his mother recalled him to Bonn, where he was visited by one of those fits of melancholy to which he was always subject; he suffered from asthma, and thought that he too was threatened with consumption.

When the Elector reconstituted his theatre in 1788, Beethoven entered the orchestra as violin player; in that capacity he served some four years, making the acquaintance of a large number of operas of all schools. By this time he was contributing materially to the income of the family; his father was giving way more and more to drink, and in 1789 he was pensioned off, half his salary being paid to him henceforth, the other half going to Ludwig as the new head of the family.

The young man's life must have been hard and cramped; even at this time he felt his own power and originality, and Bonn must have come to seem too small a field for the full development of his talents. Already, however, he had made friends who were, in various ways to be of the greatest service to him then and for many years after.

One of the most respected residents of the town was Frau von Breuning, who, at the age of twenty-eight, had been left a widow by the death of her husband, the Court Councillor von Breuning, who perished in a fire in the palace. She was well-to-do and lived in a fine house with her four children. One of these, Stephan, who was born in 1774, had been a pupil of Ries, the violinist, at the same time as Beethoven; and the two boys soon became fast friends. Beethoven was a constant visitor at the house, where he was treated by Frau von Breuning — a woman of high character, sound sense, and great tact and forbearance — as one of the children of the family; she could generally manage the wayward, moody, obstinate young genius when no one else could do anything with him.

Another friend and benefactor of these and later days was Ferdinand Ernst Gabriel Count Waldstein, a young scion of one of the noblest of the Austrian houses. He was born in 1762, and was therefore eight years older than Beethoven, whose acquaintance he seems to have made on a visit to Bonn in 1787. He not only loved music but practised it very competently. He was one of the first to sense the coming genius in Beethoven, and both with his purse and by his influence he did much to ease his path through these critical years of adolescence. The young musician was already, in spite of the disadvantages of his humble birth and the bad record of his father, a welcome guest of more than one rich house. With two of his well-to-do pupils, Jeannette Honrath and Maria van Westerhold, he fell deeply in love; the former, however, married the later Field-Marshal Greth, while Maria became the wife of Baron Friedrich von Elverfeldt.

Already Beethoven had become so outstanding a figure in the local musical life that it was felt he ought to try to establish himself, at any rate for a time, in one of the greater musical centres. He was known as a remarkable pianist, and his compositions, which as yet, of course, circulated only in manuscript, had convinced a good many thoughtful connoisseurs that he would prove to be the successor of Mozart, who had died in 1791.

Perhaps it was in large part through the good offices of Count Waldstein that Beethoven received permission from the Elector, in the autumn of 1792, to betake himself to Vienna for the purpose of further study under Haydn. His letters of the time show that he contemplated a return to Bonn sooner or later, but as events turned out he was never to see his native place again; Vienna remained his home for the rest of his days.

An indication of the esteem in which he was held is to be found in the inscription made by Waldstein in the album which, in accordance with the practice of the time, was presented to him, with suitable messages, by his intimate friends on his leaving Bonn: " Dear Beethoven! You are going to Vienna in fulfilment of your long-frustrated wishes. The Genius of Mozart is mourning and weeping over the death of her pupil. She found a refuge but no occupation with the inexhaustible Haydn; through him she wishes to form a union with another. With the help of assiduous labour you shall receive *Mozart's spirit from Haydn's hands.* Your true friend, Waldstein. Bonn, October 29, 1792." [2]

Beethoven arrived in Vienna about the 11th November. At first he was supported by the Elector, and when the composer's father died, on the 18th December, the 100 thalers of the latter's pension was granted as salary to the son. But evil days were dawning for the Elector as for so many other German princes. The new French Republic was at war with the German State, and when the French armies crossed the Rhine in the autumn of 1794 the Elector and his Court took to flight. The ultimate arrangement come to as regards Beethoven seems to have been that he was granted indefinite leave of absence from Bonn, but without salary until he should be recalled.

He was now strong enough, however, to stand on his own feet. His fame had preceded him, his social recommendations were valuable, his patrons were influential, and this protégé of the Elector was bound to be well received by the latter's nephew, the Emperor of Austria. For a long time he lived in the same house as Prince Carl Lichnowsky, one of the numerous members of the Austrian aristocracy who were passionately interested in music.

Almost all these grandees maintained private musical establishments of one kind or another. Sometimes, as in the case of Haydn's patrons, the Esterhazys, it was a complete concert orchestra, together with soloists; in others, sufficient instrumentalists for the accompaniments to the Mass in the private chapel; in others, an ensemble of string or wind players for the " table music "; in others, a quartet or sextet that met regularly for practice. Vienna at that time was rich in music of all sorts, operatic, church, and instrumental; but it was the last-named that was rapidly coming to be regarded as the specific Viennese contribution to the history of the art, and it was destined to find its culmination in Beethoven, though the tradition was still carried on, more than half a century later, by Brahms and Bruckner.

[2] The translation of this and other contemporary documents in the present " Life " is that of Thayer.

Beethoven was in great demand as teacher, piano soloist, improviser, and composer; in 1796 and 1797 a number of his works appeared in print, including the song " Adelaide," the Three Trios (op. 1), the three early piano sonatas dedicated to Haydn, the quintet for strings (op. 4), the two 'cello sonatas (op. 5), and the E flat piano sonata (op. 7). The originality and audacity of his early works were a great attraction to music lovers of the time.

A countryman of ours, William Gardiner, made the acquaintance in Leicester, in 1793, of a manuscript trio in E flat (op. 3, not published till 1797); Gardiner himself played the viola part in it. " This composition," he afterwards wrote, " so different from anything I had ever heard, awakened in me a new sense, a new delight in the science of sounds. . . . When I went to town [London] I enquired for the works of this author, but could learn nothing more than that he was considered a madman and that his music was like himself." Elsewhere he speaks of this first experience of Beethoven's music as " a new sense to me, an intellectual pleasure which I had never received from sounds."

Beethoven was making a good income and living well, perhaps by way of reaction against the privations of his early years; at one time he permitted himself the luxuries of a horse and a personal servant. He still had, to some extent, his two younger brothers on his hands, but as they grew older they became more able to take care of themselves. In 1795 they both settled in Vienna. The elder of the two, Carl Caspar, had been trained in music, and was soon able to maintain himself fairly comfortably by teaching; the younger, Johann, had been apprenticed to the Bonn Court apothecary, and now became an assistant in an apothecary's shop in Vienna. He prospered as the years went on, and ultimately bought and carried on successfully a business of his own.

Beethoven at this time was a man of great bodily strength, illimitable ambition, vast self-esteem, and a strength of character that very often showed itself as immovable obstinacy. On his first settling in Vienna he took lessons from old Haydn, but the setting star and the rising one appear to have agreed none too well. Beethoven, though he realised the need for more technical study, was already conscious of his gifts as a composer, and no doubt chafed at being pegged back by his master and kept at dry contrapuntal exercises. Haydn, for his part, was probably too much occupied just then to have much time to spare for close personal attention to this fiery young pupil who was always straining at the pedagogic leash.

In after-years Beethoven said that though he had had lessons from Haydn he had learned nothing from him; and he seems to have worked with a greater will under his next master, Albrechtsberger; but it must have been difficult all along for him to live, as it were, a double musical life during these years, a pupil in private and a much-sought-after composer and piano virtuoso in public. From the opera composer Salieri he also took lessons, mostly in the art of writing for the voice.

His friend Ries wrote long afterwards concerning this period of Beethoven's life: " I knew them all well [i.e. his three masters]; all three valued Beethoven highly, but were also of one mind touching his habits of study. All of them said Beethoven was so headstrong and self-sufficient that he had to learn much through harsh experience which he had refused to accept when it was presented to him as a subject of study."

He made his first appearance in Vienna as composer and performer on the 29th March, 1795, when he played the solo part in his piano concerto in B flat; while on the 31st he played in a Mozart concerto (probably the D minor) after the first part of a performance of *La Clemenza di Tito* that had been got up by Mozart's widow. In February 1796 he went concertising in Prague and Berlin; it is probable that the King of Prussia, Frederick William II, offered him a Court appointment, which he refused.

During this period there was more than a touch of arrogance about him: the rough giant had not yet been tamed by misfortune and suffering. His manners were none of the best, and it was sometimes only by the exercise of the greatest tact that his friends, who admired and loved him, could avoid a quarrel. Prince Lichnowsky cheerfully submitted to having his domestic arrangements upset by the caprices of the erratic young composer, and even

went so far as to tell his servant that if Beethoven's bell and his
own rang at the same time he was to attend to Beethoven first.

The huge explosive force of the young genius, bursting as he
generally was with the pride of his own strength, could with difficulty be held in check by his will. He was careless of other people's
feelings, yet exceedingly prone to take offence himself; but his
repentance was usually as quick and as sincere as his anger.
An undated letter he wrote about this time to his friend Wegeler
is typical of his alternations between unreasoning rage and almost
incoherent remorse:

" Dearest! Best! In what an odious light you have exhibited me
to myself! I acknowledge it, I do not deserve your friendship.
You are so noble, so considerate, and the first time that I arranged myself alongside of you I fell so far below you! . . . You
think that I have lost some of my goodness of heart, but, thank
heaven! it was no intentional or deliberate malice which induced
me to act as I did towards you; it was my inexcusable thought-
lessness which did not permit me to see the matter in its true light.
Oh, how ashamed I am, not only for your sake but also for my
own. . . . Oh, let me say for myself, I was always good, and
always strove to be upright and true in my actions — otherwise
how could you have loved me? Could I have changed so fear-
fully for the worse in such a short time? Impossible; these feelings of goodness and love of righteousness cannot have died for
ever in me in a moment. No, Wegeler, dearest, best, oh, venture
again to throw yourself entirely into the arms of your Beethoven;
trust in the good qualities you used to find in him; I will guarantee that the pure temple of sacred friendship which you erect
shall remain firm for ever; no accident, no storm shall ever shake
its foundations — firm — for ever — our friendship — pardon —
oblivion — a new upflaming of the dying, sinking friendship — oh,
Wegeler, do not reject this hand of reconciliation. Place yourself
in mine — oh God! — but no more; I am coming to throw myself in your arms, to entreat you to restore to me my lost friend.
And you will give yourself to me, your penitent, loving, never-
forgetting Beethoven again."

He was nearing his thirtieth year, and was superbly conscious of his gifts and his growing importance; and it is interesting to speculate as to what would ultimately have become of him had the whole course of his outer life not been changed about that time by the oncoming of deafness. He would certainly have made virtuoso tours all over Europe; as he himself says in a later letter, but for his deafness he would have travelled over half the earth by now.

He found plentiful favour in Vienna, but also abundance of opposition; for Vienna was the southern German Mecca of musicians in those days, and new-comers of great ability were anything but welcome to the people who had already attained to vested interests there. Beethoven would be doubly unwelcome — as a stranger from the outside world, and as a performer and composer of exceptional talent.

As was the custom in those days, he often measured himself, in drawing-rooms, against this or that local or visiting pianist as performer and improviser; and the universal verdict was that though others might surpass him in grace and style, he had no equal for fire and power and the gift of moving the heart. But his manners towards his rivals and his audiences were hardly calculated to endear him to either.

A contemporary account in a musical journal (1799) shows him in rivalry with a young pianist, Joseph Wölffl, two years younger than himself, whose exquisite piano playing had won for him a large number of admirers, so that the town was divided between his partisans and those of Beethoven. The writer praises Wölffl's ease, precision, and clearness, and his graceful expression in adagios, while Beethoven bears the palm for brilliance and intellectual power. The article concludes thus: " That Wölffl likewise enjoys an advantage because of his amiable bearing, contrasted with the somewhat haughty pose of Beethoven, is very natural."

Ludwig, indeed, himself confesses that he had no use for certain people except so far as they could be of service to him. "I value them," he says in one of his letters, " only by what they can do

for me. . . . I look upon them only as instruments upon which
I play when I feel so disposed." His self-esteem was a byword in
the town: old Haydn's humorous way of asking after him was,
" Well, how goes it with our Great Mogul? "

Beethoven was in great demand by the publishers, he was recognised as, in some respects, the greatest pianist of the day, and
he felt a titanic force of creation within himself; so it is hardly to
be wondered at if, judged by ordinary social standards, he lost
his head occasionally. The most tolerant of all with him were his
aristocratic patrons; probably it was easier for them to smile at
his rudenesses, his gaucheries, and his fits of temper because, after
all, the social gulf between him and them was too great ever to
be completely bridged. It was people in the middle walk of life,
and still more his colleagues and rivals, who found his arrogance
and brusquerie most trying. He was, in fact, torn asunder by two
opposing elements of his nature. On the one hand he took as his
ideal a life of love and service to mankind; on the other he found
himself forced by the very strength of his body and spirit, neither
of which could tolerate even a hint of subjection, into exaggerated
expressions of independence.

He anticipated Nietzsche's doctrine of the Will-to-Power:
" The devil take you," he writes to one of his friends (Zmeskall),
" I want none of your moral [precepts], for Power is the morality
of men who loom above the others, and it is also mine." It must
have been in some such mood as this that he made his famous
answer to the lady who asked him if he went to hear Mozart's
operas: " I do not know them," he said, " and I do not care to
hear the music of others lest I forfeit some of my originality."

The painters and the sculptors have gone on idealising more
and more, during the last hundred years, the portraits and busts
of Beethoven; they show him not as he really was, but as they
imagine the composer of the Ninth Symphony and the Mass in D
and the last quartets *must* have been. His contemporaries did
not see him like that, and especially the contemporaries of the
first half of his life, before any of his supreme masterpieces had
been written.

He was plain and pock-marked, while his manners never lost the roughness of his first upbringing. But plain as he was, he had, for a time, aspirations to be a buck; he had hardly settled in Vienna before he bought himself fashionable clothes and took lessons in dancing, though the attempt to become a dancer was soon given up. He was as susceptible to flattery as he was resentful of an injury, or a supposed injury; and unfortunately he more than once got into the hands of the wrong people who knew how to work upon his vanity. But with all his obvious failings he won the utmost devotion from the many friends who could not help seeing the fundamental bigness not only of the musician but of the man.

None of them had any doubt that out of this somewhat cubbish young fellow was to come the greatest composer of the new day; and Prince Lichnowsky's settlement upon him of an annuity of 600 florins until such time as he should obtain a worthy and profitable official post was typical of the length to which his admirers were prepared to go in order to give his genius every opportunity.

If ever there was sexless music in this world it is that of Beethoven; nowhere does it play upon the merely sensuous side of mankind, while at its best it soars into heights that are above and beyond sex, heights upon which only the spirit at its purest can breathe. But Beethoven himself, especially in his early manhood, was of a notably amorous nature.

His life-long friend Wegeler said of him: " The truth as I learned to know it, and also my brother-in-law Stephan von Breuning, Ferdinand Ries, and Bernhard Romberg, is that there was never a time when Beethoven was not in love, and that in the highest degree. . . . In Vienna, at all events so long as I lived there, Beethoven was always in love, and occasionally made a conquest which would have been very difficult if not impossible for many an Adonis."

During the period we are now considering he made a proposal of marriage to the beautiful Magdalena Willmann, a native of Bonn who had made a reputation as a singer and was at the time engaged at the Vienna Opera. Thayer, the biographer of Beethoven, met, in 1860, a daughter of Magdalena's brother Max, who told him she had often heard her father speak of the affair. When Thayer asked her why her aunt had refused the composer, she burst out laughing and said, " Because he was so ugly, and half crazy! "

During these years he was writing a great deal of music of all genres, and a considerable portion of it was published. It is not always possible to determine precisely when a particular work of his was written, owing to his habit of dropping a work for a time and taking it up again, and also owing to the fact that the date of publication does not necessarily indicate the date of composition; but we know certainly that among the works of 1798–9 are the three trios for strings (op. 9), the five piano sonatas of op. 10 and op. 14, the Sonata Pathétique (op. 13), the three violin sonatas (op. 12), the first two piano concertos, the First Symphony (which was performed on the 2nd June, 1800), and a number of variations.

To the next year belong the ballet *The Men of Prometheus,* the six quartets of op. 18, the septet (op. 30), the B flat piano sonata (op. 22), the third (C minor) piano concerto, and the oratorio *The Mount of Olives;* and to 1801 the violin sonatas op. 23 and op. 24, the piano sonatas in A flat, E flat, C sharp minor, and D major (op. 26, op. 27, Nos. 1 and 2, and op. 28), the C major quintet (op. 29), and other works. The C sharp minor sonata is the one that afterwards became known as the " Moonlight," and quite a number of people believe to this day that it was meant as a sort of declaration of romantic love for Beethoven's pupil the Countess Giulietta Guicciardi. The truth is that the title of the " Moonlight " was not affixed to it till long after, and then not by Beethoven; that the work was prompted by the reading of a poem by Seume, in which a girl kneels at the altar and prays for her sick father; and that although the sonata is certainly dedicated to Giulietta it was not written for her. To Giulietta he had given a rondo, but as he afterwards wanted this for another person he begged it back from the former and gave her this sonata in exchange.

The whole course of Beethoven's outer life and his spiritual development were changed by the deafness that, by the period to which we have now arrived, had already become of the greatest seriousness. Its inexorable progress made the career of a travelling virtuoso henceforth impossible; he was thrown back more and more upon composition as an outlet for his activity, and driven further and further inwards upon himself.

Neither the precise date nor the precise cause of the malady can now be determined. As to the latter, two legends may be disposed of at the commencement. One is that in 1796 Beethoven, coming indoors on a hot summer day, stripped to the skin and stood by an open window to cool himself, thus bringing on a dangerous illness that ended in deafness. The other came from Charles Neate the English pianist, to whom Beethoven told, in 1815, a strange story of how a tenor had given him a great deal of trouble over an opera aria, which had had to be re-written three times to suit him. Just when Beethoven was congratulating himself on having got rid of him, the tenor returned. Beethoven sprang up in a rage and threw himself at full length on the floor: when he arose he found he was deaf. There can be no question of Neate's *bona fides;* so we are simply left wondering at Beethoven's motives in telling him so fantastic a story.

The trouble seems to have begun about 1799. The first symptoms he seems to have disregarded; but in a year or so he had become thoroughly alarmed at his condition, and by 1801 he had to give up the idea of touring as a pianist. For as long as he could he concealed his misfortune from everyone, even his closest friends, partly out of sensitiveness, partly because he was afraid his Vienna enemies and rivals would use the knowledge to his detriment.

We have the first full account of the matter from his own hand in a letter of 29th June, 1801, to his friend Wegeler. Worldly matters, he says, are going well with him; Lichnowsky has settled on him the annuity we have already mentioned; " besides I have six or seven publishers, and might have more if I chose; they no longer bargain with me — I ask, and they pay."

But his " evil demon," his " bad health," is continually putting a spoke in his wheel. For three years his hearing has steadily been getting worse, for which he blames his "wretched bowels." (All his life he suffered from a sort of dysentery.) He has tried various doctors, some of them moderately sensible, others, in his opinion, asses; under the latest of them the dysentery has improved, but he still suffers from a continuous whistling and buzzing in the ears, day and night. " I can say I am living a wretched life; for two years I have avoided almost all social gatherings because it is impossible for me to say to people: ' I am deaf.' If I belonged to any other profession it would be easier, but in my profession it is an awful state, the more since my enemies, who are not few, what would they say? "

At the theatre he has to sit near the stage to hear the actors; at a little distance the high tones of instruments and singers escape him, and at a further distance he does not hear at all. He can hear the sounds of a conversation in low tones, but not the words; and when people shout it is intolerable. His friends, who do not know his real condition, put it down to absent-mindedness. " I have often cursed my existence: Plutarch taught me resignation. If possible I will bid defiance to my fate, although there will be moments in my life when I shall be the unhappiest of God's creatures." Wegeler is not to mention the secret to anyone, not even to his wife (Eleanore von Breuning).

In 1802, walking in the country with his pupil Ries, the latter drew his attention to a shepherd who was piping on a home-made flute: Beethoven could hear nothing, and became silent and morose.

He spent the summer of this year at Heiligenstadt, a village close to Vienna, where he could be at once in the country and within easy reach of Vienna and his physician. For a time his courage seems to have failed him, and he penned an extraordinary document that is known as the Heiligenstadt Testament. It was addressed to his brothers, but was never sent to them, though it is evident from the condition of the manuscript that he had made a fair copy with the greatest care: it was found in a bundle of papers bought, after his death, by the publisher Artaria. A curious and inexplicable feature of the document is that nowhere does he mention his brother Johann by name. The Testament must be given in full:

"For my brothers Carl and   Beethoven.

"O ye men who think or say that I am malevolent, stubborn or misanthropic, how greatly do ye wrong me, you do not know the secret causes of my seeming, from childhood my heart and mind were disposed to the gentle feeling of good will, I was even eager to accomplish great deeds, but reflect now that for 6 years I have been in a hopeless case, aggravated by senseless physicians, cheated year after year in the hope of improvement, finally compelled to face the prospect of a *lasting malady* (whose cure will take years or, perhaps, be impossible), born with an ardent and lively temperament, even susceptible to the diversions of society, I was compelled early to isolate myself, to live in loneliness, when I at times tried to forget all this, O how harshly was I repulsed by the doubly sad experience of my bad hearing, and yet it was impossible for me to say to men speak louder, shout, for I am deaf.

"Ah how could I possibly admit an infirmity in the *one sense* which should have been more perfect in me than in others, a sense which I once possessed in highest perfection, a perfection such as few surely in my profession enjoy or ever have enjoyed — O I cannot do it, therefore forgive me when you see me draw back when I would gladly mingle with you, my misfortune is doubly painful because it must lead to my being misunderstood, for me there can be no recreation in society of my fellows, refined intercourse, mutual exchange of thought, only just as little as the greatest needs command may I mix with society, I must live like an exile, if I approach near to people a hot terror seizes upon me, a fear that I may be subjected to the danger of letting my condition be observed — thus it has been during the last half year which I spent in the country, commanded by my intelligent physician to spare my hearing as much as possible, in this almost meeting my present natural disposition, although I sometimes ran counter to it yielding to my inclination for society, but what a humiliation when one stood beside me and heard a flute in the distance and *I heard nothing* or someone heard *the shepherd singing* and again I heard nothing, such incidents brought me to the verge of despair, but little more and I would have put an end to my life — only art it was that withheld me, ah, it seemed impossible to leave the world until I had produced all that I felt called upon to produce, and so I endured this wretched existence — truly wretched, an excitable body which a sudden change can throw from the best into the worst state — Patience — it is said I must now choose for my guide, I have done so, I hope my determination will remain firm to endure until it pleases the inexorable parcae to break the thread, perhaps I shall get better, perhaps not, I am prepared.

" Forced already in my 28th year to become a philosopher, O it is not easy, less easy for the artist than for anyone else — Divine One thou lookest into my inmost soul, thou knowest it, thou knowest that love of man and desire to do good live therein. O men, when some day you read these words, reflect that ye did me wrong and let the unfortunate one comfort himself and find one of his kind who despite all obstacles of nature yet did all that was in his power to be accepted among worthy artists and men.

" You my brothers Carl and   as soon as I am dead if Dr. Schmid is still alive ask him in my name to describe my malady and attach this document to the history of my illness so that so far as is possible at least the world may become reconciled with me after my death. At the same time I declare you two to be the heirs of my small fortune (if so it can be called), divide it fairly, bear with and help each other, what injury you have done me you know was long ago forgiven.

" To you, brother Carl, I give special thanks for the attachment you have displayed towards me of late. It is my wish that your lives may be better and freer from care than I have had, recommend *virtue* to your children, it alone can give happiness, not money, I speak from experience, it was virtue that upheld me in misery, to it next to my art I owe the fact that I did not end my life by suicide — Farewell and love each other — I thank all my friends, particularly *Prince Lichnowsky* and *Professor Schmid* — I desire that the instruments from Prince L. be preserved by one of you but let no quarrel result from this, so soon as they can serve you a better purpose sell them, how glad will I be if I can still be helpful to you in my grave — with joy I hasten towards death — if it comes before I shall have had an opportunity to show all my artistic capacities it will still come too early for me despite my hard fate and I shall probably wish that it had come later — but even then I am satisfied, will it not free me from a state of endless suffering? Come when thou wilt I shall meet thee bravely — Farewell and do not wholly forget me when I am dead, I deserve this of you in having often in life thought of you how to make you happy, be so ——

" LUDWIG VAN BEETHOVEN.

(Seal.)

" HEIGLNSTADT (*sic*),
October 6th,
1802.

" For my brothers Carl and   to be read and executed after my death.

" Heiglnstadt, October 10th, 1802, thus do I take my farewell of thee — and indeed sadly — yes that beloved hope — which I brought with me when I came here to be cured at least in a degree — I must wholly abandon, as the leaves of autumn fall and are withered so hope has been blighted, almost as I came — I go away — even the high courage — which often inspired me in the beautiful days of summer — has disappeared — O Providence — grant me at last but one day of pure *joy* — it is so long since real joy echoed in my heart — O when — O when, O Divine One — shall I feel it again in the temple of nature and of men — Never? — no — O that would be too hard."

But the fit of despair seems to have been of short duration; Plutarch perhaps helped him to win the mastery over himself and to refrain, at the last moment, from sending the document to his brothers. That his strong spirit could not have dallied long with these moods of self-pity is shown by the list of remarkable works he wrote or completed in 1802: it includes the second symphony, the three violin sonatas of op. 30, the first of the piano sonatas numbered op. 31, the sets of Variations, op. 34 and 35, and the Bagatelles, op. 33. He also saw a number of works through the press.

It was known that Beethoven possessed certain bank shares in his last years. After his death the certificates for these were looked for everywhere in vain, until one of his associates and confidants, Holz, told the searchers of a secret drawer in Beethoven's desk. There they found not only the certificates but some letters. One of these has caused more speculation than anything else in connection with him. The document consists of a letter with two postscripts, written in lead pencil on two pieces of note-paper. They are here quoted in full:

" July 6, in the morning.

" My angel, my all, my very self — only a few words to-day and at that with pencil (with yours) — not till to-morrow will my lodgings be definitely determined upon — what a useless waste of time. Why this deep sorrow where necessity speaks — can our love endure except through sacrifices — except through not demanding everything — can you change it that you are not wholly mine, I not wholly thine. Oh, God! look out into the beauties of nature and comfort yourself with that which must be — love demands everything and that very justly — *thus it is with me so far as you are concerned, and you with me.* If we were wholly united you would feel the pain of it as little as I.

" My journey was a fearful one; I did not reach here until 4 o'clock yesterday morning; lacking horses the post-coach chose another route — but what an awful one. At the stage before the last I was warned not to travel at night — made fearful of a forest, but that only made me the more eager and I was wrong; the coach must needs break down on the wretched road, a bottomless mud road — without such postilions as I had with me I should

have stuck in the road. Esterhazy, travelling the usual road hither-
ward, had the same fate with eight horses that I had with four —
yet I got some pleasure out of it, as I always do when I successfully overcome difficulties.

"Now a quick change to things internal from things external!
We shall soon surely see each other; moreover, I cannot communicate to you the observations I have made during the last few days
touching my own life — if our hearts were always close together
I would make none of the kind. My heart is full of many things
to say to you — Ah! — there are moments when I feel that speech
is nothing after all — cheer up — remain my true, my only treasure, my all as I am yours; the gods must send us the rest that
which shall be the best for us.

"Your faithful LUDWIG.

"*Evening, Monday, July* 6.
"You are suffering, my dearest creature — only now have I
learned that letters must be posted very early in the morning.
Mondays, Thursdays, — the only days on which the mail-coach
goes from here to K. You are suffering — Ah, wherever I am there
you are also. I shall arrange affairs between us so that I shall
live and live with you, what a life!!!! thus!!!! thus without you
— pursued by the goodness of mankind hither and thither —
which I as little try to deserve as I deserve it.

"Humility of man towards man — it pains me — and when
I consider myself in connection with the universe, what am I and
what is he whom we call the greatest — and yet — herein lies
the divine in man. I weep when I reflect that you will probably
not receive the first intelligence from me until Saturday — much
as you love me, I love you more — but do not ever conceal your
thoughts from me — good-night — as I am taking the baths I
must go to bed. Oh, God! so near, so far! Is our love not truly a
celestial edifice — firm as Heaven's vault.

"*Good-morning, on July* 7.
"Though still in bed my thoughts go out to you, my Immortal

Beloved, now and then joyfully, then sadly, waiting to learn whether or not fate will hear us. I can live only wholly with you or not at all — yes, I am resolved to wander so long away from you until I can fly to your arms and say that I am really at home, send my soul enwrapped in you into the land of spirits. — Yes, unhappily it must be so — you will be the more resolved since you know my fidelity — to you, no one can ever again possess my heart — none — never — Oh God, why is it necessary to part from one whom one so loves and yet my life in W [Vienna] is now a wretched life — your love makes me at once the happiest and the unhappiest of men — at my age I need a steady, quiet life — can that be under our conditions?

" My angel, I have just been told that the mail-coach goes every day — and I must close at once so that you may receive the L. at once. Be calm, only by a calm consideration of our existence can we achieve our purpose to live together — be calm, — love me — to-day — yesterday — what tearful longings for you — you — you — my life — my all — farewell — Oh continue to love me — never misjudge the most faithful heart of your beloved L.

ever thine
ever mine
ever for each other."

As will be seen, the letter bears no definite date and no indication of place; and the unravelling of the mystery has exercised the wits of numberless investigators. The " Immortal Beloved " is held by some to have been the Countess Giulietta Guicciardi, with whom Beethoven was undoubtedly in love when she was his pupil (in 1801), at which time she would be about the age of seventeen. In November 1801 he writes to Wegeler of his lonely and sad life for the last two years, by reason of his bad hearing, but says that now a change has been wrought " by a dear, fascinating girl who loves me and whom I love." For the first time he feels that marriage might bring him happiness, but " alas, she is not of my station — and now — it would be impossible for me to marry."

This girl was almost undoubtedly Giulietta. It is unlikely that her family would have countenanced the marriage in any case; and in 1803 she married a Count Gallenberg. Beethoven referred to the affair nearly twenty years later, in a conversation with his friend Schindler, who had called on Gallenberg in connection with the score of *Fidelio:* " I was much loved by her, — more than ever her husband was. . . . She was born Guicciardi. She married him before he went to Italy. When she came to Vienna she sought me out in tears, but I scorned her."

It was natural to assume that this must have been the lady to whom the " Immortal Beloved " letter was written, but the evidence is now generally recognised to be against the theory. Other names that have been suggested are those of Therese Malfatti, who in 1806 or 1807 (the probable date of the letter) would be a girl of only thirteen or fourteen, Amalie Sebald, and the Countess Therese von Brunswick, a young cousin of Giulietta. The sole clue to the year is that afforded by the " Monday, July 6." The only years in which July 6th was a Monday were 1795, 1801, 1807, and 1812; and for various reasons none of these years can come into the question except 1807. Thayer, however, believes that Beethoven, as was not unusual with him, made a mistake of a day in the heading of the postscript, and decides that the year was 1806, in the summer of which year the composer was in Hungary, and that the " Immortal Beloved " was Therese von Brunswick, the daughter of a Hungarian nobleman. After the problem has been looked at from every possible angle, Thayer's solution of it remains the most credible.

In 1803 Beethoven left behind him his period of brilliant apprenticeship and showed himself a master. Remarkable as the second symphony was, it was far outdistanced by the third (the Eroica) that was written in 1803, a year that saw also the production of the Kreutzer violin sonata and other works.

The oratorio *The Mount of Olives* was given on the 5th April, 1803, at a concert the programme of which included also the first and second symphonies and the C minor piano concerto; audiences of that day thought nothing of monster programmes of this kind, though they generally tired towards the end of the concerts. Beethoven's popularity was so great that he could charge double prices for some seats, triple for others, and quadruple for the boxes: his profits amounted to 1,800 florins. George Thomson, of Edinburgh, the collector of Scots folk-melodies, entered into negotiations with Beethoven for the composition of six sonatas on Scots airs, but the composer's demand of 300 ducats was twice what Thomson was prepared to pay. Some years later Beethoven made arrangements for Thomson of various Scots and other songs.

In this same year Beethoven took to live with him his brother Carl, who proved very useful as a negotiator and secretary in the many dealings with publishers. Carl was rather a pompous ass, but the absurd self-importance that breathes through some of his letters to publishers may be partly accounted for by his sense of his brother's high standing in the musical world. Carl, by the way, married, on the 25th May, 1806, Theresia Reiss, the daughter of a well-to-do upholsterer; on the following 4th September there was born to the couple that son — another Carl — who was to be so grievous a trouble to the composer in his last years.

The year 1805 saw the production in Vienna (on the 20th November) of Beethoven's solitary opera *Fidelio,* the success of which was more than dubious; it was badly rehearsed, and some of the singers were inefficient. The work ran to only three performances.

It has been said that Beethoven's disgust at this reception of his opera made him resolve never to touch the genre again, but this is not true. He was continually searching, in the next few years, for a suitable text; he coquetted for a time with a *Macbeth,* and would have taken up Goethe's *Faust* had he been able to find someone who could make a good libretto out of it. At various times in later years he composed three overtures for *Fidelio* in addition to the one that was played at the first performance. The comparative failure of *Fidelio* was due mainly to the city's having been emptied of a number of the more well-to-do families because of the swift advance of the French upon it; it was entered by the enemy on the 13th November.

In the autumn of 1806 Beethoven suggested to the new management of the Court Theatre that he should be engaged, at a
fixed salary of 2,400 florin per annum plus certain gross receipts,
to supply at least one opera and an operetta each year. The offer
was not accepted; Beethoven's deafness must have been felt to be
too great a disability in an opera-house. To soften the blow of the
refusal, one of the directors, Prince Esterhazy, commissioned
from him the Mass in C, which was given at the Prince's house,
Eisenstadt, on the name-day of the Princess, 13th September.

In the main, the record of the years 1806, 1807, and 1808, like
that of their immediate predecessors, is one of incessant creation;
among the works of this period are the fourth, fifth, and sixth
symphonies, the Rasoumovsky quartets, the *Coriolan* overture,
the fourth piano concerto, the 'cello sonata (op. 69), the two
trios of op. 70, and the Choral Fantasia. Count Rasoumovsky, the
Russian Ambassador at Vienna, was a man of great wealth and
decided musical gifts. Into the quartets that he commissioned of
Beethoven the composer introduced a couple of Russian folk-
tunes. The Count formed a first-rate quartet ensemble for practice in his palace: the great Schuppanzigh was the first violin, the
Count himself the second, Weiss the viola, and Linke the 'cello.

By this time Beethoven had become less sensitive about his
deafness, which could no longer be concealed from the world, but
his bad temper and his arrogance showed no signs of improvement.
In 1808 he quarrelled with his brother Johann, the apothecary,
because the latter dared to ask him for money he had lent him.

Johann wanted to buy a house and shop in Linz, the purchase-
money for which he had difficulty in scraping together. Beethoven
took offence and swore he would never write to his brother again.
As usual, it was utterly impossible for him to believe that when
a difference of opinion arose anyone could be in the right but
himself. Johann, by the way, did very well out of his shop the
next year, when he secured a contract for the supply of medicines
to the French army that was in the neighbourhood.

One of the tasks of recent biographers of Beethoven has been
to clear a number of people of the aspersions cast upon them by

the composer. The earlier tendency was to assume sympathetically that he was always right and the others always wrong; but a sober study of the documents proves that in most cases it was Beethoven who was in the wrong. His combination of almost complete ignorance of the world, bad health, quick temper, touchiness, and suspicion made it inevitable that he should again and again take offence where none was intended, and give wounds that it sometimes took years to heal.

His pupil Czerny, in later years, energetically combated the legend that had got about that Vienna had behaved badly to Beethoven. The truth is, say Czerny, that even as a youth he had received extraordinary consideration and respect from the highest aristocracy there. " Later, too, when he estranged many by his hypochondria, nothing was charged against his often very striking peculiarities; hence his predilection for Vienna, and it is doubtful if he would have been left so undisturbed in any other country. It is true that as an artist he had to fight cabals, but the public was innocent in this. He was always marvelled at and respected as an extraordinary being, and his greatness was suspected even by those who did not understand him."

He was indeed difficult to get on with, and his deafness and self-absorption made him particularly difficult in practical matters, especially conducting. In 1808 he had somehow or other so angered the orchestra that the men, while willing enough to play his works, would do so only on condition that he should not be present at rehearsals. He could not hear everything distinctly, and when he was conducting he was so lost in his dreams that he could not be trusted to count correctly, or to give proper leads.

It was shortly after the affair just mentioned that the orchestra broke down under him during a concert performance of the Choral Fantasia: Beethoven stopped them and compelled them to begin again. The men naturally felt humiliated and resentful; but Beethoven had the grace afterwards to admit that his own absence of mind was the cause of the disaster, and to apologise to the orchestra. Yet in spite of his glaring faults of character and temper there was a something about him that endeared him to his friends. Ries tells us that he was a thoroughly good and kind man, the victim of his own whims and impulsiveness; his anger with anyone would vanish as soon as he found they were in trouble, and he was always ready to assist any charitable undertaking, of which there were necessarily many during the war. When he was in a good humour people found him irresistible.

It has been remarked that while he poured out work after work in the decade from 1800 to 1810, from 1810 to 1819 his output was, for him, curiously small. It is true that during this period he was much engaged in proof-reading and in business correspondence concerning his music, but not notably more so than in the earlier years. There may possibly have been a little physical and intellectual fatigue after the great exertions of the previous decade; but his comparative inactivity between 1810 and 1819 was no doubt due largely to his mind being preoccupied with other things than music, and especially love and finance.

In 1810 we find him becoming very particular about his clothes and his appearance once more: he seems to have proposed marriage — it is thought to Therese Malfatti, now of the age of about seventeen — and to have been considerably depressed by a refusal. A little while later he is seen taking great pleasure in the company of Marie Bigot, Amalie von Sebald, and other ladies; and some investigators hold that the " Immortal Beloved " letter really belongs to 1812, the object of his passion then being that Therese von Brunswick of whom mention has already been made.

It was in 1810 that he met one of the most extraordinary young women of the day, who, like most of the other women in Beethoven's life-story, has been the cause of much research, still more speculation, and yet more diversity of opinion. This was Elizabeth (Bettina) Brentano, the young sister of his friend Clemens Brentano; she is generally referred to, however, by her married name of von Arnim.

She was a young person of considerable intelligence and great literary skill, who exercised a curious fascination upon Goethe, with whom she was corresponding at this time. She made Beethoven's acquaintance in the spring of 1810. By her own account he took to her so promptly as to have long talks with her in which he expressed himself with a fluency and at a length that must have been uncommon with him. She has been roundly accused of inventing these conversations; but the probability is that in her letters to Goethe she merely gave the dressing of her own vivacious style to Beethoven's remarks. He certainly could never have talked as she makes him talk; but he as certainly can be conceived as giving utterance to the ideas that form the basis of her dashing literary performances.

In 1839, twelve years after his death, there were printed in a German journal "Three Letters from Beethoven to Bettina." Over these a stormy controversy has raged. Their genuineness has been denied, asserted, re-denied, and re-asserted *ad infinitum;* but the general opinion is now that the second at least — of which the autograph is in existence — is genuine, while the other two may have been flights of fancy on Bettina's part, based, perhaps, on actual conversations with the composer. Whatever be the truth of the matter, there can be no question of the great interest that Beethoven, like many other eminent men of the day, felt in this remarkable young woman.

It was while Beethoven was taking a " cure " at Teplitz in 1812 that he and Goethe were able to gratify their long-standing wish to meet each other. The poet wrote to his wife, after their first meeting: " A more self-contained, energetic, sincere artist, I never saw: I can understand right well how singular must be his attitude to the world." In a later communication to his friend Zelter he says: " His talent amazed me; unfortunately he is an utterly untamed personality, and altogether in the wrong in holding the world to be detestable, but who does not make it any the more enjoyable for himself or others by his attitude."

During the visit to Teplitz there occurred the famous scene that has so often been described. Teplitz was full of notabilities that season. One day after Beethoven had been boasting to Goethe of his high-handed dealings with monarchs and princes they met the whole Court, including the Empress of Austria and the various Archdukes. Beethoven said to the poet, " Keep hold of my arm;

let them make room for us, not we for them." Goethe refused;
he stood on one side, and complied with the etiquette of the day
by standing with his hat off till the Empress had passed. Beethoven walked through the party with his arms folded and his
hat "only slightly tilted." The Archdukes, who had more native
good breeding than he had, and considerably more *savoir faire*,
merely smiled pleasantly and made way for the licensed eccentric.

The incident has been rather strangely supposed to illustrate
Beethoven's contempt for rank. On the contrary, his frequent
rudeness to rank was a sign of how much, in reality, it counted
with him. At an early stage of his career he had been greatly
angered by being put at another dining-table than that of the
highest ranks of the company; but his anger was soon appeased
when room was made for him at this very table. It never seemed
to occur to him that his deliberate rudeness to certain highly
placed people, such as the Archduke Rudolph, who became his
pupil, was made possible and safe for him only by a breeding and
good humour and kindly tolerance on their part that were lacking on his.

Towards the end of 1808 he was offered the post of Kapellmeister by Napoleon's younger brother Jerome, who had been
made King of Westphalia. The salary was 600 gold ducats; the
duties were light, and Beethoven was disposed to accept the offer.
When this became known in Vienna it was felt that it would be
discreditable to lose him merely because the city could not offer
him a permanent official post. Accordingly three of his chief patrons, the Archduke Rudolph, Prince Lobkowitz, and Prince Ferdinand Kinsky, undertook to provide him with a yearly sum of
4,000 florins until he should receive an appointment of the same
value; should no such appointment be received, or should Beethoven be incapacitated by old age or accident, the annuity was to
be for life.

The Archduke's share of the guarantee was 1,500 florins, Lobkowitz's 700, Kinsky's 1,800. In return Beethoven pledged himself
to make his domicile in Vienna or some other Austrian city, and
not to leave it except " for such times as may be called for by his

business or the business or the interests of art, touching which, however, the high contributors must be consulted, and to which they must give their assent." The agreement was dated 26th February, 1809.

Beethoven, during the negotiations, had shown himself anxious to be appointed to a Kapellmeistership at the Austrian Court, and it was understood that if at any time he should receive such an appointment he should forgo as much of his claim on the 4,000 florins as his salary would amount to. It must have been evident to everyone but himself that with his deafness and his faults of temper and manner it was out of the question that he should be given a position of authority in any opera-house; Jerome's desire to have him at Cassel was merely the desire to have the acknowledged greatest of living musicians to ornament his Court. He would hardly have been of much practical use.

When it was understood that he was not going to accept the Cassel appointment, it was offered to his pupil Ries at a smaller salary. Ries sought Beethoven out to find out if he had really refused the offer, and to ask his advice; but when, with great difficulty and after a delay of some weeks — during which even his letters on the matter were not answered — he at last found Beethoven, the latter simply said, in a cutting tone, " So — do you think that you can fill a position that was offered to me? " He was cold and haughty.

The next morning, when Ries called for an explanation, he was told by the servant that his master was not at home, though Ries could hear him playing in the next room. Ries took the servant by the throat and hurled him aside, and forced Beethoven to listen to him. After he had explained the situation, Beethoven simply said, " I did not understand that it was like that; I was told you were trying to get the appointment behind my back." Ries assured him that he had not yet even replied to the invitation, and then Beethoven volunteered to put things right. It was now too late, however; the appointment had been given to someone else.

In May 1809 the French armies were approaching Vienna (the city surrendered on the 12th), and Beethoven's pupil and patron the Archduke Rudolph left Vienna with his mother the Empress; Beethoven's grief at parting from him found expression in the first movement (" Farewell ") of the sonata " Les Adieux, l'Absence, et le Retour " (op. 81a); the " return " of the Archduke took place on the 30th January, 1810.

One economic result of the war was a forced loan on all rentals, that penalised Beethoven in common with other householders. Another was that in 1811 the Austrian Government had to issue a " Finance Patent " reducing money values to one fifth.

It used to be thought that Beethoven's annuity was thus automatically reduced from 4,000 florins to 800; but seemingly under the scale that was established it was reduced only to $1,612\frac{9}{10}$ florins. His patrons, being honourable men, would willingly have made up the difference. Rudolph did so; but Kinsky first of all fell into arrears with his payments, and then, in November 1812, was thrown from his horse and killed. Beethoven's claim against his estate for the full original annuity could not, of course, be admitted by the executors till a court of law had sanctioned it; so that, with one thing and another, he received nothing at all under the Kinsky part of the agreement from 3rd November, 1812, to 31st March, 1815. Lobkowitz had almost ruined himself in theatrical management, and from him nothing was received from September 1811 until April 1815. Beethoven flew into his usual temper, and, forgetting past benefits, spoke of his unfortunate patron as " that rascal Lobkowitz."

An act of Beethoven's in the autumn of 1812 was destined to have dire consequences for himself in the future. One of his curious little weaknesses was his passion for interfering in the private lives of his brothers. Johann, the apothecary, was at this time a man of thirty-five years, and no doubt thought himself fully competent to look after himself in the ordinary affairs of life. Ludwig thought differently.

Johann's new house in Linz being too large for him, he rented part of it to a physician from Vienna, who brought with him his wife's sister, Therese Obermayer, by all accounts a more than ordinarily attractive woman. In Johann's case the attraction was so strong that from being his housekeeper, as she was at first, she became his unmarried wife.

Most people would have said that this was nobody's affair but his own. When Ludwig heard of it, however, he descended upon Linz and on Johann, and with an air of authority demanded that the liaison should end. Johann naturally resented this officious interference on the part of his musical brother from Vienna. His opposition only developed Ludwig's natural obstinacy. He first saw the local Bishop about it, then the civil authorities, and actually obtained an order to the police to remove the girl to Vienna by a certain date if she should not have left Linz of her own accord by then. A quarrel ensued between the brothers, and the result of it all was that Johann, to keep the girl with whom he was in love, married her on the 8th November. There was nothing for it but for the defeated Ludwig to return to his camp in mortification. When the marriage turned out unhappily, as it did in later years, Johann was able to hurl at his brother the reproach that it was all his work.

Untaught by this lesson not to interfere with the private affairs of his relations, Ludwig was to bring further trouble upon himself in the years to come by his attitude towards the wife of his other brother, Carl. This latter, by the way, thought he was dying of consumption in the spring of 1813, and made a written "declaration" asking the court to appoint Ludwig guardian of his son. Carl recovered, however, perhaps as a result of an improvement that took place about that time in the state of his finances; for he too, being a Government official, had suffered by the war.

In 1813, and at intervals for some years afterwards, Beethoven thought seriously of going to England, where he was highly thought of, in quest of further fame and, what was still more important, money. On the 21st June, 1813, Wellington won the battle of Vittoria, and a certain Maelzel thought he ought to turn this resounding event to profit.

Maelzel, whose name is now remembered chiefly in connection with his metronome, was a clever inventor. He had recently produced a " Panharmonicon," a sort of military orchestra worked by a bellows, the general principle of the thing being that of the barrel-organ — i.e. a revolving cylinder with pins. On this instrument various works were played, to the great delight of the simpler members of the public.

Maelzel wanted something from the greatest composer of the day, and persuaded Beethoven to write for the Panharmonicon a descriptive piece entitled *Wellington's Victory*, now more generally known as *The Battle of Vittoria;* it was to have *Rule, Brittania* and *God Save the King* in it. Maelzel soon saw the commercial possibilities of the overture, and, with his eye ultimately on London, got Beethoven to arrange it for the orchestra, in which form it was a huge success in Vienna. In the course of the next few months *The Battle of Vittoria* was the cause of a quarrel with Maelzel, whom Beethoven was imprudent enough to sue; the matter ended, a few years later, in each of them agreeing to pay half the expenses incurred by Beethoven's action. The project for a visit to London with Maelzel naturally fell through.

In February 1815 Sir George Smart gave *The Mount of Olives* in London, following it up with *The Battle of Vittoria*, which became so popular that Smart netted £1,000 out of it. The final result of some correspondence between Beethoven and his English friends was that the Philharmonic Society ordered from him three concert overtures, for which he was paid 75 guineas. Instead of sending them, however, three new works, as they had expected, he sent them three old ones, *King Stephen, The Ruins of Athens,* and the *Namensfeier* (written for the name-day of the Emperor). These were, for him, inferior works, and as they would have made a poor impression on audiences that had learned to admire the Fifth Symphony, it was impossible to perform them, and the Society naturally felt somewhat aggrieved at Beethoven's conduct.

His dealings with England as a whole, indeed, though financially profitable to him, hardly add to one's respect for him as a man. In the spring of 1816 he had arranged with the London publisher Birchall for the sale of the English rights of publication of the trio in B flat, the G major violin sonata, and the piano arrange-

ments of *The Battle of Vittoria* and the Seventh Symphony, for
the sum of £65. Before he would sign the agreement on these lines
that had been forwarded to him, Beethoven sprang on Birchall
a demand for an additional £5 — £2 10s. extra for the trio, £1 10s.
for copying, and £1 for postage. Birchall sent the £5, but the incident got Beethoven in bad odour in the London publishing world.
When Neate went round trying to sell on Beethoven's behalf the
three overtures, he was everywhere cold-shouldered; Birchall's
blunt answer to him was, " If you gave me them for nothing
I would not print them."

In the summer of 1817 the Philharmonic Society approached
him again through his old pupil Ries, who was then living in
London. The Society offered him 300 guineas (100 in advance
for travelling expenses) to go to London the next winter with two
new symphonies. Beethoven demanded an *extra* 100 guineas for
travelling expenses, and payment of 150 guineas at once. The
Society refused his terms and repeated its own, which he accepted;
but instead of getting on with the expected Ninth and Tenth Symphonies, he settled down to the composition of the big B flat piano
sonata (op. 106).

He was always pleading poverty at this time, but was probably
not so poor as he made out. Matters with the Kinsky executors
were settled in March 1815 by the payment to him of 2,479
florins and the arrangement of an annuity on new terms; from
then to the end of his life he received 1,500 florins per annum
from the Archduke, 1,200 from the Kinsky estate, and 700 from
that of Lobkowitz. The latter's revenues were now out of his
control; in twenty years or so he had dissipated an enormous fortune in the patronage of art. " Although," he wrote generously in
1814 to the Archduke, " I have reason to be anything but satisfied with Beethoven's behaviour towards me, nevertheless . . . I
am rejoiced that his truly great works are beginning to be appreciated." He died in December 1816, in his forty-third year.
Another generous friend, Prince Carl Lichnowsky, had died in
April 1814.

Beethoven's anxiety about money during these and the later

years was the result in large part of the new responsibilities that had fallen upon him in connection with his nephew Carl. The latter's father had died on the 16th December, 1815: the cause of death was consumption, but Beethoven, with his usual suspicion of people he did not like — and he probably never disliked any-one so much as he did his brother's widow — thought he had been poisoned and insisted on a post-mortem!

The elder Carl, by his will made two days before his death, appointed Ludwig guardian of his son; but he added a codicil to the effect that as he had learned that Beethoven proposed to take the boy entirely away from his mother and bring him up himself, " and inasmuch as the best of harmony does not exist between my brother and my wife," his wish was that the boy should not be taken away from his mother but remain with her as long as " his future career " permitted, the guardianship, there-fore, to be a joint one; " wherefore," he ended up, " for the wel-fare of my child, I recommend *compliance* to my wife and more *moderation* to my brother. God permit them to be harmonious for the sake of my child's welfare! This is the last wish of the dying husband and brother."

One of the most unfortunate of Beethoven's little weaknesses was his passion for adopting a high moral tone towards other people. *They* were invariably in the wrong, while he, on his own admission, was a model of uprightness; in his differences with the London people, for instance, in which the faults, as posterity is bound to recognise, were all on his side, they were all rogues and liars, while his own conduct seemed to him impeccable.

The fact that the widow Beethoven was known to be not ex-actly a model of chastity was enough to justify him, in his own eyes, in ousting her from the half-share in the guardianship of her child that the father had so earnestly desired. Within a few days of his brother's death he applied to the courts for the full guardianship — alleging the widow's immorality — and succeeded in January in obtaining the necessary order. The boy was then nine years old.

Beethoven at first sent him to the school of one Giannatasio del Rio, in Vienna, then to a parish priest in Mödling, hard by, and then took him into his own house. He placed every possible obstacle in the way of the mother's seeing her son, and did all he could to prejudice the child against her — even encouraged him to speak ill of her; his conduct in this respect led to the parish priest's dismissing the boy as an undesirable associate for the other children at the school. In August the widow moved the court to give her authority to care for the child and attend to his up-bringing; after several hearings her appeal was rejected in October. In December, however, Carl ran away from his uncle to his mother, and the whole affair came into court once more.

No one can doubt Beethoven's perfect honesty in the matter from his own point of view. He had a high ideal of his duty towards his dead brother and towards the young life that had been partially entrusted to him. But neither can there be the slightest doubt that he, a bachelor and by temperament a solitary, was hopelessly unfitted, by nature and by circumstances, for the sole care of a child. He was incapable of regulating his own domestic affairs; his quarrels with his landlords and servants were notorious. His way with the boy alternated between infinite tenderness and a severity that sometimes approached brutality. It was said that Carl's food was not all that a child of that age needed, and that his person and his linen were neglected. The ageing musician, almost quite deaf, morose, quarrelsome, and self-absorbed, was hardly all that a spirited child wanted in the way of home companionship.

At the trial he was asked whether he would rather live at his uncle's or at his mother's. His answer was that he would like to live at his uncle's if he had but a companion, as his uncle was hard of hearing and he could not talk to him. Was he often alone? he was asked. His reply was, When his uncle was not at home he was left wholly alone. His uncle, he said, treated him well, thrashing him only when he deserved it, but after his return from his flight to his mother his uncle had " maltreated " him and threatened to throttle him. He had indulged in disrespectful remarks about his mother in the presence of his uncle because he thought that was the way to please him.

The court hurt Beethoven's pride by sending the case down to the magistracy. A certain deference seems to have been paid to him in the belief that the Dutch " van " was the equivalent of the German " von," and therefore a title of nobility. This was shown not to be so. A story has long been current that, when asked for documentary proofs of his nobility, Beethoven pointed in turn to his head and his heart, and said, " My nobility is here and here." It is always regrettable to have to destroy a romantic legend, but it must be said that there is no warrant whatever for this story in the court report of the case, the questions and answers in which are given verbatim.

The wretched affair, with all its dire consequences to Beethoven's health and pocket and work, dragged on until the summer of 1820. It came before the magistracy and the upper court again and again. Beethoven's appeals and petitions, it must be confessed, breathe a somewhat offensive self-righteousness. He harps alternately upon the wickedness of everybody who is opposed to him and on his own moral perfection. The Mödling priest, as we have seen, had not approved of his way with Carl. This was sufficient for Beethoven to write to the magistracy that this priest was " despised by his congregation " and " suspected of being guilty of illicit intercourse."

At first the right to regulate the boy's education was left to Beethoven, but in March 1819 he resigned his guardianship, " persuaded to take the step, it is fair to assume," says his impartial biographer Thayer, who unearthed all the court records of the affair, " by the magistrates, who, in the end, would have been obliged to remove him." A certain Councillor Tuscher assumed the responsibility at his request; when Tuscher resigned it a couple of months later, ostensibly on the ground that he could not spare the necessary time for it from his official duties, but perhaps in reality because he saw that the magistracy was on the widow's side, he came in for the suspicion and abuse that were sure to be the lot of everyone who took a line that was unpleasing to Beethoven.

The latter now notified the magistracy that he would resume his guardianship, but he was not allowed to do so. The court went thoroughly into the history of the various educational experiments that had been tried upon the boy, and found that he had suffered by being " subject to the whims " of his uncle, and " tossed like a ball from one institution to another." The mother was now to be guardian, as she had all along had a legal right to be, but some honest man was to be appointed co-guardian with her.

Once more Beethoven flung himself into the fray, making his accustomed lurid charges against the moral character of the widow, but objecting strenuously to " her false statements and lies " about himself. His appeal was rejected, whereupon he took the case to a higher court, which, of course, asked for a report from the magistracy.

The latter gave its reasons for its decision — Beethoven's deafness and notorious hatred of his sister-in-law made him an impossible guardian; the mother was by law entitled to the guardianship; her marital infidelity in 1811 had nothing to do with the present case; there was nothing in Beethoven's allegations of " injurious disturbances and interferences " on her part, for it was only natural that a mother should want to see her child once a fortnight or once a month, and to be assured that his clothes were good and clean; these and other things could only seem " injurious " in Beethoven's eyes, but the rest of the world would expect a mother to enquire about her child more often than that. The magistracy's report censured Beethoven for his habit of making reckless and unproven charges; the one definite thing he brought forward was the misconduct of 1811, all the rest being " unproven chatter " that was simply evidence of his passionate hatred of the widow.

So it went on and on until the court decided in Beethoven's favour, he and one Peters being appointed joint guardians. The widow appealed to the Emperor, who confirmed the judgment of the court in July 1820. That the widow was no better than she ought to be was indicated by the fact that she gave birth to another child while the case was being fought.

The magistracy seems to have taken the common-sense view

that the mother had in any case a natural right to a say in the management and the education of her child, that this natural right had been made a legal right by the codicil to her husband's will, and that however benevolent Beethoven's intentions might be, he was in almost every way unfitted for the task he desired to take upon himself.

Little else need be chronicled of these years. When the Congress of Vienna met in 1814 to decide the affairs of Europe after the first fall of Napoleon, Beethoven received from the monarchs and notabilities assembled there such deference as had never previously been the lot of any musician: " he was," we are told, " the object of general attention "; " all strove to do him homage."

It was in this same year that Beethoven made the acquaintance of Anton Schindler, a youth of eighteen years who was then studying the violin with Beethoven's friend Schuppanzigh. Schindler, as the years went on, fastened himself more and more on Beethoven, and in the end became, in fact if not in name, a sort of private secretary and factotum. He was a good-hearted if not particularly intelligent man; he made himself a little ridiculous, after the composer's death, by having " Friend of Beethoven " printed on his visiting cards. He published a biography of the master in which fancy so often takes the place of fact that it took half a century of careful research on the part of other biographers to get to the real truth of many things; some of his fictions are in circulation in the ordinary Beethoven biographies even to this day.

Fidelio was revived in May 1814, with a new overture in E major, which, however, was not ready until the second performance.

The chief works written by Beethoven during the latter years of the period we have just been considering were the E minor piano sonata (op. 90), the cantata *The Glorious Moment,* and the overture in C (op. 115) in 1814, the 'cello sonatas in C major and D major (op. 102) and the choral and orchestral *Calm Sea and Prosperous Voyage* in 1815, the piano sonata in A major (op. 101) and the song-cycle *To the Distant Beloved* in 1816, and part of the great B flat piano sonata (op. 106) and of the Ninth

Symphony in 1817, with further work on these two and on the Mass in D in 1818 and 1819.

It will be seen from the above list that Beethoven's productiveness had slowed down considerably. There were various reasons for this — the disputes over his nephew, frequent ill-health, a new feature of which was eye trouble, but above all a slackening of the pace of composition; as his ideas grew more profound they cost him far more labour in the shaping of them. This was especially true of the Ninth Symphony and the Mass in D, each of which occupied him, off and on, for some years.

In the summer of 1818 his friend and patron and pupil the Archduke Rudolph had been appointed Archbishop of Olmütz, his installation being fixed for the 20th March, 1820. Of his own prompting Beethoven began work upon a great Mass for the occasion; but he took so long over it, almost sweating blood over some parts of it, that the installation ceremony was over long before it was finished; it was first performed (or rather portions of it) at a concert in Vienna on the 7th May, 1824.

For admirers of the master's genius the negotiations with publishers over this Mass constitute the saddest chapter of his whole life. We have seen how his curious standard of honour in business matters got him into trouble with the London publishers in 1816; Neate, who was then acting as his agent in London, received a letter from a publisher that contained the sentence, " For God's sake, don't buy anything of Beethoven! " It has to be recognised frankly that his dealings in the affair of the Mass are irreconcilable with any ordinary standard of commercial probity, still less with his constant bestowal of moral certificates on himself, and still less again with the nature of the magnificent work on which he was then engaged.

No fewer than four publishers had the promise of the Mass at the same time; he took money in advance on the strength of some of these promises; and in the end not one of these publishers received the work. His letters are full of flat misstatements of fact. It is only our love and reverence for the great artist that makes us, when speaking of this affair, soften our language to an extent we should not dream of doing in the case of an ordinary business man; but there is no escaping and obscuring the evidence, and the verdict of one of his German biographers — "the conscientious reporter cannot ignore facts which lie notoriously before him, and hard as it may be, cannot acquit Beethoven of the reproach that his conduct was not in harmony with the principles of strict justice and uprightness" — certainly does not err on the side of immoderation.

Though not so short of money as he tried to make out — for he clung tenaciously to his seven bank shares for the future benefit of his nephew — his income had undoubtedly diminished of late. He was, as we have seen, brooding a long time over his big works, and he could no longer turn out smaller ones so rapidly as in his younger days. He was becoming more and more eccentric, more and more oblivious to the hard facts of the outer world.

In 1820 he was arrested as a vagrant, the police officer refusing to credit the story that this crazy ragamuffin was the great Beethoven. He suffered a good deal from rheumatism and jaundice; the latter was probably the first unmistakable hint of the malady of the liver that was to carry him off six years later. The one thing that never deserted him was his conviction that he had a sort of divine mission to regulate the lives of his relations; and we find him once more interfering in the domestic affairs of his brother Johann, whose wife had proved to be as unchaste as Carl's.

Johann had prospered so exceedingly that he had bought a nice property at Gneixendorf, where he spent his summers, coming to live in Vienna in the winter. His naïve vanity prompted him to style himself "Johann van Beethoven, Land Proprietor," which his brother countered ironically with "Ludwig van Beethoven, Brain Proprietor." In the summer of 1822 he sought a reconciliation with Johann, who could be helpful to him in business matters; but their relations were always being disturbed by his suspicions. His life at this time was a wretched one; in his world of dreams no one could give him companionship, while in the outer world he was in incessant conflict with landlords and servants — all of whom, of course, were "rascals" and "liars" and

" swindlers " — and involved in endless correspondence with publishers.

In the spring of 1822 he met in Vienna Rossini, who was then
the idol of Europe. It was said at one time that Beethoven had
refused to see the young world-conqueror, but Rossini, years after,
said that this was not the case; they met, but conversation was
practically impossible by reason of Beethoven's deafness and
Rossini's ignorance of German. In the following April, Franz
Liszt, then a boy of eleven or so who was exciting wonder as a
piano prodigy, visited Vienna; whether, as the story used to run,
Beethoven attended his concert and afterwards kissed him cannot
now be definitely decided.

The Mass was finished in 1822. Instead of having it published,
Beethoven conceived the idea — or let it be suggested to him — of
offering it for subscription to the various Courts in manuscript
copies. He received in all ten orders for it; included in the list
were the King of France (Louis XVIII, who also sent him a gold
medal), the Czar of Russia, the Kings of Prussia, Saxony, and
Denmark, and Prince Galitzin.

The last-named was a young Russian enthusiast for music who
lived in St. Petersburg. He was a fanatical admirer of Beethoven,
and it is in large measure to him that we owe the last great quartets
of the master. In November 1822 he commissioned from him one,
two, or three string quartets, for which the composer was to fix his
own price; Beethoven named fifty ducats for each. In the early part
of 1824 he turned his attention once more to the question of the
publication of the Mass. He passed over all the publishers with
whom he had so compromised himself in the previous years, and
offered it simultaneously to Schott of Mainz and Probst of
Leipzig; it was ultimately issued by the former.

Towards the end of 1822 *Fidelio* was revived once more, and
was so successful that the theatre management commissioned from
him another opera. This was never written, the composer being
unable, in spite of all the trouble he took, to find a libretto that he
thought suitable. It was in November 1822 also that the Philharmonic Society of London offered him £50 for a manuscript

symphony, and though Beethoven protested he could get more from other nations he accepted the commission. Anton Tayber, the Imperial Chamber Composer, died at this time, and Beethoven petitioned to be appointed his successor. The position, however, was allowed to expire with its last occupant.

There is comparatively little to record either of his life or of his works during his last three or four years. The *Bagatelles* (op. 126) were written in 1823, and the three string quartets that were the first-fruits of Prince Galitzin's commission (in E flat, op. 127, in B flat, op. 130, in A minor, op. 132) belong to the years 1824-5; to these have to be added the C sharp minor (op. 131) — which Beethoven thought his greatest quartet — the F major (op. 135), and the *Grand Fugue,* which was originally intended for the finale of op. 130. The Ninth Symphony was finished in February, 1824; it had occupied the composer's mind for ten years, while the idea of a setting of Schiller's *Ode to Joy* (which forms the choral ending) dates from 1793. His sketch-books and his letters show that he had projected a tenth symphony.

As there was some talk of Berlin's getting the first performance of the Ninth, thirty of his most influential admirers addressed to him a public petition to let Vienna have that honour. After a momentary outburst of rage at the publication of the letter he consented; and the work was given on the 7th May, 1824, at the same concert that saw the first performance of some portions of the Mass in D. The performance was rather a poor one, but the enthusiasm was immense.

Either at the end of the whole work or after the Scherzo there occurred the incident that has been so often described — the deaf composer being turned round by the contralto soloist, Fräulein Unger, to see the applauding crowd. After the fifth outburst of applause the Police Commissioner shouted " Silence! " three rounds of acclamation being all that the Emperor himself and his family were supposed to have. Owing to the heavy expenses and other circumstances the profit from the concert was only 420 florins, while a second concert a few days later resulted in a deficit; Beethoven promptly charged the management and his friend

Schindler with having cheated him! The symphony was given in London for the first time by the Philharmonic Society on the 29th March.

The score he dedicated to the King of Prussia, from whom, in spite of his professed contempt for rank, he was anxious to receive a decoration. He wanted to wear, at the Vienna performance of the Ninth Symphony, the gold medal given him by the King of France, but was persuaded not to do so, as the weight of it would have pulled his collar down. The King of Prussia sent, instead of the expected decoration, a diamond ring — or so it was stated in his letter. What arrived, however, was a single-stone ring of a " reddish " colour that was worth only 300 florins, paper money. There is reason to believe that at some point or other this had been substituted for the ring actually sent.

The nephew Carl had been placed first at a school, then at the Vienna University (1823–5). His uncle wanted him to be a teacher of languages, but the young man's inclinations were towards either the army or commerce — a choice that distressed the composer greatly. In 1825 Carl was placed at the Polytechnic Institute for further study, and lodged with a government official named Schlemmer. He was fond of pleasure, especially dancing and billiards, and there seems no reason to doubt that he had got into undesirable company and run up debts. His uncle had no idea how to manage him; the young man, just beginning to taste the delights of life, was especially irked by his small allowance for pocket-money and by such restrictions as not being allowed out at night without a written permission from Schlemmer.

On the 30th July, 1826, as near as we can establish the date, he tried to put an end to his miseries by blowing out his brains; but though he fired with a pistol in each hand he inflicted only a comparatively harmless skull wound. The event almost broke up Beethoven completely; he loved the boy passionately in his own way, and could not see as clearly as his friends could how unfitted he was to play the rôle of guardian. Every possible attempt was made to minimise the scandal and to mollify the police, and as soon as Carl was convalescent he and his uncle went to stay with the latter's brother Johann on his estate at Gneixendorf (28th September).

It was curious that Beethoven should have been willing to stay in the same house with the woman of whose moral character he had so low an opinion, but bad as she was in some respects she seems to have been normally sensible and broad-minded in others. During his stay with Johann, Beethoven tried to induce him to disinherit his wife and leave all his money to Carl.

A great deal of fiction has been written about these last months of Beethoven's life, Schindler being answerable for much of it. He was anxious, after the composer's death, to magnify his own importance in the great man's life, and he was liberal in accusations against other people who were rather more in the picture at that time than he liked. Johann has been accused, without any evidence, of being niggardly with firewood, etc., during Ludwig's stay with him, and of having sent him back to Vienna in an open carriage and thereby caused him to catch the chill that was to prove fatal.

The immediate cause of the journey was a letter that Johann handed to his brother (conversation, of course, being almost impossible, by reason of the composer's deafness), at the end of November 1826; in this he pointed out, quite sensibly, that the sybaritic Carl was settling down lazily to a life of ease in the country, and that the co-guardian Breuning had urged the necessity of getting him back to town and making him settle down to the serious business of a re-start in life; in the lad's own interests, therefore, Johann urged that Ludwig ought to take him to Vienna at once. There seems to have been a final quarrel over the question of the will, and then Carl and his uncle set out on Friday, 1st December. Johann could not lend them his closed carriage, as his wife had recently taken it with her to Vienna. The pair arrived in town the next day.

Part of the journey had undoubtedly been done in an open conveyance in bad weather, and Beethoven slept on the Friday night in an unwarmed bed in a wretched village inn. A fever seized him in the night, and by the time he arrived home he was plainly very ill, though he does not seem to have taken his condition seriously for another two or three days, when he sent for Holz, a young man to whom he had become greatly attached a couple of years before, and who had, in large part, taken Schindler's place as factotum — a circumstance which did not commend him to the latter gentleman.

The story used to be that Carl, who had been told to bring a physician, forgot to do so for several days, but thought of it at last and turned the commission over to a marker in a billiard-room he frequented, and that the marker, being himself taken to a hospital some time later, happened to remember the matter and spoke of it to the physician, Dr. Wawruch.

This is merely one of Schindler's many fictions concerning these last days. Wawruch was called in on the 5th December. Beethoven turned against him, as he always did sooner or later against his doctors, and others were called in to help him from time to time. There could have been little hope from the first of saving the sick man. He probably weathered a pneumonia in the first week or two, and then the old stomach and liver troubles asserted themselves. Jaundice came, and then dropsy, for which he was tapped four times between the 20th December, 1826, and the 27th February, 1827. Johann had arrived on the 10th December, and thereafter was in constant attendance on his brother, together with Holz, Schindler, and other friends.

Some two years before this, a German living in England, one Stumpff, gathering from Beethoven's conversation that he admired Handel above all other composers, had resolved to send him the complete edition of the latter's works as soon as it became available. The forty volumes of Dr. Arnold's great edition arrived in February, and gave the sick man much pleasure.

On the 8th February he wrote to thank Stumpff, reminded him of the Philharmonic Society's desire to give a concert for his benefit some years before, and suggested that such a concert now would be very welcome to him. The Society's reply was to remit £100 to him, " to be applied to his comforts and necessities during his illness," and further assistance was promised if necessary.

(Beethoven was, as usual, concealing the real state of his finances; he stubbornly refused to touch his bank stock, which he wanted to go intact to Carl.)

The sick man, on the 18th, while expressing his deep gratitude for the gift, asked the Society not to abandon the idea of a concert, from the proceeds of which the £100 could be deducted, and promised to compose for it a new symphony, " which lies already sketched in my desk," a new overture or whatever other work the Society might desire.

About this time also he read through a number of Schubert's songs, and recognised the remarkable genius they displayed. Schubert himself visited him a week or so before his death.

It had been decided to place Carl in the army, so that he might acquire some of the discipline he so sorely needed; and the young man left to join his regiment at Iglau on the 2nd January. He never saw his uncle again. The day after his departure Beethoven wrote a letter to Dr. Bach declaring Carl to be his sole legatee, but the will proper was not signed till two days before his death. After the fourth operation he seems to have been convinced that there was no longer any hope for him.

The long death-struggle set in on the 24th March and lasted two days: death took place at five o'clock in the afternoon of the 26th. The powerful frame and the still undamaged lungs fought to the last. Just before the end, a flash of lightning and a violent thunder-clap seemed to rouse the unconscious man, in whose throat the death-rattle had been heard since three o'clock; he opened his eyes, lifted his right hand, and held his clenched fist aloft for several seconds: it was an appropriately characteristic gesture for a Beethoven to die to. There is a touch of pathetic irony in the fact that the only person present at his death, with the exception of Anselm Hüttenbrenner, was his brother Johann's wife.

The story has already been told in an earlier page of the tardy discovery of the bank certificates in a secret drawer in his desk, along with a portrait of Therese von Brunswick and the letter to the " Immortal Beloved." His estate was valued at what, in sterling values before the late war, would be about £3,000.

The funeral took place on the 29th. The schools were closed, and a crowd of 20,000 people gathered in the square in front of the house. One of the torch-bearers was Schubert. The body was taken to the cemetery in the village of Währing, close by; over the grave was erected a pyramid with the one word BEETHOVEN.

During the nineteenth century the grave became so neglected that in 1863 the Vienna Society of the Friends of Music had the body exhumed and re-buried. In 1888 Beethoven's remains and those of Schubert were taken to the Central Cemetery in Vienna, and laid in their final rest side by side.

Carl inherited not only Beethoven's estate but that of his uncle Johann, who died in 1848, leaving him 42,000 florins; Johann's wife had died twenty years before. Carl died in 1858, leaving a widow and several children. The family sank lower and lower in the social scale during the next couple of generations, and the last of the Beethovens is said to have been enrolled during the Great War in the Austrian Territorials, where he served as a butt and a drudge for his comrades, and to have died of paralysis in a Vienna garrison hospital in January 1918.

BEETHOVEN took up various operatic schemes during the course of his life, but only one of them came to fruition. It has often been said that his genius was essentially symphonic rather than operatic; but that opinion was not held by Beethoven himself. He was always anxious, for financial as well as artistic reasons, to make a success in the theatre; and if *Fidelio* remains his only opera that is merely because he was never afterwards able to find a libretto that really appealed to him.

In 1803 there was great rivalry in operatic circles in Vienna. The Court Theatre was under the direction of Baron Braun, while the rival theatre, the Theater-an-der-Wien, was being run by Emmanuel Schikaneder (1751–1812), a strange creature (he died insane), a jack-of-all-trades, singer, actor, dramatist, theatrical manager, and what not, who is now remembered mainly for the fact that he was the instigator and part librettist of Mozart's *The Magic Flute,* and the man most directly answerable for the train of events that led to Beethoven's *Fidelio.*

Vienna, in the early years of the nineteenth century, had become sated with frivolous opera, and had shown signs of turning to a more serious style. Cherubini had made a success in Paris with his *Lodoiska,* and in March 1802 Schikaneder produced the work at the Theater-an-der-Wien. The Court Theatre countered this move by producing Cherubini's *The Water Carrier* and *Medea;* but the shrewd Schikaneder stole a march on it again by bringing out *The Water Carrier,* under the title of *Graf Armand,* a day before the Court Theatre.

Cherubini being obviously the man of the hour, Baron Braun went to Paris early in 1803 to secure him exclusively for his theatre. It became necessary for Schikaneder to find an equally strong counter-attraction, and his choice fell on Beethoven, whose reputation had been growing in Vienna for several years. It is true that he had not yet written an opera, but his music to the *Prometheus* ballet a couple of years before had proved popular. Schikaneder saw to it that in March 1803 a preliminary announcement of a coming opera by Beethoven appeared in one of the newspapers; and that the commission had actually been given to the composer is evident from the fact that, in accordance with the practice of the time, he was given lodgings in the theatre.

In February 1804 the Theater-an-der-Wien was sold to Baron Braun, and Beethoven had apparently to leave his lodgings. Baron Braun first of all installed at the Theater-an-der-Wien Josef Sonnleithner, the secretary of the Court Theatre; but when the latter retired in August, Baron Braun handed over the direction of the theatre to Schikaneder once more, and the invitation to Beethoven to compose an opera was repeated.

The libretto of the opera first commissioned from Beethoven was to have been by Schikaneder himself, but what the title of it was we do not know. Certain sketches for the opera, however, were found among Beethoven's papers after his death, among them a trio in G major that was afterwards worked up into the duet between Leonora and Florestan, "Oh blissful hour, oh joy of heaven! " in the second act of *Fidelio*. Perhaps the reason for Beethoven's not having made greater progress with the commission was that he was not deeply interested in the subject, whatever it was. It was otherwise with the commission given him by Baron Braun; this appealed to him so greatly that the score was completely finished by the summer of 1805.

In those days there was no copyright in operatic libretti, and it was a common practice for a poet, a composer, or a theatrical manager to appropriate any subject that had proved to be a success elsewhere. The original of *Fidelio* was an opera entitled *Léonore, ou l'Amour Conjugal*, that had been produced in Paris on the 19th February, 1798. The text of this was by Jean Nicolas Bouilly (1763–1842), a lawyer who had written a number of successful libretti, including that for Cherubini's *The Water Carrier*. The composer was Pierre Gaveaux (born 1761), a tenor singer who had taken to writing music, and, after having composed more than thirty operas, died mad in 1825.

The possibilities of the subject soon attracted the attention of the pirates in other countries. It was set afresh, to Italian words, by Ferdinando Paër (1771–1826), under the title of *Leonora, ossia l'Amor Conjugale,* and produced at Dresden, where Paër was at that time Kapellmeister, on the 3rd October, 1804. At that time, as we have seen, Beethoven was already engaged on his own opera on the subject, the text being provided for him by Josef Sonnleithner.

The work was first performed at the Theater-an-der-Wien, under the title of *Fidelio,* on the 20th November, 1805; it was in three acts. It had bad luck from the commencement. Napoleon had occupied Vienna only a week before; most of the Viennese either avoided the theatres or were unable to get to them from the suburbs, and the audience was mainly composed of French officers and soldiers, who naturally would understand very little of a work in a strange tongue. After the third performance, on the 22nd November, Beethoven withdrew the opera.

His friends, a few of whom had seen one or other of the performances, felt that sundry changes would be necessary before the work could hope to become a great success. The composer, who was always very difficult to manage in affairs of this kind, was persuaded to meet a number of friends in December, at the house of his patron Prince Lichnowsky, for a frank discussion of the opera in its present form and equally frank suggestions as to how it might be improved.

The meeting lasted from seven in the evening till one o'clock the next morning. Princess Lichnowsky played the score on the piano, accompanied from memory by the violinist Clement, who was at that time leader of the orchestra at the Theater-an-der-Wien; among others present were Beethoven's brother Caspar, his friend Stephan von Breuning, the poet von Collin, for whose tragedy on the subject of Coriolanus Beethoven later wrote his overture bearing that title, two of Mozart's brothers-in-law — the actor Lange and the bass singer Meier, who had taken the part of Don Pizarro in the opera — the official theatre poet, Friedrich Treitschke, and a young man twenty-two years old, Josef August Röckel (1783–1870), who had just joined the Theater-an-der-Wien as tenor, and who was already cast for the part of Florestan in the projected revival of the opera, in place of the ageing Demmer, who had sung the part in the first production.

With difficulty Beethoven was persuaded to consent to the sacrifice of certain numbers, and to the reduction of the opera from three acts to two by Stephan von Breuning. In this form it was produced on the 29th March, 1806, again under Beethoven, and, against his wish, once more under the title of *Fidelio;* the libretto issued at the time bears the title of *Leonora, or the Triumph of Wedded Love.* The only change in the cast was the substitution of Röckel for Demmer. (This Röckel, by the way, was the father of the August Röckel who was so closely associated with Wagner in the revolutionary days of 1848 and 1849.)

Beethoven had worked so hard and conscientiously upon the opera that there was time for only one orchestral rehearsal before the performance, a fact that he characteristically failed to take into consideration when blaming the players for certain short-comings.

The work, in its recast and abbreviated form, looked like becoming a great popular success when, on the 10th April, after the fifth performance, Beethoven withdrew his score. The always suspicious composer not only believed that there was a cabal against him in the theatre, but got it into his head that he had been cheated in the matter of his royalties. He rushed off with his charge to Baron Braun, whose tact had almost smoothed the angry Ludwig down when an unfortunate comparison with Mozart brought the interview to a stormy end.

During the years immediately following, and indeed until the end of his days, Beethoven sought anxiously for a book for another opera, but without success. He was all the more anxious to try his luck again in the theatre because *Fidelio,* on its next revival, proved a decided attraction. In 1814 three of the officials of the Court Opera were granted a benefit, the choice of the work being left to them, so long as it did not cost the theatre anything. In view of the great respect in which Beethoven was held in Vienna at that time, and his undoubted drawing power, they decided to ask him to grant them permission to revive *Fidelio*. He consented, and once more worked over the opera afresh, the many changes in it this time being made by Treitschke.

On the 23rd May, 1814, the opera was given at the Kärnthner-thor Theatre, in two acts, in the final form in which we now possess it. Beethoven conducted the first performance, but as his deafness and his abstraction were very marked at this time, the Kapellmeister Umlauf stood behind him for safety's sake, and it was to Umlauf that the orchestra really looked for direction. The sixth performance was for the benefit of Beethoven himself.

Of the success of the opera this time there could be no doubt; it was taken up by one German town after another and, aided by a succession of great Fidelios, of whom the best known were Wilhelmina Schroeder-Devrient and Lilli Lehmann, has remained to this day one of the most revered monuments of German music. It was given in London, in German, in 1832, with Schroeder-Devrient as Leonora, and in English, with Malibran, three years later. In 1851 it was given in Italian, with Cruvelli as Leonora and Sims Reeves as Florestan; and on this occasion Beethoven had the inestimable privilege of having his spoken dialogues set to recitative by the composer of *The Bohemian Girl*.

There were no less than four overtures to the opera known to our fathers, and the numbering of three of them is rather confusing. At the first production, in 1805, the overture played was, in essence, that known now as the *Leonora No. 2*. On the occasion of the 1806 production the overture was the version of this known as the *Leonora No. 3*. In 1806, with a view to a performance in

Prague that never came off, Beethoven simplified the *No. 3* into what is known as the *Leonora No. 1* overture, which remained in manuscript until five years after the composer's death, when it was published as "an overture in C, Opus 138," by Haslinger in 1832.

For the revival of 1814 Beethoven wrote an entirely new overture in E major, always known as the *Fidelio* Overture. As this was not ready for the first performance, however, the overture played on that occasion was that to *The Ruins of Athens,* a play for which Beethoven had written some incidental music in 1811.

The matter was yet further complicated by the discovery in 1926 of another version of the *Leonora No. 2,* the manuscript of this being found in the archives of the Leipzig publishers, Breitkopf & Härtel. The composer's own manuscript of the *Leonora No. 2* appears to be lost; we know it only from a copy by another hand that is now in the Prussian State Library in Berlin. In the manuscript recently found in the Breitkopf archives, which differs at sundry points from the published version of the *No. 2,* alterations and abbreviations seem to have been made by Beethoven's own hand; this version was probably the overture actually played at the performances of 1805, and so represents the composer's final conception of the *No. 2.* The newly discovered overture was played for the first time in England at a British Broadcasting Company's concert, under Hermann Scherchen, of Frankfort, in February 1927.

When a composer leaves no less than four overtures to the one opera, there is bound to be some difference of opinion as to which of them should be used in the theatre. There has been a good deal of controversy over the four overtures to *Fidelio,* but it has settled itself, like most controversies, by a mixture of reason and compromise.

A number of people contend that the proper overture to play is the *Leonora No. 3,* on the grounds that it was the *Leonora* overture that Beethoven originally wrote for the opera, and of the three versions of it the one known as *No. 3* is undoubtedly the greatest. Against this it can be urged that the *Leonora No. 3* is not only too colossal in itself as a prelude to the opera — for after it the scene of light comedy with which the opera opens is apt to seem a little tame — but, in a sense, the overture makes the opera itself appear almost superfluous. This, in essence, was Wagner's theory; he held that everything that is vital in the dramatic and spiritual idea of the opera has been said with such point and force and concentration in the *Leonora No. 3* that the opera itself is only a dilution of this in two acts.

The partisans of the *Leonora No. 3* further say that the necessity for the so-called *Fidelio* overture, in E major, has now disappeared. There were two good reasons why Beethoven should have written it in 1814 — it was easier for the orchestra than any of the others, and it was easier for the average audience of that day to understand; but the *Leonora No. 3* is now part and parcel of every orchestral player's repertory, while it is thoroughly familiar to every concert-goer.

All this is quite true; but in spite of it the *Fidelio* overture is now always played as an introduction to the opera, while the *Leonora No. 3* is generally played later, either between the first and second acts or between the first and second scenes of the second act. On the relative advantages and disadvantages of these last two methods of procedure we shall have something to say later.

The *Fidelio* overture commences with five allegro bars in which we have foreshadowed the curt theme that will afterwards form the principal subject:

This is succeeded by an adagio phrase for the horns, followed by the clarinets:

Both No. 1 and No. 2 are then repeated in another key, after which there come some soft harmonies in the strings, which gradually work up to a fortissimo and then die away again into a triplet ornamentation to No. 2 in the wind. The allegro proper commences with the full version of the theme already hinted at in No. 1:

It is developed for a little while on Mozartian lines, Beethoven's object evidently being to keep it as simple as possible, and in time it merges into the second subject:

These two main subjects, with the little subsidiary matter attached to them, are worked out in the most transparent fashion, Beethoven, as might be expected, drawing a good deal of significance from the pronouncedly rhythmic figure shown in No. 1.

Near the end there is a short adagio episode in which No. 2 is heard once more, entwined about with triplets as before; then Beethoven seizes again upon the rhythm of No. 1, alters the time to presto, and finishes off the overture with a feverishly joyous coda.

Although the *Fidelio* overture has nothing like the dramatic power and the close programmatic detail of the *Leonora No. 3*, it also, in its way, summarises the opera, triumph evidently being achieved at the end over the darker influences hinted at in No. 2.

For the proper understanding of the story we have to know what is supposed to have happened before the opera begins. Pizarro, a cruel, tyrannical man, is the Governor of a prison not far from Seville. He has been thwarted in some of his evil plans by a high-minded and incorruptible political opponent, Florestan, and having seized upon the latter's person he has secretly thrown him into one of the deepest dungeons in the prison.

Nobody knows whither Florestan has disappeared; but his faithful wife, Leonora, has a suspicion that he has been put away by Pizarro, and in order to discover whether he is in the prison she has dressed herself as a young man, assumed the name of Fidelio, and obtained the post of assistant to the chief gaoler, Rocco. Not only has Fidelio, by his assiduousness, won the confidence of Rocco, but he has inspired love in the heart of the gaoler's pretty daughter Marcelline, who is in turn loved in vain by Rocco's doorkeeper, the young Jaquino.

When the curtain rises we see the courtyard of the prison. In the background is the tower of the castle, by the side of which runs a high wall; entrances and exits through this are made by means of a small gate, which it is the business of Jaquino to open and close. On the left of the stage from the spectator are prison cells; the numbered doors are encased with iron, and barred and bolted; the windows are also barred. On the right is the castle garden, entry to which is through a row of iron railings. In the left foreground is the door leading to Rocco's quarters, and in front of this, when the curtain goes up, Marcelline is standing at a table, busy ironing; near her is a brasier, on which she warms the iron from time to time.

By the gate in the back wall is Jaquino's little hut: he spends part of his time opening the gate every now and then to people who come in with parcels, partly in running up to Marcelline's table and making love to her.

The music of this opening scene forms a complete contrast to that of the remainder of the opera; it is couched in the light Mozartian vein. Approaching Marcelline and rubbing his hands together, Jaquino compliments himself and her on being at last alone, so that they can talk about marriage:

The indifferent Marcelline goes steadily on with her work; the subject is not as interesting to her as it is to him. While he urges her to show a more friendly spirit towards him and name the day, she merely chaffs him about his eagerness.

He is just suggesting that they might get married in a few weeks when there comes a loud knocking at the door:

" To the devil with this eternal knocking! " cries Jaquino; " it always comes just when I am getting things nicely going." While he is opening the door, Marcelline confides to us how truly sorry she is for him. His devotion is hopeless, for all her love has been given to Fidelio.

Jaquino, having finished at the door, returns, and after asking
" Where was I? " plunges into his favourite subject once more,
while Marcelline ejaculates resignedly, " Here he is; he is going
to begin all over again! " Finally losing patience, she tells him he
is making her life a burden to her, and assures him that she will
never marry him, either to-day, to-morrow, or in the future; she
is sorry for him, she says aside, but she has to be firm with him.
When she mentions Fidelio in her aside, during Jaquino's absence
at the door, a tender little phrase comes out in the oboe and
bassoon:

She is just protesting that she has never given him her promise
when the knocking is again heard, and, Jaquino being called away
to his duties again, Marcelline expresses her relief at the welcome
interruption in a little coloratura. When Jaquino returns, a spoken
dialogue follows. If this isn't the two hundredth time he has
opened that door to-day, he says, his name is not Kaspar Eustach
Jaquino! Anyhow he can settle down now to a little talk. But just
then there is another knock, and after that another. After this last,
the worried Jaquino hopes for a little peace; but he has no sooner
settled down than Rocco's voice is heard calling him from the
garden. " Let him wait! " he says angrily; " now about our
love — "

Marcelline interrupts him; he must go at once, because her
father will want news of Fidelio. Jaquino shows signs of jealousy
at this name; but as Rocco calls him more peremptorily than before he is forced to go, promising Marcelline, however, that he will
be back in a couple of minutes. He goes through the door into the
garden, and Marcelline, left alone, tells us again how sorry she is
for him: she was really fond of him until Fidelio came into the

house, but since then everything within her is changed. She sings
a tender little aria:

(8) Andante con moto

O day   of joy, when wilt thou bless This
O wär   ich schon mit dir vereint, und

heart in hope con - fi - ding!
dürf - te Mann dich nen-nen!

in which she looks forward to the day when she shall be married
to Fidelio, although, like a good German maiden of the end of
the eighteenth century, she blushes to confess that her mind runs
on such a subject. But this does not prevent her from painting an
intimate little picture of their life together — a quiet little house,
days of honest toil, and evenings of affectionate communion
together.

She is interrupted by the entry of Rocco and Jaquino, the latter
carrying some garden tools, with which he goes into Rocco's house.
The gaoler tells his daughter that he is anxiously expecting
Fidelio, who has gone to fetch some letters that the Governor is
awaiting, and to fulfil other commissions. Perhaps he has been
detained at the smith's, opines Marcelline. Just then there is a
knocking at the door; Jaquino goes to open it, Marcelline gives
an eager cry of " Here he is! " and Leonora enters.

It is a testimony both to the moving seriousness of the story
in itself and the skill with which Beethoven has treated it that
we never become conscious of anything humorous in the situation
of Marcelline hoping to marry one of her own sex.

Leonora wears a dark doublet, a red vest, dark pantaloons, high
boots, and a broad belt of black leather with a copper buckle. On
her back is a sort of knapsack, and in her hands she carries some
chains, which she throws down by Jaquino's hut. At her side a
metal case hangs by a cord. She looks tired and hot, and Marcelline, with an ejaculation of sympathy, runs to her as if to wipe

her face with her handkerchief. Bidding her wait a moment, Rocco
helps Leonora to get rid of her heavy equipment, while Jaquino
moves backwards and forwards, keeping the others under observation all the while.

Leonora confesses that she is indeed hot, for she has had to
hurry; the smith had been a long time repairing the chains, but at
least he has done the job well; none of the prisoners will be able
to break them! She gives Rocco the bill for twelve piastres, and
the gaoler, running his eye over it, congratulates Fidelio on his
zeal and economy; in the six months during which he has had
charge of the commissariat he has saved the prison more money
than Rocco could have done in a whole year. In an aside he surmises that Fidelio is so attentive to business because he is in
love with Marcelline. He shall have his reward, says Rocco, glanc-
ing from Fidelio to Marcelline and back again; and the somewhat embarrassed Fidelio has to protest that whatever he does
is done solely from a sense of duty.

Rocco goes to examine the chains, and Marcelline, who has
been watching Fidelio all this while with visibly increasing emotion, begins one of the most famous numbers of the opera. It is a
canon — that is to say, each voice takes up the original phrase
after an interval. Marcelline is full of the thought that Fidelio
loves her:

When the whole of the eight-bar phrase is finished, Leonora takes
it up; she is uneasy about this love of Marcelline, that threatens
to be dangerous. When Rocco strikes in, it is to muse upon the
happiness that the future holds for this affectionate pair; while

Jaquino, who enters last, tells us that his hair is standing on end
at the thought that Marcelline's father is agreeable to her marriage with Fidelio.

A modern composer would, of course, have found another
melody for Jaquino's sentiments than for those of Marcelline or
Fidelio; but the epoch in which Beethoven wrote paid less attention to these minutiæ of musical realism; the form is allowed to
dominate the expression, and the canon is so delightful a piece of
music that we cannot find it in our hearts to quarrel with Beethoven on abstract theoretical grounds.

The canon being finished, Jaquino goes back into his hut, and
Rocco, turning to Fidelio, tells him that, though he knows little
about his antecedents, he is so pleased with him that he will welcome him as a son-in-law, whereupon Marcelline eagerly interjects, " And how soon, dearest father? " Rocco smiles indulgently
at her anxiety. Very soon, he says, they will have a little more
leisure to think about it; as they know, the Governor is now paying them the usual visit of inspection; he will be gone again in a
few days, and then they can decide about it. " The day after his
departure, then," says Marcelline, greatly to the embarrassment
of Leonora, who, however, has to feign delight as well as she can.

It is time now that Rocco, as one of the principal characters,
shall have his aria, and, taking as his cue the remark that love is
not the only essential to a happy marriage, he breaks out into a
song in praise of money:

(40) **Allegro moderato**

Life   is   no - thing with - out
Hat   man   nicht auch Gold   bei,

mo - ney, Anxious cares be - set   it round;
- ne - ben, Kann man nicht ganz glücklich sein,

the sovereign cure for most of the evils of the world.

There may be something in Rocco's philosophy, says Leonora,

but to her thinking the true source of wedded happiness is the union of two hearts that are attuned to each other. Then, checking her earnestness, she changes the subject. There is one sign of Rocco's favour that she would be glad to have, but, to her sorrow, she sees that he withholds it from her. Apparently she does not enjoy his full confidence; she often sees him go into the subterranean cells of the prison, and come back out of breath and exhausted. Why does he not allow her to accompany him? It would give her so much gratification to help him at his work and share his hardships.

Rocco tells her that he has the strictest orders not to let anyone else whatever into the cells, but he confesses that the heavy work is becoming too much for him at his age. Still, although the Governor is very strict, perhaps he will be able to obtain from him permission to let Fidelio accompany him. But there is *one* cell, he continues, in which he will not be able to let Fidelio enter, however much he may trust him. " Perhaps, father," says Marcelline, " that is the prisoner of whom you have sometimes told me." Leonora cautiously asks if this prisoner has been there long. " Over two years," replies Rocco. " Two years? " cries Leonora excitedly; and then, mastering herself, she adds, " He must have been a great criminal." " Or else, which comes to the same thing," answers Rocco, " he must have had powerful enemies."

" Does no one know then," asks Marcelline, " who he is and whence he came? " The gaoler replies that the prisoner has often wished to speak to him about all this, but he has checked him, for the less a gaoler talks to his captives the better; he can do a prisoner little good, while he, for his part, may be tempted into saying more than is discreet.

However, this particular prisoner will not trouble him very long, for his days seem numbered. For the last month, on the Governor's orders, Pizarro has been giving him less and less food; during the last twenty-four hours he has had nothing to eat but two ounces of black bread and half a cup of water; he has no straw to lie on, and no light but that of a lamp. Marcelline begs her father not to take Fidelio to him, for the young man would not be able to endure the sight; but Leonora demands why not, for she has strength and courage.

Rocco strikes Fidelio approvingly on the shoulder, and the violins give the signal for a trio. To an energetic phrase:

Leonora declares that her courage is equal to anything, Rocco congratulates her on her spirit, while Marcelline assures Fidelio that her love will console him when he comes back, sad at heart, from the cells. Within the set form imposed by the older style of ensemble, the varying feelings of the three characters are admirably expressed.

There is a beautiful touch at the finish of the trio. While Marcelline speaks of her own tears of happiness flowing at the thought of her union with Fidelio, Leonora speaks of the bitterness of *her* fears; and Beethoven gives the appropriate expression and colour to each phrase by the simple device of alternating a major with a minor interval:

It is time, says Rocco, to take to the Governor the documents that Fidelio has brought from the town; but just then a march is heard:

signalising the coming of Pizarro. Leonora gives Rocco the little case containing the documents, and goes with Marcelline into the house.

The main gate is opened by guards; officers enter with a detachment of soldiers, Pizarro follows, and the gate is closed again. Pizarro gives his orders to the officers: there are to be three guards set on the ramparts, six men day and night to watch the drawbridge, as many to overlook the garden, and anyone who approaches the moat is to be brought before him at once. He takes the dispatches from Rocco and runs through them. The usual recommendations or complaints, he says; if he were to bother about all that, he would never finish. But he recognises the writing on the cover of one of the letters. Opening it, he goes to the foreground, Rocco and the guards withdrawing to the back.

He reads the letter: " I have to inform you that the Minister has been told that the state prison under your charge contains several sacrifices to the caprice of power. He means to set out to-morrow and surprise you with an enquiry. Be on your guard." Ah! he says, if the Minister were to discover that in the prison is that Florestan whom he believes to have been long dead, that Florestan who thought of exposing Pizarro to the Minister, and on whom he has now wreaked his vengeance! He must act boldly and quickly. In a vigorous aria:

he pours out his hatred upon Florestan, who once almost achieved his ruin; but now his own hour of triumph is at hand. Softly, from the background, comes a chorus of the guards, who whisper to each other, " He speaks of death and wounds! Let us go on our round; this must be some affair of importance."

Resuming ordinary speech again after his aria, Pizarro makes vigorous preparations to secure his safety. Calling the captain, he tells him to mount to the tower with a trumpeter, not to take his eyes off the road from Seville, and as soon as he observes a coach with outriders approaching to see that the signal is given him. " At once, understand, at once! " he repeats; " you will be answerable to me with your head."

The captain goes without a word, and Pizarro imperiously orders the guards to follow him. Calling Rocco to him, he scrutinises him sternly for a while and then, deciding that the gaoler's help is necessary, throws him a purse and promises him he shall become a rich man if he does as he is told. " What must I do? " asks Rocco. " Murder! " replies Pizarro:

and Rocco shrinks back in horror. Pizarro becomes more urgent. Is he a man? he asks Rocco with a touch of contempt; if so, instead of trembling and babbling as he does he will see to it that, for the Governor's sake and for the safety of the State, a certain offender is put out of the way.

Sinister effects come out in the strings:

as Pizarro's blood-lust increases. Rocco, he says, must know the prisoner he means. " Is it the one," asks the gaoler, " who can hardly be said to be alive, for he is a mere shadow? " " It is he," replies Pizarro grimly. Rocco must set to at once and dig a grave in the cell; then he is to call Pizarro, who will enter masked; one blow, and the prisoner is silenced for ever:

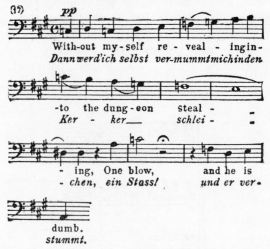

A sinister effect is made by the bare octaves that accompany the phrase, the sudden fortissimo discord:

that precedes the words " One blow! " the silence that follows as
Pizarro produces his dagger, and the pizzicato of the basses to the
words, " and he is dumb! " While Pizarro continues to pour out
his hatred on Florestan, the horrified Rocco thinks that after all
death will be preferable to the life this unhappy prisoner is now
living; the dagger will bring him release.

Pizarro goes into the garden, Rocco following him; when they
have left the stage, Leonora comes on in the greatest agitation and
breaks into the recitative of the famous aria, " Thou monstrous
fiend! " " What would you? " she asks the absent Pizarro; " does
the voice of humanity, the call of pity, no longer move your tiger's
heart? " Yet the more his rage and hate foam like the waves of an
angry sea, the more she is sure that through the dark clouds the
rainbow will soon pierce; and Beethoven realistically suggests the
waves by a rolling figure in the lower strings, and the rainbow
by soft chords high up in the wood-wind.

The theme of the adagio of the aria that follows is a cry to
Hope to shed its last rays on her now in the hour of her deepest
weariness:

(19) Adagio

Oh ___ hope, thou wilt not let the
Komm Hoff - nung, lass den letzt-en

star,___ Of sorrowing love ___ bedimm'd for
Stern, den letzten Stern der Müden nicht er-

e - ver!
- bleich-en,

As the tempo changes to allegro, opening with a fanfare in the
horns, the music takes on a more vigorous character as she speaks
of her resolution to be strong for the sake of him she loves, him
for whom she has already borne so much: the very stride of the
intervals of the melody is eloquent of courage:

(20)

Ich folg' dem in - nern Trie - be,
A heaven-ly voice doth guide me,

ich wan - ke nicht, mich stärkt die
I shall not fail, love will pre -

Pflicht der treu - en Gat -
-vail, thou hope hast ne'er

- - - - ten - lie - be
de - nied me.

As she speaks of the wickedness that has caught Florestan in its toils we hear again the dissonant diminished seventh that accompanied Pizarro's cry of " Murder! " :

Wo Bös-heit dich in Fesseln schlug,
Where hate in - human laid the snare

(21)

After a renewed expression of ecstatic faith in her mission she goes into the garden, and Marcelline enters from the house, followed by Jaquino. He is once more pressing his love on her, saying mournfully how well it was with them before this Fidelio came on the scene; and she infuriates him by her assurance that with him she had never been more than friendly, while she loves Fidelio deeply and intends to marry him. Rocco and Leonora return from the garden.

Rocco in kindly fashion warns Jaquino to think no more about Marcelline, while Leonora abruptly changes the subject. She has often begged Rocco, she says, to let the poor prisoners out to enjoy the garden, and always he has alternately promised and put it off. To-day it is so beautiful, and the Governor is not likely to return: will he not grant her request now? He urges that he has not the Governor's permission; but Marcelline thinks perhaps her father can do Pizarro some service that will placate him. "Some service?" says Rocco. "You are right, Marcelline: I will risk it"; and he tells Jaquino and Fidelio to open the cells, while he himself goes to the Governor. He enters the garden, while Jaquino and Fidelio unbolt the prison doors.

There comes out slowly a pitiful crowd of wasted figures, some, scarcely able to walk, supported by others, all of them hardly capable at first of moving their cramped limbs, and shading their eyes from the unaccustomed light of the sun. In the famous Prisoners' Chorus they sing of their joy at escaping for a moment from their living tombs into the clear air of day: at one point an officer appears on the rampart, and huddling together they exhort each other to speak softly, for they are overlooked and overheard; the effect in the theatre is indescribably moving. The prisoners pass slowly off into the garden, followed by Jaquino and Marcelline.

Rocco, who has meanwhile returned, is asked by Leonora how he has fared with Pizarro. All has gone well, he replies: he has told the Governor of Fidelio's desire, and Pizarro has consented both that he shall marry Marcelline and help the gaoler — that very day, indeed, he shall descend with him into the lower cells. Leonora gives a great cry of joy.

They are to go at once, says Rocco, into the cell of that prisoner of whom they talked before. "Is he to be released, then?" asks Leonora. "No," answers Rocco with his finger on his mouth; he will indeed find release, but in the grave, and that grave Fidelio is to help him to dig. "He is dead, then?" says Leonora; and when Rocco replies, "Not yet! not yet!" she shrinks away from him in horror, asking, "Is it your duty, then, to kill him?" The gaoler assures her: "No, my good young friend, don't tremble like that; Rocco does not hire himself out as a murderer. The Governor himself will go down there; all we two have to do is to dig the grave." "Perhaps the grave of my husband," Leonora murmurs aside: "could anything be more terrible?"

Greatly as Rocco dislikes the job, it has to be done; the grave is to be made in the ruined cistern in the floor of Florestan's cell. He would gladly spare the shivering Fidelio this ordeal, but the task is too much for his own unaided strength. The later stages of the duet are carried out to the accompaniment of an expressive orchestral melody, commencing thus in the clarinets and bassoons:

(22)   **Andante con moto**

It is one of the most effective passages in the whole score.

While Rocco is again offering to undertake the work alone, and Leonora is once more assuring him that her strength is equal to the trial, they are interrupted by Marcelline and Jaquino, who run in with the news that the officer has told the Governor of the liberty granted to the prisoners, and that he is coming thither in a fury.

Rocco, comforting himself with the thought that, let the tyrant say what he will, he has done a good action, braces himself to meet the storm of Pizarro's wrath, which soon bursts over him. Rocco stammers out an excuse about the warmth and beauty of the spring day, and it being the name-day of the King; then he softly suggests that a little indulgence may without danger be granted to the other prisoners, seeing that the Governor's vengeance is about to fall crushingly on one of them. Pizarro, somewhat appeased by this reflection, bids him get on with the business of the grave, and gives orders that the prisoners are to be driven back. They come in from the garden, singing a pathetic farewell to the sunlight. Marcelline and Leonora secretly sympathise with them, and Leonora and Jaquino, having shepherded them all into the prison, bolt the doors of the cells. The music dies down and down, in an expressive diminuendo, to a few simple chords in the wood-wind and horns, which are clinched by a shudder in the kettledrums as the curtain falls.

The second act opens in Florestan's wretched cell, which is very

faintly lit by a lamp. In the ground on the left of the stage is a
disused cistern, covered with stones and earth. In the background, through latticed openings in the wall, we see the steps of a
staircase leading down from above to the door that gives access
to the cell. Florestan is sitting on a stone seat; he is fettered to
the wall by a long chain.

His misery and the gloom of the cell are graphically described
in a fairly long orchestral introduction, in which the kettledrums
again play an expressive part:

The opening words of Florestan's recitative, "Heaven! what
darkness here! What silence full of horror!" have been severely
criticised as a dramatic blunder on the part of the librettist; it is
urged, and with reason, that as the prisoner has been in the cell
for two years he is hardly likely to be commenting on its darkness
and the silence at this juncture; the librettist has clearly forgotten this fact, and only remembers that it is we who are being
shown the darkness and made conscious of the silence for the first
time. The perception of this little blunder, however, does not make
Florestan's cry any less moving to us. His trust, he says, is in
Heaven, against whose will he does not murmur.

The opening strain of his aria:

is one that will be familiar to those who have heard the *Leonora
No. 3* overture in the concert-room. In the very bloom of his

youth, he says, happiness has fled from him; he dared to speak
the truth, and these chains are his reward. But he bears his woes
with patience, for soon his course will be run, and he is consoled
by the thought that he did his duty:

(25)

That fair vi - sion soothes my an-guish,
Süs-ser Trost in mei-nem Her-zen.

As the tempo merges from adagio into allegro an oboe melody
steals upward over a throbbing accompaniment, and then plays
like an aura round Florestan's melody, in which, in a kind of
exaltation that, though it seems to border on frenzy, is touched
throughout with a calm ecstasy, he speaks of the soft air that
seems to murmur round him, and of the rosy vision in which he
sees an angel coming to him and bringing him consolation — an
angel in the form of Leonora, who leads him aloft to the freedom
of heaven.

The rapture of the music dies away into a few soft harmonies,
and as he sinks down exhausted on the stone seat, covering his
face with his hands, we see in the background Rocco and Leonora
descending the stairs outside. Beethoven has treated the scene
that immediately follows in the form of " melodrama " — spoken
dialogue interspersed with short descriptive orchestral passages,
among which we hear again No. 22, as well as a snatch of
oboe melody taken from Florestan's vision of the coming of
Leonora.

Rocco and Leonora have with them, besides the apparatus for
the grave-digging, a lantern and a pitcher of wine. They speak in
undertones, Leonora especially being chilled to the heart by the
cold and darkness of the vault. Rocco points out the sleeping
prisoner, and Leonora tries in vain to catch a sight of his features.
They must get to work quickly, says Rocco; and throwing down
the bunch of keys that hangs at his belt and taking a mattock
from the trembling Leonora he goes down to his waist in the
cistern and begins to clear away the stones and earth from it.

Leonora all the while is trying to pick out the prisoner's features in the darkness.

The muted strings softly beat out a series of throbbing triplets, while underneath them a restless figure is given out in the gloomy tones of the double bassoon:

(26) Andante con moto

Against this sinister orchestral background Rocco and Leonora, both of them now working, converse in low tones. Leonora nerves herself for the ordeal, and swears that whoever the unhappy prisoner may be she will release him.

Rocco stops for a moment to refresh himself with a drink, and just then Florestan awakes and raises his head, but without turning it in their direction. Bidding Leonora take his place in the cistern, Rocco enters into conversation with Florestan. Has he been resting for a while? he asks; and when Florestan replies " Rest? How should I find rest? " Leonora is unable to recognise him with certainty from his voice alone. But when the prisoner turns his face to the gaoler to reproach him with his eternal indifference to his sufferings, Leonora knows at last that it is her husband, and she sinks almost unconscious on the edge of the grave.

Rocco tries to excuse himself: he only obeys the orders that are given him. Florestan asks him, as presumably he has done before, who is the Governor of this prison, and now Rocco thinks it safe to tell him it is Pizarro. Florestan repeats the name in horrified astonishment, and Leonora, raising herself gradually summons all her strength and courage. The following conversation ensues:

Florestan: " O send as soon as you can to Seville, and ask for Leonora Florestan — "

Leonora: " O God! he does not know that she herself is now digging his grave! "

Florestan: " Tell her I lie here in chains."

Rocco: " It is impossible, I tell you. I would only ruin myself, without having been able to help you."

Florestan: " Then if I am condemned to end my life here, let me at least not die thus by degrees."

Leonora (springing up and supporting herself by the wall): " O God, can this be borne? "

Florestan: " For pity's sake give me a drop of water. That is very little to ask of you."

Rocco, moved in spite of his profession, tells him that he cannot do that, but he will give him a drop of wine from his pitcher, which Leonora brings him at his bidding. Florestan looks at her and asks, " Who is this? " " My assistant, and in a few days my son-in-law," replies Rocco. He hands the pitcher to Florestan, who drinks it and thanks him:

This strain is developed into a trio, during which Leonora takes a crust of bread from her pocket and asks Rocco's permission to give it to Florestan. The gaoler, after a momentary refusal, consents; Leonora, deeply moved, offers the crust to Florestan, who seizes her hand and presses it to his breast with words of thanks, and then devours the bread.

The trio over, Rocco masters himself and remembers his duty. Going to the background and opening the door, he gives a whistle as signal to Pizarro. " Is that the omen of my death? " asks Florestan; and Leonora, in great agitation, replies, " No, no! Be calm, dear prisoner! " " O my Leonora! " he cried: " shall I never see thee again? " Leonora holds herself back with a mighty effort of self-control. " Be calm," she says insistently to him again; " do not forget that whatever you may see and hear, there is a God in heaven "; and she goes towards the cistern.

Pizarro enters, closely wrapped up in his cloak. In an assumed voice he asks Rocco if everything is ready, and being assured that it is, he tells Rocco to send his assistant away. Leonora moves to the background, and then creeps round in the shadow towards Florestan, all the while keeping her eyes on Pizarro. The latter mutters to himself that he must get rid of both his assistants that very day, so that no one may ever know of the murder.

Rocco asks him if he shall remove the prisoner's chains; he is told to release him only from the stone to which he is fettered. Drawing a dagger, Pizarro tells Florestan that his hour has come, but before he dies he shall know who it is that slays him. Throwing back his cloak he reveals himself as that Pizarro whom Florestan had tried to overthrow; and in his blood-lust he gloats over his victim, who, in answer to the Governor's cry, " Pizarro now stands before you as avenger! " calmly replies, " Before me stands a murderer! "

Pizarro raises the dagger and is about to throw himself on Florestan when Leonora gives a shriek, and, running forward, stands between the two men. Pizarro hurls her aside; returning, and once more throwing herself protectingly in front of Florestan, she cries, " Kill first his wife! " — a thrilling moment in the theatre, as the words ring out without any orchestral accompaniment.

The others ejaculate in astonishment, " His wife? " Turning to Florestan she cries, " Yes, I am Leonora! " Then, to the others, " I am his wife, I have sworn solace to him, and distruction to you! " Recovering himself, Pizarro sets himself to sweep this new danger from his path. He is about to stab both Florestan and

Leonora, when the latter draws a pistol from her doublet and, presenting it at him, cries, " Another word and you are dead! "

The situation is of itself dramatic enough, coming as it does after the long scene of doubts and fears and anguish that has led us up to it; but what immediately follows has hardly a parallel for effect in the whole range of opera. Just as Pizarro recoils from the pistol there is heard, behind the scenes, the trumpet-call:

that Pizarro had ordered to be given as the signal of the coming of the Minister. There is a fateful pause; then, as a great theme floats out in the flute and 'cellos:

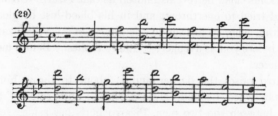

the four voices blend for a moment. Leonora, throwing her arms round her husband, cries, " God be thanked! Thou art saved! " Florestan echoes her words, while Rocco and Pizarro seem stunned.

The trumpet rings out its warning again, and Jaquino, followed by two officers and soldiers with torches, appears on the staircase and announces that the Minister is already at the gates of the prison. Rocco, greatly relieved at the turn events have taken, orders

the soldiers with the torches to come down and light the Governor
out. The interrupted quartet is resumed, and at the end of it the
frustrated Pizarro departs, leaving Florestan and Leonora, after a
brief dialogue in which the former tells how she came from Seville
and entered the prison service as a man, to express their joy in
an eager, rapturous duet:

the melody of which is taken from an unfinished opera of Beethoven's youth.

[In the libretto, Rocco returns after the duet, congratulates
(in spoken prose) the reunited pair, and tells them that the Minister has a list of all the prisoners, and has ordered Jaquino to
bring them before him. Florestan's name alone is not on the list;
he has evidently been a victim of the personal rancour of Pizarro.
This episode is usually omitted in performance, the curtain falling
on the duet.]

The final scene shows us the parade-ground of the prison, in
which is a statue of the King. The guards march in and form an
open square. They are followed, from one side, by the Minister
(Don Fernando), Pizarro, officers, and a crowd of people; while
from the other side come the prisoners, conducted by Jaquino
and Marcelline.

The prisoners kneel before the Minister, whom both they and
the people greet in a chorus of praise. He speaks to them of the
good King's clemency and sense of justice. Rocco pushes his way
through the crowd, accompanied by Florestan (still in chains) and

Leonora, at the sight of whom Pizarro gives an ejaculation of angry dismay, while Don Fernando is astonished to see again his friend Florestan, whom he had thought dead, and his wife Leonora in a man's costume.

In spite of Pizarro's protests he insists on hearing the whole story. Pizarro tries desperately to involve Rocco in his crime, but the gaoler has no difficulty in exculpating himself. At the command of the Governor, Pizarro is led away by the guards, Leonora unlocks the fetters of Florestan, who falls in her arms, and the opera ends with general rejoicing and a chorus in praise of the constancy of woman in general and of Leonora in particular.

The great *Leonora No. 3* overture commences with an adagio introduction in which, after an arresting unison phrase:

the wood-wind gives out the theme of Florestan's song in prison (No. 24). The anguish and the hopes and the heavenly vision of the prisoner are painted in the remainder of the adagio, and with the coming of the mighty theme of the allegro:

we seem to see Leonora hastening to the rescue. This theme is worked out at length in connection with another:

and is followed by the trumpet-call behind the scene (No. 28), which is succeeded, as in the opera, by the long-drawn No. 29. Another long development ensues, till we come to a rushing mighty wind in the strings, heralding a presto coda that is a great cry of triumph and joy, with the Leonora theme (No. 32) dominant at the end.

This colossal overture, the greatest thing of its kind ever written, is sometimes played between the first and second acts. The disadvantage of this plan is that by anticipating the trumpet-call the effect of this in the succeeding scene is diminished. Sometimes the overture is given between the prison scene and the finale; and in this case we feel that something of the thrill that the trumpet-call always gives us in the concert-room is now lost, because we have already heard it in its proper place in the opera.

GIOACCHINO ROSSINI

GIOACCHINO ROSSINI was born at Pesaro on the 29th February, 1792. His father, Giuseppe, the town trumpeter, got into trouble with his compatriots in 1796, owing to his sympathies with the French republicans, and had to find a new means of livelihood. His wife, though illiterate, had voice enough to get engagements as an opera singer; Giuseppe played the horn in the orchestra; and occasionally Gioacchino helped, either with his voice (until it broke) or as accompanist.

As a child he had been taught the rudiments of music, and in his early teens he entered the Bologna Conservatoire, where he received such musical education as was usual in the Italy of that time. He already realised his own marvellous facility, and had no great appetite for severe study. Through an influential friend he received his first operatic commission in 1810, when he produced *La Cambiale di Matrimonio* ("The Matrimonial Market") at Venice. Other commissions soon followed, and he won a big success with *La Pietra del Paragone* ("The Touchstone") at Milan in 1812. *Tancredi* and *L'Italiana in Algieri* followed in 1813, and *Il Turco in Italia* in 1814. In 1815 he made the acquaintance of Barbaja, the Naples impresario, who engaged him as his musical director, with the obligation of writing two operas a year; the first, *Elisabetta, Regina d'Inghilterra*, was a great success.

The year 1816 saw the production in Rome of the *Barber of Seville* (5th February), which, after an inauspicious first performance, soon became enormously popular. Rossini returned to Naples to work out his contract with Barbaja. *Otello*, the third act of which was for many years regarded in many quarters as the high-water mark of European operatic composition, was given on the 4th December, 1816. *La Cenerentola* (" Cinderella ") was produced in Rome on the 25th January, 1817, and *La Gazza Ladra* (" The Thieving Magpie ") at Milan on the 30th May. Rossini had now written fifteen operas in four years, while his total output for the eight years 1815–23 was twenty. He continued to fluctuate between serious and comic opera and oratorio. *Mosè in Egitto* was given at Naples in 1818, and *Semiramide* at Venice in 1823.

Long before this latter year his fame had spread all over Europe, and on the termination of his Naples engagement in 1821 he accepted an invitation to go to Vienna and produce his *Zelmira*. He remained six months in the Austrian capital, where, apart from his triumphs in the theatre, his wit and charm of manner made him highly popular in society. He heard the Eroica Symphony, was overwhelmed by it, and sought and obtained an introduction to Beethoven; but little was said at the interview, owing partly to Beethoven's deafness, partly to the fact that neither of them understood very much of the language of the other.

In 1823 Rossini went to Paris, then to London, then (after a visit to Italy) to Paris again, where he was made Director of the Italian Opera, a post which he held for about two years. For Paris he wrote *Le Comte Ory* (1828) and *Guillaume Tell* (1829). Though he was then no more than thirty-seven years old, and he had still nearly forty years of his life before him, he wrote no more operas. He still wrote small works for the church and the salon, and one large one, the *Stabat Mater* (Paris, January 1842).

In the years immediately following the production of *Guillaume Tell* he travelled a good deal, finally settling at Bologna, where he took an amount of trouble that was quite exceptional with him over the reform of the Conservatoire. He had always lived well rather than wisely, and about this time his health began to fail, his chief ailments being stone and neurasthenia. In May 1843, after suffering for many years, he underwent an operation in Paris that restored him to health for a time. When it failed again, he left Bologna finally for Paris (in the spring of 1855); the change of air and a hydropathic treatment benefited him greatly, and for the next twelve years his health on the whole was good.

His first wife was Isabella Colbran, who had been both the leading prima donna and the mistress of Barbaja of Naples. Rossini separated from her in 1837, and she died in October 1845; in August 1846 he married Olympe Pélissier, who had already cared for him for some ten years.

The town of Paris presented him with a plot of land in Passy, on which he built himself a house, and his remaining years were spent between this and his apartment in Paris. He continued to write innumerable little pieces for himself and for his friends' albums: some of these have been pieced together in our own day to make the Russian ballet *Le Boutique Fantasque*. On the 12th February, 1868, *Guillaume Tell* was given for the five hundredth time at the Paris Opera, and the occasion was made the pretext for a general act of homage to him; he was serenaded in his Paris apartment by the Opera orchestra, chorus, and some of the soloists. He died of pneumonia at Passy on the 13th November, 1868.

Rossini was an inveterate joker, and the stories told of his wit and humour are almost innumerable. One of the best is in connection with an early opera of his, *Il Figlio per Azzardo*. The story goes that as he did not like the libretto, which had been forced on him by the impresario, Rossini revenged himself by turning the whole thing into nonsense — in each bar of the overture the second violins had to strike the lamp-shade with their bows, the bass part was written absurdly high, the soprano part absurdly low, and so on. No doubt there was some fun at the time, but one suspects that the joke was largely worked up by Rossini in conversation in later years. The score as we now have it hardly bears out the details. A revised version of the opera, under the title of *Il Signor Bruschino*, was produced at Paris in 1858. It is one of the best of Rossini's less-known works.

He was said to have made ironical and somewhat malicious

comments on Wagner, but Rossini indignantly denied having uttered them. The two men met in 1860, and in an interesting article on Rossini written after the latter's death, Wagner spoke of him as " the first truly great and reverable man I had as yet met in the world of art."

THE BARBER OF SEVILLE

THE French dramatist to whom we owe the original texts of
The Barber of Seville and *The Marriage of Figaro* was
one of the most remarkable products of the eighteenth century.
His real name was Pierre Augustin Caron. He was born at Paris
on the 24th January, 1732, and being the son of a watchmaker he
himself graduated in that trade. In his early twenties he managed
to secure a post in the King's household, where he taught the harp
to the daughters of Louis XIV. In 1761 he purchased the title of
Secretary to the King, and with it a patent of nobility, in virtue of
which he called himself in future Caron de Beaumarchais.

The upstart was regarded with none too favourable an eye by
some exclusive members of the genuine aristocracy, but his unfail-
ing wit and assurance — not to say impudence — carried him
triumphantly through most of his little encounters with them. In
addition to his literary activities he dabbled in trade and speculation during a great part of his life, making large sums and not
infrequently losing them again; during the war of the French
colonies with England he supplied arms to the United States, and
became the creditor of the new country for large amounts which
were never paid him, though his family received, thirty-six years
after his death, 800,000 out of the 2,280,000 francs that were
admitted to be owing to him. In 1764 he went to Spain to champion the cause of one of his sisters who had been jilted by a
Spaniard names Clavigo. Out of his experiences in this affair he
made his first play, *Eugénie* (1767).

He was twice married, in 1757 and in 1768, in each case to a widow, in the first case being left a widower after a year of marriage, in the second after two years. In 1770 he became involved in one of the most famous lawsuits of the eighteenth century. A certain Comte de la Blache accused him of fraud in connection with the business affairs of his uncle, an old banker, and claimed from him 139,000 livres. Beaumarchais fought the case, both in the courts and in the Press, with infinite wit and ingenuity. The first verdict went against him; he appealed, and won, but lost a third trial and found himself, for a time, practically ruined.

His comedy *The Barber of Seville* appeared in 1775, and was a tremendous success. He wrote *The Marriage of Figaro* shortly afterwards, but it was not performed until 1784. In 1787 he produced a curious opera *Tarare*, the fruit of certain theories he had upon the new possibilities of this genre; it was set to music by Mozart's rival in Vienna, Salieri. After living for some time in magnificent style in a great house in Paris, he was ruined by the revolution, and at one time was actually in prison. He died in 1799.

In view of the uses to which musicians later put the two great comedies, it is interesting to recall that Beaumarchais himself originally planned *The Barber of Seville* (in 1772) as a sort of opera in four acts, the music in the sung portions being mostly from Spanish folk-songs. One of his friends, the Prince de Conti, told Beaumarchais that he thought the preface gayer than the play itself, and advised him to remodel the latter and make a comedy of it. In this form it was first produced in 1775. The work, by the way, had been refused by the Comédie Italienne; the chief actor at that establishment, Clairval, had himself once been a barber, and the Parisian wits could have been trusted to take full advantage of the opportunity this would have afforded them had he played the Barber's part.

Figaro was apparently not set to music until Mozart took up the subject in 1786. But *The Barber of Seville* had been set ten years before this by the Italian Paisiello (1741–1816) — almost immediately, as will be seen, after the publication of the play. This previous opera on the subject proved a bit of an embarrassment to Rossini. It is probable, indeed, that the subject was no choice of his own, but was forced upon him by the Roman impresario. This gentleman had latterly been having a good deal of trouble with the local police, who refused him permission to stage one subject after another because it was held to be dangerous in the political state of Italy at that time. Finally the distracted impresario suggested Beaumarchais' comedy; and the Roman Governor seems to have fallen in with the proposal out of sheer fatigue with the whole bothering business. Besides, as the subject had already been set by Paisiello, it was presumably harmless.

Rossini, however, appears not to have been particularly pleased at the impresario's choice. He knew the passion of the Italians for taking sides, and the general estimation in which the venerable Paisiello was held; and he foresaw trouble for his own opera. To put himself in the right in advance, he wrote to Paisiello advising him courteously of his intention to set the *Barber*. The old composer replied to the young one in a letter that was a blend of politeness and irony. He had not been particularly pleased at the success of Rossini's *Elisabetta* in Naples, and no doubt already had the suspicion that a dangerous new star had come above the Italian opera horizon. But he maintained the courtesies of the polite world; he told the young man, with mock gravity, that it gave him much pleasure to approve of the choice of the Roman papal police. No doubt he hoped that the work of the presumptuous new-comer would be a failure.

Rossini astutely saw to it that the contents of Paisiello's letter became known all over Rome, and in addition he introduced the libretto with a note in which he expressed his respectful admiration for the old public favourite. He thought it prudent also to give his own work the title not of *The Barber of Seville*, but of *Almaviva, or the Vain Precaution*.

His wary diplomacy, however, was not of much avail with the Roman public. The opera had a stormy reception at its first performance on the 6th February, 1816. A number of malcontents regarded it as an impertinence on Rossini's part that he

should have set the text at all after Paisiello; others were outraged
by the novelty of some of Rossini's proceedings — for it must be
remembered that in his day the young Rossini was regarded as an
audacious musical innovator, almost a red revolutionary. Altogether they found the new *Barber* rather disturbing.

The partisan audience was only too delighted when, in addition to the many things that outraged its æsthetic sensibilities,
something happened to provoke laughter. At one point in one of
Almaviva's arias a string of his guitar snapped; at another, a cat
that was not in the cast strolled across the stage; at another,
Basilio became entangled in his robe; and each contretemps of
this kind was an occasion for joyous hissing and hooting. Rossini,
who conducted at the first performance, was so upset by the attitude of the audience that he left the theatre as soon as he could,
and many years after he told Wagner that he feared he was going
to be assassinated. But the next night the audience gave the opera
a fair hearing, and at the third performance the success of the new
work was assured.

It seems almost incredible that a work of this size could have
been written in thirteen days, as is alleged, yet the dates confirm the story. Rossini's facility, indeed, was so great that had
he really been put to it he could probably have finished the work
in a day or two less. When Donizetti was told that the opera had
been written in thirteen days, " Yes," he said, " but then Rossini
always was a lazy fellow! "

Rossini, it is true, saved himself a little trouble here and there
by using up material from his older works. The original overture
has disappeared; but in the library of the Paris Conservatoire
there is a manuscript score of the opera with an overture that is
identical with that used by Rossini for two other operas of his —
Il Turco in Italia and *Sigismondo;* and it is a fair presumption
that this was the overture heard at the first performance of the
Barber. The sprightly overture which is now published and played
with the opera is really that to *Elizabetta;* and Rossini had already used this in two earlier works, *L'Equivoco stravagante*
(1811) and *Aureliano in Palmira* (1814). There were other

borrowings from others of his works, which we shall note in the appropriate places.

It was quite a common thing in the eighteenth century and the early nineteenth for an opera composer to economise his labours by drawing upon earlier works that had not succeeded in establishing themselves; he probably did not see why a good thing should be lost to the world merely because the world had not had the good sense to take it to its heart at once. It is amusing to read that the Roman audience of 1816 found in the borrowed *Elisabetta* overture a summary of *The Barber of Seville;* they persuaded themselves that in one part they could hear the scoldings of old Bartolo, in another the lamentations of Rosina, and so on.

Rossini, who always took the gayest possible view of every situation, told Wagner, many years after, that for the score of the *Barber* he was paid twelve hundred francs, plus a nut-coloured coat with gold buttons, of which the impresario made him a present in order that he might be able to cut a decent figure in the theatre. The coat Rossini valued at a hundred francs — total thirteen hundred francs; and as the composition had taken him only thirteen days, this was at the liberal payment of a hundred francs a day. " So you see," he said, " that I was really getting quite a big wage. I swaggered about it before my father, who, when he was the public trumpeter at Pesaro, was paid only two francs fifty centimes a day."

ACT I

The first act shows an open square in Seville. On the left is the house of Doctor Bartolo, the old guardian of the fair Rosina; as he hopes to marry the young lady himself he keeps her as secluded as possible, and at present the windows are barred and the blinds drawn. It is early morning.

Count Almaviva, a rich young Spanish nobleman, has come with a band of musicians to offer Rosina an aubade; but for the moment he himself is not visible. The musicians are led in by his

servant Fiorello; all make a great point of secrecy and quietness,
and keep on singing "Softly, softly," no more loudly than the
exigencies of opera call for. Count Almaviva appears, learns from
Fiorello that everything is ready for the aubade, and, while the
musicians are tuning their instruments, breaks out into an aria
in which he exhorts the slumbering fair one to rise and graciously
allow the dawn to set about its normal business. The music is very
florid; a faint idea of its technical difficulty can be gathered from
the opening bars:

Dawn, with her ro - sy man - - - - tle,
Ec - co ri - den - te in cie - - - - lo

Stands at the gate of morn - ing,
Spun - ta la bel - la au - ro - - ra,

Night's gloom a - far is dri - ven, Yet...............
E tu non sor-gi an - co - ra, E...............

thou art slum - b'ring still!...............
puoi dor - mir co - si?...............

and from the following passage taken from the middle section:

un - - til...... I have...... told her my
oh......... dol - ce con - ten - to, che e-

heart...............
gual...............

she.......................... en˙ - - - - - - chants,
no,........................ non - - - - - - ha,

This aria, by the way, was added to the score after the first performance; Rossini adapted it from a chorus in an earlier oratorio of his, *Ciro in Babilonia* (*Cyrus in Babylon*).

Almaviva fancies he sees Rosina at the window, but Fiorello, whose eye is not affected by love, assures him he is mistaken; meanwhile the morning is advancing, and it would be prudent, he thinks, to get rid of the musicians. The Count is far too much of a grandee to come into personal contact with these hirelings; he hands his purse to Fiorello, who in turn distributes the money to the musicians. This he does on such a liberal scale that instead of going off promptly they take quite a considerable time kissing the hands and the cloak of the Count and bowing to him, meanwhile expressing their humble thanks in a chorus which runs to such length that, after many vain attempts to persuade them to retire, the Count is reduced to driving them away.

The Count now bids Fiorello also leave him. Each morning he has seen Rosina at her window, and he assumes that she has also seen him, in which case she can hardly doubt that it is love for her that has brought him here. His intentions, he assures us, are strictly honourable; he intends to marry the lady. While he is indulging in these reflections a voice is heard without, singing a gay " La, la, la." The Count, who does not wish to be detected, hides under some arches — for it is now daylight — in order to observe the new-comer.

A riotously merry strain (No. 3) breaks out in the orchestra, and Figaro trips in, still singing his joyous " La, la, la! " Suspended from his neck is a guitar. He is full of the sense of his own importance. " Make way," he cries, " for the factotum of all the town! ":

I'm......... the fac - to - tum of all the
Lar - - go al fac - to - tum del - la cit -

town, .   make   way!
- tà,   lar - go.

Morning has come, and everybody must be off to his business.
What a pleasant life is that of the barber — a barber such as he —
a barber of quality! He is the most fortunate of men, for he is
everywhere in demand:

al - ways in luck where good for - tune is
for - tu - na - tis - si - mo per ve - ri -

rife, La le ran la la le ran la la re la re la
- tà, La le ran la la le ran la la re la re la

la la ran la la ran la.

There is no profession in all the world, indeed, to compare with
that of such a barber as he, for besides his services with scissors
and razor he is the confidential adviser of all sorts of people,
cavaliers and ladies alike:

Ear - ly and late,   for all who re -
Pron - to a far tut - to, la not - te, fi

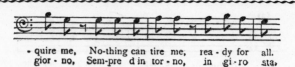

- quire me,   No-thing can tire me,   rea - dy for   all.
gior - no,   Sem-pre d in tor - no,   in gi-ro   sta,

In such request is he that he gets no rest, either day or night; one man calls for his wig, another to be shaved; another wishes to be bled, another sends him off with a billet-doux. The multiplicity of their cries distracts him; one at a time, he begs them, for pity's sake — " Here I am; Figaro here, Figaro there, ready, aye, super-ready, as quick as lightning." For all that he counts himself the most fortunate of mankind:

(6)

Ah bra - vo,,   Fi - ga - ro, bra - vo, bra -

- vis - si - mo, ah bra-vo,   Fi - ga - ro, bra - vo, bra -

- vis - si - mo, thou art   a   fa - vour - ite   of
          a   te for - tu - na, a te for -

For-tune, thou art a   bar - ber of great re - nown.
- tu - na,   a   te for - tu - na non man-che - rà.

The aria is the finest specimen in existence of the Italian humorous bass aria — a genre that was in great vogue in the eighteenth and early nineteenth centuries, when Italian basses were expected to have almost the vocal agility of sopranos. It need hardly be said that the " Largo al factotum " can be taken at its proper pace only in Italian, with its large proportion of vowels to consonants.

Still full of his own importance, even after he has finished his superb aria, the bright fellow goes on to tell us further in a recitative how much in demand he is; it is a subject on which, we feel, he could discourse for ever. Life is glorious, he says, when one is as famous as he is: without him not a girl in Seville could find a husband; to him comes the little widow who would like to be married again. And it is all so easy, for what with his comb and his razor by day, and his guitar at night, he is admitted everywhere.

By this time it has struck the Count that the features of this breezy new-comer are familiar to him, while it occurs to Figaro also that he has seen the Count somewhere. They recognise each other, and the Count, who is in the town incognito, and wants to remain so — for reasons that so intelligent a person as Figaro will grasp at once — asks the barber to be careful how he addresses him before others; no " Your Excellency " or anything of that kind! He sees that Figaro can be very useful to him in his enterprise with Rosina; and he tells him how one evening on the Prado he saw a lovely girl, the daughter, as he thinks, of a certain senile doctor, and fell in love with her. He now spends his days and nights under her window, hoping for a sign of recognition. " That window? And a doctor? " says Figaro. " How lucky! "

The Fates are indeed on the side of the Count; as Figaro puts it in his own picturesque language, the cheese has dropped right on to the macaroni! For in that very house is not he, Figaro, barber, coiffeur, surgeon, herbalist, druggist, vet, and confidential man in general? Moreover, the young lady is not the Doctor's daughter, but only his ward.

Just then the balcony window opens, and Figaro retires under the portico. Rosina is seen on the balcony. She has come out hoping and expecting to see the young man who has been following her for days; in fact, she has a letter for him. But old Bartolo appears most inopportunely. " What is that paper? " he asks. " Oh, nothing," says Rosina; " merely the words of an aria taken from the new opera, *The Vain Precaution*." The Count, hidden in the street below, chuckles over her wit, and Figaro, who is a connoisseur in these matters, slips in a quiet word of praise of Rosina's guile. She lets the letter fall, and, pretending that this was an accident, sends Bartolo out to retrieve it; meanwhile the Count has picked it up and again hidden himself.

Bartolo, unable to find the letter, is not satisfied with Rosina's innocent explanation that the wind must have carried it away. His suspicions are aroused; he orders her in, and threatens to have the balcony walled up on the morrow. Rosina goes indoors, and the Count and Figaro read the letter, which runs thus: " Your assiduous attentions have excited my curiosity. My guardian is just going out; as soon as he is out of the way, find some ingenious means of letting me know your name, your position, and your intentions. I can never appear on the balcony without my tyrant following me; but be sure that everything that it is possible to do will be done to break her chains by the unfortunate Rosina."

While Figaro, in answer to the Count's enquiry, is explaining that this tyrannical guardian is a suspicious and grumbling old miser who hopes both to marry Rosina and to secure her money, the Doctor himself comes out. He calls out to Rosina, within, that not a soul is to be admitted but Don Basilio, who, should he call, is to be kept waiting. He locks the door from the outside and goes off, muttering that he must see to this marriage of his at once. This is too much for the Count, who has caught Bartolo's last words. Who is Basilio? he asks Figaro. Basilio, replies the barber, is hand-in-glove with Bartolo. He is a person very much down at heel, a hypocrite, a born intriguer, and a cunning matchmaker; at present his duty in the house is to teach Rosina music.

The Count and Figaro work out a plan of campaign. For the present Rosina is not to know the Count's name or rank; he would first learn whether she loves him for his own sake. Figaro sees Rosina behind the curtain, and exhorts the Count to take the first step towards her affections by singing her a ballad. This he does, and under cover of a charming song:

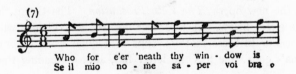

(7)

Who   for   e'er 'neath thy win - dow is
Se il mio   no - me   sa - per voi bra o

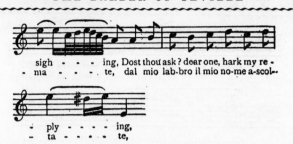

sigh - - - ing, Dost thou ask? dear one, hark my re -
- ma - - - te, dal mio lab-bro il mio no-me a-scol --

ply - - - - ing,
ta - - te,

conveys to her that his name is Lindoro, and that he faithfully
adores her. The naïve pun runs more smoothly in the Italian:

" Io son Lindoro
Che fido v'adoro."

Rosina finds the song and the sentiments so much to her taste
that she begs him to go on, which the Count does, with a second
stanza in which he tells her that Lindoro can offer her no treasure,
but only a heart full of sincere love. Rosina has just begun to
reply to him when she disappears from the balcony, evidently having been interrupted from inside the house. The Count impatiently
declares that he must see her at once or he will go crazy; Figaro
must come to his aid; let him put his boasted wits to work and
find a means to introduce him into the Doctor's house. The Count
promises him all the money he will require, and Figaro breaks out
into a song in praise of gold as the source of all inventiveness:

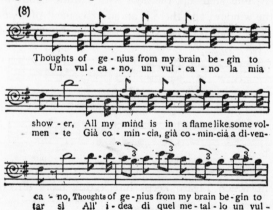

(8)

Thoughts of ge - nius from my brain be - gin to
Un vul - ca - no, un vul - ca - no la mia

show - er, All my mind is in a flame like some vol -
men - te Già co - min - cia, già co - min-cià a di-ven-

ca - no, Thoughts of ge - nius from my brain be - gin to
tar sì All' i - dea di quel me - tal - lo un vul -

show - er, and like some vol - ca - no
ca - no la mia men - te in - co -

all.................. my mind is......... in.
- - min - - - - - cia a di - ven - tar.

After a little cogitation, Figaro decides that the best way for
the Count to gain access to Bartolo's house will be in the disguise
of a soldier; a regiment is expected in the town that very day, and
it will be easy for the Count to pretend that he has been quartered
upon the Doctor. The pair express their delight at this happy idea
in a duet based on the rollicking second part of No. 8. But the
gold has not yet finished its beneficent work in Figaro's fertile
brain. Another idea has occurred to him: the Count, in addition
to being a soldier, had better pretend to be drunk, for who would
suspect a spy in a drunken man? The suggestion appeals to the
Count, and once more they give vent to their joy to the same
strain as before. " But where," asks the Count, " can I find you
when I want you? " Figaro gives him, at great length, his address
in a sprightly aria, in which he tells him that he lives at No. 15
on the left, four steps up, the door with a white band; five wigs
hang in the window, and there is an advertisement of a wonderful
pomade. The Count expresses his satisfaction in a jubilant song:

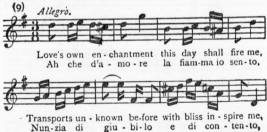

(9) *Allegrò.*

Love's own en - chantment this day shall fire me,
Ah che d'a - mo - re la fiam-ma io sen - to,

- Transports un - known be-fore with bliss in - spire me,
Nun - zia di giu - bi - lo e di con - ten - to,

throughout which Figaro keeps interjecting more directions as
to his address, and expressions of his delight at the shower

of gold that is going to descend on him. At the conclusion
of the duet Figaro enters Bartolo's house, and the Count goes
off.

The scene changes to a room in Bartolo's house, the windows of
which are closed with venetian blinds. Rosina is there, holding a
letter in her hand. A few preliminary bars in the orchestra depict
the flutterings of her little heart; then she breaks into the famous aria " Una voce poco fà," that is so beloved by every prima
donna:

(The opening words of the aria are, in a rough translation, " A
little while ago a voice resounded in my heart: my heart is already touched, and it was Lindoro who dealt it the blow.") She
assures the absent Lindoro that she will marry nobody but him.
Then she proceeds ingenuously to describe her own charming
qualities: she is respectful, obedient, affectionate, easily ruled —
so long, of course, as nobody crosses her will, when she turns into
a viper:

When this happens she will stop at nothing to get her own way:

But if you cross...... my will, or what I
Ma .se mi toc - - ca - no dov' è il mio
do............... take ill, like a - ny
de - - - bo - le, sa - rò u na
vi - per...... I........ will...... turn,
vi - pe - ra........ sa - - rò,

The aria is extremely difficult, and is therefore in great favour with prime donne; but in spite of the florid character of the writing, which on the surface seems intended only to give opportunities for vocal display, it is a perfect expression of the character of Rosina. It is evident from the words that it should be sung only by coloratura sopranos who can suggest not only to the ear but to the eye a kittenish creature of sixteen — which is Rosina's age in the opera.

The aria over, she has just come to the conclusion that she will give the letter, which she now seals, to Figaro to take to Lindoro, when the barber most opportunely enters. Figaro, for his part, has a message for her; but before he can deliver it, Bartolo is heard returning, and Figaro hides, while Rosina retires. Bartolo comes in cursing Figaro for a scoundrel, for with his medicines he has upset the whole house since morning. He calls in his servants Berta and Ambrogio, and tries to pump them to discover if the barber has been talking to Rosina; but he can get no sense out of either of them, for Berta has been given something that keeps her sneezing all the time, while Ambrogio has had a narcotic and can do nothing but yawn.

Basilio now enters. Bartolo tells him that he means to speed

matters up and marry Rosina the next day; but Basilio has a
secret for him — he has seen the great Count Almaviva lurking in
the neighbourhood. They at once conclude that this must be the
unknown who has been dangling round after Rosina. The crafty
Basilio has a sovereign plan for getting rid of the Count —
calumny, which, skilfully employed, can always be trusted to
bring the strongest down! He explains his meaning to Bartolo in
the celebrated " Calumny " aria, in which he describes how, in
the mouth of a master, detraction begins with a whisper so faint
as to be hardly noticeable, then swells to a zephyr, then to a gale
that destroys the victim. The aria is a masterpiece of characterisation; the gradual swelling of the chorus of calumny from a breath
to a devastating hurricane is represented by a long crescendo in
the orchestra, the following phrase being repeated again and again,
starting *piano* and rising to a huge *fortissimo:*

And yet, appropriate as the music is to the words, it is really another of Rossini's borrowings from his early operas: it is adapted from the *Sigismondo* of 1815.

Good, they will employ calumny when necessary, says Bartolo; but meanwhile time presses. The first thing to do is to draw up the marriage contract; when once he is Rosina's husband he will know how to put a stop to her flirtations. The pair go out, and Figaro and Rosina come forward. The barber tells her of the plan that is afoot, and Rosina assures him that Bartolo will have his hands more than full with her. Figaro tells her of a cousin of his, a handsome young man, just completing his studies, who has fallen in love with her; and he discloses his scheme for bringing this " Lindoro " into the house.

After a little affectation of maidenly reserve, Rosina consents to listen to Figaro's suggestion that she shall write Lindoro just a couple of lines saying that she expects him. It turns out, however, that the letter is already written! She takes it from her pocket and gives it to Figaro, who compliments her on her smartness. In a lively duet Rosina expresses her delight at the prospect of meeting Lindoro, while Figaro comments sarcastically on the artfulness of woman.

As Figaro comes out, Bartolo enters. He wants to know what Figaro had called about that morning. Rosina fences with him. Bartolo goes to the heart of the matter with a question — did not Figaro bring her a reply to the letter she sent by the window, that alleged aria from *The Vain Precaution?* This disconcerts her for the moment. And why, the prying Bartolo goes on, those ink-stains on her finger? Rosina is ready with her reply; she scalded her finger this morning, and applied the old-fashioned remedy of a little ink. " But there were six sheets of paper on the desk this

morning," Bartolo continues relentlessly, "and now there are only
five." " The other one? " replies Rosina. " Oh, I took that to
wrap up some sweets for Marcellina." " But this pen," says
Bartolo, " has it not just been used for writing? " " Oh, yes,"
says Rosina; " I used it to draw a flower on my embroidery."

Baffled at every turn, Bartolo bids her hold her tongue, and
breaks out into an aria in which he pompously warns her not to
attempt to impose on a man of his quality:

(14) *Andante maestoso.*

To a man of my im--portance Dare you
A un dot-tor del-la mia sor-te Que-ste

of - fer such ex - cu - ses?
scu - se, si - gno - ri - na!

The concluding phases of his aria:

(15) *Vivace.*

Mark, my la - dy, for the
Si - gno - ri - na, un' al - tra

fu - ture, I, Don Bar - to - lo, have
vol - ta Quan - do Bar - to - lo an - drà

said it, I per - force will save your
fuo - ri, Si - gno - ri - na, un' al - tra

cred - it, I, Don Bar - to - lo, have
vol - ta, Quan - do Bar - to - lo an - drà

said it, I per - force will save your
fuo - ri, La con - se - gna ai ser - vi -

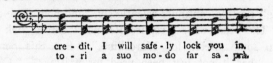

cre - dit, I will safe - ly lock you in,
to - ri a suo mo - do far sa - prà,

are not only an amusing expression of petulance, but an admirable
example of the rapid Italian patter-song of the period.

He rails and storms at her for a long time, and then goes out.
Rosina follows him, after declaring that the only effect of his
tyranny will be to make her defy him all the more. The Count
now enters, in the guise of a soldier, and Bartolo returns. The
Count, pretending to be drunk, cannot remember the Doctor's
name accurately, and makes several grotesque shots at it; but he
is certain that he has been quartered upon him. Rosina returns,
and the Count manages to pass the word to her that he is Lindoro.

A scene of lively stage intrigue follows. Bartolo, to the momentary dismay of the Count, produces a document giving him exemption from quartering; while he was looking for it the lovers
have managed to get in a few furtive words with each other. Still
playing the drunken rowdy, the Count pitches the document
away, and declares his fixed intention of remaining where he
is. He drops a letter, upon which Rosina lets her handkerchief
fall. Then, pretending to see the letter for the first time, he
picks it up along with the handkerchief and gives them both to
Rosina.

The servant Berta now comes in, and the five indulge in an
elaborate quintet. Rosina tries tears for the melting of Bartolo's
rage, and the Doctor, who has caught sight of the letter, is for a
moment softened; meanwhile the Count, with sword drawn, keeps
up his feigned drunken bluster. Figaro enters with his barber's
basin under his arm; he has heard the noise, he tells them, down
in the street, where a crowd has gathered. The Count and Bartolo
soon get at cross-purposes again, but before the quarrel has gone
very far a loud knock is heard at the street-door. An officer of the
guard enters with his soldiers. Bartolo complains of the conduct
of the drunken soldier who has forced his way into his house,
and the officer is about to arrest the Count when the latter takes

him aside and shows him the insignia of his nobility. This, of
course, alters the whole situation so far as the officer is concerned; though when the curtain falls, after a very long and
brilliant ensemble, in which everyone insists noisily upon his own
point of view, matters seem to be left for the time being very
much as they were.

ACT II

The second act shows the library in Doctor Bartolo's house,
containing a harpsichord, on which is some music. The Doctor has
been making enquiries about the rude soldier, and finds he is not
known to the regiment he claimed to belong to; and Bartolo suspects that he is an agent of the prowling Count Almaviva. There
is a knock at the door, and the Count enters, this time disguised
as a music-master. He pretends that he is Don Alonzo, a pupil of
Basilio, and has come to give Rosina her usual lesson in place of his
master, who is confined to the house with illness. The motive on
which his dialogue with Bartolo is founded is exquisite in its oily,
ironical politeness:

(16)

Andante moderato.

(Peace and joy be on this dwelling!)

Bartolo is very suspicious, but the supposed Don Alonzo partly wins his confidence by telling him that in Almaviva's lodging, which happens to be his also, he has found a letter from Rosina to the Count which Alonzo now hands to Bartolo. Perhaps, Alonzo hints, by means of this letter it may be possible to persuade Rosina that her lover has been faithless. " Calumny! " says Bartolo to himself: " an apt pupil of his master Basilio! " The Count, however, has got himself into a bit of a mess; his tongue, in the embarrassment of the moment, has outrun his common sense. But for the moment he gains his end, which is to see Rosina; Bartolo brings in his ward, and the assumed Alonzo pretends to give her her lesson, Bartolo listening and watching.

To the Count's accompaniment at the harpsichord Rosina sings a rondo from *The Vain Precaution,* but soon she breaks off into an appeal to Lindoro to help her, which the Count promises to do. This is the famous Lesson Scene; it has long been the custom for the prima donna at this point to sing anything she likes, her preference, of course, being for an aria, however irrelevant to the play or the period, that will allow her to show off her virtuosity. The selections have ranged from " Robin Adair " and " Home, Sweet Home " to the Mad Scene from Donizetti's *Lucia di Lammermoor,* and to things even madder than that.

Bartolo does not think much of the song. Music, he says, is going to the devil in these days; in his young days it was much better — had more tune in it — which he offers to prove by singing a favourite ditty of a preceding generation. He has hardly got through more than half a dozen lines, however:

(17)

Come where the wood will screen...... us, My sweet-est of Ro - si - - nas

Quan - do mi sei vi - ci - - na, A - ma-bi - le Ro - si - - na

when he is annoyed to find that Figaro, who has entered with his basin under his arm, is imitating him behind his back.

Figaro insists on shaving Bartolo at once; no other day will do, as he is in such demand all over the town. His engagement book for the morrow is full. He has to shave and cut the hair of all the officers of the regiment that has just come to town; the old Marchese Andronica wants her blond wig dressing; the young Count Bombè's top-knot needs attending to; to Bernadone, the lawyer, who yesterday fell ill of indigestion, he must give a purgative; to say nothing of other engagements. No, to-morrow is quite impossible; the shaving of Bartolo must be done to-day.

Figaro, having obtained Bartolo's keys, goes to get the shaving utensils, and a great crash is heard " off," as if all the crockery in the house were being broken. Bartolo rushes out to see what has happened, and returns with Figaro, crying out that owing to the barber's clumsiness his best dishes and wine-glasses have been smashed. It has all been a ruse on the part of Figaro, who has seized his opportunity to take from the bunch the key of the balcony. He proceeds to shave Bartolo, but has not got very far with the business when, to everyone's amazement, the supposedly bed-ridden Basilio enters.

The situation is a critical one for the conspirators. The Count saves it by taking Basilio aside and persuading him that he is very ill and ought not to have ventured out of the house with such a fever on him; Figaro feels Basilio's pulse and confirms the awful diagnosis — it can't be anything less than scarlet fever. Basilio does not know what to make of it all until the Count surreptitiously passes him a purse, which, welcome as it is in itself, still fails to elucidate the matter completely for him. But at last, by dint of hard work, the company manages to persuade him that he really is ill, and in a most amusing ensemble he is persuaded to go home and get to bed.

Figaro now resumes the shaving of Bartolo, placing himself in such a position as to hide the lovers, who hurriedly arrange for an elopement at midnight, the Count now having the key. While trying to explain to Rosina the use he has been compelled to make of her letter, he happens to raise his voice a little too high, and Bartolo overhears him. He escapes from Figaro, and, after railing at them all, drives them out. Then he calls for Ambrogio and Berta; the former he sends to Basilio, bidding him come at once, while Berta is to go downstairs and see that no one else enters. On second thoughts he decides that as he cannot trust anybody, he had better go himself; his doing so allows Berta to have the stage to herself for a few minutes, during which she sings a pleasant little song that has no great bearing on the action.

This over, and Berta having left the stage, Bartolo and Basilio enter. The Count's trick as " Alonzo " is exposed by Basilio, and it becomes clear to Bartolo that the supposed music-master was another emissary of the marauding Count; while Basilio is sure that it was the Count in person. Bartolo sees the need for prompt action, and sends Basilio away to bring a notary to draw up the marriage contract. Then a bright idea occurs to him; calling Rosina, he hands her the letter that has been given him by the Count, which, he says, is a proof that her lover has another mistress. Rosina recognises the letter as her own, and having learned how it has come into Bartolo's hands, she assumes that Lindoro has betrayed her, and, the viper in her replacing the kitten, she vows vengeance on him. She is now willing to marry Bartolo; and she confides to him the plan of Lindoro and Figaro to come for her at midnight. Bartolo tells her to go to her room and locks the door while he runs for the police, and the wretched Rosina obeys.

There is a short orchestral interlude, depicting a storm. When this is over the shutters open, and Figaro and the Count, both wrapped in cloaks, while Figaro carries a lantern, enter by the window. The Count's transports at the sight of Rosina are soon ended; she turns on him and abuses him roundly for his treachery. The time has now come for him to reveal himself; throwing back his cloak he appears in the rich dress of a nobleman, and he explains that he is not Lindoro but Almaviva. The happy pair indulge in a very florid duet, the general character of which may be gathered from the following phrases:

(18) ROSINA.

O what bliss, no more we mar-
Al-la fin de' miei mar-

sev - er,........ O........ what......
ti - ri,........ al - la........

ALMAVIVA.

O what bliss, no more we miei......
Al - la fin de' miei......

bliss,........ no........ more....... we........
fin........ de'........ miei...... mar......

sev - er!
mar - ti - ri!

while Figaro impatiently exhorts them to put an end to their
billing and cooing and make their escape before it is too late;
through the window he has seen two people carrying a lantern.

As time is obviously pressing, they delay no longer than is necessary to sing a trio expressive of their anxiety to get away at once.
This is the famous " Zitti, zitti " trio, that goes at a tremendous
pace that is only possible with the Italian words. The Count
begins it, Rosina and Figaro taking up the melody in turn after
him, and then the three voices uniting:

(19)

Zit-ti, zit-ti, pia-no, pia - no, Non fac-
-cia-mo con-fu-sîo - - ne,

("Sh! sh! softly! softly! we mustn't make a noise! Let us go quickly by the balcony ladder.")

When at last they make up their minds to leave in a hurry, they find, to their dismay, that the ladder has disappeared. All seems lost. While they are hiding and wondering what they can do, Basilio enters, bringing with him the notary. Figaro takes charge of the new situation: stepping forward, he reminds the notary that he has been ordered to draw up a marriage contract between Count Almaviva and his (Figaro's) niece. By a fortunate chance, the parties happen to be here, so if the notary has the contract with him they can proceed. Basilio asks where Bartolo is, but the Count, taking him aside, offers him a ring, and at the same time showing him a pistol, promises him a couple of bullets in his head if he does not behave as he should do. Basilio says he prefers the ring, and, with Figaro, witnesses the marriage contract.

The ceremony over, the Count kisses Rosina's hand, while Figaro takes Basilio into his arms in a grotesque embrace. Just then, Bartolo enters with an officer and a patrol of soldiers. He bids the officer arrest Almaviva and Figaro as thieves. The Count, for the moment, refuses to give the officer his name, but presents Rosina as his wife, which staggers Bartolo. The officer becoming importunate and a little aggressive, the Count discloses his name, to the vast astonishment of Bartolo. His protests are in vain: the Count, in a florid aria, tells him that resistance is useless, that Rosina has escaped from his clutches. A second aria, in which he assures Rosina of his undying love, is accompanied by the felicitations of the company — except Bartolo, who now rounds on Basilio. The latter admits his defection from the cause, but pleads that the Count had, in his purse, arguments that were quite irresistible. What chiefly annoys Bartolo is that he himself, by removing the ladder, should have made the marriage certain; it was, as Basilio ironically reminds him, a vain precaution. Bartolo is placated by the Count's gift to him of Rosina's dowry, and everyone now being satisfied, the opera ends with a joyous ensemble.

Rossini's immortal work is the finest flower of the older Italian musical comedy.

WILLIAM TELL

T HE case of Rossini is one of the most curious in musical history. Although he lived to the age of seventy-six, his career virtually closed with the composition of *William Tell* at the age of thirty-seven.

It is true that his *Stabat Mater* appeared in 1842, and a *Messe Solennelle* in 1865, and that from time to time during the latter half of his life he wrote a number of vocal and pianoforte trifles; but it was in the opera-house that he had made his great reputation, and, though he lived until 1868, the opera-house saw no more of him after 1829.

The majority of Rossini's operas have passed so completely out of the repertory of most theatres that it is difficult for people to-day to realise that in his own time he was regarded as a daring innovator. Responsible critics of his epoch spoke of him very much as the critics of a later day spoke of Wagner — the unapproachable master who had created a new heaven and a new earth in opera; while devotees of the older school shrank from him as a sort of operatic Bolshevist.

All this is rather hard for the plain man to understand nowadays, the reason being that, knowing little or nothing of the Italian opera before Rossini, he has no basis of comparison. As a matter of fact, Rossini altered the form and the spirit of Italian opera in a way and to an extent that must have been rather disturbing to the conservative minds of his own day.

It was not merely that he wrote better and livelier and stronger music than his predecessors and contemporaries. He broke away, bit by bit, from a good deal of the older formalism of structure; he shortened the long and dreary recitatives that were common in the older opera — and only tolerable there because nobody listened to them, preferring to chatter or eat ices all the time — and substituted for these a more animated and natural musical dialogue; he did a great deal to break the preposterous tyranny exercised by the singers over the composer, putting it out of their power to deface his melody with their " ornaments " by himself writing out in full the coloratura with which he desired his melodies to be embellished; he made opera in many ways more natural and self-sufficing; he developed the expressive power of the choral ensembles, and placed them not merely, as was customary before his time, at the end of an act, but wherever they were called for by the dramatic necessities of the story.

All this may sound somewhat obvious nowadays; but in the early years of the nineteenth century these were real reforms that it took some courage to carry out; and we can well understand the consternation of old-fashioned music lovers like Lord Mount Edgecumbe, who were convinced that Rossini and his imitators were ruining opera.

At the age of thirty-seven Rossini had written thirty-seven operas, and thirty-four of these had been produced within the space of fourteen years — not a bad record for a man who was regarded as constitutionally one of the laziest of mankind. His last opera to be written expressly for Italy was *Semiramide,* which was produced in Venice in 1823.

It is clear from this, and from the work or two that preceded it, that in his own dashing, unreflective way Rossini was heading towards a more serious conception of opera; and it was probably for this reason that his last Italian works did not at first meet with such favour as some of his earlier productions had done. By 1823 he was the most talked-of composer of his epoch. He was still only thirty-one, and there was every probability that, with a change of environment and the impact of new influences, creating new ambitions, his mind and his art would undergo further developments.

In the late winter of 1823 he went to London, where a new opera had been commissioned from him. He remained in England until the following July. The opera, owing to the bankruptcy of the theatrical manager, was never produced, and, indeed, seems not to have been written, apart from the first act; but Rossini made himself immensely popular in Society by the charm of his personality, and he and his wife, who was a singer, were in great demand for concerts. He charged handsome fees, and when he went to Paris in July 1824, he carried away with him some seven thousand pounds — more than he had earned in all the preceding years of his life.

In Paris he was engaged as musical director of the Théâtre Italien for eighteen months at a salary of twenty thousand francs. He performed his duties very conscientiously, and produced some of his own works that had not previously been given in France. When his agreement expired, he was retained in Paris, where his possible future services to French opera were regarded by the Government as being valuable, by a continuation of his salary of twenty thousand francs under the guise of a pension.

The conditions in Paris, then looked upon as the leading city for opera, were very different from those he had been accustomed to in Italy, and they probably set him thinking hard. The result was that gradual change in his conception of opera that culminated in *William Tell*. Pure lyrical singing had never been the strong point of the French; writers like Rousseau, indeed, had argued that the French would never be able to sing like the Italians because their language was not made for singing. But the French had always shown more liking than most nations for the dramatic side of opera, and, in addition, the Paris Opera, with its large Government subvention, was able to spend large amounts on careful rehearsal and elaborate production.

For the Grand Opera he recast and partly rewrote two of his Italian operas — *Maometto*, which became the *Siege of Corinth* (1826) and *Moses in Egypt* (1827). His next work for Paris was *Count Ory*, in which he had the benefit of the co-operation of so skilled a librettist as the famous Scribe. This opera, in which

Rossini incorporated some of the music from an Italian opera, *The Journey to Rheims* (written for the coronation of Charles X in 1825), was produced in 1828.

Rossini was evidently ripening for a serious work on a bigger scale than anything he had yet attempted; and it was a great pity that just when his powers were at their height he should have allied himself with a singularly poor pair of librettists. He took an unusual amount of pains over the composition of *William Tell*, retiring to the country house of his friend Aguado, the banker, at Petit-Bourg. In these quiet surroundings he completed in six months the whole of the piano portion of the work, leaving only the orchestration to be added on his return to Paris.

A new type of opera subject was coming into fashion; people were tired of classical mythology and wanted to see the life of their own time on the stage, or something that they could correlate with this. Liberal ideas were also in the air, as a result of the political and social fermentation of the time; liberty and democracy were idealised, and tyrants were in bad odour.

In 1828, a year before the production of *William Tell*, Auber had made a great sensation with his *Masaniello,* that deals with the revolt of the Neapolitans against their Spanish oppressors. The extraordinary excitement created by this work may be gathered from the fact that a performance of it in Brussels in August 1830 led to risings that ended in the expulsion of the Dutch from Belgium. It was quite in accord with the spirit of the times, then, that Rossini should become enamoured of the story of *William Tell,* which had lately become known in France through a translation of Schiller's German play upon the subject.

He chose for his librettist, or had chosen for him by others, a certain M. de Jouy, an inferior dramatist of the day who had made something of a reputation for himself in musical circles by writing the libretti for *The Vestal, Fernand Cortez,* and other operas of Spontini's. Jouy's vanity made him think more of himself than of the composer.

He turned out in the first place a long poem of some seven

hundred verses that seemingly had the minimum of relation to
the stage. Rossini finding this text impossible, a M. Bis was
called in to get the text into a better shape. Precisely what Bis
did with the libretto is not known, but he is generally credited
with the second act, which is undeniably the best of the five. But
Bis, like Jouy, found that Rossini had a will of his own in these
matters; and both librettists were worried by his incessant demands that the verses should be reshaped to suit his musical ideas.
In the end they came to regard themselves as very aggrieved
persons.

Like the Leicestershire squire, Charles Jennens, the author
of the text of the *Messiah,* who thought that Handel had let him
down rather badly — " I have with great difficulty made him
correct some of the grossest faults in the composition, but he
retains his overture obstinately," he wrote to a friend — M. de
Jouy and M. Bis regarded themselves as great dramatists whose
masterpiece had been ruined by the caprice and stupidity of a
mere composer.

They thought it necessary, in the interests of their own reputa-
tions, to publish the libretto with an explanatory preface. From
this it appears that of the libretto as it was originally written several scenes had been cut out in obedience to Rossini's demands,.
the place of certain others had been changed, and some verses
had been put in only because Rossini insisted on them for music
that was already in his head. They candidly admitted that some
of their lines were not up to the highest poetic standard, but they
pleaded in extenuation that the rhythm of these had been fixed for
them in advance by the composer. However, they said, they
thought it advisable to publish the libretto in its final form, because the spectators would have a natural desire to know what the
opera was about, and in the theatre the instruments often made
it impossible for them to catch the words.

They ended up with an artful compliment to Rossini as the only
" creator " of the opera. They were thus safely on the side of the
angels if the work turned out to be a success, while if it proved
a failure they had cunningly left it to be inferred that it was all

Rossini's fault for not having accepted their masterpiece as it originally stood.

As a matter of fact, a third hand had been made use of by Rossini — that of Aguado's secretary, Armand Marrast, who had put the finishing touch on many a line that the composer had found impossible.

The work was produced at the Opera on the 3rd August, 1829. Its fate was curious. After an enthusiastic reception, and in spite of the general recognition that it was not only Rossini's masterpiece but a significant sign of the times, the public enthusiasm gradually cooled. It was given in its proper form fifty-six times. Then it was shortened to three acts by the omission of the third and the telescoping of the fourth and fifth into one; and at last the second act alone came to be given as a sort of curtain raiser.

There is a well-known story of the Director of the Opera meeting Rossini one day and saying to him, with the evident desire to please him, "To-night, Master, we play the second act of *William Tell* again." "What! the whole of it?" was Rossini's ironic reply.

In 1837 the part of Arnold was taken up by the great French tenor Duprez, whose fine performance of the part restored the work to temporary popularity. In London it was given in 1839 and again in 1848; but Henry Chorley, writing in 1861, had to record regretfully that, in spite of its showing Rossini's genius at its best, it never managed to take hold of the general public in this country.

Chorley, who had a great admiration for Rossini's genius, and considerable insight into it, has some shrewd remarks on the subject. He thinks that Rossini relied so much on his musical invention as to be far too careless about his libretti. "It would appear," he says, "as if the greatest of Italians had taken a despotic pride in choosing a subject without reference to dramatic treatment, and without a leading female interest, always of the first importance to opera, be the part long or brief." "The music, however," he prophesies, "will grow so long as music lives and lasts. Year by year will be more and more seen the rare characteristic beauty royally showered over the work from its earliest to its latest note." He thinks that the reason the public preferred the operas of inferior composers such as Donizetti was that these afforded more " scope for action."

It certainly looks as if Rossini had been culpably careless about the dramatic aspect of the story; and if it be true that he rejected the libretto of *The Jewess* (afterwards composed by Halévy), which Chorley calls " the most powerful opera book in the modern list," choosing instead of it the relatively feeble *William Tell* of M. de Jouy, the charge appears to be a just one.

There has been a vast amount of speculation as to the reasons for Rossini's never taking up operatic composition again after *William Tell*. It is said that he was piqued by the failure of the public to take to its heart what he knew to be the best of his works; that he was jealous of the growing vogue of Meyerbeer; that he had made so much money (he was given many a good Stock Exchange tip by his friends the Rothschilds) that he could indulge his natural bent towards indolence; that he wanted, in the years following the production of *William Tell*, to live in Italy with his old father, who, not knowing a word of French, would have been unhappy in Paris; and so on.

There may be something in each of these explanations with the exception of that relating to Meyerbeer; although, while Rossini was probably incapable of the meaner form of jealousy of his powerful rival, he may have realised that only a colossal effort on his own part could suffice to stem the Meyerbeer tide, and he may have preferred not to run the risk of another failure.

But Chorley makes a suggestion as to Rossini's abstention from opera for the remaining years of his life that may be the correct one, and in any case is interesting: " The strange, obstinate retirement from creation of such an artist as Signor Rossini," he wrote about 1861, while the composer was still alive, " in the prime of his powers, with *Guillaume Tell* just made, and myriads of fancies still unexpressed, has always reminded me of nothing so much as of the old story, true in the main, which, however, has been added to and coloured and lectured on till small truth, it may be, is left in it — the story, I mean, of the man who left his wife in pique, without bidding her farewell, and who dwelt, for a long term of years undiscovered, in a house on the opposite side of the street, long after her agony of wish to discover him had died out in blank hopelessness. After holding out for a certain time, pride forbade him to go home.

" Who has ever weighed the strength of perversity, the self-punishment of the implacable, or the comfort of their conviction that if the outer world suffers by it, so much the better! Thus it may be that the perpetual reference to, and solicitude concerning Signor Rossini during the past thirty years, the anxiety to be allowed to hope that his last words were not said, the return to his best operas (in spite of the feeble stories), after one and another writer have been praised, become wearisome, and been laid by, may have amounted to so many incitements to persistence in the course of musical perversity, by which we have lost so much. No stranger story is, at all events, recorded in the annals of art, with respect to a genius who filled his own world with its glory, and then chose to vanish ' not unseen.' "

The period of the opera is the beginning of the fourteenth century, when the Swiss were trying to free themselves from Austrian rule; and the central episode in it is of course the old story — or rather the legend, for it is found in other places at other times — of the shooting of an apple from the head of Tell's son. Rossini had more than once in the earlier part of his career flown in the face of tradition by giving an important part to a bass, and he makes a baritone of William Tell, who is really the main hero of the opera. There are two other Swiss patriots, Arnold, the tenor, and Walter Fürst, a bass.

The chief soprano is Mathilde, a Princess of the Austrian house. Hedwiga, Tell's wife, is a mezzo-soprano, and Jemmy, his little son, is of course a soprano. Gesler, the oppressive Governor of Schwitz and Uri, is a bass, as is also Arnold's father, Melcthal. The minor characters are Rudolph, a captain of Gesler's guards, who is a tenor, a fisherman named Ruodi, also a tenor, and Leuthold, a herdsman, who is a bass.

The overture, which had been the joy of both the concert-goer

and the opera audience for the last hundred years, is really a
little symphonic poem. A certain eminent musician of the present
day, when he was asked to go to a festival of modern Swiss music,
replied, " Modern Swiss music? There isn't any. The only piece
of decent Swiss music ever written is the overture to *William Tell.*"
Swiss music or not, it is excellent music.

The preliminary *andante* paints the piece of a pastoral scene.
The opening theme, which must have been a daringly original piece
of colouring in its day, is entrusted to five solo 'cellos with the
double basses:

This is followed by a second theme:

the development of which is interrupted for a moment by a soft
roll in the kettledrum, a presage of the coming storm. The succeeding *allegro* paints the storm itself; commencing with soft hurrying figures in the strings and veiled wood-wind harmonies it works
up to a pelting *fortissimo* tempest; from time to time we hear

high up in the wood-wind, the piccolo being especially prominent, staccato notes that seem to fall like raindrops.

The storm rises to its height, spends its fury, and disappears as gradually as it came, with murmurous *tremolandi* in the strings, and little flicks in the flute that suggest streaks of clear blue coming into the heavy sky. Then the English horn gives out a *Ranz des vaches:*

(The *Ranz des vaches* is the call that the Swiss herdsman blows on the Alpine horn to his cattle to call them from the lower to the higher pastures in June. Rossini is said to have used some ten or twelve *Ranz des vaches* in the score of *William Tell;* he probably culled them from a book on the subject by one Tarenne, published in 1813.)

The call is answered by the flute in the higher octave, and a romantic series of calls and echoes ensues. Then comes another melody for the English horn:

which in time is succeeded by a development of the main call (No. 3). As this dies away, the trumpets seize upon the B natural and ring out a brilliant fanfare in the key of E major, the relative remoteness of which from the preceding key of G major is splendidly effective. The trumpets are answered by the horn, and to the strains of a lively galop:

a hunting party comes upon the scene. The second strain of the galop:

is as exhilarating as the first. The remainder of the overture is devoted to brilliant repetitions and developments of these two themes.

The curtain having risen, we see the shores of the Lake of Lucerne. On the right is William Tell's châlet; on the left a waterfall, spanned by a little bridge. Jemmy, Tell's little son, is practising with bow and arrows; his mother, Hedwiga, sits in front of her house plaiting a basket. She keeps looking now at her son, now at her husband, alternately delighting in the happiness of the one and concerned about the other; for William Tell, leaning on his spade, obviously has something on his mind.

Peasants engaged in one occupation or another are scattered about the stage; some of them are festooning with green three small châlets, the future residences of three newly wedded couples, for this is the day on which, according to the ancient usage, three marriages are to be made and blessed by the elder of the community. A brief orchestral introduction, with a melody that commences in the violins:

paints a charming picture of the pastoral scene. The peasants celebrate the beauty of the day and the interest of the occasion in a chorus:

after which there comes from the fisherman Ruodi, who is in his boat on the lake, an invitation to his lady love to accompany him on an excursion:

The light orchestral accompaniment to this changes to gloomier colours as, the first stanza of Ruodi's song being finished, William Tell, in an aside, contrasts the youthful fisherman, singing of his happiness and his love, with himself, racked by the thought of the oppression to which his beloved country is subject; " while he sings, Switzerland weeps for its liberty." Ruodi continues his song, which is made the text of a quartet between himself, Jemmy, Hedwiga, and William Tell.

the patriot asks the young man the cause of his perturbation and exhorts him to remember his duty to his country. Arnold breaks out into a passionate cry to Mathilde:

and this and a counter-motive of Tell's are worked up in admirable style. In answer to Tell's further appeals to his patriotism, Arnold, pointing to the châlet, bids Tell remember the danger he may bring upon those he loves; Tell's reply is that he knows this only too well, but he knows also the weight of the chains under which his country groans.

The horns of Gesler's hunting party (No. 13) are heard again, and a final appeal from Tell goads Arnold into a cry that he too will go forth and brave the insolent oppressor, although within himself he is still torn between love for his country, his father, and Mathilde:

Heav'n,   thou   know'st ·how   Ma -
ciel,__   tu   sais   si   Ma -

- til - da I trea - sure!
- *thil - de m'est chè - re!*

The three bridegrooms appear, followed later by the three brides, and the stage gradually fills with people, to the accompaniment of a simple pastoral melody:

(17) **Allegro**

Hedwiga calls upon old Melcthal to bless the rite; the bridal pair kneel before him, and all join in a chorus based on the following melody:

(18) **Andante**

against which we hear, from time to time, the melancholy ejaculations of Arnold.

Gesler's horns are heard again in the distance, and Arnold slips away unperceived by the others. Tell, in spite of the expostulations of his anxious wife, tries to goad his compatriots into revolt, and then departs in search of Arnold. To a graceful melody:

(19) **Allegretto**

the peasants shower congratulations and good wishes upon the
married pairs, and there follows the inevitable ballet. Jemmy,
having distinguished himself in the archery contest, is fêted in a
chorus:

(20)

Chil-dren of hard - y Na - ture,when -
En-fans de la na-tu-re, le

- e'er the foe ad - van - ces,
sim-ple ha - bit de bu - re

while the archers march round the stage.

The joyous proceedings are interrupted by the sudden cry of
the herdsman Leuthold, who pauses in exhaustion and leans upon
a bloody axe. In excited accents he tells the horrified crowd that
his only daughter having been carried off by one of the Austrian
soldiers, he has cloven the miscreant's skull with his axe. He
implores Ruodi to ferry him over to safety on the opposite side
of the lake, but the fisherman refuses, on account of the danger
from the rocks and the strength of the current.

At this point Tell returns, his search for Arnold having been
unsuccessful. Outside are heard the voices of the Austrian soldiers
clamouring for their prey, and Leuthold makes another despairing
appeal for help. Learning of Ruodi's refusal, Tell himself offers to
row the herdsman across; as the boat leaves the shore, the chorus,
to an expressive orchestral accompaniment, sings a typically Ros-
sinian prayer to Heaven to aid the fugitives.

A threatening theme that has been heard in the orchestra
before the prayer makes its reappearance as Rudolph, Gesler's
captain, enters with the soldiers. He has hardly had time to demand that Leuthold shall be given up to him when a great cry
of thankfulness goes up from Hedwiga, Jemmy, and the others
as the boat is seen to have reached the opposite shore safely. All
refuse to tell the name of the escaped man; and Melcthal, having

defied Rudolph, is arrested, Rudolph breaking into a furious
threat of vengeance upon the Swiss:

The strain is taken up by the others in turn, and worked up into
one of those imposing finales in which Rossini delighted. The villagers try to rescue Melcthal, but are held back by the soldiers'
spears. Melcthal is being dragged off roughly as the curtain falls.

The setting of the greatly admired second act is a pine forest
on the heights of Rütli, commanding the Waldstetten lake. It is
night. The stage fills with hunters bearing torches, some carrying
the trophies of the hunt. The hunting motive associated with
Gesler (No. 13) is heard in the orchestra, and the chorus break
out into a vigorous song in praise of the joys of the hunt:

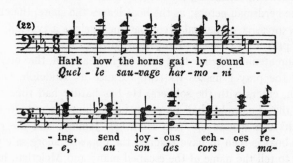

>   - bound   - ing,
>   - ri   - el,

In the distance is heard the song of the shepherds bringing their flocks down into the valley, and their evening song merges into the chorus of hunters, which, however, is soon resumed. No. 13 is heard once more in the horns; it is the call to return, and the hunters leave the stage, the horns dying away across the lake.

After an expressive orchestral introduction, admirably suggestive of the romance of the forest by night, Mathilde enters. During the hunt she has caught sight of Arnold, and believes he may have followed her to this secluded spot. After an introductory recitative she sings the once famous aria " Sombre forêt ":

(23) Andantino

> Oh   lone-ly wood, in thy dark syl-van
> *Som - bre fo - rêt, dé-sert triste et sau-*

> bow - ers, let me for - get world-ly
> *- va - ge, je vous pré-fère aux splen-*

> care and an - noy,—
> *-deurs des pa - lais,—*

in which she tells us that she prefers love under the simple conditions that Arnold can offer her to the splendours of the court. No matter how sincere her emotion, a leading lady in opera has her rights, and so Mathilde's aria contains a fair amount of brilliant coloratura.

The aria concluded, Arnold enters, and after some characteristically French compliments and excuses on the part of each of them, Arnold confesses his love and implores Mathilde to command him, if she so wishes it, to abandon even his country and his father

for her. A confession on her part that she returns his love draws
from him a tender melody:

which is worked up into a duet that was the admiration of our
grandfathers.

The pulse of the music quickens as Mathilde urges her lover:

to return to the field of battle and win a glory that shall ennoble
him in the eyes of the world and justify her choice, which he
consents to do.

Someone is seen approaching, and Mathilde hastily quits Arnold, promising to meet him again at dawn next day in the ancient
chapel. The new-comers are Tell and Walter Fürst. They enter to
the accompaniment of an orchestral phrase:

which, as will be seen, is a curious anticipation on Rossini's part
of the theme representative of Faust in Liszt's *Faust Symphony*:

(27) Lento

The two patriots reproach Arnold for his indifference to his country's woes and his infatuation with the alien Princess. Arnold
declares his intention of leaving so hopeless a country to find
distraction and glory in war, and is upbraided by Tell:

(28)   Allegro maestoso

While ev-'ry true-heart-ed Swit-zer is
Quand l'Hel-vé-tie est unchampsde sup-

groan-ing to see op-pres-sion rule the
-pli - ces ou l'on mois-son-ne ses en -

land,
-fants;

for his desertion of his native land to join the ranks of its enemies.

Arnold reiterates his resolve, but is pulled up by Fürst, who,
to the strain of No. 28, hints at a fresh crime on Gesler's part that
calls for Arnold's presence at the funeral rites. The young man
learns that his father has been executed for his defiance of Gesler,
and he is filled with remorse:

(29)

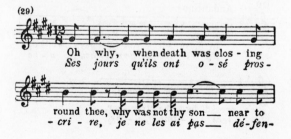

Oh   why,   when death was clos - ing
Ses   jours   qu'ils ont   o - sé   pros-

round thee, why was not thy son ___ near to
-cri - re,   je ne les ai pas___ dé-fen-

save?
-dus?

While he is giving full vent to his anguish the others, blending their voices with his in a trio, rejoice at these signs of a change of heart in him.

Arnold has now only one thought, that of vengeance. The others tell him to be present that night at a gathering of patriots who are planning a revolt; and after another vigorous trio in praise of vengeance and liberty there is heard a soft roll in the kettle-drums, followed by a call in the horns, this by some *pizzicato* notes in the 'cellos and basses, and this in turn by a march-like, but as yet very quiet, melody in the strings:

All this is the prelude to the famous scene of the Gathering of the Cantons.

The patriots come upon the stage stealthily — first of all the men of Unterwald, then the men of Schwitz with a tune of their own:

In these sor - row-ful days, — while op -
En ces temps de mal - heur, — u - ne

-press'd by the stran - ger,
race é - tran - gè - re,

and finally the men of Uri. The music of the three Cantons is admirably differentiated, but all of it is kept within the same frame, as it were, the air of caution and secrecy that has dominated this final scene from the commencement being consistently maintained.

The groups are greeted by Tell and Walter as they arrive, and the men of Uri address Tell in a strain:

that is taken up by the others and worked up into a massive chorus.

There is still a touch of fear in the hearts of some of the men. William Tell, in a series of vigorous recitatives, reanimates their courage, and he is seconded by Arnold, who, rousing himself from the stupor into which he had fallen, vows that he will avenge the death of his father. At last they all clasp each other's hands, and, led by Tell, they swear to rise against their tyrant, and invoke the wrath of Heaven on any traitor there may be in their midst.

Few scenes in the opera of the early nineteenth century could be counted upon to thrill the audiences of that day as this scene of the Gathering of the Cantons did.

The real heroes of Rossini's opera are of course William Tell and the Swiss people, and it would have been better had the composer and the librettists kept the great national movement in the forefront of their picture, as Moussorgsky did in *Boris Godounov*. But in Rossini's time the main attractions in opera were still the leading soprano and the leading tenor, to each of whom due opportunities for display had to be given.

It is to this convention that we owe the opening scene of the third act, which takes place inside a ruined chapel in the grounds of the Governor's palace at Altdorf. Arnold has come to take farewell of Mathilde; she learns, however, that he is not going to the wars as he had promised, but is remaining to avenge his murdered father. Mathilde, realising that it was by Gesler's orders that old Melcthal was killed, bids farewell to hope in an agitated aria:

but, she assures Arnold in some brilliant coloratura:

she will always, under the worst blows of fate, preserve the memory of her rescuer and lover.

Wildly she conjures him to flee from the murderous Gesler, but still to remember her in a foreign land. He cries that it is his father that he will remember, and their voices blend in an excited duet, the burden of it being that, in renouncing their love, they have given Melcthal more than their life.

The scene changes to the market place of Altdorf. The occasion is the celebration, at Gesler's orders, of the centenary of the Austrian rule in Switzerland. Gesler's castle is in the background; in front of it is a raised seat for the Governor. In the centre of the stage is a banner bearing Gesler's arms, and surmounted by a hat. Gesler's soldiers hail him in a martial chorus:

while after them the peasants praise the gentle and beloved Mathilde.

After a proud fanfare in the trumpets, Gesler arrogantly demands that, as a sign of their subjection, the people shall salute the hat as if it were himself; and the Switzers are compelled to file in front of the hat and to bow to it.

Addressing the people from the steps of his throne, Gesler tells them that it is now a hundred years since the Austrian power deigned to exercise its lordship over them: let them accordingly celebrate the occasion with song and dance; "This is my will." This is the cue for a series of brilliant ballets and a march of the soldiers, interspersed with choruses in praise of Mathilde. One of the ballets:

has a genuine Tyrolese flavour.

All goes well until Rudolph notices that William Tell has not done homage to the hat. He roughly orders him to demean himself, but Tell refuses. The Switzers at this give an apprehensive cry; and Rudolph draws Gesler's attention to Tell's defiance of his commands.

Tell is brought before the Governor, and again refuses to obey the degrading order, let Gesler threaten him as he will. Rudolph now recognises Tell as the malcontent who helped Leuthold to escape across the lake. He is seized by the soldiers: in tender accents he exhorts his little son to leave him, but Jemmy bravely replies that his place is there, to die, if need be, in his father's arms.

After an expressive ensemble Tell bids the boy go to his mother and take the message that the beacons are to be lighted on the mountains as the signal to the three Cantons to raise the standard of revolt. But in the affection of Tell for his child Gesler sees an opportunity to intensify the pleasure of his vengeance. Throughout the land, he says, Tell is known as a skilled archer; let an apple be placed on his son's head; if Tell can pierce the apple with his arrow he shall be set free, but if he fails, both he and his child shall die.

Tell weakens for a moment and appeals for mercy; but when the pitiless Gesler orders the son to be killed he gives way completely and humbles himself before the tyrant; whereupon Gesler taunts the once intrepid archer and boatman with his weakness. It is Jemmy who restores Tell's courage; taking his father's hand and placing it on his breast, he bids him feel how calm his heart is; it will not quail under his father's arrow. Proudly declaring, " I am still William Tell! " the father demands his bow and arrows. Bending down, he selects two arrows, one of which he conceals in his clothes; at this point one of Mathilde's pages slips away and runs towards the castle.

Gesler orders Jemmy to be bound, but the boy proudly refuses; if he is to die he will die free. The Switzers break out into a cry of anguish: even the sight and the words of this innocent child do not disarm the tyrant's vengeance! Jemmy exhorts his father to take courage, and the trembling Tell, his eyes dim with tears, receives permission from Gesler to embrace his son.

A troubled theme in the 'cello:

winds its way in and out of the orchestra as Tell feverishly orders Jemmy to fall upon one knee:

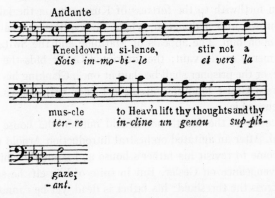

to remain immovable, and to look up and offer a prayer to Heaven. The sight of the arrow may affright his childish eyes; the slightest movement will be fatal; let him think of his mother, who is awaiting them both.

Jemmy returns to his original position, and the apple is placed on his head. Tell gives a dull and hopeless look around him, and as his eyes fall on Gesler his hand almost unconsciously feels for the concealed arrow; then, mastering himself, he shoots, and the apple. flies from Jemmy's head. The Switzers give a cry of joy, while Gesler curses this fresh misadventure. Jemmy runs to his father and throws himself into his arms; Tell, blinded by emotion, is hardly able to recognise him. To restore him Jemmy unfastens his mantle, and the second arrow falls to the ground. Tell admits, in reply to Gesler's question, that, if the first arrow had failed, he had intended the second for the tyrant; and the furious Gesler orders Rudolph to arrest him.

Mathilde enters with her ladies upon a scene of wild confusion, the soldiers clamouring for the death of Tell and Jemmy, the trembling Switzers stammering out their fears, and Gesler gloating over the savage revenge he is contemplating. In spite of Mathilde's protests, he orders Tell and his son to be taken and thrown into a dungeon. But Mathilde puts a protecting arm round Jemmy, and on this point Gesler has to give way.

With regard to Tell, however, he is inflexible; the patriot is to be taken forthwith to the fortress of Kussnach, on the lake, and there thrown into a dungeon, where the reptiles can sate their hunger upon him. The appeals of Mathilde and the Switzers for further mercy are in vain; the infuriated Gesler bids the people disperse, or the prisoner shall be slain at once. Clanking his chains, Tell curses Gesler loudly; and the act ends with the usual imposing ensemble.

The scene of the fourth act is laid outside the house of old Melcthal. After an agitated orchestral introduction Arnold enters; he has come to revisit his father's house and strengthen his longing for vengeance on Gesler. But in spite of himself, he says, he cannot cross the threshold; his father is dead, yet he cannot enter the ancestral house! We surmise, however, that his real reason for not entering the house is that he has to sing an aria; for the first tenor, like the first soprano, has his inalienable rights. His aria:

is a dolorous lament over his father and the happy days of his childhood.

After his final roulade, cries of " Vengeance! Vengeance! " are heard from the Switzers behind the scenes. Soon they enter in wild excitement; they have heard that William Tell has been imprisoned, and they are summoning their compatriots to arms to help him.

Arnold encourages them: " No more futile fears! No more sterile tears! Gesler must perish! " He and the other patriots take heart from each other's words, and Arnold, in a final brilliant aria that is soon worked up into an ensemble:

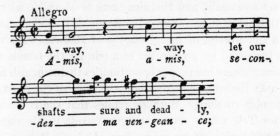

calls upon them to follow him to Altdorf and rescue William from the tyrant's hands. In the course of his exhortation there comes from time to time a soaring phrase:

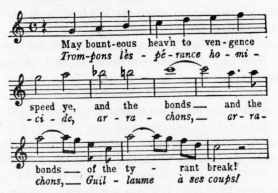

that must have made an electrifying effect in the great days when tenors were tenors.

The final scene takes place on the shore of the Lake of Lucerne,

Tell's cottage being visible on a hill in the distance. A storm is raging, but the distracted Hedwiga cannot be restrained by the women who surround her from setting forth to see Gesler, to intercede with him for her husband. She is just lamenting that she has neither husband nor child left to her when the voice of Jemmy crying, " My mother! " is heard outside, and the boy himself appears, brought thither by the protecting Mathilde, who is followed by her pages.

Jemmy assures her that, thanks to Mathilde, his father will soon be set free again, and Hedwiga turns to Mathilde with a cry of gratitude. Mathilde returns Jemmy to his mother, praising him as a son worthy of her. Jemmy and Hedwiga take up the strain in turn, and we are treated to a trio for the female voices, in which each singer has proper opportunities to distinguish herself.

Why, asks Hedwiga, has Mathilde, the pride of the court, come to her humble dwelling? Mathilde replies that she is there as a hostage for Tell, whose return she guarantees. But is there any hope, asks Hedwiga, of his rescue from Altdorf? It is only then that she learns that Tell is not at Altdorf, but on the lake — the lake over which a storm is now gathering. Jemmy goes off to rouse the patriots, while Hedwiga, falling on her knees, offers up a prayer for her husband, in which she is joined by Mathilde and the other women.

Precisely how William Tell has escaped we do not know, but we learn from Leuthold, who now rushes in, that, although the boat is being tossed about by the tempest, Tell's hands are free, and he is handling the helm with his usual skill. All run to his aid. Another storm is painted in the orchestra, and after a while Hedwiga and Jemmy return, bringing with them Tell, who is delighted to see that not only has Jemmy, no beacon being available, given the signal to the patriots by setting fire to the ancestral roof, but has saved his father's bows and arrows from the burning.

Taking them from him, Tell says significantly, " Now, Gesler, thou canst come! " Just then the pursuing Gesler and his soldiers appear on the rocks above. Fitting an arrow to his bow, Tell takes aim at Gesler, who falls dead into the lake. The soldiers fly, and

Hedwiga, Jemmy, and Tell give thanks for their deliverance. Walter Fürst and the other patriots enter; they have been aroused by the signal of the burning house, and have come, they say, to be led against the tyrant. Tell bids them seek his tomb in the lake, but not to rejoice too soon, for until Altdorf is taken their liberties are still not safe.

At this point Arnold and the remainder of the Swiss patriots enter with the news that the castle has fallen, and Arnold presents to Tell the banner that, in the third act, floated in the grounds of the castle. Appropriately enough, the storm has now passed away, and in the clear air the mountains and the lake are seen glistening in the sun. All take the transformation as a happy presage of Switzerland's new-found liberty, and the opera ends with a chorus in praise of freedom.

INTERESTING as Weber's life is in itself, it is still more interesting for the fullness of the light it throws on musical conditions in Germany at the end of the eighteenth century and the beginning of the nineteenth, and on the change to modern conditions in the latter part of his career. Short as his life was, Weber seems to sum up in himself an older and a newer German world. His earliest years were spent in much the same *milieu* as Mozart's; when he died, the German operatic stage was practically set for the entry of Wagner.

For a long time before Carl Maria's birth the Weber stock seemed to have been trying to produce a musical genius. It was a breed with plenty of vitality and a certain amount of musical and dramatic talent, and was no doubt fairly represented by the two male representatives of it that immediately preceded the composer.

The family had at one time been of some standing in Austria, but by the middle of the eighteenth century had come down in the world, and from having estates of its own was reduced to taking service on the estates of others. It always prided itself on the " von " in its name — the composer's father was particularly proud of it — and this symbol of petty nobility generally gave Carl Maria a certain social standing, and at times may have made his path in life rather smoother than it might have been without it.

We first meet with Carl Maria's father, Franz Anton, and the latter's brother, Fridolin, when both were in the service of the Elector of the Palatinate, who maintained an excellent theatre and an exceptional orchestra at Mannheim. Fridolin, who soon gave up the stage for a legal post, became the father of Mozart's future wife, Konstanze, and of that Josefa Weber who married the Vienna actor Hofer and sang the part of the Queen of Night in the first production of *The Magic Flute;* Mozart and Carl Maria von Weber were thus cousins by marriage.

Franz Anton, a vain, handsome, bumptious, pleasure-loving, restless young man, left Mannheim to fight in the Seven Years' War. He was wounded at Rossbach, left the army, and was given a post at Hildesheim in the civil service of the Elector of Cologne. In 1758, at the age of twenty-three, he married Maria Anna von Fumetti, a maiden a year or so younger than himself, the daughter of the departmental chief; and Fumetti having obligingly died shortly before that event, Franz Anton, in addition to getting a nice little dowry with Anna, stepped into the old man's official shoes. Just as at Mannheim, where he had been engaged to sing and make music, he pined to be at the wars, so now that he had official duties to perform he neglected them for his fiddling. In the course of time he became so unsatisfactory to his employer that in 1768 he had to be pensioned off.

For some years yet he remained at Hildesheim, but in 1773 he resolved to take the road as musician and actor, dragging his wretched family everywhere with him. Poor Maria Anna, her father's fortune long since squandered by her crazy husband, died in misery in 1783.

It had always been Franz Anton's desire to see one or other of his children turn out to be some such musical genius as Mozart was; and to this end he betook himself to Vienna in 1784 in order to place his two elder sons as pupils of Haydn. The boys were lodged with a family named von Brenner, one member of which was a pretty daughter of sixteen, named Genofeva. The fifty-year-old Franz Anton married this girl in August 1785 and took her to Eutin, where he had been domiciled for some time, and where he now obtained the somewhat humble post of town musician.

On the 18th December, 1786, there was born to him a son, Carl Maria, a child so sickly that he was four years old before he could walk; he suffered from a disease of the right hip-bone that in after-life lamed him permanently.

Franz Anton, who by this time had come down very much in the world, dragged his second wife about with him and a company of vagrant players from town to town as he had done his first. In 1797, after years of wandering, they found themselves at Salzburg, and there, in the following year, the poor young Genofeva, worn out with hardships and disappointments, died of consumption. In less than a year the irrepressible old Franz Anton was engaged to a widow named von Beer, but for some reason or other he did not this time get as far as matrimony.

In pursuance of his pet scheme for raising a genius in the family, he forced his youngest son's musical education from the first. Carl Maria soon became a good pianist, sang prettily, and composed profusely in an amateurish kind of way; it is true he had lessons in harmony and counterpoint from various teachers, including, when he was about eleven years old, Michael Haydn (the younger brother of the more famous Joseph), but he received nothing like the rigorous grounding that Leopold Mozart gave the little Wolfgang. Franz Anton wanted quick and spectacular results.

At the age of thirteen the boy was initiated into the mysteries of lithography by Aloys Sennefelder, the inventor of that art, and a friend of Carl Maria's father. In Sennefelder's case, necessity was certainly the mother of invention. As no publisher could be found to undertake the printing of his literary works, he looked about for a cheap means of reproducing the written page himself, and hit upon the process of transfer from stone. Franz Anton thought he saw not only money in the new invention but an easy way of giving his wonder-child's compositions to the world; and the boy took to lithography with such enthusiasm that he managed to improve on the inventor's idea at certain points. But his father and Sennefelder quarrelled, and the association came to an end.

While the Webers were in Freiberg in Saxony, in November 1800, Franz Anton managed to bring about a performance of his son's juvenile opera, *The Forest Maiden*, but neither there nor at Chemnitz, where it was given a fortnight later, did the work make any impression. Nor had he any better luck with *Peter Schmoll and his Neighbours* (Augsburg, 1803); the final " number " in this ultimately became the final chorus of Weber's last opera *Oberon*, while the overture to *The Forest Maiden* was later used for *Silvana*.

The boy was turning out a good deal of music at this time, and the proud father must have been more certain than ever that he would prove to be a second Mozart. In 1803 he took him to Vienna and placed him in the care of the Abbé Vogler — one of the strangest figures of the day, half genius, half charlatan, who enjoyed an enormous reputation in certain musical circles and was heartily despised in others. He assuredly had a great influence on Weber, both in 1803 and later. In the summer of 1804 Vogler was asked to nominate someone for the post of conductor at the Breslau Opera. He recommended his pupil Weber, and thus at the age of seventeen and a half the boy found himself suddenly placed in a position of considerable authority.

He remained in Breslau until the autumn of 1806. He naturally had difficulties with the singers and players, some of whom resented having so young a man set over them; and perhaps, in his youthful reforming zeal, Weber was not always as tactful as he might have been. But he did excellent work, insisting on thorough rehearsal for every opera he produced, and he learned a good deal that was to be useful to him later. He was obviously predestined for the stage, though some years were to elapse before he could fully realise himself there as either composer or conductor.

In 1805 he nearly came to a premature end by drinking some corrosive acid used by his father for experiments in engraving. The careless old man had left the bottle on the same table as a flask of wine; a friend who had called on Weber by appointment fortunately arrived in time to summon a doctor, but Weber's throat and mouth were terribly burnt, and his singing voice never regained its former power or quality.

He was always romantically susceptible to women, and in

Breslau he became entangled, largely out of chivalry, with an unhappily married woman singer connected with the theatre. She seems to have been the first cause of the heavy debts he gradually accumulated, and that hung like a millstone round his neck for years.

In the autumn of 1806, through the instrumentality of a Fräulein von Belonde, maid of honour to the Duchess Louise of Württemberg, he was invited to visit the Duke and Duchess at their seat in Carlsruhe, Silesia. The Duke was one of the many German princelings of the time who maintained in their feudal states a theatre and an orchestra of their own. Weber's affairs had been going badly before this: he had given up his post at the Breslau theatre, and on account of the war with France pupils had become very scarce. A concert tour as pianist that he had planned fell through for the same reason.

The kindly Duke accommodated not only the composer but his father and his aunt, and Weber spent some happy weeks at Carlsruhe making music with the Duke and the ladies of the Court. Even when the Duke had to leave to join the army the Duchess delayed as long as possible the breaking up of the happy circle. But as the winter wore on, the economic consequences of the war became more and more serious, till in the end the Duke was forced to disband his theatrical and musical forces. He made whatever provision was possible for each of them, and Weber he recommended to his brother, Duke Ludwig of Württemberg, who was just then in search of a new private secretary. Weber reached Stuttgart, where Duke Ludwig lived, on the 17th July, 1807. The two years and a half that he spent there were useless to him as an artist, but were the turning-point in his life as a man.

The situation at Stuttgart was a peculiar one. The King (Frederick, husband of Charlotte Matilda Augusta, daughter of George III of England) was a coarse and brutal egoist who sacrificed the whole kingdom to his pleasures, squeezing every thaler he could out of his subjects, and often ruining the countryside with his hunts without paying the unhappy peasants anything in compensation.

Württemberg was at that time in alliance with France, and there was a heavy drain on the manhood of the little State to provide the army with soldiers. As no one could count on exemption unless he happened to be in the service of the Court, the natural result was that Court posts of the most nominal kind were eagerly sought after and handsomely paid for, the money going into the pockets of a few crafty and unscrupulous favourites of the King.

Frederick, in spite of the economic troubles of the country, maintained an enormous Court establishment, the sole pursuit of everyone connected with it, from himself downwards, being pleasure. He was essentially an able man, but incurably coarse in his speech, violent in his temper, and crudely overbearing in his ways. He was almost unbelievably corpulent: he projected so far in front that it would have been impossible for him to feed himself at table had not a space been cut in the board to accommodate the promontory.

The great thorn in his flesh was his brother, Duke Ludwig, a man of some fifty-one years when Weber made his acquaintance. Ludwig's hopes of becoming King of Poland having been frustrated, he had settled down in Stuttgart with a wife and large family; there he lived as extravagantly and dissolutely as his brother, who detested him cordially, and whom he plagued incessantly for money.

Weber was not accredited to Ludwig in any musical capacity; he was to be simply the Duke's private secretary and comptroller of the household. He had to raise money when and how he could, use his diplomacy to stave off importunate creditors, and, when necessary, squeeze something out of the reluctant King to pay the Duke's debts and provide for his pleasures.

The King, as we have said, had no liking for this troublesome and expensive brother of his, and he soon conceived a strong dislike for his emissary; he disgorged unwillingly when pestered by Weber for money, and vented his spleen in the foulest language on the head of the poor secretary. The young man detested him with equal ardour, and one day, unable to bear his insults any longer, he played a prank on him that might have had very serious consequences. Leaving the King's presence one day in great irritation after an unusually stormy scene, in which he had been bespattered with insults, he was accosted by an ill-favoured old woman who asked him where the room of the royal washerwoman was. " There," said Weber, pointing to the door through which he had just come. The King, as it happened, hated to be anywhere near old and ugly women. He fired some of his choicest curses at the frightened creature, who told him she had been sent in by the young gentleman who had come out. Weber was at once arrested and imprisoned, though Duke Ludwig's influence soon obtained his release.

The King bided his time, and a year or so later found the opportunity to strike a decisive blow. Weber's father, then nearly seventy-five, had suddenly descended on him in the spring of 1809: he was as proud and vain as ever, but with less control over himself now than he had ever had; it seems likely, indeed, that neither physically, mentally, nor morally was he quite normal.

One day towards the end of 1809 Weber discovered, to his horror, that his father had misappropriated a sum of money that the Duke had handed to his secretary to pay off a mortgage on his Silesian estate; the old man had already sent the money to Carlsruhe to liquidate some of his own debts. Carl Maria begged one Höner, the landlord of a tavern in Schweiberdingen, to lend him 1,000 florins, but was refused. The malversation of the funds being discovered by the Duke, there was nothing for Weber to do but to tell him the whole story and promise repayment as soon as possible. Shortly afterwards one of the Court servants, Huber, approached Weber and told him that he could get him the desired loan from Höner if he himself (Huber) were paid a small commission. Weber foolishly made the agreement and received the money without asking just how it had been raised.

As it turned out, the knavish Huber had gulled Höner with the story that for the sum of 1,000 florins he would use his influence with the Duke's secretary to save Höner's son from being drafted into the army; and when, in spite of this, the boy was called up in the following January, Höner naturally made a fuss about it.

The affair came to the ears of the King, who was in a state of perpetual fury over the evasions of military service that he knew to be practised, and the secret cause of which he suspected to be Court bribery and corruption. He was rejoiced to find that at the bottom of the flagrant case that had just been brought into the light of day was the detested secretary of his detested brother.

On the night of the 9th February, while Carl Maria was in the theatre, making arrangements for the forthcoming production of his *Silvana*, he was arrested by gendarmes. The next morning he was brought before the King. The story was told in outline by Weber's son, Baron Max von Weber, in the biography of his father that he published in 1864–6, but it was only a few years ago that the Württemberg palace archives were consulted by a more recent biographer for further light on the case.

Weber's rooms had been searched while he was under arrest, and he was now asked to account for the presence there of two silver candelabra and other articles belonging to the Duke; according to Baron Max they had been lent by the Duke to his secretary. When the case of Höner was gone into, it soon became evident that the Duke himself was deeply concerned in the whole scandal of evasion of military service; and it was no doubt the necessity of saving his brother's face that made the King reluctantly break off the proceedings and send Weber back to prison.

The young man found hardly a friend anywhere: the Duke no doubt thought it imprudent to interfere, and even the young actress, Gretchen Lang, with whom Weber was deeply in love, deserted him in the hour of his need.

On the 18th February the King, unwilling to stir up any more muddy waters in connection with the Höner affair, ordered Weber's release; but he was promptly re-arrested on the application of his many creditors. These, in the end, saw the wisdom of accepting his promise to repay them when he could; it seems probable, too, that the King, who was anxious to get rid of Weber, gave the creditors a hint that it would be indiscreet on their part to insist on his being sent to the debtors' prison and kept there indefinitely. So Weber and his father were sentenced to perpetual banishment from Württemberg, and on the morning of the 26th February, 1810, they were conducted to the frontier by a police official, their sole possessions being some personal linen and forty gulden. The official, however, secretly handed Weber another twenty-five gulden that had been raised by the one friend, Danzi, who still believed in him.

He had lived a hectic life in Stuttgart, and, as we have just seen, had piled up fresh debts there. The experiences of this February were a lesson to him and a blessing in disguise. He pulled himself together sharply and resolved henceforth to regulate his life rationally, not to put his trust in either princes or women, and to devote himself to his art.

On the day of his deportation he began a diary that he kept up almost without intermission to the day of his death; on the last day of this year, 1810, he wrote in it: " Since with the 26th February a new epoch in my life began, I regard that date as the beginning of the year for me. God has indeed given me many vexations and adversities to contend with, but has always brought me into the company of good men who made life worth while for me again. Truly and tranquilly I can say that in these ten months I have grown *better:* my sad experiences have taught me; I have at last become regularly industrious."

From Stuttgart he went for a time to Mannheim, where he met Vogler again, and began a lifelong friendship with one of the Abbé's pupils, the young Jacob Meyer Beer (son of the rich Berlin banker Beer), who was afterwards known to fame as Giacomo Meyerbeer. On the 17th September, 1810, Weber's opera *Silvana* was produced at Frankfort before only a small audience, the town having been drawn to the superior attraction of a balloon flight by one Madame Blanchard.

A charming one-act opera by Weber, *Abu Hassan,* was given at Munich on the 4th June, 1811, with great success. A concert tour in company with the celebrated clarinettist, Bärmann, for whom Weber wrote several works, was interrupted for a while by a sojourn at Gotha, at the Court of the eccentric but art-loving Duke Emil Leopold; then the tour was resumed, and in February 1812 the two artists found themselves in Berlin, where *Silvana* was given on the 10th July. Weber's father had died on the 16th of the previous April. From September to December was spent in a return visit to Gotha, and after a short visit to Leipzig Weber arrived in Prague on the 12th January, 1813.

In Prague a new phase of his life was to be accomplished. He was invited by Liebich, the manager of the local opera, to become musical director of that institution, which for some time had been on the down grade. Weber accepted the post, and soon showed that, apart from composition, his true *métier* was that of operatic conductor and producer. By unremitting work and the utmost rigour with himself and his forces he soon achieved a high standard of performance, though naturally the loftiness of his ideals and the strictness of his discipline made many enemies for him in the theatre.

While he was thus developing rapidly as an artist, however, he had still some way to go before he could achieve mastery of himself as a man. In spite of his good intentions he became entangled with an actress named Therese Brunetti, the wife of a dancer belonging to the company. Therese was completely self-seeking, immoral, and unscrupulous, and not even faithful to Weber, for she distributed her favours wherever there was a good market for them. Torn between love and contempt for her, Weber passed a miserable time, and there is no saying how the affair might have ended had not a certain Caroline Brandt come upon the scene.

This young singer had played the chief part in *Silvana* on its first production in Frankfort in 1810; she was then between seventeen and eighteen years old. Weber engaged her, purely on her artistic merits, for the Prague Opera, where she made her début on New Year's Day, 1814.

Gradually the modesty and virtue of the young girl, and the simplicity of her home life with her mother, began to exercise a charm on Weber; and after a final disillusionment as regards the worthless Therese Brunetti he was accepted as Caroline's lover.

Whether, at first, he contemplated going as far as matrimony seems to be doubtful, judging from a letter of his to his friend Gänsbacher of the 15th July, 1814, in which he speaks of his fondness for " Mlle Caroline Brandt," but assures his friend that he is still of his old opinion that if an artist is to give his whole soul to his art he must be a celibate. The pair became formally betrothed, however, in 1815.

The course of their love ran anything but smoothly for a considerable time, for Weber's prospects were not particularly brilliant, and neither Caroline nor her mother took kindly to his demand that on marriage she should cease to appear in public; while Caroline seems to have been at this time of rather a touchy nature, and to have found plenty of causes for sharp criticism of and disagreement with her lover.

During 1813 and 1814 Napoleon's power was visibly declining, and the new German aspiration towards independence found vent in a great number of patriotic poems, the most striking of which were those of the young Theodor Körner, who was killed in the battle of Gadebusch in 1813.

In 1814 Weber set some of Körner's poems to music that at once became recognised everywhere as the one predestined musical expression of them. These settings were taken to the heart of the German people, and especially of the students, and were a strong factor in the popularity that was before long to come Weber's way. A patriotic cantata of his, *Kampf und Sieg (Conflict and Victory)*, written to celebrate the victory of Waterloo (18th June, 1815), was not performed until the 22nd December of that year, at a concert in Prague for the composer's benefit.

A difference of opinion between the theatre committee and himself led to his giving up his post at Prague in April 1816, the resignation to take effect at the end of the following September. During his three and a half years in the town he produced sixty-one operas, thirty-one of them being novelties.

The reasons for his resignation were set forth in a letter to Liebich that has recently been published for the first time. He draws the impresario's attention to the many difficulties of the post: the *personnel* of the institution is not first-rate, yet the public is always demanding something new; the consequent strain on the conductor has been immense, and his health will bear it no longer; further, this incessant routine labour in and about the theatre leaves him neither time nor energy for imaginative work, and as " it seems to me a higher thing in art to work as a composer for the whole world than to labour as musical director for the pleasure of a particular public, I must not let the years in which my strength may still remain in me slip by unused."

He has taken especial care, he says, to leave the property of the opera and the documents relating to it in such perfect condition that his successor will be able to see his way clearly from the commencement; and he ends by saying that though his contract entitles him to the usual three months' holiday he will be satisfied with only an occasional brief visit to Carlsbad.

Evidently Weber, where art was concerned, was one of those incurable idealists whose self-sacrificing instincts and passion for perfection are taken advantage of and exploited by people with a stronger sense of reality. He had grossly overworked himself in Prague, to the serious damage of his health; in later years he was to overwork himself in Dresden to such an extent as to bring him to his death before he had reached his prime.

The Intendant of the Berlin Opera, a sincere admirer of his, Count Brühl, tried to induce the King of Prussia to take Weber into his service as Kapellmeister, but the traditions of the Prussian Court in music were predominantly Italian, and moreover Weber's musical association with the movement for popular freedom did not commend him to the King, so that the latter passed the German over in favour of the Italian Spontini.

Weber went to Berlin in June to superintend the rehearsals of his cantata *Kampf und Sieg,* and though the success of the work was enormous — even the King being compelled to admire it — his petition for the title of Royal Court and Chamber Composer (which would have been useful to him in the concert tour he was then planning) was rejected. Brühl, in a memorial to the King, ventured to lay stress on the fact that Weber " is undoubtedly one of the first among living German composers, and as a conductor there are few who can compare with him anywhere, while in Berlin there is not one who can come near him "; but the royal reply was that the granting of the title might raise in Weber expectations which there was no prospect of being realised. For the moment, then, Brühl, who never wavered in his devotion to Weber, could do no more.

The direction of the Leipzig Opera was offered to Weber, but this he declined. In Carlsbad, in July, he met Count Heinrich Vitzthum, the Intendant of the Dresden Opera, who had ideas for the encouragement of German opera in the Saxon capital, and knew that Weber, both by the pronouncedly German quality of his mind and his great gifts as conductor and organiser, was the man he and the cause needed. He ultimately managed to secure Weber's appointment at Dresden, and after a visit of Weber to Prague in September, in which vain attempts were made to induce him to resume his theatrical work there, he arrived in Dresden in January 1817.

In the preceding November he had completed his A flat and D minor piano sonatas and other works, and Caroline Brandt, who had been singing in " guest " parts in Berlin, realised for the first time, by the great honour in which Weber was evidently held there, that this lover of hers was actually a great man — not merely a gifted operatic conductor, but, in many people's opinion, the man of the hour so far as German opera was concerned. The future, then, seemed to Weber and her particularly promising.

But in Dresden the disillusionment soon began. The Court traditions in music had been Italian ever since the middle of the eighteenth century, and the royal house being Catholic by religion, the association with Italy was exceptionally close. The King and the Saxon aristocracy had no sympathy with the democratic attempt to found a German Opera. The Court was honeycombed with Italians, and the Italian influence in the opera-house was all-powerful, the German *Singspiel* (play with music), being banished, as an inferior bourgeois *genre,* to the smaller suburban theatres.

The King's chief minister was Count Einsiedel, a rigid bureaucrat who, like his royal master, looked with uneasy suspicion on anything that savoured of a national spirit in either politics or art; and Weber, as we have seen, had made himself a *persona non grata* to the more reactionary German Courts by his settings of Körner's stirring patriotic poems, that were now in the mouth of every German with nationalist longings.

When Weber arrived in Dresden he found that he was not to be placed on an equality with the Italian Morlacchi as " Kapellmeister," but given the lower title of " Musical Director of the German Opera." He protested to Vitzthum against this slight, but was persuaded to let matters continue as they were until a favourable opportunity should come to assert himself with more chance of success.

He was formally introduced by Vitzthum to the singers and the orchestra, and made a speech in which, after asking for their confidence, he said, " On the other hand, as your leader, I expect from you unconditional obedience: I shall be just, but also, without distinction of persons, inexorably strict towards everyone, and most of all towards myself." While keeping his word in these respects in the theatre, he was friendly enough with his forces in private life.

In comparison with the Italian Opera he had a poor set of singers, especially the women, and the chorus was inefficient. But by the sternest discipline and incessant hard work he brought his material to a pitch of competence that surpassed expectations: he took under his charge not only the singing and the orchestral playing but the stage production; and the orchestra in particular soon realised his superiority to Morlacchi both as conductor and as musician.

He had always had a penchant for literature, and in his Prague days had made a point of preparing the public for a new work or a new production by an elucidatory article in the local newspaper. He opened his first season at Dresden with Méhul's *Joseph,* because that work requires only one female singer and makes little demand on the chorus; and two days before the performance, which was fixed for the 30th January, 1817, he published in the local *Abendzeitung* an address " To the Art-loving People of Dresden." Such an act on the part of a Court servant had never before been dreamed of; and while the Dresden public realised that the new conductor was going to be a law to himself, the Court looked askance at this spirit of independence.

The story of the next few years is one of eternal struggle inside the theatre and outside it. Bit by bit he raised the standard of performance and made himself the centre of the national ideal in music; but he had to contend with constant intrigue on the part of the Italians and the aristocracy, the cold, immovable, bureaucratic spirit of Einsiedel, and the antipathy or indifference of the monarchy. He repaid the treachery and ill-will of the Italians with courtesy and kindness: when Morlacchi's oratorio *Isacco* was given, he wrote a helpful analysis of it, and again and again he undertook his intriguing colleague's duties for him at grievous cost to his own health.

Weber married Caroline Brandt in Prague on the 4th November, 1817, and brought his bride to Dresden on the 20th December. A couple of months before this, the King, unable any longer to turn a blind eye to his ability and assiduity in the theatre, the Church, and all the Court functions for which music was required, had confirmed his appointment for life.

A girl was born to him in December 1818, but lived only a few months. A son, Max Maria, afterwards a famous railway engineer and his father's biographer, was born on the 25th April, 1822.

In 1810 Weber had come across the story of *Der Freischütz* in Apel's *Gespenter Geschichten* (*Ghost Stories*), and was so taken by it that he and a friend worked it up into an opera libretto. He was unable to proceed with the composition at that time, however, and the project seems to have faded from his mind. In 1817 the desire to write an opera awoke in him again, and, as luck would have it, during his search for a subject in co-operation with his friend Kind he once more came upon Apel's book. His old enthusiasm for the story revived. Kind put the text together in quick time in the February of that year, but though the subject occupied Weber's thoughts perpetually it was not until the spring of 1820 that he was able to complete the writing down of the music. The opera was originally given the title of *The Trial Shot;* this was afterwards altered to *The Hunter's Bride;* it was on the suggestion of Count Brühl that in the end it was given the same title as Apel's well-known story.

Brühl had hastened to secure the new work for Berlin. He had not given up hope of placing Weber in the Prussian capital, but his plans in this regard were frustrated by the King's appointment of Spontini; he could be helpful to Weber, therefore, only as composer.

The Italian, who came with a great reputation from Paris, took precedence of Weber with his *Olimpia,* which was produced on the 14th May, 1821; the work relied largely for its effect on the splendour of its spectacle — there were thirty-eight trumpets on the stage in one scene, and the triumphal car was drawn by real elephants — but it failed to attract the public when the first novelty of it had worn off.

Der Freischütz was given on the following 18th June; four hours before the performance was timed to begin the opera-house was besieged. In the packed house were many celebrities, including Heinrich Heine, Mendelssohn, and the novelist E. T. A. Hoffmann; the Court, however, was conspicuous by its absence.

Weber, who conducted the performance, was given a great ovation when he stepped into the orchestra. The brilliant and novel overture was encored. The first act, in which nothing of particular importance seemed to happen, and in which no female characters appeared, was somewhat coolly received; but from that point onward the enthusiasm steadily increased, and at the end there could be no doubt that not only Weber but German art had scored an unexampled triumph. On the very morning of the production of *Der Freischütz* Weber calmly finished the *Concertstück,* which is really a piano concerto with a programme; he played it at a concert he gave in Berlin on the 25th July.

He received about this time an invitation to become

Kapellmeister at Cassel at a salary of 2,500 thalers, but although this was a thousand thalers more than he was getting in Dresden he declined the offer. An application for an increase of his Dresden salary was rewarded by a grudging grant of an extra 300 thalers, Morlacchi being simultaneously given the same increase.

Der Freischütz was given at Dresden on the 26th January, 1822; but though it was as great a success there as it had been in Berlin, the Court would not confer the smallest decoration on him.

His friend Kind, angry at what he thought the excessive praise given to the mere composer of *Der Freischütz* at the expense of the librettist, parted from him and refused to be reconciled, so that for the libretto of his next opera, *Euryanthe,* Weber had to go to one Wilhelmine von Chezy, a local lady whose literary ability was not quite the equal of her ambitions. She put together for him a text so obscure and absurd that the new opera, in spite of a flattering reception at its first performance in Vienna, under Weber, on the 25th October, 1822, had to be written down as a failure.

Weber was exceedingly mortified when the bitter truth had at last to be faced. He had been nettled by some criticisms of *Der Freischütz* in which that work was patronisingly referred to as a *Singspiel:* in *Euryanthe* he wanted to show the world that he had it in him to write a full-length grand opera without any spoken dialogue; and the failure of his new work was a terrible blow to him. His stay in Vienna, however, brought him one great experience — a long and intimate conversation with Beethoven.

In 1820 he had begun a comic opera, *The Three Pintos:* he set this aside to work at *Euryanthe,* and it remained unfinished at his death.

On his return to Dresden, where a second son, Alexander Victor Maria, was born to him on the 6th January, 1825, his health visibly worsened: in the fifteen months between October 1823 and January 1825 he wrote nothing but one small song. In 1824 he received an invitation to write an opera for Paris, a libretto by Desangriers, *The Wrath of Achilles,* being suggested; but the affair came to nothing. His eyes were bent on England, where he knew he was very popular.

Charles Kemble, the London impresario, asked him to write a new work for Covent Garden, and after the subject of *Faust* had been rejected in favour of that of *Oberon,* the offer was accepted, Kemble agreeing to pay him £1000.

Weber had been told by his doctor that his consumption had by now made such inroads on him that even with complete rest he could hope for only five or six years more of life, while if he persisted in working he would be dead within a few months. He deliberately chose to write and produce *Oberon* in order that his wife and children might be, to some extent, provided for after his death.

With his customary thoroughness he learned English well enough to be able to conduct the correspondence with London in that language. The libretto of the new opera was put together by Planché. Weber began work on it in January 1825. The composition of it was interrupted sometimes by ill-health, sometimes by visits to other towns (he produced *Euryanthe* at Berlin on the 23rd December, 1825), and it was January 1826 before the score was virtually complete.

He set out for England on the 16th February, 1826, in company with Fürstenau, the flautist of the Dresden orchestra, who had promised the anxious Caroline to look after him. After a week in Paris he reached London on the 5th March. He was lodged in Sir George Smart's house in Great Portland Street, where he received every possible kindness and attention.

Weber had heard of the large sums that Rossini had made in England by performing in fashionable houses, and had hoped for similar luck himself. In this, however, he was disappointed, his earnings of this kind being very small. Rossini, besides being the most popular opera composer in Europe, was a man of charming address, who could make himself at home in any society; but the average hostess and her guests found nothing particularly attractive in the sickly little German Kapellmeister. His success with the public, however, was great, both at the concerts that he conducted and in Covent Garden, where *Oberon* was produced on the 12th April. He conducted eleven further performances himself.

On the 26th May he gave a concert on his own account, but for one reason and another connected with the amusement-life of London it was only poorly attended. The last piece on the programme was the *Euryanthe* overture; after conducting this, Weber collapsed in the arms of Fürstenau. He was taken to Smart's house and anxiously cared for.

The next day he felt so much better that he hoped to be able to attend the performance of *Der Freischütz* that was to be given on the 5th June for his benefit. But it soon became clear not only to others but to himself that if he was ever to see his dear ones again he must give up everything and set out for Germany as quickly as possible; so he determined to leave London on the 6th June.

On the night of the 5th he went to bed at ten o'clock, after having shaken hands with all his friends and thanked them for their love; Fürstenau helped him to undress and would have slept in his room, but Weber rejected the offer. At twelve o'clock, when Sir George Smart's party broke up, the light in his room was already extinguished. The next morning he was found dead in his bed, sleeping peacefully with his right hand under his head; according to the doctors he had been dead some five or six hours.

The grievous news stirred London's sympathies. A committee was formed to raise funds for the embalming of the body and for the funeral, so that nothing need be spent of the money he had so hardly earned for his wife and children. He was buried in the Church of St. Mary, Moorfields, on the 21st June, Mozart's Requiem being sung at the service.

In later years another coffin was placed on his, obliterating the inscription on the plate, so that it was only by the Weber crest on the side that the coffin could be recognised. An English admirer, W. H. Grattan, had a silver plate put on it in 1840.

In the following year a Dr. Gambihler, of Nuremberg, who had visited the tomb in London, issued an appeal to the German nation to bring the remains of the national musical hero back to Germany. This was done in 1844, the body being taken to the Catholic cemetery in Dresden on Sunday the 14th December of that year. A vault had been designed by the architect Semper — a vault in which Weber's second son, who had died of measles, had been buried only a fortnight before. The funeral music for Weber, compiled by Wagner from motives from *Euryanthe,* was performed by torchlight on the night of the 14th. The next day the body was laid in the tomb; speeches were made by Wagner and others, and some music specially composed by Wagner accompanied the burial.

DER FREISCHÜTZ

[Carl Maria von Weber]

*D*ER FREISCHÜTZ is one of the most significant works in the history of German opera.

Most of the German courts had, from the middle of the eighteenth century, shown a preference for Italian over German art, and the court of Saxony was no exception to the rule. Weber's life at Dresden was one long struggle against these musical invaders, who had on their side the royal family, most of the aristocracy, and a fair number of the people. Weber was hampered and humiliated in every conceivable way in his work as director of the despised German opera, and it was only his unquenchable idealism and patriotism that sustained him.

Der Freischütz did not immediately extinguish the Italian influence in Germany, but it gave it a blow from which it never recovered. The new opera was thoroughly German from start to finish, in its subject, its characters, and its settings no less than in its music. The German people delightedly recognised themselves and their own country in it at every point. It summed up for them all their secret aspirations towards an art of their own, and its colossal success was not merely a tribute to the genius of Weber but a symbol of a nation's awakening. The only musical event comparable to the episode in modern Europe is the success of Glinka's *Life for the Czar* in Russia.

Weber first met with the subject of *Der Freischütz* in 1810, in Mannheim, in a collection of tales by Apel. He saw the operatic possibilities of it at once, and at his request his friend Dusch set about turning it into a libretto. For one reason or another, however, the scheme was dropped for some seven years — fortunately so, for the long interval gave Weber time to mature as a musician.

In Dresden he took the subject up again in 1817, the poet this time being Friedrich Kind (1768–1843), a rather vain and over-ambitious man of letters who for once did something that has kept his name alive. He did not, as is generally supposed, merely work on the basis of Apel, but went back direct to the old folk-tale. He placed the action in the period following the Thirty Years' War, thus avoiding possible difficulties with the censorship on account of some features of the story, and he practically re-created the tale and the characters in a way of his own.

The title first projected for the opera was *The Trial Shot;* later this was changed to *The Huntsman's Bride.* It was apparently on the suggestion of Count Brühl, the Intendant of the Berlin Opera, that almost at the last moment the work was re-named *Der Freischütz.* For this title there is no real English equivalent. Literally it means " The Free-shooter," but that term carries no very definite meaning in English, for which reason it is best to retain the German title. The basis of the story is the pact that certain individuals, according to the saga, were accustomed to make with a sinister figure known as the Black Huntsman, in virtue of which they received, in return for their souls some day, seven magic bullets, warranted to bring down anything that walked or flew. Six of the bullets obeyed the will of their possessor, but the destination of the seventh rested with the Black Hunts-man himself.

It took Kind only about a week to do his part of the work, but Weber turned the poem over in his mind again and again before attacking it. It was not until July 1817, more than four months after the text had been given to him, that he wrote the first num-ber, which was the duet between Agathe and Aennchen in the second act. He seems to have worked the music out in detail in his head, going over it time after time, rejecting this, improving that, before setting anything down on paper. Next to nothing of the opera was written during the rest of 1817, the whole of 1818, and the greater part of 1819. It was not until September of this last year that he settled down continuously to the writing of it. It was finished, down to the overture, in May 1820.

Weber had made the poem his own in more senses than one. At first Kind wanted to share with him whatever profits the as yet unwritten opera might bring. Weber, however, who had had experience of the trouble that this sort of arrangement sometimes brought between collaborators, urged Kind to sell him the book outright, which he eventually did for thirty ducats. When the opera turned out to be so colossal a success, Kind's vanity led him to believe that too little credit for it went to the poet and too much to the composer. Weber generously offered him a portion of his profits, but this the poet refused coldly. The friendly relations between the pair gradually changed to indifference, and finally, on Kind's part, to enmity, so that for the text of *Euryanthe* Weber had to go to another librettist, Frau Wilhelmine von Chezy, who provided him with a book so poor that it has dragged Weber's fine music down with it.

Originally *Der Freischütz* was in four acts. The first consisted of two scenes. The former of these shows a Hermit's house in a forest. Near it is a rough altar, behind which stands a cross, surrounded by white roses. It is nearly evening. When the curtain rises the old Hermit is seen praying before the altar. He has had a dream of the devil lurking in the darkness and stretching out his horrible hand towards an unspotted lamb, Agathe, and then trying to ensnare her bridegroom, Max. The holy man implores the grace of Heaven for the innocent pair. He is just reflecting anxiously that he has not seen Agathe for three days when she appears, bringing him a pitcher of milk, and followed by her cousin Aennchen, who carries a little basket of bread and fruit. Aennchen having gone out, the Hermit asks after Max, and learns that he is uneasy about the shooting trial that is to take place on the morrow. The Hermit tells Agathe that he is anxious in another way for them both. Some danger, he thinks, threatens them — so, at least, he surmises from his dream.

He exhorts Agathe to preserve the purity of her heart, and she, in return, begs him to remember her in his prayers. As she is leaving him he recalls her; an inner voice bids him not let her go without a gift. He turns to the rose bush, the first cutting of which had been brought to him long ago by a pilgrim from the Holy Land: each summer he collects and presses the leaves, to which the peasantry attribute supernatural powers of bodily healing and preservation from harm. He gives Agathe some of the roses as a bridal gift, and dismisses her with a further exhortation to be simple and virtuous.

Weber appears to have had his doubts as to the desirability of opening the opera with these two scenes, but Kind insisted on their retention, declaring that without them the work would be like a statue with its head cut off. Weber, however, consulted his fiancée, Caroline Brandt, on whose sense of the stage he always relied; and she was emphatic in her judgment. " Out with these two scenes! " she wrote; " plunge right into the life of the people at the very beginning of the opera; start with the scene in front of the tavern."

Thus fortified in his own opinion, Weber approached Kind again; he pointed out to him the novelty of the scene at the commencement of the second act, which would make so excellent an opening; to begin with the Hermit would be to give too much importance to a minor character; further, the music he would have to sing would call for a first-class bass, and as a voice of this kind would be indispensable for another of the characters also, and not many German theatres could be trusted to be so rich in first basses, it would be policy to cut these two scenes out entirely. In the end Kind gave in. His pride of authorship, however, made him print the discarded first act in later years, and in 1871 one Oskar Möricke set it to music, using motives of Weber's own. There can be no doubt that the opening of the opera has been improved by the sacrifice of these two scenes; but it is also true that without them the *dénouement* is not of itself fully intelligible.

THE OVERTURE

The overture is one of the world's masterpieces of its genre. It was a striking novelty for its time. With rare exceptions, such as Mozart's use of the music of the Supper Scene for the andante introduction to the overture to *Don Giovanni,* composers until then had not drawn upon the themes of the opera. Weber began a new genre with the overture to *Der Freischütz,* without which, in all probability, we should never have had such overtures as those to *Tannhäuser* and *The Mastersingers.*

Further, Weber was not only a born musical dramatist but a very original and skilful orchestral colourist; and the overture to *Der Freischütz* has a depth and brilliance and variety of tone to which there was nothing to compare in any previous operatic overture.

It commences with an adagio prelude that breathes the very spirit of the romantic German forest. The strings and wood-wind arrest the attention with a preliminary phrase:

after which, over a soft rustling in the violins, supported by solid harmonies in the lower strings, the horns give out a two-part melody that seems born out of the very nature of the instrument:

As this dies away, the violins and violas break into a sort of shuddering tremolando, with the clarinets adding their own deep colour to it; the double basses (pizzicati) and the timpani strike in with sinister reiterated notes, and the 'cellos break out into a wail:

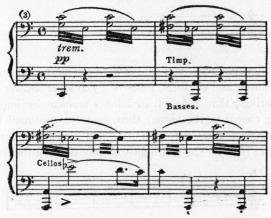

The horror rises to a climax and then dies away almost into silence. In these dozen bars we have already the revelation of a new genius in German opera.

The tempo now changes to *molto vivace,* and after some bars of agitated syncopation, drawn from Max's aria in the first act, at the point at which the Black Huntsman appears in the background, the clarinets give out the melody to which Max sings the words " What evil power is closing round me? "

This merges into the theme, given out by the full orchestra fortissimo, to which, in the grisly scene in the Wolf's Glen in the second act, Max cries out his terror at the horrors around him:

This section culminates in a wild upward and downward rush in the strings, flutes, and clarinets, followed by another sinister tremolo in the strings, that is punctuated for a moment by imperiously arresting chords in the horns; then, over the continual tremolo, a solo clarinet gives out, fortissimo and *con molta passione*, a theme that is like a shaft of light suddenly piercing the darkness:

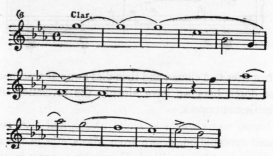

and after a short transitional passage the violins and clarinets sing the melody of the final part of Agathe's aria in the second act:

in which she speaks of her confidence in the ultimate happiness
of Max and herself.

We thus have already presented to us the vital essence of the
drama — its setting in the depth of the German wood, the intrusion of the powers of evil, the horror and despair of Max, the
trustful innocence of Agathe, and the final triumph of simplicity
and goodness. The remainder of the overture is a symphonic
working-out of the material here shown. After the sinister No. 3
has been heard for the last time there is a dramatic silence for
two bars, then a solitary plucked note in the 'cello and basses,
then another long pause, followed by a huge crescendo in the full
orchestra and a final triumphant statement of Agathe's melody
(No. 7), this time in the broad C major tonality in which the
overture opened.

ACT I

When the curtain rises for the first act we see an open place
before a tavern in a forest. Max is sitting alone at a table in the
foreground, with a tankard before him and his gun in his arm.
In the background is a target, surrounded by a crowd of peasants.
Just as the curtain goes up, Kilian, a rich peasant (bass), is firing
at the target; shouts from the crowd — " Bravo! Well fired!
Splendid! " — greet his success. Max (tenor), who till now has
kept his forehead sunk in his clenched hand, strikes the table
heavily and cries, " Good luck, peasant! " while the others break
out into a chorus of praise of Kilian. The crowd lines up for a
procession, while Max asks himself in a gloomy, puzzled kind of
way what has happened to him that his skill as a marksman has
deserted him.

A procession is now formed, headed by a band of village musicians playing a rustic March. After them come peasant lads, carrying pewter vessels as trophies; Kilian, the victor in the contest,
decorated with flowers and a ribbon, on which is stuck the stars
that he has shot from the target; a boy with the remains of the
target on a short pole; marksmen, several of whom have stars
on their caps, carrying guns; and women and girls. They all march

round, and as they pass Max they point mockingly at him, bow, whisper, and laugh among themselves. At last Kilian stands before him, makes a sign to the others, and breaks out into a derisive song; the others echo his taunts.

Max springs up in a rage, draws his hanger, seizes Kilian by the chest, and orders him to leave him in peace. The others press around him, and just then Cuno, the head ranger, enters with Caspar and several huntsmen with guns and spears. Cuno (bass) demands to know what the trouble is, and Kilian, who has been released by Max, but is still a trifle scared, tells him that all he has been doing is to chaff, in accordance with time-honoured custom, the man who never hits the mark; it has come to something when the peasant beats the huntsman at his own game! Max, in great mortification, has to admit that the charge is true; and Caspar, one of the foresters (bass) who is senior to Max, mutters to himself, " Thanks, Samiel! " (He himself is in love with Agathe, but having been refused by her, he hates her accepted suitor, Max, and has sold himself to Samiel, the Black Huntsman, to get the better of his rival.)

Cuno cannot make it out at all: here is Max, supposed to be the best shot in the place, who has not brought down claw or feather for four weeks. Caspar, who knows quite well why, comes forward with a glib explanation; someone must have cast a spell over Max, and to break it he will have to stand next Friday at a cross-road, draw a circle round himself with his ramrod or a bloody knife, and call three times on the Black Huntsman. Cuno indignantly orders him to be silent: " I have long known you for what you are," he says — " an idler, a glutton, and a cheater at dice. Take care that I don't think still worse of you! " Caspar makes a grovelling apologetic gesture, and Cuno warns him that if he speaks another word he will dismiss him.

Then, turning to Max, Cuno bids him also be careful. He wishes him well, but if he fails to win the prize to-morrow he loses the hand of Cuno's daughter, Agathe, and with it the succession to Cuno's post. Strange to say, the others, though they have heard of the ordeal of the trial shot, do not know precisely how and why it came about. They appeal to Cuno to tell them the story, which he proceeds to do, for the audience's benefit, no doubt, as much as for that of the people on the stage.

It seems that Cuno's great-great-grandfather (also named Cuno) was one of the Prince's bodyguards. One day the hounds started a stag on which a man was tied — the usual punishment in those days for one who broke the forest laws. The Prince, moved to pity, promised that whoever should kill the stag without wounding the man should be made a hereditary forester and given a house.

The original Cuno, more out of compassion than from a desire for the reward, fired at the stag and brought him down without inflicting any more injury on the man than some scratches on the face from a thorn bush. But, says Cuno with a meaning glance at Caspar, it was then as it is now: the evil one always sows tares among the wheat. The enemies of the former Cuno told the Prince that the deed had been accomplished by means of magic — Cuno must have used a " free " (or magic) bullet. (" I thought so! " interjects Caspar; and then, to himself, " Help, Samiel! ")

Kilian explains to the others what a " free " bullet is; his grandmother had told him all about them: six hit the mark, but the seventh belongs to the evil one, who directs it where he will. The Prince, Cuno continues, then ordered that each of the original Cuno's successors should undergo a shooting trial on the day when the ycung man is to marry his betrothed, who must be of irreproachable character and must appear in a virginal wreath of honour. All this having been satisfactorily explained, Cuno breaks up the gathering, telling Max that he expects him again before sunrise at the Prince's house.

(This long conversation, like all the others in *Der Freischütz*, is carried on in spoken dialogue.)

There follows a short ensemble in which Max sings of the foreboding with which he looks forward to the morrow's trial; Cuno bids him collect himself, for everything now depends on his skill; the others add an occasional word of encouragement; and Caspar insinuates a hint that there are other powers than that of his own

hand and eye that he can call to his aid. Cuno shakes Max by the
hand, and, with a final heartening word to him, goes out with
his huntsmen, who sing a chorus in praise of the hunt. It is
growing dark. Kilian, a rough good fellow, wishes Max the best
of luck the next day, and invites him into the tavern, to drive away
his melancholy with a glass and a dance with the girls; but Max
being too depressed for anything of that kind, Kilian and the
others leave him, some of them waltzing their way into the inn.

Max, left alone, declares that he can bear his evil fate no longer:
for what crime, he asks in despair, is he being made to pay? Then
he breaks out into the famous aria " Durch die Wälder ":

Thro' the fo-rests, thro' the meadows, Joy was
Durch die Wäl-der, durch die Au-en, zog ich

wont_ with_ me__ to__ stray:
leich - ten __ Sinns da - hin!

in which he describes how easily life used to run with him — how
everything he aimed at fell to his gun, and in the evenings, laden
with booty, he would return to find Agathe waiting for him at her
window with a loving look. It is now quite dark. " Has Heaven
then forsaken me? " he asks, and as he speaks the words Samiel
appears from a thicket in the background — a huge figure in dark
green and flame-coloured garb, his face a dark yellow, a cock's
feather in his hat.

We hear the typical Samiel music in the orchestra (No. 3).
Samiel disappears, and Max's thoughts turn again to Agathe,
whom he sees in imagination at her open window, waiting for his
footsteps, and confident of his triumph; but her gesture of greeting receives no answer. Once more his gloom overmasters him.
The orchestra gives out the agitated syncopated figure already so
familiar to us in the overture, and to the melody of No. 4 he
speaks of his doubts and despair. Will no ray come to pierce the

night in his soul? Does blind fate rule? Is there no God? At his first words of despair Samiel reappears in the background and crosses the stage with great strides; but at the word " God " he gives a convulsive start and disappears.

Caspar now enters, accosts Max with assumed good-fellowship, and orders wine from the inn, telling the serving-maid to chalk it up to him, which she evidently does unwillingly and untrustingly. He drops something out of a phial into Max's glass, and mutters his usual " Help, Samiel! " whereupon the Black Huntsman's head looks out from the thicket — much to the terror of Caspar, who ejaculates, " You here? " He assures Max that he was only speaking to himself, and at last forces him to drink by pledging the Head Ranger — a toast which it is impossible for Max to refuse. Then Caspar breaks out into a rough drinking-song:

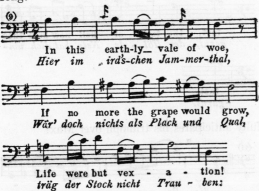

In this   earth-ly— vale of woe,
Hier im   „ird's-chen Jam-mer-thal,

If   no   more the grape would   grow,
Wär' doch   nichts als Plack und   Qual,

Life   were but vex - a - tion!
träg der Stock nicht   Trau - ben:

Nor can Max refuse the second toast that Caspar proposes — to Agathe; nor the third — to the Prince.

Max, feeling unaccountably uneasy, would now go home, but Caspar holds him back while he offers to help him to fire a shot that will ensure his happiness and Agathe's the next day. He thrusts his gun into Max's hands, points hastily to an eagle that is a mere speck in the night sky, and tells him to fire. As Max does so a peal of harsh laughter is heard. A huge eagle falls dead at their feet; Caspar plucks out some of its largest feathers and puts them on Max's hat. How has it been done? asks the astounded Max. Caspar laughs at him — as if Max did not know that this was a free bullet! It was his last, he assures Max; but he knows how to get more; Max must meet him at midnight in the Wolf's Glen. At first Max is appalled at the thought of being in that haunted place at such an hour; but deceived by Caspar's protestations of goodwill, and full of the thought of Agathe, he at last consents. After he has left, Caspar breaks out into an aria in which he calls on the powers of evil to make sure of their coming prey:

and gleefully anticipates his triumph over Max:

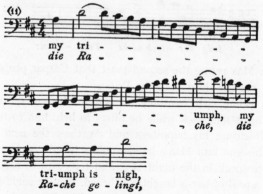

As he leaves the stage the curtain falls.

ACT II

The second act opens in a room in Cuno's house in the forest, hung with tapestries and trophies of the chase. On one side of it is a table with a lamp and a white dress trimmed with green. On the wall is a picture of the original Cuno. On the other side of the room from the table is Agathe's spinning-wheel. Agathe, in an undress, has a bandage on her head; we learn that the picture has fallen and hurt her. Aennchen is standing on a stool, hammering in a nail to hold up the picture. She is a care-free girl of unquenchable good spirits and a roguish, teasing disposition, while Agathe, as befits an affianced bride, is much more inclined to sentiment. There is a charming duet between the two, in which each expresses her own character; and afterwards Aennchen sings of the gloom of the old house they are in, and expresses her preference for brighter scenes and a gay wooer.

Agathe tells Aennchen of her visit to the Hermit that morning and how he warned her of a danger threatening her: the falling picture and the wound were evidently the fulfilment of his presentiment. She will take care of the consecrated roses he gave her; and to preserve them Aennchen proposes to put them outside the window, in the cool night air. Aennchen would then go to bed, but Agathe refuses to go until she has seen Max.

Aennchen having left her, taking with her the roses, Agathe muses upon the sorrow that always goes hand in hand with love. She draws aside the curtain in front of a balcony and looks out into the starry night. Stepping out on the balcony, she raises her hands in prayer, and breaks out into the universally known aria, " Leise, leise, fromme Weise ":

in which she commends herself to the protection of Heaven. Why does Max tarry? she asks. She hears a footstep and sees a form among the pines, and her pulse quickens. Jubilantly she waves a white handkerchief, but Max does not yet see her. Is that a nosegay in his hat, and does it mean that he has been successful in the contest? She returns into the room and gives full expression to her joy and hope:

She sings of her rapture to the strain of No. 7, and turns to meet Max, who enters hurriedly, looking pale and troubled; at the same moment Aennchen re-enters from the other side.

Agathe is a little disturbed to find only an eagle's feather in Max's hat instead of the expected trophy. He tells her that by a marvellous shot he has brought down a great eagle. She explains about the fallen picture and the wound on her forehead, and he protests that he must away at once to the Wolf's Glen; he has shot a stag there in the dusk, he says, and must bring it in, or the peasants may steal it. The two girls are horrified at the thought that he is going to the haunted glen at night, but in spite of their entreaties he takes himself off, only pausing at the door for a tender little duet with Agathe, in which he implores and she grants him forgiveness for having grieved her, while the light-hearted Aennchen comments on the situation in her own fashion:

The scene changes to the Wolf's Glen. All that happens from now to the end of the act is in the pure spirit of the German romanticism of the early years of the nineteenth century, when people loved to frighten themselves with the thought of mysterious magic forces at work all round them.

We see a fearsome hollow between high mountains, from one of which a waterfall runs down. The full moon is shining; a storm is gathering. Near the front is a tree blasted by lightning — it has rotted away from the inside, and has a phosphorescent glow; on a gnarled branch a great owl with fiery eyes is sitting; on other trees are ravens and other forest birds.

Caspar, without a hat and in his shirt sleeves, is busy making a circle of black stones, in the middle of which is a skull; a few steps away are an eagle's wing, a bullet-mould, and a crucible. Over a mysterious shudder in the orchestra, a bass chorus of invisible spirits sing on one note, a gruesome snatch about a bride that is soon to die, while other voices break in every now and then with a cry of " Uhui! " which is punctuated by a similar hoot in the wood-wind:

Just as Caspar finishes the circle a clock in the distance begins to strike twelve.

Caspar draws his hanger, and at the twelfth stroke thrusts it into the skull; then, raising the hanger with the skull on it, he cries, " Samiel! Samiel! Appear! " and replaces skull and hanger in the middle of the circle. Samiel appears in a fissure in a rock and asks, " Who calls me? " Caspar grovels before him. His time is up to-morrow: will not Samiel prolong it if he brings him another victim — his friend Max, who is in quest of free bullets? " Six shall make him, seven break him," says Samiel. " The seventh is thine," answers Caspar eagerly: " direct it from his own gun to his bride, and so drive both him and her father mad." Over Agathe, says Samiel regretfully, he has as yet no power; but he is inclined to listen to the proposition so far as Max is concerned, and to grant Caspar another three years' grace if he can ensnare the other. To-morrow it must be he or thou! " This dialogue, sung by Caspar, spoken by Samiel, is carried on to an appropriately descriptive orchestral accompaniment.

Samiel disappears; Caspar rises and wipes the sweat from his forehead. The hanger and skull have disappeared; in their place a small hearth with glowing coals has risen out of the earth. Caspar refreshes himself with a draught from his hunting-flask; the coals burning low, he throws faggots on them and blows on the fire; the owls and the other birds, as though in sympathy, raise and lower their wings, and the fire smokes and crackles. Max now becomes visible on one of the rocks; he bends down towards the glen, and in a recitative describes his horror at the darkness, the ghostly forms, the whirring night birds, and the blasted tree.

Determined that nothing shall daunt him, however, he climbs

down a little way and stares fixedly at the opposite rock, where, in
the moonlight, stands the spirit of his mother, clothed in white.
" Thus she was in her coffin," he says in terror; " thus she lies in
her grave! With a warning glance she implores me to go back! "
Laughing nervously at his fears, and calling aside on Samiel for
help, Caspar bids him look again, when he will see better what it
was that frightened him. The figure of his mother disappears, and
in its place stands the form of Agathe. Her hair is loose, she is
strangely decked out with straw and leaves: she has the air of
one distracted, and seems as if she were about to throw herself
down into the waterfall. Crying out that he must follow her, Max
descends to where Caspar is, whereupon the form of Agathe
vanishes.

" Here I am," says Max; " what is it I must do? " The moonlight grows dimmer. Fortifying him with a draught from his
hunting-flask, but refusing to drink himself, Caspar tells him to
come within the circle, which, he says, is a sure wall against the
spirits, whether of heaven or of hell. Whatever Max may see or
hear he is to remain calm; if someone came to help him, even were
it a black rider on a black horse, striking fire from his hooves, what
would that matter? Not without some disturbance can the hidden
powers be brought to bestow their treasures on mortals. Only
when he sees Caspar himself trembling is Max to come to his aid
and repeat his call — otherwise they both will be lost.

By now the moon has sunk to a mere point in the night sky.
Caspar picks up the crucible, orders Max to watch him, that he
may learn the art, takes the necessary ingredients from his pouch
and throws them in one by one, enumerating them as he does so:
" First the lead; some broken glass from church windows, which
can easily be got; some quicksilver; three bullets that have already
found their mark; the right eye of a hoopoe; the left eye of a
lynx. *Probatum est!* And now a blessing on the bullets! " To the
sinister chords shown at the commencement of No. 3 he prostrates
himself three times to the earth and invokes Samiel, exhorting him
to " bless the deed, seven, nine, and three, that the bullets
mighty be."

To an appropriately hair-raising tremolando in the strings of the orchestra, and eerie cries in the wood-wind, the contents of the crucible begin to ferment and hiss, and give out a greenish-white flame. A cloud passes over what is left of the moon, so that the only light on the scene now comes from the fire on the hearth, the eyes of the owl, and the putrescent wood of the tree.

" One! " says Caspar, as he casts the first bullet and drops it out of the mould; and an echo repeats the word, as it does all the later ones. Night birds fly down, gather round the circle, and hop about flapping their wings.

" Two! " A black boar crashes through the thicket and runs panting across.

" Three! " says Caspar, now greatly agitated. A storm rises, breaks the tops of the trees, and sends sparks flying from the fire.

" Four! " Caspar counts anxiously. The rattling of wheels, cracking of whips, and trampling of horses are heard. Four wheels, throwing out fiery sparks, roll across the stage, so rapidly that neither their real shape nor the coach they carry is visible.

" Five! " says Caspar, still more nervously. The barking of dogs and the neighing of horses fill the air, and in the heights there is a rush of ghostly hunters on foot and on horseback, with stags and hounds; invisible voices sing in chorus on one note, accompanied by a pelting rhythm in the orchestra. " Woe! Woe! " cries Caspar: " the wild chase! " The scene becomes completely dark.

" Six! Woe! " cries Caspar. The sky becomes completely black. The hitherto contending storms crash together and burst with fearful lightnings and thunders. Rain falls in torrents. Dark blue flames spring from the earth; will-o'-the-wisps appear on the hills; trees are torn up crackling by the roots; the waterfall foams and rages; pieces of rock are hurled down. From every quarter there comes a tumult in the air; the earth seems to totter.

" Samiel! Samiel! Help! " shrieks Caspar convulsively. " Seven! Samiel! " Caspar is thrown to the earth. Max, who is also tossed hither and thither by the tempest, leaps out of the circle, seizes a branch of the blighted tree and screams, " Samiel! " The storm begins to die down. Samiel, the Black Hunter, appears where the

tree was. He seizes Max's hand and cries in a terrible voice, " Here
I am! " Max makes the sign of the cross and falls senseless. In
the distance a clock strikes one. There is a sudden silence. Samiel
has disappeared; Caspar is still lying with his face to the earth;
Max raises himself convulsively, and the curtain falls.

ACT III

The third act commences with a vivacious orchestral introduction, in the course of which we hear a merry tune in the horns:

When the curtain rises we see a wood, bathed in sunlight. Two
of the Prince's huntsmen enter. They congratulate each other on
the fineness of the day that has followed so fearful a night: in the
Wolf's Glen especially, they think, the devil himself must have
been loose; branches the thickness of a man have been split
like canes, giant firs are turning up their roots towards the skies;
everyone knows whose work that was! Max, somewhat heated,
enters with Caspar. The two couples greet each other, and one
of the huntsmen tells the other, aside, to be polite to Max, who has
just fired three marvellous shots; if he goes on like that he will
one day be head master of the hounds.

The pair having gone out, Max turns feverishly to Caspar and
demands the lucky bullets. " Three for me, four for you! " says
Caspar; " could a brother divide more fairly? " " But I have only
one," says Max. " The Prince had his eye on me. I made three
wonderful shots. What have you done with the bullets? " Caspar
takes two magpies out of his hunting-pouch and throws them behind a bush. " You see," he says, " two have gone on these. What

do I care about the Prince's game? " " But you still have another
bullet," says Max urgently; " give it to me." " I should be a fool,"
replies Caspar; " one for me, one for you; I am keeping it for you
for the trial shot." " Give me your third! " cries Max passionately.
" I can't! " says Caspar.

Max is beside himself; but just then a third huntsman enters
and tells him that the Prince wishes to speak to him at once;
there has been a dispute as to the range of his gun. When he has
left, Max once more urgently demands the third bullet of Caspar,
who refuses to give it to him even if he were to beg for it on his
knees. Max calls him a rascal and hastens away. " Well and
good! " says Caspar when he is alone. " Soon the sixth bullet will
be fired " (he loads his gun), " and then the seventh for the trial
shot! Ha ha! Splendid! May the lovely bride get it! There's a
fox out over there: let him have the sixth in his skin." He raises
his gun to his shoulder as he goes out, and the shot is heard as the
curtain falls.

In performance the foregoing scene, which is carried out
entirely in spoken dialogue, is often omitted; and the third act
commences with the next scene, which takes place in Agathe's
chamber in the forester's house — an old-fashioned room, but
neatly furnished. On one side there is a little domestic altar, upon
which stands a vase containing the bouquet of white roses. Agathe
is alone; she is in a white bridal costume with a green band in her
hair. When the curtain rises she is kneeling at the altar; then she
rises, comes forward, and in a tone of fervent piety breaks into a
deeply-felt aria:

in which she expresses her confidence in the loving protection of Heaven.

When she has finished, Aennchen enters, also in bridal dress, but without any flowers. (It is important that neither Aennchen nor any of the other bridesmaids should carry flowers, so that Agathe, for her bridal adornment, has to take the holy roses, that confer immunity against the magic bullet.)

The sprightly Aennchen rallies her more serious friend in the usual way. She notices that Agathe has been crying: well, " bridal tears and morning showers, according to the proverb, don't last long." And speaking of rain, there has been enough in the night to wash the old house away. " And Max," said Agathe, " in the wood in all that tempest! " She has had a fearful dream — that she was changed into a white dove, flying from branch to branch. Max fired at her and she fell; but the white dove had vanished, she was Agathe again, and at her feet a great black bird of prey lay weltering in its blood!

Aennchen claps her hands. " Charming! Charming! " she says. It is all very easily explained. Last night Agathe was working late at her wedding-dress, and no doubt she was thinking of it before she went to sleep: that accounts for the white dove. She had started back from the eagle's feathers in Max's hat: that explains the bird of prey. Agathe, however, is not so easily pacified, so Aennchen, anxious to turn her mind from its gloomy thoughts, sings her the story of how her old aunt once had a fright: just as she was going to sleep she saw and heard a monster creeping towards her with eyes of fire, rattling a chain. She called for help, but when the servants came with lights they found it was only Nero, the watch-dog.

Agathe, at this unexpectedly absurd *dénouement*, turns away in vexation, but gradually yields to Aennchen's loving entreaties to be happy in the thought of what the day is to bring her. Then Aennchen runs off to fetch the bridal wreath, which she has left below. As she is going, the door opens, and the bridesmaids enter, whom she tells to cheer up the bride. This they proceed to do in the famous " Jungfernkranz " (Bridal Wreath) chorus that quickly became one of the melodies that every German knew:

(18)

The   bri-dal wreath for   thee we bind, With
Wir   win-den dir den   Jung-fern-kranz, mit

silk - en thread of__   a - zure,
veil - chenblau - er__   Sei - de,

Aennchen, returning with the box containing the wreath, brings the news that ancestor Cuno has been at his pranks again: he has fallen from his nail a second time, and Aennchen has nearly tripped over him. Agathe sees another evil omen in this, but Aennchen asks her what was more likely to happen on such a night as last, when the house was shaken from top to bottom by the wind. Kneeling before Agathe and presenting the box to her, she starts the chorus off on their song again.

They have hardly begun, however, before they are interrupted by a startled cry from Agathe. She has opened the box, and found in it only a silver wreath for the dead — a mistake on the part of the old servant who had been sent to the town for the wreath. The bridesmaids are embarrassed: Agathe is distressed at this fresh omen of evil; she recalls once more the Hermit's foreboding. Aennchen takes the Hermit's white roses from the vase and binds them into a garland; then, bidding the bridesmaids begin their song again, she takes Agathe by the hand and leads her through the door, the others following in couples.

The scene changes. Hunting-horns are heard in the orchestra, and, the curtain having risen, we see a romantically beautiful landscape. On one side are the tents of Prince Ottokar, where the court notabilities and guests are banqueting; on the other side are the huntsmen and beaters, also feasting; behind them are piled-up heaps of game. Prince Ottokar is seated at table in the principal tent; Cuno is at the bottom of the table. Max is standing near Cuno, but outside the tent, leaning on his gun; on the opposite

side Caspar is watching behind a tree. A vigorous hunting chorus
is sung, to a melody that has already been heard in the introduction to the third act, prefacing No. 16:

The music is worked out with an appropriate wealth of colour,
especially in the horns, No. 16 also being drawn upon for refrain.

The Prince then rises and recalls the company to the serious
business of the day. He approves Cuno's choice of a son-in-law;
the young man pleases him. He tells Cuno to bid Max be ready,
which the old forester does with a sign. " But where is the puppet? " says Caspar to himself, adding his customary, " Help,
Samiel! " He climbs up into the tree and looks around. Ottokar
turns to Cuno and asks him where the bride is; he has heard so
much good of her that he is keen to make her acquaintance. Cuno
tells him that she should be here presently, but asks whether the
trial shot may not take place *before* she comes; the young lover
has been a trifle unfortunate of late, and the presence of the bride
may unnerve him.

The Prince laughingly remarks that Max seems to be hardly
cool enough for a huntsman: " When I was watching him from a
distance he fired three master-shots; but since I had him called
he has done nothing right." Cuno has regretfully to admit that
this is true, though, he adds, until quite lately Max was the best
shot of them all. The genial Prince doubts whether Cuno and himself would have done any better on their wedding-day, but all the
same the old custom must be adhered to. Raising his voice so that
Max may hear him, he smilingly asks Cuno whether he has not
an older huntsman to whom the preference used to be given.

While Cuno, in some embarrassment, is stammering a reply, Max mutters to himself, " Caspar has perhaps still his last free bullet. He might perhaps — " and then he hastily loads his gun, and ejaculates, " Once more and never again! "

Ottokar tells Cuno that the time has come to settle the matter, and he turns to Max with a " Come, young fellow! One shot like the three you fired this morning, and you are safe! You see that white dove on yonder branch? It's an easy mark. Fire! " Just as Max raises his gun to his shoulder, Agathe, Aennchen, the bridesmaids, and others come into view, just where the white dove is sitting. Agathe cries out, " Do not fire! I am the dove! " The bird rises and flies towards Caspar's tree; Caspar hastily climbs down. Max fires at the dove, which flies away. Agathe and Caspar both give a shriek and fall to the ground, and the chorus break into a cry of horror.

Agathe is picked up and led to a small mound in the foreground; Max falls on his knees before her. She soon recovers consciousness, and all give a joyous shout of " She lives! Praised be the powers above! " Then attention is directed to Caspar, who is struggling convulsively, bathed in his own blood. " I saw the Hermit beside her," he says; " Heaven has won, my time has come! " Agathe is by now sufficiently restored to join with Max in a brief duet, which is taken up by the rest of the company.

Meanwhile, unseen by these, Samiel has risen from the earth behind Caspar. " Thou, Samiel, here already? " Caspar asks. " Is this how thou keepest thy promise to me? Take then thy prey! I defy my doom! " Then, raising his hand, " Accursed be Heaven! And accursed be thou! " He falls to the earth in a convulsion, and Samiel vanishes. All are horrified at this strange last prayer of a dying man; but they agree that Caspar was always given to evil ways, and that the judgment of Heaven has at last overtaken him. The Prince orders them to take the miscreant's body and throw it into the Wolf's Glen, and a few of the huntsmen carry it away.

Then the Prince turns to Max, and in grave tones charges him to clear up the mystery. Max kneels before him and makes his

humble confession of wrong-doing — the four bullets he has fired
that day were " free " bullets, cast in association with the dead
Caspar. All are astonished and shocked. The Prince angrily ban-
ishes him for ever from his dominions; never shall he have Agathe's
pure hand.

Max breaks out into reproachful self-pity, and Cuno and Agathe
both intercede for him, the chorus later supporting their plea.
But the Prince is immovable: Max must either flee the land or
go to prison. Just then the Hermit enters majestically, and all
salute him respectfully, the Prince baring his head: if this is the
holy man of whom he has heard such good report, he will be
guided by him; let the Hermit, then, pronounce judgment.

The Hermit, to slow and solemn music, preaches them a little
sermon on the fallibility of all mankind and the virtue of tolerance;
which among us has the right to throw the first stone at any
sinner? Let the trial shooting be abolished from that day, and as
for Max, since his heart was always good and true, let him be put
upon a year's probation; after that, if he is what he used to be,
let him be given Agathe's hand. The Prince consents; Max and
Agathe blend their voices in a cry of gratitude and hope; and
the whole company express their satisfaction in a chorus based
on the melody of Agathe's air in the second act, that has played
so large a part in the overture (No. 7).

CHARLES LOUIS AMBROISE THOMAS, one of the masters of French operetta, and with a certain gift for bigger things, was born at Metz on the 5th August, 1811.

His father and mother, both of whom were musical, kept a school of music, and it was from them that he received his first instruction in the art, commencing at the age of four; at seven he took up the violin and the piano. In 1828 he entered the Paris Conservatoire, his master for the piano being Zimmermann, the father-in-law of Gounod. He won the first piano prize in 1829, the first harmony prize in 1830, and the Prix de Rome in 1832. Among the compositions he sent to the Conservatoire from Rome, in accordance with the conditions of the prize, was a duet that earned the praise of Berlioz in one of his *Gazette Musicale* articles.

In Rome, and during the years immediately following his return to Paris, he composed a quantity of chamber music, some songs, a Requiem Mass, and other works; but, as with all French composers until comparatively recently, the only road to fame and fortune for him lay through the theatre.

Influence obtained for him in 1834 an introduction to the Opéra-Comique, where he made his début with the one-act operetta *La Double Échelle*. This was successful, and between that year and 1860 he produced a large number of operas, operettas, and ballets at both the Opéra-Comique and the Opéra.

The most successful of these works were *Mina* (1843), *Le Caïd* (1849), and *Le Songe d'une Nuit d'Été* (1850). In the first of these there were no choruses and no bass or baritone soloist, the three men's parts being all written for tenors. *Le Caïd,* a sprightly and musicianly work, had a great vogue for more than thirty years: a critic of the time aptly characterised Thomas's muse as " a well-brought-up young lady who elects to play the *cocotte*." In *Le Songe d'une Nuit d'Été*, Queen Elizabeth was presented as in love with Shakespeare. *Raymond* (1851) ran for only thirty-four performances, the opera being dragged down by its libretto, which was an absurd version of the story of the Man in the Iron Mask.

Thomas may have been partly consoled for the failure of *Raymond* by the fact that a few months previously he had been elected to the Institut in the place of Spontini, who had died in January of that year. Among the other ten candidates for the vacant seat was Berlioz. Thomas received thirty votes, Niedermayer five, Batton three, and Berlioz not a single one.

From 1837 to 1851 Thomas had produced a new stage work practically each year. Others followed in 1853, 1855, and 1857, and then, perhaps feeling a little tired and discouraged, he was silent for nearly six years. He had no great hopes of the success of his next work, *Mignon* (17th November, 1866); at the final rehearsal he assured a friend that the opera would not run to fifty performances. His pessimism, however, was groundless. The new work proved to be a great favourite from the first: on the evening after the production he happened to be at a concert in the Cirque des Champs-Élysées, where the audience rose to its feet to applaud him. *Mignon* turned out to be one of those works that make the fortune both of the author and of the theatre; by 1894 it had had a thousand performances at the Opéra-Comique alone.

Thomas never quite managed to repeat this colossal success, though *Hamlet* (1868) became very popular also. The part of Ophelia in this was created by Christine Nilsson. Hamlet, in the original version, was a tenor; but the chief tenor at the Opéra-Comique — Gueymard — proving unequal to the rôle, Thomas turned the part into one for a baritone, to be played by the celebrated Faure, who achieved a triumph in it.

Auber died in 1871, and Thomas, thanks to the success of *Mignon* and *Hamlet,* was elected to succeed him as Director of the Paris Conservatoire. His administrative duties seem to have taken up an undue proportion both of his time and his energy, and after *Hamlet* he did little creative work of any importance. Partly by reason of the inane treatment of Dante's famous story by the librettists, partly because of the weakness of the music, *Françoise de Rimini* (1882) was a complete failure; the Prologue to the opera alone had a touch of the old quality about it. Thomas had no better luck with the ballet *La Tempête* (1889), which soon disappeared from the stage.

He was the first composer to live to see the thousandth perform-ance of one of his works. As an old man of eighty-three he was present on the 13th May, 1894, at the thousandth performance of *Mignon* at the Opéra-Comique, when he was given an ovation by a distinguished audience. The grand cordon of the Legion of Honour was conferred on him by the President of the Republic, he being the first musician to receive that high dignity. A medal, re-producing the famous Mignon of the painter Ary Scheffer, was struck in commemoration of the celebration.

On the evening following the thousandth performance of *Mignon* there was a gala performance at the Opéra-Comique. The pro-gramme, apart from the *Marseillaise*, consisted entirely of Am-broise Thomas's works, including the *Raymond* overture, a duet, and a chorus from the *Songe d'une Nuit d'Été* (sung by the solo-ists and chorus of the Opéra-Comique and a number of Con-servatoire pupils), a cavatina from *Raymond* (sung by the tenor Clément), the always popular Gavotte and some vocal numbers from *Mignon*, two arias and a chorus from *Psyché*, and a ballet and a scena from *Hamlet*.

In the last twenty-five years of his life Ambroise Thomas be-came very serious and self-centred and very much of a solitary: one of his contemporaries described him at this time as a " Verdi solennel." His mind ran a good deal on the idea of death, and a quarter of a century before the end came he had prepared a granite tomb for himself on a storm-swept island off the Breton coast that he had bought. He died in Paris on the 12th February, 1896, and was given a public funeral at Montmartre, an eloquent funeral oration being pronounced by Massenet.

MIGNON

THE story of *Mignon* was derived, though somewhat remotely, by the French librettists from the novel of Goethe, *Wilhelm Meister's Apprenticeship and Travels,* upon which Goethe commenced work in 1777, though the book was not completed till nearly twenty years later, in 1796.

Partly by reason of the time its composition had taken him, partly because he had no gift for construction in this kind of work, the telling of the story is extremely confused; the strangest of incidents happen, and they link up with each other in the strangest of ways. But if Goethe could not design a novel he had an exceptional insight into character, and the majority of the portraits in the book are vital to this day. Widely as the French librettists have departed from the original, some knowledge of this is necessary to an understanding of the opera.

Wilhelm Meister is a young man who, after a disillusioning love affair with an actress named Mariana, goes out into the world in search of happiness, wisdom, and knowledge of himself and others. His tastes are in the direction of the theatre, and he himself experiments later both as actor and as author.

During the course of his travels he falls in with two stranded actors, Laertes and Philina, the latter a light-hearted coquette who takes nothing seriously, living solely for flattery and pleasure. She is one of Goethe's most convincing figures; a curious thing is that though he credits her with hardly a single admirable trait, and though scarcely any of the other characters in the book have a good word to say for her, she makes a decided appeal to us.

Later Wilhelm meets with a company of rope-dancers, who have with them a mysterious young creature whom, at first, Wilhelm has difficulty in pronouncing to be either boy or girl. As a matter of fact she is a girl in boy's clothes. " He reckoned her about twelve or thirteen years of age; her body was well-formed, only her limbs gave promise of a stronger growth, or else announced a stunted one. Her countenance was not regular, but striking; her brow full of mystery; her nose extremely beautiful; her mouth, although it seemed too closely shut for one of her age, and though she often drew it to a side, had yet an air of frankness, and was very lovely. Her brownish complexion could scarcely be discerned through the paint."

To the questions of Wilhelm and Philina she gives curt, enig-matic answers. When they ask her name, she replies, " They call me Mignon." When asked how old she is, she answers, " No one has counted." To the question, " Who was thy father? " she replies, " The Great Devil is dead." One day the master of the rope-dancers beats her because she will not perform the egg-dance; Wilhelm rescues her and buys her from the showman for thirty crowns. All that the man can tell him is that she fell into his hands at the death of his brother, who, by reason of his skill in his pro-fession, had been called the Great Devil.

Wilhelm takes the child about with him and begins to educate her, though nothing will induce her to change her boy's clothes for those of a girl. Though he does not know it, she is deeply in love with him, and suffers agonies when other women, such as the flirtatious Philina, pay him attention.

One day Wilhelm hears her sing a song — " Know'st thou the land where lemon trees do bloom? " — that is a cry of longing for some mysterious land of sunlight, thick with myrtle and laurel, and where there is a large house with a tall pillared porch, and marble statues in the hall that look down on her. Each stanza of the song ends with the cry, slightly varied, " 'Tis there, 'Tis there! oh my beloved, I with thee would go! " Wilhelm, after question-ing the child, comes to the conclusion that the land of which she speaks must be Italy, but he can get no more out of her.

Another mysterious character who joins the company is an old Harper, the victim of an incurable melancholy; he too sings a number of songs that have become treasures of German poetry, and, like those of Mignon, have been set to music by several of the great German song writers.

Wilhelm afterwards meets with a company of actors, with whose productions he associates himself. Among them is a woman named Aurelia, who has with her a little boy named Felix, with whom Mignon forms a close companionship. One day the house is discovered to be on fire, and in a vault in the garden Mignon comes upon the old Harper, who, after having lit some straw, is on the point of sacrificing Felix with a knife. The Harper is taken charge of by a clergyman, and is visited from time to time by a physician, who can extract from the melancholy old man no information about himself; the physician, however, discovers that he is oppressed with a sense of guilt, fancies that he brings misfortune wherever he goes, and believes that death, to be unwittingly brought about by a boy, is constantly impending over him.

Later Wilhelm goes to reside in the castle of a gentleman named Lothario, in whose neighbourhood lives a certain Natalia, who, by one of those extraordinary coincidences that abound in the story, turns out to be the sister of a boy named Friedrich, who, in the earlier part of the story, has been the jealous slave of Philina. Wilhelm also meets one Theresa, to whom Mignon and Felix (the latter, by the way, has meanwhile turned out to be the son of Wilhelm and Mariana) are sent to be taken care of.

Natalia has original ideas on the education of little girls, a number of whom she constantly has about her. On the birthday of two twin sisters among these, she plans a little tableau in which the girls, as a reward of virtue, are to receive a present from an angel. Mignon is dressed for the angel's part in a long white dress, with a golden girdle round her waist and a golden fillet on her hair. When the tableau is over she refuses to let them divest her of her angel's robe, and sings a beautiful little song that has been set to music by various German composers, but by none so touchingly as by Hugo Wolf:

" Such let me seem till such I be;
Take not my snow-white dress away;
Soon from this dust of earth I flee
Up to the glittering land of day. . . ."

Finding Wilhelm one day in the arms of Theresa, Mignon clutches at her heart and falls dead. She is buried, with great ceremony, in a room in the castle, and an Abbé who is of the company injects " a balsamic substance " into her veins, so that, as she lies in the angel's dress, she seems to be only asleep. The Abbé tells them that in her last days she used frequently to kiss an image of the Crucified which was tattooed on her right arm. He raises the dead girl's sleeve to show the company this, and an old Italian Marchese recognises Mignon as his niece.

Later he tells them the whole strange story. The Harper, it seems, is his long-lost brother Augustin. Their parents had also had a daughter, Sperata, whose birth, however, had been concealed, the child being brought up in the country, and only an old friend of the family (whose child she was given out to be) and the confessor were in the secret. Augustin and Sperata, not knowing their true relationship, had fallen in love with each other, and Mignon was their child.

After vain attempts by their friends to separate the pair, Augustin had been decoyed into a cloister; yet although they had managed to convince him that Sperata was his sister, he refused to give her up. From Sperata the secret was kept, though the confessor had induced her to consent to a separation from Augustin, having convinced her that her union with a priest (for such Augustin was) was a sin. The child was taken from her and committed to the charge of a family that lived on the sea-shore; there the wild little thing led a life of the greatest freedom, climbing the rocks, running down to the ships, and delighting to change clothes with boys. She would run away for miles into the country, and her guardians would think she was lost; when she returned she would stop to rest at a large country-house in the neighbourhood, where she would run up and down the great hall, looking at the statues.

One day she went out and did not return; her hat was found swimming on the water, and it was supposed that in clambering up the rocks she had fallen into the sea. As a matter of fact, she had, as we know, been kidnapped by the rope-dancers. In the course of time, Sperata died, and Augustin escaped from the cloister. He had already become subject to melancholia, and was perpetually tormented by an illusion in which he saw a boy standing at the foot of his bed, with a bare knife, threatening to kill him.

In the later stages of the story the Harper is cured; he divests himself of his long beard, and goes about clothed and in his right mind. From the clergyman's laboratory he has taken a bottle of laudanum, and this figures in a mysterious episode in which Felix is at first thought to be poisoned, though a lucky accident has saved him. The next morning Augustin is found lying dead in bed, having cut his throat with a razor; it seems he had found in the Abbé's room a manuscript in which his story was recorded, and, filled with horror, he had poured laudanum into a glass of milk, intending to drink it. But a feeling of revulsion had come over him; setting down the glass untasted he went out into the garden, and on his return found Felix filling up the glass out of which he had apparently been drinking.

It had so happened, however, that the boy had drunk from the milk bottle, not from the glass, and had at first told a fib about it, because he had previously been scolded for touching the bottle.

If all this seems somewhat incoherent, the reader is asked to lay the blame to the charge of Goethe, who, as has been said, though an admirable painter of character, constructed a long story with difficulty. Let us now see the form the story of Mignon assumes in the opera.

Of Goethe's many characters only seven remain, and the names and natures of two of these are changed in a way that is a trifle confusing at first. Wilhelm, Laertes, Philina, and Mignon remain very much as we know them already, except that their mentality has become considerably more French than German; Wilhelm in particular is no longer the earnest, brooding, self-questioning young Teuton of the original, but an elegant young man of the Parisian *beau monde*.

In Goethe's story there is a certain Jarno, a curious, cynical figure whom we first meet as the man of affairs of a certain Count in whose house the actors are engaged to give a performance, and later as the confidant of Lothario. In the French opera there is no corresponding character, but the name Jarno is given, for some mysterious reason or other, to the chief of the gipsies who have possession of Mignon. By a similar freak of fancy the name Lothario is given to the Harper. To crown all, the opera has, as we shall see, a doubly happy ending.

THE OVERTURE

The overture is, in the main, a pot-pourri of some of the leading melodies of the opera. It begins with a slow introduction, in which, after a hint of Mignon's unhappiness, and a succession of arpeggios that may no doubt be taken to have reference to the Harper, we hear the melody of Mignon's song, " Know'st thou the land? " (see No. 12). This is followed by the brilliant Polonaise sung later by Philina (No. 21), with its gay after-strain (No. 22).

ACT I

The curtain rises, to some lively music, on the courtyard of a German tavern, where, seated at tables, drinking and smoking, the worthy citizens of the place are enjoying themselves. The inn is on the left of the stage; a flight of steps runs up from the courtyard to a balcony, from which a little door with a glass window gives access to the first floor of the inn. To the right is a shed. While the citizens are singing their festive chorus:

Bons bour-geois et no - ta - bles,   As-

- sis   au tour des   ta - bles,   Fu -

- mons,   fu-mons, tran - quil - le-ment,

Et bu-vons en fu - mant.

a harp is heard preludising, and soon Lothario, the old Harper, appears upon the scene. He tells us in his song — which he accompanies upon his harp — that he wanders from place to place searching for the child who, he feels in his heart, still lives. The citizens know the old wanderer well; they make him sit down with them, fill his glass for him, and break into their chorus once more.

A number of peasants of both sexes now break in, bidding the others make room for the gipsies, who make their appearance to the accompaniment of a gay march in the orchestra:

Two ragged gipsies drag in a cart containing the poor possessions of the troupe; at the back of the cart Mignon is sleeping on a sheaf of straw.

One of the gipsies takes a violin and motions to the others to commence the dance, which is accompanied by oboe and tambourine:

Some of the older citizens comment ecstatically on the beauty of the eyes of the gipsy girls:

and swear that their own wives could not dance better. Laertes and Philina have meanwhile come out upon the balcony to see the show, and Philina, who is in a state of perpetual effervescence, carols light-heartedly to the rhythm of the dance.

The bagpipe-like *loure* to which the gipsies have been dancing changes to a waltz:

the strain of which is taken up by Philina, while the chorus also join in from time to time. The spectators throw money to the performers; and Jarno, having thanked them, promises that Mignon shall now perform her egg-dance.

He orders Zafari, the fiddler, to " produce his best concerto," and the others to spread their finest carpet on the ground; then, approaching the cart and waking Mignon, he bids her get up and begin. To appropriate music:

(6) Allegro moderato

one of the gipsies spreads a wretched faded old carpet on the ground, and on this a boy places several eggs. Mignon, holding in her hand a bouquet of wild flowers, comes down from the cart and advances to the centre of the stage. Philina, from the balcony, asks Jarno what this poor child is who seems to be cursing the gipsy for having awakened it; is it a boy or a girl? " Neither the one nor the other, fair lady," replies Jarno; " it is neither boy, girl, nor woman; it is Mignon "; whereupon Philina and the others laugh heartily.

The unhappy Mignon, perturbed by all these eyes fixed on her and the rough laughter, summons up strength enough to defy Jarno and refuse to dance. He takes a stick from one of the gipsies, and as Mignon still refuses in spite of his threats:

(7)

Dan - se, Mi-gnon, Dan - se, Mi-gnon, Mé -

-chant dé-mon.　　On mon bâ-ton sau-

-ra te mettre à la rai-son,,

he raises his stick to beat her; but as he does so, Lothario runs to her and throws his arms protectingly around her. Jarno thrusts the old man back angrily and is again about to chastise Mignon when Wilhelm, who has just appeared upon the scene followed by a servant carrying his portmanteau, throws himself on the gipsy and holds back his arm. He induces Jarno to see reason by presenting a pistol at his head, while Philina pitches him her purse; Jarno finds both arguments irresistible.

Mignon divides her bouquet in two, giving one half to Wilhelm and the other to Lothario in token of her gratitude; and this portion of the scene ends with a little ensemble in which Mignon, who has withdrawn a little from the others, prays to the Virgin for protection:

(8) Andante

O Vier-ge, mon seul es - poir, _ Pro-

- té - ge ta cré - a - tu - re,

While Lothario, his eyes fixed on vacancy, describes a vision of a knight in heavy armour, on a black horse, whom he apparently sees in a forest at night, Wilhelm speaks of the strangeness of the adventure that has just befallen him, Philina betrays a lively interest in the handsome young stranger, and Laertes twits her upon her curiosity. Lothario and the chorus go off at the back, Jarno and the gipsies, accompanied by Mignon, making their way to the shed at the right. Philina points to Wilhelm and says something to Laertes, whereupon the latter descends by the outer staircase of the inn and accosts Wilhelm, Philina meanwhile retiring to her room.

Laertes, in the politest French fashion, with several changes from complete naturalness to the emphatic theatrical grand manner, introduces himself as an actor out of work. He compliments Wilhelm on his gallant defence of Mignon, and when the young man smilingly waves the compliment aside, declaring that anybody else in his place would have done as much, Laertes assures him that this is not the opinion of the charming lady who was lately on the balcony and whose name is Philina. Wilhelm in return introduces himself as a rich young man in his twentieth year, who has just left his university and is making a tour of the world.

How different Ambroise Thomas's Wilhelm is from the super-serious young hero of Goethe is shown by the aria he sings at this point:

He is his own master, he declares, and his one object in life is to go laughing through the world, singing like a joyous bird. His heart, he continues in the most urbane French manner, " is not rebellious to the sweet pleasure of love," and if the opportunity should come his way:

he is quite prepared for an amorous adventure, though so far he has not succeeded in meeting with his ideal. This aria is sometimes

omitted in performance, which is a pity, for it gives us the key
to Wilhelm at the outset.

Laertes, in his character of a more experienced and more cynical man of the world, mock-seriously felicitates him on still
possessing so many of the illusions and hopes of youth. He himself, he says, has been married and regretted it; and he warns his
new friend against falling into the universal snare. He seems, however, Wilhelm ventures to remark, to be getting on very nicely
with the lady on the balcony. Laertes repels the insinuation vigorously: God forbid that he should be in love with Philina; each of
them knows the other too well for that! She is foolish, vain, more
fickle than fortune, more changeable than the moon; but she has
wit and beauty, and is altogether the most delightful demon in
the world; having delivered himself of which judgment he raises
his glass and toasts the lady — at Wilhelm's expense.

Philina, who has overheard this conversation, now approaches,
and tapping Laertes on the shoulder with her fan, asks if he has
anything to add to so charming a portrait. Brushing Laertes' description of her aside with the laughing remark that he is one of
those men who profess to despise women because he knows he
cannot interest them, she sets herself, in the most open manner,
to fascinate Wilhelm, who, for his part, is more than half-way
already towards being her slave.

While the orchestra pours out a stream of easy badinage:

(11)   Andantino con moto

Laertes ceremoniously introduces them to each other and shows
Wilhelm how to present his bouquet to Madame, and after a delightful trio Philina departs on the arm of Laertes, with a final
coquettish glance at Wilhelm.

Mignon now comes out from the shed, kisses Wilhelm's hand,
and thanks him for his intervention on her behalf. In reply to his
many questions she tells him that the only name she has is Mignon,
that she does not know her age, that she has no mother, and that
" the Great Devil is dead." Of her infancy she has only one mem-

ory — of being seized one evening by rough men as she was wandering on the shores of a lake. If she were to be set free, Wilhelm asks, to what beloved country would she wend her way? This gives Mignon the cue for her simple but expressive song " Know'st thou the land? "

Con - nais-tu le pa-ys où fleu-rit l'o-ran-ger? Le pa-ys des fruits d'or et des ro-ses ver-meilles,

one of the most popular of operatic melodies.

The land she would seek for, she says, is one where the sun is warmer and the sky bluer than here; it is there, she cries in the refrain of the song:

C'est là que je vou-drais vi-vre, Ai-mer, ai-mer et mou-rir! C'est là que je voudrais vi-vre, c'est là, oui c'est là!

that she would like to find love and die. This enchanted land must be Italy, thinks Wilhelm; but the strange little creature can tell him nothing more.

Jarno now comes out from the shed, and after being threatened by Wilhelm consents to sell Mignon for what he paid for her. The two men go into the inn to conclude the bargain. Mignon is clapping her hands for joy when Lothario enters. He has come, he tells her, to take his leave; the swallows are flying south, and he must follow them. This gives Mignon the cue for another song. Taking the harp from Lothario, and surprising him by the dexterity with which she touches the strings, she sings a pleasant little ditty to the swallows:

(14)   Andantino con moto

Lé - gè - res hi - ron - del - les, Oi -

- seaux bé - nis de   Dieu, —

in which she is afterwards joined by Lothario. From behind the scenes comes the merry laugh of Philina; Mignon, who is apparently already a little jealous of her, remarks, " That woman again! " and withdraws with Lothario into the shed.

Philina re-enters, this time with her young admirer Frederick, who has nearly killed his horse racing after her. She is keeping him at the proper distance, handling him like the accomplished coquette she is, when Wilhelm and Jarno return. When she compliments Wilhelm on his generous deed in buying Mignon, Frederick shows signs of jealousy at her obvious interest in the new-comer, and Philina, delighted to have the opportunity of playing the two men off against each other, introduces them; but before the danger can develop they are interrupted by Laertes, who runs in flourishing a letter that has arrived for Philina.

She reads it aloud to the company; it is from Frederick's uncle, Baron Rosemberg, inviting her and Laertes and the other actors to his castle to give an entertainment in honour of the visit of

Prince Ulric de Tieffembourg: the letter ends with effusive compliments to Philina, and the information that the Baron's carriage will come for her shortly, and if the charming one resists she will be carried away by force.

The offer, of course, is accepted, and Philina proposes that Wilhelm shall accompany them, assuming the rôle of author to the troupe. Having planted this new barb in the susceptible heart of Frederick she ascends the staircase and enters her room; Frederick curses her and the Baron, seizes his hat, and rushes out with a half-threat to Wilhelm. Laertes, having shaken Wilhelm's hand and advised him to accept the invitation, follows Philina.

While Wilhelm is thinking over this, Mignon returns, to place herself at the service of her benefactor. His offer to place her with some good people of the town whom he knows fills her with dismay; she suggests that she shall follow him dressed as a boy — anything so as not to be separated from him. He tells her this is impossible, whereupon she sadly turns to Lothario and declares she will go with him.

The old Harper, opening his arms, welcomes the suggestion with delight; they two will live in freedom under the open skies. He is taking Mignon away when Wilhelm, fearful of the future this opens out to the waif, declares that he will take her with him, and Mignon gives a cry of joy. Just then the actors, of both sexes, come upon the scene, accompanied by Philina, Laertes, Jarno, the other gipsies, the citizens and the peasants; and the actors, delighted at the prospect of an engagement and something to eat, take leave of the villagers in a lively chorus. Philina gaily invites anyone who loves her to follow her:

(15)

Qui m'ai - me me sui - ve! Et

toi, Dieu des ___ a - mours,

and poor little Mignon feels a pang in her heart as she recognises, in Philina's bouquet, the flowers that she herself had earlier given to Wilhelm. Wilhelm soothes her, but is obviously fascinated by Philina. Mignon takes leave of Jarno, whom she forgives for all his cruelty to her, and the scene ends with friendly adieux all round.

ACT II

Between the first and second acts there is an orchestral intermezzo, consisting of the dainty gavotte:

(16)

that has become one of the most popular numbers of the opera.

When the curtain rises we see Philina in the dressing-room allotted to her in the castle; the table is covered with flowers and letters, and Philina, who is seated at the toilette table, looking at herself in the glass, is evidently very pleased with both herself and her situation. Laertes, who enters almost immediately, is equally delighted with life; he has all the wine he wants, at someone else's expense. Philina is sure that Wilhelm will follow her; and she has hardly said so when the young man appears, followed after a little while by Mignon, whom Laertes, to his surprise, finds waiting at the door as he is going out.

He has already explained to Wilhelm that the play they are going to perform that evening is *A Midsummer Night's Dream,* by " a certain Shakespeare, quite a good poet." Philina is to be Titania, and Wilhelm is sure to be enchanted with her. " Au revoir, my dear sir! Adieu, my fair one! " says the actor as he leaves; " I leave you with him, I leave you with her."

Mignon enters, dressed as a page, and is greeted with a touch
of ill-humour by the jealous Philina, who sarcastically bids her sit
down and warm herself, after which she will perhaps favour them
with the egg-dance. Philina professes to be vastly amused at the
solicitude Wilhelm and Mignon show for each other; Mignon
swallows her chagrin as best she can, while Wilhelm, answering
the actress in her own tone of lively banter, offers her his services.
At her command he brings her the candelabra from the chimney-
piece and places it on her toilette table, where she seats herself
and proceeds to embellish herself for the evening, Mignon meanwhile watching them both gloomily without stirring from her seat.

Philina is looking forward ecstatically:

Je crois en-ten-dre Les doux com-
-pli-ments, Et la voix ten-dre De vingt a
-mants.

to her success, the general admiration, the compliments of old and
young. Wilhelm tries to draw a serious expression of love from her,
but she only fences with him, showing him a bracelet that has
been given her by the Prince, and offering to present him to the
Baron. Wilhelm presses a kiss upon her hand, whereupon Mignon,
who has been feigning sleep, betrays herself to her rival by
a start.

Philina goes out on Wilhelm's arm, and Mignon, left to herself,
and being the heroine of a light, not a serious, opera, comes to the
conclusion that it is foolish to repine, and that the best thing she
can do is to submit and make the best of the situation.

She examines with great interest the lovely furniture and fittings
of the room, and innocently assumes that the secret of Philina's

charm must be in the pots and bottles on her toilette table. She gets rid of her paleness by putting on some rouge, and is so pleased with the effect that she breaks out into a little song about a poor gipsy lad who, though he wears a smile, is sad at heart because his master does not appreciate him: the song is called a " styrienne " and has a characteristic gipsy refrain:

Like Marguerite in *Faust* she cannot believe that the new face she sees in the glass is hers; and, no doubt by way of contrast between her present state and her past, she sings the bagpipe air (No. 3) to which the gipsies made their first appearance in the opera.

But no, she concludes sadly on looking at herself in the glass again, she is still not Philina; the actress must have other secrets than these to make herself so beautiful. May not the secret be in her dresses? for Mignon reflects that, for Wilhelm, she herself is hardly a woman. She goes into a cabinet on the left that evidently contains Philina's clothes, just as Frederick enters hastily through the window. The charming air that follows, in which Frederick, to the tune of the gavotte (No. 16), sighs out, like another Cherubino, the desires of his half-awakened amorous little heart, was added to the original score for Madame Trebelli when the opera was produced in London.

Wilhelm enters in search of Mignon. The young man and the boy, each of whom is astonished and irritated to find the other in Philina's room, soon get at cross-purposes and have just commenced a duel when Mignon, dressed in one of Philina's robes, rushes between them, guarding her master. Frederick is greatly

amused at the sight; magnanimously refusing to distress the girl
by putting an end to Wilhelm's life, he spares his rival for the
present, and goes out laughing.

Wilhelm is grateful to Mignon for the anxiety she has shown
on his account, but having now seen her in a woman's dress he
explains to her very seriously that the situation has become a
little delicate; he cannot very well keep a young person of this
kind about him as a page, and in spite of her mournful query,
" Then you would send me away? " and her bitter suggestion that
it is at the wish of Philina, he persists that he will have to take her
elsewhere, where she will be well looked after. She throws herself
disconsolately into a chair, and, in a gracefully tender little air:

he bids farewell and counsels her not to weep, for Heaven will
protect her; no doubt she will find her country and her family
again, and with them the road to happiness; as for himself, he
will preserve the tenderest recollection of her, and will hope that
some day they will meet again.

If they must part, she replies mournfully, she prefers to be free again. She will go back to her old life and her gipsy clothes, becoming Mignon once more; God and the Angels will protect her, and she will dance for her crusts. He offers her his purse, but this she declines, asking nothing of him but that he will give her his hand to kiss in farewell.

Philina returns, accompanied by Frederick, who has told her, as a great joke, of Mignon's escapade. The actress ironically compliments Mignon on her newly-acquired style, and offers, as the dress suits her so well, to give it her; whereupon Mignon first of all angrily tears the ribbons from it, and then, bursting with rage, runs back into the cabinet. Philina ironically remarks that anyone would think the child was jealous of her — a remark that sets Wilhelm thinking. But just then Laertes, to the strain of the gavotte, comes in dressed for the play as Prince Theseus, and calls them to the theatre, where the performance is about to begin.

Wilhelm, still turning the word " jealous " over in his mind, offers his arm to Philina and leads her out; Frederick, following them with his eyes, declares that he would willingly assassinate his fortunate rival. He is not the only one who is animated by these amiable sentiments: Mignon, returning dressed in her boy's clothes, rushes away crying, " That Philina! How I hate her! "

The next scene shows us a part of the park adjoining the Baron's castle. On the left is a lake, on the right a conservatory lit up from within. Music and applause are heard behind the scenes. Mignon, advancing from among the trees, listens to these sounds and soliloquises upon her unhappy lot: she is alone and unhappy, while her detested rival is basking in the smiles of the man she loves. She sees the lake, and its tranquillity attracts her; she will seek eternal peace beneath its waters.

She is just about to throw herself in when from behind the trees comes the sound of a harp, and the thought of the old Harper and his affection for her recalls her to life. She addresses Lothario by his name. The old man, looking at her tenderly, asks, " Is it thou, Sperata? " " No," she replies; and Lothario, repulsing her gently, finds that he has been deceived again, for this is only the child who wanted to follow him — Mignon. The two unhappy creatures pour out their woes to each other in a tenderly expressive little duet.

A clapping of hands that comes from the theatre behind the scenes turns Mignon into a fury. Why, she asks in her frenzy, does not God strike the detested Philina with His thunder, and destroy this hated palace with fire? She rushes away among the trees, leaving the dangerous word "fire" ringing through the half-crazed mind of the old Harper. Repeating the word after her in a bewildered sort of way, he leaves the stage just as the door of the conservatory opens and the theatrical audience and the actors come forth, accompanied by Philina, Frederick, the Prince, the Baron, and the Baroness.

The performance has been a triumph for Philina, and all crowd round her, offering their congratulations in a sparkling chorus:

Philina takes their homage as a matter of course. Yes, she says, for this evening she is indeed Titania, the Queen of the Fairies, and — pointing to her magic wand — this is her golden sceptre, and these — showing her wreaths — are her trophies; and she breaks out into a brilliant vocal Polonaise:

the difficulty of which may be gauged from a note in the
score to the effect that " if the singer finds it impossible to
sing the Polonaise, a cut must be made to the finale." The
aria abounds with technical difficulties of all sorts, and has a
sprightly middle section, describing the will-o'-the-wisps following Titania's chariot, that gives opportunities for light staccato
singing:

(22)

staccato

La trou-pe fol - le des lu-tins   Suit

— mon char qui vole et dans le nuit   Fuit!

Her Polonaise finished Philina turns to Wilhelm and coquettishly reproaches him with having neglected her during the evening; her chief object seems to be to kindle the jealousy of
Frederick again, which she soon succeeds in doing. Wilhelm, however, is preoccupied and uneasy; he tells Philina that he has been
looking everywhere in vain for Mignon, and the actress, with the
pouting comment, " So she whom you were seeking, sir, was not
I? " takes the young man on one side.

The librettists now apparently think it is time to make use,
after their own fashion, of the episode of the fire in which the
Harper was concerned in Goethe's story. Coming close to Mignon,
Lothario whispers to her that she can not be happy; her wish has
been fulfilled; he has lit the fire that will bring the castle down
in ruins. Mignon has only time for an ejaculation of incredulous
horror when Wilhelm and Philina return; and the latter, in order
to get rid of Mignon, asks her to prove her zeal by going into the
theatre and bringing her the bouquet she has left there — the
bouquet given her by Wilhelm. The young man protests, but
Mignon, apparently thinking it is his wish that she should go,
hastens to the conservatory.

She has hardly left the stage when Laertes rushes in with the

announcement that the theatre is in flames. All give a cry of
horror; even Philina is for a moment sobered; while Wilhelm
hurries after Mignon, in spite of the efforts of Laertes to hold him
back. The servants take away the torches they had brought with
them when the company flocked on the scene, so that the stage is
now dark, and the red flames of the fire are seen licking the glass
panes of the conservatory.

Through the general commotion Lothario tries to make himself
heard with a repetition of the song with which he made his first
appearance in the opera, declaring that he is convinced his long-
lost one lives, and that it is time for him to wander off again
in search of her. The glass of the conservatory falls in with a
great crash, and shortly after Wilhelm reappears panting, carrying
the fainting Mignon in his arms; he had reached her, it seems,
just as the flames were seizing on her. He places her on a bank; in
her hands she clutches the little bouquet of withered flowers. All
give a great cry of " Saved! " and the curtain falls.

ACT III

In the third act we see the French librettists taking up Goethe's
various loose threads and tying them in a way that is decidedly
their own.

Apparently Mignon has been brought by Wilhelm to Italy to
recover from the effects of her adventure in the blazing conservatory. We see a gallery containing statues; to the right is a window
overlooking the landscape, and at the back a closed door. Outside
is heard a pleasantly melodious chorus:

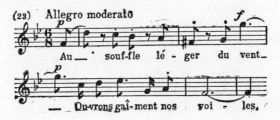

(23) Allegro moderato

Au — souf-fle lé - ger du vent —

— Ou-vrons gaî-ment nos voi - les,

of people about to embark upon a placid sea. Lothario enters and
sings a gentle cradle-song:

for Mignon, who, her fever relieved, has at last fallen asleep in
an adjoining room. Wilhelm enters with a servant carrying a lamp.

Turning to the window, the servant explains, for Wilhelm's
benefit and ours, that the next day there is to be a festival on the
lake, and that alone among the houses of the neighborhood the
palace in which they now stand will not be illuminated. For it has
a tragic history: years ago the child of the house was drowned, the
mother died, and the father, crazed with grief, left Italy for ever.
The house is for sale, and if it suits Wilhelm he can buy it. Dismissing the servant with the remark that he will give his decision
tomorrow, Wilhelm turns to Lothario and expresses his joy at the
favourable turn in Mignon's health, which he puts down to her
having been brought back to her native air. To-morrow, he says,
he will buy for her this Cipriani palace.

At the word " Cipriani " Lothario gives a start; then he advances towards the great door at the back of the scene, and tries
to open it. That room, Wilhelm explains to him, has been closed
for fifteen years. Lothario repeats the words after him as if dazed,
then, turning towards a door on the left, passes through it with the

air of a man who has suddenly remembered something. Wilhelm,
who cannot understand his strange actions, opens the door on the
other side and contemplates the sleeping Mignon. From the graceful little song he sings:

(25) Andantino

El - le ne croy-ait pas, dans sa can -
-deur na-ï - ve, Que l'a-mour in-no-cent
qui dor-mait dans son cœur,

we learn that Mignon has become conscious of the love that previously was only an unconscious stirring within her; but she is
apparently somewhat frightened of him, and will tell him nothing
of the cause of her secret sorrow. He can only hope for the spring
and the sunshine to open her heart to him.

He is interrupted by the servant bringing him a letter, which
Wilhelm reads aloud. It is from Laertes: "Philina follows you;
fly — already she is here!" the melody of "Know'st thou the
land?" (No. 12) is heard softly in the orchestra as Mignon comes
in from the room on the right; she does not see Wilhelm, who has
withdrawn a little. The convalescent girl rejoices in the beauty and
warmth around her. But the place stirs old memories in her; surely
she has seen something like this before in her dreams? She gives
an appealing cry of "Lothario! Wilhelm!"

Her lover runs to her; she throws herself into his arms, and
sings of her new-found happiness:

(26)   Allegro moderato

Je suis heu - reu - se! l'air m'en-

She no longer fears death, she says: and Wilhelm taking up her words, bids her live for love; she must drive from her memory for ever the recollection of the old unhappy days:

But she still cannot believe that he loves her: is not his heart given to Philina? He has no sooner assured her that he has never loved Philina, and that she is far away from them, when the voice of the coquette is heard outside singing the showy " I am Titania " (No. 21). Mignon's jealousy flames out once more, and is apparently exasperated by the confident coloratura in which Philina keeps indulging outside.

In vain Wilhelm tries to console Mignon; she falls in a faint, and on recovering consciousness still refuses to be convinced. The only one who loves her, she says, is Lothario, whose footsteps she declares she hears in the room at the back.

Wilhelm assures her that nobody can possibly be there, but he has no sooner spoken than Lothario appears on the threshold of the open door. He is transformed; he is dressed in rich black velvet, and carries in his hand a small coffer. Advancing slowly, he gives the astonished Wilhelm " greeting to this my house," and, informing him that he was once the master of this splendid palace — a statement which Wilhelm attributes to the derangement of his intellect — he hands Mignon the casket, bidding her open it. She does so, and finds in it a child's scarf, embroidered with gold and silver. It was, Lothario tells her, Sperata's and the name arouses vague memories in Mignon.

Searching the casket again, she finds first of all a coral bracelet that is now too small for her arm, though, Lothario tells her, it was once too large for the little Sperata. Then Mignon finds at the bottom of the casket a prayer-book, from which, says Lothario, Sperata was accustomed to spell out her evening prayer.

Reading from the book, Mignon begins with clasped hands a prayer to the Virgin, but soon, to the astonishment of Lothario, she lets the book fall and continues from memory. In wild exaltation she cries to them to tell her where she is. " In Italy," replies Wilhelm. The name recalls further memories to her, and running into the room at the back she cries that the picture of her mother is hanging there.

She and Lothario throw themselves into each other's arms with ejaculations of " My daughter! " — " My father! " and the three voices blend in a cry of joy. But the still frail body almost gives way under its happiness: Mignon faints again, Wilhelm opens a window, and as the orchestra softly gives out the theme of " Know'st thou the land," he confesses his love. She takes up the refrain of the song, " Ah, 'tis there I would live, 'tis there I would love and die! " It is to this melody, worked up into a little trio, and followed by a brief coda, that the opera ends.

Volume III

STORIES *of the* GREAT

OPERAS

~~~~~

VERDI (*1813–1901*) TO PUCCINI (*1858–1924*)

THE first thing the young Giuseppe Verdi did when he had made a little money by his early operas was to buy three or four houses, with the land pertaining to them, in the country near his native place. It was significant of much in his nature and his life.

He himself said on one occasion, " I am and always will be a Roncole peasant "; at another time he declared that he would have become a farmer had he been strong enough. Out of the land and houses first purchased there gradually grew a magnificent estate, to which, in his later years, Verdi gave perhaps more time and thought than to his music, seeing to the buying and the feeding of his own cattle, planning and superintending improvements, and keeping a sharp eye on lazy or careless workmen. There was the strength of the fields in his hardy frame, that endured eighty-eight years, and out of which, at the age of nearly eighty, could come the amazingly youthful *Falstaff;* there was something also of the hardness and the sombreness of the peasant in his outlook upon life until near the very end.

In 1813 the province of Piacenza, in the north of Italy, was French territory, and it is in French that the record of the birth of Verdi was made out. It runs thus:

" In the year 1813, on the 12th day of October, at nine o'clock in the morning, before me, the mayor of Busseto, civil officer in the commune of Busseto aforesaid, in the department of Taro, appeared Verdi, Charles, aged twenty-eight years, innkeeper, domiciled at Roncole, who presented to us an infant of the male sex, born on the tenth of the current month, at eight hours in the evening, son of the declarer and his wife Luisa Utini, spinner, domiciled at Roncole, and to which he declared his wish to give the Christian names of Joseph Fortunin François. The said declaration and presentation made in the presence of Romanelli Antoine, aged fifty-one years, usher to the mayor, and Cantù Hiacinte, aged sixty-one years, door-keeper, domiciled at Busseto, who, after the present act had been read to the appearer and the witnesses, have signed with us.

" Antoine Romanelli, Verdi Carlo, Hiacinte Cantù, Vitali."

Busseto is a small town some seventeen miles from Parma, between that town and Piacenza; Roncole is a tiny village (at that time the population was only a couple of hundred) three miles from Busseto. Carlo Verdi kept a small inn that was also a sort of village stores.

In 1814, when the struggle of Europe against Napoleon was approaching its end, the territory was invaded by the Russians and Austrians. In Roncole the savage soldiery butchered as many of the inhabitants as they could lay their hands on, including women and children. Some of the women took refuge in the church, but were pursued and slain even there. One of them, with a child a few months old in her arms, found her way into the sacristy, and thence, by way of a narrow staircase, to the belfry, where she hid until danger was over. It was Luisa Verdi, who thus saved for the world the future composer of *Aida* and *Otello* and *Falstaff*.

Little Giuseppe grew up a very serious child. His parents were not musical, and there were no opportunities of hearing music in the village except in the church and from itinerant fiddlers; one of these, a certain Bagasset, is said to have been remembered and protected by the composer when he became rich and famous.

At the age of seven the boy became an acolyte in the village church, and one day he was so absorbed in the musical part of the Mass that he forgot to hand the priest the water, for which little lapse the saintly man kicked him down the altar steps. He was taken home pale and bruised and bleeding, and when his parents asked him what was the matter his only reply was, " Let me learn music. "

The father's first step was to buy him an old spinet, upon which the child, to his great delight, managed to pick out some agreeable chords. Trying to hit upon them later, and not succeeding in doing so, he vented his wrath on the instrument with a hammer. A piano tuner from Busseto, named Cavalletti, had to be called in to repair the damage; he refused to take any payment for his work, but pasted in the inside of the spinet a piece of paper with these words: " I, Stephen Cavalletti, have repaired these jacks and hammers, and put on the pedals, of which I make him a present together with the jacks, seeing how well disposed the young Giuseppe Verdi is to learn to play this instrument, and this of itself is payment enough for me." Verdi kept the old spinet in the days of his prosperity.

Giuseppe received the rudiments of a musical education from the village organist, Baistrocchi, and made such progress that in time he was able to succeed his dead master, at the munificent salary of 40 lire (about 30s.) per annum. This post he occupied from about his twelfth to his eighteenth year. During the earlier part of this period he attended a school at Busseto, lodging with a shoemaker at about threepence a day, and walking to Roncole each Sunday for the service. One dark and stormy Christmas Eve he fell into a ditch and could not get out, but was luckily rescued by a passer-by. He soon became very popular with the peasants, and when the bishop proposed to oust him from the organ in favour of a protégé of his own, the people broke into the sanctuary and demanded his retention.

His father used to visit Busseto periodically to buy his stores from a well-to-do shopkeeper named Antonio Barezzi, and sometimes Giuseppe used to carry out his father's orders for him. Barezzi grew to like the boy, and took him, at the age of about ten, into his shop.

Barezzi was a keen musician; he played the flute and clarinet and was the president of the local Philharmonic Society, the rehearsals of which were held in his house. Verdi thus heard a good deal of music, and got valuable experience in the copying of scores and parts, besides playing piano duets with his patron's daughter Margherita. At the same time he was learning Latin from a canon in the place, Pietro Saletti, and taking lessons in music from the Busseto organist, Ferdinando Provesi, who was also conductor of the Philharmonic Society. Provesi gave up both posts to Giuseppe when the latter was sixteen. Verdi was now a person of some importance in the little town; he wrote a goodly number of songs, piano pieces, church music, and marches, the last-named being played with great applause by the Busseto municipal band.

Beginning to feel the tiny town rather too small for his ambitions, he applied for the post of organist at the Church of St. James, Soragna, but in spite of Provesi's recommendation he was unsuccessful. The general feeling in the town, however, was that he ought to be helped to make a career elsewhere, and so, at the age of eighteen, a Busseto benevolent institution made him a grant of 300 lire a year for three years, to which Barezzi added a contribution of his own. He was to go to Milan first of all to study. He lodged there with a nephew of Saletti, and made application to be allowed to enter the Conservatoire.

A great deal of unnecessary fuss has been made by some of the biographers about his rejection; it has been cited as yet another illustration of the stupidity of official musicians where a budding genius is concerned. But on enquiry it turns out that there was nothing whatever stupid about the action of the authorities. By the rules of the institution, pupils were to be under fourteen years of age; Verdi, in 1832, was over eighteen. A point would have been stretched in his favour had he shown especial ability as a pianist, which Verdi did not. To accept him as a pupil for composition alone would have been justifiable only if he had shown outstanding aptitude in that line, which again he did not at that time. The authorities therefore saw no particular reason to set aside the rules of the Conservatoire in his case.

Depressed, but not discouraged, the young man became the

pupil of the composer Lavigna, who at that time was the cembalo player in the orchestra of the Scala Theatre. Verdi was put through a serious course of harmony and counterpoint, and studied closely a quantity of old music, especially that of Palestrina and Marcello; but no doubt Lavigna's instruction was especially valuable to him in the field of opera, for the old theatrical hand, with his experience of this form of art from the inside, would be a sure guide to what was effective.

A chance for the young Verdi to distinguish himself came when Marini, the conductor of the Milan Philharmonic Society, took fright at the idea of producing Haydn's *Creation,* which had been insufficiently rehearsed, and suggested that Verdi might be able to carry the concert through. This he did with great success.

When his three years' term was nearing its end, Provesi died, and Verdi thought it advisable to return to Busseto and ask for the vacant post. Musical affairs in Busseto, however, as they are in most places, were largely a matter of local politics. The clerical party was all for a certain Ferrari; the anti-clericals and the musicians, in the main, for Verdi. Thanks to the support of a couple of bishops, Ferrari gained the appointment.

To compensate Verdi the municipality conferred on him the title of " Master of the Commune and the Monte di Pietà of Busseto "; the people were on his side, and his music, as played by the municipal band, became more popular than ever — so popular that frequently the band had to perform in the neighbouring villages. He and Margherita Barezzi had long been in love with each other, and though his income as yet was exceedingly small, he was so respected by Barezzi that the latter willingly consented to the marriage, which took place in 1835. During the following two or three years two children were born, a daughter and a son.

Verdi had brought back with him from Milan a libretto by the young poet Solera, on the subject of *Oberto Conte di San Bonifacio,* on which he had been working hard all this time. He hoped to have it produced at Parma in the autumn of 1837, but to his disappointment it was rejected by Granci, the local impresario. Terminating his engagement at Busseto, Verdi went with his wife and children to Milan early in 1839, hoping to place the opera at the Filodrammatici Theatre, of which his friend Marini, who had been the means of procuring the libretto for him, was a director.

Another disappointment awaited the young composer; Marini was no longer in control of the theatre. As the result of his efforts, however, he managed to get his friend's opera accepted for the spring of 1839 at the Scala, where the director was the famous Merelli. Once more Verdi was disappointed; soon after the rehearsal had commenced the tenor fell ill, and a production of the opera was impossible.

Verdi was by now so discouraged and depressed that he thought of giving up the idea of an operatic career and returning to Busseto for the rest of his days. He was only dissuaded by the entreaties of his wife and by Merelli's promise to give *Oberto* the following season on a profit-sharing basis. It was, in fact, produced at the Scala on the 17th November, 1839. Its success, according to Verdi himself, was " not very great, but good enough." Already, in this first work, most of the characteristics of the later Verdi are to be distinguished, especially his rather rude vigour.

The opera must have made some impression on the public, or the publisher Ricordi would not have bought it, nor would Merelli have commissioned two more works from the young composer.

The first of the two new operas was to be a serious one, but Verdi had hardly started upon it when Merelli told him that the financial condition of the theatre called for a comic opera. A libretto entitled *Il finto Stanislas* by Felice Romani, was given to the composer, and a new title — *Un Giorno di Regno* (*A Reign of a Day*) — given to it. And now misfortune began to accumulate upon the young musician's head. He became subject to heart attacks that hindered him in his work. Being short of money to pay his rent, and there not being time for him to obtain it from Busseto, he asked Merelli for an advance on his contract, but was refused. The situation was saved by his wife pawning her jewellery.

" After that," said Verdi later, " my great troubles began. At the beginning of April [1840] my little boy fell ill: the doctors could not make out what it was he was suffering from, and the poor little fellow died in the arms of his distracted mother. As if this were not enough, a few days afterwards my little girl fell ill in her turn, and she too died. And, as if this were still too little, my poor wife was seized with a violent inflammation of the brain, and on the 3rd June a third coffin left my house! I was alone, alone, alone! In barely two months my three dear ones had left me for ever; my family was exterminated! In the midst of these terrible griefs I had to write a comic opera! *Un Giorno di Regno* did not please; part of the fault lay no doubt with the music, but part also with the performance. With my soul tortured by my domestic misfortunes, chagrined by the non-success of my work, I felt certain that it was hopeless to look to art for consolation, and I decided I would compose no more."

In after-life Verdi had more than once the mortification of feeling, on a first night, that his audience was not completely with him; but none of these experiences hurt him so much as that of *Un Giorno di Regno*. No doubt the public reception of the work wounded him the more deeply because it seemed like a lack of sympathy with him in his terrible domestic troubles. Be that as it may, the memory of this experience rankled in him for many years.

As late as 1859 we find him, in a letter to Ricordi, complaining that the public had " maltreated the work of a poor sick young man, worried by the shortness of time, and with his heart bruised by his awful misfortunes; had it, I will not say applauded, but endured the opera in silence, I could not have found words enough to thank them." The critics often dealt roughly with him in later years, but he seems to have borne their displeasure stoically; perhaps no later experience of this kind could seem so cruel to him as the first.

His resolution not to compose again was broken down, in part, by Merelli, who one day slipped into his coat pocket a libretto by Solera on the subject of Nebuchadnezzar, which Verdi could not resist reading, and which so greatly appealed to him that after another effort to keep to his resolution he succumbed to Merelli's wiles.

The new work was given at the Scala on the 9th March, 1842; the tenor was the famous Ronconi, and the soprano Giuseppina Strepponi, who later became the composer's second wife. This time there could be no question about the success of the opera; people became aware that a new spirit had come into Italian opera. Rough, coarse, even vulgar as this spirit was at times, not only in *Nabucco* but in many of the later operas, no one could fail to perceive the tremendous energy of it.

And it came at the right time: Rossini had ceased operatic work some time before, and even the Italian musical world was beginning to feel a trifle weary of the gentle sentimentalities of Bellini and Donizetti. It did not object to sentimentality in itself — far from it; but it wanted a new turn given to the traditional Italian sentimentality, and this Verdi supplied. His youthful vigour, for all its coarseness and commonplace — perhaps even because of these — gave the Italian operatic public a shaking such as it had not had in the theatre for many years. *Nabucco* was the real beginning of Verdi's career.

The most successful number in it, perhaps, was a chorus of the captive Hebrew people, *Va pensiero sull' ali dorate* (*Fly, thought, on golden wings*). When Verdi took this libretto out of the pocket in which Merelli had placed it and threw it on the table, it chanced to open at this passage; the words and the situation seized at once on his imagination and impelled him to read the whole libretto. The chorus was a great success even at the rehearsals, and the north Italian people, who were then under the heel of Austria, soon came to take the words and the music as an expression of their own aspirations towards freedom.

One sure sign that *Nabucco* was the opera of the hour was the fact that all the chief theatres of Italy took it up at once; another was that Ricordi gave the composer 3,000 Austrian lire for the publishing rights. Of the 3,000, half, by the terms of the contract, belonged to Merelli, who, however, returned 1,000 lire of his share to Verdi.

After this, Verdi's operas came in rapid succession, as will be seen from the following list:

I Lombardi, produced at Milan, 11th February, 1843.

Ernani, produced at Venice, 9th March, 1844.

I due Foscari, produced at Rome, 3rd November, 1844.

Giovanna d'Arco, produced at Milan, 15th February, 1845.

Alzira, produced at Naples, 12th August, 1845.

Attila, produced at Venice, 17th March, 1846.

Macbeth, produced at Florence, 14th March, 1847.

I Masnadieri, produced at London, 22nd July, 1847.

Jerusalem (a new version of *I Lombardi*), produced at Paris, 26th
    November, 1847.

Il Corsaro, produced at Trieste, 25th October, 1848.

La Battaglia di Legnano, produced at Rome, 27th January, 1849.

Luisa Miller, produced at Naples, 8th December, 1849.

Stiffelio, produced at Trieste, 16th November, 1850.

It will be seen that not a year passed without the production of
a new Verdi opera, while in some years two were brought out,
and in one year three; the grand total is thirteen in eight years.
Not all of them were successes; the weakest of them were *Giovanna d'Arco* (*Joan of Arc*), *Alzira, Il Corsaro* (founded on
Byron's *Corsair*), *Stiffelio,* and *I due Foscari* (founded on Byron's
play). The resounding successes were *I Lombardi alla Prima Cro-
ciata* (*The Lombards at the First Crusade*), *Ernani* (which was
taken up by fifteen theatres in the first nine months), *Attila,
Macbeth,* and *Luisa Miller* (the story taken from Schiller's play
Cabal and Love).

Verdi was always a good business man — scrupulously honest,
and never going back on his word, but thoroughly competent to
deal with publishers, impresarii, farmers, and shopkeepers —
and the gradual rise in the scale of his terms is a sort of barometer
of his success with the public.

After *Nabucco* had proved so popular he was invited to write
the new carnival opera for the Scala. He asked Giuseppina Strepponi what he ought to demand: her advice was, in essence, to get
all he could, but to be careful not to go too far. He asked 8,000
Austrian lire (about £270) for *I Lombardi,* and got them

without difficulty. For the *Corsaro* he received from the publisher £800, for *Luisa Miller* (from the Naples theatre) £500; for *Aida,* in 1871, from the Khedive of Egypt, £6,000.

These sums represent merely the right to first performance or publication; in addition there were royalties from other theatres and incidental perquisites of all sorts, such as the fees paid to the composer for conducting occasionally. Verdi soon became very comfortably off, and in his later period he was exceedingly rich.

The peculiar conditions of the time helped him a good deal. There was something in this vigorous music of his that the Italians, then chafing under the foreign yoke, felt to be peculiarly expressive of themselves. Music is the one form of human thought that the most censorious censor cannot deal with; and the Austrian censors, who could suppress or imprison poets and politicians and journalists who ventured to speak about Italian freedom, could do nothing against a melody that the people took to their hearts and sang in the streets with the conviction at the back of their minds that it voiced their desire for freedom.

There were other ways also of dodging the censorship. So far as the censor could, he vetoed any reference to liberty in a play, a poem, or an opera; but the forbidden subject could generally be introduced, in opera at any rate, by a side door; nor could any censor prevent an audience from reading into seemingly harmless words about this ancient event or that a reference to the Italian conditions of the day. It was thus that the audience applied the prayer of the captive Hebrews, in *Nabucco,* to themselves, and the censorship could find no real cause for offence.

The subject of *I Lombardi* is merely that of two Lombard brothers, Pagano and Arvano, the former of whom, after killing his father and falling in love with his own brother's wife, flees to Palestine and becomes a holy hermit. The Lombards go to Palestine on a crusade, and the Saracen chief, Acciano, captures Arvano's daughter Griselda. She is loved by Acciano's son, Oronte, who decides to become a Christian. Arvano, seeking counsel, visits the supposed hermit, who has a plan by which Antioch will be surrendered to the invaders. This is done, and most of the Saracens are killed except Oronte, who returns to Griselda disguised as a Lombard. The lovers escape together but are pursued; Oronte is fatally wounded, and dies — a convert — in Pagano's cell. Pagano goes with his brother to the siege of Jerusalem, and receives a fatal wound; before dying he discloses his real name.

On the surface it is just one of those highly coloured melo-dramas in which Verdi delighted; but the authorities from the beginning had the suspicion that beneath the surface there was a political intent, and sure enough the modern Lombard audience saw themselves in the old Lombards and the old Lombards in themselves. There were allusions in the libretto to the *Pio,* i.e. the pious man (Pagano) — for instance, the pilgrims " rejoiced at the invitation of the *Pio* "; the Italians took a delight in asso-ciating this personage with Pio Nono (the then Pope, Pius the Ninth).

The police thought they had an excuse for prohibiting the opera in the numerous representations of religious matters — baptisms, conversions, and so on — that it contained; and so the Austrian Archbishop of Milan set the chief of police to work. The latter gentleman happened to be musical, and when Verdi and the man-agement refused to alter the libretto as the Archbishop desired, the chief of police tactfully compromised; he asked that " Salve Maria " should be substituted for " Ave Maria." His request was granted, and all was well.

In *Ernani,* again, there was in the original libretto a conspiracy scene. This, of course, would never do; it might put dangerous ideas into the heads of the people! So the police insisted on the withdrawal of the scene, and Verdi and his librettist had to re-cast the story at this point. The subject of *Ernani* is derived from Victor Hugo's drama *Hernani,* and the setting is in Spain. In one of the choruses of the opera there is a reference to the " Lion of Castile " (Castiglia): the singers used to substitute " Caprera " for " Castiglia," and " Italia " for " Iberia," while in-stead of " Honour and glory to Carlo Magno " they would sing " Honour and glory to Pio Nono," or even " to Carlo Alberto."

In 1847, two years after its production at Milan, *Giovanna d'Arco* (*Joan of Arc*) was given at Palermo, which was then under the foreign rule of the Bourbons. It was thought that, even in the mouths of the contemporaries of Joan of Arc, it would not be safe to allow such dangerous words as " country " and " liberty "; so alterations had to be made in the " book," and the title of the opera was altered to *Orietta di Lesbo*.

Sure enough the people seized upon anything and everything in the libretti of the Verdi operas that could be twisted into some sort of bearing on politics: in *Macbeth*, for instance, the chorus " The betrayed country calls upon us with tears " never failed to evoke a patriotic demonstration.

The Battle of Legnano, dealing as it did with the exploits of the Lombard League against the German Emperor Friedrich Barbarossa, was of course recognised as a thoroughly patriotic subject; it was to its patriotism, indeed, as much as its music, that the opera owed its great popularity. The Italian audiences used to grow delirious at the performances of it; it came, it will be remembered, in 1849, a year in which revolution was in the air in a great part of Europe. By this time Verdi and his librettist felt safe enough to refer to their country by name instead of indirectly: the " book " contained such lines as " Long live Italy, a sacred pact binds her sons together! " and " Let us swear to chase the tyrants of Italy beyond the Alps." Later the censor insisted on the title of the opera being changed from *The Battle of Legnano* to *The Siege of Haarlem;* but the more the pseudo-Dutch chorus, in the new version, sang " Viva Olanda " the more the public sang " Viva Italia."

Verdi had no liking for politics; he believed that all men should cease to strive for party and work only for the good of the country. He was a great admirer of patriots like Manzoni, and at the request of the latter he set to music, in 1848, a patriotic poem commencing " Sound the trumpet, wave the yellow-and-black flag," and sent it to his friend with the words, " May this hymn soon be sung, to the sound of cannon, on the plains of Lombardy."

It took courage to do this, and also, in the same year, to add his signature to a manifesto that was issued asking the help of

France against Austria: this latter act might easily have led to his exile. But he never thought much of politicians, and though he could not refuse Cavour's request to let himself be elected a deputy of the Italian Parliament in 1861 — for the statesman wanted the House to be representative of all that was good in the life of the country — he took his seat only once or twice.

In 1874 King Victor Emmanuel created him, by decree, a Senator; but Verdi put in only one appearance — on the occasion when he took the oath. But though he was neither a politician nor an admirer of politicians he was intensely patriotic, especially in his early manhood; and in his way he did as much as almost any man to bring about Italian freedom and unity.

While other thought could be suppressed, musical thought, as we have said, is free. The people were quick to recognise this; and Verdi's music became a rallying cry for the nation. By a curious chance, the letters of his name constituted the initial letters of " Vittorio Emmanuele, Rè d'Italia," and the nation found, to its delight, that it could thus shout out indirectly the name of its future king while ostensibly only shouting " Viva Verdi."

But Verdi all this time was making another reputation besides that of patriot. It may have been his good luck to have been born just when and where he was, and to have come to maturity just when the Italian people wanted a composer to express their own feelings about liberty; but Verdi would not have become what he was to the Italian people unless his music, as well as his patriotism, had been just the thing they wanted.

It was a period of growing national strength, and Verdi's music had an almost rude strength as its chief characteristic. Neither Rossini, Bellini, Donizetti, Mercadante, nor any of the other composers of that generation could have taken Verdi's place in the Italy of the eighteen-forties and fifties; their music lacked the driving power of his.

Some of the critics of the time, and especially the English critics, have been severely censured since then for having written so disparagingly about him. But when we come to look into the matter for ourselves we find that they were not so grievously to blame. It is very easy to be wise after the event. *We* know the master-Verdi of *Aida, Otello,* and *Falstaff,* and so we can afford to smile tolerantly at the many absurdities and vulgarities in the early Verdi. But the critics of 1840 to 1850 could hardly be expected to have a prophetic vision of the future — to see that bit by bit Verdi would purge himself of all his weaknesses and coarsenesses, and in his old age write three masterpieces that would be the quintessence of all that had been best in him from the first.

Had Verdi died in, say, 1855, we should now be looking at his music through very different eyes. The critics of the early period could only deal with this work as they saw it, and it must be admitted that there was a good deal in it to set them against it.

To begin with, he had an undue partiality for gloomy, even violent, subjects. His was always a very serious mind, and there can be little doubt that the deaths of his wife and children turned his natural seriousness into downright gloom for a good many years. His operatic subjects got on the nerves of some of the more sensitive of his hearers, who found them rather too full of blood and thunder, of battle, murder, and sudden death.

The Two Foscari is the story of a Venetian blood-feud, with all its trimmings of assassination, imprisonment, and torture. The subject of *Attila* is the stabbing of the hero by Odabella, the daughter of one of the Roman lords who had been killed in battle by the barbarian invader. The subject of *Macbeth* is sufficiently well known to British readers; it can hardly be called a cheerful one. In *I Masnadieri (The Brigands),* one brother conspires against the other, drives him out to become a robber, and tries to marry his betrothed — almost starving to death, by way of a little side activity, his own father. The good brother revenges the wrongs of the family on the bad brother, and then, instead of marrying his betrothed like a sensible man, becomes unreasonably horrified at the thought that he is a brigand and an outlaw, and stabs her to the heart.

Luísa Miller, the heroine of another of these early operas, has two lovers, Rodolfo, the son of Count Walter, the big person of

the village, and Wurm, the Count's chief man. Luisa favours
Rodolfo without knowing his rank. Wurm, in his rage at being
rejected, tells the whole truth both to the Count and to Luisa's
father, who is an old soldier. The Count thereupon claps the
father in prison and bids his son marry one Federica; but Rodolfo
secures the old soldier's release by a bit of blackmail: the Count,
it seems, has committed a murder, and Rodolfo threatens to
publish the fact.

After some rather muddled intrigue, in which everybody looks
like having to marry someone he or she doesn't want to marry,
Rodolfo takes poison because Luisa has written, at Wurm's dictation, a letter in which she rejects Rodolfo and chooses his rival.
Luisa too takes a drink from the cup, but before dying tells of
Wurm's plot. The other characters rush in, and Rodolfo manages
to stab Wurm before lying down to die with Luisa.

The reader will know the stories of *Rigoletto, Il Trovatore,* and
La Traviata, and will remember that the first is a lurid story of
seduction and villainy, ending in the jester's murder of his own
daughter, and that in the second the daughter of a gipsy woman
who had been burned for witchcraft steals the younger son of
the lord who did the deed and brings him up as her own child,
teaching him to hate his own blood-brother. The two fall in love
with the same girl; the elder brother has the younger executed,
whereupon the gipsy tells him in triumph how, unconsciously, he
has revenged her and her mother, and the girl dies of a dose of
poison.

In the third, a fashionable " unfortunate " (" La Traviata "
means literally " the lapsed and lost one ") ruins the life of a good
young man, develops consumption, and dies in his arms in the
last act. *The Sicilian Vespers* — still to anticipate our biographical
story a little — deals with a well-known historical massacre. The
subject of *Un Ballo in maschera* (*A Masked Ball*) is the assassination of King Gustavus of Sweden. In *Simone Boccanegra* the
Doge of Venice of that name, who has had an illegitimate child
by the daughter of a previous Doge, dies of poison.

There are lighter episodes, of course, in some of these operas, but the general atmosphere of them all is gloomy. Life is seen in convulsions; everything is a little overdone. This accounts, in large part, for the prejudice felt against Verdi by the more classically minded critics in England; Chorley, the famous critic of the *Athenæum,* summed up *Luisa Miller* as " fire, faggot, and rack," and the description holds good of a great many of the early Verdi operas.

The classically and fastidiously minded, again, were repelled by many things in Verdi's early music — his frequent commonplace, his occasional downright vulgarity, his fondness for having his ranting melodies shouted out in unison, as if he were having the dreadful tune printed in underlined capitals, his frequent convulsiveness of rhythm, and above all the noise of his orchestration.

These things hardly mattered to the Italian audiences, which loved to concentrate on the big thumping tune and take it home with them and sing it in the streets, and the more loudly the orchestra and the singers bellowed the tune at them the more easily they picked it up. But in non-Italian countries the insistence seemed a trifle excessive. Yet though some of the English critics rarely found a good word to say for Verdi, our public, in the main, liked him; they shuddered a little at his rowdinesses and brutalities, but they could not help being impressed by his rough strength.

The first opera of his to be heard in London was *Ernani,* which was given at Her Majesty's Theatre on the 8th March, 1845, a year after its production at Venice. It rather staggered its first English audience, but quickly became popular, and received more performances than any other opera that season. Both *Nabucco* and *I Lombardi* were given in London in 1846.

In England, of course, it was not permissible to stage a story from the Bible; so *Nabucco* appeared under the title of *Ninus, King of Assyria.*

I due Foscari was given in London in 1847, *Attila* in 1848, and *Luisa Miller* in 1858. *I Masnadieri* was written specially for Lumley the impresario of Her Majesty's Theatre, who had for a long time been trying to get a " first production " of an opera

by the young composer who was setting Italy on fire. At first
Verdi thought of *King Lear,* but though there is evidence that he
wrote some music for this, the opera was never completed. *I Masnadieri* was based on a play by Schiller — *The Robbers.* The
London cast was vocally almost an ideal one — Jenny Lind,
Lablache, Gardoni, Coletti, and Bouche. The work, however, was
not a success; both libretto and music were at fault. But what
went most against it in London was the fact that Lablache — a
genial colossus of a man, with a bass voice on the same generous
scale as his person — had to play the part of an emaciated prisoner
in the last stages of starvation. The spectacle was too much for
the sense of humour of the audience.

That Lumley, even after the partial failure of *I Masnadieri,*
still thought Verdi the man of the future in Italian opera was
shown by his offering him the post of conductor at Her Majesty's
for three years at an excellent salary, and the promise of the
production of a new opera of his each year.

Michael Costa was leaving Lumley for the rival house at Covent
Garden, and the impresario of Her Majesty's needed a strong
counter-attraction. But Verdi could not accept the offer, as he
was under engagement to write two new operas for Italy.

We must now resume the interrupted story of Verdi's life.

All composers who had long lives show three "periods" or
"styles." The division is only a rough one, and here and there a
work may come that it is difficult to allot confidently to either
of two periods; but in the main it holds good.

In the first period the artist is struggling to find himself. In
the second he is thoroughly master of himself as he then is. In the
third he is at first not quite so sure of himself, for he is developing
mentally more rapidly than he is technically; but in time he develops a new style to fit his new thought, once more attains complete mastery of all his forces, and does his greatest work. Thus
Wagner's first style extends from *The Fairies* and *The Ban upon
Love* to *The Flying Dutchman,* his second embraces *Tannhäuser*
and *Lohengrin,* while his third contains *The Ring, Tristan, The
Mastersingers,* and *Parsifal.*

Verdi's first style is represented by the operas we have lately been considering. His second style includes three works of very much the same kind that came one on the heels of the other — *Rigoletto*, *Il Trovatore*, and *La Traviata*, — and five operas that show, along with a great deal of the old Verdi, decided anticipations of the greater Verdi of the last years. The list of his works between the *Stiffelio* of 1850 and the *Aida* of 1871 runs thus:

Rigoletto, produced at Venice, 11th March, 1851.
Il Trovatore, produced at Rome, 19th January, 1853.
La Traviata, produced at Venice, 6th March, 1853.
Les Vêpres Siciliennes, produced at Paris, 13th June, 1855.
Simone Boccanegra, produced at Venice, 12th March, 1857.
Aroldo, produced at Rimini, 16th August, 1857.
Un Ballo in maschera, produced at Rome, 17th February, 1859.
La Forza del Destino, produced at Petersburg, 10th November, 1862.
Macbeth, produced at Paris, 21st April, 1865.
Don Carlos, produced at Paris, 11th March, 1867.

Aroldo was a new version of the unsuccessful *Stiffelio* of 1850, and the *Macbeth* a new version (with a ballet) of the opera of the same name that had been produced in 1847. We are thus left with eight new works, covering a period of sixteen years.

It will be seen that Verdi was producing more slowly as the years went on, not because his fountain of inspiration was running dry but because the greater works of his middle and later period required a longer time for gestation. The first three of these eight operas were produced within ten years — *Il Trovatore* and *La Traviata*, indeed, within two months of each other. After that, in place of the old record of at least one and sometimes two operas a year, there is an interval of two (and on one occasion three) years between each two successive works. After *Don Carlos* the periods of gestation became still longer, as the following list shows:

Aida, produced at Cairo, 24th December, 1871.

Otello, produced at Milan, 5th February, 1887.

Falstaff, produced at Milan, 9th February, 1893.

Between *Aida* and *Otello* he produced a second version of *Simone Boccanegra,* at Milan, on the 24th March, 1881.

It was with *Rigoletto, Il Trovatore,* and *La Traviata* that Verdi unmistakably conquered the world. The success of these three works was incredible, especially that of *Il Trovatore,* the melodies of which were ground out by every barrel-organ in Europe.

La Traviata had at first some opposition to overcome in England, where the highly moral people were up in arms at the idea of putting a lady of easy virtue on the stage, and the newspapers were full of the nonsensical leading articles and still more non-sensical "Letters to the Editor" that are common on occasions of this kind.

The ever-pompous *Times* thundered against "the foul and hideous horrors" of the opera; and even less rigid moralists found the story "improper," as Ibsen was found improper and foul and hideous and horrible half a century later.

But nothing could check the triumphant course of the work. It began badly at Venice, it is true; on the day after the first performance Verdi wrote to his friend Emmanuele Muzio, "Yesterday *Traviata* — fiasco. Is the fault mine, or the singers'? Time will show." The laughter of the first-night audience, however, was due to the spectacle of the twelve-stone soprano who played Violetta trying to convince them that she was in the last stages of consumption. Once this little defect in the casting had been remedied, all was plain sailing for the opera.

These three operas were the turning-point in Verdi's career. In these the energy of his temperament had come to its finest possible expression along the old lines; the problem before him now was both to find new lines for it and to tame its somewhat excessive exuberances. This, in one way or another, and with varying success, he did in the later works of his second period.

There were still a good many outbursts of the old brutality and vulgarity; but there were also many touches that showed a finer sensibility and an ability to get his effects with the fingers instead of with the fist.

The Sicilian Vespers falls between two stools; it was written for Paris, and Verdi tried to cross his own Italian manner with that of the French " Grand Opera " of Meyerbeer. In spite of its initial success, the work has not survived on the stage. (When it was given in Italy, by the way, the censor insisted on the title being changed; it accordingly became *Giovanna di Guzman*.) *Simone Boccanegra* contains some excellent music, but the libretto dragged it down. Ten years after he had written *Aida* Verdi recast *Simone Boccanegra*, but the new version succeeded no better than the old. The double failure must have been a great disappointment to him, for there is some of his best work in this opera.

With *The Masked Ball* and *The Power of Destiny* he made yet another step forward in his art; in the best passages of these two operas there are clear hints of the coming of the change in him that was one day to reveal itself complete in *Aida*. It is in *The Masked Ball* that the aria " Eri tu " occurs — so beloved of baritones, professional and amateur. The truly fine moments of *The Power of Destiny* are dragged down by the weaker, and by a somewhat confused " book."

After this work, Verdi allowed his mind to ripen in a long silence; it was five years before he again appeared before the public with a new work — *Don Carlos* — and after that there was another interval of five years before *Aida* appeared. *Don Carlos* was the second opera that he wrote specially for Paris, and once more the necessity of conciliating French tastes hampered him a little; he had to make five acts of the work, and to surrender to the French passion for the ballet. But so pronounced, here and there, is the advance on his previous work that some critics regard not *Aida* but *Don Carlos* as the true beginning of his third period.

Before we continue the story of Verdi as an opera composer we must digress a little to consider his works in other genres. His true vein, needless to say, was the opera; but from time to time he made an excursion into other fields, with varying success. A few songs of his early and middle period have been published, together with a string quartet (written in 1873 at Naples, when the rehearsals of *Aida* were held up for a time by the illness of a singer), a *Pater noster*, an *Ave Maria* (both in 1880), and in the last years of his life (after 1897), another *Ave Maria* for four voices (in a peculiar scale that he called " enigmatic "), a *Stabat mater*, a *Te Deum*, and the *Laudi alla Vergina* (songs in praise of the Virgin). But his great work in the sacred field is the *Requiem*.

About 1867–8 his thoughts ran much on the subject of death. His father died on the 15th January, 1867, and his early benefactor Antonio Barezzi on the 27th July. On the 13th November of the following year Rossini died. Four days later Verdi wrote a letter to his publisher Ricordi, suggesting that all the most eminent of living Italian composers should collaborate in a Mass to be sung on the first anniversary of Rossini's death. The idea found favour, and the Mass was written by Verdi and twelve other composers who were then " eminent," but whose very names are unknown to the ordinary music-lover of to-day. Verdi took the final number of the Mass — the *Libera me*.

The work was never performed: the impresario Scalaberni put difficulties in the way of granting the services of his choir and orchestra in Bologna, while the proposed conductor, Angelo Mariani, would not co-operate because his vanity had been hurt by his omission from the list of selected composers.

One day Verdi's friend Mazzucato happened to see the score of the Mass at Ricordi's, and was so moved by the *Libera me* that he wrote to Verdi expressing his admiration. Verdi, in his reply, spoke of a half-wish that some day he might compose the whole Mass. The impulse to do this came to him some years after, when Manzoni died.

Verdi had always felt the profoundest love and reverence for Manzoni, whose novel *I Promessi Sposi* (*The Betrothed*) he thought the finest of modern books. He met Manzoni in 1868, and some time later he wrote to his close friend, the Countess Clara

Maffei, " What could I say to you about him? How could I explain the inexplicable, agreeable new emotions awakened in me by the presence of this holy one, as you call him? I would have knelt before him, if man could worship man. . . . When you see him, kiss his hand for me, and assure him of my whole veneration."

Before this, in 1867, he had written, " How I envy my wife, who has seen the great one! But I doubt whether, if I come to Milan, I shall have the courage to introduce myself to him. You know well how great is my reverence for this man, who, in my opinion, has written not only the greatest book of our day but one of the greatest that ever came from a human brain. And it is not only a book but a solace for humanity. I was sixteen years old when I read it first. Since then I have read many other books, my esteem for which has changed or perished as I grew older — and several are very famous ones. But for this book my enthusiasm remains undiminished — nay, it has even increased with my knowledge of mankind, because this book is true, as true as truth itself. Oh, if artists could only understand this truth, there would be neither musicians of the future nor musicians of the past, neither veristic, realistic, nor idealistic painters, neither classical nor romantic poets; but simply true poets, true painters, true musicians."

On the 22nd May, 1873, he hears of Manzoni's death. " Now," he writes, " everything is ended! And with him goes the purest, the holiest, the highest of our celebrities. I have read many articles on him; none of them speak of him as is his due. Many words, but little innermost feeling! Even disparagements are not lacking! Even of him! . . . What an evil race we are! "

Verdi resolved to erect a monument of his own to Manzoni's memory — a Requiem Mass for the first anniversary of his death. Thus from the *Libera me* of the Rossini *Requiem* and from the death of Manzoni grew the great *Requiem*. It has often been reproached with being operatic rather than religious music. But Verdi was a man of his time and of his race, and it was in terms of drama, of humanity, that he saw the *Requiem*, rather than in terms either of Church dogma or of German musical tradition. He was as sincere in this music as in everything else he wrote.

The first performance of the work was given in the church of San Marco, Milan, on the 22nd May, 1874, Verdi himself conducting. Three days later he conducted it again in the Scala Theatre, and he presided at the first English performance of the Mass in the Albert Hall, on the 15th May, 1875.

One other non-operatic work of his has to be mentioned before we resume the main thread of his life. A musical work was wanted for the great International Exhibition of 1862, and this, under the title of *L'Inno delle Nazioni* (*Hymn of the Nations*) was provided jointly by Auber, representing France, Meyerbeer, representing Germany, Verdi, representing Italy, and Sterndale Bennett, representing England. It was not given at the Exhibition, however, owing to the action of Costa, but was performed at Her Majesty's Theatre on the 24th May, 1862. Verdi was present, and had to come forward to take the applause: it was his first appearance in London since he had produced *I Masnadieri* in 1847.

Verdi was never a great traveller. He had spent some time, at various periods of his life, in Paris and London, and had called at various German towns on the way; but he loved the solitude of his country estate better than the acclamations of the crowd, and above all he disliked the sea.

It was for this latter reason that he did not attend the production at Cairo, on the 24th December, 1871, of *Aida*. The work had been commissioned by the Khedive, Ismail Pasha, at a fee of £6,000, to inaugurate the new Cairo theatre. The production was a magnificent one, no expense having been spared in the matter of chorus, costumes, and scenery. *Aida* was given at Milan in the February of 1872, and came to Covent Garden four years later; wherever it was given it was recognised as the master's finest work.

Because the music flowed on continuously, without the old-fashioned separation into arias, duets, choruses, and so on, and for other reasons, the cry was raised that Verdi had been influenced by Wagner. The truth was that all this was a natural development on Verdi's part. He remained, as indeed he did to the end of his career, Verdi and an Italian. But Wagner may have contributed indirectly to make *Aida* what it was. Wagner's music had been steadily conquering the world during the last few years; and the resounding success of *Lohengrin* in Bologna in 1872 showed that Italy, no less than Germany, France, and England, was beginning to fall at the German's feet.

In face of this gradual penetration of Italy by Wagner, Verdi may have felt that it behoved him to show that there was another solution of the operatic problem than that put forward by his rival, and that, admirable as the Wagnerian orchestral symphonic methods might be for Germans, the true method for Italians was the historic Italian one of glowing vocal melody with an orchestral support.

His confidence in himself and in Italian art was justified; it is from *Aida* in 1871 that the renaissance of Italian opera dates. But *Aida* must have seemed to the world his swan-song, so long was his silence after it. To the world's amazement he broke this silence sixteen years later, and at the age of seventy-four produced *Otello*, in which the advance even on *Aida* was notable. Still greater was the world's surprise when, six years later still, the old man of eighty sprang upon it his first comedy, and a comedy fit to rank with the *Mastersingers*.

Verdi had always been attracted to Shakespeare, and we have seen him twice handling the *Macbeth* subject and making a tentative beginning at *King Lear*. But in those days he lacked the librettist who could forge for him the true link between himself and Shakespeare. In his old age he found the man he wanted in Arrigo Boïto, later the composer of *Mefistofele* and *Nerone*. Boïto was a better poet than composer, and he ranks among the best librettists in the whole history of opera.

It was a piece of singular good fortune both for Verdi and for the world that at the height of the musician's imaginative and technical powers he should meet with a poet who could place Shakespeare at his service in a form thoroughly practical for the operatic stage. Both in *Otello* and *Falstaff* Boïto has condensed the Shakespearean action in the most skilful manner, besides often coming astonishingly near the original in his own language.

Verdi had worked at *Falstaff* for some time in secret. Vague rumours of it filtered down to the outer world from time to time, but few of those who heard them took very seriously the idea of a man who was nearing his eightieth year writing his first comic opera. The secret was let out in 1890, when, at a dinner given by Ricordi to Verdi and Boïto, the latter stood up and drank to the health of the *Pancione* (the fellow with the big paunch).

The news spread quickly: a friend wrote to Verdi for information on the subject, and received the following reply:

" What shall I say? For forty years I have wanted to write a comic opera, and for fifty I have known *The Merry Wives of Windsor*. But . . . the usual ' buts ' invariably stood in the way of the fulfilling of my desire. At last Boïto has settled all the ' buts ' and given me a lyrical comedy libretto that is like no other. I amuse myself setting it to music, without plans of any kind and without even knowing whether I shall ever finish it. I repeat: I amuse myself. Falstaff is a rascal who does all sorts of villainous things, but always in a diverting way. He is a type. There are many other types in the work, which is comic from first to last. Amen."

The first performance, at Milan on the 9th February, 1893, drew musical celebrities from all parts of the earth. The Falstaff was Maurel, who had already distinguished himself as Iago in *Otello*. From the beginning the opera was recognised as one of the three or four supreme masterpieces in comic music. Verdi, at the conclusion of the performance, was called before the curtain again and again; a huge crowd accompanied his carriage back to his hotel, and refused to leave until the master appeared on the balcony.

Charles Villiers Stanford, who was present at the performance, and who saw the composer afterwards, testified that even in this moment of supreme triumph he never lost his usual modesty and dignity: " so devoid was he of all self-assertion that he even expressed his regret that so vast a concourse of strangers should have taken the trouble to come from all parts of Europe for the *première*, and declared that he preferred the earlier days of his career, when his operas were accepted or rejected on their merits alone, and when the test was independent of any considerations of personal popularity. A glance at his honest eyes was enough to satisfy the hearer that these were his true convictions and no affectations of humility."

Verdi had still eight years to live. He spent them between his estate of Sant' Agata, his house in Genoa, and Milan. The land and three or four houses he had bought at Busseto nearly half a century before had developed into a splendid estate, which Verdi himself, for the most part, managed down to the smallest details.

He loved his solitude, and was always with difficulty persuaded to leave it; and it was characteristic of him that for his town habitation in the winter he did not choose one of the larger or more frequented cities, such as Milan, Venice, Rome, Naples, or Florence, but the relatively unmusical town of Genoa, where he would be least likely to be always meeting people who would want to talk to him. Everyone in Genoa knew him, of course, but everyone knew also of his desire to be left alone; and though, when he entered his usual café, the whole company would rise in his honour, his privacy was respected.

From first to last he had been very self-centred — not selfish, for a more generous heart never existed, but simply anxious to live his own life in his own way — and without any illusions as to the general nature of mankind. Least of all had he any illusions about the operatic public.

" You are surprised," he wrote to Ricordi in 1859, " at the ill-behaviour of the public? It does not surprise me in the least. The public is always happy when it has a chance to make a scandal. When I was twenty-five I had illusions and believed in its courtesy; a year after, the veil fell from my eyes, and I saw with whom I really had to do. Some people make me laugh when they point out to me, with reproach in their eyes, that I owe much to this or that public! It is true: at the Scala *Nabucco* and *I Lombardi* were applauded — whether on account of the music, the singers, the orchestra, the chorus, the setting, the fact was that altogether it was a play that deserved applause. But hardly more than a year before that this same public had maltreated the opera [*Un Giorno di Regno*] of a poor, sick young man, who had been badly handled by circumstances, and whose heart was lacerated by a terrible misfortune. The public knew it all, but this did not avail to restrain its rudeness. Since that time I have never seen *Un Giorno di Regno*, and no doubt the opera is poor; but who knows how many that were no better have been tolerated and perhaps applauded?

"Oh," he continues in words we have already quoted, " if the public at that time had, I will not say applauded this opera, but even received it in silence, I should not have been able to find words enough to thank it. . . . I do not condemn it; I accept its censure and its hooting under the condition that I am not asked to give thanks for the applause. We poor gipsies, showmen, or whatever we are, are forced to sell our labours, our thoughts, our intoxications, for gold; and for three shillings the public buys the right to applaud or hiss us. We must submit."

An Italian sculptor of the day, Giulio Monteverde, who knew Verdi well, said that his deep-set eyes had a peculiar phosphorescence, which affected people who were even at too great a distance from him to see his features clearly. Those phosphorescent eyes looked out upon the world and men steadily and calmly, a little sombrely, and free from all illusions.

Verdi never tried to delude either himself or others over the reception of his works. In 1843, an hour or two after the production of *I Lombardi*, he wrote to a friend: " It has been a big fiasco: a really classical fiasco. Everything in it was either disliked or just tolerated, with the exception of the Cabaletta in the vision scene. That is the simple but true story, and I tell it to you without either joy or grief."

Verdi's music shows none of the drastic changes in style that are observable in the music of one or two other composers who had long lives. He developed marvellously; but his development was simply the gradual bettering of a style that, in essence, remained the same from the beginning of his career to the end of it. He was influenced singularly little by the music of other men, especially among his foreign contemporaries; indeed, he gave comparatively little attention to any music but his own. He took no pleasure in reading new music, and would not let Ricordi send him the publications of the firm. There was hardly any music to be found in his house; he liked to hear his guests play the piano, or take part with them occasionally in a duet, but they had to bring their own music with them. It was neither pride, nor vanity, nor indifference; it was simply the unconscious assertion of the instinct that for his own spiritual growth the thing most needed was that he should be left alone.

And as he was in his art, so he was in his life. He was considerate and generous, but he would brook no interference from anyone in his private affairs. He provided handsomely for his father on his estate, but when the old gentleman tried to take a small part in the management of this, he was gently but firmly warned off.

Verdi lived for some years, without being married to her, with the singer Giuseppina Strepponi, whom we have seen advising him in business matters at an early stage of his career, and for whom he had the greatest respect. His one-time Busseto patron and father-in-law thought it his duty to remonstrate with him in the matter. Verdi, though he loved Barezzi and never forgot his early obligations to him, promptly put him in his place; that a good woman who, like himself, loved solitude and was independent, chose to bind her life to his, what concern was this, he asked, of anyone but their two selves? He married Giuseppina, by the way, in 1859. There were no children of the union.

In the theatre he was respected but not greatly liked, for he was merciless to his singers, refusing, after he had become a power, to let a work of his go before the public until it had been rehearsed to his satisfaction. With his publishers and with impresarii, as with farmers and cattle dealers and gardeners and merchants, he was firm in the assertion of his rights, for he saw no reason to allow other people, and especially publishers, to grow rich by his exertions; but he was impeccably straight in all his dealings.

As a patriot he suffered, like most other Italian patriots, when, after the French had liberated the country from Austria, the liberators themselves fell below his ideal of international conduct. But he was deeply distressed at the defeat of France in the war of 1870; and he saw, with his usual clear-sightedness, the danger to the world of the increasing self-consciousness of German culture, and especially the militarist spirit of Prussia.

" In their veins," he wrote to a friend, " there still flows the old Goth blood; they are of a measureless pride, hard, intolerant, scorners of everything that is not Teutonic, and of a greed that knows no bounds. Men with heads but no hearts: a strong, uncivilised race." And some of his words were almost prophetic: " The European war cannot be avoided, and we shall be devoured. It will not come to-morrow, but it will come; a pretext is easy enough to find; Rome, perhaps, or the Mediterranean. And is there not also the Adriatic Sea, that they have already begun to call the German Sea? "

Honours, had he cared for them, would have come to him in abundance during the last twenty years of his life; but to Verdi these things meant nothing. He refused the title of Marquis of Busseto. When the Minister of Public Instruction sent him the decoration of Commander of the Crown of Italy he returned it with the words, " Why has this been sent to me? Evidently there has been a misunderstanding. I decline it."

In the last years of all he had moments of pessimism. " Born poor, in a poor village," he wrote at the age of eighty-two, " I had no means to learn anything. They gave me a miserable spinet, and a little while after, I began to write notes . . . notes on notes . . . nothing but notes! That is all. The worst of it is that now, at eighty-two, I very much doubt whether the notes are worth anything! It is a pang for me, a desolation! "

On the 14th November, 1897, Giuseppina died; she had sung in his *Nabucco* in 1842, and had lived to witness his final triumph with *Falstaff*. On the 29th July, 1900, King Humbert was assassinated; the deed filled Verdi with horror. Queen Margherita wrote a " Prayer," and it was suggested to Verdi by his friend the Countess Negroni-Prati that he should set it to music. He declined, giving as his excuse his great age and the difficulty of finding an adequate musical expression for the words. That the idea of the composition had appealed to him, however, was shown by the fact that after his death there were found on his piano some phrases sketched out to the words of the " Prayer."

His strength was now beginning to fail him, and his solitude, instead of being a strength to him as it once was, became a source of melancholy. He left Genoa towards the end of 1900 for Milan. In January he wrote to a friend, " Although the doctors tell me I am not ill, I feel that everything tries me: I can no longer read or write; my sight is not good, my hearing is worse still; and above all, my limbs no longer obey me. I do not live; I vegetate. What is there for me to do in the world? "

On the 21st January, 1901, while he was dressing in his room in the Hotel Milan, he had a stroke that paralysed his right side, and he fell back on his bed. For six days the sturdy old body fought with death, and the struggle was a grievous one; the end came on the 27th. In his will he expressed the desire to be buried " very modestly, either at dawn or at the evening *Ave Maria*, without any music." His wish was respected; his remains were laid beside those of Giuseppina in the " House of Rest " for musicians, to which Verdi had bequeathed the royalties from his works. There were other charitable bequests; the remainder of his huge fortune was left to his cousin Maria, the wife of Alberto Carrara, of Busseto.

THE story of Verdi's *Rigoletto* was taken from Victor Hugo's play *Le Roi s'amuse,* which was first produced in Paris in November 1832; and the best approach to the opera is through the poetic drama, because in that way one or two points become clear that are a little obscure in the opera. We shall therefore first of all tell the story as it unfolds under Victor Hugo's hands.

The scene of the play is Paris in the early twenties of the six-teenth century; and the King who " amuses himself " is the famous pleasure-loving Francis I. His pursuit of the ladies of his court is not always relished by their husbands and fathers; and one of the husbands who has least cause to be pleased with him is a certain M. de Cossé.

In the opening scene of the play we find the King telling a few of his courtiers of one of his recent amorous adventures; he is in the habit of going about in disguise, and latterly he has seen each Sunday a charming young bourgeoise who, he has discovered, lives in the cul-de-sac Bussy, just by M. de Cossé's large house. She is guarded by a forbidding old duenna, and the curious thing is that each evening a man of a most mysterious air enters the house, closely wrapped up in a cloak.

More courtiers enter while the King is speaking, among them is Triboulet, the King's jester, an ill-favoured hunchback. He is hated by all the courtiers because of his biting tongue and his malicious glee over the depredations of the King among the wives and daughters of the nobles.

After a scene of cautious flirtation between the King and Madame de Cossé, during which the husband of the latter is jeered at by Triboulet, an old man in mourning enters. This is M. de Saint-Vallier, the father of Diane de Poitiers, who has been seduced by the King. His plain speaking does not commend itself to Francis, who orders Saint-Vallier to be arrested. The servile Triboulet laughs at the old man, who turns on him and curses him: " Valet with a viper's tongue, you who thus make jest of the sorrow of a father, be accursed! "

Before this climax has been reached, however, one of the courtiers, M. de Pienne, has taken some of the others aside and imparted to them a delicious piece of news. He has discovered that the ugly and deformed Triboulet keeps a young mistress, whom he visits each night wrapped up in a dark cloak; de Pienne has hit upon the discovery by accident while he was rambling near de Cossé's house. Triboulet has heard nothing of this conversation, and when later he sardonically advises the King, in de Cossé's hearing, to abduct the latter's wife and if necessary behead the husband, de Cossé gladly joins in the plan of the courtiers to take revenge upon Triboulet by the kidnapping of his pretty mistress.

The second act takes place in the deserted cul-de-sac Bussy. On one side of the road are the gardens belonging to the large de Cossé mansion; on the other side is a modest house, with a wall that encloses a little courtyard. In the wall is a door that gives on the street; on the wall is a narrow terrace covered with a roof supported by arcades in the Renaissance style. The door of the first story of the house gives on to this terrace, which communicates with the courtyard by a staircase.

It is evening. Triboulet, closely wrapped up in a cloak and with nothing in his dress now to indicate his profession of buffoon, appears in the street, and is making his way towards the door in the wall when a man dressed in black, and with a huge sword showing through his cloak, accosts him. Triboulet is meditating, very ill at ease, on the curse of Saint-Vallier. His first impression is that the man in black is a beggar; but the stranger reveals him-

self as a professional assassin, one Saltabadil, whose occupation it
is to dispose, on suitable terms, of anyone who may be obnoxious
to his employer of the moment. His services are at Triboulet's
command if ever he should need them; his terms are half payment in advance, the other half " after," as he puts it. Triboulet
having assured him that he has no occasion for his services at
present, Saltabadil retires, after having told the buffoon where he
can be found if he should be wanted.

Triboulet, still brooding uneasily upon the old man's curse, goes
into the courtyard through the street door, which he carefully
locks after him; then he indulges in an embittered soliloquy upon
his evil fate as a buffoon. Other men, he says, are at liberty to
indulge themselves in their grief; *he* must always be prepared to
laugh at the bidding of the heartless, capricious King, and to submit to cruel jokes upon his deformity. His young daughter Blanche
comes out, followed by her attendant, Dame Bérarde. Blanche's
mother is dead, and the girl, who has only recently been brought
from the provinces to Paris, does not know either the name or
the profession of her father, who now anxiously warns her again,
as he has often done in the past, not to show herself in public.
Blanche assures him that she never goes out except to church,
when she is always accompanied by Bérarde. Triboulet tells
Blanche that he has to leave her at once, to " resume his collar ";
and once more he warns Bérarde to keep the door to the street
locked.

Having opened the door he looks apprehensively up and down
the road, and while his back is turned the King, who has meanwhile crept up in the growing darkness, slips into the courtyard.
The light of the lantern held by Bérarde happens to fall for a
moment upon Triboulet, and the King, with a laugh, recognises
him as his buffoon, Triboulet puts Bérarde through a last cate-
chism; she is sure, he hopes, that when she goes to church with
Blanche nobody follows them. Bérarde assures him that his fears
are groundless, and Triboulet at last goes away, carefully closing
the door behind him. When he has gone, the King comes forward
and by means of lavish gifts overcomes the hypocritical scruples

of Bérarde. Blanche already loves the handsome young stranger whom she has seen regarding her from afar in church and on the way homeward. " You are not, I hope," she says to him, " a lord or a gentleman, for my father dreads them both." The King assures her that he is only a poor scholar, by name Gaucher Mahiet.

Just then voices are heard in the road, and Bérarde hurriedly lets the King out through the house, after he has deposited a kiss upon the eyes of Blanche. The voices in the road are those of the courtiers, who are wearing cloaks and masks and finding their way about by a dark lantern, for it is now completely night. A servant carries a ladder. Blanche appears for a moment upon the terrace, breathing the beloved name of Gaucher Mahiet to the night. She is at once recognised by de Pienne, and the others comment favourably upon the beauty of this supposed mistress of Triboulet. Blanche having re-entered the house, the courtiers proceed with their plan, which is to enter by means of the ladder, carry off the lady, and present her to the King in the morning.

Just then, however, Triboulet returns, still repeating gloomily to himself, " The old man cursed me! My secret! Something troubles me! " The night is so dark that he does not see the courtiers, into one of whom he bumps; they, however, recognise him by his voice when he asks, " Who goes there? " M. de Cossé is for killing the jester, but the others prefer the more humorous kind of revenge they have already planned. They address him by name, tell him who they are (with the exception, of course, of de Cossé), and pretend they have come to abduct Madame de Cossé.

In this plan Triboulet, becoming the King's buffoon again in a moment, is willing to join. They put a mask on him, bandage his eyes unknown to him, and set him to hold the ladder, by which the others mount to the terrace. They enter the house, and a moment after one of them reappears in the court and opens the street door from the inside; then the others come out carrying Blanche, who is half-clothed and gagged. When they have gone, Triboulet, who has got tired of waiting, tries to remove his mask and finds that his eyes have been bandaged; as he tears away both bandage and mask he sees, by the dim light of the lantern which has been left behind, something white on the ground; he picks it up and recognises his daughter's veil. Turning round, he sees that the ladder is against the wall of his own house, and that the door into the courtyard is open. He rushes in like a madman, and a moment after reappears dragging with him Dame Bérarde, who, like Blanche, has been gagged by the conspirators. He looks at her in a sort of stupor, tears his hair, and utters wild, inarticulate cries. At last, finding his voice, he cries out, " The curse! " and falls fainting to the ground.

The third act takes place the next day in the ante-chamber of the King at the Louvre. The courtiers are chuckling over the success of their scheme when the King enters in a magnificent morning négligé. He is accompanied by de Pienne, who has told him of the appetising morsel that has been brought for him — the pretty mistress of the detested Triboulet, as they all think. The trembling Blanche is brought in, and in the King she recognises the supposed poor scholar with whom she has fallen in love. The courtiers having been dismissed, the King endeavours to overcome the apprehensions of Blanche, who, however, flies in terror through a door that, as it happens, leads into the bed-chamber of the King. He pursues her there, and the returning courtiers laugh cynically over the latest turn of events.

Triboulet now enters. He has a suspicion that his daughter has been brought to the Louvre, and he looks round furtively in every direction, scanning also the faces of the courtiers, but trying to disguise his inquietude; the others observe him with an air of hardly concealed amusement. A gentleman of the court enters with the news that the Queen wishes to see the King upon an important affair of state. The courtiers, unwilling to have their scheme thus spoiled, first of all try to persuade him that the King is not yet up, and when he shows incredulity at this they tell him that his majesty has gone hunting. " What! " says the gentleman, still more incredulously, " without pages and without huntsmen? "

Triboulet, who has heard the dialogue, now understands every-thing: in a voice of thunder he cries out, " She is here! She is here with the King! " He furiously demands his daughter, and the courtiers for the first time learn, to their astonishment, his true relationship to the abducted girl. He turns on them fiercely and in a series of impassioned monologues curses and insults them; then, his spirit for the moment breaking, he appeals humbly to their sympathy. All is in vain; the courtiers maintain a stony silence.

At last the door in the inner room opens violently, and the distracted Blanche rushes out and falls into the arms of her father. Triboulet commandingly orders the courtiers out, and, overawed by his unaccustomed air of authority, they obey. Blanche makes her broken-hearted confession, and the jester, turning towards the inner chamber, curses the debauched King and threatens him with vengeance. There is a stir in the background; a guard enters, conducting Saint-Vallier to the Bastille. As he is passing out he stops, turns towards the King's room, and apostrophises the absent monarch; his curse, he says, bitterly, has failed; not a voice has been raised in his support, not a sign has come from heaven; " this King will prosper! " Triboulet, as the curtain falls, looks Saint-Vallier in the face, and says, " Count! you deceive yourself. You shall be avenged! "

The fourth act takes place partly inside and partly outside the house of Saltabadil, a wretched hovel in a deserted place on the outskirts of Paris, near the river. Inside the house is Saltabadil, who is seated at a table polishing his sword-belt. Outside are Triboulet and Blanche. The latter, in spite of all that has happened, in spite even of her father, still loves the King, and is sure that he loves her. She reminds her father that he has promised to forgive him; but Triboulet assures her that for the last month he has only been feigning forgiveness in order to gain time to perfect his plan for revenge. Would she still love the King, he asks her, if she discovered that he no longer loved her? " I do not know," she replies; " he loves me, he tells me he adores me; only yesterday he told me so." " Very well, then! " says Triboulet grimly, " look there! " He points to one of the many cracks in the walls of the hovel. Blanche looks through it, and says, " I

see only a man " — Saltabadil, whom of course she does not
know.

Triboulet, in a low voice, bids her wait a moment. Just then
the King, dressed plainly as an officer, appears in the room, having entered it from inside the house. Blanche recognises him with
a shudder, and during the whole of the following scene looks
through the crack in the wall, hearing and seeing everything that
passes, and pitiably shaken. The King, in the course of his amorous adventures, has come upon Saltabadil's good-looking sister,
Maguelonne, whom he now demands to see. He gaily sings the
celebrated stanza written by the historical Francis I:

> " Souvent femme varie,
>   Bien fol est qui s'ye fie.
>   Une femme souvent
>   N'est qu'une plume au vent."

(" Variable is woman; he is a fool who puts faith in her; woman
is like a feather on the wind.")

Saltabadil places on the table a bottle of wine and a glass and
strikes two blows on the ceiling with the pommel of his long sword
by way of calling his sister down; when she has entered he goes
out by the door in the wall, closing it after him. He sees Triboulet,
who comes towards him with a mysterious air and whispers something to him. Blanche, who is still intently observing what is going on inside the hut, does not hear their conversation. " Is he to
live? " asks Saltabadil. " Your man is in our hands — in there."
Triboulet sends him away for a while, and Saltabadil disappears
slowly behind the parapet overlooking the river. Meanwhile inside
the hovel the King is carrying on a flirtation with Maguelonne,
whom finally he takes on his knee, addressing her in low tones.

Blanche can bear no more; she turns, pale and trembling, towards Triboulet, who asks her how the idea of revenge appeals to
her now. She has been so distressed and horrified that she consents, for the moment, to her father doing whatever he will, and
Triboulet thanks her with a wild cry of joy. He discloses his plan
to her; she is to hurry home, change into male costume, which he

has already provided for her, take money and a horse, and without losing an instant set out for Evreux, where he will join her the day but one following; above all, she is on no account to return here, for something terrible is about to happen. Frozen with fear, she begs him to come with her, but he refuses, and after embracing her sends her away with a final strict injunction to do his bidding.

When Blanche has gone, Triboulet makes a sign to Saltabadil, who returns. The light is now fading fast. Triboulet counts out ten gold crowns to Saltabadil, promising him the remaining ten when the deed has been done. " Have no fear," says Saltabadil; " it will rain within the hour, and the storm and my sister between them will keep him here." Triboulet promises him to return at midnight. Saltabadil assures him there is no necessity for that, as he himself can throw the corpse into the Seine; but Triboulet having told him that he wishes to perform this agreeable office himself, Saltabadil promises to deliver the body to him in a sack. " All shall be done as you desire," he says. " But what is the name of this young man? " " His name? " replies Triboulet; " and would you know mine also? His name is Crime, and mine is Chastisement." Saltabadil, left alone, muses to himself for a moment on the queer ways of mankind (he is a philosopher and an artist in his way), and then re-enters the hut.

Thunder is heard in the distance. The King does not mind the coming storm in the least, as he intends, he says, to occupy Saltabadil's chamber that night; Saltabadil is graciously informed that he can sleep in the stable, or go to the devil, or do whatever else he likes. Maguelonne, who has a sort of feeling for this gay, impudent young gallant, appears to sense a coming evil, and in a low voice she tells him to go away; but he laughs at her. Saltabadil lights a lamp and conducts the King to the squalid upper room, where he leaves him.

The King, who is very tired, is seen to stretch himself out on the wretched bed, where he soon falls asleep. In the lower room Saltabadil and Maguelonne, while the tempest rages outside, now discuss the situation. Maguelonne is unwilling that harm should come to so charming a young man; but Saltabadil puts forward the unanswerable argument of ten gold pieces in the pocket and ten more to come; and at his bidding Maguelonne ascends the stairs and comes back with the sleeping King's sword.

Meanwhile Blanche, dressed in a man's riding-clothes, with boots and spurs, has again appeared outside, and once more, through a crack in the wall, she listens to the gruesome conversation. Again Maguelonne appeals to her brother not to kill the young officer, but Saltabadil's only reply is to push towards her an old sack and order her to mend it.

Maguelonne suggests as an alternative scheme that Saltabadil should kill the hunchback when he returns, but Saltabadil indignantly rejects the proposition as a slur on his professional honour: " What do you take me for, sister? Am I a bandit, am I a thief, to kill a client who pays me? " Maguelonne's next suggestion is that he shall fill the sack with a faggot of timber; but this also is rejected by Saltabadil as impracticable: the client could not be so easily imposed upon. As a last resort Maguelonne, determined to defend the supposed officer, places herself before the staircase and bars the passage to her brother, who is thus forced to reopen the discussion. Finally he proposes a compromise: Triboulet will be returning at midnight; if before that hour someone else should come, a passing traveller or whoever it may be, Saltabadil will kill him and place his body in the sack; the client, on such a night of tempest and darkness as this, will not know one corpse from another.

Blanche, who has heard the whole of this conversation with growing terror, tries to make up her mind to sacrifice herself for the King, but finds it very hard to die by violence before she is sixteen. The clock strikes a quarter to twelve. Saltabadil, declaring that time presses, is about to ascend the staircase to do the deed, when Maguelonne, with tears in her eyes, implores him to wait a little longer. These tears decide Blanche. " What! " she says, " this woman weeps, while I, who could succour him, remain here! Since he no longer loves me, there is nothing for me but to die, so let me die for him."

But the thought of the physical details of the killing terrifies her: " If only I knew how I should be struck! If only I would not suffer! They may strike me on the face! " Steadying herself by a great effort, she at last summons up courage enough to knock at the door. Unaware, of course, that she can hear them, Saltabadil and Maguelonne discuss this fortunate chance that has befallen them. " It is a young man," says the sister, as Blanche demands shelter for the night. " He will pay a fine sum for it! " says Salta-badil grimly, in Blanche's hearing; and Maguelonne answers, " Yes, the night will be a long one! " Saltabadil asks his sister to give him his knife, which, in sight of Blanche, he sharpens.

The pair hurriedly make their plans; Maguelonne is to open the door, while Saltabadil conceals himself behind it. The door is opened and Blanche enters, her last horrified thought being that the sister is helping the brother in the crime. " Pardon me, O God! " she cries. " Pardon me, my father! " As she steps over the threshold of the hut Saltabadil's arm is seen to lift the dag-ger, and the curtain falls.

In the fifth act Triboulet, who has returned at midnight, re-ceives the sack from Saltabadil, and pours out over it a long mon-ologue of triumph over his enemy. He bends over the sack, and in the frenzy of his hatred strikes the corpse within it. Just as he has dragged the sack to the parapet in order to throw it into the river the door of the hovel opens; Maguelonne comes out, looks round her anxiously, re-enters the hut, and returns with the King, to whom she conveys by signs that the coast is clear. She goes in again and closes the door, while the King takes the path she has indicated to him.

At the moment Triboulet is about to throw the sack into the water he hears the King's voice in the distance singing once more his gay " Souvent femme varie." At first his dazed mind takes it to be an hallucination; but when he hears the song a second time he realises that somehow he has been duped. He returns to the house, which he finds completely closed except for the upper windows. He runs his hands anxiously over the sack, for it is so dark that he cannot see anything, though his touch has told him that there is a human body within it, and one with spurs. (The

King, it will be remembered, was in officer's dress.) He draws his poniard and feverishly rips open the sack from top to bottom, but still cannot distinguish what it contains. At last, by a flash of lightning, he recognises the face of his daughter. She is still alive, but in answer to his passionate entreaties to be told how this catastrophe has come about she can only say faintly, " It is all my fault; I deceived you. I loved him too much; I die for him."

The frenzied father rushes to the ferry bell and strikes it furiously; a crowd rushes in, among them a coachman with his whip in his hand. Triboulet clutches him convulsively and begs him to seize him and place his head under the coach wheels. Then, a reaction coming, he refuses to believe that Blanche is dead; he takes the body in his arms and holds it tenderly like a mother holding a sleeping child. At last a physician enters. Triboulet appeals to him to say that she has only fainted. The physician answers, " She is dead! " and Triboulet, with a wild cry of " I have killed my child," falls insensible.

Verdi seems to have made the acquaintance of Victor Hugo's play about 1849. The violent subject appealed instantly to his sombre nature, and he gave his friends no rest till a libretto had been constructed for him by Piave; the title of the opera was to be *La Maladizione* (" The Curse ").

Difficulties soon arose with the censorship, as they had done in Paris in 1832, when, immediately after the production of the play, the Théâtre-Français was forbidden by the authorities to continue to perform it. Victor Hugo brought an action in defence of his right of free speech, and the affair created the greatest excitement at the time. The story was no doubt rather highly spiced for some tastes, but the charge of immorality — the ostensible reason for the ban upon the drama — was probably only a pretext; the real cause of offence seems to have been the representation of a French monarch in so unflattering a guise. Victor Hugo, in a vigorous preface to the published edition of the play, defended himself eloquently against the charge of immorality, and the passage dealing with Triboulet remains to this day the best analysis of that complex character.

" This," says Hugo, " is the basis of the play. Triboulet is

deformed; Triboulet is unhealthy; Triboulet is a court buffoon —
a triple misery that makes him malicious. Triboulet hates the King
because he is the King, the noblemen because they are noblemen,
and men in general because they do not all have a hump on their
backs. His sole pastime is to keep the courtiers and the King for
ever clashing with each other, using the stronger to break the
weaker. He depraves the King, corrupts him, brutalises him; he
urges him to tyranny, to folly, to vice; he unleashes him among
the families of his courtiers, incessantly pointing out a wife to seduce, a sister to abduct, a daughter to dishonour. The King in
the hands of Triboulet is merely an all-powerful puppet who
smashes in pieces every life that the buffoon gives him to play
with.

"One day, during a fête, at the very moment when Triboulet
is urging the King to abduct the wife of M. de Cossé, M. de Saint-
Vallier forces his way into the presence of the King and reproaches
him before them all with the dishonour of Diane de Poitiers. Triboulet derides and insults this father whose daughter has been
taken from him by the King. The father raises his arm and curses
Triboulet. From this the whole action of the piece is evolved. The
true subject of the drama is *The Malediction of M. de Saint-Vallier*.

"Listen. We are in the second act. On whom has this malediction fallen? On Triboulet the King's fool? No. On the Triboulet
who is a man, who is a father, who has a heart, who has a daughter. Triboulet has a daughter; everything centres in that. Triboulet has only his daughter in the whole world. He conceals her from
everyone's eyes in a secluded house in a deserted quarter. The
more he spreads contagion and debauchery in the town, the more
he keeps his daughter isolated and walled up. He brings up his
child in innocence, faith, and modesty. His greatest fear is that
she shall be touched by evil, for he, the soul of malice, knows too
well all the suffering that evil brings. Well, the malediction of the
old man will strike Triboulet in the only thing in the world that he
loves — his daughter.

"This same King whom Triboulet is always inciting to rape will

ravish Triboulet of his daughter; the buffoon will be struck down
by Providence exactly in the same manner as M. de Saint-Vallier
was. Then, his daughter seduced and lost to him, he will set a
snare for the King to achieve his vengeance, but it is his daughter
who will fall into the snare. Thus Triboulet has two pupils, the
King and his daughter, the King whom he trains up to vice, his
daughter whom he brings up in virtue. The one will be the destruction of the other. He means to abduct Madame de Cossé
for the King, but it is his own daughter whom he helps to abduct.
He means to assassinate the King to avenge his daughter, but it
is his daughter whom he slays. There is no half-way house in this
chastisement; the malediction of Diane's father is accomplished
on the father of Blanche. It is not for me to say whether this is or
is not a dramatic conception, but most emphatically it is a moral
one."

It was no doubt the political rather than the moral implications
of the story that perturbed the Austrian censor also. (Italy at
that time, it will be remembered, was under the domination of
Austria.) During the years 1848 and 1849 a revolutionary spirit
was stirring over the greater part of Europe, and it was not considered advisable that a king, even one who had lived some three
hundred years before, should be shown to the Italian people in so
unfavourable a light.

For a time it looked as if Verdi and his librettists would have
to give up their plan; but Verdi was thoroughly in love with the
subject — he used to say in after years that *Rigoletto* was one of
the best libretti that had ever been given him — and he obstinately
refused to set any other text for the impresario who had commissioned the opera. A compromise was at last arranged. The action was transferred from the Paris of the sixteenth century to
the Mantua of about the same period; and Francis I became the
Duke of Mantua. The names of all the other characters were
changed; Triboulet became Rigoletto, Saltabadil became Sparafucile (*fucile*, a gun, *sparare*, to discharge), M. de Saint-Vallier
became Count Monterone, Blanche became Gilda, Maguelonne
became Maddalena, and so on. Everybody's face being saved by

these simple means, the opera was produced at Venice on the 11th March, 1851, and quickly became a European success.

The opera follows the prose play so closely that in the remaining portion of this analysis we need dwell, for the most part, only on the points of difference between the two, and on the more specifically musical effects. Verdi and his librettist were quick to see that some of the most effective situations in the play could be touched in with very much higher lights and deeper shadows by means of music.

For example, the father's curse could be made much more sinister by means of the brass of the orchestra; far more dramatic point could be given to the ballad sung by the King in the tavern, and again as he is leaving it; while only an art such as music could do complete justice to the double scene inside and outside the hut in Victor Hugo's fourth act, for only in music can a number of characters all say different things at the same time with results agreeable to the listeners. Seldom has the superiority of the musical over the spoken drama in certain respects been more conclusively demonstrated than in the splendid quartet in the third act of *Rigoletto*.

The overture commences with the grim motive of the Curse in the brass:

Beginning softly, it is worked up to a tornado of tone, and succeeded by a wailing motive:

after which the theme of the Curse is heard again. The curtain
rising, we see a brilliantly lit room in the ducal palace, with other
rooms opening off it at the back. In these latter there is dancing,
and a number of festive strains reach us successively from a band
behind the scenes:

The Duke comes forward accompanied by one of his courtiers,
Borsa, whom he tells of the pretty girl he has lately been pursuing,
who lives in an obscure by-way, in a house to which a mysterious
man is admitted each evening. The Duke sings a gay song, in
which he professes his contempt for the lovers who remain faithful to one love; his own rôle is that of the bee who goes sipping
from flower to flower:

Que - sta o quel - la............. per me pa - ri
In my heart all............ are e - qual - ly

so - no A quant' al - - tre d'in - tor - no....
che - rish'd. Ev - 'ry thought of ex - clu - sion...

.... d'in - tor - no mi ve - - do.
.... with - in me I smo - ther.

To the courtly strains of a minuet the Duke makes love to the Countess of Ceprano (Madame de Cossé in the play), and as the pair go out arm-in-arm, Rigoletto makes malicious sport of the fretful Ceprano. After he has left the stage a peregodino (peregourdine) is danced, after which the lively music of the commencement of the opera is heard again as Marullo enters and tells his fellow-courtiers, with great glee, of his discovery that the ill-favoured Rigoletto has a pretty mistress. The Duke returns with Rigoletto, and the buffoon again rouses the anger of the courtiers by his malice; they express their sentiments towards him in a chorus in which they swear to have vengeance. The following quotation gives, in skeleton, an idea of the structure:

Ah sem - pre tu spin - gi lo
Ah yes,...... of thy jests...... we

Ven - det - - ta!
Yes, ven - - geance!

scher - zo all' e - stre - mo, quell',
all......... have grown wea - ry, the

Ven - det - - - ta!
Yes, ven - - - geance!

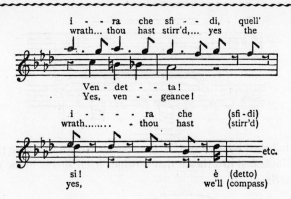

The top voice is that of the Duke, warning Rigoletto that some day his mocking tongue will get him into trouble; the "Vendetta!" is the cry of the courtiers; while Rigoletto, in a part not shown here, derides them, safe, as he thinks, in the protection of his master. But the dancers flock in from the other room, and for the moment all is gaiety once more.

There is a sudden change of colour as old Monterone forces his way in, to reproach the Duke with the seduction of his daughter. Rigoletto takes upon himself the agreeable task of answering and deriding the old man, and once more we see the superiority of music over speech for certain dramatic purposes; the dramatist can make use only of words, while the musician can call into play also the graphic resources of the orchestra, which is here an extra voice taunting the unhappy old man. Monterone delivers his curse, under which Rigoletto cowers; and the act closes with a chorus of the courtiers, in which we can detect signs that they too have been a little unnerved by the episode. Finally Monterone is led out between two halberdiers, and the curtain falls.

The next scene is outside Rigoletto's house, as described in the analysis of Hugo's play. Rigoletto, enveloped in his cloak, enters, still brooding upon Monterone's curse:

He is followed by Sparafucile, the sinister nature of whose profession is indicated in a theme that unwinds itself slowly in the muted lower strings:

This theme is worked up in the orchestra with a gruesome suggestiveness that would be impossible to words alone. Sparafucile gives Rigoletto his name in a phrase that, in its blending of the sinister and the bluff, is very characteristic of him:

and reiterating his promise of willing help should his services be required, he goes slowly off.

Rigoletto, left alone, bitterly compares himself with the assassin; the other stabs with his sword, he with his tongue. The malediction occurs to him once more, and he pours out his hatred upon the Duke and the courtiers, who, for their sport, have made him the vile, self-loathing thing he is, with a soul as crooked as his body. The music takes a lighter turn as Gilda comes towards him in the courtyard. She greets him lovingly, and implores him, as she has evidently done before, to tell her something of her mother, whom she has never known. The buffoon tells her how, hideous and malicious as he was, he was loved by a beautiful angel, who died soon after Gilda was born; and the pair indulge themselves to the full in the luxury of grief, mostly expressed in the sobbing phrases in which Verdi specialised at that time.

Rigoletto still refuses to give his daughter his name or any other information about himself, as he is surrounded, he says, by enemies whose loathing for him he secretly dreads. He feverishly makes Gilda promise to respect his wish that she shall not be seen abroad, and Gilda, with a little pang of conscience, conceals from him the fact that she has lately been followed by a handsome young stranger. As Rigoletto opens the door to look out nervously into the street, the Duke slips into the courtyard, where he soon recognises his jester. Rigoletto bids his daughter a tender farewell and departs.

Gilda now expresses to old Giovanna (Bérarde) her remorse at having deceived her father, but Giovanna, who has already been bribed by the Duke, makes light of her compunction. The Duke emerges from his hiding-place, and having dismissed Giovanna makes ardent love to Gilda, commencing with an aria that is one of the favourite show pieces of the Italian tenor who happens to be sure of his notes round about the high B flat:

E il sol dell' a - ni - ma, la vi-ta è a-mo - re, Sua
Sun of the soul, a di-vine in - spi - ra - tion, Is

vo - ce è il pal - pi - to del no - stro co - re,
love, that par - a-dise, thro' all cre - a - tion.

Gilda, in return, pours out her maiden ecstasies with a due regard for the established rights of a coloratura soprano. Giovanna returns hastily, having heard voices in the street; and the Duke makes a hurried exit through the house, leaving Gilda to sing her famous rhapsody to Gualtier Maldé, by which name the supposed poor young student has made himself known to her. This is the famous aria " Caro nome," which commences thus:

Ca - ro no - me che il mio

cor Fe - sti pri - mo - pal - pi - tar.

It is too often made, especially in the concert-room, a mere vehicle for technical display. It is not only this, however; it is in addition an admirable piece of dramatic expression, the spontaneous outpouring of a young heart that feels for the first time the ecstasy of love. The following variation upon the main melody, for example:

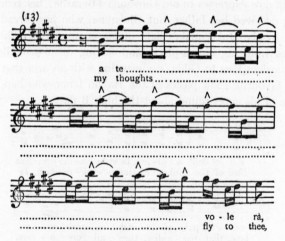

a te...
my thoughts...........................

vo - le rà,
fly to thee,

is not merely coloratura; in its delighted flutterings it is psychologically true to the character of the young girl. She goes into the house, reappears (to sing a coda to her aria) on the verandah with a lantern, by the light of which she follows her lover down the

street, and finally makes a very effective exit, her voice trailing off
into the distance.

Rigoletto, still with the curse in his mind, returns in the darkness and is accosted by the courtiers, who set about their conspiracy to the following theme in the orchestra:

which, throughout this scene, makes a mysterious background for
the furtive dialogue. The masking of Rigoletto and the abduction
of Gilda follow as in Hugo, except that the conspirators, true to
the tradition of Italian opera, do not carry out their plan at one
stroke, but indulge in a chorus on the subject, in which, at some
length, and with a fair body of tone, they exhort each other to
be not only cautious but swift and quiet. As Rigoletto, having
dragged out Giovanna, realises what has happened, he falls fainting to the ground, while the orchestra blares out the inexorable
motive of the Curse.

The second act opens in the ante-chamber of the palace, where
the Duke is lamenting his loss of Gilda the night before, just
when he thought he had won her. He had returned to Rigoletto's
house after his hasty flight, but found it locked up and apparently
deserted. He expresses his determination to rescue her in a short
aria that shows a more serious side to his character than we are

conscious of in Hugo's drama. The courtiers enter, and in joyous accents tell him of the success of their exploit of the night before — how they fooled Rigoletto with a story that it was Ceprano's wife they were abducting, and then made off with his own pretty mistress, whom they have brought to the palace. The Duke receives the news with joy, and his lyrical outburst once more indicates that he is more truly in love with Gilda than the King is in *Le Roi s'amuse*. The seriousness of his rapture, indeed, somewhat puzzles his courtiers, who have never seen him in this mood before.

As the Duke goes out hastily through the centre door, Rigoletto enters, trying to conceal his inquietude under an air of gaiety. This is his great scene in the opera. While the courtiers secretly amuse themselves at his expense, he passes through every phase of anger and entreaty, the many changes of mood following rapidly upon each other. The prevarications of the courtiers with the messenger from the Duchess at last put him on the track of the truth. Cursing them, he attempts to make his way through the centre door, but is repulsed; nor are his supplications of any more avail.

At last Gilda rushes out from the room on the left and throws herself into the arms of her father. In pathetic accents she tells him the story of her innocent deception of him and her present betrayal. He comforts the poor child, and tells her that they must leave the palace that day. Just then Monterone passes across the stage, accompanied by the halberdiers who are conducting him to prison. His brief, bitter comment that the Duke, for all his sins, is apparently protected by heaven is supplemented by a wild outburst from Rigoletto, who promises to take vengeance for both of them.

It is more particularly in the third act (corresponding to Victor Hugo's fourth) that we see the advantage the musician has over the poet in the treatment of a subject of this kind. The accumulation of horrors, the contrast and combination of effects, the suggestion of atmosphere, particularly during the storm — in all these points the opera has a tragic power to which the original drama cannot lay claim.

The scene is that described in connection with *Le Roi s'amuse,* with the substitution of Mantua and the Mincio for Paris and the Seine. There is a brief dialogue outside the inn between Rigoletto and his daughter, in which the latter confesses that she still loves the Duke. Bidden by her father to look through a fissure in the wall, she sees the Duke, who retires within the tavern, where he sings the famous " La donna è mobile " — the Italian equivalent of King Francis's " Souvent femme varie ":

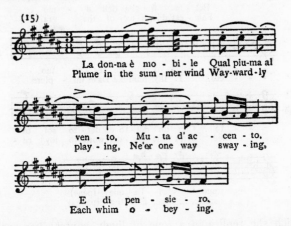

It is an admirable expression of the careless gaiety of the young Duke, who, for all the ardour of his pursuit of women, has no illusions as to the stability of their affections. The rhythm of this song was an original one for the time, and Verdi had a premonition that it would become immensely popular. The greatest pains were taken to prevent the song becoming known before the first performance; the tune was even kept from the tenor's knowledge until very near the performance, and he was threatened with dire pains and penalties if he sang it outside the theatre. Verdi was right; the tune was in the mouth of all Venice the next day, in that of all Italy the following week, and of all Europe in a very little while after.

Inside and outside the tavern everything takes place very much as in Victor Hugo. Sparafucile, after a word with Rigoletto, goes

off in the direction of the river while the Duke makes love to the
pretty Maddalena, a pert coquette who fences dexterously with
him. The climax of the scene comes with the famous quartet.
First of all the Duke breaks out into a broad melody in praise of
Maddalena:

(16)

Bel - la fi - glia dèll' a - mo - -
Fair - est daugh - ter of the   gra - -

- - - re, Schia - vo són de' vez - zi tuo -
- - - ces, I thy hum - ble slave im - plore

- - - i; Con un det - to un det - to sol tu
thee. With one ten - der word to joy re -

etc.

puó - - i Le mie (pene)
- - - store...... me, End the (pangs)

to which she replies in a tone of lively banter; her sparkling
phrases are interrupted by interjections from Gilda on the other
side of the wall:

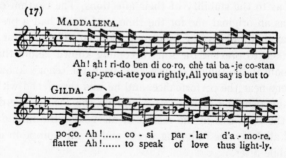

(17)

MADDALENA.

Ah! ah! ri - do ben di co - ro, chè tai ba - je co - stan
I ap - pre - ci - ate you rightly, All you say is but to

GILDA.

po - co. Ah!...... co - si par - lar d'a - mo - re.
flatter Ah!...... to speak of love thus light - ly.

Rigoletto joins in, gloomily bidding his daughter forget her love
for the Duke, and the four voices are woven into a masterly piece

of writing that has been the admiration of opera-goers for three-
quarters of a century. As a musical ensemble it falls deliciously on
the ear, yet, for all its smoothness and its technical skill, the mood
of each of the characters that takes part in it is truthfully depicted
— the despair of Gilda, the brazen light-heartedness of Maddalena, the amorous passion of the Duke, and the gloom and persistence of purpose of Rigoletto.

The jester sends Gilda home, bidding her take horse to Verona;
Sparafucile returns, and the murder is arranged and part paid for.
As Sparafucile re-enters the inn, the tempest begins to gather;
throughout the scene its howling is suggested by the ascending
and descending chromatic harmonies sung by tenors and basses
with closed mouths behind the scenes:

(This quotation shows the theme in the more extended form it
assumes in the latter course of the scene.) To the accompaniment
of this eerie moaning the situation works itself out as in Victor
Hugo. Singing a few lines of " La donna è mobile," the Duke falls
off to sleep and Sparafucile and Maddalena indulge in their gruesome dialogue in the hearing of Gilda, who by this time has returned in male attire, booted and spurred. Sparafucile, to the accompaniment of intermittent thunder and lightning, promises
Maddalena, in a nervous, savage phrase, that the first new-comer
to the inn shall pay the penalty for the Duke:

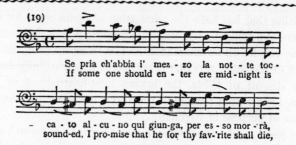

and the three voices blend for a moment, that of Gilda rising high above the others in a despairing wail:

In accordance with musical rather than strictly dramatic exiger.
cies, all this is repeated and carried to a tense climax; finally Gilda enters the tavern, and we are left to imagine the tragedy that takes place in the dark.

A brief orchestral interlude depicts first the raging of the storm at its height, then its gradual decline and final passing away, except for an occasional rumble of thunder and flash of lightning in the distance. Rigoletto returns and receives the sack from Sparafucile, but has hardly begun to give expression to his triumph when, in the distance, the departing Duke is heard singing once more his " La donna è mobile." The long monologue in which, in the play, Rigoletto savagely apostrophises his supposedly dead enemy is not included in the opera; we have in its place a thoroughly Italian duet between the father and the daughter, in which the latter first implores Rigoletto's forgiveness for having deceived him, and then promises to pray for him in heaven, by her mother's side:

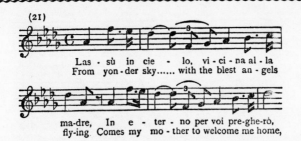

(21)

Las · sù in cie - lo, vi - ci - na al · la
From yon - der sky...... with the blest an - gels

ma-dre, In e - ter - no per voi pre-ghe-rò,
fly-ing. Comes my mo - ther to welcome me home,

while the broken buffoon sobs out his anguish and despair, and at last falls senseless on the body of his child.

LA TRAVIATA

THE theme of Redemption by Love was not the Wagnerian specialty it is generally supposed to be. Victor Hugo had already touched upon it in his play *Marion Delorme* (1829), and it obtained an enormous vogue in the eighteen-fifties through the play of the younger Dumas, *La Dame aux Camélias,* in which a beautiful courtesan engaged the sympathies of the time first of all by loving greatly, then by dying opportunely and gracefully.

Alexandre Dumas's novel was published in 1848, and was so much to the taste of the French public that in the following year he treated the subject again in the form of a play. This was accepted by a Paris theatre, but it closed its doors before the play could be performed. The work was then accepted by the Vaudeville, but owing to the usual difficulties with the censor and with certain highly placed political personalities it was not until the 6th February, 1852, that it was produced. Owing to the nature of its subject, it was many years before it was thought safe to give the play in England.

Marguerite Gautier, the Lady of the Camellias, was drawn from a fashionable courtesan of the period whom Dumas had known well. Her real name was Alphonsine Plessis, which she changed, for professional purposes, to the more high-sounding one of Marie Duplessis. " She was tall and very slender," says Dumas in a preface to the play, " with a pink-and-white complexion. Her head was small, her eyes were long, like those of a Japanese, but refined and vivacious, her lips were cherry-red, and she had the loveliest teeth in the world. She looked like a piece of Dresden china.

"In 1844, when I saw her for the first time, she was at the summit of her opulence and in the full flower of her beauty. She died in 1847, of consumption, at the age of twenty-three. She was one of the last and the few courtesans who had a heart; no doubt that is why she died so young. She lacked neither intelligence nor disinterestedness. She died poor in a luxurious apartment, that had been seized by her creditors. She had a native distinction, she dressed with taste and walked with grace, almost with nobility. She was sometimes taken for a woman of good society; to-day [Dumas was writing in 1867, and had a poor opinion of the contemporary fashionable world] the mistake would have been general. She had been brought up on a farm."

Dumas goes on to tell us that Marie Duplessis did not have all the pathetic adventures he attributes to Marguerite Gautier, though no doubt she would have liked to have them. "If she did not sacrifice her all to Armand," Dumas continues in his witty way, "it was because Armand did not wish her to. To her great regret, she acted only the first and the second acts of the play. These she commenced afresh again and again, as Penelope recommenced her weaving; with this difference, that it was in the day that Marie destroyed what she had begun in the night."

The camellias were Dumas's own invention, but readers of the novel attributed them to the original of the character; and the tomb of Alphonsine Plessis in the Montmartre cemetery was surmounted by a sculptured bunch of camellias in a glass.

Dumas's play is in five acts. In the first, we see Marguerite in her own home in Paris, in the company of a number of women of her own type and their protectors. Opposite to her lives a friend, Prudence, whom, through the open window, she invites to supper. Prudence replies that she has two young men with her who have asked her to supper; one of them, Gaston Rieux, Marguerite already knows; the other is a friend of Gaston. Marguerite invites the three to supper in her own house, and the young friend, Armand Duval, is presented to her.

He is, it seems, the son of a M. Duval, a Receiver-General; his mother has been dead three years. Gaston and Prudence tell Marguerite that although Armand has never met her before he has been in love with her for the last two years, going wherever he can hear her spoken of by those who know her, and lately, when she was ill in bed for three months, he had called every day to enquire after her, though without leaving his name. Marguerite remembers this romantic incident, and calls Armand to her to thank him.

After supper, Marguerite is dancing a polka when she suddenly stops, out of breath. She assures the others that it is only a passing indisposition, and, begging them not to allow it to interfere with their pleasure, sends them into another room. She looks at herself in the glass, is horrified at her paleness, gives a sigh, puts her head in her hands, and leans her elbows on the chimney-piece. She is roused from her mournful reverie by Armand, who has returned quietly. He declares his love for her and implores her to take care of her health, as a first condition of which she must abandon the feverish life she lives at present; and he asks to be allowed to take care of her like a brother.

She likes the idealistic and obviously inexperienced young man, but tells him it is quite impossible for her to abandon her present mode of living, and advises him, in his own interests, to think no more of her, for she is nervous, sick, and sad — or else gay with a gaiety that is sadder than melancholy itself — and exceedingly extravagant.

Armand and she had better be just friends; he has a good heart and is deserving of love, but is too young and too sensitive for the world in which Marguerite lives; let him choose some other woman for his mistress, or else marry a virtuous girl. As for herself, she has never loved anyone. He receives, however, permission to call again, and when he has left her it is evident that the sincerity of his affection has somewhat moved her.

In the second act, which also takes place in Marguerite's house in Paris, she proposes that he shall spend the summer with her in a country house she has acquired from an elderly duke who is one of her admirers. The high-minded young man at first rejects the proposal, but Marguerite assures him that the duke's interest in her is of the purely platonic kind, and after various revulsions of mood on the part of each of them the matter is arranged. Marguerite is conscious of loving for the first time; she is weary of her hectic life in Paris, and she is fascinated by the prospect of an idyll in the country.

In the third act we see the lovers in their nest at Auteuil, where, after a fortnight of bliss, Armand accidentally learns from Prudence that Marguerite is disposing of her diamonds and horses in order to meet the expenses of the establishment.

Armand has had an intuition that something of the kind was happening, and already he has arranged with his notary to sell the reversion of his interest under his mother's will; the papers have been prepared, and he sets off at once to Paris to complete the transaction, bidding Prudence conceal from Marguerite the reason for his absence.

To a friend, Nichette, Marguerite later confides that so ideally happy is she with Armand that she has no desire to resume her old life in Paris. She proposes, with the money acquired by the sale of her luxurious establishment there, to take a small lodging in town for herself and Armand, where they can live quietly and simply, " the world forgetting, by the world forgot "; their summers they will spend in some modest dwelling in the country.

A visitor is announced, whom Marguerite assumes to be her business man, bringing her papers for signature. It proves, however, to be M. Georges Duval, the father of Armand. He is a little distant and uncomplimentary to her at first, for he believes her to be an evil woman ruining his son by her luxury; the father has received from his lawyer a letter advising him that Armand has made an assignment of part of his income to Marguerite.

She soon convinces him that she has known nothing of this, and, handing him the act of sale of her diamonds, carriages, and so on, proves to him that he has been mistaken in his estimate of her character and of the relations between her and his son. But while welcoming the revelation that she really loves Armand, none the less he has to ask a sacrifice of her. His only other child, a daughter, is about to marry a young man of good family whose relations threaten to break off the engagement unless Armand, by abandoning Marguerite, wipes out the stain that this liaison has brought upon the Duvals.

At first Marguerite does not quite understand; she thinks that all that is necessary is that she and Armand shall separate, for respectability's sake, till the marriage is over, and then resume their association. M. Duval makes it clear to her that the separation must be final, and at last, with her heart breaking, she consents, though she rejects the father's proposal that she shall bring about a rupture by telling Armand she no longer loves him; this, she says, he will never believe.

Having dismissed M. Duval, she is engaged in the difficult task of writing an explanatory letter to Armand when the young man himself enters. He has received a letter from his father, telling him that his intrigue has been discovered, and that M. Duval will see him that evening to have an explanation of the affair with him. Armand is dependent upon his father, but if necessary, he informs Marguerite bravely, he will work.

He is a little curious as to the letter Marguerite is writing; but she puts him off by saying that it contains something about which she cannot speak to him directly; it is a proof of her love that she is giving him, and she begs him not to ask her anything more about it. He assumes that it has to do with the sale of her property in Paris; and he now tells her that he has already heard of her sacrifice on his behalf, so that her secret is a secret no longer. She bursts into tears and leaves him, saying she will go into the garden while he has the interview with his father.

A little time after, convinced that his father will not call that evening, he sends a servant to ask Marguerite to return, but discovers that she has left the house. Then a messenger brings him a letter from Marguerite; having read it he gives an angry cry; turning round, he sees his father, and throws himself sobbing into his arms.

The fourth act takes place in the house of Olympe, a friend of Marguerite's and of the same profession. Armand enters, and re-

ceives with glacial calm the news that Marguerite is expected at
the party. She is now living, it seems, with a M. de Varville, and
her existence is more feverish than ever; Prudence, who tells
Armand this, is afraid, indeed, that her way of living is in a fair
way to shortening her days.

Marguerite enters later with Varville, and smiles timidly at
Armand, who gives her a coldly courteous recognition. Varville
and Armand engage in a game of cards, and Armand wins persistently; the two men are on the verge of a quarrel, and Armand
promises his opponent his revenge later, in any way the latter
may choose.

When the company has left the salon for an inner room, Marguerite and Armand are left together. She implores him to leave
the house before he provokes Varville too far, for she does not
want a duel on her account. He consents to do so on one condition
— that she will leave with him. This she declares to be impossible.

He entreats her passionately to fly from Paris with him and resume their old quiet life together, but she can only reply that an
abyss separates them, and she implores him to forget her. Seeing
no other way out of her difficulty, in her distraction she tells
him she loves Varville. Throwing her to the ground, Armand goes
to the door and recalls the guests from the other salon. " You see
this woman? " he cries. " Do you know what she has done? She
sold all she possessed to live with me, so much she loved me. That
was fine, was it not? And do you know what I have done? I behaved like a cur. I accepted her sacrifice without giving her anything in return. But it is not yet too late for me to repent, and I
have returned to make everything good. Be witnesses, all of
you, that I no longer owe anything to this woman! " and he
throws a handful of banknotes in her face. Marguerite gives a cry
and falls back senseless; Varville calls Armand a coward, and the
guests are seen separating the two men as the curtain falls.

The fifth act shows us Marguerite in her bed; she is very ill,
and, though the doctor doles out the usual professional comfort to
her, we gather that her days are numbered. She takes from her
bosom and reads aloud a letter from M. Georges Duval, in which

he tells her that he has heard of the duel between his son and M. de Varville; the latter has been wounded, but is now out of danger. Touched by her devotion and her sacrifice, M. Duval has written to Armand, telling him the whole truth; and his son will come to ask her pardon for both of them. It is six weeks since she received this letter, and there is still no word from Armand.

He enters shortly afterwards, full of remorse, and passionately implores her forgiveness; his father, he tells her, knows her now for what she is, and, the sister having been married, he consents to their union. The happy Marguerite calls for her outdoor clothes, but the effort to walk is too much for her; she falls exhausted on the sofa, and, recognising now that her fate is sealed, she gives Armand a little medallion with her portrait, which, if ever he should marry, he is to give to his wife, telling her that it is the picture of one who prays daily in heaven for them both. She dies happy, and the last words pronounced upon her are those of her friend Nichette, who has arrived during the death-scene — " Sleep in peace, Marguerite! Much will be forgiven you, for you have greatly loved! "

La Traviata was a failure at its first performance (Venice, 6th March, 1853). For this the singers are mainly held responsible — the soprano in particular; she was exceedingly stout, and the audience rocked with laughter in the last act, when the doctor announced that she was in the last stages of consumption and had only a few hours to live.

In spite of the Lord Chamberlain's ban on Dumas's play, the director of Her Majesty's Theatre seems to have had no obstacle placed in the way of his producing the opera there in 1856. But there was a great outcry in some quarters against the " immorality " of it. Clergymen preached against it, *The Times* stormed at it; and no doubt all this publicity was an excellent thing for the box office.

Henry Chorley boldly suggested that the excitement was worked up by interested parties; indeed, one of the managers of the theatre publicly defended the story " as conveying a salutary warning to the young men of our time." Chorley's objection to the opera was not so much that it was immoral as that Dumas's play was by its very nature unfit for music. " Consumption for one who is to sing! A ballet with a lame Sylphide would be as rational! " But rational or not, the opera soon became a universal favourite, and is still one of the most popular works in the Italian repertory.

Dumas's *La Dame aux Camélias* is good, sound theatrical stuff; though the characters, for a great part of the time, do and say the sort of thing that is done and said only in the theatre, the stage effectiveness of it all cannot be denied. Necessarily many of the details of the action and a good deal of the subtlety of the psychologising disappear in the opera, for music has to simplify both the incidents and the motives of a drama and concentrate upon the salient emotional moments of it. Verdi's heroine reasons less than Dumas's, but is much more emotional and impulsive.

Verdi was very much alive to the dramatic developments of his time, and there can be no doubt that he meant *La Traviata* to be the contemporary musical equivalent of the play. At its first production the opera was placed in the then present time, and one of the reasons for its unfavourable reception is said to have been the revolt of the Italian audience against the unaccustomed spectacle of operatic characters in contemporary costumes. It was found necessary to put the period of the opera back to about 1700; and perhaps this ante-dating of the subject reconciled some hearers to the risky story. In modern productions the setting is always that of the original place and period — the Paris of the eighteen-forties. As in the case of *Rigoletto*, Verdi and his librettist (Piave) changed the names of all the characters; Marguerite became Violetta Valery, Armand Duval became Alfredo Germont, and Varville became the Baron Douphol. Necessarily something of the first heat of the music has died out of it in the course of time, and the colours have faded; but we can still see how bent Verdi was on painting to the life the feverish atmosphere in which Violetta lived, and it takes only a slight effort of the imagination to realise how exciting this nervous music must have been to the mid-century audiences that heard it for the first time.

The Prelude, short and simple as it is, has a programmatic significance. It opens, *adagio* and double *pianissimo*, with a theme in the minor that is associated later with Violetta's malady:

This is succeeded by a broad *cantabile* melody:

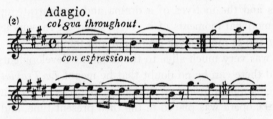

which we shall meet with again later; it is Violetta's cry of love for Alfredo.

When the curtain rises we see Violetta's salon in Paris, in which a brilliant party is in progress. Violetta is with her guests, and she makes, for a prima donna, a singularly modest vocal entry, for the scene has hardly begun before we hear her, in a phrase that lasts only a few bars, exhorting her guests to enjoy themselves to the full. The opening of the opera is not unlike that of *Rigoletto;* the basis of the music is a succession of sparkling dance tunes, of which the following are typical:

that form a background for the conversation. Among the guests is Alfredo, who is presented to Violetta by his friend Gastone.

At the invitation of Violetta her guests seat themselves at the supper-table, and, to the accompaniment of No. 4, Gastone tells her of the romantic dumb devotion of this young man to her during her late illness, when he came day after day to enquire about her. Violetta asks him if the story is true, and he gravely admits that it is. Gastone proposes a song by Alfredo for the delectation of the company, and at the request of Violetta the young man, who has a reputation as a singer, obliges.

His song:

is a toast in praise of wine, love, beauty, and the joy of life generally. The strain is taken up first by the chorus, then by Violetta who outdoes Alfredo in her expression of the philosophy of enjoying life as madly as possible while it lasts. From another room comes the sound of a brilliant waltz, and Violetta suggests to her guests that they shall join in the dance. She is leading the way when suddenly she pauses, gives a little exclamation of pain, and seems about to faint. To the accompaniment of the waltz:

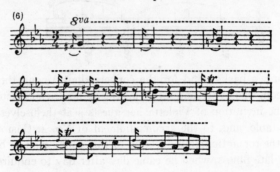

that, with its pendant:

dominates the scene for some time now, her guests break out into expressions of sympathy, while she endeavours to persuade them and herself that it is nothing and will soon pass. She asks them to leave her, assuring them that she will join them shortly.

Left to herself, she is looking with alarm at her pallor in the glass when Alfredo joins her. Greatly distressed, he urges her to give up this wild life that is killing her, promising to help her to any extent in his power. Violetta is touched by his solicitude; for the first time she hears in a man's voice the accents of genuine affection. She twits him light-heartedly for a time on the seriousness of his professions, but with the gravity that is mostly characteristic of him he assures her of the genuineness of his love:

He has loved her for a year, he says — from the day when, though as yet unknown to her, he felt himself penetrated by " that love that is the very breath of the universe, love mysterious and profound, at once the cross of the heart and its delight ":

This musical phrase recurs more than once as a motive in the course of the opera, and special note should be taken of the later part of the melody, with its expressive veiling of the harmony at the word *misterioso*:

Violetta replies that it would be better for him to leave her and forget her, for she can offer him nothing but friendship; she is incapable of a love on the heroic scale of his own.

In the windings and flutterings of her melody:

sof - - - fro un co-(si)
- barr'd me, No ten (der)

we see again Verdi's attempt to paint her realistically as a creature
of whims, given up to feverish pleasures. While she is indulging
in these roulades, Alfredo, to the strain of No. 10, steadily maintains his protestations of love.

The dialogue is broken in upon by Gastone, and the waltz
from the other room takes possession of the orchestra once more.
Violetta, in spite of herself, has been touched by Alfredo's affection. While still laying it down that it shall be agreed between
them that he shall not speak to her of love, she gives him, at parting, a flower, which, she coquettishly tells him, he can return to
her when it is faded. This, of course, he rightly takes to be an invitation to call on her again on the morrow, and he leaves her with
a new hope in his heart.

Violetta's guests now burst in *en masse* and take leave of her
in a long and bright ensemble, the burden of which is that as
dawn is breaking it is time that even such hardened pleasure-
seekers as they should go home to sleep, if only to fortify themselves for another night of pleasure.

Left alone, Violetta begins to think over the contrast between
her mode of life as typified in the chorus that has just ended and
the prospect of a calmer, sweeter existence held out to her by Alfredo. She has the remainder of the act to herself, and she occupies it in singing her aria " Ah fors è lui," which is one of the
favourite show pieces of the coloratura soprano in the concert-
room as well as in the theatre. It is strange, she says in the preliminary recitative, how Alfredo's words have struck home to her
heart. Would it, after all, be so great a misfortune for her if she
were to fall seriously in love? For it would be delightful both to
love and to know herself loved, neither of which experiences has
yet been hers. Shall she throw away this possibility of quiet happiness for the feverish follies of her present life? Perhaps, after
all, she says in the opening stages of the aria proper:

(12) Andantino.

Ah fors' è   lui   che   l'a - ni -
Was this the   man   my   fan - cy

ma   so-lin-ga ne' tu - mul - ti,
bright, Oft in the world in   dreams e'er

so - lin - ga ne   tu - mul - ti
paint-ed in hues   of   light . . . . ?

this young man is he of whom, lonely among the flattering crowds
that surround her, she has long dreamed in fancy. She remembers
Alfredo's words describing the universality and mystery of love,
and she repeats them to herself to the musical phrases to which
he has already sung them (No. 9 and No. 10). As a child she had
dreamed of a pure and simple love; can it be that at last this is
to become incarnate?

But a revulsion of feeling comes, and hastily and nervously
she puts the tempting dream aside. She is alone in Paris, with no
weapons but her beauty and her charm with which to fight the
world. She dare not allow herself to be weakened in the eternal
combat of the sexes; there is nothing for it but to plunge once
more into the giddy round of pleasure. To the former *andantino*
succeeds an *allegro brillante*:

(13) Allegro brillante.

Sem-pre li - be - ra.   degg'
Shall I   al - ways free - ly

i - o fol - leg-gia - re di gio-ja in
rang-ing, Run the   course of my ca-

gio - ja,
-*reer*,——

in which she vows herself to the eternal pursuit of new and ever
new pleasures. From outside comes the voice of Alfredo, singing
once more the words and melodies of No. 9 and No. 10. Violetta
listens for a moment, then thrusts the sweet temptation aside once
more with a cry of " Madness! Madness! " and ignoring the subtle appeal of Alfredo's emotion she delivers herself up to yet wilder
and wilder declarations that she means to be free to drain the
cup of pleasure in her own way.

Events have moved quickly between the first act and the second, for when the curtain rises again we not only see Alfredo established in the country house at Auteuil, near Paris, but we learn
from him that their idyll has already lasted long enough for the
first fever to have died out of it, to be succeeded by a phase of
calm contentment. The lovers have been three months together
in their retreat, and for both of them the great world with its noisy
joys is hardly more than a curious memory.

In a quietly moving aria:

De' miei bol-len - ti spi - ri - ti
Calm'd by her gen - tle ten - der sway

il gio - va - ni - le ar-do - re
Pas - sion for-sakes its mad - ness,

he tells how Violetta's love has tamed the turbulent passions of
his own youth. His meditations are broken in upon by Violetta's
companion, Annina, who, we learn, has just come from Paris,
where she has been carrying out Violetta's commission to dispose
of her horses and other possessions in order to meet the heavy
expenses of the country house.

There is still need of a thousand louis, Annina tells him, and Alfredo, warning her not to let Violetta know of his intentions, tells her that he himself will go to Paris and raise this sum. This has been the first revelation to him that he was living largely on the bounty of Violetta, and the young man expresses his deep dissatisfaction with himself in a passionate aria:

(15) **Allegro.**

When he has left, Violetta enters. She is a very different Violetta now from the one we saw in the first act. She is quietly dressed, has lost her hectic manner, and is not only more tranquil in mind but seemingly in better bodily health. Learning that Alfredo has gone to Paris but will return by the evening, she begins to read her correspondence, among which is a letter from one of her former companions, Flora, inviting her to a dance. She smiles as she assures us that they will await her in vain.

Just then her manservant, Giuseppe, enters with the news that a visitor has called, and, believing him to be the Paris man of affairs whom she is expecting, Violetta orders him to be admitted. It turns out, however, to be Germont *père*. The dialogue between the two runs on much the same lines as in Dumas's play, but, as time presses on both the librettist and the composer, the action is quickened and the various psychological motives telescoped, as it were. Here Germont very quickly arrives at his suggestion that, in order to secure the happy marriage of his daughter, Violetta shall make the sacrifice of her own love.

The suggestion brings up a touch of the old fever in Violetta, and her music has the typically nervous quality characteristic of Verdi in a situation of this kind as she assures Germont that he does not comprehend the immensity of the love that burns within her:

Germont, who, thanks to Verdi, is a more sympathetic character than the Duval of *La Dame aux Camélias*, is touched by her evident anguish, and grieves to have to inflict this blow on her.

To soften it, and to make the resolution easier for her, he hints that Alfredo himself may possibly tire of her some day, when the first heat shall have died out of his passion:

(The reader will note, in the demi-semiquaver figures that end almost each phrase of this aria, another phase of that curious obsession of Verdi's to which we drew attention several times in our analysis of *Il Trovatore*.) Partly because she admits to herself the possibility of this abandonment, partly out of sympathy for the young girl in the way of whose happiness she sees she is standing, Violetta consents to sacrifice herself, and Germont, deeply touched by the spectacle of her misery, breaks in again and again upon her lamentations with a consoling phrase that makes an admirable effect in performance:

(18)

Pian-gi,   pian-gi,
Mourn on!   *mourn on!*

pian - gi, o mi-se-ra,
sad   and de-spairing heart!

Having dismissed Germont, Violetta dashes off a letter to Flora, accepting the invitation, and sends for Annina. She is nerving herself to write another letter, explaining everything to Alfredo, when the young man himself returns. He asks to be allowed to see what she has been writing, but she manages to put him off. He, for his own part, is distracted with troubles of his own. He has had a severe letter from his father, whom he is momentarily expecting to call on him here in Auteuil.

Violetta declares that she will throw herself at Germont's feet and implore him not to separate them, and she passionately calls upon Alfredo to assure her that he loves her. But why is she weeping? he asks. She felt the need to weep, she replies, but now, as he can see, she is smiling again. She will go and wait for him among the flowers, where she will still be close to him; as she leaves him she breaks out into a wild cry that is the forerunner of the famous cry of Desdemona in the last act of *Otello:*

(This will be recognised as the theme that has already been used in the overture to the opera.)

Alfredo, left alone, is musing upon the depth of Violetta's love, when Giuseppe enters hurriedly with the news that his mistress has left, apparently for Paris, in her carriage, and that Annina has preceded her. Alfredo has as yet no suspicion that anything is wrong; he naturally connects Violetta's departure with the liquidation of her affairs in Paris. But on the heels of

Giuseppe comes a messenger with the fateful letter from Violetta. His brain reels under the blow; turning round, he sees his father, who has entered unobserved, and falls into his arms. In an aria:

that, old-fashioned as its sentimentality is, never fails to make its effect on an audience, the father implores his son to go back with him to the fair land of Provence in which his childhood was spent, and begin the old happy life again in the bosom of the reunited family. There is no room in Alfredo's mind, however, for any thought but that of vengeance, for he attributes Violetta's defection to the enticements of Baron Douphol.

A second appeal from the older Germont is no more effective than the first; Alfredo has now found Flora's letter on Violetta's writing-table, and, assuming that the latter will be at Flora's party, he hastens away to Paris, followed by his distracted father.

The second scene of this act takes place in Flora's drawing-room. As the opera opened with a festive scene of much the same kind, it was necessary for Verdi to avoid a mere repetition of this on the musical side. He accordingly has Flora arrange a little entertainment for her guests, consisting of a chorus of fortune-telling gipsies, followed by one of Spanish matadors; these two choruses give the composer plenty of opportunity for the display of local colour. The chief occupation of Flora's guests is gaming, and it is at one of the card-tables that the vital parts of the action take place.

Alfredo enters, somewhat to the surprise of the others, who ironically compliment him on his self-possession. Later comes Flora with Baron Douphol, who, seeing Alfredo, warns Violetta not to engage in a single word with him.

As in the play, Alfredo has a long run of luck at cards, and he loudly announces his intention of using the money to retire into the country again with one who lately left him. Both Violetta and the Baron, of course, hear his words; the former is greatly agitated, while the latter goes to try his luck with Alfredo at cards. Alfredo again wins, and offers his antagonist any satisfaction he likes.

All see that a duel is impending between the two " protectors " of Violetta, but for the moment the tension is relieved by the departure of the guests for the supper-room. Violetta remains behind in great agitation, and manages to detain Alfredo, whom she begs to do all he can to avoid a conflict with the Baron. He taunts her with the fear that he may kill her wealthy protector, but she assures him that her anxiety is rather lest he himself shall be slain. More urgently than ever she entreats him to leave the house, but he will do this only on condition that she comes with him. Tearfully she says that this is impossible; only lately she has had to abandon him in order to keep a secret promise.

Alfredo demands the name of the man to whom this promise was given; Violetta will only say that it was one who had a complete right to it. He asks her if it was Douphol, and she answers, " Yes." Seeing no way of escape from her difficulties except by braving it out, she declares that she loves Douphol, whereupon Alfredo, in blazing wrath, summons Flora and the guests from the supper-room. He tells them of his love for Violetta, of his attempt to rescue her from her former life, and of the financial obligations under which he had found himself to her; then, throwing his winnings at Violetta, he calls them all to witness that he has discharged his debt.

They all cry shame upon him for his brutality, and the elder Germont, who has just entered, heaps reproaches upon his son for his indefensible action. In Alfredo a cold fit soon succeeds the hot one; he is overwhelmed with remorse; his crime, he feels, has been too monstrous for forgiveness.

The act ends with a big ensemble, in which each of the company expresses at great length his own point of view. Musically the mass of sound is imposing enough; but as they are all talking at once it is difficult for the audience to make out what they are saying. The majority are sympathetic to Violetta; Alfredo keeps reiterating that he is consumed with remorse; Baron Douphol threatens him with vengeance; the elder Germont declares that he alone of all present knows all the beauty of Violetta's soul; while Violetta herself — almost the only one whose words are intelligible to us — assures Alfredo that some day he will know of the sacrifice she has made on his behalf, and the love that has prompted it.

The orchestral Introduction to the third act is one of the best specimens of Verdi's expressive writing in his middle period. It opens with the tenuous motive (No. 1) that we have already associated with the malady of Violetta. A sweet sadness breathes through the melodies and harmonies that follow, and at the end of the Introduction a series of broken descending phrases:

depicts realistically the ebbing tide of Violetta's life.

The action takes place in the modest apartment in Paris which Violetta, sick and apparently abandoned by most of her friends, has for some time occupied. The curtains are drawn when the scene opens, but Violetta, learning from Annina that it is seven o'clock in the morning, orders a little daylight to be let in. Annina tells her that Dr. Grenvil is here, and Violetta rises to greet this good and faithful friend; her feeble steps are accompanied by the vacillating No. 21 in the orchestra.

The doctor exhorts her to be of good courage, for she will soon be convalescent; but with a sad smile she tells him she knows this is only one of the pious fictions with which doctors try to console their patients. To Annina, when he is leaving, the doctor quietly announces that Violetta is so far gone in consumption that she has only a few hours to live.

Violetta hears festive noises in the street, and from Annina she learns that it is the Carnival. And at once she thinks of the poor and the suffering. Finding that there are still twenty louis in her purse, she bids Annina take ten and distribute them among the poor — for the remainder will be ample for her.

Annina having left her, Violetta turns to her letters. Among them is one from the elder Germont, which she reads aloud: " You have kept your word. . . . The duel took place. . . . The Baron was wounded, but is now recovering. . . . Alfredo is abroad; I have told him of your sacrifice, and he will come to you to beg forgiveness. . . . I also . . . Get well again; you deserve a better future." The reading of the letter is accompanied softly in the orchestra by the two Love motives (No. 9 and No. 10).

She waits and waits, says Violetta sadly, but they do not come! She looks at herself in the mirror, and is shocked at the ravages her illness has made in her. Sadly she bids farewell to the beautiful dreams of the past:

(22) **Andante mosso.**

Ad - di - o, _____ del pas -
All fa - ded_____ the gay

-sa-to___ bei___ so-gni___ ri -
fancies   I___ thought once___ were___

-den - ti,
re - al,

The desire for life and love surges up in her for a moment, but sorrowfully she recognises that it is useless now to cherish such a hope. She will soon die the death of the despised and forgotten — no mourning friends, no tears, no flowers upon her coffin, no cross upon her tomb.

As her voice dies away in a mere thread of tone, a bacchanalian chorus breaks in from the street; and when the revellers have moved on, Annina enters, and excitedly asks Violetta, if she is strong enough to bear good news, to prepare herself for an unexpected pleasure.

Violetta realises that Alfredo is there, and the next moment she is in his arms. They pour out their love and remorse to each other, and, health seeming to revive in Violetta, she enters joyously into his plans for a new life together in the country. They will say farewell to Paris:

(23) Dolcissimo.

Pa - ri - gi, o ca - - ra,
Charm-ing Pa-ris, once so che-rish'd,

noi la-sce - re - mo,   la vita u -
we now will leave___   Our lot's in

-ni - ti tra-scor - re - re - mo,
u - nion we no more need grieve,___

and Violetta, to the same strain, echoes his belief in the brightness
of their future.

Violetta would go to church with Alfredo, to give thanks for his
return; but when she tries to walk she collapses once more.
Bravely she tries to master her weakness, but a second attempt
to raise herself ends in a more pitiful collapse than before; and
Alfredo, greatly alarmed, sends Annina for the doctor, Violetta repeating the command and adding, " Tell him that Alfredo has returned, and that I want to live again." To Alfredo, however, she
softly confesses that hope has abandoned her.

With a last feverish effort she appeals to God not to let her
die so young, just when she is so near to happiness:

and Alfredo mingles his tears and appeals with hers.

At the conclusion of their duet the elder Germont enters, and
takes Violetta to his breast as a daughter. She tells him and the
doctor that it is now too late, and Germont, seeing that she is
indeed doomed, reproaches himself bitterly for all he has done
to her. She calls Alfredo to her and gives him a miniature of herself, showing her as she was in healthier and happier days. This he
is to give to the modest maiden he will some day marry, and tell
her that Violetta, among the angels, is praying for her and him.
The Love motive (No. 9) peals out softly in the orchestra once
more. The consumptive has a last sweet illusion of new life cours-
ing through her veins; she gives a great cry of " Oh, I shall live
again! Oh joy! " and falls back dead. Somewhat inexplicably,
Verdi does not set Dumas's final words, but contents himself
with a rather conventional little ensemble.

THE first in order of composition of Verdi's operas to keep the stage to our day was *Rigoletto,* written when Verdi was nearing his fortieth year. Less than two years later came *Il Trovatore,* the work with which his reputation as the leading Italian composer of the day was established beyond dispute.

Verdi found the subject for his new work in a drama, *El Trovador,* by the Spanish writer Gutiérrez. He seems to have met with this about 1850, before he had become acquainted with the play of Victor Hugo's from which he drew the plot of *Rigoletto;* but it was not until after that work was off his hands that he turned his attention seriously to the Spanish subject.

His librettist on this occasion was Cammarano, but Verdi himself, as usual, had a good deal to say in the matter. He suggested various alterations in Cammarano's book, and it is to his own keen sense of the stage that we owe what is not only one of the most striking situations in *Il Trovatore* but one of the most telling effects in all Italian opera — the union of Leonora's voice with that of Manrico in the *Miserere* scene.

It was more especially the very original character of Azucena, with its mixture of fanatical love and equally fanatical hatred, that fascinated Verdi; indeed, it was mainly owing to the difficulty of finding a singer to come up to his ideal for this part that he hesitated for a while as to the choice of a theatre for the first production. By this time Verdi, of course, had open to him any opera house in Italy, to say nothing of Paris and London. Venice had asked for a new opera from him, but Venice had no singer who came up to his requirements for *Il Trovatore*.

For the part of Manrico he wanted a tenor of exceptional power and brilliancy of tone; while for Azucena he desired a contralto of a peculiarly deep, sombre colour that should also be capable of expressing passion when required. He at last found his various ideals, or something approaching them, in Rome; and so it was at the Apollo Theatre, Rome, that the work was first given, on 19th January, 1853.

It was a great success from the first; by the end of 1854 Paris had produced it, and in May 1855 it appeared at Covent Garden, where it laid solidly the foundations of Verdi's great popularity in England. *Il Trovatore*, however, did not make its way without a good deal of severe criticism. The unredeemed gloom of Verdi's mind and his insistence on rather crude horrors, which had already been evident in several other works of his, were not to everyone's taste. The effect of these features of his operas has faded a good deal with familiarity and the passage of the years; but we can guess that they must have been rather strong tobacco for the people who met with them for the first time.

There was a good deal of violence in Verdi's musical style also, which shocked the easy-going audiences who had been used to the paler music of the majority of his Italian predecessors and contemporaries. He was regarded by many good souls as likely to achieve the complete ruin of Italian opera; no one could foresee that this rather crude-minded man of forty, whose art seemed to be one long-drawn-out spasm, would develop, in another twenty years or so, into the sensitive artist of the finer parts of *Aida*, and then into the master who gave the world the noble *Otello* and the supremely delicate *Falstaff*.

Henry F. Chorley, the musical critic of the *Athenæum*, who was a much abler man in his line than he is credited with being by people of to-day who have never read a single page of him, probably expressed the average critical opinion of the time when he said that " there is a mixture of grandeur in portions of Signor

Verdi's operas, alternated with puerilities, which is impossible to be outdone in its triteness and folly." He pointed out how the impression made by Verdi's music on the English public when *Ernani* was produced in London (in 1845) had gradually weakened when it became evident that in the three operas that followed — *Nabucco, I Lombardi,* and *I due Foscari* — " the strain and violence were repeated."

" It became obvious," he continues, " that the new composer relied on effect, not sound knowledge; that he preferred ferocious and gloomy stories; that rant, in short, was the expression most congenial to his genius. In his earlier operas this vigour was borne out by a naked ferocity of instrumentation, which had a certain attraction when it was heard for the first time." Chorley went on to point out that Verdi had obviously made earnest attempts to vary his idiom and to temper the crudenesses of it, but, he concludes, " the style to which he has chosen to cling and abide, the style of a bad musical time, ill wrought out in Italy, has remained essentially the same in all — spasmodic, tawdry, untruthful, depending on musical effects of a lower order and coarser quality than those of any Italian predecessor."

While taking the view that Verdi " is generally the most *untender* of Italians, past, present, (let it be hoped) to come," Chorley does justice to the best parts of *Il Trovatore,* and decides that " Signor Verdi is not, however, to be disdained, as a shallow or perversely insincere man should be. It is evident — howsoever incomplete may have been his training, howsoever mistaken his aspirations must have proved, and thought to have been and to be — that he *has* aspired." Further, " what there is good in his music betokens a certain elevation of instinct and ambition, with most paltry musical culture, working with poor executants, and during an epoch of artistic decay." Later, Chorley spoke of *Il Trovatore* as " the work in which his best qualities are combined, and in which indications scattered throughout earlier productions present themselves in the form of their most complete fulfilment."

All this is not, in essence, unjust. But Chorley did not think the work would live, because, good as the music was of its type, the libretto was an impossible one; most people in the theatre failed, it seems, to get the hang of the story, which is hardly to be wondered at. Chorley was wrong on this point, however; the incoherence of the plot and the violence of the situations have not stood in the way of the survival of *Il Trovatore*. The fact is that its faults are the faults of genius — a genius, it is true, that had not yet quite understood and tamed itself, but that went to its goal with a vigour and a certainty that were beyond any other Italian opera composer of the time.

The scene of the opera is laid in Spain. There is no overture — merely a roll in the drums, a wild outburst in octaves in the orchestra, and then a horn call, the whole occupying only twenty bars. Then the curtain rises, showing a vestibule in the Palace of Aliaferia, in which household the Count di Luna obviously holds some office the nature of which is not made clear to us. We gather later that Leonora is also located in the Palace, as companion to the Queen.

There is a good deal in the story of *Il Trovatore* that is not made clear by the stage action, but only by way of narration on the part of someone or other; while there are sundry little points in the plot upon which we have to exercise our powers of conjecture. At the back of the stage, soldiers are walking up and down, while near the doorway at the side are a number of the Count's retainers, seemingly guarding the place against a mysterious Troubadour who of late has been serenading Leonora from the garden.

The Count himself is in love with Leonora, and spends the night watching beneath her window, rent asunder, as the chorus assures us, by jealousy. The retainers themselves are on the point of falling asleep under the strain of their vigil, and have to be roused by Ferrando, the Count's trusted man. They ask Ferrando if he will not tell them, in order to keep them awake, the story of the Count's brother Garzia. One would have thought that everybody within fifty miles of the place would have known it by this time, for the tragic misfortune of the Count's household could hardly have been kept a secret from the whole countryside; but perhaps the retainers are kindly feigning ignorance of the matter in order that we in the audience may be told what is necessary for our comprehension of the coming drama.

The soldiers join in the request of the retainers, and Ferrando begins his story in an easy conversational tone. The former Count di Luna, it appears, had two children, both boys; the nurse of the younger used to sleep by the cradle. One fine morning she woke up and found a sinister-looking old gipsy-woman gazing at the child:

Swar-thy and threat-en-ing, a gip-sy wo-man Bear-ing of fiend-ish art sym-bols in-hu-man,

Ab-biet-ta zin-ga-ra, fo-sca ve-gliar-dal Cin-ge-va i. sim-bol-i, di ma-li-ar-da,

In this narration of Ferrando's we already meet with a marked peculiarity of Verdi's style at this epoch — the tendency to repeat a melodic formula *ad infinitum*. Having written the group of four semiquavers shown in the third bar of our quotation, he is obsessed by it for the remainder of the song. It is seen again in the following typical phrase:

Spell-bound the nurse watch'd at first the bel-dame hoar-y,

D'or-ror com-pres-sa la nu-tri-ce

com-pres-sa è

and in this:

(3)

And quick-er than now— I can
Ed ec - co, in me - no che

tell— you the sto - ry, The
lab - bro il di - ce, i

ser - vants of the cas-tle one and all came
ser - vi, i ser-vi ac-cor-ro-no, i ser-vi ac-

has-ten-ing to her as - sist-ance,
- cor-ro - no in quel-le so -glie;

The shrieks of the nurse, it seems, had brought the servants, who, with threats and curses, drove the gipsy away. The old woman made the excuse that she had merely come to cast the infant's horoscope; but the fact was that from that day he sickened. At this the chorus make appropriate signs of horror. Resuming his discourse, Ferrando tells them that the sorceress was pursued, captured, and burnt at the stake. Her daughter, however, escaped, and with her disappeared the child. Ferrando has no doubt that the gipsy, for revenge, had burnt him to death, for next morning a heap of calcined bones was found in the remains of the pyre.

" And what about the father? " ask the listeners. Ferrando tells them that the old Count had never been able to get it out of his mind that his child was still alive, and on his deathbed he made his other son take an oath to search without intermission for his lost brother. Of the witch who took the child, nothing has been seen or heard from that fatal day. It is the one object of the faithful Ferrando's life to find and punish her; and long ago as the affair happened, he is certain he would know her again if he saw her.

But he has still more horrors in store for his fascinated audience. It seems that the spirit of the burnt gipsy still haunts the place; when the night is dark it hovers about in all sorts of unearthly shapes — sometimes on the housetops, in the form of a hoopoe or an owl, sometimes in that of a crow. A servant of the old Count who had struck the woman had died in terror. She visited his room in the shape of an owl and stared at him; at midnight a savage howl was heard, and the poor man went mad. Just then, when seemingly the listeners' nerves can stand no more, a bell in the Palace strikes twelve, and all join in a cry of " A curse upon the witch! " Then the servants take up their position by the door once more, the soldiers retiring to the back of the stage.

The scene now changes to the garden of the Palace; on the right is a marble staircase. The moon is shining. Leonora, followed by Inez, her confidante, enters by way of the staircase. Inez is trying to recall her mistress to a sense of her duty; the Queen has been desiring her attendance. Leonora, however, can think and talk of nothing but the pain of passing another night without seeing the serenader who has made so romantic an impression on her.

As it is necessary for the audience to know something of this personage, Leonora, in response to a request from Inez, obligingly tells the story of how she first met him. It was at a tournament, at which there had entered a knight in sombre armour, whom no one knew, for there was no device on his shield. He overthrew all the other knights, and it fell to Leonora's lot to place the wreath of victory on his brow. Then civil war broke out in the land, and she saw him no more. She mourned him for a time, and then a strange thing happened. One night a voice, accompanied by a lute, serenaded her from the garden, murmuring her name; running to the porch, she recognised in the melodious Troubadour the knight of the tourney. The melody of Leonora's solo is typical of Verdi at this period:

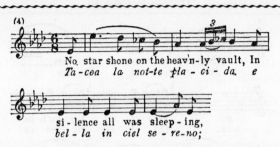

No star shone on the heav'n-ly vault, In
Ta-cea la not-te pla-ci-da, e

si-lence all was sleep-ing,
bel-la in ciel se-re-no;

Inez fears that trouble will come of all this, and implores Leonora
to forget the Troubadour; but Leonora assures her that that is
impossible; and she breaks out into the brilliant *cabaletta* that in
those days was the almost indispensable ending to a slow aria:

The love my heart o'er-flow —
Di ta-le a-mor che dir —

-ing, No earth-ly word can ren — der,
-si mal può dal-la pa-ro — la,

The burden of her song, which affords plentiful opportunities
for the display of vocal technique, is the unchanging fidelity of
her heart to the still unknown singer. Inez expresses the pious
wish that Leonora may never regret it, and the pair ascend the
steps into the Palace.

A few bars of slow and solemn music are heard in the orchestra,
and the Count di Luna appears. He has come into the garden, as
usual, to indulge himself in the luxury of thinking about Leonora,
whose light he sees in her window. After a short recitative, in
which he announces his resolution to see her, he is about to ascend
the staircase when he hears the sound of a harp preludising.
Soon the Troubadour's voice is heard, in a short but melodious
apostrophe to Leonora:

(6)

Nought up-on earth is left
De - ser-to sul - la ter -

me,   Fate of all joy hath be-
- ra,   Col rio de - sti - no in

- reft ____ me, But one heart firm and
guer - ra, E so-la spe-me un

pure,   but one heart firm and   pure,
cor,   E   so-la spe-me un   cor,

but one heart firm and pure ___ de-sires the
E so-la spe-me un cor, ___   un cor al

Trou - ba - dour.
Tro - va - tor.

The Count is at first a little apprehensive, but finally jealousy
and rage get the upper hand of him. He wraps himself up closely
in his cloak as Leonora rushes out from the Palace with a cry of
delight, and, making a mistake that is pardonable in the bad
light, throws herself into the Count di Luna's arms instead of
those of the Troubadour. This is one of several little things in the
stage action that are apt to perplex the spectator who is seeing
the opera for the first time.

Even the Troubadour, who is concealed among the trees, does
not all at once quite get the true sense of the situation. It wrings
from him a reproachful " Ah, unfaithful one! " The familiar
voice, coming from an unexpected quarter, makes Leonora pause;
and just then the moon comes through the clouds and reveals a

knight with closed visor. Leonora now recognises her mistake, and, leaving the Count, throws herself at the feet of Manrico, whom she assures of her eternal devotion. The Troubadour accepts her assurances, while the indignant Count, breathing vengeance, demands that his mysterious rival shall make himself known. Raising his visor, the Troubadour declares himself to be Manrico.

The Count is astonished at his audacity in appearing there, for this Manrico, being in league with Urgel, the enemy of the State, has been proscribed and a price has been put upon his head. Manrico tauntingly dares the Count to call his guards and have him arrested, and the Count angrily assures him that the hour of his doom has arrived. He orders the Troubadour to follow him that he may punish him with his own hands, and he gives expression to his rage and hatred in a short aria in which once more we see Verdi's tendency to repeat a melodic figure:

the group of four quavers shown in bar 4 being repeated in phrase after phrase. In the trio that follows, Leonora exultingly confesses her love for Manrico, while the latter hurls back the Count's threats in his teeth. Finally the two men rush out with drawn swords, while Leonora falls fainting to the ground.

The second act shows us a gipsy encampment in the Biscayan mountains. Inside a ruin, by a fire, Azucena is seated; on a low couch by her side lies Manrico, wrapped in his cloak, his helmet at his feet, his sword in his hand. Scattered about the stage are gipsies engaged in their various avocations, the girls dancing, the men working at the forge. The strong and piquant local colour of this scene, which was something novel in the middle of the nineteenth century, made a great impression on the audiences of the time. A supposedly gipsy strain, plentifully bestrewn with trills, is first of all heard in the orchestra:

This is followed by another piquant melody, to which a gipsy colouring is given by means of the triangle:

Then the men of the chorus, accompanying their song at times with their hammers, break out into the famous Anvil Chorus, the rude energy and sheer noise of which must have been rather startling to the more classical-minded opera-goers of the eighteen-fifties:

Later there comes a vigorous melody:

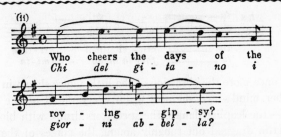

in which the women join with the men. The burden of the song is the solace brought into the male gipsies' life by the company of the female of the species. The women pour out wine for the men, and the racy, bouncing chorus is repeated.

All this while Azucena has been oblivious of what has been going on about her. Huddled over the fire, she is brooding upon the past; never does the memory of her mother's dreadful fate leave her, and in spite of her love for Manrico, who, as the spectator has probably already guessed, is the missing son of the old Count di Luna, the dominant passion of Azucena's strange nature is revenge.

The psychological motives, it must be confessed, are not made absolutely clear. It is a little difficult to understand why, having reared Manrico from childhood simply as an instrument by which she may consummate her vengeance upon the house of di Luna, Azucena should have allowed herself to develop for him an affection like that of a mother for her own child; nor again why, feeling this affection as she does, she should still be willing to sacrifice him for the sake of the old blood-feud. However, in opera we must perhaps not enquire too closely into things of this kind.

At present Azucena's mind is occupied with the vision of her mother at the stake; this is the subject of the song into which she now breaks, at first in a quiet voice, as if talking to herself, the other gipsies gathering round her:

the _____ cru - el mul - ti - tude
la _____ fol - la in-do - mi-ta

(Note once more the obsession of the little figure shown in bar 3.)

In her mind's eye she sees again every detail of the terrible scene — the leaping flames, the spectators drunk with blood-lust, the victim dragged out roughly among the curses of the crowd, the rough tieing of the old woman to the stake, and the ferocious glee of her executioners as she perished in the flames. The chorus comment mournfully upon her story, and Azucena, turning towards Manrico, sings in an impressive undertone her mother's final words, " Avenge thou me! " — a mysterious saying that Manrico has often heard from her lips but has never been able to understand. The incident passes by, and the normal life of the camp is resumed. One of the gipsies tells the others that now the day has broken it is time for them to go forth and seek their bread in the neighbouring village, and the chorus, putting away their tools, go out singing the melody of the Anvil Chorus (No. 11).

We now come upon another of those explanatory interludes in which, through the peculiar construction of the libretto, *Il Trovatore* is so rich. It would be natural to assume that Manrico, as a member of the tribe since his childhood, knows the remainder of the story by now; but as the audience does not yet know it, it is necessary for him to ask Azucena to enlighten him on the subject, which she proceeds to do, giving an air of verisimilitude to the affair by explaining that it is Manrico's frequent absence at the wars that has kept him in ignorance of the matter until now.

She tells him of what lay behind the story she had only hinted at in her song — how her mother had been charged with sorcery and with laying the evil eye upon the old Count's son. They burnt her, she says, on the very spot on which Manrico is now standing, and the young man starts away with an exclamation of horror. When they dragged her mother in chains to the stake, Azucena, with her own little son in her arms, had followed weeping. The brutal guards had made it impossible for her to speak to her mother, and all that the latter could say was the "Avenge thou me!" that has haunted her from that day to this.

"And did you avenge her?" asks Manrico. "I stole the Count's child," replies Azucena; "I brought him to this spot, where the pyre was still burning." But when the child burst into exhausted weeping, pity overcame her. Then once more the dreadful sight at the stake filled her mind; she lost her reason, and in the flames she saw her victim burning; but when she looked around her she saw — not her own child but that of the hated Count; her own had perished, and it was she who had thrown him into the flames! Manrico gives a cry of horror, and Azucena finishes her story in a kind of brooding wail:

(13)

Ah! let me think on that
Sul ca - po mi - o le

day no more, the re-
chio - me sen - to driz-

-mem - brance is death, I can no
-zar - si an-cor! driz - zar - si an-

more, I can no more.
-cor! driz - zar - si an - cor!

in which we realise how necessary it is that the player of the part should have in her voice the deep, rich, dark contralto tones that Verdi so desired. Azucena falls down exhausted, and Manrico for a while is dumb with horror and amazement.

In any other environment but that of Italian opera one would have expected Manrico by this time to leap to the inevitable conclusion. All he does, however, is to ask, "But am *I* not thy son? Who, then, am I?" Azucena staves off his curiosity with a curt

"Thou art my son!" and though Manrico would ask her further questions, she closes the discussion with an evasive remark to the effect that when she recalls the circumstances of her mother's death her mind becomes confused, and foolish words rise to her lips. Has he not always found her a tender mother? To her he owes his life, for when he was left for dead by his comrades in the fight at Pelilla did she not bring him back to life and heal his wounds?

Manrico proudly recalls the historic fight, and how, though stricken down by many wounds, they were all in his breast; he alone of the thousands there that day had kept his face turned to the enemy. That was the day the cruel Count di Luna had fallen upon him with his troops, and though he fell, he fell like a hero. In single combat between the two men, Manrico had had the Count at his mercy. Why did he spare him, then? Azucena asks. Manrico — a good psychological point, this — does not really know; all he remembers is that some feeling stronger than himself withheld his arm when he might have struck the fatal blow:

(14)

I as-sault-ed, He feeb-ly de-fend-ed, At my mer-cy the foe lay ex-tend-ed.
Mal reg-gen-do all' a-spro as-sal-to, ei già toc-co il suo lo a-ve-a.

Azucena regrets this clemency, and exhorts Manrico, if ever he should have the Count at his mercy again, to be pitiless and strike him to the heart. This Manrico promises to do.

Just then a prolonged horn call is heard behind the scenes; it is the signal for a message from Manrico's trusty follower, Ruiz. The messenger enters with a letter. While Azucena, still absorbed in her gloomy memories, sits unconscious of everything about her, Manrico reads the letter, which conveys two pieces of information to him — first, that the Prince, his master, orders him to come at once to defend the fortress of Castellor, which has just been captured; the second, that Leonora, who has been told that Manrico has died of his wounds, is about to forswear the world and enter a convent.

Manrico, greatly agitated by the latter news, sends the messenger in hot haste to saddle his horse, puts on his helmet and snatches his cloak, and is on the point of leaving Azucena without explanation when she appeals to his love for her and the memory of all she has done for him as a mother. To a vigorous melody:

he replies that he must fly at once to Leonora, and in spite of her efforts to detain him he makes his exit in hot haste.

It appears that the Count di Luna has also heard of Leonora's resolution to take the veil, for in the next scene, which takes place at night outside the convent, we find him, Ferrando, and others of his followers concealed as far as possible in their cloaks. We learn from the Count's conversation with Ferrando that when the news of Manrico's death came he thought he was at last sure of Leonora, but she had sprung upon him a fresh pretext for refusing him her hand — her intention to enter the cloister. But he swears in his usual violent way that he will not give her up, and he describes his passion in the celebrated aria " Il balen ":

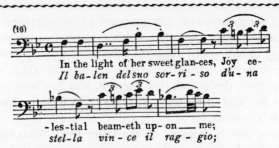

In the light of her sweet glan-ces, Joy ce-
Il ba-len del suo sor-ri-so d'u-na

-les-tial   beam-eth up- on ___ me;
stel-la   vin - ce il rag - gio;

that was probably the most universally popular operatic melody of the middle of the nineteenth century; everybody sang or whistled it, every barrel-organ played it.

After he has assured the universe again and again that one glance from Leonora, and that alone, could dissipate the tempest that rages in his heart, a bell is heard inside the convent. It announces the coming celebration of the rite that is to remove Leonora from the world of men. The now desperate Count declares that he will seize her before she can reach the altar. He bids Ferrando and the others conceal themselves among the trees, which they proceed to do, singing the while, *sotto voce,* a little chorus assuring him of their swiftness and secrecy. The Count pours out his feelings in a vigorous aria, declaring once more that he will allow no one to take Leonora from him, and the chorus, at appropriate moments, echo his sentiments.

A chorus of nuns is now heard, singing to Leonora of the sad deceptions of the world that she is about to give up, and the peace that awaits her in the convent, where no temptation can assail her. Between the stanzas of their song the Count and his concealed followers break in with hectic assurances that never shall Leonora belong to anyone but him.

At last Leonora enters, accompanied, of course, by Inez, who is lamenting that she is to be for ever parted from her mistress. The sorrowful Leonora tells her that her trust now is in Heaven alone, and she is just about to pass through the convent gates when the Count rushes forward and tells her that " the only altar she shall approach is that of Hymen." He has scarcely had time to announce to the astonished Leonora his intention of carrying her

off when the Troubadour also appears. Leonora, almost fainting,
falls into the arms of the lover whom she had believed to be dead,
and voices her ecstasy in a short snatch of song:

(17)

Can I__ be-lieve the
E deg - gio e pos - so

vis - ion blest, And art thou here be-
cre - der-lo,__ Ti veg-go a me d'ac-

- side me!
- can - to!

the broken melody of which suggests vividly, in the true Verdian
style, the palpitations of her heart. The Troubadour and the
Count hurl defiances at each other, and a brilliant ensemble is
built up, in which, in addition to the three principals, Inez, Ferrando, the followers of the Count, and the nuns all join.

The pace and the temperature of the music increase. Ruiz enters
with the news that Urgel has been victorious, and the Troubadour
is about to lead Leonora away when the maddened Count draws
his sword and attacks him. The Count is disarmed by Ruiz and
the others, and can express his rage only in a passionate cry of
hatred. The scene looks like ending in a conventional ensemble;
but Verdi has still a card up his sleeve. After the whole company
have united their voices once more he suddenly silences them,
and after a pause the voice of Leonora steals in with a tender
reminiscence of her song of happiness when she fell into Manrico's
arms.

In the interval between the second act and the third we are to
suppose that Manrico has brought Leonora with him to the fortress of Castellor that he has been ordered to defend. We see the
towers of the fortress in the distance; the stage itself is occupied
by the Count di Luna's camp, conspicuous in which is the Count's

own tent, from the top of which a banner is floating. The soldiers are engaged in various occupations, some polishing up their weapons, others finding consolation for the hardships of a soldier's life in dice.

Ferrando tells them that the Count means to attack Castellor the following day; if they succeed in taking it, the booty, he can promise them, will be rich. The soldiers demand only to be led to the combat, and express their martial spirit in a bouncing chorus that was also one of the delights of our grandfathers:

(18)

Cla - ri-ons blow-ing and bu - gles re-
Squil - li, e cheg-gi la trom - ba guer-

-sound-ing Call us forth to the fight and to
, rie - ra, chia-mi all' ar - mi, al-la pu - gna, all'as-

glo - ry,
-sal - to,

The Count enters, a prey, as usual, to the most hectic emotions; he is torn between the madness of his love for Leonora and rage at the thought that she is at present in the arms of his hated rival. He is just calling Heaven and men to witness that very soon he will separate them when a confused noise is heard " off," and Ferrando enters with the news that the soldiers have come upon a wandering gipsy who, as soon as she caught sight of them, had tried to escape. Suspecting her to be one of the enemy's spies, they captured her, and have brought her to the camp as a prisoner. So far Ferrando himself has not seen the woman; he has only been told of the affair.

The commotion draws nearer, and at last Azucena, her hands tied, is dragged in by some of the soldiers; she is resisting vigor-ously and calling for help. She is brought before the Count, who interrogates her sternly. Where is she going? he asks. She replies that she does not know, for it is the way of the gipsy to be always in movement, with the sky above for tent and all the world for country. " Whence do you come? " the Count asks. " From Biscay," she answers — a reply that sets something stirring uneasily in the Count's mind, for at the back of it always is the dreadful story of the burning of his brother by the witch.

Ferrando too finds a sinister suspicion creeping into his mind. This suspicion deepens as Azucena tells them that she is travelling in search of a dearly loved son who has left her. Has she lived long among the Biscay mountains, the Count asks her. Yes, a long time, replies Azucena. Then does she remember an event that happened some fifteen years before — the death of the young son of the Count? Taken by surprise, Azucena stammers, " And thou — who art thou? " " I am his brother," replies the Count.

Azucena anxiously denies that she has ever heard the story and is hoping that they will release her, when Ferrando bursts out that this is the very woman who committed the crime of fifteen years before. She denies it, but the Count, also convinced, furiously orders the guard to bind her more tightly. In her despair she cries out, " And thou comest not, O Manrico, my son, to the aid of thy unhappy mother! " The discovery that he now has in his hands the mother of his detested rival is a great joy to the Count. Azucena turns on them in savage defiance and invokes the vengeance of Heaven upon them; they in their turn heap objurgations on the head of one who has been guilty of the double crime of murdering the Count's brother and being the mother of the Troubadour. Finally, she is led away by the soldiers, the Count and Ferrando enter the tent, and the curtain falls.

The next scene of this act takes place in a hall in the fortress of Castellor. Manrico and Leonora are about to be united, but the latter cannot shake herself free of the terrors of the situation. At daylight, Manrico tells her, he is expecting the assault of the Count's army: he hopes to be victorious, but if, he assures her in an expressive aria, he should fall, their souls will meet again in heaven. The second half of the aria:

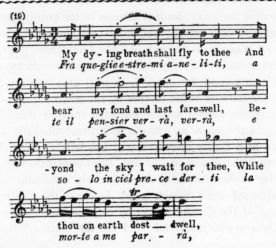

My dy - ing breath shall fly to thee And
Fra que-glie e-stre-mi a-ne - li-ti,   *a*

bear   my fond and last fare-well,   Be-
te il   pen-sier ver - rà,   ver-rà,   *e*

-yond   the sky I wait for   thee, While
so -   lo in ciel pre - ce - der - ti   la

thou on earth dost __ dwell,
mor-te a me   par. - rà,

has a peculiar soft charm; it reminds us in a curious way of some
of Sullivan's melodies.

An organ in the chapel strikes in with a few solemn chords, and
on their way to the chapel Leonora and Manrico blend their aspirations and their oaths of eternal love in a short duet. This is
interrupted by Ruiz, who enters in haste with the news that
Azucena has been captured by the enemy and is to be burnt in
the pyre that has already been lighted for her, and that can be
seen from the window of the hall.

The music becomes feverishly excited as Manrico tells Leonora
that the gipsy is his mother. Making a desperate effort to collect
his scattered senses, he sends Ruiz out to collect his men; then he
breaks into the famous aria " Di quella pira " that has been a
favourite show-piece for more than seventy years with the tenors
who can believe themselves equal to its difficulties:

Trem-ble ye   ty - rants,   I will chas-
Di quel-la   pi - ra,   l'or-ren-do

-tise   ye
fo - co

The literal sense of the opening lines is, " The dreadful flames of this pyre inflame my every fibre "; and the aria is in part a declaration of Manrico's resolution to rescue his mother and wreak vengeance on her captors, in part a passionate farewell to Leonora. The music is full of the pounding energy characteristic of Verdi, and the melody once more shows his peculiar tendency to keep repeating a figure — the four semiquavers shown in bars 2 and 4 of our quotation reappear in one phrase after another.

Robust — or robustious — Italian tenors are in the habit of ending the aria with a mighty high C from the chest, which is always sure to bring the house down. There is no warrant in the score, however, for this display of virtuosity and vanity. Verdi did not want the action to be interrupted at this crucial point by applause, however well the singer may deserve it. The moment Manrico has finished, his soldiers, who have returned with Ruiz, break in on the scene with a vigorous cry of " To arms! " Above the mass of choral and orchestral tone rises the voice of the distracted Manrico, crying, " Unhappy mother! I fly to save thee, or to die with thee! " Finally he rushes out, followed by Ruiz and the others, the trumpet sounding the call to arms.

The fourth act shows Verdi's genius at the greatest height to which it attained in this, his middle period. It is still one of the most effective pieces of work in Italian opera.

We are to understand that in the interval between the third and the fourth acts Manrico has been taken prisoner while attempting to rescue his mother, and she and he have been thrown into the same dungeon in the Palace of Aliaferia. The curtain having risen, we see a wing of the Palace, with a high tower, the windows of which are secured by iron bars. It is night. After a slow and gloomy orchestral introduction Leonora and Ruiz enter, closely wrapped up in cloaks. Ruiz, in an undertone, points out the tower to her as that in which the prisoners are lying. Leonora having dismissed him, she apostrophises, in a recitative, the breezes of the night, bidding them carry her sighs to her captive lover. This is the burden of the expressive aria that follows:

She has come to save Manrico by offering herself to the Count; and she exhorts the breezes never to let Manrico know of the pain that racks her heart. She has already fixed her eyes significantly upon a ring, evidently containing poison, which is to be the means of her deliverance when her purpose has been attained.

From the adjacent chapel the death-bell sounds, and we hear a male-voice chorus singing the solemn *Miserere*: " Mercy on the soul that is near to its setting out upon a journey from which there is no returning; grant it Thy mercy, O divine goodness; let it not fall into the pit of hell! "

Then, over heavy, palpitating chords in the orchestra, that seem like blows of fate:

the voice of Leonora is heard:

her song terminating in one of those sobbing refrains to which Verdi was so partial:

She is answered, with an effect that the years have been unable to diminish, by the voice of the Troubadour from the tower:

(26)

Ah! send thy beams, Au-ro - ra,
Ah! 'che la mor-te o-gno - ra

Light me to ear-ly death, Waft her my
è ___ tar-da nel ve-nir a chi de-

pray-er Waft her my la-test breath, I leave
-si - a, a chi de-sia-mo-rir! ad-di -

thee, Leo-no - ra, Ah, I leave thee.
- o, ad-dio, Leo-no - ra ad-di - o!

("Ah! How slow is death in coming to him who desires to die! Farewell, Leonora, farewell! ")

The same musical pattern is repeated in what immediately follows. Leonora, to the same melody as before, and over the same accompaniment (No. 23), now mourns the intelligence that the *Miserere* has brought her of the coming death of her lover; Manrico exhorts her not to forget him; and she sobs out her assurance that she is his for ever.

The voices of Manrico and the chorus having died away, Leonora, in an agitated aria, declares her resolution to make a last attempt to save her lover's life. She withdraws herself to one side as the Count enters, followed by some of his attendants. To the latter he gives his final instructions — at dawn the son is to be beheaded, the mother burned at the stake.

The attendants go into the tower, and the Count reflects for a moment upon the situation; he is perhaps exceeding the powers entrusted to him by the Prince, but it is his fatal love for Leonora that is driving him insanely on. But where is she now? After the taking of Castellor she disappeared, and he has had no further tidings of her. " Ah! cruel one, where art thou? " he cries, and Leonora, coming forward, answers, " Here, in front of thee! "

The Count can hardly believe his eyes or his ears. In a rapid dialogue between the two, Leonora tells him that she has come to ask for mercy for Manrico. She must be raving, he replies, to think that he would show any pity to his rival; Heaven has put in his hands the opportunity for revenge, and he means to use it to the full. In an expressive duet she implores him to let her die in place of Manrico, a suggestion that only goads him to still greater fury, for the clearer she makes it that she loves the Troubadour, the more overwhelming are his hatred and his desire for revenge.

The Count makes as if to go, but Leonora clings to him in a last appeal for mercy. He tells her that there is no price on earth that could be paid for the saving of Manrico, and angrily bids her leave him. " There is one price only," she replies, " and that I offer thee." " What is it? " asks the Count. Holding out her hand to him she answers mournfully, " Myself! " she will marry him, she assures him, if he will allow her to enter Manrico's dungeon with the news of his release.

Having made her swear this, the Count calls a guard and gives him an order; meanwhile Leonora furtively drinks the poison from the ring, and mutters, in a low tone, " Thou shalt have me, but cold and dead! " When the Count at last turns to her and gives her his promise that Manrico shall go free she breaks out into a wild cry of joy, the musical quality of which may be judged from the following quotation:

(27)

The pow - er that on high doth reign_ a-lone, my_ pur - pose_ know - eth,

ma coi_ fre-quen-ti pal - pi - ti_ mer-ce_ ti_ ren - de il co - rel

In the duet that follows, while she is abandoning herself to the ecstasy of the thought that Manrico is saved, the Count almost incredulously congratulates himself on his good fortune in at last obtaining possession of Leonora. They enter the tower, and the curtain falls.

The final scene shows us the dimly lit dungeon in which Manrico and Azucena are confined; she is lying, sleepless and exhausted, on a pallet, and Manrico is sitting by her. Vainly he tries to console her; the gipsy, used to a life in the open, cannot breathe in this suffocating air. But her gaolers, she says, have no power over her; already she feels the cold hand of death on her forehead; when they come for her they will find her a corpse, cold and silent. Then a sort of delirium seizes her, and she cries out in terror that her executioners are coming to drag her to the stake. " Oh, save thy mother! " she cries.

Manrico tries to assure her that no one is coming, but Azucena cries out again in terror of the fire; in the orchestra we hear the motive (No. 12) that accompanied her recital, in the second act, of the burning of her mother, and we realise again that the memory of this has never faded from her mind. Once more she runs over the horrid scene in her imagination, describing how the flames rose above her mother, how her scorching hair sent up sparks to heaven, how her tortured eyes started from her head; and with a frenzied cry of " Ah! Who will free me from this atrocious sight? " she falls into the arms of Manrico. He implores her, if she loves him, not to give way to these terrors, but to try to sleep.

Composing herself on the couch, she says she will try to sleep and forget, but if the horrible vision should pass through her mind again he is to awake her. In an exquisitely consoling phrase he promises to do so, and Azucena, half sleeping, half waking, sings the pathetic aria " Home to our mountains! " in which she dreams of happy days for them again, he singing and accompanying himself on his lute, she sunk in tranquil slumber:

(28)

Home to our moun-tains thou yet shalt
Ai   no-stri   mon - ti   ri - tor - ne -

take— me, No fear or sor - row,
- re - mo, L'an-ti-ca pa - ce
there shall o'er - take thee
i - vi go-dre - mo!

Manrico bends over her lovingly, and gradually her tired spirit finds rest in sleep, the orchestra accompanying the last phrases of the duet with a gently lulling figure in the muted strings:

(29)

While Manrico is still kneeling beside the pallet, the door opens and Leonora enters. At first he thinks it must be a delusion due to the gloomy light of the cell. " It is I, Manrico, my Manrico! " she says. She tells him she has come to save him, and, pointing to the door, bids him fly at once — without her. This he cannot understand, and gradually his suspicions are aroused. From whom has she purchased his freedom, and at what price? Her silence gives him the answer; " I understand! It is my rival! Thou has sold thyself! " In feverish accents she implores him not to doubt her, but to make his escape at once. Manrico's reproaches and Leonora's appeals rise in intensity, and into the tissue of their duet Verdi weaves a strain of touching pathos when the brooding voice of Azucena strikes in with her dreamy " Home to our mountains! "

Meanwhile the poison has been working in Leonora. In broken accents she makes a last appeal to Manrico to save himself, but he dismisses her with curses. At last she falls to the ground, and as he raises her she confesses that she has taken the poison. " Feel my hand," she says, " it is cold; but here, in my breast, here is a terrible flame! " While she is in her last agony, and Manrico is pouring out his remorse at having doubted her, the Count enters and surveys the scene from the threshold.

Realising that he has been duped, he makes a signal to the guards, who lead Manrico away. The Troubadour cries out a wild farewell to Azucena, who, only half awake, does not at first grasp the situation. " Manrico, my son, where art thou? " she asks. " He has gone to his death! " says the Count. He drags Azucena to the window, and fiendishly makes her watch the execution of Manrico. " It is done! " he cries in triumph. With her last breath Azucena shrieks out " He was thy brother! " and falls senseless to the ground. The Count gives an exclamation of horror, and after a few crashing chords in the orchestra the curtain falls.

With all its faults, *Il Trovatore* remains a remarkable work. Its vigour may sometimes become roughness, but as to the vigour there can be no question. Moreover, Verdi has plainly tried to give a different musical physiognomy to each of his characters. There may be touches of exaggeration in the portraiture here and there, but all the same we feel that the characters are alive, and that each of them moves by his own mechanism.

Leonora is equally different from, say, the Gilda of the *Rigoletto* of a couple of years earlier and the Violetta of *Traviata*. Manrico is always polished and chivalrous; while the Count di Luna is always violent almost to the point of insanity, so morbid is his hatred of the Troubadour for the one part and the gipsy woman for the other. And in Azucena Verdi has drawn a character so vitally human and so consistent that it will bear close analysis even to-day.

AIDA

BETWEEN the ages of twenty-nine and fifty-four, that is
to say, between the years 1842 and 1867, Verdi produced
twenty-four operas, including the three of his middle period
that made him beyond cavil the first Italian opera composer of his
day — *Rigoletto* (1851), *Il Trovatore* (1853), and *La Traviata*
(1853).

As he grew in years and experience his rate of production
slowed down considerably. Between the *Simone Boccanegra* of
1857 and the *Ballo in maschera* of 1859 two years elapsed, between *Un Ballo* and *La Forza del Destino* three years, and between this last and *Don Carlos* five years. After that it was not
for another four years, in 1871, that Verdi appeared before the
world with a new work.

It is sometimes said that *Aida* was written for the opening of
the new opera house at Cairo; but that is a mistake, the theatre
having been inaugurated some two years before the production of
the opera, to celebrate the opening of the Suez Canal. The
Khedive, Ismail Pasha, had asked Verdi to write an opera expressly for the Cairo theatre, but the composer had refused. He
had even resisted, during a visit to Paris, the blandishments of
his friend Camille du Locle, who was apparently intended to be
the librettist of the proposed work.

But some time later du Locle sent Verdi a sketch of an opera
plot by the celebrated Egyptian archæologist Mariette Bey, and
the subject at once captured the composer's imagination. This

Mariette was a French employé in the department of Egyptian antiquities in the Louvre. In 1850 he had been sent by the Louvre authorities to Cairo to search for Coptic manuscripts. He became, however, more interested in the remains of Memphis than in manuscripts, and obtained permission to remain in Egypt a further four years and devote himself to archæological research. For his services in this direction he was made Inspector-General of Egyptian monuments, and received the title of Bey.

As we have said, Verdi had no sooner seen the sketch of the story of *Aida* — which is said to be founded on an episode in Egyptian history discovered by Mariette — than he was on fire to set it to music. The contract was quickly concluded, Mariette acting on behalf of the Egyptian Government.

Verdi set out the main terms in a letter to du Locle of the 2nd June, 1870. The composer was to have the libretto made at his own expense, it becoming, of course, his property. He was to send, also at his own expense, someone to rehearse and conduct the opera at Cairo, and he was to reserve the right to the libretto and the music for every country in the world but Egypt. For the Egyptian concession he was to be paid a hundred and fifty thousand francs. In a further letter to du Locle of a couple of months later Verdi made the further stipulation that, if the production of the opera at Cairo in January 1871 should fail to take place from any cause for which he was not answerable, he should have the right to give the opera anywhere else six months later.

Perhaps this clause was the result of the Franco-German War, which was then in progress; Mariette was unable to leave Paris during the siege, and as the arrangements for scenery and costumes had been left in his expert hands, it must have been evident to the level-headed and business-like Verdi that there was a considerable chance of the Cairo production not being ready at the appointed time. In the last-mentioned letter to du Locle we find him asking the latter to request payment of the first fifty thousand francs due to him under the contract; two thousand of these are to be given by du Locle, at his discretion, to funds for the wounded French soldiers, and the remaining forty-eight thousand invested in Italian funds.

In December 1870, Draneth Bey, the director of the Cairo theatre, heard that Verdi had given permission to the Scala theatre, Milan, to produce *Aida*. Thereupon he wrote to Verdi, courteously pointing out that the delay in the production of the opera at Cairo was due entirely to the fact that the siege of Paris made it impossible for him to get the costumes and decorations that had been ordered, saying that the delay in the production was as prejudicial to the theatre as to the composer, and appealing to Verdi's loyalty and delicacy not to insist upon the strict letter of his agreement, as it was naturally the Khedive's desire to have the first performance of the opera that had come into being through his commission.

Replying on the 5th January, 1871, Verdi said that when he made the arrangement with the Scala to give *Aida* in February he did not know that Mariette Bey was in the besieged Paris, and with him the costumes, etc., intended for the new opera. Under the circumstances, of course, he would not insist on the strict letter of the agreement, but at the same time he had to point out that the Scala director counted on being able to give *Aida* during the carnival season of 1871-2.

This point being amicably settled, the next to be dealt with was the engagement of artists for the new opera. The conductor at the Cairo theatre, Nicola de Giosa, seems to have been hurt at the news that Verdi was sending the conductor Emanuele Muzio to Egypt to superintend the rehearsals and the production.

In a tactful letter of the 5th January, 1871, Verdi points out to de Giosa that the right to do this is conferred upon the composer by the agreement, and that, a modern opera being a complex of so many elements, all of which are vital to the total effect, it is necessary for the production to be under the control of someone who has studied the work with its author.

The negotiations with regard to the singers were prolonged and difficult; sometimes a singer, for financial reasons, would make trouble, sometimes a name that had been suggested would not commend itself to Verdi, who, for all his courtesy, would never yield an inch in matters that concerned his art. In his letters we find him again and again pointing out to Draneth Bey that the new opera demands an exceptional cast — an absolutely first-rate soprano, mezzo-soprano, tenor, and baritone, and two good basses, and that all of them must be good actors as well as fine singers. He was particularly worried over the selection of the Amneris; he insisted that the singer of the part must be a genuine mezzo-soprano, not a soprano, and that in addition to an exceptional voice she must have a commanding dramatic personality.

Everything having been satisfactorily settled at last, the opera was sumptuously produced in Cairo on the 24th December, 1871, before an audience gathered from every part of the world. Verdi himself was not present; he always disliked the sea — the voyage from France to England being the greatest nautical adventure he ever attempted — and he objected to being fêted.

A fortnight or so before the production he received a letter from Filippo Filippi, the leading Italian musical critic of the day, saying that the Khedive had invited him to Cairo for the rehearsals and the first performance of *Aida*, and asking if he could be of any service to the composer there.

Verdi replied to him at once with his usual frankness. Thanking him for his offer, he uncompromisingly rejected it; he had no desire for journalistic *réclame*. " It seems to me," he said, " that under these conditions art is no longer art, but a trade, or a pleasure party, or a hunt, or anything else you like," notoriety, if not success, being now sought for at all costs. The only sentiment, he says, that all this inspires in him is one of disgust and humiliation. " I always remember joyfully my early days, in which, with hardly a friend, without any talk about me, without any preparations, without influence of any sort, I presented myself to the public with my operas, prepared to be shot at, and more than happy if I succeeded in creating some sort of favourable impression. But nowadays what an apparatus for an opera! Journalists, artists, chorus, directors, professors, etc. etc. — all think they must bring their own stone for the building of the edifice of *réclame,* to pile up a number of petty miseries that can add nothing to the merit of an opera, nor do anything to obscure its real value. It is deplorable, profoundly deplorable! "

The opera was next given at Milan on the 8th February, 1872, in New York in the following year, and at Covent Garden on the 22nd June, 1876. Verdi was delighted with the success it won everywhere; he rightly felt that Italian opera had done something to justify its existence in the face of the Wagnerism that then seemed to be sweeping everything before it.

In some accounts of the origin of *Aida* we read that " the original sketch of the libretto was developed in French prose by M. Camille du Locle, who worked under the eye of the composer at Busseto, and thus had the advantages of his advice and criticism. It was then translated into Italian verse by Signor Ghislanzoni." This account, however, does not entirely cover the whole facts as made known to us through Verdi's letters.

From a letter to his publisher, Ricordi, on the 25th June, 1870, it would seem that when he was in Paris at the end of 1869 or the beginning of 1870, after he had refused to accept a commission for an opera, du Locle had sent him a printed sketch of a story by " an important and anonymous person," and that having read the sketch he was willing to set to music a libretto on the subject. Du Locle then visited him at Sant' Agata, where the two went over the sketch together, Verdi suggesting various alterations. Verdi thought at first that all the Italian librettist would have to do would be to turn the French prose into Italian verse. He suggested Ghislanzoni for the purpose, offering to pay him well, the libretto to be the composer's property. Ricordi arranged matters with Ghislanzoni, and then the latter's troubles began.

Verdi took his new task perhaps more seriously than he had taken any before. He sought information from various quarters as to Egyptian and Ethiopian geography and history, the mysteries of Isis, and so on. He was not disposed, as he might have been in his earliest days, to accept anything within reason that called itself a libretto. What he now wanted was a thoroughly effective dramatic poem.

He must have worried Ghislanzoni considerably with his frank criticism of the latter's verses, his suggestions for alterations at this point or that, and his occasional demands that fresh verses should be written to fit in with music already composed. He did his best to gild the pill, tactfully begging Ghislanzoni to understand once for all that he was not criticising his poem *as* a poem, but merely giving his opinion upon it as adapted to stage effect; but all the same we feel that Ghislanzoni must have had rather a bad time.

In one of his letters Verdi writes: " If I am to give you my opinion frankly, I must say that the scene of the consecration does not appear to me to have turned out as well as I had expected. The characters do not always say what they ought to say, and the priests are not sufficiently priest-like. Further, it seems to me that you have not found the *parola scenica* [i.e. the manner of expression adapted strictly to the stage], or, if you have it, it is buried beneath the rhyme of the verse structure, and therefore does not come out as clearly and cleanly as it ought to do."

In another letter he urges Ghislanzoni to say what he has to say in fewer words, especially in the recitatives. He insists on the necessity of the *parola scenica* wherever the action is brisk: " I do not know if I make myself clear when I speak of the *parola scenica;* I mean the sort of speech that defines and clarifies the situation."

In the scene in which Amneris surprises Aida's secret from her by first of all telling her that Radames has been killed and then that Radames lives, Ghislanzoni originally had some lines that may be roughly translated thus: " Now fix your eyes firmly on mine and lie to me if you dare. Radames lives." " This," says Verdi, " is less theatrical than these words — ugly, if you like — ' With a single word I will tear your secret from you. Look at me; I have deceived you; Radames lives! ' You will reply, no doubt," he continues, " ' And what about the verse, the rhyme, the strophe? ' Well, I do not know what to say; but when the action demands it I would fling overboard rhythm, rhyme, and stanza; I would write blank verse in order to express the essentials of the

action clearly and concisely. In the theatre it is sometimes necessary that the poet and the composer should have the talent for
writing neither poetry nor music."

Sometimes, on fire with the subject and unable to wait for
Ghislanzoni's text, Verdi would dash off the music to the scene
as he saw it, and then ask the librettist to find words to go with
the music. The correspondence was a long and trying one on both
sides, and Ghislanzoni must have been relieved when his ordeal
was over.

The brief orchestral introduction, which is the finest operatic
prelude ever written by Verdi, commences with the sad, appealing
theme of Aida high up in the violins:

A short but exquiste development of this is followed by the fateful motive representative of the Priests of Isis:

This is developed contrapuntally for a few bars, but just as it is
getting into its stride, as it were, it is swept aside by the Aida
motive, which, after being put through some exquisite metamorphoses, soars to a triumphant climax and then dies away in the
heights.

When the curtain rises we see the magnificent hall of the King's
palace in Memphis. At the back is a great gate through which are
visible the temples and palaces of the town, and, beyond these,
the pyramids. Two characters are seen in consultation —Ramphis, the High Priest of Isis, and Radames, a young captain of
the guard. Egypt, it seems, is once more at war with Ethiopia,
the King of which is now threatening Thebes and the valley of the
Nile. After a few lines of dialogue, in which the Priest, looking significantly at Radames, declares that the goddess Isis has

already named the soldier who is to lead the Egyptian armies, Verdi plunges at once into the more lyrical substance of the story.

Ramphis having left the stage, Radames faintly hopes that it may be he who has been chosen; he sees himself in anticipation victorious, his return to Memphis in triumph — here the brass rings out with a magnificent fanfare:

and the beautiful Aida won for his own. His love for Aida is expressed in an aria that, coming thus early in the piece, is a severe trial for the composure and the technique of any tenor:

(This Aida is the slave of the King's daughter Amneris, who is also in love with Radames. Although no one at the Court knows it, Aida is Amneris's equal in rank, being the captured daughter of the Ethiopian King.)

Amneris already suspects that Radames and her slave love each other. The Princess enters at the conclusion of the aria, and reading in Radames's face his exultation at the prospect of his

appointment, she asks him whether there is not room in his heart
for a gentler emotion also; has he no other desires in Memphis,
no other hopes? His confusion and hesitation in answering confirm her suspicions, and in the orchestra we hear the agitated
motive of Amneris's jealousy:

Aida enters, to the accompaniment of her typical theme, and
Amneris notices how disturbed Radames is at the sight of the
slave. Disguising her feelings, she addresses Aida in honeyed
tones, assuring her that she is as much sister to her as slave, and
asking her to confide to her the secret of her tears. Aida assures
her that she is grieved at the thought of the war, the gathering
hosts, and the misery that is in store for the country. When Amneris asks her if she is sure that no other care oppresses her,
Aida casts down her eyes and tries to conceal her emotion. A
brief trio ensues, in which each character speaks in an aside, Amneris warning Aida that her secret is known to her, Aida be-
moaning her unhappy fate, and Radames apprehensively noting
the suspicion and anger in Amneris's eyes. The whole trio is
dominated by the motive of Amneris's jealousy (No. 5).

The King now enters, accompanied by his captains, guards,
ministers and priests, and Ramphis. Martial fanfares peal out in
the orchestra as a prelude to the King's address, which is to the
effect that grave news has reached him from Ethiopia. The messenger who has brought the news is commanded to come forward,
and he tells how the sacred soil of Egypt has been raided by the

barbarous Ethiopians, its fields laid waste, its harvests burned; and now, emboldened by their easy victory, the predatory hordes are marching on Thebes under the leadership of a fierce and indomitable warrior — their King, Amonasro. At this name Aida cries aside, " My father! "

Already, continues the messenger, through the hundred gates of Thebes the Egyptians have poured themselves upon the invader. All the men cry out for war, and the King, turning to Radames, tells him that by the will of Isis he has been appointed leader of the Egyptian armies. The King invokes the patriotism of his followers in a spirited melody:

(6) Allegro maestoso

Su! del Ni - lo al sa - cro
Up! of Ni - lus' sac - red

li - do ac - cor - re - te, Egi - zii e-
ri - ver guard the shores, E-gyp-tians

- roi,
brave,

that is taken up by all on the stage with the exception of Aida, who, in an aside, laments that inexorable fate should have made her love one who is compelled to be her country's foe. Amneris presents a standard to Radames, and bids him " return as victor "; the cry is taken up by the others, and to the strain of No. 6 in the orchestra all march off the stage, leaving Aida alone.

Bitterly she repeats Amneris's words, and in a long scena she describes the emotions that are contending in her breast — love for Radames, love for her own country, desire for its victory, and the hope of being restored to her father and her former high station. For a moment the thought of her father and her country comes uppermost:

L'in - sa - na pa - ro - la o
Ye gods_watch-ing o'er_ me, those

Nu - mi sper - de - te!
words deem un - spo - ken!

and she calls upon the gods to humble the Egyptian army in the dust. Then, to the melody of No. 1, she remembers her love for Radames and all the consolation it has brought her in her captivity. In a sad, sweet melody:

Allegro giusto poco agitato

I sa - cri no - mi di pa - dre, d'a-
Those names so ho - ly, of fa-ther, of

-man-te nè prof - fe - rir pos - s'i - o,
lo-ver, No more dare I now ut-ter

she bewails the unhappy division of her heart between her father and her lover, and ends with a pitiful cry to the gods:

Nu - mi, pie - tà del mio sof-
Mer - ci - ful gods, look from on

- frir! Spe - me___ non v'ha
high! Pi - ty___ these tears

pel mio do - lor
hope - less - ly shed

to look down in mercy on her, and a wailing prayer to Love to break her heart and let her die.

She goes out slowly, sobbing out her appeal for pity, and the scene changes to the interior of the temple of Vulcan at Memphis. It is lit from above by a mysterious light; at the sides are long rows of columns that recede into the dark distance. There are statues of various deities, and in the centre of the stage, on a carpet-covered platform, is the altar, surmounted with its sacred emblems. The fumes of incense arise from golden tripods. Ramphis is standing near the altar. From the priestesses among the columns comes a fascinating invocation to the god Phthà; it is accompanied by the harps, and its unusual intervals give it a strange exotic quality:

The invocation, which is broken here and there by a broadly harmonised melody for Ramphis and the priests, always terminates with a striking refrain:

The music is full of an intriguing religious mystery, which persists also through the ritual dance of the priestesses that follows:

During the dance Radames enters, unarmed, and goes to the altar, where a silver veil is placed on his head, while the High Priest, in solemn tones, tells him that the fate of Egypt has been placed in his hands by the gods, and bestows on him the sacred sword that shall bring terror and death to his enemies. Turning to the god, Ramphis sings a solemn prayer for protection:

(13) Grave

Nu - me, cu-sto-dee vin - di - ce
Hear us, oh guardian de - i - ty,

di ques-ta sa - cra ter - ra,
our sac-red land pro-tect - ing,

The melody is taken up in a higher key by Radames, and then by the priests; the priestesses strike in with the melody of No. 10, followed, as before, by No. 11; and it looks as if Verdi were about to build up an end-of-the-act ensemble of the usual brilliant kind. Towards the finish, however, the voices are hushed almost to inaudibility, as if the participants in the ritual were awed by the presence of the god; then, after a long silence, all give a great cry of " Mighty Phthà! " and the curtain falls.

The second act is concerned both directly and indirectly with the triumphal return of Radames from the war — directly in that the elaborate second scene is devoted to the pageant of the return itself, and indirectly in that the first scene brings to a crisis the secret rivalry of Aida and Amneris and discloses to the latter the slave's secret.

The first scene shows us a hall in Amneris's apartments; she is being attired by her slaves for the coming reception of the armies; young Moorish slaves wave great feather fans about her. The slaves sing the praises of the all-conquering Radames, Amneris breaking in from time to time with an ecstatic cry:

(14)

Ah! vie - ni, vie-ni, amor mio, rav-
Ah! come___ love, come love, let thy voice

-vi - va - mi d'un ca - ro accen-to an -
thrill   me with ac-cents dear once

- cor,   d'un ca - ro accen - to an - cor!
more, with ac-cents dear once more!

While the adornment of Amneris still proceeds, the young Moorish slaves regale their mistress with a piquant dance, after which the song of the Egyptian slaves is resumed, with Amneris completing it as before.

Softly the 'cellos give out the Aida motive, and Amneris, seeing the young captive approach, sends her attendants away. Tortured with jealousy as she is, she means to surprise Aida's secret from her. She begins cautiously and cunningly. With counterfeited affection she commiserates with Aida on the defeat of her people and assures her of her own love as some consolation for the misfortunes of her race. Aida replies that she can never be happy, far from her native land and in ignorance of the fate of her father and her brothers. But time, rejoins Amneris, will bring healing with it, and something more potent even than time — love. The word thrills Aida, and her typical motive becomes unusually animated as she sings of love's mingled joys and anguish.

Looking at her fixedly, Amneris, to the accompaniment of an insinuating phrase in the orchestra:

(15)

invites her to tell her all that is in her heart. Is there not some warrior in the Egyptian army to whom she has given her love? Fate is not equally cruel to all; and even if the fearless leader has fallen on the field. . . . At this, Aida betrays herself with a cry of pain. Amneris assures her that Radames has been slain by the Ethiopians, and so she is avenged on her enemies.

Aida's wailings at this news leave Amneris no longer in doubt. " Tremble! " she says vehemently; " I have read your heart; you love him; deny it not! " Then, as Aida tries to stammer out a denial, Amneris resumes, " One word more and I know the truth. Look me in the face: I lied to thee; Radames lives." Thereupon Aida, unable to disguise her relief, falls upon her knees and gives a fervent cry of thanks to the gods.

Amneris now throws off the mask. Does Aida, then, love Radames? So does she; the slave's rival is a Pharaoh's daughter! For a moment Aida's pride is in danger of betraying her; drawing herself up haughtily she is about to say that she too is of royal blood, but she checks herself in time, and falling at the feet of Amneris implores pardon and pity. It is true that she loves Radames, she sings in a touchingly beautiful melody, and this love is all she now has in the world, while her mistress is powerful and happy. Amneris repulses her with angry insults; she holds, she says, the vile slave's fate in her hands, and her heart is filled with the fury of hatred and vengeance.

Just then a fanfare is heard behind the scenes, followed by a patriotic chorus of Egyptians to the melody of No. 6. Aida sends up a last despairing cry — Amneris's fury, she wails, will soon be assuaged, for this slave's love that angers her will soon be extinguished in the tomb; but the inappeasable Amneris only reiterates her insults and threats of vengeance. The moving scene ends with a reiteration of Aida's former cry of misery (No. 9) with its pitiful sobbing ending.

The scene changes to a vast avenue of the city of Thebes. On the right of the spectator is a throne with a gorgeous canopy; on the left is the temple of Ammon; at the back is a triumphal arch. The stage is full of people excitedly awaiting the coming of the victors.

To stirring processional music, that begins softly and gradually works up to a climax, the King enters, followed by priests, officers, standard-bearers, and others. Next comes Amneris, with Aida (in a state of profound dejection), and other slaves. The King takes his seat on the throne, Amneris places herself at his left hand, and the people break into a vigorous chorus in praise of Isis and Egypt and the King:

The superb pageantry of the music is interrupted for a while by a softer strain from the women, which is followed by a fugued treatment, as usual, of the motive of the Priests (No. 2). This motive is admirably expressive of a rigid, overbearing priesthood; one realises that no mercy is to be expected by anybody who comes into conflict with its interests and its inexorable will.

Then the Egyptian troops enter, preceded by trumpeters playing a magnificent march theme on their long silver trumpets:

While the march is being played the troops defile before the King; then the trumpeters take up their station at the sides of the stage, leaving the centre for a group of dancing girls, who, in a piquant ballet, bring in the spoils of the conquered.

The splendour of the pageant increases as more troops enter, with war-chariots, banners, religious vessels, and images of the gods. No. 16 is given out once more, but with still fuller tone and still more gorgeous colour, the women's strain that previously followed it also being taken up by the whole of the people. At the height of the jubilation, as the hard motive of the priests is heard tearing its way through the general tissue, Radames enters, under a canopy carried by twelve of his officers. The King comes down from his throne and embraces the hero, hailing him as the saviour of Egypt; Radames kneels before Amneris, who places on his brow the crown of victory.

The King offers to gratify any wish that Radames may have, but the hero first of all asks that the captives may be brought in. It is to the Priests' motive (No. 2), sung softly by Ramphis and the others, that the Ethiopian captives enter, surrounded by guards; last of all comes Amonasro, dressed as an officer.

At the sight of him Aida impulsively cries, "My father!" and embraces him. Amonasro has only time to whisper to her a warning not to disclose who he is when the King orders him to come forward. "I am her father," says Amonasro in gloomy, dignified accents; "I fought, I was conquered, I sought death in vain." Pointing to his uniform, he says that he is an officer who fought against fortune for his own King, who fell on the field of battle. He ends with an appeal to the King:

(18)

Ma tu Re, tu sig-no - re pos-
But oh, King, in thy po - wer trans-

-sen-te, a co-sto-ro ti vol-gi cle-
-cen-dent, spare the lives on thy mer-cy de-

-men - te
-pen - dent

to show clemency to those who are now in his power, for who can say what turn fortune's wheel may take on the morrow?

Aida, the prisoners, and the slaves take up the appeal, but the priests cry out to the King to harden his heart and send his captives to their death. On these motives Verdi builds up one of his most imposing ensembles, in which all on the stage take part.

Meanwhile Radames looks sadly and lovingly at the weeping Aida, and Amneris regards them both jealously. Radames reminds the King of his promise, and asks that the Ethiopian prisoners may be granted their life and freedom. The priests protest against this clemency, and Ramphis warns Radames of the danger of releasing these hardened warriors, in whose hearts will be only one thought, that of vengeance; but Radames replies that their last hope has perished with the death of Amonasro. Ramphis then demands that at least Aida's father shall be retained as a hostage, and to this compromise the King consents. In his gratitude to the victor he gives Amneris to Radames, declaring that they shall jointly reign over Egypt after him; and Amneris, aside, cries: "Now let the slave rob me of my love if she dares!"

The chorus of jubilation (No. 16) breaks out once more, and over it is heard the voice of Aida bewailing this destruction of all her hopes; Amneris exults in her triumph, while Radames, dismayed at his undesired good fortune, declares that not even the throne of Egypt outweighs Aida's love.

The librettists and composers who plan gigantic ensembles do not always realise that with half a dozen people singing half a dozen different sets of words the spectator is not likely to hear them all; so it is not surprising that the important words of Amonasro to Aida do not come over to the listener. He is bidding her not to give up hope, for vengeance upon their enemies will surely come and the fortunes of their country be restored. The vocal ensemble is completed by a last triumphal statement of No. 17 in the orchestra as the curtain falls.

The psychological interest of the third act centres mainly in Aida.

The scene is the banks of the Nile, with palm trees growing

everywhere. It is night, and a bright moon is shining. On the summit of a rock, half-hidden among the trees, is the temple of Isis.
From within the temple comes a softly-breathed chorus of priests
and priestesses singing to Isis, " Immortal Mother and Spouse of
Osiris, goddess who implanted chaste love in the human heart."
A boat approaches the shores; from it descend Amneris, Ramphis,
some veiled women, and guards.

The High Priest has brought Amneris to the temple on the eve
of her bridal, to pray the favour of the goddess who knows all
the mysteries of the human heart. " I will pray," says Amneris in
reply to his exhortation, " that Radames may give me all his
heart, as mine will be sacred to him for ever." All enter the temple,
where Amneris is to pray until the dawn, the others guarding her.
The chorus of priestesses and priests inside is heard again, and
for a few moments the stage remains empty.

Then, accompanied by her typical motive, Aida, closely veiled,
enters cautiously. She has appointed to meet Radames here. If
he comes only to bid her a last farewell, then, she says as she
turns towards the river, she will find a tomb beneath the dark
waters of the Nile, where perhaps there will be peace for her,
peace and forgetfulness. Never, she sighs, will she see her beloved native land again; and she sings a long and moving song
as she dwells in recollection upon its loveliness:

(19)

O cieli az - zur-ri, o dolci au-re na - ti - -ve,
O skies ce - ru-le-an, breezes soft blow - -ing,

There is an equally exquisite second strain to the song:

(20)

O ver-di col - li o pro - fu-ma-te ri - ve
Sweet sloping ver-dure by streams so softly flow - ing

The aria is the most perfect lyrical expression Verdi had ever
achieved till then. It is, in essentials, the traditional show piece
of the soprano; but, like every other traditional operatic form in

Aida, it is lifted high above all conventions; the *prima donna* has the fullest opportunities to show off her range and her technique, yet there is not a bar that is not perfectly congruous with the character and the situation.

As the orchestra, the aria being concluded, is sighing out the exquisite No. 20, Amonasro enters. It seems that he has been waiting for this opportunity to speak in secret to his daughter; for nothing escapes his eye, and he sees that she and Radames love each other, and that she is now awaiting him here. Her rival is the daughter of the Pharaohs, " an accursed, detested race, to us always fatal." " And I," replies Aida sadly, " I am in her power — I, Amonasro's daughter! "

Not in her power, rejoins Amonasro, if Aida wills it otherwise; he can show her a way by which she can vanquish her powerful rival and possess herself again of her country, her throne, and her love. Father and daughter, commencing with Amonasro:

(21)

Ri - ve - drai le fo - . res - te imbal-sa-
Once a - gain shalt thou on our bal - my

-ma- te,   le fresche val - li, i nostri templi
for - ests, our verdant valleys, our golden temples

d'or!
gaze!

join in wistful remembrances of their beloved country — its balmy forests, its green valleys, its golden temples; there Aida will find happiness in the arms of the man she loves.

Turning from this ecstatic picture, Amonasro darkly bids her remember how the Egyptians descended on their country and profaned their homes, temples, and altars, tore the young women from husbands, lovers, and fathers, and slew the mothers, the children, and the old men. Too well does she remember it all, replies Aida; and Amonasro, seeing how she is moved, confides his plan to her.

The Ethiopians are arming for another fight; success is certain if only they can discover one thing — the path that the Egyptian army will take. Radames is again to command the Egyptians; he loves Aida — the inference Amonasro leaves Aida to supply for herself.

At first she rejects the suggestion, but Amonasro savagely reminds her of what will follow upon her refusal — another victory of the Egyptians, more rapine and misery for Ethiopia. The blood of her country will be upon Aida's head; the dead already rise from their graves to reproach her, and among the phantoms is one that stretches towards her her withered arms and curses her; it is her mother! Roughly he repulses her: she is no longer his daughter; she is only the slave of the Pharaohs. She gives a cry, drags herself to the feet of her father, and, to an accompaniment the syncopations of which express her agitation, she assures him that she is still his daughter and that he may count upon her to save her country, even at the cost of her love: he approves her resolution in a phrase:

(22)

Pen - sa che un po - - po-
*Think that thy race*_____ *down-*

- lo, vin - to, stra - zia - to
trampled by the conq'-ror

of a splendid expansiveness.

Hearing Radames approaching, Amonasro, with a final exhortation to his daughter to be brave, conceals himself among the palms, where he can overhear everything that follows. Radames enters with a cry of rapture at seeing Aida again:

Pur ti ri - veg - - go, mia dolce A -
I see thee again,   my sweet   A -

- i - da
-*i* - *da*

She holds herself a little aloof from his transports; true that he loves her, she says, but how can he hope to escape from the net woven round him by the love of Amneris, the will of the King, the trust of the people, and the anger of the priests?

To the accompaniment of a figure in the orchestra that, restrained as it is, has still the true martial quality about it, but perhaps the quality of a war that is as yet only in anticipation, he unfolds to her the plan he has conceived. The Ethiopians have risen once more and invaded Egypt; he is again the leader of the Egyptian armies; when next he returns victorious he will prostrate himself before the King, open out his heart to him, and tell him that the only reward he wants is permission to unite himself with Aida.

The agitated motive of jealousy (No. 5) is heard in the orchestra as she warns him of the fury of Amneris, who will certainly call for vengeance on her, her father, and her country. He will defend her, replies Radames; but she assures him that it will be in vain. But if he really loves her, another plan is open to them — to fly together. She paints in glowing colours the delights of their life in her own country, while Radames hesitatingly declares that it would be hard for him to forget the land that gave him birth, the land for which he has fought, the land in which he first won honour.

The musical picture she paints of the loveliness of Ethiopia is one of alluring beauty. Radames still hesitating, however, she turns on him, vows he does not love her, and bids him to go to

where Amneris is awaiting him at the altar. This decides him; in
an impassioned phrase:

(24)

Si   fug - giam da que - ste
Yes   we'll   fly these walls now

mu - ra, Al_ de - ser_ to in-siem fug-
ha - ted, In_   the_ de - sert hide our

-gia - mo;
trea - sure,

he takes the resolution to fly with her, and their voices blend in
a rapturous duet.

They are hastening away when Aida suddenly pauses. " Tell
me," she says, " which path we must take to avoid the soldiers? "
" We will take," he says, " the path that we have chosen to attack the enemy by; it will be deserted until to-morrow "; and in
answer to her further question he tells her that the path is by way
of the gorges of Napata. Thereupon Amonasro emerges from his
hiding-place and cries triumphantly, " By the gorges of Napata!
There will my soldiers be; I am Aida's father and Ethiopia's
King! "

The astounded Radames cannot at first believe what he has
heard, but Aida implores him to be calm and listen to her. He
cries out distractedly that his honour is destroyed:

(25)

Io   son di - so - no - ra - to!
My name for e - ver bran - ded!

and that for Aida he has betrayed his country; and he cannot
be quietened either by Aida's entreaties or by Amonasro's

assurance that no guilt attaches to him, for it was the will of Fate.

Amonasro invites him to come with him beyond the Nile where his warriors are gathered, and where love shall crown his de- sires. He is dragging Radames off when Amneris, with a cry of " Traitor! " comes out of the temple, followed by Ramphis, the priests, and the guards. Amonasro draws his dagger and throws himself on Amneris, but is held back by Radames. At a word from the High Priest the guards seize Radames, who calls to Aida and Amonasro to save themselves by flight. The guards pursue the escaping pair, and Radames, with a heroic gesture, surrenders himself to Ramphis.

One of the strong points in the *Aida* story is the fact that it in- cludes two women's parts of equal importance. In the third act our interest centred mainly in Aida; in the first scene of the fourth act it is the psychology of Amneris that claims our attention; while in the last scene of all Aida again takes the foremost place.

The first scene of the fourth act takes place in a hall in the King's palace. On the right is a passage leading to the prison in which Radames has been confined; on the left is a large door that leads to the subterranean hall of judgment. The feverish, cat-like motive of Amneris's jealousy (No. 5) is given out by the orchestra, and we see Amneris crouching in misery before the door on the left.

From her recitative we learn that her hated rival and her father have escaped, while Radames is awaiting sentence from the priesthood as a traitor. " Yet no traitor is he," she says; " that he revealed the secret of the army he intended only flight — flight with her "; and her jealousy suddenly flames into rage as she cries, " Traitors all of them! To death with them! To death! " Then she suddenly checks herself. " What am I saying? " she wails. Amneris loves him still, with a desperate, insane love that is destroying her life. If only he could love her! She will make a last effort to save him.

She orders the guards to bring Radames to her. She makes a passionate, despairing appeal to him:

Già i sa-cer-do-ti a-du-nan-si
Now to the hall the priests proceed,

ar - bi-tri del tuo fa - to;
where judgment thou art wait-ing;

The priests, in whose hands his fate lies, she tells him, are now
sitting in judgment upon him; yet there is still a way by which he
may be saved — she will kneel at the foot of the throne and beg
for mercy for him. To the melody of No. 26 he replies sombrely
that to his judges he will make no attempt to exculpate himself,
for in the sight of neither gods nor men does he believe himself
to be vile; it was merely from his careless lips that the fatal
secret escaped; his thought was pure and his honour unstained.
He has no desire to live, for he has lost everything that made life
sweet.

In a broad melody that comes from the better part of her nature:

Ah!___ tu dei vi - ve - re!
Ah ___ no! con-sent to live!

Si, all' a - mor mio vi - vra - i;
Live, of all my love as - sur - ed;

Amneris implores him to live for her sake and for the sake of
the love she will give him. Taking up her own melody, Radames
cries that for Aida's sake he has betrayed his country, and Aida,
he says, to the mournful strain of No. 26, has been put to death
by Amneris.

But she tells him that Aida still lives: in the rout of the

Ethiopians Amonasro was killed, but Aida escaped, and there has been no further news of her. Softly and gently Radames invokes the protection of the gods upon Aida; may she get safely back to her own country and never know that he has died for love of her.

Amneris implores him to forget Aida, but Radames refuses life on such terms. The frenzied Amneris warns him of the fate in store for him now that he has turned into rage the love of the woman who might have saved him; but he is unmoved by her threats of vengeance, and declares that death will be welcome, since he dies for Aida. Amneris, overcome, falls upon a chair, and Radames is conducted out by the guards.

The hard, implacable theme of the priests comes out in the lowest tones of the orchestra:

and is developed in a slow, inexorable way as Amneris, in despair, curses this jealousy of hers that has sent Radames to his death and condemned her to eternal misery. The priests cross the hall to enter the chamber below, and at the sight of them she shudders and covers her face with her hands. " He is in their power," she mutters numbly; " it was I who threw him to them — I, myself! "

From below, in the subterranean hall, come the voices of Ramphis and the priests (unaccompanied by the orchestra) praying the gods to send down the spirit of justice among them. Radames, escorted by the guards, crosses the hall and goes below; as she sees him pass, Amneris cries distractedly, " Oh, who will save him? "

From the crypt we hear Ramphis solemnly indicting Radames for his offences; he betrayed the secrets of his country to the enemy; he deserted the camp the very day before the battle should have commenced; he has broken his faith, been false to country, King, and honour.

Solemnly Ramphis, from time to time, exhorts him to defend himself, and the exhortation is repeated by the priests; while Amneris keeps breaking in with despairing appeals for mercy; in one of her cadences:

(29) Allegro

Nu - mi, pie - tà, Nu - mi, pie -
Ah spare him, heaven, ah spare him

- tà! -
pray!

we recognise the old familiar Verdi of the sobbing cadence, but here it has an expressiveness and a dignity it never achieved in any of the earlier operas.

There is an extraordinary solemnity and fatefulness in the monotone of Ramphis and the other priests, but even more awe-inspiring are the silences that follow each exhortation to Radames to speak. As he persists in remaining silent, judgment is pronounced upon him; his shall be the death of all traitors — he shall be entombed alive beneath the altar of the god he has flouted. As the sentence is pronounced, the orchestra, rising to its topmost height, gives out a wailing theme of the type shown in No. 29, and Amneris shrieks out a curse upon these relentless priests who call themselves the ministers of the gods and who can never get blood enough to sate them.

The priests, coming out of the crypt, file slowly across the stage, and Amneris again assails them with insults and curses. They are punishing the guiltless, she cries. " Priest! " she hurls at Ramphis, " this man whom you are murdering, you know was once loved by me. The curse of a tortured heart will be upon your head with his blood! "

To all her ravings and wailings the priests only reply, with monotonous and implacable iteration, that the man is a traitor and must die. Ramphis and the priests having gone out, the maddened Amneris raises her hands and her voice in a last passionate appeal to the gods to avenge her, and the curtain falls.

The effective arrangement of the stage in the final scene was Verdi's own idea. He had already experimented with the divided stage in *Rigoletto,* but there the division was vertical, the scene representing both the inside and the outside of a house. In this last scene of *Aida* the stage is divided horizontally. The upper section shows us the interior of the temple of Vulcan, bathed in a bright light and glittering with gold. The lower section is the crypt in which Radames is awaiting death — a vast, gloomy place, the pillars of which are supported by colossal statues of Osiris with crossed hands. In the temple two priests, as the curtain rises, are lowering the stone that seals up the apartment below.

Radames, in the dark crypt, hears the fatal stone closing over him, and laments that he will see Aida no more. He hears a groan, and for a moment fancies he sees a beloved phantom; but it is Aida herself, who, having learned her lover's fate, has come to share death with him. He cries out in horror at the thought — she, so beautiful and pure, to die in the flower of her age for love of him! Aida, in an ecstasy of abandonment that is near madness, greets the radiant death that is hovering over them. She sees heaven opening above them, that heaven in which their immortal love will truly begin.

In the temple above, a solemn ritual is being conducted by the priests and priestesses, who, as the slow dance goes on, sing the invocation to Phthà that we have already quoted as No. 10; it is followed, as before, by No. 11. " It is the joyous dance of the priests," says Radames. " It is our hymn of death! " answers Aida. Radames makes a desperate attempt to move the stone that closes in the vault, but all his strength does not avail; and resignedly the lovers set themselves to await the inevitable end.

Aida bids farewell to the world in a strain of spiritualised ecstasy:

Radames takes up the words and the melody after her; the
final strain:

is their *Liebestod,* a mystical anticipation of the flight of their
souls to the eternal day.

The further course of the duet is blended with the chorus of
the priests and priestesses above. Amneris, in mourning, enters the temple, and throwing herself on the stone that closes the
vault, sobs out a broken farewell to Radames and a prayer to Isis
for his soul. Aida at last falls dying in the arms of Radames. Amneris keeps on intoning her appeal to Isis, the priests invoke great
Phthà once more, and the curtain slowly falls as the orchestra, the
strings seeming to soar to the skies, gives out slowly a last
reminiscence of the ecstatic Nos. 30 and 31.

Aida may be regarded as the culminating point of the older
Italian opera. It makes use of nothing but the long-familiar apparatus — spectacular singing, gorgeous stage settings, and the
ballet — but it lifts each of these factors up to its highest possible point of expression, and, on that high level, blends them in
a perfect unity.

VERDI'S work, like that of most composers who had a long life, falls into three fairly well-defined "periods." The first, extending from 1839 to 1850, contains some sixteen operas, among which the modern reader will recognise the titles of no more than two or three — *I Lombardi, Ernani,* and *Luisa Miller.* His rate of production slowed down as he grew older and became more thoughtful. The second period (1851–67) contains only ten operas, several of which, however, still keep the stage: among them are *Rigoletto* (1851), *Il Trovatore* (1853), *La Traviata* (1853), *Un Ballo in Maschera* (1859), *La Forza del Destino* (1862), and *Don Carlos* (1867).

During the next fourteen years Verdi wrote only one new opera (*Aïda,* 1871), though in 1881 he revised an earlier work, *Simone Boccanegra.* There are hints of the coming of the third period in the later works of the second, but its real beginning is in *Aïda.* Sixteen years elapsed between this work and *Otello* (1887), while the third opera of the third period, *Falstaff,* was not produced till 1893, when Verdi was eighty years old.

For so thoroughly dramatic a composer as Verdi good stage subjects and skilled librettists were necessities. He was not badly served by some of his earlier librettists, but it was not until he collaborated with Arrigo Boïto (1842–1913) that he found his ideal. Boïto, besides being a man of great culture, was enough of a genuine poet to turn out better libretti than the ordinary theatrical "poet" could do, and enough of a musician to understand what goes on in a composer's mind when he is writing an opera.

Boïto himself wrote music, though he was never more than a

cultured amateur in it; his *Mefistofele* (1868; revised version 1875) keeps the stage to-day by virtue of its subject, its impressive stage scenes, and the genius of certain great basses who play the part of Mephistopheles, rather than as the result of anything original or notable in the music. His posthumous *Nerone*, that was produced with great pomp in Milan three years or so ago, is also insignificant musically but theatrically imposing. We need have no quarrel with Boïto, however, for not being a better composer. If he had been, he would probably have been too busy setting his own libretti to want to write libretti for anyone else; and in that case he and Verdi might never have come together. Boïto's highest claim on the gratitude of music lovers is that he provided the great Italian master with the " books " of his last two operas — two of the best libretti that have ever been placed at the service of a composer.

We may perhaps regard it as a piece of good fortune for Verdi that he did not meet Boïto earlier in his career. He would no doubt have had one or two better Shakespearean libretti than that of the *Macbeth* of 1847, but he himself, at that time, would not have been musically ripe for them. The gods acted wisely in keeping the thirty-years-younger Boïto in reserve for him till he had attained to complete mastery of his ideas and his technique.

Boïto's adaptation of Shakespeare's *Othello* is an exceedingly skilful piece of work. Music requires more room to spread itself, if we may use the expression, than speech does, because its very essence is the elaboration and intensification of emotion; where the poet can say " I love you " in three words, the musician will need anything from ten bars to ten pages to say it in *his* way. A previously existing full-sized drama therefore calls for drastic concentration before it can be made fit for opera: the only exception we know is *Pelléas and Mélisande*. Debussy has set Maeterlinck's drama to music line by line; but he only manages to do so by writing the greater part of his opera in a sort of recitative, avoiding the big emotional expansions that other composers delight in.

The five acts of *Othello*, then, had to be boiled down considerably for operatic purposes. It would be difficult to imagine the

thing being better done than as Boïto has done it. He often keeps
so faithfully to Shakespeare that the musical phrase that Verdi
has written to the Italian words can be sung also to the English
words, or to words singularly close to these. Boïto has also been
most skilful in his compressions and condensations of the original.
Sometimes two or more scenes will be rolled together in his con-
jurer's palm, as it were, and then when his hand is opened we
find a single scene that contains the essence of the others. For
instance, no one who knows his Shakespeare would think an opera
on this subject complete if it did not contain something at least
of Othello's famous speech to the Senate, in which he tells how he
wooed and won Desdemona by regaling her with the story of his
campaigns and the dangers he had run. A less expert librettist
than Boïto would have done one of two equally unsatisfactory
things: he would either have omitted this altogether or wasted a
great deal of valuable time by devoting a whole act to the scene
before the Senate. Boïto begins his opera with Othello and Desdemona already married, and in the course of a short love-duet
between them in the first scene he makes their minds run back
upon his wooing of her. In Shakespeare Othello says:

> " She loved me for the dangers I had
> passed,
> And I loved her that she did pity
> them."

In the opera the pair go over it all in retrospect and in dialogue
form. " When you told me," says Desdemona, in effect, " of your
exiles, your adventures, your long miseries, I listened to you in
rapture." " I described for you," Othello answers her, " my bat-
tles, my going into the deadly breach . . ." And so on between
the two until the lyrical interchange culminates with Othello's:

> " You loved me for the dangers I had
> passed,
> And I loved you that you did pity
> them,"

to which Desdemona replies, to the same musical phrase:

> " I loved you for the dangers you had
> passed,
> And you loved me that I did pity
> them."

The substance of the whole of Shakespeare's long independent scene is thus given us in a few swift and very telling strokes. In the later parts of the opera there is a similar condensation and telescoping, so to speak, of the scenes in which Iago slowly casts his net round Othello, Desdemona, and Cassio.

Shakespeare's opening scenes in Venice are dispensed with: the whole action of the opera takes place in Cyprus. The first scene shows us a tavern on the quay, with the battlements and the sea in the distance. It is night, and a hurricane is raging. There is no overture; the curtain rises after a few tremendous bars that sufficiently paint the tempest. The chorus, with Montano and Cassio, are anxiously watching Othello's ship battling with the waves and wind, and praying for its safety. Iago thinks and hopes the ship is lost, but he has hardly spoken when the chorus break out into a great cry of " She's safe! She's safe! " and a few moments later Othello appears upon the fortifications, followed by his soldiers and sailors. " Exult! " he cries; " the Ottoman pride is buried in the sea; to us is the glory under heaven! After our arms came the tempest and destroyed them! "

Othello's cry of victory lasts only a dozen bars, but they constitute perhaps the most difficult first entry for a tenor in the whole of opera; they require enormous vocal power and a tremendous stage personality. Verdi wrote the part of Othello for Tamagno, a great bull of a man who had one of the hugest voices ever heard on the stage.

The crowd follows up Othello's ejaculation with a chorus of victory, during which the storm dies completely away. The crew of the ship come up from the shore and carry arms and baggage into the citadel, while the populace come from behind the fort with pieces of wood, with which they make a fire. Against this moving background Iago talks to Roderigo on the lines that will be familiar to the reader who knows his Shakespeare: Iago gives

vent to his hatred of Othello, promises Roderigo possession of
Desdemona, and pours out his scorn and envy of Cassio, who has
now entered and taken his place among a group of soldiers.
Iago's—

"And I,—God bless the mark!—his Moorship's ancient," is
set to a subtly ironic phrase:

The fire is now blazing away merrily, and neither Verdi nor his
librettist, being Italians, can resist the temptation for a chorus on
the subject: this is one of the three or four cases in *Otello* in
which the conventions of the older Italian opera assert themselves.
When the chorus is over and the fire has died down, Iago, Roderigo, Cassio, and a few other soldiers are seen at a table; some
are sitting, some standing. Iago exhorts the company to drink,
forces wine on Cassio in spite of the latter's refusals of it, and
breaks out into Boïto's version of the song "And let the canikin
clink." Verdi has found the perfect musical expression for the
lines—a rollicking melody with a refrain:

("Drink with me.")

that has almost a drunken jollity and yet a touch of the sinister about it.

The chorus take up the song; Cassio becomes tipsier and tipsier, and tries to sing the first phrase of it himself but fails at it, to the amusement of the others. Montano comes in to tell him he is expected for sentry duty on the bastion. Roderigo provokes Cassio by laughing at him for being drunk, and a fight ensues between the two, followed by Cassio's assault upon Montano when the latter intervenes. During the excitement Roderigo is sent off by Iago to raise the town, and the noise soon brings out Othello, who orders the combatants to put down their arms, demands an explanation, listens to Iago's hypocritical story of how the quarrel began, and cashiers the repentant and sorrowful Cassio with the words, " Never more be officer of mine."

Desdemona, who also has been disturbed by the tumult, now enters. Othello dismisses everyone, and the pair break out into the love-duet which, as we have said, covers most of the ground of Othello's speech to the Senate in an earlier scene in Shakespeare. The ramparts of a fort may seem an odd place for two lovers to choose to pour out their hearts to each other in, but opera is opera. Anyhow, in view of the beauty of the music, we are not inclined to be too critical of dramatic probability. The phrase to which Othello sings:

" You loved me for the dangers I had passed," etc., runs thus:

Desdemona takes up the melody and the words (with the necessary changes in the pronouns); and the lovers feel the cup of their happiness to be brimming over.

The duet comes to a quiet, ecstatic end with the lovely theme of the " Kiss ":

that will be used again with poignant effect in the final moments
of the opera. The pair go into the castle with their arms about each
other, and the curtain falls.

The scene of the second Act is laid in a room on the ground-
floor of the castle, with a garden at the back and porches at the
sides. There is a brief orchestral introduction, based on the smooth,
sinister, insinuating music that, when the curtain rises, accompanies Iago's advice to Cassio to beg Desdemona to intercede for
him with Othello. Cassio goes out; Iago follows him with a look
of contempt, and delivers himself of his famous " Credo." He believes only in a cruel God who has made him in his own image.
" From some vile germ was I born; I am wicked because I am a
man, and feel the elemental mud in my being. I believe that the
good man is only a bantering comedian, and everything about
him — tears, kisses, sacrifices, and honour — nothing but falsehood. After all this absurdity comes Death. And then? And
then? Death itself is nothing, and heaven only an ancient idle
tale." This " Credo," of course, is Boïto's invention. The key to
Verdi's subtle and terrible musical commentary on it is given in
the motive that prefaces it in the orchestra:

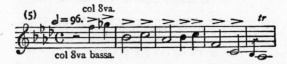

Desdemona comes into the garden with Emilia; Iago draws
Cassio from his place of retirement in the porch, and sends him to
her. Iago conceals himself in the porch on the left, gazes at the
pair fixedly, and pretends not to see Othello on the latter's entry.

As in Shakespeare, he skilfully works up the Moor's suspicion by means of hints and ejaculations, and Verdi's music is as subtle as the words; note, for instance, the insinuating melodic line of the query: "Did not Cassio know Desdemona in the first days of your love?" —

(6) ♩=84.

Cas - sio, nei pri-mi dì del vos tro-amor, De- . . sde-mo-na non co - no - sce - va?

and the creeping, serpent-like phrase to which Iago sings the equivalent of Shakespeare's —

> "It is the green-eyed monster, which
>   doth mock
> The meat it feeds on":

(7) pp

Eun' i - dra fo - sca, li-vi-da, cie - ca, col suo ve - le - no sè stes - sà at-tos - ca.

The dialogue between the two, which is treated throughout in masterly fashion, is marred somewhat by another hark-back on Verdi's part to the methods of the older opera type: he must have a chorus at this point, so he introduces a number of maidens, children, Cypriot and Albanian mariners, and so on, who surround Desdemona and offer her flowers; by way of local colour, they accompany their song with the *guzla* (a kind of mandoline) and other instruments.

The chorus over, Desdemona graciously dismisses her admirers and comes forward to Othello, with whom she intercedes on behalf of Cassio. Othello tries to shelve the question, but she insists. She takes out her handkerchief and tries to bind up Othello's head, but he throws the handkerchief to the ground. It is picked up by Emilia, from whom, later, it is snatched by Iago, during a quartet of the characters in the course of which Desdemona protests her love for Othello, while the latter fancies he sees their golden love trampled in the mud. Desdemona withdraws sadly with Emilia, and Othello gives full cry to his grief, ending with the famous " Othello's occupation's gone! " Iago, pretending to reassure him, subtly adds fuel to his suspicions; his " I lay with Cassio lately . . ." is a masterpiece of insidious suggestion. The scene ends with Othello's oath of vengeance, in which " honest Iago " insists on joining him.

The third Act takes place in the great hall of the castle, at the back of which is a colonnade. The orchestral introduction is based on the phrase to which Iago has lately sung, " It is the green-eyed monster " (No. 7). When the curtain rises, Othello and Iago are seen in the hall. From the colonnade a herald announces that the look-out has signalled the Venetian galley that is bringing the ambassadors to Cyprus. Othello dismisses the herald, turns to Iago, and bids him continue what he was saying. Iago advises him to conceal himself and observe Cassio with Desdemona. Meanwhile Iago goes out as Desdemona enters; his last words to Othello are to remember the handkerchief.

The dialogue between Desdemona and Othello is at first conducted on lines of high courtesy; but the atmosphere becomes disturbed when Desdemona speaks of Cassio. Othello tells her he feels his old malady coming upon him, and begs Desdemona to bind his head for him. The handkerchief that she produces will not do; he asks for the one he had once given her as a pledge of his love, the charmed handkerchief that an Egyptian woman had given his mother: woe to her if she has lost it! If she has, let her look for it at once! Desdemona believes he is merely feigning in order to turn her from her advocacy of Cassio; she harps upon her own theme until the maddened Othello takes her under the chin and by the shoulder and forces her to look at him. In answer to his tortured questions she protests that she is his chaste and loving wife. His mood softens for a moment into pity for himself and her; then his fury rises, and hurling a last insult at her, he orders her away. When she has gone, he breaks out into a pitiful lamentation over his lost happiness: he would, he says, have borne uncomplaining the worst misfortune with which it would have pleased heaven to visit him, but not this — to have had the illusion that sustained his soul and heart destroyed. His final cry, commencing with the phrase:

(8) ♩ = 60.

Spen-to è quel sol, quel sorriso, quel rag - gio che mi fa
vi - vo, che mi fa lie - - - to!

(Extinguished is that sun, that smile, that ray, that gives me life, that gives me gladness!)

is of a heart-rending pathos. Then his jealousy takes possession of him once more, and he resolves first to wring a confession from Desdemona and then to kill her.

He conceals himself as Cassio enters. Iago goes to meet the latter and gets him to speak gaily of his mistress Bianca; Othello, not having heard this name, which was spoken softly by Iago, of course assumes that it is his amour with Desdemona that Cassio is describing so light-heartedly. Cassio produces the mysterious handkerchief that Iago has caused to be left in his room, and Othello needs no more evidence to confirm his suspicions. Trumpets ring out, followed by a discharge of cannon — the signal of the arrival of the Venetian ship; Iago urges Cassio to go before the hall fills with people.

When he has gone, Othello emerges from his hiding-place and, as in Shakespeare, summarises his whole emotion in the one grim question, " How shall I murder him, Iago? " He nominates Iago his lieutenant, and asks him to bring him a poison that night; but Iago counsels him rather to suffocate Desdemona in her bed, and the justice of this mode of vengeance appeals to Othello. First, however, to avoid suspicion, Desdemona is to be shown to the legates. Iago goes to bring her, and Othello places himself in position to receive the Venetian dignitaries, who now enter, along with Desdemona, Emilia, soldiers, Roderigo, Lodovico (Desdemona's uncle), and others — finally also Cassio.

After a short chorus of greeting, Lodovico hands the Senate's message to Othello, who respectfully kisses the parchment and then opens and reads it. While he is doing this, the others engage in conversation: Desdemona tells them how her heart is oppressed, and Iago hypocritically hopes that Othello's anger against her will leave him. But when, still anxious to serve the dismissed lieutenant, she says to Iago, " You know how true my affection is for Cassio," Othello, still ostensibly reading, hisses *sotto voce* at her a command to check her tongue, and then, unable to control himself any longer, bursts out with a " Silence, devil! " that horrifies them all. He gives the herald an imperious demand to bring Cassio to him, and then quietly bids Iago watch both Desdemona and Cassio when the latter comes.

Othello announces the will of the Senate that he shall return to Venice, his place in Cyprus to be taken by Cassio. Lodovico begs him to say a word of comfort to Desdemona, but his only reply is, " We set sail to-morrow! " Then, in a gust of rage, he seizes Desdemona and, to everyone's horror, throws her to the ground. Emilia and Lodovico raise her, and she pours out her sorrow in long, touching musical phrases that are continued through the elaborate ensemble that follows. Othello, at the end of it, hurls himself at the company and imperiously orders them to depart. Desdemona runs to him with a cry of " My husband! " but he repulses her with a curse. The stage empties, except for Othello and Iago. Othello, foaming, cries out " Blood! " raves about the handkerchief, and falls in a swoon. " My poison works! " says Iago. Outside, the crowd shouts " Long live Othello! Long live the Lion of Venice! " Iago looks at the prostrate form of the Moor, and with a fiendishly derisive gesture points to it and says " Behold the Lion! " as the curtain falls.

The fourth Act commences with a short orchestral prelude based on the " Willow " song that Desdemona sings later (see No. 9).

When the curtain rises, we see Desdemona's bedchamber. A lamp burns before an image of the Madonna that stands over a faldstool. It is night, and the room is dimly lit by a candle on a table. Desdemona tells Emilia how Othello has ordered her to await him, and in touching tones bids Emilia to lay on her bed her wedding sheets, and —

> " If I do die before thee, prithee
>   shroud me
>   In one of those same sheets."

" I am so sad, so sad," she sighs, and, seating herself mechanically before the mirror, she breaks out into the tale of the " maid called Barbara " and her song of " Willow," which begins thus:

goes on to the mournful cry of " Willow ":

and ends with the Italian equivalent of " Sing all a green willow must be my garland ":

(11) Can - tia - mo! can - tia - - mo!

Three other verses of the ditty she sings, interrupting herself from time to time to give Emilia orders. In the third stanza she sighs " Poor Barbara! ":

(12) Po - ve - ra Bar - ba - ra!

After the fourth verse she bids Emilia " Good night," and the maid turns to depart; but hardly has she done so than a premonition of coming evil overmasters Desdemona, and she bursts out into a heart-rending cry of " Emilia, farewell! ":

(13) Ah! E - mil - ia, E - mil-ia, ad - dio, E -
- mil - ia, ad - di - - - o!

The wild passion of it, the unexpectedness of it, and the sudden *fortissimo* of the orchestra make this simple phrase the most terribly poignant moment in the whole work.

Emilia embraces her and goes out. Left alone, Desdemona kneels at the faldstool, sings a quiet, touching prayer to the Virgin, and then lies down in the bed. A secret door opens, and Othello appears; as he slowly and furtively makes his way down the stage he is accompanied by some most sinister phrases low down in the double basses: it is as if some great fearsome beast were stalking its prey in the darkness. He lays his sword on the table, pauses before the candle, looks for a moment at Desdemona, then puts out the light, makes his way to the bed, pauses again, draws the curtain aside and contemplates the sleeping figure. Thrice he kisses her, while we hear in the orchestra the earlier " Kiss " motive. Desdemona awakes. Othello accuses her of loving Cassio and of having given him the prized handkerchief; bids her not perjure herself on her deathbed by denying it, and suffocates her in the midst of her prayers and cries.

As he stands contemplating her, a noise is heard without. Emilia knocks and feverishly demands entrance. When at last Othello has admitted her, she cries out that Cassio has killed Roderigo, but that Cassio still lives; and from the bed is heard a choked cry from Desdemona. " O falsely, falsely murdered! . . . A guiltless death I die! Farewell! " " She lies! " says Othello; " 'twas I who killed her."

Emilia passionately scorns his story of Desdemona's guilt with Cassio, runs to the door and calls frantically for aid. Lodovico, Cassio, Iago, and others enter. Emilia denounces her husband's perfidy, and Montano rushes in with the news that Roderigo, before he died, has exposed Iago's wiles. The villain flies Othello takes up his sword, but at the bidding of Lodovico lets it fall again. He goes to the bed, utters over Desdemona a last pathetic monologue, draws a dagger from his doublet and stabs himself. With the last of his strength he kisses her, to the strain of the " Kiss " motive, and the curtain falls.

CHARLES FRANÇOIS GOUNOD

C HARLES FRANÇOIS GOUNOD was born in Paris on the 17th June, 1818. His father, an engraver and lithographer of repute, died when he was five years old. His mother, of whom he was passionately fond, exerted a great influence upon the soft, impressionable nature of the child who was left entirely in her charge. She supported herself and her two children at first by continuing her husband's business as a lithographer, and afterwards by teaching the piano. To her Charles François owed the rudiments of his musical education; for his general education he attended the Lycée Saint-Louis.

His bent towards music had asserted itself at a very early age, and he was no more than thirteen, and still at the Lycée, when he begged his mother to let him adopt the art as a career. His mother, however, wisely kept him at his general studies for some years longer, and it was not until he was eighteen that he was allowed to enter the Conservatoire, where he became the pupil of Halévy for counterpoint and fugue, and of Lesueur for composition. He entered three times for the Prix de Rome. The first time he was placed second; the second time he failed completely; the third time, in 1839, he won the coveted prize with a cantata, *Fernand*. The next three years he spent, in accordance with the terms of the prize, mostly in Rome, visiting Germany on the way back to his own country.

He was all his life of a deeply religious temperament, and in 1846 there was some question of his entering the Church, a temptation which he managed in the end to withstand. During the years immediately following 1846 he wrote a Mass in G, four numbers from which were performed at St. Martin's Hall, London, under John Hullah, on the 15th January, 1851. This was the beginning of Gounod's long and close association with England.

He dallied with various forms of composition, including the symphony, but, like every other French composer of that time, he had to look to the theatre for a career, and for the theatre he was only in a minor degree fitted by nature. He had an abundant flow of pleasing music of several kinds, but the one kind that was mostly lacking in him was the dramatic. Hence the large number of his stage works that were either partial successes or complete failures. In Rome he had attracted the attention of the great singer Pauline Viardot, who later asked him to write something especially for her. The result was Gounod's first three-act opera, *Sapho*, which, no doubt owing to the influence of Madame Viardot, was produced at the Paris Opera in 1851. The work did not keep the stage, in spite of a remodelling, in two acts, some seven years later; all that the ordinary music lover of to-day knows of it is the aria " O ma lyre immortelle." A second stage work, *Ulysse* — choruses and incidental music for a five-act tragedy by Ponsard (1852) — was no more successful; this, too, was revised and put on again in 1854, but without breaking its ill-luck.

A third opera, *La Nonne Sanglante*, produced in Paris in 1854, ran only to eleven performances. A comic opera, founded on Molière's *Le Médicin malgré lui* (in the English version *The Mock Doctor*), produced in 1858, was fairly successful. It was not until he was nearly forty-one that Gounod made a success, and that a world-wide one, with his *Faust* (Paris, 19th March, 1859); in this he was for once fortunate enough to find a story strong enough in itself to hold his charming lyrical music together.

After that came another sequence of failures and semi-failures: *Philémon et Baucis* (1860), *La Reine de Saba* (1862) (given in

English under the title of *Irenej*, *Mireille* (1864), *La Colombe* (1866), *Cinq Mars* (1877), *Polyeucte* (1878), *Le Tribut de Zamora* (1881), and *Sapho* (1884) (a third version, in four acts, of his first opera, 1851). One enduring success broke the monotony of these discouragements — *Roméo et Juliette* (1867).

All this while Gounod had been devoting considerable attention to religious music, with occasional excursions into lighter moods, to one of which we owe the delightful *Funeral March of a Marionette*. The Mass in G had been followed in 1855 by the Saint Cecilia Mass, and this by some nine other Masses. In addition he wrote, concurrently with his operatic works, an immense quantity of music for the Church or associated with religious words. In his later years he became more and more absorbed in religion. The *Redemption* was begun in 1868, but not finished until 1881; it was first performed at the Birmingham Triennial Festival of 1882. *Mors et Vita* was produced at Birmingham in 1885. His last work was a *Requiem* (1893). It is interesting to recall that his motet *Gallia* was produced at the Albert Hall, London, at the opening of the International Exhibition of 1871, and that out of the English choir that he created later to perform in the newly opened Albert Hall there developed what is now known as the Royal Choral Society.

To this large output has to be added some forty sacred songs (among them the famous *Nazareth*) and over two hundred secular songs, two symphonies, three string quartets, a number of piano and organ works, and the well-known *Meditation* on the first Prelude of Bach's " 48," which was written about 1854.

He had fled to London from the German invasion of France in 1870, and the English capital remained his home for the next three years. Here he formed that association with Mrs. Weldon that was at first a consolation and a stimulus and afterwards a sore trial to him. His friends managed to tear him away from the " sorceress " in the summer of 1874, and to plant him in his native country again. The lady, a prey to the traditional fury of the woman scorned, made it impossible for him ever to enter

England again without having to face a lawsuit and probable arrest.

He was working at his *Requiem* one afternoon in the October of 1893, in the company of a pupil, Henri Büsser, when he was attacked by a congestion of the brain, and fell forward on the piano. He died three days later, on the 18th, at Saint-Cloud. He was given a State funeral.

THE Faust legend is a very old one, and is probably, even in the earliest form in which it has reached us, a composite from various sources. Marlowe reduced the story to dramatic form in *The Tragicall History of Doctor Faustus* (1604). Towards the end of the eighteenth century, for some reason or other, the legend took possession of a great many of the most serious minds in Germany. It was a period of profound spiritual change, and the idealists seemed to recognise themselves in the old mediæval figure who was broken in his attempt to " read the riddle of the painful earth."

A writer of 1784 says that Goethe " undertook his work at a time *when in every quarter of Germany* Fausts *were announced as forthcoming;* and I know that he completed it. I have been positively informed that he only delayed his publication in order that the other *Fausts* might appear." We know, in fact, of something like thirty other treatments of the legend in Germany during the long period, lasting some sixty years, in which Goethe was working out his own vast plan.

The great poet probably first conceived the idea of a work on the subject when he was about sixteen — certainly before he was twenty. Nothing of it saw the light, however, until 1790, when certain scenes from the First Part of *Faust* as we now have it appeared. It was not until 1808, when Goethe was fifty-nine years old, that the complete First Part was published. He had long been working at intervals at the colossal Second Part, but it was not until he was seventy-five that he settled down seriously to the completion of this. The gigantic project was at last carried out to the appointed end in July 1831, a month or so before the poet's eighty-second birthday. He sealed the manuscript up, not wishing it to be published until after his death. He died on the 22nd March, 1832.

Few English people of the present day can boast of an acquaintance with the Second Part of Goethe's *Faust*. It is probable, indeed, that most people to-day are indebted entirely to Gounod's opera for their knowledge of the legend.

The libretto that Gounod has set to music corresponds in its essentials with the First Part of Goethe; this shows us the weary old philosopher who has given up in despair the hope of ever receiving an answer to his question as to the meaning of life, persuaded by Mephistopheles to sell his soul in return for the renewal of his youth, and then falling in love with Marguerite, who is afterwards executed for the murder of their child. In answer to Mephistopheles' malicious " She is judged! " a celestial voice cries out " She is saved! " and the First Part ends with the devil disappearing with Faust. In the slowly spun Second Part we see the gradual redemption of Faust through his unselfish love of humanity; the situation is summed up in the final song of the Angels who soar into the higher atmosphere, carrying the immortal part of Faust:

> " The noble spirit now is free,
>   And saved from evil scheming:
> Whoe'er aspires unweariedly
>   Is not beyond redeeming.
> And if he feels the grace of Love
>   That from on High is given,
> The Blessed Hosts that wait above
>   Shall welcome him to Heaven! "

It was inevitable that a subject of this kind should attract musicians — Beethoven at one time thought of taking it up — and it would probably be impossible to-day to enumerate all the musical settings of the legend. Schumann, in what, on the whole, is his finest work — *Scenes from Goethe's Faust* — has made a not unsuccessful attempt to combine the essentials of both Goethe's realistic First Part and his mystical Second. Berlioz, in his *Damnation of Faust,* treated the subject from a standpoint entirely his own, his work ending with a macabre " Ride to the Abyss."

Wagner, in his young days, projected a Faust Symphony, but did not proceed with it further than the first movement, which, in a later revision, we now possess as the *Faust Overture.* Liszt treated the subject in the form of a symphony, with a mystic chorus at the end of the last movement. In our own day, Busoni has given a new turn to the story in his posthumous opera *Doktor Faust.*

Gounod's *Faust* was produced for the first time at the Théâtre Lyrique, Paris, on the 19th March, 1859, and was at first only moderately successful. It quickly established itself in public favour, however, and in a very short time had overrun all Europe, including even Germany, which had come to regard itself, in a special sense, as the guardian of the Faust subject. It has been said, though with what truth we do not know, that it was the overwhelming popularity of Gounod's *Faust* that held Wagner back from the completion of his own work. Reading between the lines of his autobiography, we can perhaps see that Wagner was anything but pleased with this success of a French composer in what was regarded as a specifically German subject. During the troublous days of the production of *Tannhäuser* in Paris in 1861, Gounod boldly championed the cause of Wagner. " As an acknowledgment of this," says Wagner, " I presented him with the score of *Tristan and Isolde,* being all the more gratified by his behaviour because no considerations of friendship had been able to induce me to hear his *Faust.*"

Gounod's opera was, in its first form, an *opéra comique.* This term does not necessarily denote a comic opera, but merely an opera in which the non-lyrical portions are carried on by means of spoken dialogue; Bizet's *Carmen,* for instance, is an *opéra comique* in spite of the tragic nature of the subject. When *Faust* was taken to the Paris Opera, on the 3rd March, 1869, the spoken portions were replaced by music, and it is in this later form that *Faust* has come down to the present generation. The librettists of Gounod's opera were Jules Barbier and Michel Carré, the former a prolific French dramatist of some ability, the latter a minor man of letters who had already produced a little play entitled *Faust et Marguerite*. Barbier had a good deal of skill in the manufacture of opera texts, and was greatly in demand in Paris for this class of work; among the best known of his other " books " are those for Meyerbeer's *Dinorah* and Ambroise Thomas's *Hamlet*.

We have rather contradictory accounts of the origin of *Faust*. Gounod tells us in his autobiography that during one of his nocturnal rambles while he was living as a student in Rome there first occurred to him the idea of a setting of the Walpurgis Night scene in Goethe's poem, and that for many years after he jotted down any idea which he thought might be useful if ever he should compose an opera on the subject. One would think, therefore, that he is entitled to be believed when he says that, having made the acquaintance of Barbier and Carré in 1856, he asked them to collaborate with him and suggested *Faust*, an idea which pleased them both. That he had had the idea of an opera on the subject of *Faust* in his mind since his Roman sojourn appears to be beyond dispute; but he was perhaps in error in saying that it was he who suggested *Faust* as a subject for collaboration with Barbier and Carré.

Barbier's own story is that he had conceived an admiration for the genius of Gounod, whom he regarded as a coming man, and that having met him by accident one night on the boulevard, he asked to be allowed to write a libretto for him, and suggested *Faust* as a subject; whereupon Gounod said animatedly, " Ah! my dear sir! I have had that in mind from my earliest years! "

Carvalho, the director of the Théâtre Lyrique, who first produced *Faust,* gives us yet another version of the matter. He tells us that he met Gounod at a performance of an opera by Massé towards the end of 1866, and reproached him in a friendly way with not having brought a work to him for production at his theatre. " There is nothing I should like better," Gounod replied; " but what am I to do? Find me a subject! " " Well," said Carvalho, " do me a Faust "; and he continues, " That was thirty-five years ago, but I can still see the astonishment and delight in his eyes. ' A Faust,' he cried. ' Why, I have had that in my stomach for many years.' I give his reply verbatim; I have never forgotten it. We fixed up a meeting next day with Jules Barbier and Michel Carré, and it was decided that Gounod should begin work on *Faust*."

Barbier, by the way, had already offered a libretto on the subject to Meyerbeer, who refused it because, as a good German, he was outraged at the thought of turning the great national poem into an ordinary stage show.

Carré entered into the scheme with some reluctance; he thought the plot " worn out " by that time, and not particularly well suited to the theatre. His own share in the libretto seems to have been a small one. In his *Faust et Marguerite* there had been a version of the song about the King of Thule, and this was incorporated in the Gounod libretto; apart from this, his only contribution, so far as we can make out, was the song of the " Calf of Gold " in the second act, which was the final survivor of no less than thirteen experiments on Gounod's part.

It has been said that when the new opera was ready, the authors first offered it to Roqueplan, the director of the Paris Opera, who refused it, declaring the subject to be " out of date." His successor, Royer, also declined it, his reason being that there were not sufficient opportunities for scenic display in it. But whether *Faust* came to Carvalho in the first place or in the third place, it is certain that he agreed to put it on at the Théâtre Lyrique, in the Boulevard du Temple. But ill-luck still pursued it. A *Faust* by a dramatist named Dennery was put on at another theatre in the immediate vicinity, and it would have been injudicious to embark on the opera until this was out of the way. It was to keep Barbier and Gounod from chafing during the many months of waiting that Carvalho commissioned them to write *Le Médecin malgré lui,* which was produced in January 1858.

Meanwhile, though the part of Marguerite was being studied by Madame Ugalde, Carvalho's wife, who was also a singer, had taken a fancy to it, and Madame Ugalde had to be compensated with the leading part in an opera by another composer. Carvalho, after the fashion of theatrical managers, made all sorts of criticisms and suggested all kinds of alterations, some of which the authors had to accept: the church scene in particular was placed now before the love scene, now after it, and then before it, and then after it again. Carvalho's own account of the matter, in his *Memoirs,* is that originally the opera " was too long, and the performance would never have finished."

Gounod was very well pleased with his singers during the rehearsals, especially Madame Carvalho and Balanqué, the latter of whom played Mephistopheles. Gounod had hoped for great things from the tenor, Guardi, but the latter fell ill during the rehearsals, and the part had to be given to a provincial tenor, Barbot.

It was during the rehearsals that Carvalho managed, though with great difficulty, to persuade Gounod to cut out certain sections from the opera, especially a duet, at the beginning of the Kermesse, between Marguerite and Valentine, during which Marguerite gave her brother the little cross that figures later in his duel with Faust. Carvalho's objection was a rational one: he argued that the part of Marguerite would be much more effective if the spectators saw her for the first time as she crosses the stage and rejects the advances of the stranger Faust, instead of first appearing earlier in a somewhat unnecessary scene with her brother. There were also cut out a song in which Valentine praised the beauty of his sister, and the whole of the scene in the Hartz mountains, which was so long as to be quite impossible in a single evening. In place of the song of Valentine's just mentioned there appeared the Soldiers' Chorus, which had already been written by Gounod for another opera, *Ivan the Terrible,* which was never finished.

Almost at the last minute there were difficulties with the censor, who raised objections, on religious grounds, to the cathedral scene. Carvalho, who was at first in despair, got out of this difficulty in a highly ingenious way. One of Gounod's greatest friends and admirers was Monseigneur de Ségur, the Apostolic Nuncio at Paris. Partly out of liking for the composer, partly out of love of music, this dignitary attended all the final rehearsals.

One day, when the censor was raising his old objection in the theatre itself, Carvalho, who had Monseigneur de Ségur in his own box, said, " Well, we have with us Monseigneur de Ségur, the Apostolic Nuncio. Let us go to him, and I will ask him, before you, his opinion on the question whether the susceptibilities of Rome are likely to be hurt by the cathedral scene." They approached the Nuncio and put the question to him, and he replied, " But, Monsieur Carvalho, I should like all the theatres to have scenes like that. What! suppress the cathedral scene? Who on earth asked you to do that? " The censor went away quite satisfied. Carvalho, however, had very sagaciously omitted to mention to him that the Papal Nuncio was blind.

It is sometimes said that *Faust* was a failure on its production. That is not true; the work, containing so much that was new, certainly did not take the Parisian public by storm all at once, but it had a steadily growing success, and fifty-seven performances of it were given during the first year.

Gounod, in his autobiography, says, " The success of *Faust* was not overwhelming, yet so far it has been my greatest success in the theatre. Does this mean that it is my best work? I am absolutely unable to say; but in any case it confirms what I have already said on the matter of success, namely, that this is rather the result of a certain concurrence of fortunate circumstances and favourable conditions than a proof and a measure of the intrinsic value of the work itself. What wins the favour of the public at first is what lies on the surface of the work; but it is in virtue of what lies beneath that it maintains and strengthens its position. A certain amount of time is required to grasp the expression and the infinity of detail that make up the drama.

. . . I would call it a sensation rather than a shining success. The musical habits of the public, of the singers, and of the critics, and consequently of the publishers, were somewhat upset by it; the only publisher who nibbled at it was Monsieur Colombier, who had the magnanimity to offer us, for a work of five acts, the fabulous sum of four thousand francs! Our delicacy recoiled before so generous a proposition."

The publisher Heugel is said to have accepted the score, and then declined it under pressure from his partner. At last a friend of Gounod, Prosper Pascal, found a small publisher, Choudens, who had just started in a modest way. Pascal persuaded him to put practically the whole of his capital, ten thousand francs, into the purchase of *Faust*. The lucky investment laid the foundations of the fortunes of the house of Choudens, and must have paid for itself thousands of times over.

We have seen that for a fairly considerable time in the early part of his life Gounod coquetted with the idea of entering the Church. The impulses driving him in the direction of religion were probably more emotional than intellectual; his spiritual aspirations, in fact, were only the other side of his general longing for love. In this respect he strongly resembled Liszt, who all his life fluctuated between a very real appreciation of women, wine, and song, and a desire to live in a world entirely spiritual.

In 1857 Gounod seems to have passed through a final emotional crisis, for we read in a letter of Berlioz to Escudier of the 8th October of that year: " I expect you have heard of the new trouble that has descended on the Zimmermann family: poor Gounod has gone mad; he is at present in the asylum of Dr. Blanche, and his reason is despaired of." The Zimmermanns were his wife's family, with whom he was at that time living. He had been out riding in the morning. During dinner he suddenly went very pale, burst into tears, and went to his own room. The others followed him, and found him in a faint on the floor. He became possessed with the idea that his mother was ill, and insisted on being taken to Paris. No sooner had he arrived there than he had to take to his bed, where he became so delirious that at first a cerebral fever was feared. The convulsion passed; but as his reason still seemed affected, it was thought prudent to take him to the establishment of Dr. Blanche, where he stayed ten days or so.

By the 18th the French papers could announce the end of an illness that had caused considerable sensation in Paris. It seems likely that round about this period Gounod's physical, mental, and spiritual forces were all working at a white heat, and it is to this incandescence — an incandescence to which he never quite attained at any later epoch of his life — that we owe both his temporary breakdown and his *Faust*, which is the quintessence of all that is best in his genius.

Faust has become so familiar an object to the modern world, and so much has happened in music since 1859, that it takes a slight effort of the historical imagination to realize how overwhelming was the effect it produced upon its own generation.

For its day it was an exceedingly original and a very disturbing work. The more serious Germans did their best to disparage it; they could not reconcile themselves to so predominantly sensuous a treatment of a subject which, for them, was mainly spiritual and philosophical. But nothing could stay the triumphal progress of the opera even in Germany.

If we want to see how Gounod impressed his more intelligent contemporaries, we cannot do better than turn to the English critic, H. F. Chorley, of the *Athenæum*. Chorley, who had heard Gounod's *Sapho* in 1851, declared it to be "the best *first* opera ever written by a composer, Beethoven's *Fidelio* (his first and last) excepted." He described the special characteristics of Gounod as consisting in " a certain placid grandeur of line, a richness of colour, not perhaps sufficiently various, an elegance and tenderness of melody which belonged to no preceding model." Gounod, in fact, created almost as much stir in the musical world of his day as Wagner did. He was the subject of not only disparaging but wrathful criticism in some quarters, while Chorley made bold to declare, about 1862, that he " is now one of the very few individual men left to whom musical Europe is looking for its pleasure."

Chorley's article upon *Faust* is too long to reproduce in its entirety here; the reader will find it in his *Thirty Years' Musical Recollections,* and a perusal of it will prove very instructive. In those days *Faust* was not what it has become now, a coin that has been somewhat worn by its constant passing from hand to hand for more than half a century. It was fresh from the mint, and the people who heard the opera for the first time were better qualified than we are to detect the many features of it that were audaciously original.

The love-duet Chorley describes as " a real love-duet, if there was ever such a thing written; one of those inspirations which might have been born among the dews of a summer twilight, and the scent of flowers, and the musical falling of distant waters. The brief *adagio* which contains the full confessions of the pair has a luxury of tenderness and beauty which are unsurpassable." Our modern conception of love-music has been altered by the duet in the second act of *Tristan.* In comparison with the terrific fire of that, the love-music of *Faust* may seem to us to-day to inhabit a world of a rather lower temperature; but Chorley was right — at the time when *Faust* appeared there was no operatic love-music to compare with this either for sweetness or for depth of passion.

We see once more the difference between that age and this in our attitude towards the Soldiers' Chorus as compared with that of the generation of 1860. For us, the chorus has been somewhat cheapened by popularity; to the people who heard it for the first time it was a thrilling expression of communal feeling. Chorley says of it: " The return of the regiment is one of those seizing pieces of music which are instinct with fire. I shall never forget the riotous enthusiasm which burst out when this magnificent chorus, to which an army of myriads might sweep on its way to victory, electrified the ears of the Théâtre Lyrique on the night of the first performance of the opera. I feel it thrill in my pen as I write."

Goethe's poem begins with a Prologue in Heaven, in which Mephistopheles pours out his scorn upon man, and particularly on " the gleam of heavenly light which Thou hast lent him ":

> " He calls it Reason — thence his powers increased,
>   To be far beastlier than any beast."

Humanity is so vile and so stupid that he has " scarce the heart to plague the wretched creature." The Almighty asks him if he knows Faust. Mephistopheles replies:

> " Forsooth! He serves you after strange devices:
>   No earthly meat or drink the fool suffices:
>   His spirit's ferment far aspireth;
>   Half-conscious of his frenzied, crazed unrest,
>   The fairest stars from Heaven he requireth,
>   From Earth, the highest raptures at the best,
>   And all the Near and Far that he desireth
>   Fails to subdue the tumult of his breast."

The Almighty replies that though Faust is still in confusion as to his service under Him, some day he is certain to find the light. Thereupon Mephistopheles bets the Almighty that he can seduce the soul of Faust. The Almighty gives him permission to try, but prophesies his failure:

> " A good man, through obscurest aspirations,
>   Has still an instinct of the one true way."

These last two lines are vital for an understanding of Goethe's poem. It is clear from these that the First Part of it describes only the preliminary stage of Faust's trial; the full meaning of the Almighty's words does not become evident until, at the end of the Second Part, Faust has redeemed himself by love and good works. It is for this reason that the musicians who have had a sure understanding of the significance of Goethe's poem as a whole, like Schumann and Liszt, have tried to round off their *Fausts* somewhat in the manner of Goethe's.

The French librettists and the French composer, on the other hand, ignored the mystical philosophy of the poem. They were content with a Faust who, after the restoration of his youth, has an ordinary love-affair with Marguerite, which ends in a way in which a great many love-affairs do, and at the finish, though

Marguerite, in spite of her crime, is saved by her essential purity, the spectator is sent away with the impression that Faust becomes the property of Mephistopheles for all time.

The opera has no formal overture, but only a short Introduction, the first part of which (*adagio molto*) paints the melancholy philosophical broodings of Faust, while the second consists of a simple statement of Valentine's aria in the second act. This aria, " Even bravest heart may swell, In the moment of farewell," was written for Charles Santley when the opera was produced in English at Her Majesty's Theatre in 1864; so that the Introduction as we now have it is an afterthought.

The *adagio* has always been recognized as the most truly Faust-like music in the whole opera. It commences with an arresting fortissimo chord, followed by a pianissimo unfolding of a contemplative theme:

One of the most noticeable peculiarities of Gounod's style is the immediate repetition of a phrase, or a group of phrases, in another key, generally a higher one than the first. We see this love for the sequence (to give its technical term) on the opening page of *Faust:* the whole of the matter quoted as No. 1 is instantly repeated, the fortissimo chord being this time A flat instead of F, and the succeeding theme also being given out a minor third higher. A second theme:

hints further at the doubts and difficulties that beset the soul of Faust. This theme is taken up and developed fugally:

rising to a climax and then dying away. Old-fashioned music-lovers in the eighteen-sixties shook their heads solemnly at this Introduction, the harmonies of which seemed to them dangerously revolutionary.

The music, which began in the key of F minor, has now swung
itself round into F major, in which key we hear Valentine's song:

A few placid bars, of which the following, with its flowing triplets,
is typical:

bring the Introduction to an end. It will be seen that there is
nothing in this short and unassuming prelude to justify the charge
of " Wagnerism " that was hurled at Gounod by some of his
agitated contemporaries.

The curtain rises on Faust's study, a narrow, lofty, gloomy
Gothic chamber. Faust, an old, bearded man, is poring over his
folios and crucibles. The brief orchestral prelude to the scene is in
the vein of the genuinely Faust-like music we have already heard;
the basis of it is the following theme:

which, in accordance with Gounod's practice, is repeated again
and again in higher keys, mounts to a climax, and finally dies
away in exhaustion. Faust, in a recitative, describes his weary
vigils, in which he has sought in vain for an answer to his enquiries

as to the meaning of the universe. When, in a more glowing passage, he speaks of his great age and yet his inability to find refuge in death, we have the first hint of Gounod's dramatic limitations; the music in itself is charming in its lyrical way, but it is hardly the kind of music we should expect an old philosopher like Faust to be singing under such circumstances.

As if in mockery of his cares, the orchestra gives out a merry dance-tune, for it is Easter Day, and all the world is rejoicing:

Faust resumes his lament; night is passing away, another day is about to dawn; he calls upon death to come in its pity and end his strife. Then he comes to a sudden resolution. If death thus avoids him, why should he not go forth and seek it? He bursts into a joyous song of greeting to his last and brightest day:

Once more the lilting strain of human delight in the joys of earth is heard (No. 7, now given to a distant chorus of female voices).

As he raises to his lips the goblet that has so often been drained by his fathers, another merry tune is heard without, this time from the men who are going to the fields. They end with a call to "Rejoice and pray," and the "Pray" is taken up and echoed by Faust in a kind of ironical despair. If he prays, who is there to hear him? Who will give him back his youth, with its love and its faith? In a revulsion of feeling he curses everything that has formerly given him pleasure — his hopes, his ambitions, his learning. He calls upon the powers of evil to come to his aid, and at once, to the accompaniment of some sinister chords:

Mephistopheles appears, gaily dressed as a rich nobleman, with sword by his side and a cloak thrown over his shoulder. We have to take his own word for it that his purse is full of money. Faust, suddenly chilled with terror, bids him begone, but Mephistopheles ironically pleads for politer treatment. He can grant Faust his heart's desire. Shall it be gold? Faust contemptuously asks what value gold would be to him. Glory then, perhaps? Mephistopheles enquires. No, not glory either. There is only one thing that Faust longs for — the return of his youth; and he breaks out into a song of love of beauty and passion:

The accommodating devil is quite willing to satisfy Faust's desire in this respect also. Faust asks what the fee will be, and Mephistopheles assures him that that is a mere trifle, hardly worth talking about; up here he will be Faust's humble servant, but down there Faust must wait on him. Seeing him waver at this, Mephistopheles plays his last and surest card. He causes a vision of a beautiful woman to appear: it is Marguerite at her spinning-wheel. The orchestra gives out one of the themes of the later love-duet (See No. 27); Mephistopheles again promises Faust all the delights of youth and love for which he longs, and the old philosopher at last signs the fatal bond. He is at once transformed into a young cavalier, and his first question is, " When shall I see her again? " " To-day," Mephistopheles promises him; and the pair indulge in a joyous duet on the theme shown as No. 10, at the conclusion of which the curtain falls.

The second act shows us a Kermesse, or rustic merrymaking, in the market-place of a small German town. The orchestra gives out a gay theme:

which is quickly taken up by the basses of the chorus, representing the students; their song is in praise of drink. One of them, Wagner, carries on the melody as a solo:

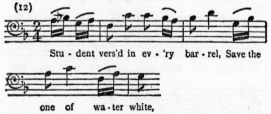

Stu - dent vers'd in ev - 'ry bar - rel, Save the

one of wa - ter white,

the students taking up his phrase after him.

They are followed by the soldiers (second basses), who sing of the delights of capturing any citadel, whether pertaining to girls or to more scientifically fortified places; the tune that characterises the soldiers is given not to the voices but to the orchestra:

To these succeed the citizens (first tenors):

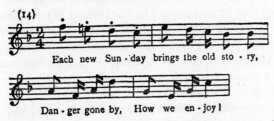

These old philosophers are content, they assure us, to sit under the trees and watch the boats going along the river, drain their goblets, and let the worrying and fighting be done by younger people.

The girls then break in:

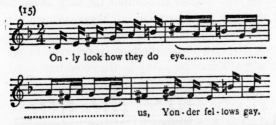

and their melody is taken up in a higher key by the students (second tenors) to the words "How those merry girls do eye us; we know what it means." Finally the tune is sung by the old men (the second sopranos, in a piping voice), who have observed the by-play between the students and the girls and think that they themselves are more deserving of the attentions of the latter. By way of finish, the drinking song (No. 11) is given out sonorously by the first basses, generally reinforced by the orchestra, while the other characters, in a piece of charming ensemble writing, carry on their own merry by-play.

Valentine now enters, contemplating a medallion that his sister Marguerite has given him. He is about to go to the wars, but believes that no harm will come to him so long as he is protected by this charm, which he hangs round his neck, singing the while the aria already mentioned, "Even bravest heart may swell." Wagner accosts him, demanding the cause of his gloom; Valentine replies that he is oppressed by the thought of the young sister whom he is leaving behind him with no one to care for her, their mother being dead. A young boy of the company, Siebel, promises to take Valentine's place as protector of Marguerite, and, this load being removed from Valentine's mind, the party gives itself up to jollity once more.

Wagner attempts the historic "Song of the Rat," without which no *Faust* can be considered complete, but has hardly got past the first couple of lines when he is politely interrupted by Mephistopheles, who has meanwhile come upon the scene unobserved. (Faust follows later.) Like the amiable and well-bred gentleman he is, the Prince of Darkness asks to be allowed to make one of the party; he begs Wagner to continue the song he has begun so well, and after that he himself will sing the company a better one. Wagner, however, exhorts him to begin his own performance at once, which Mephistopheles courteously proceeds to do. There is an outburst of demoniac jollity in the orchestra:

(16)

after which Mephistopheles plunges into his " Calf of Gold " song, which is in praise of gold as the true ruler of the world:

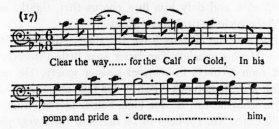

The song, after the first phrase, is accompanied in the orchestra by the swirling figure seen in the treble part of No. 16.

The words and the melody are so much to the taste of the company that at the finish all take them up with Mephistopheles. Then they begin to reflect about the matter; the song strikes them as a strange one, but Valentine finds the singer of it stranger still. Wagner opines that Mephistopheles' throat must be dry after this vocal effort of his, and offers him a glass. But a sinister atmosphere now begins to settle upon the scene. Mephistopheles, glancing at Wagner's hand, professes to be horrified by the presage he reads in its lines; if Wagner goes to the wars, he will be killed. Siebel is also anxious to test the prophetic power of the stranger, and asks to have his hand read: Mephistopheles crushes him with the announcement that every flower he touches shall wither. A further cynical hint to Siebel to " Look to your nosegays for Marguerite " brings in the fiery Valentine, who resents this use of his sister's name. Mephistopheles turns on him and tells him in sinister tones to beware, as his slayer is already awaiting him.

The mysterious stranger now puts the glass to his lips, but throws it away in disgust and offers to provide the company with something better. He puts his magic upon the barrel that constitutes the sign of the inn, and bids the company choose whichever wine they fancy while he proposes the health of Marguerite. Valentine, infuriated at this fresh impertinence, draws his sword and tries to attack Mephistopheles, but finds his weapon powerless in his hand. Realising now with whom they have to deal, the soldiers and citizens point the crosses of their swords toward Mephistopheles, and defy him in a chorus that, rightly enough, has a certain ecclesiastical tinge about it.

Valentine and the citizens leave the stage, still pointing their crosses at Mephistopheles. The latter is a little disconcerted at first, but soon recovers his normal sinister gaiety. He turns to Faust with a contemptuous " Bah! " for the rabble, and asks his companion what he can do for him. Faust, to the strain of the youthfully eager No. 10, begs to be taken to the lovely girl who has been shown to him in his cell — or was it only a figment of his imagination, the result of sorcery? Mephistopheles assures him that she is real enough, but that he will find it anything but easy to overcome her virtue. As he speaks of her being under the protection of Heaven we hear in the orchestra a motive:

which we shall meet with again later. Gounod, as will be seen, had imbibed a good deal of the Wagnerian doctrine of leading motives.

Mephistopheles, with a renewed assurance that he is Faust's slave on earth, promises that he shall see Marguerite soon.

The orchestra now gives out a preliminary hint of a waltz,

and the populace enter once more and dance to the strain of the famous waltz melody, that is given to the orchestra:

the chorus accompanying it with a tune of their own. A charming effect of double rhythm, it will be observed, is obtained by syncopating the melody across the bars, while the accompanying instruments maintain the regular one-two-three of the waltz. This number has lost none of its charm in nearly three-quarters of a century, and its gaiety must have been intoxicating to the audiences that heard it for the first time.

Mephistopheles and Faust, the latter all impatience for the arrival of Marguerite, stand aside and watch the happy crowd. Siebel is also waiting for her to come: but he is too young and shy to declare his passion. He expresses his sentiments to the accompaniment of a tune that carries on the waltz very happily, yet somehow or other concentrates the attention of the moment not on the dancing crowd but on Siebel:

Then, when Marguerite at last enters, yet another change comes over the spirit of the waltz. Here again we can now see Gounod's superiority as a craftsman to the other French opera composers of his time; the music to the scene has been unbrokenly continuous from the beginning, yet with all sorts of changes of mood and atmosphere.

Siebel rushes forward with a cry of " Marguerite," but is ironically hedged off by Mephistopheles. Faust approaches Marguerite, and courteously offers to escort her home.

(21)

High-born and lovely maid, forgive my humble du - ty

She declines the offer with equal courtesy, disclaiming all title to the compliments he has paid her beauty, and passes off the stage, followed by Faust's passionate cry of " Angel of Heaven! I love thee! " Faust, in reply to Mephistopheles' query how he has fared, tells of his rebuff, and Mephistopheles once more sardonically promises his help. The girls of the chorus whisper among themselves at this strange happening: Marguerite has refused the attentions of a young and handsome nobleman! Gounod once more shows genius at this point: on the surface the orchestra seems still to be developing the same waltz as at the commencement, but the strain has a different colour each time the circumstances change.

The chorus soon forget the incident and plunge into the delights of the waltz again, till the curtain falls on the swirling groups.

When the curtain rises for the third act we see Marguerite's garden, with her humble cottage on the right. At the back is a high wall, with a door leading into the street. A brief orchestral introduction paints for us the calm of a beautiful summer evening, with a suggestion of a tremor in the air. But suddenly this mood changes. Gounod's marking of the new six-eight movement is " Allegretto *agitato* " — a point that is too often missed by both conductors and hearers. When Siebel enters it is not merely, as

is generally supposed, to bring flowers for Marguerite and sing a
pretty song over them. We have to bear in mind Siebel's rôle all
through the opera — that of guardian of Marguerite, a guardianship prompted at first by his own love, then confirmed by Valentine's committal of her to his charge while the brother is at the
war.

Now Siebel has been greatly perturbed by the sinister stranger
in the second act, with his prophecy that every flower he touches
— the nosegays he is so fond of offering to Marguerite — shall
wither. Siebel wishes to put the prophecy to a test. The *agitato* in
the marking is therefore important: it gives us the clue to the
frame of mind in which the boy hastens to the garden, dimly conscious of an evil that is threatening both him and Marguerite. The
spasmodic phrases in the orchestra as he enters are intended to
suggest his agitation.

He sings a simple little song of love:

(22)

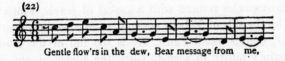

Gentle flow'rs in the dew, Bear message from me,

as he contemplates the nosegay he has brought. Innocent as the
melody is, his perturbation is indicated in the accompaniment. He
finds the flowers withered. So the stranger was right! Near by him
is a statue of the Virgin, with a little bowl of holy water. In this
he dips his fingers, and finds, to his joy, that the next posy he
plucks is unharmed. As he speaks of Marguerite coming each
evening to the statue to pray, we hear again the motive of the
" protection of Heaven," as we might call it (No. 18). He sings
his little song once more, this time with a stouter heart.

Faust and Mephistopheles enter. Faust's mind is more than
ever concentrated on Marguerite now that he is in her garden and
feels her presence in the beauty of the flowers; No. 10 is heard
again in the orchestra. Mephistopheles accosts Siebel ironically,
and the timid boy flies in terror. Faust would be alone with his
dreams, and Mephistopheles leaves him, declaring that he will

bring a present for Marguerite that will more than match the simple offering of Siebel.

Left alone, Faust breaks into his famous cavatina, " All hail, thou dwelling pure and lowly! ":

(23)

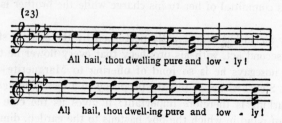

(Note, in the instantaneous repetition of the first phrase a tone higher, that love of the " sequence " on Gounod's part to which we have already referred.) The cavatina is a fine specimen of continuous lyrical development, and to this day it is without a superior in its own *genre* in French opera.

Mephistopheles returns with a casket of jewels, which he deposits, by the side of Siebel's nosegay, at Marguerite's door. Now, however, doubts assail Faust. He is too full of the thought of Marguerite's purity to wish to carry the adventure any further, and he begs Mephistopheles to leave with him. The tempter laughs at him, but humours him for the moment in order that the evil charm may work.

As the pair retire, Marguerite enters from the cottage, her thoughts running on the handsome young stranger who had accosted her at the fair. Who can he be? What is his name? She seats herself at her spinning-wheel and sings, in a sort of reverie, the ballad of " King of Thule ":

(24)

That her mind is on the adventure rather than on the song is shown by her unconsciously interrupting it every now and then to muse upon the grace of Faust's bearing and the kindliness of his looks, and her own embarrassment at the meeting. Then her thoughts turn to Valentine and to her own loneliness. She takes up Siebel's nosegay and sings tenderly of the faithful boy.

But now the casket, with its key lying by it, has caught her eye. Her curiosity is too much for her; she opens the box, and woman-like she is fascinated by the jewels it holds. She decks herself with them, seeing herself no longer as poor and humble Marguerite, but as a king's daughter. This idea is the theme of her " Jewel Song," another of the numbers in *Faust* that has lost not a particle of its first freshness: it is a perfect expression of the emotions of a girl, still little more than a child, dazzled by the sight of gems and overcome by the thought of all they will mean to her.

Her old guardian, Martha, now enters, and Marguerite has hardly had time to show her these new-found treasures when Faust and Mephistopheles come upon the scene. Mephistopheles takes charge of the old woman, first telling her that her husband has died and sent her his blessing, and then making grotesque love to the simple old soul, who is vain enough to think she has fascinated a fine gentleman. We hear first this couple and then Faust and Marguerite dialoguing, while occasionally the voices blend in a quartet.

The whole scene is a masterly piece of writing of its kind; the music flows on with logical coherence, yet each of the four characters is clearly differentiated from the others, not only in the

solo passages but in the ensembles. Marguerite confides to Faust
the sadness of her own lot — her mother and her dearly-loved
little sister dead, her brother at the war. Night is coming on, and
she begs Faust to leave her, while he implores her to accept his
love. They pass off the stage for a moment, leaving the scene to
Mephistopheles, who, in a sinister monologue, calls upon night to
draw around the lovers and complete his evil work.

Faust and Marguerite return, and the love-duet proper begins with an ardent melody from Faust:

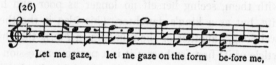

(26)

Let me gaze,   let me gaze on the form   be-fore me,

It is taken up by Marguerite, who, to test her lover, plays prettily the old game of " He loves me, he loves me not," with the
petals of a flower, their final answer being " He loves me! " The
music slows down to *adagio,* breaks into a new and more passionate strain (afterwards taken up by Marguerite):

(27)

O   ten - der   moon,   O star-ry Heav'n,

that may be regarded as the central and highest peak of the duet.

Again Marguerite implores Faust to leave her:

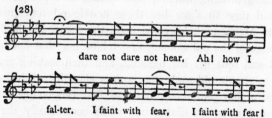

(28)

I   dare not dare not hear,   Ah! how I

fal-ter.   I faint with   fear,   I faint with fear!

and Faust responds with a cry to her beauty and innocence (No.
23 in the orchestra). Marguerite promises to see him on the morrow, and Faust lets her leave him and re-enter the cottage — a
weakness for which he is derided by Mephistopheles. Faust's
better nature still urges him to fly, but the devil holds him fast

and points to the window of the cottage. This slowly opens; Marguerite leans out, and, believing herself alone, pours out all her rapture to the night — " He loves me! " she says again and again. " At morn! At morn! Oh, speed the night away! He will return! Come! " A passionate motive in the orchestra accompanies her ecstatic cries:

(29)

The intoxicated Faust rushes to her with a wild cry of " Marguerite," and the mocking laughter of the triumphant Mephistopheles is heard through a last orchestral outpouring of No. 29.

The fourth act contains two scenes — the return and death of Valentine, and the church-scene. The former should come first, but in some productions it is placed last, because of the effectiveness and popularity of the Soldiers' Chorus.

By now it has become known in the town that Marguerite has had a lover and is about to become a mother. After a brief, melancholy orchestral prelude, we see Marguerite's girl-companions passing her by with a jeering song of lovers who " love and ride away and never return." She reflects sadly that she too was once only too ready to censure the frailties of other women; now, when she craves for sympathy and pity, everyone scorns her. Gounod here fails us somewhat; the music he puts into Marguerite's mouth has not the depth of expression we have a right to expect at so critical a moment in the drama.

Siebel, who alone remains faithful, now enters. Though he is but a boy in years, he says, he has the heart of a man: he will seek out the seducer and kill him. But Marguerite still loves Faust, and will hear no evil of him. She will go before the altar and pray; as she quits the stage we hear in the orchestra a reminiscence of one of the phrases from the love-duet in the preceding act. (The song of Siebel in this scene, " When o'er thy joying shone the pure sun of gladness," is another of the later additions to

the original score; it was written for the London production of
1864.)

A cheering crowd runs upon the scene, welcoming the soldiers
returning victorious from the war; they sing a breezy, rousing
song. Among the soldiers is Valentine, who catches sight of Siebel.
Valentine learns from the boy that Marguerite is in the church,
praying, he has no doubt, for him; but how greedily she will listen to the tales of the war that he has to tell her! The soldiers,
with plenty of support from the orchestra, sing the vigorous and
effective Soldiers' Chorus, at the end of which all march off the
stage, leaving Valentine and Siebel.

The former is all impatience to reach his home and tell his
tale and celebrate his safe return in a goblet; but Siebel holds
him back. His troubled manner and evasive answers at last arouse
the suspicions of the soldier; and when he is implored to " forgive
her," he is just about to brush the boy aside and make for the
cottage when Faust and Mephistopheles appear. The devil, who is
in excellent spirits, would enter the cottage and find Marguerite,
but the remorseful Faust bids him be still: already he has brought
too much misery on the girl. Then why stay in her neighbourhood? asks Mephistopheles; are there not other beauties waiting
for him? Laughing at Faust for his weakness in still loving Marguerite, Mephistopheles declares that he will bring her out with
a song. His mocking serenade:

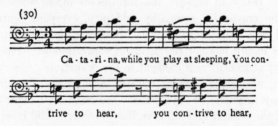

(30)

Ca - ta - ri - na, while you play at sleeping, You con-
trive to   hear,   you con - trive to hear,

is a song supposed to be addressed to a certain Caterina by her
lover, asking her to admit him: the singer, however, warns her
to " lock thy heart like a prison till thou hast a ring! " The song
is punctuated by bursts of derisive laughter from Mephistopheles.

Valentine, who, in the background, has heard the serenade, realises its bearing upon his sister. He steps forward, and we enter
upon the trio that is one of Gounod's best efforts in the whole
opera. " What is your will with me? " he asks Mephistopheles.
" With you? " the devil replies; " nothing! It is not for you my
serenade was intended. " " For my sister, then! " cries Valentine; and Faust learns, to his horror, that this is Marguerite's
brother. Mephistopheles mocks the young soldier with great
politeness: has something upset him, or is it that he does not like
the song? Valentine brushes the banter aside, and furiously demands to know upon which of the two he shall be avenged for the
wrong done to his sister. Faust has no stomach for the fight, for
he feels that Heaven will be on the side of the avenger; but
Mephistopheles urges him to take up the challenge. Valentine
contemplates sadly the charm that Marguerite once gave him,
curses it, and throws it from him — an action that is ironically
approved by Mephistopheles. Swords are drawn, and the two
men clash: aided by Mephistopheles, Faust deals Valentine a mortal wound, and the pair hasten away.

It is now night. The noise has aroused Martha and the other
neighbours, who enter hurriedly. They raise the dying man, who
bids them have no care for him, for he knows his end is near:

Marguerite runs to him, but he repulses her: " Her shame has
slain me! Her fine seducer's sword has sent her brother home! "
To long, wailing phrases in the orchestra, Siebel and the others
implore him to forgive her, but in vain; Valentine warns her that
some day, after the life of sin to which she is now committed, her

end also will come; and with his dying breath he curses her. The four bars of unaccompanied choral music with which the people pray for the peace of his soul are singularly moving; once more we see how readily Gounod finds the right expression for a religious mood.

The scene changes to a side-chapel in a great church in which a service is being held, while Marguerite pours out her broken-hearted penance before the altar. Some rising and falling chromatic chords suggest impending evil; then the organ gives out a solemn phrase. Marguerite prays for mercy, but is mocked by Mephistopheles (invisible, of course, to her, his voice seeming to be simply that of her own conscience), who denies her the right to pray, and calls upon the demons to terrify her, which they do (basses behind the scene crying threateningly "Marguerite!"). Mephistopheles reminds her of the days of her innocence, of her fall, and of the damnation now awaiting her; his biting phrases are sung to the accompaniment of the organ in the remoter part of the church:

(32)

A chorus behind the scenes, representing the church choir, thunders out, along with the organ, the words of the old Latin hymn, " Dies iræ," though not to the old plainsong melody always associated with that poem. Marguerite's emotions are suffocating her, but Mephistopheles is relentless. At last she bursts into a passionate appeal to Heaven for mercy, her voice soaring above those of the choir. Mephistopheles claims her as his own for ever; she gives a shriek and falls senseless to the ground, where she is found by the congregation as it streams out of the church to the final strains of the organ.

The last scene shows us Marguerite in prison: her misfortunes have driven her mad, and in her frenzy she has killed her child. The orchestral prelude opens with a passage that, in its majestic severity, seems designed to depict the inexorableness of the law as well as the sadness of Marguerite's fate. Then we hear a sound of galloping, and Faust and Mephistopheles enter. The latter is bent on acquiring the soul of Marguerite along with that of her lover. The warder has been put to sleep, and Mephistopheles has obtained admittance with his keys; but what he has to do must be done before the break of day, or it will be too late. The scaffold on which Marguerite is to pay the penalty of her crime is ready, and if Marguerite is to escape she must come quickly. Mephistopheles goes out, leaving Faust to prevail on Marguerite to fly with him. He contemplates her sleeping form for a time, his heart full of remorse and love. Then he wakens her. She breaks out into a cry of love for him:

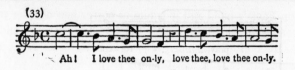

Ah! I love thee on-ly, love thee, love thee on-ly.

Death on the scaffold has no terrors for her now. Faust takes up the melody, and urges her to escape with him and commence a new life of happiness.

But now her crazed mind begins to wander. Faust and the prison are no longer realities to her; she begins to live again in the happy scenes of the past. Very softly the orchestra gives out the theme of the waltz from the second act, and she recalls her first meeting with Faust at the fair. She runs over in her memory his first greeting and her modest reply to it (No. 21). Then she is in her own garden once more, with Faust pouring out his love to her. The distracted Faust again and again implores her to fly with him while there is time, but she no longer has either the power or the wish to move. Mephistopheles enters, and bids Faust either come with him or stay and perish with her. Marguerite sees him, and recognises him for what he is — the symbol of all evil. Once more we hear the horses stamping in the yard, impatient to be gone. Marguerite turns to Heaven as her only refuge; her ecstatic song:

Ho-ly an-gel, in hea-ven bless-ed my spi-rit
longs with... thee to rest!

is given out three times, each time a tone higher. The voices of Faust and Mephistopheles blend with hers, the former trying to convince her that he has come to save her, the latter, more and more excitedly, urging Faust to make his own escape, as dawn is on the point of breaking. Her frenzy increasing, Marguerite sees blood on Faust's hand and bids him in horror begone. Her prayer has been heard: a celestial choir sings "She is saved," and proclaims salvation for all sinners who repent. Mephistopheles makes his escape, taking with him only one of his hoped-for victims — Faust.

GEORGES BIZET.

ALEXANDER CÉSAR LEOPOLD BIZET was born at Paris on the 25th October, 1838. His father was a teacher of singing; his mother was the sister of a pianist who married the famous singing teacher François Alexandre Delsarte. The boy's godfather invariably called him Georges; the name was adopted by the family, and it is as Georges Bizet that he is now always known.

He entered the Paris Conservatoire at the age of nine, and quickly became recognised as one of the most promising students of that institution. He studied the piano under the celebrated Marmontel, and counterpoint under Zimmermann, the father-in-law of Gounod; sometimes the future composer of *Faust* himself gave the boy his lesson. Later he worked under Halévy, the composer of *The Jewess*. He carried off many prizes, showed extraordinary facility in all kinds of directions, and in particular became a pianist of the first order. His sight-reading, especially of orchestral scores, was also remarkable.

In 1857 he shared with Lecocq the prize for an operetta on the subject of *Doctor Miracle;* for a time both works were given in the same evening at the Bouffes Theatre. In this same year Bizet won the coveted Prix de Rome with a " lyric scene " entitled *Clovis et Clotilde.*

In Italy he studied Rossini, Cimarosa, Mozart, and other composers of comic opera, as well as some of the serious German masterpieces. One of the works he sent home, in accordance with the terms of the prize, was an opéra bouffe, *Don Procopio,* set to

Italian words. The score, after having been lost for some years, was discovered long after his death, and the opera was produced for the first time at Monte Carlo on the 6th March, 1906.

The three months from August to October 1859 he spent in Naples, where he suffered seriously from a throat trouble to which he was always subject, and which, in all probability, was the root-cause of his early death. On his return to Paris he found more opportunities of gaining a hearing than fall to the lot of most composers of his age. An orchestral suite of his had been given at the Institut in 1861, and a commission from Carvalho, the director of the Théâtre Lyrique, produced the opera *The Pearl Fishers,* which was brought out on the 29th September, 1863. It ran to only eighteen performances.

He had no better luck with his immediately succeeding stage works. The libretti of some of them were lacking in dramatic interest, while his own talent seemed to be less dramatic than lyrical. The score of *Ivan the Terrible* (a subject that had attracted Gounod for a time) he burned. *The Fair Maid of Perth,* produced by Carvalho on the 26th December, 1867, was withdrawn after twenty-one performances, and *Djamileh* (22nd May, 1872) after ten. His other works of this period included an orchestral suite, *Souvenirs de Rome,* that afterwards became the *Roma,* another suite, *Jeux d'Enfants,* that had been originally planned for piano duet, and an overture *Patrie* (15th February, 1874).

In 1872 Carvalho gave up the Théâtre Lyrique for the Vaudeville, where he produced Alphonse Daudet's drama *L'Arlésienne.* For this he asked Bizet to write certain musical numbers. The play had no more than fifteen performances, but Bizet's music, arranged for the concert-room, soon became very popular. *Carmen* was produced at the Opéra-Comique on the 3rd March, 1875. It is generally supposed that the opera was a failure, and that the disappointment killed Bizet. Neither statement is true. *Carmen* was fairly successful from the first with the public, however severe some of the critics may have been on it. Between the date of its production and February 1876 it had fifty performances. Then it disappeared from the bills, to be revived, after it had become popular all over the world, on the 21st April, 1883. This time there could be no doubt as to its success: in Paris alone the work had 1,000 performances during the next twenty years.

Three months after the first production Bizet died suddenly at Bougival, near Paris, on the 3rd June, 1875. His death was in no way the result of the reception of *Carmen*. He had been persistently overworking for years, and the immediate cause of death was either heart failure or an embolism, with an abscess in the throat as contributory cause. He left an unfinished opera, *The Cid*.

His wife, whom he had married on the 3rd June, 1864, was the daughter of his master Halévy.

In addition to the works here enumerated, Bizet wrote a number of songs and piano pieces, and collaborated with Legouix, Jonas, and Delibes in a work, entitled *Marlbrough s'en va-t-en guerre*, that was staged in the Athenée Theatre, Paris, in 1867; Bizet contributed the music to the first of the four acts. The best of the songs, perhaps, is the *Adieux à l'hôtesse arabe;* but though Bizet could write such original and expressive melodies in his theatrical works, the detached song was not his vein. Nor have his piano works any particular distinction, with the exception of the twelve charming pieces for four hands, *Jeux d'Enfants;* they show his genius, in 1870, just ripening for the masterpieces of his later years.

Bizet was a passionate admirer of Wagner, and fought for him at a time when there was in many French musical circles a strong prejudice against him. It was perhaps the knowledge of this that made some of the critics of the time profess to see a Wagnerian influence in some of Bizet's later works, for it is difficult for us to-day to detect any such influence. Bizet was undoubtedly stimulated by Wagner's example, but he was too original a genius to become a mere imitator of the great German; whatever he took from Wagner he assimilated and made part of himself. When Nietzsche turned his back on his former idol, Wagner, he tried to set up *Carmen* as the model of what opera should be, and the example of everything that Wagner's music dramas were not. One phrase of Nietzsche's has become famous — " Music must be Mediterraneanised " — meaning that it must get away from the fogs and mists and philosophising of the North. *Carmen* is certainly the ideal music of the type Nietzsche had in view.

CARMEN

I T will probably be a long time yet before the legend dies that
Carmen was a failure at first, and that the failure was the
direct cause of the death of Bizet.

There is no truth in either part of this pathetic story. Bizet, it
is true, went away from the first performance somewhat depressed. But it is not at all an uncommon occurrence for composers to feel a little depressed after the first performance of a
work in which they have put their whole heart and soul, and of
which the reception did not quite come up to their fevered expectations; and Bizet was already an ailing and monstrously overworked man, an easy prey to depression.

There was necessarily a great variety of critical opinion upon
the new opera, as there is upon every new work of any originality,
and if a good deal that the critics wrote about *Carmen* after the
first performance reads very stupidly now, it must be remembered
that the musical Press of Paris in the eighteen-seventies included
a greater number of stupid and self-sufficient nonentities than have
ever exercised the functions of musical criticism in Paris or any
other town before or since.

At the first performance the first act was very warmly received, but the enthusiasm declined sensibly through the three
remaining acts. For this there were special reasons which we
shall consider later. But there is no justification whatever for
regarding the opera as a failure at its début. One of the librettists,
Ludovic Halévy, has told us that " after the vexatious *première*

the performances went on, but not, as has been said, before empty houses; the receipts, on the contrary, were respectable, and generally in excess of those for the other works in the repertory. Little by little, at each of the performances of *Carmen*, there was an increase in the number, at first small, of the admirers of Bizet's work. Things went on thus during the months of March, April, and May. Bizet left for the country, sad, but not discouraged."

That the opera found favour with the public is evident from the fact that by the 18th June — that is to say, only three months and a half after its production — it had reached its thirty-seventh performance at the Opéra-Comique. It was put on again at the commencement of the new season, and by the 15th February, 1876, had attained its fiftieth performance. It is true that it then disappeared from the boards of the Opéra-Comique for seven years, but operas cannot be given in theatres unless the directors so will it, and it happened that the director of the Opéra-Comique was not particularly enamoured of *Carmen*. But while the work was thus falling into neglect in Paris it had already commenced its triumphal career over Europe.

On the 23rd October, 1875, it was produced in Vienna with great success, and with still greater success at Brussels on the 3rd February, 1876. It was revived in the French provinces in 1878. In that year it was given in France, at Lyons, Marseilles, Angers, and Bordeaux; in Belgium, at Ghent; in Russia, at St. Petersburg; in Italy, at Naples and Florence; in Germany, at Mainz and Hannover. On the 25th June of the same year it was performed, in Italian, at Her Majesty's Theatre, London. On the 5th of the following February the Carl Rosa Company produced it in English.

By 1883 Parisians were asking themselves why this characteristically French opera, that had been so enthusiastically received everywhere else, should not be heard in Paris also; and public opinion ultimately forced the Opéra-Comique to revive the work on the 23rd April, 1883. That production does not seem to have been a particularly good one; and the real revival of *Carmen* in Paris dates from the 27th October of the same year, when the original Carmen, Galli-Marié, appeared in the title-part once more.

There were several reasons why the opera was a little slow in making its way at the very first. For its time it was a very original work, that cut clean across the routine of the Opéra-Comique at several points. It lacked the happy ending that the audiences at that respectable institution had become accustomed to. Its musical texture was rather too closely woven and continuous for some of the listeners of that day, and brought on Bizet the usual charge of Wagnerism.

It is significant that the " numbers " greeted with most applause at the first performance or two were those in the more conventional form — the duet between Don José and Micaela in the first act, Escamillo's song in the second, and Micaela's song in the third. Both the audiences and the singers of that day were fettered by conventions that we of to-day find it a little difficult to understand; when Colonel Mapleson produced *Carmen* at Her Majesty's Theatre in 1878, the Don José, Campanini, took a dislike to his part because the only number in the opera that could be said to approach a love-duet had to be sung with the *second* lady of the piece. Italian tenors of that time were not accustomed to this sort of thing: it looked to them like disrespectful treatment.

The subject, again, was not only new and a little disturbing for some sober tastes, but presented difficulties for both producer and artists. In the front of the house a good many susceptibilities were shocked by the novel spectacle of women smoking on the stage; while on the scene itself not only was there an absence of convincing ease about the efforts of the chorus girls to manage their cigarettes in the first act, but the results are said to have been physically distressing in the case of some of the ladies.

The bourgeois morals of the Paris of 1875 were shocked at some of the incidents in the opera, and the charge of immorality was freely levelled against *Carmen,* as it had been sixteen years earlier against Gounod's *Faust.* The Opéra-Comique was a very decorous theatre, and its habitués found the realism of *Carmen* rather too strongly flavoured for their taste. It is said, indeed, that a chief reason for the first antipathy to the opera on the part of many of the Parisians was the very realistic performance of Galli-Marié, who stressed the wild and sensual element in the character of Carmen.

It is highly probable, indeed, that she played the part as she understood it not simply from the libretto, but from the short story of Prosper Mérimée — one of the world's masterpieces in its genre — on which the book was based. The Carmen of Mérimée is a very different character from the Carmen of Halévy and Meilhac. Mérimée shows her as a captivating gipsy woman completely lacking in moral qualities. She is a creature of the wilds, who knows no law but that of her own appetites. She can love, but refuses to be fettered by any man after she has wearied of him. She is not merely the romantic associate of smugglers; she is, when opportunity serves, a very common sort of thief. She has no scruple in compassing or conniving at the death of any man who stands in the way of the realisation of her desire of the moment. She is not immoral; she is simply non-moral — a superbly vital and fascinating animal that knows no law but that of the wilds.

The character has been considerably softened down by the librettists, and successive performers of the part have gradually toned down even the crudities that remained in the French libretto, till the part of Carmen has, in our day, become more or less an agreeable and pretty convention.

The libretto does not follow the original story with any great exactness. There is no Micaela in the original; the character had to be invented partly in order to provide a contrast of colour in the women's voices, partly in order to ingratiate Don José with the audience by showing him to be simple and virtuous at bottom, always longing, until Carmen comes across his path, for the domestic virtues of his native village.

There is no Escamillo in the original; this character is an expansion and variation of a picador named Lucas, with whom Carmen has one of her passing flirtations. Le Dancaïre and Le Remendado are not the comic-opera smugglers shown us in the opera, but two business-like and serious-minded members of the band of brigands with which José becomes connected. Both come to a violent end some time before the conclusion of the story. Le Remendado is wounded in a fight with the pursuing soldiers: José wishes to save him, but Garcia, the one-eyed husband of Carmen at the moment, unwilling to lose time over an act of mere humanity, calmly empties his revolver a dozen times into the wounded man's head, with the object of making his face unrecognisable to the pursuers. Le Dancaïre is killed in a later mêlée with the emissaries of justice. Garcia is killed by José in single combat.

José, driven mad by jealousy, both loving Carmen and hating her, unable to live with her and unable to face the prospect of life without her, urges her to fly with him to America, where they can begin a new life. Carmen refuses scornfully; she no longer loves José, and is too proud to pretend that she does, even to save her life. José kills her, but not during the bull-fight, as in the opera, but in a secluded valley, after having visited a hermit and asked him to say a mass for the soul of one who is about to die.

Almost from the beginning of their association Carmen has told José that it is written in the book of fate that he shall kill her and that he will be hanged. Both prophecies come true; after stabbing Carmen and burying her in the valley, he gives himself up, and it is his story to a traveller, while he is in prison awaiting execution, that Mérimée has told us. Apart from these differences, the opera follows the story fairly closely, though some of the incidents are transposed, others telescoped, and others developed at greater length. In the original, Carmen, in her quarrel in the cigarette factory, draws her knife and slashes an S across the face of a girl who has offended her; if Galli-Marié played the part along these lines, one can hardly be surprised at the taste of 1875 being a little shocked at the realism of it.

The Prelude commences with the lively strain which, in the

last act of the opera, accompanies the preparations for the bull-fight.

It is followed by a tune of a slightly quieter kind, though in the same vein:

after which No. 1 is resumed for a moment. Then, without warning, the music makes a transition from the key of A to that of F, an abrupt proceeding that greatly scandalised the academic purists of the time; and after a few preliminary chords to mark the key the orchestra gives out softly the melody that terminates Escamillo's song in the second act:

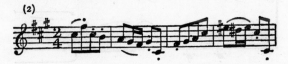

It is repeated in rather louder tones, and then, by a modulation as swift and unexpected as the earlier one, we are switched back into A major again, in which key No. 1 is heard as before. Then the tempo slows down from *allegro giocoso* to *andante moderato*, and underneath a tremolando in the strings we hear the motive that throughout the opera characterises the fascination of Carmen and the fatality associated with her:

(4)

This is at once repeated in a higher key, and for a moment it looks as if Bizet were about to develop it symphonically at some length; but he suddenly cuts it short with a crashing chord in the full orchestra, and after a longish silence the curtain rises.

The scene is a square in Seville. On the right is the door of the tobacco manufactory; on the left are the quarters of the guard; at the back is a bridge. When the curtain rises, the brigadier Moralès and a number of soldiers are grouped before the door on the left, while the square is filled with promenaders.

Throughout the opera Bizet shows an incomparable art in painting the movement of a scene; and of this art we have a fine example in the orchestral introduction and the chorus of dragoons, who comment brightly on the animation of the crowd and the drollery of the life around them. Another characteristic of the opera is that even the minor characters in it are given good music to sing; Moralès is only one of the soldiers, and has next to nothing to do with the working out of the plot, yet almost every phrase that Bizet puts into his mouth is significant and charming.

Micaela appears in the background, and the sight of her brings out all the gallantry of the dragoons. A delicate little phrase comes tripping out in the orchestra:

to the accompaniment of which Moralès draws the attention of his companions to the pretty new-comer. He asks her whom she is seeking; she replies, with the simplicity of manner that becomes an operatic blonde, " I seek a brigadier." " A brigadier? Behold me! " says the gallant Moralès. Micaela, however, makes it clear to him that what she is in quest of is not the species but a particular specimen of it, by name Don José; does Moralès know the name? They all know him well, Moralès replies, but he is not here; in fact, he does not belong to their company, but he is due shortly, with the guard that is coming to relieve Moralès and the others. Meanwhile will not the pretty maiden rest herself a while in the guard-house?

Micaela rejects the flattering offer, even after Moralès has assured her that she will be perfectly safe; and with a finer irony than we should have thought a good village maiden capable of she employs Moralès's own words and his own musical phrase for her reply that she will return when " the mounted guard comes to replace the descending guard." The soldiers becoming still more pressing in their invitation, Micaela thinks it prudent to seek safety in flight.

In the English version Moralès remarks, " The bird has flown; it was wise, I own "; but in the French he is much more philosophical; what he says is, " The bird has flown; well, let us console ourselves and resume our pastime of observing the crowd "; and the scene is appropriately rounded off with a chorus of Moralès and the soldiers on the lines of their first one.

A trumpet is now heard behind the scenes playing a military call in the distance; this is echoed by a trumpet in the orchestra, and the dragoons stand to attention before the guard-house. Right up at the top of the orchestra a perky little theme comes out, to the accompaniment of which the relieving guard marches in, accompanied by a troop of street-urchins. Behind these are the lieutenant (Zuniga) and the brigadier (Don José); behind these again come the dragoons. The two groups of guards range themselves opposite each other, while the boys, doing their best to look and behave like soldiers, sing of their valuable services to an ungrateful country in thus accompanying the guard:

(6)

When the soldiers mount on guard, We march with them
A - vec la gar - de mon-tan-te.   Nous ar - ri - vons,

man for man,   Trumpets! ring out our re - ward,
nous voi - là!   Son - ne trompette éc - la - tan-te!

Plan, ra - ta-plan, plan,   ra - ta - plan.
Ta ra - ta ta, ta   ra - ta ta.

Their song, and the orchestral accompaniment to it, are rather like genuine military music seen, as it were, through the wrong end of the telescope — a burlesque in miniature of the real thing. Moralès tells Don José that a charming young girl in a blue skirt, with blonde plaits hanging down to her shoulders, has been enquiring for him. "It must be Micaela," says Don José. The street-urchins give another imitation of the soldiers and go off, their perky little tune trailing off in the distance with them.

Zuniga is evidently a stranger to Seville. Is not that big building opposite, he asks Don José, the place where the cigarette girls work? "It is indeed," Don José replies; "and certainly nowhere else will you see girls of such light behaviour." Already, in this little remark, we see that Don José is a very serious and good young man from the country, who does not at all approve of either the manners or the morals of the cigarette makers. "But at least," Zuniga continues, "they are pretty?" "Lieutenant," replies the serious Don José, "I know nothing about that; I do not trouble about these gallantries." Zuniga replies chaffingly that he knows what it is that occupies the thoughts of Don José — a young girl with plaited hair, in a blue skirt, who answers to the name of Micaela. Don José admits the soft impeachment: he loves her; as for the work-girls and their beauty, well, here they are, and Zuniga can judge for himself.

The factory bell is heard, and the cigarette girls enter, followed by a number of young men. The latter make love to the girls:

(7)

'Tis the mid-day bell,   loud-ly, gai-ly ring-ing,
La cloche a son - né;   nous, des ou-vri - è - res,

For the pret - ty girls   we im - pa - tient wait. .
Nous ve-nons i - ci   guet-ter le re - tour;

whose only response is to sing a charming little chorus in praise of smoking; the music swings and curls as seductively and lullingly as the smoke they blow into the air from their cigarettes. This is the scene that was rather spoiled at the first performance by the unfamiliarity of the chorus girls of that epoch with the technique of smoking. Their expressions of delight in the novel pastime apparently failed to carry conviction to the audience.

But there is one, the men say, who has not yet appeared — La Carmencita! The words are no sooner out of their mouths than Carmen enters to the accompaniment of an appropriately impudent flourish in the orchestra, derived from No. 4. The men greet her enthusiastically, protesting that all are her slaves, and asking her to name the day when she will love them all. Simple as Carmen's reply is, it is one of the most effective first speeches made by any character in opera. When will she love them all? Upon her word, she does not know — perhaps never, perhaps to-morrow, but certainly not to-day; as she says this she throws a meaning glance at Don José. Light-hearted as her words and the music are, there is already a touch of the sinister in them. To the rhythm of the Habanera she tells the men that love is a bird that will not be captured; if it does not want to be caught, neither prayer nor caresses will bring it:

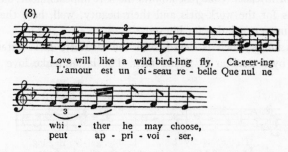

(8)

Love will like a wild bird-ling fly, Ca-reer-ing
L'amour est un oi-seau re - belle Que nul ne

whi - ther he may choose,
peut ap - pri - voi - ser,

This man, she says, speaks well, while this other is silent, and it is the latter that she prefers. Love is like the gipsy in that it knows no law; "you may not love me, but I love you; and if I love you, then beware!" Like a bird, love takes wing just when you imagine you have caught it. Now it is in the distance, and you wait in vain for it to come to you; then, when you expect it no longer, it is there! You think you hold it, and it evades you; you try to evade it, and it lays hold of you. And always her song takes up the mocking refrain, " You may not love me, but I love you; and if I love you, then beware! " Bizet founded this charming and expressive song on one by a practically unknown Spanish composer, Yradier.

The young men repeat their protestations that they are all Carmen's slaves, and gather round her. She, however, after a momentary glance at them, turns to Don José, who, indifferent to all women but Micaela, is making a chain for his sword. She looks at him fixedly, hesitates for a moment and turns towards the factory, then retraces her steps, stands in front of Don José, takes from her bosom a flower, and throws it in his face. Then she runs with a laugh into the factory, while the cigarette girls mock the brigadier with a phrase from the Habanera.

The factory bell is heard a second time, and the cigarette girls and young men leave the stage. The soldiers enter the guardhouse, leaving Don José alone on the stage. He picks up the flower, that had fallen at his feet, and in the orchestra we hear a reminder of the theme of the fatality of Carmen (No. 4). He is astounded at the effrontery of the woman, but cannot deny that the flower is pretty and that its scent is strong; as for the woman, well, if there are witches, she certainly is one! While he is indulging in these reflections he hears his name called, and finds, to his joy, Micaela before him. She has come, he learns, with a message from his mother, who sends him also a little money and — this, like a modest blonde, she can hardly bring herself to avow — a kiss from the mother with Micaela as the intermediary:

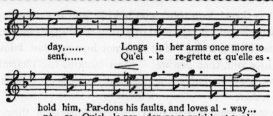

Micaela gives Don José the consigned kiss, and he breaks out into
a simple song of love for his mother and the village in which
his childhood was spent:

The whole of the music of this scene is a reversion to the pleasant
lyrical vein characteristic of the Bizet of *The Pearl Fishers* and
The Fair Maid of Perth. There is a cut in the English edition here.
In the French original the thought of Carmen crosses Don José's
mind, and we hear her motive in the orchestra. With a shudder
he reflects that he was on the point of becoming the prey of " this
demon " from whom he has been saved by his mother and
Micaela's kiss. Micaela anxiously asks him, " What demon? What
danger? " José does not give a direct answer. " Let us speak of
you," he says; " when do you return? " Micaela replies that she
is returning the same evening; to-morrow she will see his mother
again.

Don José, to the melody to which Micaela has announced his
mother's message (No. 9), sends back a loving answer, and he
returns her kiss through the instrumentality of Micaela. Then
follows a repetition of No. 10, which is developed in a little duet.
The object of the cut in the English version has no doubt been
to avoid a good deal of somewhat unnecessary repetition; the cut,
however, has the disadvantage of depriving us of the significant
moment in which we are first made to realise the sinister spell
that Carmen has already thrown over Don José.

Micaela having left him, Don José reads the letter in silence,
accompanied in the orchestra by No. 9, softly phrased in caressing
sixths:

"Have no fear, mother," he says; "your son will obey you. I
love Micaela and will take her for my wife; as for your flower, vile
sorceress ———"; but before he can finish the sentence there is
a great outcry in the wings. Cigarette girls and soldiers flock upon
the stage, and in an ensemble of incessant hubbub the girls, chattering like magpies, appeal to the soldiers to take their part
against Carmen.

There has been a quarrel in the factory. One of the girls, La
Manuelita, happening to say that she thought of buying an ass,
Carmen ironically recommended her to buy a broom instead.
Manuelita having made an appropriately acid reply to this pleas-
antry, she and Carmen had fallen upon each other and torn out
each other's hair.

When Zuniga can at last hear himself speak among the hullabaloo he sends Don José and a couple of soldiers into the factory to discover the cause of the trouble. The girls continue the argument at the top of their voices, some laying the blame on Carmen, others on Manuelita, till at length the soldiers clear them all away. This scene also is curtailed in the English version.

Carmen appears at the door of the factory in the company of Don José, the two soldiers following. Don José makes his report to Zuniga; there has been a quarrel, followed first of all by insults and then by blows, and a woman has been wounded by Carmen. Asked by Zuniga what she has to say in her defence, Carmen merely hums an insolent refrain:

(12)

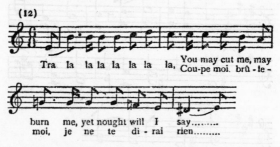

Tra la la la la la la la, You may cut me, may
                         Cou-pe moi. brû - le -

burn me, yet nought will I say.........
moi, je ne te di - rai rien.........

Seeing the impossibility of bringing her to reason, Zuniga commits her to prison, where, if she likes, she can continue her song. The chorus give a pleased cry of " To prison! " whereupon Carmen raises her hand to strike one of the girls who is near her. Remonstrated with again by Zuniga, Carmen hums her tune more impudently than ever (Bizet's directions are *avec la plus grande impertinence*). It is a great pity, says Zuniga regretfully, for she is a very nice girl; but she will have to be taught sense; so to avoid further breaches of the peace he orders her hands to be tied behind her back.

The dialogue that follows between Carmen and José (the others having left the stage) is in the form of recitative in the original; the change to spoken dialogue was made later, with, it must be admitted, a considerable gain in effect. Carmen begins to exercise her wiles upon Don José; he will not take her to prison, she assures him, because he loves her; that flower she had hurled at him — oh yes, he can throw it away now if he likes, but it has already exercised its sorcery!

Forbidden by the agitated José to speak to him again, she says in that case she will commune with herself, for thought, surely, is free! In an exquisite seguidilla:

Close by the ramparts of Se - - -. - ville,
Près des remparts de Se - vil - - - le,.

Dwells my good friend Lil - las   Pas - tia......
Chez mon a - mi Lil - las   Pas - tia......

she describes how she will dance and sing and look for a new lover in the tavern of her friend Lillas Pastia, near the ramparts of Seville. For there is not much pleasure in being alone, she says. Having quarrelled yesterday with her lover, she must now find another. A dozen gallants are besieging her, but she will have none of them; her heart is free; does anyone want it?

The scandalised brigadier again bids her be silent; has he not forbidden her to speak to him? She is not speaking to him, Carmen replies, she is merely musing to herself. She is thinking of a certain soldier who loves her, and whom she in her turn might be able to love. He is not a captain, not even a lieutenant; he is only a brigadier, but that is good enough for a gipsy like her. The charm of the flower has already worked; Don José feverishly asks her whether, if he does what she wishes, she will keep her promise to love him. She gives her word, and as he unties the rope that binds her hands she sings once more, at first softly, then triumphantly, of the delight of dancing the seguidilla and drinking manzanilla at Lillas Pastia's. The scene is a little masterpiece of characterisation; the music perfectly expresses the wildness of

Carmen, her gipsy longing for freedom and movement, and the undercurrent of fitful passion there is in her.

Zuniga enters with the order for Don José to transport his prisoner; as he gives it to him he advises him to keep a close eye on her. Carmen in a low voice tells Don José what he is to do; on the way she will give him a sudden push, whereupon he is to stumble and leave the rest to her. Completely at her ease again now, she turns to Zuniga, laughs in his face, and hums once more her impudent little refrain, " You love me not, but I love you; and if I love you, then beware! " She sets out with Don José and the soldiers; when she arrives at the foot of the bridge she carries out the plan arranged with Don José and makes her escape, to the general delight of the crowd.

The second act commences with a short orchestral introduction based on the little song sung by Don José on his entry later (see No. 19, pp. 220–1). When the curtain rises we see a room in the tavern of Lillas Pastia, which is the meeting-place of the band of smugglers of whom Carmen, when not engaged in other immoralities, is occasionally one. Carmen and two of her girl-companions, Frasquita and Mercédès, are sitting at the table with Zuniga and other officers of the dragoons. Gipsy girls are dancing:

(14)

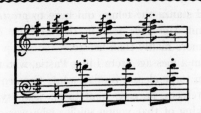

Carmen, to the same rhythm, sings a gipsy song:

Frasquita and Mercédès joining her in a piquant refrain:

At the end of the third stanza the tempo quickens to *presto,* and Carmen, Frasquita, and Mercédès join in the whirling dance, which has broken out more madly than before.

Frasquita brings them a message from Lillas Pastia, who thinks it is time for the tavern to be closed. Zuniga wants Carmen to go with them; when she refuses, he gives vent to his jealousy; evidently she is still thinking of that young soldier who was put in prison on her account. Well, he is free now, he says; whereupon Carmen gives a little cry of joy, and she and her two companions politely but ironically dismiss the men.

There is a cry, however, behind the scenes of " Hurrah! The Toreador! Hurrah! Escamillo! " A torchlight procession is passing, Zuniga tells them, in honour of the conqueror at the Grenada bull-fight; he invites them all to drink to Escamillo's successes, past and present. The toreador enters and is greeted joyously by them all. He thanks them for their toast in the famous " Toreador's Song," which describes the scene in the arena and the fight with the bull. A great deal of the superb effect of the song comes from the strength of the very original rhythm:

(17)

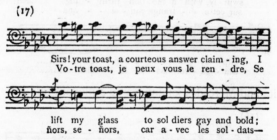

Sirs! your toast, a courteous answer claim - ing, I
Vo - tre toast, je peux vous le ren - dre, Se

lift my glass to sol diers gay and bold;
ñors, se - ñors, car a - vec les sol - dats—

To each stage of the graphic description of the bull-fight is appended a refrain in the major, in which the toreador turns to thoughts of the bright eyes that are fondly regarding him and the impressionable hearts awaiting him. In this refrain, the melody of which has already been heard in the Prelude to the opera (No. 3), the other principals and chorus join. At the end of the last verse is an exquisite effect that is too often omitted in performance, owing to the difficulty of finding, for the parts of Frasquita and Mercédès, chorus girls with sufficient beauty of voice and confidence in their own powers; the texture of the passage is shown in the following quotation:

In the English version the words are " For thee awaits." In the French, however, the whole passage is sung to the words "L'amour" (" Toréador, l'amour, l'amour t'attend! "). Mercédès first sings the words, and is answered expressively by Escamillo. Frasquita repeats the little phrase at a slightly lower pitch, Escamillo answering her also. Finally Carmen, with a glance at Escamillo, strikes in with her expressive contralto tones; Escamillo returns the glance and echoes her phrase in the deeper tones of his own register, and then the whole company carry the refrain to a vigorous conclusion.

Escamillo has been greatly taken with Carmen, whom he now sees for the first time. He asks her her name, that he may breathe it in his next hour of danger. Carmen tells him, but fences with his enquiry whether it is permissible for him to love her. He can if he likes; he can hope if he likes; but that is all the consolation she will give him. Zuniga, finding it impossible to persuade Carmen to go with them, goes out with a threat to return; to which Carmen's only reply is, " You had better not! "

Escamillo makes his exit with great pomp, to the melody, in the orchestra, of the chorus to his song; and the girls, who have now been joined by the two smugglers, Le Dancaïre and Le Remendado, settle down to the discussion of business. The men are hoping to bring off some excellent *coups,* but for these they need the assistance of the women, for, they assure them, there is nothing like women when the affair calls for dexterity and trickery. They all express this admirable sentiment in a quintet that is a miracle of light-fingered characterisation.

Frasquita and Mercédès are willing to join the band at once, but Carmen holds out. It is in vain that the men appeal to her; she persists in her refusal, finally giving her reason — she is in love again. Le Dancaïre and Le Remendado compliment her in a phrase of exquisite irony, but remind her that it would not be the first occasion on which she had been able to reconcile the delights of love with the call of duty. Answering them in their own ironic tone, Carmen tells them that normally she would be delighted to set out with them, but this time it is impossible, as love comes first with her, duty being second. For nimbleness of wit and grace of style this scene is without a parallel in opera.

Off the stage Don José is now heard singing, unaccompanied, a little song in praise of the dragoons of Alcala:

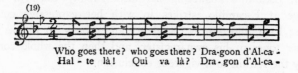

(19)

Who goes there? who goes there? Dra-goon d'Al-ca -
Hal - te là!   Qui   va là?   Dra - gon d'Al-ca -

la ?......   What brings thee here de - clare,
la !......   Où t'en vas - tu par là,

Dra - goon d'Al - ca - la ?......   I ride forth to -
Dra - gon d'Al - ca - la ?......   Moi, je m'en vais

night, For at the moon's first light, A
fai - re mor - dre la pous - siè - re

ri - val I must fight.........................
A mon ad - ver - sai - - - - - - re.

A dragoon of this martial quality, Le Dancaïre and Le Remendado opine, would be an excellent recruit for their band; will not Carmen try to enlist him? She promises to make the attempt, and the smugglers leave as Don José enters, free at last after his two months' imprisonment. But he has not grieved, he assures Carmen; for her he would willingly have served much longer. He tells her he adores her, and at once his jealousy is roused when he learns that the officers of his regiment have been in the tavern and that the gipsies have been dancing for them. But now, she says, she will dance in *his* honour; this she does to the accompaniment of her castanets:

(20)

La...,............. la   la.............. la...

la......................, la... la............ la......

but she has hardly begun when there comes from a distance the
faint sound of a bugle blowing the retreat:

The soldier in Don José compels him to listen; he stops Carmen
and draws her attention to the call. The wild creature claps her
hands with joy; it is melancholy, she says, to dance without an
orchestra; truly this music has fallen from the skies! And she resumes her dance and her castanet playing. All this time the retreat has been increasing in loudness, as if the soldiers were
drawing nearer to the tavern, and Bizet dexterously combines the
bugle-call with the song and dance of Carmen:

At last Don José stops her again; the soldier in him has asserted
itself peremptorily; it is necessary, he says, for him to get back to
the barracks. To her stupefaction she realises at last that he is
serious. Then the tiger-cat comes uppermost in her; she turns on

him viciously, calls him by the derisive name of " Canary " (an allusion to the yellow tunic of the Spanish dragoons), picks his helmet and sword up from the table and hurls them at his head, and contemptuously bids him, poor-spirited creature that he is, to go back to his barracks. He makes a sad attempt to justify himself, protesting that no woman has ever had the empire over his heart that Carmen has:

Ah ! cru-el 'tis, Car-men, to mock my pi-teous state.
With ach-ing heart I go,

C'est mal à toi Car-men, de te mo-quer de moi !
Je souff-re de par-tir,

but her only reply is another outburst of savage mockery; the thought that the mere sounding of the retreat should have made a soldier forget *her* drives her to frenzy. This, then, is his conception of love!

Don José feels that the time has come to play what he hopes will be a sure card. He takes from his breast the flower that Carmen had thrown at him in the first act, shows it to her, and launches into the " Flower Song ":

See here, thy flow-'ret trea-sur'd well,...... Its o-dour cheer'd my pri-son cell,......

La fleur que tu m'a-vais je-té-e Dans ma pri-son m'e-tait res--té-e.

This flower, he tells her, has been his sole consolation during his imprisonment. Sometimes, in his bitterness, he had hated her; but against his destiny, he knows, it is useless for him to struggle.

(It is interesting to recall that the somewhat unusual modulations in the orchestra in the final phrase of the song aroused the anger of the pedants of the time.)

Carmen softens, but she is not yet sure of him; if he loved her he would follow her away to the mountains, where both would be free — he with no officer to obey, no retreat recalling him from love, the open sky above them both, the world for their country, for law nothing but their own will, and that liberty so dear to the gipsy. This she says, accompanied by interjections from Don José, in a wonderful passage in 6/8 time, through the apparent light-heartedness of which there runs a moving strain of nostalgia, the heart-hunger of the gipsy for the open:

(25)

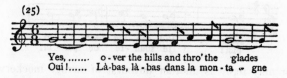

Yes, ... o - ver the hills and thro' the   glades
Oui!...... Là-bas, là - bas dans la mon - ta ⌣ gne

But once more Don José gets his brain clear of the heady fumes, and tearing himself violently from the arms of Carmen, swears that it is impossible for him to desert his flag — it would be an infamy; but when she stonily bids him go, he weakens again. He wishes to preserve his honour, but he does not want to lose Carmen. Finally he reconciles himself to the inevitable. Despairingly he bids her adieu for ever, and has just reached the door when there is a loud knocking on it, followed by a tense silence. It is Zuniga who has returned.

Recognising the danger that threatens Don José, Carmen refuses to open, so Zuniga breaks the door down. At the sight of Don José he understands everything; but, remaining a gentleman, he merely reproaches Carmen with exquisite irony; this is not very distinguished of her, he tells her; to take the common soldier when she might have had the officer, surely this is a mis-alliance! Then he turns to Don José and roughly bids him be-gone. The latter refuses. Zuniga draws his sword and attacks José, who defends himself. Carmen cries loudly for help, and the smug-glers and gipsies rush in; Le Dancaïre and Le Remendado throw themselves on Zuniga and disarm him. Then follows a scene which for the expression of polite irony in music is without its equal in the whole range of musical art. Zuniga, Carmen assures him in a tone of mocking triumph, has arrived most inopportunely, and, much to their regret, they will have to detain him for a little while for the sake of their own safety.

Le Dancaïre and Le Remendado take up the polite conversation; each of them presenting a pistol at Zuniga's head *avec*, as the score says, *la plus grande politesse*. They regret to be compelled to take him with them when they leave the tavern; but, after all, what is it but a pleasant little promenade? He will consent, of course? The following quotation will give an idea of the graceful wit of their exhortation to him:

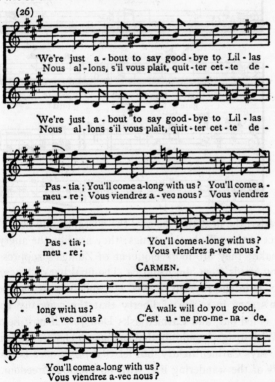

(26)

We're just a-bout to say good-bye to Lil-las
Nous al-lons, s'il vous plaît, quit-ter cet-te de-

We're just a-bout to say good-bye to Lil-las
Nous al-lons s'il vous plaît, quit-ter cet-te de-

Pas-tia; You'll come a-long with us? You'll come a-
meu-re; Vous viendrez a-vec nous? Vous viendrez

Pas-tia;
meu-re;

You'll come a-long with us?
Vous viendrez a-vec nous?

CARMEN.

long with us?   A walk will do you good,
a-vec nous?   C'est u-ne pro-me-na-de.

You'll come a-long with us?
Vous viendrez a-vec nous?

Zuniga, like the gallant and well-bred officer he is, answers them in their own polite style. Their arguments, he assures them, are perfectly irresistible; nevertheless, he continues, still with imperturbable courtesy, but with the hint of a threat in it, his time will come, and then let them beware! —

(27)

But   have a care!.....
Mais   gare à vous!....

my   turn   will   come!......
gare à vous   plus   tard!.......

The reader, the next time he sees the opera, should note the sinister effect of the trills in the strings; they are like the angry hissing of a snake; they are more eloquent of Zuniga's suppressed rage than any words from him could be. The final bar of No. 27, it will be seen, is in the rhythm of No. 25; and it is to the melody of Carmen's song in praise of liberty that the company continues. Zuniga is led out, and Carmen asks Don José if now he will join them. With a sigh he admits that he has no choice. He is not very gallant, says Carmen lightly, but let that pass; once he has tasted the joys of the wandering life, with its precious freedom, he will

long for no other. The gipsies and the smugglers take up the joyous refrain, and the curtain falls.

Between the second and third acts there is played a charming
orchestral intermezzo:

which was originally written not for *Carmen,* but for *L'Arlésienne.*
Delightful as it is in itself, it must be confessed that it is more appropriate to its original environment than to the stage of *Carmen*
at which we have now arrived.

But we are soon plunged again into the real *Carmen* atmosphere when the curtain rises for the third act, showing a wild spot
in the mountains. A number of smugglers are lying on the ground,
wrapped up in their cloaks. The orchestra gives out an expressive
and curiously enigmatic march, to the accompaniment of which
the gipsies enter. They sing an exhortation to each other to be
watchful of the dangers that surround them; in the music there is
something almost sinister that harmonises well with the scene.

While Le Dancaïre and the others go to make sure that the
course is clear, Carmen asks Don José the cause of his gloom. He
tells her he is thinking of a good and brave old woman who still
believes him to be an honest man; and we hear in the orchestra
No. 11 once more. "Who is this woman?" asks Carmen contemptuously. It is his mother, he tells her. That a man, once a
soldier and now a smuggler, should have scruples about his mother
is something that Carmen cannot understand. In the orchestra we
hear the motive of fatality (No. 4) as she advises him to leave not
only the band, but her. If she breathes the word "separation"
again, he begins — and then breaks off. "You would kill me, I
suppose?" Carmen answers tranquilly. "You look at me, but
you do not reply. Well, no matter, destiny is lord!"

Frasquita and Mercédès now bring out their cards and set themselves to play, singing the while a graceful duet:

Now, pret-ty cards, we've plac'd you du - ly,
Et main-te-nant par - lez mes bel - les,

Now, pret-ty cards, we've plac'd you du - ly,
Et main-te-nant par - lez mes bel - les,

Each of the girls reads her prospects in the cards — for Frasquita a young lover who carries her off on his horse into the mountains, for Mercédès a lover who is old but very rich, and who installs her in an almost royal château. Frasquita's young lover becomes a famous chieftain with a hundred brave followers; Mercédès's elderly admirer does even better — he dies, leaving her a rich widow.

Carmen, who has a premonition of coming tragedy, now consults the cards on her own account. She turns up first diamonds, then spades. She recognises that this means death — she first, afterwards Don José. In a gloomy monologue she tells herself that the cards never lie; if the sign they have given is death, you may play the game twenty times, but it is still " Death " that they will pitilessly repeat. Frasquita and Mercédès, intent only on their own more amusing affairs, break in upon her sombre reflections with their gracious little melody (No. 29), and, for finale of the scene, Bizet works Carmen's gloomy ejaculations most cleverly into the tissue of their lighter phrases.

Le Dancaïre returns with news that the band must now try to pass the frontier; the coast is fairly clear, but there are three government officials about who must be evaded. The smugglers go out carrying their merchandise, leaving Don José to guard some of the bales. The three women express their confidence in their ability to manage the customs men:

(30)   FRAS. & MERCÉDES.

As   for   the   guards, 'tis our af-
Quant   au   doua - nier, c'est notre af -

CARMEN.

As for the guards, that's our af-fair,   'tis our af -
Quant au douanier, quant au douanier, c'est notre af -

- - fair,............   E - ver...... they seek......
- - fai - re! Tout comme un au - -

- - fair,........   E - ver........ they
- - faire! Tout comme un au - tre, il

to please the fair,   And   al - (ways)
il aime à plaire. Il   ai - (me)

seek   to   please the   fair,
aime   à   plai - - - re.

The chorus take up the melody, and, judging from the noise they
make, they are evidently quite free from apprehension on the
score of the authorities.

When they have all left the stage, and Don José has also gone
to occupy his observation post, Micaela enters. She has heard
that Don José is now one of the smugglers, and she has sought
him out, in spite of the danger, to bring him another message
from his mother, and to exhort him to leave the sorceress who
has enslaved him. Her big aria, " I said naught should frighten me
here " :

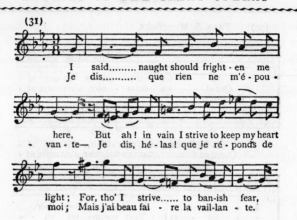

(31)

I said........ naught should fright - en me
Je dis........... que rien ne m'é - pou -

here,   But ah! in vain I strive to keep my heart
- van - te— Je dis, hé - las! que je ré - ponds de

light;   For, tho' I strive...... to ban-ish   fear,
moi;   Mais j'ai beau fai - re la vail-lan - te.

is a fine piece of writing, but it is perhaps a little over-elaborated
for the dramatic situation; however, the operatic soprano must
not be denied her rights.

Micaela and Don José catch sight of each other simultaneously; but Don José mistakes her for an enemy and fires, fortunately missing her. As she runs away in terror, Escamillo comes
in, looking with rueful amusement at his hat; Don José's bullet
has just missed his head. José enters and challenges him, and
Escamillo makes himself known. He has come, he says, to find a
woman with whom he is madly in love. Her name is Carmen; a
little while ago, he believes, she had a passing affair with a soldier
who deserted on her account, but all this is over now; Carmen's
affairs never last more than six months. " Those who come to take
our women away from us," says the irritated Don José, " must
fight for them."

Escamillo, very self-possessed and somewhat vain, as becomes a
toreador, declines to take Don José seriously, though he is quite
willing to fight him for Carmen. The pair are soon separated by
Carmen and the others, and Escamillo's tone at once changes from
the bellicose to the ironical. The game for the moment, he tells
Don José, is even; the deciding round can be fought any time
his opponent likes.

Le Dancaïre asks him to be good enough to take himself off,

as the smugglers must be getting on their way; and Escamillo, before leaving, cordially invites them all to his next bull-fight at Seville. "They who love me will come," he says, with an eloquent glance at Carmen. This is too much for Don José, who starts forward angrily, his menacing gesture being indicated by the sudden fortissimo shown in the following quotation:

(32)

They who love me will come!.........
Et qui m'ai - me y vien - dra!...........

(to Don José.)

my friend, keep yourself still !............
l'a - mi, tiens toi tran - quil -- .- le !

Escamillo, with cold courtesy, bids him be tranquil, and makes his departure to the accompaniment in the orchestra of a slow version of the refrain of the "Toreador's Song" (No. 3). Don José tries to hurl himself again on Escamillo, but is held back by the smugglers. He cries wildly to Carmen, "Have a care, Carmen! I can endure no more!" But he is interrupted by Le Dancaïre, who urges the necessity of immediate departure.

Just then, however, they perceive what they take to be a spy;

it is Micaela. She is brought in; Don José recognises her, and, in reply to his enquiry why she has ventured into such danger, she tells him, to the melody of No. 9, of the mortal illness of his mother, to whom she implores him to return.

Carmen sardonically recommends him to do so, for it is clear, she says, that a smuggler's life will never suit him. The jealous José cannot bear the thought of leaving her to Escamillo; he wildly swears he will never leave her till death separates them; but his resolution is broken down when Micaela, playing her last card, tells him that his mother is on the point of death. " I will go," he cries to Carmen, " but we shall meet again "; and we hear the fateful No. 4 once more in the orchestra. As he is going out with Micaela the voice of Escamillo is heard in the distance singing his " Toreador's Song " again. Carmen tries to run to him, but Don José, with a threatening gesture, bars her path. The curtain falls to the strain of the " Smugglers' March " as the band makes its preparations for departure.

The fourth act is prefaced by an entr'acte against the dramatic appropriateness of which nothing can be urged; it is the best possible introduction to the atmosphere of the bull-ring that envelops the whole of the fourth act.

This brilliant piece of writing is apparently based on a genuine Spanish *polo* (an Andalusian song and dance). One French author claims that Bizet took his theme from a *polo* sung with guitar accompaniment by a student under the window of his lady-love in an opera entitled *El Criado fingido* (*The Supposed Servant*), a musical comedy written in 1804 by Manuel Garcia, the founder of the celebrated family of singers and teachers. No score of this opera is to be found in any of the libraries, and as the writer to whom we owe the information admits that, though he had a score in his possession at one time, it is no longer there, we cannot test the truth of his statement.

The *polo* on which Bizet has obviously worked, however, has been published in various collections of Spanish folk-songs. He may possibly have seen it in print somewhere, but it is more probable that he had heard it sung by some wandering musician; in any case his treatment of the chief theme is so personal that the whole entr'acte may really be regarded as his own invention.

The curtain having risen, we see an open place in Seville; at the back are the walls of the circus in which the bull-fights take place; the entrance to this is closed. The stage is crowded with vendors of fans, oranges, programmes, water, cigarettes, and wine; among them are Zuniga, Frasquita, and Mercédès. The itinerant traders, in a lively chorus, try to sell their wares to the passers-by.

The toreadors enter and are greeted with enthusiasm by the crowd, the children being prominent with the melody already heard in the Prelude and quoted as No. 2, while of course large use is made of the typical toreador motive (No. 1). Finally, the great star of the occasion, Escamillo, enters, and is enthusiastically greeted with a chorus to the melody of No. 3. With him is Carmen, brilliantly dressed and radiant with happiness. To a tender melody, packed with those sixths which Bizet loved to employ to express sentiment, he tells her that soon she will have cause to be proud of him if she loves him.

(33)

If thou lov'st   me Car - men,   If thou
Si tu m'ai - mes Car - men,   Si tu

lov'st me   Car - men.
m'ai - mes   Car - men.

She replies, to his own melody, that she does love him; may she die if she has ever loved anyone so much! Their brief colloquy is put an end to by the entry of the Alcade, accompanied by the Alguazils; these officials enter the circus, the crowd following them.

Mercédès approaches Carmen and whispers a word of warning to her. She has seen Don José hiding among the crowd, and now she points him out to Carmen. The gipsy has no fear; she is anxious, indeed, to speak to him and make an end of it all. Mercédès repeats her warning in still more urgent tones, and is supported by Frasquita; but Carmen merely replies that she has no fear. Finally the two girls follow the crowd into the arena, and Carmen and José find themselves face to face and alone.

An air of fatality broods over the scene that ensues. Carmen, with a secret conviction that her end is near, is still unshakeably courageous. Don José, however, has come not to threaten her, but to make a last broken appeal to the memory of her love for him. Will she not forget the bitter past and join him in another life under other skies, far from Spain? Carmen replies inflexibly that it is impossible; between herself and him everything is finished; she is incapable of lying, she declares. He implores her once again while there is yet time; will she not save him, and herself with him? " No," she replies. " I know well that the hour has come. I know well that you will kill me. But whether I live or die, never will I be yours again." He repeats his passionate appeal, and for a moment the two voices blend in a deeply moving duet.

The distracted José makes a still more desperate appeal to her. If she will only love him again he will resume the life of a bandit and do anything she wishes. Her sole reply is, " Never will Carmen be yours again! Free she was born, and free she will die! "

Just then the crowd in the arena, to the music of No. 1, breaks out in a shout of praise of Escamillo. Carmen, hearing this, makes a joyous gesture, and attempts to enter the circus; but Don José, who has never taken his eyes off her, places himself in front of her and bars the way. Jealousy has added the last coal to the fire of his passion. He extorts from her a wild cry that she loves Escamillo, even though the confession means her death.

As the shouts within the circus break out again she tries once more to escape, but once more Don José stands in her way. He is now completely beside himself; has he imperilled his salvation, he asks her wildly, only that she may laugh at him in the arms of Escamillo? Never will he allow that! Carmen angrily bids him

either strike her down or let her pass. For the last time he asks
if she will follow him; her reply is to take from her finger the
ring he had once given her and throw it in his face. Again the
chorus in praise of the toreador is heard, and once more Carmen
tries to escape; but at the gate Don José meets her and strikes
her dead; then he kneels beside her in an agony of grief. The
crowd rushes in, and we hear for the last time, in all its power,
the motive of fatality (No. 4):

Don José gives himself up with a last magnificent cry of love for
his adored Carmen:

The orchestra, with a great crescendo, completes his phrase, and
the curtain falls.

OFFENBACH was not the actual creator of the modern French operetta. That distinction belongs to one Hervé (1825-92), a composer, conductor, librettist, singer, scene painter, and many other things, whose real name was Florimond Ronger. But it was Offenbach who took up the genre and gave it its enormous vogue during the Second Empire and afterwards.

Jacques Offenbach was by birth a German. He was born in Cologne on the 20th June, 1819, his father, whose real name was Juda Eberscht, being a chorister of the local synagogue. His father gave him his first instruction in music. It was the paternal wish that he should specialise in the violin, but Jacques's predilection was for the 'cello, which instrument he cultivated in secret until he attained a certain proficiency on it.

In his fifteenth year he and his brother went to Paris, where Jacques, in spite of the rule that forbade foreign students admission to the Conservatoire, somehow or other managed to enter that august institution by a side-door. At the same time he obtained, at a salary of 83 francs a month, a post among the 'cellos of the orchestra of the Opéra-Comique, where he and a companion, Seligmann, used to amuse themselves during the performances by playing all sorts of pranks with the music, such as stopping when they liked and beginning again when they liked, missing out every other note, or playing their part in another octave than the right one.

In 1838, after about three years' service at the Opéra-Comique, he left the orchestra and supported himself as best he could by doing musical hack-work of every sort. Not making a commercial success of this he took up his 'cello again, and toured as a virtuoso of sorts through Germany and England.

On his return to Paris he married a Spanish girl, Herminie de Alcain, and for a long time was hard put to it to maintain a very modest establishment. When the revolution broke out in Paris in 1848 he retired to Germany, whence he returned in 1849. A friend of his, Arsène Houssaye, had just been appointed Director of the Théâtre-Français. He was ambitious to effect many reforms in the historic theatre, one of them being the maintenance of a better orchestra than had been customary there, and the provision of better music. He engaged Offenbach as his conductor at 6,000 francs a year.

Offenbach remained at the Théâtre-Français several years, attending to the entr'acte music in general and the incidental music to certain plays, and occasionally contributing some little thing of his own; one of these, the *Chanson de Fortunio,* became a great favourite.

It was about this time that Hervé began to make Paris talk to him and his sprightly operettas. Offenbach was quick to see the possibilities of the style, and when, in the summer of 1855, a tiny theatre in the Champs-Elysées that had lately been used by the scientist Lacaze became vacant, he managed somehow or other to scrape up enough money to obtain a lease of it. His licence from the Government permitted him to produce musical plays with not more than three or four characters at the outside, a limitation which irked him for a considerable time.

He opened the theatre, which he called the Bouffas-Parisiens, with a little piece entitled *Les deux Aveugles (The Two Blind Men),* which was quickly followed by *Le Violoneux.*

The sparkle of Offenbach's music, the wit of the libretti, and the dash of the acting soon made the Bouffes the rage of Paris; *Les deux Aveugles* itself ran for more than four hundred consecutive performances. In *Le Violoneux* Hortense Schneider, the brilliant singer and actress who was the delight of our grand-fathers, and whose name is indelibly associated with that of Offen-bach, made her first appearance in his music.

In the winter the theatre in the Champs-Elysées was a little too far out of town for convenience or comfort, so Offenbach took a lease of the Salle Choiseul in the city, where he opened in December with *Ba-Ta-Clan*. Thereafter, for many years, he occupied the two theatres alternately; and in twenty-five years he wrote some hundred works, producing most of them himself.

The chief landmarks in the long story are *Orphée aux Enfers* (1858), *Geneviève de Brabant* (1859), *Barbe-Bleue* (1866), *La Grande Duchesse de Gérolstein* (1867), *La Belle Hélène* (1865), *La Périchole* (1868), *Madame l'Archiduc* (1874), *La Fille du Tambour Major* (1879), and *La Vie Parisienne* (1866). Some of these were produced at other theatres than Offenbach's own; and, to the great anger of the highbrows, he even obtained a footing at the Grand Opera with the ballet *Le Papillon* (1860), and at the Opéra-Comique with *Barkouf* (1861) and *Vert-Vert* (1869).

Offenbach gave up management on his own account in 1861, but in 1873 took over the Gaîté Theatre, where he remained as director till 1875.

Success brought him money, but money did not bring with it prudence; and in the early seventies he found himself practically ruined. To retrieve his fortunes he went on a tour in America in 1875, from which he brought back with him a hundred thousand francs and materials for a book — *Notes d'un Musicien en Voyage* (1877). During the Franco-German War an agitation was worked up against him as a German, although he had become a naturalized Frenchman as long ago as 1860. Sanity returned to the French after the conclusion of the war, and Offenbach once more became the prime musical favourite of the Paris population.

His health had never been particularly good, and he had persistently overworked himself for the greater part of his life. In his later years probably the one thing that kept him alive was his desire to write a work that should show the world that he had something more in him than the dashing Offenbach whom they knew only as a composer of operettas. This was *The Tales of Hoffmann*, which was destined for the Opéra-Comique. The work was virtually completed — it required only a slight revision by Ernest Guiraud — but before it could be produced Offenbach died after an attack of rheumatism of the heart on the night of October 4-5, 1880. His last and greatest work was produced posthumously at the Opéra-Comique on the 10th February, 1881.

THE TALES OF HOFFMANN

THE libretto of *The Tales of Hoffmann*, which before Offenbach took it up, had been offered to Gounod and several other composers, is by Jules Barbier and Michel Carré, and is founded on certain stories of the celebrated German romantic writer Ernst Theodor Wilhelm Hoffmann. (Through an error in one of his earliest manuscripts the W of Wilhelm was read as A; Hoffmann philosophically accepted the transformation, and thenceforth for the Wilhelm substituted Amadeus, one of the Christian names of his adored Mozart.)

This Hoffmann, who had an extraordinary influence not only on his own day but on most of the German poets, prose writers, and musicians of a later time, down even to Brahms, was born at Königsberg on the 24th January, 1776. His parents separated when he was three years old; his mother returned with him to the house of her parents, where, devoting herself mainly to religion, she kept very much to herself, the young Hoffmann being mostly left to the company of an aunt Sophie and an uncle Otto.

There were several lawyers in the family, and in 1792 the young Hoffmann entered the Königsberg University as a student of law, setting up in practice for himself three years later. In 1796 we find him in Glogau, in 1798 in Berlin, and in 1800 as an assessor in Posen, in which last town he married. His irrepressible satirical bent took the form of drawing caricatures of certain Posen notabilities, with the result that in 1802 he was sent, by way of punishment, to Ploszk on the Vistula. In 1804 he was in Warsaw.

All this while he had been cultivating music passionately, and in 1808 he obtained the post of musical director of the theatre at Bamberg. The theatre became bankrupt, and for some time Hoffmann had to support himself as best he could by literature and the teaching of music. He was a correspondent of the Leipzig *Allgemeine Musik-Zeitung*, for which paper he wrote some essays on music that were remarkable for their time, among them one on Beethoven's instrumental music that has become famous. For a while he was associated in Dresden with the theatrical troupe of Seconda, another member of which was that Ludwig Geyer who is supposed to have been the father of Richard Wagner.

In 1814 influential friends obtained for him a legal post in Berlin, and he seems to have performed his duties ably and conscientiously as Councillor of the Court of Appeal. He had drunk deeply and lived wildly all his life, and on the 25th June, 1822, he died of locomotor ataxy. He wrote several operas, none of which, except *Undine* (1816), is known at all to-day, and a great number of stories, most of them in the fantastic vein, interspersed with illuminative speculations on music and the other arts. Two volumes of a collection entitled *The Serapion Brethren* have been issued in English in a translation by Major Ewing.

As usual with French librettists when dealing with a German subject (we have had an example in the case of *Mignon*), Barbier and Carré have dealt very freely with their material. None of the " Tales " of the opera correspond precisely with any stories of Hoffmann's own or with that of his life. The reader who has a knowledge of German and would like to go into the matter more thoroughly for himself may welcome the following information.

The first act of the opera is based mostly on a story called *The Sandman*, which is one of Hoffmann's *Night Pieces*. The basis of the second act is one of the *New Year's Eve Adventures* (from the *Fantastic Pieces in Callot's Manner*), which contains the episode of the last reflection. Pitichinaccio, however, does not appear in this tale; he is taken from a story in *The Serapion Brethren* entitled *Signor Formica*.

The third act comes from the story *Councillor Crespel*, in *The*

Serapion Brethren. (The original of Councillor Crespel was an actual person of the Goethe epoch.) There is no Doctor Miracle, however, either in *Councillor Crespel* or in any other Hoffmann story. There is, it is true, a doctor in *Councillor Crespel,* but he is not in the least the sinister Dr. Miracle of the opera. Dr. Miracle seems to be drawn, in part, from the Coppélius of *The Sandman.* The servant Cochenille appears in a story called *The Connection of Things,* in *The Serapion Brethren;* and there is a servant Frantz in a story entitled *The Succession,* in the *Night Pieces.*

It was, of course, the idea of the French librettists alone to make Hoffmann himself the protagonist of the various adventures set forth in the Tales. There is a fair quantity of the historical Hoffmann in the Hoffmann of the opera; each is an inveterate amorist and a feverish seeker for a happiness that can never be realised.

It is unfortunate that *The Tales of Hoffmann* has come to be regarded as, in the main, a comic opera. The most casual spectator, it is true, realises that there is a tragedy in the second act; but he invariably regards the first act as highly comic, and sees only the superficially humorous side of Dr. Miracle in the first act — his jangling of medicine flasks, his magical entries and exits, and so on. Offenbach called his work " a fantastic opera." We see the melancholy Hoffmann restlessly searching for his ideal: he is accompanied in all his adventures by his faithful young friend Nicklausse, who, himself no visionary, is always trying to correct Hoffmann's fantasies and to make him see things as they really are, while opposed to him is a force for evil incarnated in turns as Lindorf, Coppélius, Dapertutto, and Dr. Miracle.

It is sometimes argued that the three chief women's parts and the subordinate one of Stella should be taken by four different singers in order to make clear to us the differences between Hoffmann's four loves. That, no doubt, would be in some respects the ideal way of producing the opera, but it would constitute a very expensive production. For economic reasons the four parts have in practice to be played by the same singer, as was done at the first performance. For the same reason various other parts are doubled or trebled, the same actor playing Lindorf, Coppélius,

Dapertutto, and Dr. Miracle, and another playing the three servants' parts — Andrès, Cochenille, and Frantz. Actually, therefore, the twenty-two characters of the opera call for only fourteen actors.

In some theatres it is the practice to omit the Prologue and the Epilogue, both of which, however, are essential for the whole understanding of the opera as the librettists and the composer conceived it.

After a few bars of orchestral prelude, the Prologue opens in Luther's tavern in Nuremberg (it should really be Berlin, but the French librettists made the change for some reason of their own that is not clear to us). The tavern is full of casks that surround a particularly huge specimen, surmounted by a little figure of Bacchus carrying a streamer on which is inscribed " At the Sign of the Nuremberg Tun." Running round the walls are shelves on which stand bottles of all shapes and sizes. In front of the big cask is a small counter. On the left is a stove, and on the right a clock and a small door concealed in the wainscoting that runs all round the room to about the height of a man. Tables and benches are scattered about the room. It is night, the only light in the tavern being that of the moon.

There is a preliminary chorus of the Spirits of Beer and the Spirits of Wine, who announce themselves as the true friends of man and the chasers away of every care. Then the Councillor Lindorf appears, followed by Andrès, the servant of Stella, an opera singer who has just come from Milan and is now performing in the Nuremberg theatre.

Lindorf is jealous of the numerous admirers of the beautiful prima donna, and finding that Andrès has a missive for one of these he buys it from him for forty thalers and then consigns him to the devil. Left alone, Lindorf finds that the letter is addressed to Hoffmann. He sarcastically comments on the queer taste of women — " Hoffmann! A poet! A drunkard! Well, well! " He opens the letter and reads it: it is an apology from Stella to Hoffmann for having hurt him. She encloses the key to her dressing-room; if he loves her, he can come to her there.

Lindorf sings a song in which, while frankly confessing that he has no beauty of person, he claims to have a certain attractiveness for women and " a satanic aspect that produces on the nerves the effect of an electric battery." He attains his ends not through love but through fear. He is old, he says, but he is game, and he will get rid of Hoffmann. He knows that Hoffmann frequents Luther's tavern, and he resolves to wait for him.

Luther enters, followed by his waiters, who bustle about under his orders. When the room has been got ready for the expected company, Nathanael, Hermann, Wolfram, Wilhelm, and a number of students enter gaily, and, singing a merry chorus, treat themselves to wine and beer.

We are to understand that the tavern is in the same building as the opera-house, and that the students are making good use of the interval between two of the acts. They enthusiastically drink the health of the diva, and then enquire where Hoffmann can be. Just then Hoffmann himself enters, followed by Nicklausse.

Hoffmann, a self-absorbed idealist and a hard drinker, looks gloomy, and for some time cannot be induced to take any interest in the jokes of the students. On his way to the tavern he has seen a withered flower that reminded him of a dead love, and a drunkard lying in the mud, whose happy forgetfulness of life he has envied. To make matters worse, in the theatre, from which he also has just come, he thinks he has seen his vanished love once more, and an old wound has been reopened. Making an effort to overcome his melancholy, he declares that as life is short there is nothing for it but to make the best of it with wine and song, and at the request of the company he sings them the story of the dwarf Kleinzach, once the hideous ornament of the Court of Eisenach, who wore a cap, had a hump for a stomach, and a nose blackened with snuff; when he walked his legs went clic-clac, and his waggling head cric-crac.

He is just about to describe Kleinzach's face when his mind wanders, and in a sort of dream he describes his vanished love, with her blue eyes and white throat and her sweet voice whose echo resounds for ever in his heart. His astonished friends ask him if he is still talking about Kleinzach, and pulling himself together with a smile, Hoffmann goes on with the maliciously humorous description of the dwarf.

His song finished, he curses the vile beer of the tavern and demands punch. The lights are extinguished, and Luther lights an immense bowl of punch, the blue flame illuminating the whole scene. Hoffmann and Lindorf soon get at cross-purposes, and exchange insults that are none the less deadly for their politeness and wit.

Hoffmann tells the company that Lindorf is his evil genius: if he plays cards, he loses; if he drinks, it goes down the wrong way; if he loves — here Lindorf interrupts him with a malicious laugh: so he is in love, then, sometimes? Hoffmann admits the soft impeachment, but pours scorn on the innamorate of the others. His own love is Stella, who is " three women in one, three souls in one; artist, innocent girl, and courtesan; not a mistress but three mistresses, three charming enchantresses who have shared my life." Would they like to hear the story of his mad loves? They welcome the suggestion and take their seats to listen to the story.

Just then Luther enters with the news that the curtain is just about to rise, but all protest that they prefer to hear the Tales of Hoffmann. Luther takes his place at the counter, and Hoffmann, seating himself on the corner of a table, commands silence. " The name of the first," he says, " was Olympia! " and the curtain falls.

The three acts that follow are played on the plane of reality, but we are to understand all the time that we are listening to Hoffmann's stories of his three great loves.

The first act deals with his love for Olympia, who, although he did not know it, was only a mechanical doll.

In the English edition the setting is said to be " a doctor's room." This is one of the very few errors in an admirable translation. In the original the room is described as " un riche cabinet de physicien " — that is to say, the room of a physicist or natural philosopher. It is the room of Spalanzani, an eager experimenter in the mechanical. It so happens that he has just constructed a marvellous doll, Olympia, that is as like life as makes no difference. It is true that Olympia's conversation is restricted to the single word "Yes," but in every other respect she is as large and as natural as life. She is entirely Spalanzani's work with the exception of the eyes, which are the secret of a pseudo-friend and scientific rival, Coppélius; and this dual property in Olympia is very irksome to Spalanzani.

When the curtain rises we see that the back of the scene is closed by curtains, which, as we afterwards discover, are drawn in front of a corridor. On the sides of the stage are various doors, also closed by curtains. We see Spalanzani lifting up the curtain from one of these doors and contemplating admiringly the as yet invisible Olympia. He not only feels an artist's joy in his work, but hugs to himself the thought that by means of Olympia he will make good the five hundred ducats that he has lost through the bankruptcy of the Jewish banker Elias; the only fly in his ointment is the thought of the demand that Coppélius may make on him for his share in the rights of paternity.

Spalanzani has evidently passed off Olympia upon Hoffmann as his daughter, for when the young man enters, Spalanzani, rather to Hoffmann's mystification, while praising Olympia, speaks enthusiastically of the triumph of physics. He calls his servant Cochenille, and bids him prepare the lights and champagne for the coming party.

Master and servant go off, and Hoffmann, alone, muses upon the delightful prospect of life with the beauty who is now sleeping in the next room. He gently raises the curtain and contemplates her. He is interrupted by the entry of Nicklausse, and quickly lets the curtain fall.

Nicklausse, who is always the embodiment of the common sense that Hoffmann lacks, twits his friend on his infatuation. Does the lady know that Hoffmann loves her? Hoffmann has to reply "No!" "Then write to her," advises Nicklausse. "I dare not," replies Hoffmann. "Then speak to her," continues Nicklausse; and Hoffmann can only reply that that also is dangerous. "Then sing to her." Hoffmann puts aside the suggestion; it seems

that Monsieur Spalanzani does not like music. "No," says Nicklausse, laughing ironically; "Spalanzani is all for physics";
and he sings a delicious little song about a little doll with enamel
eyes and a little brass cock with which it used to amuse itself,
pretending it loved it: the reference, of course, is to Hoffmann
and Olympia.

Coppélius enters, and for a moment has difficulty in rousing
Hoffmann out of the trance into which he seems to have fallen.
When he manages to do so he shows Hoffmann the magical apparatus he carries with him, barometers, hydrometers, thermom-
eters, and above all spectacles that enable the wearer to see just
what he will, and, indeed, to penetrate to the secrets of all things,
including the hearts of women. He demands three ducats for a
pair, and the necessary money is handed over by Nicklausse on
Hoffmann's account.

When Spalanzani enters, Coppélius demands his share in the
proceeds of Olympia, for are not the eyes his? Spalanzani, wanting to make these eyes his own property, persuades Coppélius
to accept five hundred ducats for them in the form of a draft on
the house of Elias, which, he assures his fellow-scientist is sol-
vency itself. The deal is concluded, and with many compliments
and much embracing between the pair Coppélius takes his leave,
having first recommended Spalanzani to marry Olympia to
the young nincompoop who is evidently so much in love with
her.

Cochenille comes in to announce that the guests have arrived
to make the acquaintance of Spalanzani's charming daughter,
and soon the guests themselves arrive and walk about admiring
the details of the scientist's room. Spalanzani brings Olympia
in, and she excites the liveliest curiosity in the guests, who praise
her face and her figure. "Oh, she is adorable!" ejaculates Hoffmann; and Nicklausse adds an ironic "Charming, incomparable!"

Spalanzani begins to vaunt his daughter's talents. She has a
rare gift for music, it seems, and will be delighted to oblige the
company. Cochenille brings in a harp, and, to Spalanzani's

accompaniment, Olympia sings, in the true staccato style of the mechanical doll, a sentimental little ballad that contains some coloratura of an exquisitely appropriate kind.

The song being finished, Cochenille takes away the harp, and the guests crowd round and compliment the singer as guests do on these occasions; Olympia thanks them prettily with a movement first of the right hand, then of the left. A servant announces that supper is served, and the guests gradually make their way through the corridor at the back into the supper-room. Meanwhile Hoffmann has approached Olympia to ask if he may have the pleasure, and, in response to a touch on the shoulder from Spalanzani, the doll squeaks " Yes! " Spalanzani, however, assures the young man that she will not eat anything; whereupon the satiric Nicklausse murmurs " Poetic soul! " The mechanism looks like running down: Spalanzani winds Olympia up and leads her to a sofa upon which he plants her; then he goes to supper with his guests.

Hoffmann and Olympia are left alone. He pours out his romantic soul to her, and, happening to touch her now and then on the shoulder, she manages to ejaculate her usual " Yes! " He takes her hand in his and chances to touch a spring, whereupon Olympia gets up, flutters about the stage for a while, and then runs through the door at the back without raising her hands to part the curtains. Hoffmann, thinking he has somehow or other offended her, is about to follow her when Nicklausse appears at another door and intercepts him. Nicklausse tries to bring his infatuated friend to his senses: his adored one, so people say, is not only dead but was never alive! But Hoffmann is impervious to reason: he runs out after Olympia, and the devoted Nicklausse has to follow him.

Coppélius now comes on in a furious temper; he has discovered that Elias is bankrupt and that the draft Spalanzani gave him is worthless. Declaring he will have his revenge on the swindler he slips into Olympia's room. The company returns to dance, and Hoffmann waltzes with Olympia, to the admiration of all. They dance off the stage in one direction and return in another, Olympia making the pace madder and madder until Nicklausse, who tries to stop them, is thrown violently on to a chair. Spalanzani stops Olympia at last by pressing a spring, and Hoffmann falls dazed upon a sofa.

" Enough, enough, my child," says the scientist, and Olympia answers with her eternal " Yes! " He turns her towards the door on the right and gives her a push, whereupon the doll, giggling " Ha! ha! ha! ha! ", trips off the stage.

Nicklausse and the others are attending to Hoffmann when Cochenille rushes in in great agitation: the man with the glasses is there! As Spalanzani runs to Olympia's room there is a horrible sound of smashing machinery, and Coppélius returns, laughing triumphantly. Hoffmann hurries away to see what has happened, while Spalanzani and Coppélius begin fighting and blackguarding each other. Hoffmann returns, pale and overcome, cries " An automaton! " and falls exhausted on a sofa. Nicklausse bends over him, while the company, echoing Hoffmann's cry of " An automaton! " break into derisive laughter at his expense.

It is perhaps inevitable, but all the same a pity, that in performance the comic elements of this scene should overpower the fantastic. We ought to be amused at the antics of the doll, but we ought not to forget the tragical in Hoffmann's situation: we should try to see him as the idealist coming to wreck through his inability to distinguish between his fancies and reality.

The second is the undeniably tragic act of the opera. The scene is laid in Venice, where a fête is being held in a palace overlooking the Grand Canal. We see a balustrade, a staircase, lustres, and rich furnishings. It is the house of Giulietta, a rich courtesan, whose guests are standing about or reclining on couches. From the wings come the voices of Giulietta and Nicklausse blending in the famous barcarolle — a charming song to the beauty of the night and love. The pair enter when the duet is over, and Giulietta seats herself on a divan where she watches and listens to Hoffmann, who, declaring that pleasure should not be a matter for soft sentimental sighing of this sort, breaks out into a " bacchic song " in praise of more hectic transports, the chorus joining with him in a cry of " To the devil with whoever weeps for two beautiful eyes! "

Schlemil, the shadowless man, enters with one Dapertutto, and Giulietta presents Hoffmann to the former; the rivals greet each other with ironical courtesy. Giulietta proposes cards to her guests, and goes out with them on the arm of the jealous and touchy Schlemil, leaving Hoffmann and Nicklausse alone on the stage. The faithful friend already sees danger approaching the dream-ridden Hoffmann; he has, he tells him, two horses ready saddled for an emergency. Hoffmann laughs at his fears, and the two go out.

Dapertutto, the villain of the act, now enters. He wants to compass the death of Schlemil, which he will bring about through Giulietta. Drawing a ring from his finger, he contemplates the great diamond that flashes in it; no woman, he is certain, and least of all a Giulietta, can resist a lure like this.

True enough, Giulietta comes in as if fascinated, and placing the ring on her finger, Dapertutto states his terms: she has already obtained for him Schlemil's shadow; now he wants Hoffmann's reflection. As the young man enters, Dapertutto kisses Giulietta's hand and retires. The courtesan accosts Hoffmann, who appears to be about to leave the scene (he has just lost everything at cards), and implores him to leave her, for Schlemil may kill him in her arms that night. But before he goes will he not leave her something to remember him by — say his reflection in the mirror that she hands him?

Hoffmann is at once delighted and disturbed by the romantic idea, and has just looked in the mirror when Schlemil, Dapertutto, Nicklausse, and Giulietta's admirer Pitichinaccio enter. The jealous Schlemil at once picks a quarrel with Hoffmann. " You are pale," says Dapertutto to the latter, handing him a mirror, and Hoffmann starts back in horror at perceiving there is no reflection in it. All burst into laughter at the catastrophe that has befallen him, and Nicklausse implores his friend to fly with him.

Hoffmann, however, is too madly in love to leave Giulietta, whom he both hates and adores. The courtesan blandly assures him that she adores him also, but confesses that, being a woman, she was unable to resist so magnificent a diamond as the one she is now wearing; and Dapertutto and Pitichinaccio laugh at the unfortunate young man who has been so crudely betrayed and humiliated. Schlemil, laying his hand on the hilt of his sword, promises Hoffmann a kiss not from Giulietta but from the cold steel. Nicklausse and the other guests pity Hoffmann for being so sorry a dupe. All this is said in a big ensemble, after which the gondolas arrive for the guests.

Schlemil conducts them to the water at the back of the scene, and Giulietta goes out on the left, after throwing a last glance at Hoffmann, who follows her intently with his eyes. Dapertutto remains at the back. Nicklausse, seeing Hoffmann sunk in dreams, goes to him, touches him on the shoulder, and urges him to come with him; but the young man refuses. Nicklausse is compelled to leave without him, but he promises to watch over him and be there if he is wanted.

The episode that follows is one of the most impressive in all opera. Schlemil returns to the front of the stage, and while the orchestra gives out the melody of the barcarolle he and Hoffmann have a brief dialogue, the sudden change to the spoken word having a curious effect that can be understood only by those who have experienced it in the theatre.

Earlier in the scene Giulietta has told Hoffmann that Schlemil has a key belonging to her. This key Hoffmann now demands. Schlemil refuses to give it up, and draws his sword to attack Hoffmann. Perceiving that the latter has no sword, the Mephistophelean Dapertutto politely offers him his. The two men exchange passes: Schlemil falls dead, and Hoffmann, taking the key that is suspended round his neck, runs into Giulietta's room. Pitichinaccio cynically looks over Schlemil and makes sure that he is dead; Dapertutto tranquilly picks up the sword that Hoffmann has let fall, wipes it, replaces it in its scabbard, and then moves away to the gallery overlooking the Canal. Giulietta appears at the back in a gondola, and at the same moment Hoffmann returns to the stage, in time to see Pitichinaccio enter the gondola and take Giulietta in his arms.

At last Hoffmann realises the full perfidy of the courtesan. He gives a cry of rage, and Nicklausse rushes on and drags him away, for the watch is coming. Giulietta and Dapertutto laugh at the deluded Hoffmann. " What will you do with him now? " asks Dapertutto; and Giulietta replies maliciously, " I give him to you! "

These last conversations are carried on in the speaking voice against the background of the barcarolle in the orchestra and the voices of the guests, and once more the sinister contrast between music and speech has an electrifying effect.

The third act takes place in Crespel's house in Munich (not Venice, as stated in the English edition). The room that we see when the curtain rises is strangely furnished. On the right is a harpsichord; on the left, a couch and an arm-chair. Violins hang on the walls. There are two doors at the back of the scene, and in the foreground, on the left, a window opening on to a balcony. On the back wall, between the two doors, hangs a large portrait of a woman. It is sunset.

Crespel's daughter Antonia is seen sitting at the harpsichord, singing a plaintive little romance and accompanying herself: she is thinking sadly of a love that has left her. For a moment she moves away from the harpsichord, then returns to it and accompanies her song standing up, turning over the music from time to time. Finally she falls exhausted into the chair in front of the instrument.

Her father enters hurriedly and runs to her. Anxiously and lovingly he reproaches her for having disobeyed him: has she not promised him she would never sing? It is her mother who sometimes comes to life again in her, says Antonia: when she sings she imagines it is her dead mother she hears. That, replies Crespel, is his torment: her mother, an incomparable singer, has bequeathed her voice to Antonia. He ever mourns his dead wife: may he not have to mourn the loss also of his beloved daughter! Sadly Antonia gives him her promise never to sing again, and goes out slowly.

Alone, Crespel gives himself up to despair. On his daughter's cheeks he has once more recognized the hectic flush that proclaims the disease from which she is suffering, and that music exacerbates. " It is this Hoffmann! " he cries; " it is he who has intoxicated her! I fled to Munich to escape him! "

There enters another of Offenbach's comic servants: the Cochenille of the first act stammers; the Frantz of the third act is rather deaf, and always misunderstands his master and others absurdly, giving answers that have no rational relation to the questions that have been asked him. Crespel orders him to admit no one and goes out quickly, unable to keep his temper any longer with the stupid fellow. Frantz, left alone, closes the door after Crespel and comes down the stage, where, after a short recitative of complaint against his unreasonably irritable master, he sings a little song in praise of his own perpetual patience, assiduity, and cheerfulness in difficult circumstances. Singing, he assures us, is his only refuge from his troubles. Not that he is a great success as a vocalist, as he frankly admits: his voice is well enough, but he knows his method is wrong. Anyhow, whether he can sing or not, he can dance, which he proceeds to do. But seemingly he is no more of a virtuoso in the one art than in the other, for he slips and falls, and then, having picked himself up, drops weakly into a chair just as Hoffmann enters, followed by Nicklausse.

The dialogue between Frantz and Hoffmann — who wants to know how Antonia is — runs on the usual lines of complete misunderstanding owing to Frantz's deafness. The servant goes out at last, and Hoffmann, seating himself at the harpsichord, sings a snatch of the music that is open on the stand. Antonia runs in and flings herself into his arms, and Nicklausse, murmuring, " Je suis de trop; bonsoir! " makes a tactful exit.

The re-united lovers, who have been separated by the father for some reason that neither of them can understand, revel, in a brief duet, in the thought of soon being each the other's own for ever. Then Hoffmann smilingly points out the one fault with which he has to reproach Antonia: he is jealous of her music, which she loves too much. Also smiling, the happy Antonia bids him have no fear: surely he would not, like her father, forbid her to sing? At this he is a little troubled: he does not quite understand, but he has an intuition that something is wrong; he notices how unnaturally bright her eyes are and how her hands tremble. She invites him to judge for himself whether she has lost her voice or not: she makes him sit at the harpsichord, and leaning over his shoulder she completes the song that he had begun, Hoffmann accompanying her and finally joining in the melody with her.

But the effort is too much for Antonia, who suddenly clutches at her heart and appears about to faint. She assures the alarmed Hoffmann that it is nothing, and, hearing her father approaching, slips out as Crespel enters. Hoffmann, anxious to discover the meaning of the mystery, hides himself in a recess of the window.

Crespel is just congratulating himself on not finding Hoffmann there as he had feared, when Frantz enters and announces the arrival of Dr. Miracle. Crespel cries out that the man is not to be admitted: he is not a doctor but a grave-digger, a murderer; he has killed Crespel's wife, and would now kill his daughter! But it is too late. Outside is heard the clicking of flasks that always accompanies Miracle like a sort of ghostly leading-motive, and the sinister fellow himself enters immediately, laughing horribly. " How is Antonia? " he asks. " How goes the malady she inherited from her mother? But never mind! We will cure her! Take me to her! "

In vain Crespel upbraids and insults him and tries to get rid of him. To the horror of Crespel and the watching Hoffmann, Miracle, ignoring the distracted father, draws up a chair and makes magnetic passes in the direction of Antonia's door, which opens slowly of its own accord. Miracle goes through the gestures of taking the hand of the invisible Antonia and placing her in the chair, where he asks the empty space a variety of questions which he answers himself: she is twenty, in the very springtime of life! He draws his watch and extends his hand: the pulse is irregular — a bad symptom! " Sing! " he suddenly commands, and the voice of Antonia is heard in the inner room. Miracle describes her behaviour: see how her face grows animated and her eyes flash, how she places her hand on her wildly beating heart! The door of the inner room closes abruptly, and Miracle, moving the chair back into its place, says, " Truly it would be a pity to let death have so beautiful a prey! "

In spite of Crespel's agonized protests, Miracle, jangling his flasks, offers to save Antonia; calmly ignoring everything the father says, he prescribes for her a certain medicine each morning. At last Crespel succeeds in driving him out. Hoffmann, finding the stage empty, emerges from his hiding-place and is followed by Antonia. He implores her to put out of her mind all thought of singing and the glory she wants to win by it, and out of love for him she gives him her promise. Then the happy Hoffmann leaves her, and Antonia, after following him for a long time with her eyes, muses sadly on the promise she has given: " He has become my father's accomplice! Well, tears will not avail: I have given him my word, and will sing no more."

Suddenly Miracle appears behind her, as if materialising out of space, and whispers in her ear: " Do you realise the sacrifice you have imposed on yourself? Your grace, your beauty, your talent — will you give up these merely for marriage and children? " Hoffmann, he warns her, is sacrificing her to his egoism, and then some day, when her beauty has fled, he will be unfaithful to her. He magically disappears, then swiftly reappears and bids the weeping Antonia think of her mother, whose voice speaks through him, reproaching her with ingratitude.

At this, the portrait glows and seems to come to life; and the phantom of her mother sings, " Dear child, I call you as of old; it is your mother; listen to her voice." " See," says Miracle: " She comes to life again as she hears the bravos of the crowd! " So the horrible, uncanny scene goes on till Miracle seizes a violin, plays on it madly, and goads Antonia into frenzied singing, the mother's voice making a trio with those of Antonia and Miracle.

Antonia rises hysterically to the high C as she speaks of her soul soaring to the skies; then she falls dying on the couch. Miracle, with a ghastly laugh, disappears through the earth: the phantom vanishes, the light on the portrait dies away, and the canvas resumes its normal aspect. Crespel runs in in time to receive Antonia's dying message that her mother has called her to her; he is followed by Hoffmann, whom he wildly reproaches with having killed his daughter. Blood may yet revive her! and seizing a knife that is lying on the table he hurls himself on Hoffmann, but is held back by Nicklausse, who enters at that moment. Hoffmann calls madly to Nicklausse to bring a doctor, and Miracle, suddenly reappearing, cries, " I'm here! " He feels Antonia's pulse and pronounces her to be dead. Crespel wails " My daughter! My child! " Hoffmann gives a despairing cry of " Antonia! " and Frantz, who also has entered by now, kneels and prays by the side of the dead Antonia.

The three Tales are told. While the curtain is down we hear in an orchestral intermezzo the barcarolle once more, and the scene changes to Luther's cellar, where we see Hoffmann, Nicklausse, Lindorf, Nathanael, Hermann, Wilhelm, Wolfram, Luther and the students in precisely the same places and attitudes as those in which we left them at the end of the Prologue. " That," says Hoffmann, " is the story of my three loves, the memory of which will never leave me." Luther runs in to announce that the prima donna has had a tremendous success, and Lindorf, with a glance at Hoffmann, goes out ejaculating, " He is no longer to be feared; the diva is mine! "

The company still do not quite understand Hoffmann's Tales: " What has Stella to do with these? " asks the student Nathanael. But Nicklausse understands: " Three dramas in one! Olympia, Antonia, Giulietta, are only three women in one — Stella! " At his suggestion they would all drink Stella's health, but Hoffmann, flinging down his glass in a fury, swears that at another word from Nicklausse he will smash him as he has smashed the glass. He will seek forgetfulness again from his dreams and his pain in drunkenness and folly; and at his suggestion the chorus break delightedly into the song in praise of Luther and his punch that they sang in the Prologue.

The students go out noisily, leaving Hoffmann sunk in stupor. The Muse appears to him. She alone is his faithful friend, she tells him, as the orchestra gives out softly the passionate melody that Hoffmann once sang to Giulietta. Let him take heart again, says the consoling Muse: Hoffmann the man is no more; let Hoffmann the poet be born again: she loves him; let him henceforth belong to her, and find peace from his troubles in the cultivation of his genius; " smile serenely at thy sorrows: the Muse will bless and sweeten thy sufferings; for man is great in virtue of his love, and greater still in virtue of his tears." She disappears; and to the same ardent melody Hoffmann, with a great cry, gives himself up to the Muse, whose kiss he feels on his lips and his eyes.

He sinks down with his head resting on the table. Stella enters, accompanied by Nicklausse and the students. " Asleep! " says Stella, contemplating Hoffmann. " No! dead drunk! You are too late, madame! " replies Nicklausse. Lindorf, entering, ejaculates " The devil! " and Nicklausse, turning to Stella, says, " Here is Councillor Lindorf, who awaits you! " Stella takes her cloak from the hands of her servant Andrès and throws it over her shoulders; then, taking Lindorf's arm, she pauses a few steps from Hoffmann, takes a flower from her bosom, and throws it at his feet. Hoffmann, still stupefied, follows her with his eyes. The students break once more into their noisy chorus, and the curtain falls.

ENGELBERT HUMPERDINCK

ENGELBERT HUMPERDINCK was born at Siegburg, in the Rhineland, on the 1st September, 1854.

After some preliminary studies he entered the Cologne Conservatory in 1872, working under Ferdinand Hiller. Four years later he won the Mozart Prize, which enabled him to go to Munich, where he studied at the Royal School of Music, first of all under Franz Lachner, then under Josef Rheinberger. In 1879 he obtained the Berlin Mendelssohn Prize, on the strength of which he went for a couple of years to Italy, and in 1881 the Meyerbeer Prize.

In the early days of January 1880 Richard Wagner, having finished the composition of *Parsifal* and being in poor health through that and other labours in connection with the Bayreuth theatre, went to live at the Villa d'Angri, Naples. Humperdinck, who was in Rome at the time, was an enthusiastic Wagnerian, and hearing that the master was in Naples he himself went there at the beginning of March.

He had no personal introduction, but sent in his card, on which he was fancifully described as " Companion of the Order of the Grail " — an association of young Munich musicians whose purpose was to further the cause of Wagner in general and Bayreuth and *Parsifal* in particular. He was at first refused admission by the servant, but when the disconsolate young man had reached the garden gate he was recalled; Wagner, who had been amused by the inscription on the card, received him cordially, and after a lively conversation invited him to call again on his return from the trip he was about to make to Sicily.

Humperdinck returned to Naples on the 2nd May. The next day Wagner took him and the pianist Joseph Rubinstein (who made the piano arrangement of *Parsifal*) to the Conservatory where the great man frankly expressed his dissatisfaction with the teaching and its results. He took a great liking to Humperdinck, who spent most of his evenings at the Villa d'Angri, where he assisted at many a run-through of *Parsifal* in the domestic circle.

Wagner returned to Bayreuth in November, and Humperdinck followed him there in January. Wagner sent to his lodgings each day as many pages of the full score of *Parsifal* as he had completed, and Humperdinck made a connected copy of them, thus learning, as he afterwards said, more about orchestration in a few weeks than he could have done in a conservatoire in as many years. The evenings were spent at Wahnfried in conversation and music-making, Wagner often coaching the young man in the classical works he had to conduct for the local musical society.

It was during this Bayreuth period that Humperdinck won the Meyerbeer Prize (4,500 marks) with three compositions — an overture to the *Frogs* of Aristophanes, a cantata, and an eight-part fugue for double choir. Being unwilling to leave Wagner, he petitioned the Berlin Academy of Arts to allow him to postpone the sojourn in France that was one of the conditions attached to the prize.

During the summer and winter of 1881 he assisted Wagner not only in various matters connected with the copying of the score and parts of *Parsifal*, but in the coaching of some of the singers for the work, and with the preparation of it generally for its production in the summer of 1882. In particular he took charge, during Wagner's absence in Italy in the winter of 1881–2, of the Grail choir, which he made up of the best voices from among the Bayreuth schoolboys.

When, in June 1882, the "transformation" scene in the first act was being rehearsed, it was found that the machinery that worked the revolving scenery moved so slowly that the music gave out before the transformation was completed. After several experiences of the kind, Wagner, who was exhausted with his labours over the opera, flew into a temper and declared he would have nothing more to do with the business. A critical situation was saved by Humperdinck, who wrote some extra bars that he took in fear and trembling to the master, who approved of them cordially. The music now played to exactly the right time. Later the machinery was speeded up, so that the music could be restored to the form in which Wagner originally wrote it.

After the festival of 1882 Humperdinck, in accordance with the conditions of the Meyerbeer Prize, went to Paris; thence he was called by Wagner to Venice in December to superintend the production, on Christmas Eve, of Wagner's youthful symphony, the long-lost parts of which had recently been discovered. The performance itself, however, was conducted by the composer. Wagner hoped to establish Humperdinck at the Venice Conservatoire (the Liceo Marcello), but this plan came to nothing. Humperdinck left for Paris on the 2nd January; it was his last farewell of Wagner, who died a few weeks later.

In 1885, after further wanderings, Humperdinck settled in Barcelona as teacher at the local Conservatoire. He returned to Cologne in 1887, and in 1890 joined the teaching staff of the Hoch Conservatoire, Frankfort-on-the-Main, where he remained until 1896; during this period he also acted as musical critic for the *Frankfurter Zeitung*. He had already written various works that enlarged his reputation, including a Humoreske for orchestra and two choral ballads, *The Luck of Edenhall* and *The Pilgrim to Kevlaar*. It was in 1893 that he made a resounding success with *Hänsel and Gretel;* and on the strength of this he retired to Boppard on the Rhine in 1897 to give up the bulk of his time to composition. In 1900 he accepted the directorship of a Master School for Composition in Berlin, which post he gave up twenty years later.

His chief remaining works were a play with music, *Die Königskinder* (*The Children of the King*), 1896, which he afterwards converted into an opera, *Dornröschen* (*The Sleeping*

Beauty), 1902, a *Moorish Rhapsody*, 1898, a two-act opera, *The Canteen Girl*, 1914, a ballad opera, *Gaudeamus*, 1919, a comic opera, *Die Heirath wider Willen* (*The Unwilling Marriage*), 1905, and a good deal of incidental music to various plays, including Shakespeare's *Tempest, Winter's Tale, Twelfth Night,* and *Merchant of Venice,* Maeterlinck's *Blue Bird,* and Vollmöller's *The Miracle.* He died at Neustrelitz on the 27th September, 1921. He was an amiable man, of whom it is recorded that he " left no enemies."

HÄNSEL AND GRETEL

A FTER the death of Wagner in 1883 there came a wave of
depression over opera in Germany; apparently the last
great German opera had been written, and as the Wagnerian works
became better known and passed into the ordinary repertory
there was naturally a diminution in the fighting enthusiasm that
had made the years from about 1870 to 1883 so glorious for
young people.

There were other causes for depression. From Italy there came
what seemed to many good Germans an invasion of the bar-
barians. In 1890 Mascagni's *Cavalleria Rusticana* had been produced in Rome, to be followed two years later by Leoncavallo's
Pagliacci. These two operas, which very quickly had a world-
wide success, looked like setting a new fashion in opera: the talk
was that romance, especially romance of the German order, had
had its day, and that the future of opera lay in " verism " — the
realistic stage representation of contemporary life.

A number of other Italian composers followed the fashionable
and profitable lead of Mascagni and Leoncavallo, and all over
the classical world of music there was weeping and wailing and
gnashing of teeth over the new " Italian brutality." Audiences
liked these works because they imposed no intellectual strain on
them; and a section of the Press seized upon them gladly as a
stick with which to beat the Wagnerians. And then, in 1893, the
rot, so to speak, was stopped, so far as Germany was concerned,
by a native work that was both thoroughly good and thoroughly
German.

Hänsel and Gretel took the German people back once more into the beloved land of their national stories; and it was the work of a composer with a wholly German idiom and a masterly German technique. *Hänsel and Gretel* was, of course, more than a work of the moment. If its sole or chief virtue had been that it gave the serious German musicians a rallying-point and a slogan against the Italian invaders, it would have had only a short life. But it happened, in addition, to be first-rate music of its kind. It soon became popular in other countries than Germany, and to this day is part of the ordinary operatic repertory.

In 1890 Humperdinck, then of the age of thirty-six, was living in Frankfort-on-the-Main; the days of glorious association with Wagner were long over, and he had settled down resignedly as one of the many thousands of capable men who compose and teach music in Germany.

In the spring of 1891 his sister, Frau Adelheid Wette, thought of producing a children's play in the family circle, and she asked her brother to write a tune for certain lines — the little song, " Brother, come and dance with me," that Gretel was later to sing in the first act of *Hänsel and Gretel*.

Frau Wette was so enchanted with the result that she conceived the idea of writing, with her brother's co-operation, a little opera on the subject of *Hänsel and Gretel* for a home theatre. But the more Humperdinck worked at the subject the more it grew upon him, and it soon expanded beyond the limits set it by the necessity of a production by children. The domestic play developed into a full-sized opera; it was fully sketched out by May 1891, and completely finished, including the orchestral score, during the course of the following year.

Humperdinck first offered it to the Gotha theatre, but it was rejected as unsuitable to the stage. It was then brought to the notice of Hermann Levi, at that time chief Kapellmeister at Munich, who was so enchanted with it that he decided to produce it at the Munich Opera. Almost immediately after this decision had been come to, the opera was accepted for Weimar by Richard Strauss, who was at that time located there.

The Weimar production, which had been fixed for the 23rd December, 1893, was to have been a few days after the Munich *première*. For some reason or other the Munich production had to be postponed, so that to Weimar fell the honour of the first performance of the work. Apart from Strauss, no one in the Weimar theatre seems to have taken it very seriously. The production was put down for a matinée; and so little did the Director of the theatre believe in the future of the opera that he kicked at ordering new scenery for it. But it turned out to be a decided success both in Weimar and Munich. Other towns, including Frankfort, Berlin, Vienna, Prague, and Dresden, took it up, and in a very little while it was the vogue of the day all over Germany. It was first given in London in December 1895.

The story of *Hänsel and Gretel* is founded on one of Grimm's Tales of the same title, with just a dash of another — *Brüderchen und Schwesterchen* (*Little Brother and Little Sister*). But Frau Wette has made several changes, all of them for the better so far as the sympathies and interest of a theatre audience are concerned.

In Grimm, a poor woodcutter is greatly exercised how to provide food for his two children when famine comes upon the land. His wife suggests taking them out into the thickest part of the forest, giving them one piece of bread each, and leaving them there. The good woodcutter at first will not agree to this heartless plan: the wild animals, he says, will soon come and tear the children to pieces. But his wife tells him that it is either this or death by starvation, so in the end the poor man reluctantly consents.

But *Hänsel and Gretel* have overheard the conversation. Gretel can do nothing but weep, but Hänsel shows himself to be a little man. When the parents are asleep that night and the moon is at the full he creeps out and puts as many bright pebbles in his pocket as it will hold; they look just like silver pennies. When day dawns the children are driven out into the wood by the wicked mother with a piece of bread each. Hänsel marks the way they have taken by dropping a white pebble here and there, and when night comes, and Gretel begins to cry with fear and hunger, he leads her back to the house by the light of the moon on the pebbles. The father is happy to see the little ones again, but the mother scolds them for having been so long away.

A little later there is again great scarcity, and once more Hänsel and Gretel are sent into the depths of the forest. This time, the door being locked at night, Hänsel cannot get out and pick up the pebbles again, but the next day, on the way to the wood, he marks his tracks by crumbs. On this occasion, however, the trail is lost, for though the moon is shining that night, the birds have eaten the crumbs.

The children wander about, completely lost, for three days, living on berries. At last they come to a beautiful little house built of bread and covered with cakes, the windows being made of clear sugar. It proves to be the lair of a wicked old witch, who has built it to entice little children, whom she kills and eats when they are plump enough. She locks Hänsel in a stable with a grating, meaning to fatten him up with dainties to the point of edibility, while Gretel is set to do the cooking and the housework.

Each morning the witch hobbles to the stable and tells Hänsel to put his finger out through the grating, so that she may see if he is now fat enough; but he cheats her each time by putting out a little bone. After four weeks her patience is exhausted, and declaring she will eat Hänsel the next day, she orders Gretel to light the fire and boil the cauldron. The oven is already blazing away, and the witch tells Gretel to creep in to see if it is the right temperature, her diabolical plan being to shut Gretel in, bake her, and eat her also. But Gretel says she does not know how to get in the oven, so the witch has to show her. Gretel gives her a push, bangs the oven door and bolts it, and runs to the stable and releases Hänsel.

They kiss each other and dance for joy and then go into the witch's house, which they find to be full of jewels and pearls: Hänsel fills his pocket with these, and Gretel her pinafore. When they at last find their house again, the wicked mother is dead, but the good father, who has not known a happy hour since he abandoned them in the forest, rejoices to see them. They produce their jewels and pearls, and the three of them live rich and happy ever afterwards.

It would have been a mistake to set the audience against the mother at the commencement, so Frau Wette very wisely makes the departure of the children for the forest the result of the breaking of a valuable piece of property — an earthenware jug, containing the precious supper milk. The mother, who is not bad at heart, but only poor and worried, sends them out into the wood to gather strawberries to replace the milk. At the finish it is the anxious parents who find their naughty but beloved children, while the confectionery of the witch's house turns out to be bewitched boys and girls, who are now restored to their proper form.

The story has indeed been most skilfully reconstructed for stage purposes: the incidents are delightful in themselves, while even the mother is made sympathetic, for she is not bad at heart, but only as cross for the moment as worried mothers of lively children are justified in being.

The woodcutter of Grimm becomes a broom-maker — a good fellow, who, in spite of his poverty, keeps up a stout heart and is fond of his glass; the mother, though she likes to have both her husband and her children under her thumb, is also a worthy soul at heart. The actress who plays the part should beware of overdoing the henpecking of the husband and the nagging at the children: no more of this should be done than is absolutely necessary, given the circumstances of the scene and the financial condition of the family, for the mother must not be made in the least degree unsympathetic to the audience.

In the same way the tipsiness of the husband in the first scene must not be exaggerated, as is generally done. The broom-maker is not a confirmed drunkard who forgets his obligations to his poverty-stricken household and spends his substance on riotous living, but an honest fellow who, having had an unexpected bit of good business, has celebrated the occasion by a drink or two — just enough to make him agreeably mellow. Frau Wette was always angry when the player of the father's part turned him into the conventional stage toper.

It has to be noted, finally, that whereas in Grimm it is Hänsel who does most of the thinking and acting, in the opera he is just a natural boy, the brains of the family having mostly been bestowed on Gretel, though, girl-like, she has not her brother's scruples about admitting she is scared when trouble or danger comes.

Humperdinck has succeeded wonderfully in reproducing not only the style but the spirit of the German folk-song, and of the old Church music that grew out of this; the melody (see No. 1) that appears in the Prelude, in the " Pantomime " of the angels, and on the final page of the score, where it is sung to the pious words:

"When past bearing is our grief,
    Then 'tis heaven sends relief! "

might be a chorale from the great period of German spiritual music, the 16th and early 17th centuries.

But along with this charming simplicity of soul that enables Humperdinck to place himself inside the skin, as it were, of the child, the German peasant, and the German worshipper, there goes a very skilled technique, especially of counterpoint. There are many passages in the opera that seem to the casual hearer just a flow of pleasant tune that are the admiration of the theorist for their clever combination of different melodies. In many ways *Hänsel and Gretel* reminds us of Wagner's *Mastersingers*.

The Prelude begins with the chorale in four-part harmony in the horns:

The second strain is given out by the strings:

and a broad line brings the chorale to a clinching finish:

It is followed by a merry trumpet tune in a faster tempo:

which runs into a melody sung in a slightly different form by the children in the last act to the words " The wind, the wind, the heavenly wind ":

Later comes a theme that we shall hear again at the commence-

ment of the third act, when the children are about to waken from
the sleep into which the Sandman has plunged them:

It is generally known as the Morning Motive.

Another melody is heard a little while afterwards in the oboe,
followed by the flute:

The chorale (No. 1) is then worked out on broad lines, commencing with a statement of it in the soft tones of the trombones,
and it is dexterously combined contrapuntally with other themes.

When the curtain rises we see a small room, evidently, from its
furnishing, that of a very poor household, though it should not
be shown as dirty and untidy, as is done in some theatres by
producers who have not caught the spirit of the story; the broom-
maker and his wife are indeed poor, but they are honest, hard-
working people who neglect neither their house nor their children. For the same reason Hänsel and Gretel, though their
clothes must show signs of wear and tear, should not have the
appearance of being neglected by a good-for-nothing mother.

In the background is a door, and near it a small window that
looks out on the forest. On the left is the fireplace. The profession
of the father is indicated by a number of brooms, of all sizes,
hanging on the walls. Hänsel sits near the door, busy at

broom-making — or as busy as a little fellow of his age can reasonably be expected to be; while Gretel sits opposite him by the fireplace, knitting a stocking. The couple are trying to keep up their
waning enthusiasm for their work by singing a snatch of melody:

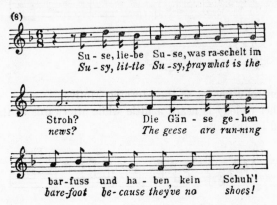

It is one of the three actual German folk-tunes of which Humperdinck has made use in his score; that several of his other melodies have been taken for folk-songs only shows how perfectly he
has caught the immemorial musical spirit of the German people.
Frau Wette has made more use of genuine children's poems than
her brother has of genuine children's songs.

No. 8 runs through most of the scene that follows, but however
expert the technical handling of the music may be, it never becomes obtrusively highbrow; invariably it is in the proper childlike vein. The concluding words of the song are to the effect that
if there is no bread, milk, or sugar, the only thing to do is to go
back to bed; and the lines remind the children how hungry they
are. If only mother would come back! Hänsel has eaten nothing
but dry bread for weeks, and that's hard luck, confound it! Good
little Gretel exhorts her brother, who is inclined to rebel against
the gods, to remember the comforting proverb that father repeats to mother when she loses heart, as seemingly she often
does: " When past bearing is our grief, Then 'tis heaven sends
relief! " This she sings to the melody of the chorale (No. 1).

All very well, says Hänsel, who is a bit of a sceptic in his way; but fine words don't fill the stomach. What a time it is since they had anything nice to eat! He has almost forgotten what egg-cakes and buttered rolls taste like! Good, resigned little Gretel tells him not to be peevish, and picking up a broom she goes through the motions of sweeping trouble and temper out of the house:

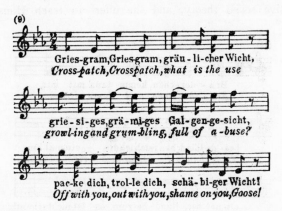

Hänsel follows her good example with the broom, and the pair work up the tune into a charming little duet.

The evil spirit having been thus expelled from the house, Gretel confides a secret to her brother: there is some milk in the jug, sent them by a kind neighbour: their mother will be sure to make them a rice pudding when she returns. Hänsel sings and dances with joy at the prospect:

He cannot resist scooping out a bit of cream and licking it up, for which bit of petty larceny he is rapped over the fingers by the scandalised Gretel. She tells him to get on with his work, so as to be able to show mother something when she comes home.

But the cream has gone to his head: it has made him a rebel against the established order of things. Work is a nuisance; better far to dance and be jolly. Gretel falls a willing victim to this subversive social theory, and she offers to teach Hänsel his steps:

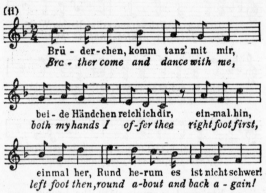

Brü - der-chen, komm tanz' mit mir,
Bro - ther come and dance with me,

bei - de Händchen reich ich dir,   ein-mal hin,
both my hands I of-fer thee   right foot first,

einmal her, Rund he-rum es ist nicht schwer!
left foot then, round a-bout and back a - gain!

He is a bit awkward, and has to be instructed in the rudiments of the art:

Mit den Füss-chen tapp, tapp, tapp,
With your foot you   tap, tap, tap;

mit den Händ-chen klapp, klapp, klapp,
with your hands you clap, clap, clap;

Bit by bit, under her expert tuition, he acquires the technique of the toes and fingers, and right foot and left foot, and offering his arm to the lady, and so on; but when she dances him round a trifle too energetically he gives her a push and gruffly declares that a man like him finds no pleasure in dancing with girls; he even points out, with devastating cynicism, that she has a hole in her stocking. But good-tempered little Gretel wins him over, and they sing and dance together with such abandon that they lose their balance and roll over on the ground, just as the door opens and the mother appears, carrying a basket, which she places on the table and proceeds to open. She scolds the abashed children — each of whom begins to put the blame on the other — for their idleness and frivolity: a nice thing, this, she and the father toiling and moiling from early morning till late in the night, while the children waste their time in play! Hänsel, who gets a box on the ear, has made no progress with his broom-making, while the depraved Gretel has not finished a single stocking! She threatens them with a stick, and in so doing manages to knock the milk jug off the table and smash it, whereupon the corrupt Hänsel cannot repress a snigger.

The poor woman, overwhelmed by this last and crowning misfortune, gives them a hint of what they may expect when father comes home, bursts into tears over the double loss of the jug and the milk, and giving Hänsel and Gretel a basket packs them off into the forest to gather strawberries for the evening meal; then, sinking into a chair, she bewails the emptiness of the larder and sobs herself to sleep.

Outside, in the distance, is heard a voice trolling a gay " tra-la-la," and soon the father enters with a basket on his back, to the accompaniment of a tune in the orchestra in the vein of No. 14. He has had a bit of luck, and is in a cheery mood. He sings ironically a song in praise of hunger — the best of all cooks, but something of a trial to the poor man all the same. Still, why not be cheerful about it, especially when you can make a good song out of it:

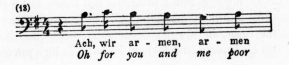

(13)

Ach, wir ar - men, ar - men,
Oh for you and me poor

with a jolly refrain like this to it:

He is so unnaturally pleased with himself and life generally that his wife naturally assumes him to be drunk, whereas he is only agreeably mellow.

These easy masculine escapes into cheerful forgetfulness, however, are not for worried wives and mothers; and she angrily and sarcastically invites him to consider their depleted larder. But he has a surprise for her. Opening the basket he shows her bacon, butter, flour, sausages, fourteen eggs (" Eggs are dear just now! ' she ejaculates), beans, onions, and a quarter of a pound of coffee, and when he turns the basket upside-down a number of potatoes fall out. He takes her by the arm and dances round with her, and even she, a confirmed pessimist, has to admit that somewhere in the sky the sun is shining.

She puts the provisions away in their proper places, lights the fire, breaks a few eggs into a saucepan, and listens to his story of how he came into the possession of all this treasure. There was a fair in the town: he saw his opportunity, went from house to house with his brooms, and sold out his stock at high prices. He is just treating himself to a drink when an idea occurs to him: where are the children? The mother, with a shrug of the shoulders, says she does not know; all she knows is that the jug is broken and the milk lost. The father brings his fist down heavily on the table; the young rascals have been at it again, have they?

His wife piles up the indictment against them: when she came home they were singing and dancing instead of working, and when she remonstrated with them she had the misfortune to smash the jug. The father gives a tolerant laugh, and then asks again where the children can be. "How do I know?" snaps the bothered mother; at the Ilsenstein, for all she knows. This perturbs the father: at the Ilsenstein, astray at night in the dark wood, where the wicked witch lives who gobbles up little children:

She rides on a besom; she is in league with the devil:

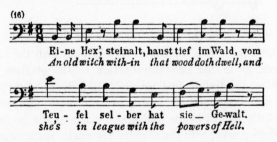

Ei-ne Hex', steinalt, haust tief im Wald, vom
An old witch with-in that wood doth dwell, and

Teu - fel sel - ber hat sie — Ge-walt.
she's in league with the powers of Hell.

and at midnight, when honest folk are asleep, she canters off on her broomstick to the witches' hunt; while her recreation in the daytime is to lure children to her lair by means of cakes and gingerbread, pop them into the oven, do them brown, and eat them.

The mother is horrified; and the anxious couple make off into the forest in search of the children, the father, in spite of his agitation, not forgetting to take his brandy flask with him.

While the curtain is down there is an intermezzo for the orchestra, descriptive of the Witches' Ride; this is mostly made up of statements and transformations of the typical Besom motive (No. 16) and a new motive that symbolises the unholy joy of the Witch:

The themes are worked up quite in the manner of Wagner's Preludes to this or that scene of *The Ring*. Towards the end, while the wood-wind continues with No. 17, the trumpet gives out a broad melody:

that commences in the softest tones of the instrument and then swells to a fortissimo, the trombones helping with the harmony. We have, as in the slow introduction to the overture to *Der Freischütz*, the feeling that we are in the depth of the German forest: soft horn-calls are heard, and the music dies away into tender little figures in the 'cellos and violas as the curtain rises, showing us a wood with the dreaded Ilsenstein, surmounted by fir trees, in the background.

On the right is a great fir tree, under which sits Gretel on a moss-covered tree-trunk; she is making a wreath of wild roses;

another garland of flowers lies by her side. Hänsel is among the bushes on the left, looking for strawberries. It is sunset.

Gretel hums to herself a simple old German folk-song:

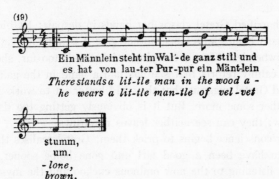

(19)

Ein Männlein steht im Wal'- de ganz still und
es hat von lau-ter Pur-pur ein Mänt-lein
There stands a lit-tle man in the wood a -
he wears a lit-tle man-tle of vel-vet

stumm,
um.
- *lone,*
brown.

to which, from time to time, Humperdinck gives a charming accompaniment. As Gretel asks, " Who can the little man be who stands there with his little black cap on his head? " she surveys the wreath critically from all sides, and, standing up, tries to put it on the head of Hänsel, who has just come out from the bushes, swinging his basket in great glee, and thinking how his mother will praise him for having filled it so full.

Gruffly, as usual, he rejects the wreath as being something fit only for a girl to wear, not a boy, and placing it on Gretel he declares that she looks just like the queen of the wood. If she is to be the queen, she says, she must have the nosegay also. Hänsel gives her this, pays her becoming homage, and hands her the basket of strawberries, telling her majesty, however, not to eat too many of them.

Somewhere from the wood comes the repeated call of a cuckoo. The children remember that the cuckoo helps himself unscrupulously out of other birds' nests, and, thinking that they cannot do better than follow so good an example, they pop the strawberries one by one into each other's mouths. They go on with this pleasant game, calling the cuckoo all the disparaging names they have learned from their elders, until Hänsel begins to help himself to the strawberries by the handful. He is called to order by Gretel, and a quarrel breaks out between them. They fight: Hänsel, who is the winner, puts the whole basket to his mouth and empties it.

The horrified Gretel clasps her hands in despair; let him wait till he gets home; won't his mother give it to him for eating all the strawberries! This is carrying a joke a bit too far, she says. Hänsel calmly retorts that she has had a hand in the game herself, and Gretel suggests that they had better set to work at once and gather some more. But it is obviously getting too dark for this now: they can see neither leaves nor fruit.

Their conscience begins to prick them: Gretel realises that she ought to have been a good girl and gone home sooner, while Hänsel, listening to the now ominous cuckoo and the mysterious rustling that has begun in the wood, and feeling decidedly afraid, confesses, with a rather embarrassed manner, that he does not know the way.

Gretel makes no attempt to hide the fact that she is scared; but Hänsel puts out his chest and swears that, being a boy, he is not afraid of anything. Gretel begins to see things — something glimmering in the darkness, something else grinning at her from the marsh, a light coming towards them. Hänsel, though his knees are trembling and his tongue cleaving to the roof of his mouth, tries his best not to seem afraid: the glimmering thing, he says, is only a birch tree, the grinning thing only the stump of a willow, the moving light only a will-o'-the-wisp. He valorously makes faces at them all, and then, going to the back of the stage, calls " Who's there? " through his hands. Echo answers " You there! "

Poor Gretel begins to be frightened out of her wits. A thick mist comes up and completely veils the background; and Gretel running under the trees, falls on her knees and hides behind Hänsel, crying, " Father! Mother! " while sinister noises come from the orchestra.

Suddenly the mist dissolves on the left, and a little grey man with a sack on his back is seen. The orchestral turmoil dies down into soft harp and violin arpeggios, a trill in the wood-wind, and soaring violin solo: then, to an accompaniment of the same transparent kind, the Little Sandman approaches Hänsel and Gretel in friendly fashion and sings his lovely little song:

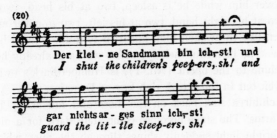

Der klei - ne Sandmann bin ich st! und
I shut the children's peep-ers, sh! and

gar nichts ar - ges sinn' ich st!
guard the lit - tle sleep-ers, sh!

every now and then throwing sand into their eyes. The burden of his song is that he loves little children and brings them pleasant sleep, and if they are good and go to sleep soon the angels come down from the stars and bring them happy dreams:

dann wa-chen auf die Ster - ne, aus
Then from the star-ry sphere a-bove the

ho - her Him- mels - fer - ne gar
an - gels come with peace and love and

hol - de Träu-me— brin-gen euch die
send the chil-dren hap-py dreams while

En - ge - lein!
watch they keep.

The melody comes out in warm, full, but still soft tones in the orchestra as well as in the voice.

The singer disappears. Half asleep, Hänsel murmurs, " Sandman

was there!" Gretel, also drowsy, does not forget the duty of
the evening prayer; and the two children, squatting down, sing
the old German child's song about the fourteen angels who keep
watch over him while he is asleep, two at his head, two at his
feet, two at his right hand, two at his left, two to cover and protect him, two to awaken him, and two to guide him to heaven's
paradise. The beautiful melody, which we have already heard in
the Prelude to the opera (No. 1), is Humperdinck's own; it is
now given out in the broad, rich key of D major.

The children sink back on the moss and fall asleep in each
other's arms. The stage becomes completely dark for a moment;
then a bright light suddenly shines through the mist, which condenses into a cloud and then shapes itself into a staircase running
up from the centre of the stage to the back.

While the orchestra works up Nos. 21 and 1 symphonically,
fourteen angels in light, flowing garments come down the staircase in pairs and arrange themselves about the sleeping children
as described in the evening prayer — two at their heads, two at
their feet, and so on, the seventh pair taking up their position as
"guardian angels," one on each side. The others then join hands
and perform a solemn dance around the group. The light gradually
grows in intensity, the angels arrange themselves in a sort of
tableau, and the curtain falls slowly, the strings of the orchestra
floating up softly into the heights.

Before the curtain rises again for the third act we hear the
sharply rhythmical motive that will afterwards be associated
with the nibbling of the children at the Witch's gingerbread
house:

It is given out first of all by the horn, answered by the oboe, and
afterwards developed, along with other fragments, in the way
Humperdinck had learned from Wagner. Later the Morning

melody that we have heard in the Overture (No. 6) sings out in the oboe, the wood-wind gives out a summons to the children to awaken, and the curtain rising shows us the same scene as at the end of the second act, except that the angels are no longer there.

Morning dawns, and the mist that envelops the background slowly dissolves. The Little Dewman (the Dawn Fairy) comes forward and shakes dewdrops from a bluebell on the sleeping pair. " I am the Little Dewman," he sings to a charming melody:

Der klei - ne Tau-mann heiss' ich, und
I'm up with ear - ly dawn-ing, and

mit der Son - ne reis' ich,
know who loves the morn-ing,

who comes with the golden sunshine and pours light into the eyes of sleeping children, and wakes them with the cool dew on their eyelids; " so up, ye sleepers, for the bright day smiles at you! "

He goes off singing, and the children begin to move. Gretel rubs her eyes, looks around her, and raises herself a little, while Hänsel lazily turns over and settles down to another sleep.

The Morning motive (No. 6) winds its way in and out in the violas and 'cellos as Gretel greets the lovely dawn and the happy little twittering birds: she imitates their " Tire-lire-li " as she wakens her lazybones of a brother. In excellent spirits he answers her " Tire-lire-li " with a " Ki-ke-ri-ki," and declares that never has he had a better sleep and never felt so well. " Listen, Hänsel," says his sister; " I have had a lovely dream." " I too! " says Hänsel. Gretel tells him how she heard a murmuring and rustling like a choir of angels singing; then came rosy clouds, and she saw a golden ladder with angels on it — beautiful angels with golden wings.

" Fourteen of them," interjects Hänsel, to the astonishment of Gretel, who thought the vision had been all her own. " Yes, indeed," says Hänsel; " I saw them too, and very lovely they were, and I saw them float away over there."

He turns towards the background as he says this and just then the last bit of mist clears away. Where before the fir trees were now stands the Witch's house on the Ilsenstein, sparkling in the rays of the fully risen sun. A little way off, on the left, is an oven, and opposite it, on the right, a large cage, both joined to the house by a fence of gingerbread figures. The children gasp with astonishment: never could they have believed that such delicious sights and odours could exist — a little house made of gingerbread and pastry, with a roof of cake, and windows of clear sugar, raisins all over the gables, and, just think of it, a gingerbread fence all round! What a lovely little castle to eat and drink in, in the company of the beautiful wood-princess who must own it:

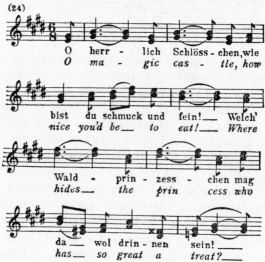

The delight of the children finds expression also in another little figure that is used a good deal later:

All is still, says the bold Hänsel; suppose they go in? But Gretel
is shocked at the suggestion — to walk into other people's houses
like that! Who knows who may live there? It must be the angels
who led them hither, says Hänsel; whereupon we hear the Angels'
motive (No. 1) in the orchestra once more. Gretel agrees, and
they cautiously approach the house on tip-toe, hand in hand.

Hänsel is just breaking off a piece of cake from the right-hand
corner when a voice is heard inside:

(26)

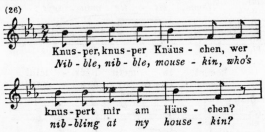

Knus-per, knus-per Knäus - chen, wer
Nib - ble, nib - ble, mouse - kin, who's

knus-pert mir   am   Häus - chen?
nib-bling at   my   house - kin?

The children are frightened, and Hänsel lets the cake fall. " Did
you hear that? " he asks. " It was the wind," says Gretel, to the
melody of No. 5, " the heavenly wind," and Hänsel thinks so
too. Growing bolder, Gretel picks up the cake and tastes it; it is
so delicious that Hänsel also has to have a bit, and they express
their rapture to the strains of Nos. 25 and 26. Surely, they say,
this must be the house of a sweetmeat maker!

Hänsel breaks a piece of cake off the wall — a bigger piece this
time; once more the voice is heard from inside asking what mouse-
kin is nibbling at the housekin; and once more the happy but a
trifle anxious pair assure each other that what they hear is the
wind, the heavenly wind. They have not noticed that the upper
part of the door of the house has opened softly and that the
Witch's head has appeared there. They go on gobbling up the
dainties, having a little quarrel now and then over the division of
the spoil; and they do not see the Witch, who, approaching
stealthily from behind, suddenly throws a rope round Hänsel's
neck.

Both children are now very scared; they ask the old woman who
she is, and demand that she shall let them go. In as honeyed

tones as she can command she tells them that she is Rosina Sweet-
tooth, while the orchestra weaves a delightful tissue of sound out
of the waltz (No. 24). She is so fond of little children, she says
(to the melody of No. 8); they are so delicious to eat — and
she caresses the shrinking Hänsel. She laughs harshly as he repulses her; then, honeying her voice again, she invites them
cajolingly into her house:

where she will give them every dainty they can desire — choco-
lates, and tarts, and marzipan, and cream cakes, and rice pudding,
and raisins, and figs, and almonds, and dates; and, like an ironic
commentary on her words, we hear the orchestra playing No. 25.

But the children distrust her, and Gretel plucks up courage
to ask what she means to do with her brother. She will fatten
him up nicely, says the Witch, and if he is a good, well-behaved
boy, she whispers in his ear, there is a great treat in store for him.

Hänsel mistrusts her more than ever. He has meanwhile managed to slip out of the rope, and calling to Gretel to follow him he
runs to the foreground. But the Witch stops them by laying a
charm on them; holding out a stick that has been hanging at her
girdle, and making the appropriate gestures, she sings the magic
spell, " Hocus pocus, witches' charm! " Dreadful things will
happen to them if they so much as move hand or foot. Do they see
the stick? The knob of this is now glowing, while the stage has
gradually become darker: " hocus pocus, bonus jocus, malus
locus, hocus pocus," she mutters as she shepherds the hypno-
tised Hänsel, who cannot keep his eyes off the shining stick, into

the cage, the lattice door of which she closes on him, whereupon, the spell being ended, the glow dies out of the knob and the stage becomes light again.

Turning to Gretel, who has been deprived of motion by the spell, she tells her to be a good little girl while Hänsel is being fattened up, and holding up a warning finger and grinning at the child she goes into the house to get things ready. While she is away, Hänsel whispers to Gretel to keep her eyes open, say as little as possible, and pretend to do whatever she is told. The Witch returns, gives a glance at Gretel to see that she is still immobilised, and proceeds to stuff Hänsel with raisins and almonds from a basket; then, with a juniper branch and more muttering of " hocus pocus," she disenchants Gretel, who is now able to move again.

In grimly caressing tones the Witch sends her into the house to set out the little dish, the little plate, the little knife, the little fork, and the little serviette for her little mouth, or else — here she gives a threatening titter — she will lock Gretel up too. Hänsel is pretending to be asleep. She quietly bids him go on sleeping till she is ready for him; meanwhile she will begin on Gretel, who is so nice and plump and tender — just the sort of dainty for a witch.

She opens the oven door and sniffs in it, and the red glow within lightens up her face. The sticks are cracking and the dough rising well. She pushes a few more sticks in and rubs her hands with glee: she will get Gretel to look in the oven, give her a push, bang the door, and soon she will be done to a turn. She is so delighted with the idea that she seizes a broomstick and rides around on it in the approved witch style, singing gaily:

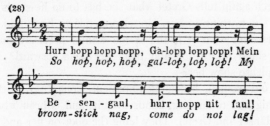

(28)

Hurr hopp hopp hopp, Ga-lopp lopp lopp! Mein
So hop, hop, hop, gal-lop, lop, lop! My

Be - sen - gaul, hurr hopp nit faul!
broom-stick nag, come do not lag!

the horns accompanying the melody with the Ilsenstein motive (No. 15).

Her song is all about the various hours of the day and night and what the witches do with them: at dawn they ride away; at dead of night, when everyone else is asleep, they are off to the witches' feast; at five and six, and seven and eight, other devilry; and nine is one, and ten is none, and much is nothing; and so on till morning again. In a delirium of joy she hops on her broomstick to the back of the stage and disappears behind the house, Gretel all the while watching her from one of the windows.

The Witch comes into view again, surrounded by lightnings, flying through the air past the Ilsenstein; at last she comes to earth again in the front of the stage, and throws the broomstick away. She hobbles to the cage and tickles the apparently sleeping Hänsel with a birch twig. He opens his eyes, and at her bidding sticks out his tongue. This looks satisfactory enough, but when he puts out a bit of stick in obedience to her order to show her his thumb she laments over his leanness and toughness.

She calls Gretel to her and sends her to get some more almonds and raisins, and while she is feeding Hänsel with these, Gretel, seizing the juniper branch, stands behind her and makes the gesture of disenchantment, murmuring the usual " hocus pocus " formula. The Witch turns round sharply and asks her what she is saying. " Only that I hope it will go well with Hänsel," says Gretel.

The Witch sticks a raisin in Gretel's mouth, and decides that the time has come to eat this dainty morsel. She tells the little girl to peep in the oven and see if the gingerbread is done: Hänsel meanwhile has managed to open the door of his cage, and when the Witch again tells Gretel what she has to do he steals out and whispers a warning to her. Gretel pretends to be stupid and not to understand what it is the Witch wants: precisely how ought she to stand on tip-toe and bend her head forward? Will the Witch please show her?

The old woman, becoming impatient, creeps up to the oven, muttering and mumbling, bends over it, and is promptly pushed in by Hänsel and Gretel. They bang the door on her and sing her a mocking farewell in a parody of her own style, the orchestra aiding and abetting them with an ironic version of Nos. 24 and 25.

The children embrace each other and break out into a joyous vocal waltz — " Hurrah! the Witch is dead, dead as a doornail! ":

(29)

Juch - hei! Nun ist die
Hur - rah! Now sing the

Hex - e tot, mau - se - tot
witch is dead, real - ly dead!

und aus die Not! ___
No more to dread! ___

They can now eat their fill, they cry delightedly, and dance to their hearts' content, and have no end of fun: hip, hip, hurrah!

All through the opera Humperdinck has been lavishing all the severest technical devices of composition on his music without ever letting the science interfere with the flow of his tunes, and now he lets himself go, as it were, in a grand final effort. If the reader will examine the following skeletonised quotation:

(30)

he will see that in the bass is the melody associated with the charm of the gingerbread house, while in the top stave the same melody is treated canonically — i.e. it follows the bass at a little distance.

In the second stave from the top is the Witch's song (No. 27), in the third stave the waltz, and in the fourth stave the melody

we already know as No. 24. In spite of the science of the construction, it all " sings " quite flowingly and naturally.

The children's waltz has gradually brought them to the house:
when they reach it, Hänsel breaks away from Gretel, runs inside,
closes the door behind him, and then throws from the upper
window into Gretel's apron apples, pears, oranges, gilded nuts,
and sweetmeats of all sorts. The oven begins to crackle loudly and
the flames mount up, until at last there is a great crash, and the
oven falls in.

In their fright, Hänsel and Gretel let their dainties drop, run to
the oven, and stand staring at it motionless. They are still more
astonished when they find around them a number of children
whose coverings of cake have fallen from them. " How came all
these little children here? " ask Hänsel and Gretel. The Gingerbread Children, who have as yet not moved, and whose eyes remain closed as before, sing softly that they are released at last (see
No. 7 in the Prelude):

and beg Hänsel and Gretel to touch them, so that they may
awake. Timorously Gretel caresses the nearest child, who opens
its eyes and smiles. At the murmured prayer of the others she
wakes them also; but still they cannot move, till at last Hänsel
waves the juniper branch and speaks the magic " hocus pocus."

The children run toward Hänsel and Gretel from all sides and
thank them in a chorus to the tune of No. 7, Hänsel strikes in
with the Morning melody (No. 6), which is worked up into a song
of praise of the Angels.

Into the joyous chorus there suddenly strikes the " Tra-la-

la-la " of the Father behind the scenes: he seems merry enough, " but if only the children were here! " he says. " Why, they are really here! " he cries as he comes into view with the Mother. Hänsel and Gretel run towards them shouting with delight, and are clasped in their parents' arms.

By now the Witch has been reduced to a big gingerbread cake, which two of the boys drag out of the ruins of the oven: they place it in the centre of the stage, and all break out into merry laughter. The Father points the moral — the wicked are always punished, and when we are in greatest need, it is then that Heaven comes to our aid. The two boys drag the Witch into the house, and all join in a last solemn singing of the chorale (No. 1):

> " When past bearing is our grief,
>   Then 'tis heaven sends relief! "

The curtain falls on a dance of the children.

The musical examples from " Hänsel and Gretel " have been reproduced by kind permission of Messrs. Schott & Co. Ltd., London.

GIACOMO PUCCINI

GIACOMO PUCCINI, who came of a musical family, was born at Lucca on the 23rd December, 1858. He received his first musical education from his father, the Inspector of the local Institute of Music, who died in 1864, when the boy was taken in hand by one of his father's pupils, Angeloni.

Giacomo showed talent at an early age, and while still a boy acted as organist at the church of San Pietro, Somaldi. In 1877 he failed to win a prize for composition offered in connection with an exhibition at Lucca, but he had his unsuccessful cantata and other works performed on his own account, and by the time he was twenty it became evident to a few discerning people in the town that his promise deserved fostering. He was accordingly sent to the Milan Conservatory, Queen Margharita defraying the cost of his education for one year, and another patron for two years more.

He entered the Conservatory in December 1880, his masters being Bazzini (the composer of the popular violin piece *The Witches' Dance*) and Ponchielli (the composer of *La Gioconda* and other operas). For his graduation piece Puccini wrote a *Sinfonia-Capriccio* that attracted a good deal of attention. This and a couple of minuets for strings and a *Hymn to Rome* are almost his whole output in non-theatrical music.

His bent towards opera was obvious, and about 1883 Ponchielli introduced him to the librettist Fontana, who collaborated with him in his first opera, *Le Villi*, in one act. With this he entered for a prize offered by the publishing house of Sonzogno, but was unsuccessful. The work, however, was put on at the Teatro dal Verme, Milan, in May 1884, and was so much to the public taste that it was expanded to two acts and transferred to the Scala the next year.

Some years of poverty and struggle followed, during which he wrote a second opera, *Edgar,* the text being adapted by Fontana from Alfred de Musset's *La Coupe et les Lèvres.* The new work, which was given at the Scala in 1889, was a failure, mainly owing to the libretto. Puccini's first notable success came with *Manon Lescaut* (Turin, 1893), but this was eclipsed by *La Bohème* (Turin, 1896), the "book" of which was by the two librettists, Giacosa and Illica, who served the composer so well in later years. The novelty, the charm, and the expressiveness of the music to *La Bohème* made it evident to all Europe that a new star had arisen in Italian opera: the succession to Verdi seemed now assured.

The opera was given in English by the Carl Rosa Company at Manchester in 1897, Puccini attending the rehearsals but not the production. In the October of the same year the opera was produced at Covent Garden, again in English, while two years later, in June 1899, it was performed at the same theatre in Italian, with Melba as Mimi. The Musetta on this occasion was Zélie de Lussan, whom the Carl Rosa management, for some strange reason or other, had originally cast for Mimi. This part, however, was played at Manchester by Alice Esty.

The Manchester rehearsals seem to have given Puccini a good deal of trouble and anxiety. There were features of English musical life with which he was making his first acquaintance, and which he found it hard to understand. It puzzled him to grasp the reason for putting the brass in a box at one side of the orchestra, and the drums in another box on the opposite side. From these little fortresses of their own these instruments made sudden disconcerting raids, as it seemed to Puccini, into the main territory of the music, and then popped back into cover again. Nor did the four-square tempi of the conductor please him. At last he had to dispense with the orchestra for a while and take himself a couple of piano rehearsals with the principals, after which all went well.

Tosca (Rome, 1900), founded on the play by Sardou, once more made him a marked man; many people disliked the work for its theatricality, its mixture of the religious and the sensuous, and its often oily sentiment; but they were compelled to confess that what Puccini did not know about the theatre was hardly worth knowing.

In 1904, at Milan, *Madam Butterfly* was produced, the libretto being based on a play by John Luther Long and David Belasco, which in turn was adapted from a novel by the former. For some reason or other the opera did not please the Milanese audience, and it was withdrawn after the first performance. It was revived in Brescia a few months later, and at once started on a triumphal career round the globe. He failed to make so enduring a success either with *The Girl of the Golden West* (New York, 1910) or *The Swallow* (*La Rondine,* Monte Carlo, 1917); but he broke fresh ground with the triptych *The Cloak* (*Il Tabarro*), *Sister Angelica* (*Suor Angelica*), and *Gianni Schicchi* (New York, 1918). These were three one-act operas in contrasted styles. The first two have fallen into unmerited neglect, but *Gianni Schicchi* has established itself a favourite. It is universally recognised as the finest piece of Italian comedy in music since Verdi's *Falstaff.*

For some years before his death Puccini had been working at *Turandot,* a subject drawn from a " fable " by Count Carlo Gozzi (1722-1806) that has been cast into various dramatic and operatic forms, from Schiller to Busoni. Puccini's constant endeavour in this was to get a Chinese atmosphere and colour that would be different from the Japanese atmosphere and colour of *Madam Butterfly.* Before he could finish the opera, a throat trouble that had been vaguely threatening for some time became serious. The doctors diagnosed it as cancer, and he was operated on in November 1924. He died a few days afterwards, on the 29th November, leaving *Turandot* unfinished. The little that remained to be done to it was added by his friend Franco Alfano, and the opera was produced at the Scala, under Toscanïni, in 1926.

PUCCINI'S *La Bohème,* the libretto of which is by Giacosa and Illica, is based on a novel entitled *Scènes de la vie de Bohème* by Henry Murger (1822-61).

The book is a faithful picture, by turn amusing, poetic, and pathetic, of life in the poor artists' and students' quarter of Paris in the eighteen-forties; the life was extremely hard, but those who lived it found many compensations in it, especially among the grisettes of the Quarter. For his book Murger, who had suffered great privations in his attempt to live by his pen, drew extensively upon his own experiences. The four chief male characters, the poet Rudolph, the musician Schaunard, the painter Marcel, and the philosopher Colline, are all more or less portraits of the author and the associates of his youth. Rudolph is, in the main, Murger himself.

A good deal of light upon the others is thrown by an amusing and little-known book, published in the eighteen-eighties, entitled *Souvenirs de Schaunard,* by one Alexandre Schanne. Until these reminiscences appeared, few people realised the historical character of many of the people and of the incidents that Murger describes. This Schanne, a humorous fellow, became a member of the Bohemian circle about 1840. In his book he jests freely about his enormous nose, the generous dimensions of which are testified to by the two portraits of himself that he gives us; in his youth, it seems, he was given the punning nickname of " Marshal Nez."

Among his Bohemian associates Schanne was generally referred to familiarly as Schannard; and it was this name that Murger gave to one of his characters when, in 1847, he published the first chapters of the *Scènes de la vie de Bohème* in the Paris journal *Le Corsaire*. The printer, however, having reversed the first *n* and made a *u* of it, and the error not being corrected, it was as Schaunard that the character was known henceforth.

Schanne practised painting, but, like many others of the young men of his day, dabbled in all the arts, including music; he actually wrote, though it was never published or performed, that famous " Symphony on the Influence of Blue in the Arts," spoken of in Murger's book, that is generally looked upon as only one of the jokes of the gay young romantics. Schaunard finished up more comfortably, though less romantically, as a manufacturer of children's toys in the Rue des Archives.

Marcel is an amalgam of two painters of the circle, Lazare and Tabar. Readers of Murger's book will remember that a good deal of fun is had out of Marcel's picture " The Passage of the Red Sea," which goes through various transformations in the hope of making it more acceptable to the exhibitions, becoming in turn the " The Passage of the Rubicon " (Pharaoh being transformed into Cæsar), " The Passage of the Beresina," and finally the " Passage des Panoramas." " Having gone so often," says Murger, " forwards and backwards between the artist's studio and the gallery, the picture knew the route so well that if it had been put on rollers it would have been able to find its own way to the Louvre."

It was Tabar, Schanne tells us, who began a big picture of " The Passage of the Red Sea "; but the expense of models and costumes being too much for his slender purse he metamorphosed it into " Niobe and her Children slain by the Arrows of Apollo and Diana," in which form it was exhibited in the Salon in 1842.

Colline is a compound of a certain Wallon and one Trapadoux: Schanne expresses the combination algebraically thus, $W+T=C$. Mimi and Musetta are compounded out of various young women who from time to time attached themselves to the Bohemians; for their names and characters and other details the reader must be referred to Schanne's book. The Mimi of the opera is also, in part, taken from another character in the *Scènes de la vie de Bohème* — Phémie, who was drawn by Murger from one Louisette, whose occupation was dyeing artificial flowers. The girls of the circle were as poor as the men, and more than one of them died of sheer privation.

The episode of Mimi's death is taken from the death of one of Murger's loves, Lucile, who died of consumption in a hospital. Murger heard of it too late to claim the body, which, according to the rules of the institution, was sent to the School of Medicine for dissection. Puccini's Mimi, as those who have seen the opera will recollect, asks on her death-bed for her muff to warm her poor cold hands.

This episode is taken from a story in the *Scènes de la vie de Bohème* entitled *Francine's Muff*. This Francine was Lucile; it was not a muff, however, but a cloth dress of which poor Lucile dreamed in her last moments. Louisette (Phémie) provided another well-known incident of the opera — that in which Colline, in order to buy medicine for the dying Mimi, goes out and sells the oldest and dearest of his friends, the overcoat into whose capacious pocket he used to cram his beloved books. Louisette, after a three months' illness, having complained that as she had no winter wardrobe she felt the cold, Schanne, who was in love with her, sold his new overcoat for thirty francs, and rigged out Louisette on the proceeds. She did not die, however, like Mimi; she tripped out on the 1st January in her new finery and never returned to Schanne.

Leoncavallo also wrote a *Bohème*, which was produced in Venice in 1897. There is a story current to the effect that Leoncavallo told Puccini one day of the subject he was working at, that Puccini went away, looked into the story and thought it would suit him, and stole a march upon his colleague by producing his own *Bohème* first. There is no truth in this libel on Puccini. The fact is that during a conversation one day on the plans that were then occupying them, each composer, to the consternation of the other, announced that he was working at an opera on the subject of Murger's book. Each of them promptly took steps, by announcing his own forthcoming opera, to guard against any charge of plagiarism.

The first scene of the opera is set in the attic that Rudolph uses as a study and Marcel as a studio. It is poorly furnished, containing little else but a table, four chairs, a small cupboard, a bed, a few books, and an easel. On the right of the spectator is a fireplace, that lacks nothing but a fire to be complete. Through the window towards the back we see a great expanse of the roofs of Paris; it is winter, and they are covered thickly with snow. Marcel is busy at the easel, painting his great picture, " The Passage of the Red Sea "; his hand, however, is so cold that he can hardly hold the brush. Rudolph, also shivering, is looking meditatively out of the window; he keeps dancing about on his toes for warmth, swinging his arms about, blowing on his fingers, and so on.

The orchestra, in a brief introduction, gives out a motive that runs through a good deal of this scene:

and Marcel and Rudolph break into a dialogue. " This Red Sea Passage," says the painter, " seems damp and chill to me, but in revenge " — this with a flourish — " a Pharaoh will I drown." Setting himself energetically to work, he asks how his colleague is faring. Rudolph points to the smoke rising from all the other houses, and humorously contrasts the devotion to business of all these chimneys with the shameful laziness of their own stove — an idle rascal that seems to want to live without work, just like a lord:

Each confesses that he is so frozen he does not know what to do with himself; Rudolph can hardly think for the cold, while Marcel's fingers are as chilly as if they had been touching " that iceberg, the heart of false Musetta."

They indulge in some profound reflections on the natures of the two sexes, and then address themselves in desperation to the problem of getting a little warmth. Marcel seizes a chair with the intention of making firewood of it, but Rudolph restrains him. A better idea has occurred to him — his own five-act tragedy, that is lying on the table! Not to be outdone in generosity, Marcel proposes making a sacrifice of his picture, but Rudolph's objection to this plan is that the cremation would make a smell. No, he will immolate his own masterpiece. He takes the first act from the bulky manuscript on the table, strikes a flint on steel, lights a candle, and the pair of them feed the stove with the sheets.

They are warming themselves with great delight in front of this bit of fire when the door at the back opens violently and Colline enters. He too is pinched with cold, and in a bad humour in addition. Taking a bundle of books out of the handkerchief he is carrying, he throws it petulantly on the table. It is Christmas Eve, and it seems that the virtuous population of Paris has a queer notion of the right way to celebrate the festival, for Colline has found the pawnshops closed. He can hardly believe his eyes when he sees a fire, and learning that it is due to Rudolph's drama he ironically congratulates his colleague on the sparkling quality of his work; its only fault is its excessive brevity.

The first act having burnt itself out, and Rudolph complaining, with a shiver, about the length of the entr'acte, another act of the masterpiece is delivered to the flames; indeed, the reception of the drama has been so enthusiastic that the gratified author sends the three remaining acts after the first two. The flames, however, soon die away again, and Marcel and Colline in mock anger, set upon the author.

Just then, through the door at the back of the scene, two boys enter, one carrying food, wine, and cigars, the other a faggot of wood. Colline takes the latter and carries it joyously to the stove, while the boys place the provisions on the table. The two Bohemians, to a strain that is cheerfulness itself:

are congratulating themselves on this sudden accession of good fortune when Schaunard enters in high spirits. The boys go out. Schaunard scatters coins about, which the others, long unused to such a spectacle, for the moment take to be merely medals. A closer inspection, however, reveals the effigy of King Louis Philippe on them. During the scene that follows, Schaunard does his best to explain how this good fortune has come to him, but the others do not listen; they are too busy putting wood on the stove and arranging the eatables on the table.

Schaunard goes maundering on and on through all their chatter, trying to tell them about an eccentric Englishman who had engaged him in an odd professional capacity. When Schaunard arrived he found that what he had to do was to play and sing to a parrot — the property of a neighbour, and a most objectionable bird — until the effect should prove fatal to it. For three days Schaunard had played himself tired and yelled himself hoarse, but without any effect on the infernal parrot. Then he made love to the servant-girl, and, having obtained from her a sprig of parsley — "the prussic acid of parrots," as Murger says — the bird's doom was soon sealed.

A newspaper is used for a table-cloth — an excellent idea, as Rudolph points out, for thus one can eat and read the news of the day at the same time. Rudolph and Marcel set the four chairs round the table, while Colline arranges the food. Schaunard having finished his story, and finding that no one has been listening to him, turns angrily on the others. He rescues the patty and the roast beef on which they have already set to work, puts them in the cupboard, and reminds his friends that though they may drink at home on Christmas Eve they must dine outside, for all Paris will be enjoying itself in the restaurants that night.

Just as they have filled their glasses with wine a knock is heard at the door. It is their landlord, Benoit, who has called for his rent. They receive him with an assumption of great cordiality, politely insist on his sitting down, offer him a glass of wine, and drink his health:

Once more be presents his account, and once more they pledge him. Marcel shows him the money on the table, and the sight of it gives him an unaccustomed respect for his tenants. Will he not join their friendly circle, they ask, and tell them all about his honoured self — his age, for example?

By this time old Benoit is half tipsy. He listens with great complacency to Marcel's account of how he saw him the other evening at the Bal Mabille with a charming young beauty; and Benoit confesses that old as he is his chief delight is still a pretty girl. He likes them small and piquant, but not lean, for lean women are cantankerous and scratchy — his wife, for example. At the discovery that the complacent old rapscallion has a wife the Bohemians break out into an expression of mock horror; the air of their chaste room must really be purified after it has been polluted by this immoral fellow. They edge the bewildered and protesting Benoit to the door and finally push him out; then they divide the money, do themselves up nicely, and Marcel, Schaunard, and Colline prepare to go to the Café Momus.

Rudolph, however, to the accompaniment of his typical motive (No. 2), tells them that he must stay awhile to finish the article he has to do for his new journal the *Beaver;* it will not take him more than five minutes. The others leave him, exhorting him to " cut short the beaver's growing tale "; and Rudolph, placing the candle on his table, takes a pen and tries to set to work.

He has just discovered that after all he is not in the humour for writing when a timid knock on the door is heard, followed by a gentle voice saying " Pardon! " and in the orchestra we hear the Mimi motive:

Rudolph having opened the door, he finds Mimi standing there with a key and an extinguished candle. She is out of breath with climbing the staircase, and is now seized with a fit of coughing.

She seems about to faint, and as Rudolph supports her and places
her on a chair she drops her candlestick and the key.

The solicitous Rudolph sprinkles a little water on her face;
she declines an invitation to sit by the fire, but takes a sip of wine.
Feeling better now, she asks to be allowed to light her candle,
which, it seems, has been extinguished by the draught as she was
climbing the staircase to her room. Rudolph lights her candle from
his own and escorts her to the door, but Mimi, returning suddenly
to the table, cries out that she has left her key behind her
somewhere:

The draught from the open door blows her candle out again, and
when Rudolph makes to light it a second time his own goes out
too, so that the room is now in darkness.

Explaining that this is very awkward, Rudolph, who has found
himself near the door, carefully closes and fastens it and politely
assures Mimi that she is not at all the tiresome little neighbour
she declares herself to be. Having knocked against the table he
places his candlestick on it, and the pair of them, sinking to their
knees, feel along the floor for the key. A sudden exclamation from
Rudolph lets us know that he has found it, but he slips it into his
pocket, and, still feeling about the floor, at last his hand falls on
that of Mimi.

(This episode is taken from Murger's story of *Francine's Muff*.
There, however, things run a little differently. When the draught

blows Rudolph's candle out he puts the matches in his pocket and pretends he has no more, while it is Francine who, at the critical moment, kicks the key under a piece of furniture.)

Everything is now prepared for the great duet. Rudolph begins with an expression of pity for the tiny frozen hand of his visitor; the phrase to which he sings, " Your tiny hand is frozen! Let me warm it into life! "

will be put to pathetic uses in the final scene of the opera, as will a little figure that is heard in the orchestra:

Mimi finds a chair, into which she drops as if overcome by emotion, while Rudolph tells her all about himself; he is a poet, he says, with plenty of wit though rather lacking in wealth; he is peculiarly susceptible to the beauty of women, and just at present, he tells her in a phrase greatly loved by the tenors, is fascinated by Mimi's eyes:

jew - els In fan-cys storehouse cherish'd
- iel - li due la - dri: gli oc-chi bel-li

And now that he has told her his story, will she not tell him hers?
Very modestly and hesitatingly she tells him that though her name
is Lucia she is called Mimi. She lives by embroidering flowers on
silks and satins; and these flowers speak to her of spring and love:

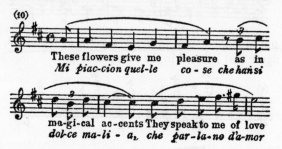

These flowers give me   pleasure   as in
Mi piac-cion quel-le   co - se che han si

ma-gi-cal ac-cents They speak to me of love
dol-ce ma-li - a, che par-la-no d'a-mor

Her life is a simple one: she lives alone and frugally in her little
attic; but when, after winter is over, the first glad rays of the
spring sun greet her, her whole heart warms under its kiss. She
ends with a naïve apology for being "such a tiresome neighbour"
and for having intruded upon him.

Just then the shouts of the other three Bohemians are heard
from the courtyard, telling Rudolph not to dawdle. Very much
annoyed, he goes to the window and opens it; a few rays of moonlight enter and brighten up the room a little. Explaining that
there are now two of them inside, Rudolph asks them to keep a
couple of places for them at the Momus, and then, turning to
Mimi, who seems transfigured by the moonlight, he breaks out
into a passionate song in praise of her beauty, to a weightier version of No. 9. Mimi has by now recovered herself and has become
coquettish. She offers to go with Rudolph to the Momus, although
he insinuates that it would be more pleasant to stay there in the
warm room. She assures him ardently that she will always be near
him. "And after we return?" he asks, whereupon she replies

archly, " Who knows? " With scrupulous old-fashioned courtesy
he gives her his arm and they pass out slowly through the door,
their voices dying away as they descend the stairs.

When the curtain rises for the second act, to the accompaniment
of a piquant melody in fifths in the orchestra:

we see a square in the Latin Quarter, on one side of which is the
Café Momus. The stage is filled with a motley crowd of citizens,
soldiers, children, students, servant-girls, and so on; all are moving about animatedly, while the shop-keepers add to the turmoil
by noisily crying their wares. Colline is standing near a rag shop,
while Schaunard is buying a pipe and a horn at a tinker's. Marcel
is among the crowd; Rudolph and Mimi are walking up and down
apart from all the others. It is Christmas Eve; little lamps are lit
outside the shops, while the entrance to the café is lit up by a
great lantern.

All on the stage amuse themselves according to their respective
fancies. Colline goes hunting for old books; Schaunard, after having obtained the desired horn from the tinker after much haggling,
blows on it vigorously; Marcel invites the girls to make love to
him; Mimi and Rudolph go into a shop to buy a bonnet to which
the former has taken a fancy. Having acquired it, she sees a necklace that she also admires; and Rudolph, finding himself out of
cash, tells her that he has an aunt who is a millionaire, and if it
should please God to take the old lady, Mimi shall have an even
finer necklace than this.

As the Bohemians have been unable to find an unoccupied
table outside the café, they go inside, and soon Colline, Schaunard, and Marcel reappear carrying a table, and followed by a
waiter with chairs. The three are joined later by Rudolph and
Mimi; the poet introduces his new friend to his old ones. Rudolph
and Mimi are obviously very much in love with each other, and

have to put up with some delicate chaff from the others. A good deal of the conversation is carried on over a basis supplied by the following theme in the orchestra:

A hawker, Parpignol, creates a momentary diversion by passing through the crowd with a barrow covered with flowers, paper lanterns, etc.; he is followed by a crowd of delighted street-arabs, chattering and squabbling. While this episode is going on the Bohemians are ordering their meal, and preparing to do themselves exceedingly well; Marcel, however, strikes a somewhat discordant note by loudly and bitterly ordering a bottle of poison. His friends are a little astonished at first, but they quite understand when they catch sight of Musetta, whose infidelity it is that has caused Marcel to take such a tragic view of life.

Musetta, a bold coquette, now enters on the arm of an admirer, a fussy and over-dressed fop, the elderly Alcindoro. To the accompaniment of the rhythm that always characterises her volatile temperament:

she shows herself off before the whole company, while Alcindoro, grumbling all the while, trots about after her like a little dog. Noticing the Bohemians at their table, Musetta tells Alcindoro to secure an adjacent table that has just been vacated; and the pair sit down, Musetta facing the café and the other table. Mimi asks Rudolph who is this pretty newcomer with the smart clothes. The embittered Marcel replies for his friend: her name is Musetta; her surname is Temptation; her vocation is that of changing one lover for another; and, like a bird of prey, her favourite tit-bit is the heart of her victim.

Musetta, for her part, is annoyed at the indifference of Marcel and the amusement she is visibly creating in the other party; and at last, her temper getting out of hand, she becomes a trifle hysterical and smashes a plate by way of relieving her feelings. Marcel, who sits with his back to her, still obstinately refuses to look round, and Musetta's rage increases every moment. It is in vain that poor old Alcindoro reminds her that there are people present and implores her to remember her manners; he only gets viciously snubbed for his pains.

At last Musetta, enraged by the comic turn the situation has now taken, changes her tactics. Still seated, but addressing herself markedly to Marcel, she sings the famous aria:

in which she extols her own irresistible charms and describes her innumerable conquests. At the end she addresses herself still more directly to Marcel, who begins to show signs of agitation; at one point he makes as if to go, but is held by Musetta's voice as by a spell. Mimi takes a great interest in Musetta, and Rudolph explains that she and Marcel had once been lovers, but that she had forsaken him for what she found more profitable game.

Alcindoro, all this time, is trying to induce Musetta to sit down and behave herself as a lady should in public. At last the voices of Musetta, Mimi, Rudolph, Schaunard, and Colline are woven together in a quintet, in which each expresses melodiously his or her sentiments. Musetta sees that the critical moment has come, and that it is necessary to get rid of old Alcindoro. She sits down again, pretends that her foot is paining her terribly, and hysterically orders Alcindoro to run to the boot-shop near by and see if he can find her a pair of shoes less torturingly tight. The Bohemians draw near to the other table, and Marcel is now visibly weakening. Musetta, having taken off her shoe and put it on the table, sends Alcindoro off to see about the relief pair. Rudolph picks up the shoe and hastily puts it under his coat, while Musetta and Marcel throw themselves ecstatically into each other's arms.

The general enthusiasm is slightly damped by the waiter bringing in the bill, which the astonished Bohemians pass from hand to hand; somehow or other there is no money in the company. The waiter also presents Musetta with Alcindoro's bill; she coolly tells him to add the two amounts together, as the gentleman who came with her will settle them both. A tattoo is heard " off," and a delighted crowd gradually fills the stage, waiting for the coming of the soldiers. At last the patrol enters, and all prepare to follow. As Musetta lacks a shoe she cannot walk, so she is carried by Marcel and Colline, much to the delight of the crowd. Rudolph and Mimi follow Musetta and the others; then comes Schaunard, blowing his horn vigorously, while the students, townsfolk, and others bring up the rear.

All very pleased with themselves, they march off to the rhythm of the tattoo. When the stage is almost empty, Alcindoro returns with a pair of shoes, carefully wrapped up. He is greeted by the waiter, who politely presents him with the double bill; at the sight of the appalling figures he drops helpless into a chair, and the curtain falls.

Between the second act and the third, matters have gone rather badly with both pairs of lovers. Rudolph and Mimi, though devoted to each other, are always quarrelling and on the point of separating; while Musetta, although Marcel is the only man she has ever really loved, is too extravagant and too fond of pleasure to remain faithful to him. So far the atmosphere of the opera has been entirely comic; from this point it takes on an ever-deepening tinge of tragedy.

The scene is the toll-gate in one of the Paris customs barriers. It is February, and everything looks bleak and bare. To the left is a tavern; to the right, one of the boulevards; there is also an entrance at this side to one of the streets leading to the Latin Quarter. From the tavern hangs a signboard which is none other than Marcel's picture " The Passage of the Red Sea," now described, in large letters, as " The Port of Marseilles." It is early morning, and lights show from the lower windows of the tavern, while every now and then we hear from this quarter laughter and the clinking of glasses. The toll-gate is closed; in front of a brazier, warming themselves, are a number of custom-house officers, while another, as the curtain rises, comes out of the tavern with wine. The brief orchestral introduction, with its bare fifths:

admirably suggests the chilliness of the hour and the time of the year.

Outside the toll-gate are a number of street-scavengers, blowing on their fingers and adopting other devices to get warm; they call out vigorously for admission, but the officials take no notice. At last one of them gets up with a yawn and opens the gate, through which the scavengers pass to the street on the right, the official closing the gate after them again. A merry chorus is heard from the tavern, and mingled with the voices of the revellers is that of Musetta carolling the strain that is typical of her (No. 14).

Paris is waking up and proceeding to work. First come the women with the milk, then a number of carters, then peasant-

women with butter, cheese, chickens, and eggs; all are admitted
by the officials and, after an examination of their goods, allowed
to go their way. At last Mimi, to the accompaniment of her motive
in the orchestra (No. 5), enters from the street on the right, and
looks around her anxiously as if not quite sure of her bearings.

When she reaches one of the plane trees that adorn the scene,
she is seized by a violent fit of coughing; recovering herself, she
approaches the sergeant and asks if he can tell her the name of
the tavern where a painter is now working. The sergeant points
to the cabaret, from which a serving-woman has just emerged.
Going up to her, Mimi asks her if she can find for her the painter
Marcel, to whom she is to say that Mimi has an urgent message
for him. The woman goes back into the tavern, and soon Marcel
comes out and greets Mimi with an exclamation of astonishment.
By this time day has come, but the light is still cold and cheerless.
Marcel tells Mimi that he has been staying at the inn for some
weeks with Musetta; to pay their footing Musetta has been teaching singing, while he — here he points to pictures of a Zouave and
a Turk painted on either side of the tavern door — has been
placing his art at the service of the proprietor.

Mimi learns that Rudolph also is in the tavern. Bursting into
tears, she appeals despairingly to Marcel to help her; Rudolph
loves her yet avoids her, for he is madly jealous. Marcel gloomily
tells her that when two people cannot agree it is better for them
to part. Mimi thinks as he does, and asks him to help herself and
Rudolph to separate; it is their own wish, yet of themselves they
find it impossible to realise it. Marcel tells her that what alone
keeps himself and Musetta together is the mirth and laughter that
form a sort of bond between them.

Marcel will waken Rudolph, he says; and he points him out to
Mimi through the tavern window, where the poet, overcome with
fatigue, is sleeping on a bench. Mimi's persistent coughing arouses
the sympathy of Marcel. At his bidding she conceals herself behind one of the plane trees as Rudolph comes out of the tavern
and hastens towards Marcel. He pours out his soul to his friend
and asks his advice; he wants a separation from Mimi. Marcel

advises him to think again, and impartially points out to the poet that he has faults of his own; he is not only jealous, but inclined to be somewhat trying, for he is suspicious, stubborn, and choleric. Rudolph then pours out all the bitterness of his heart; Mimi, he tells Marcel, is fickle, and her flirtations are an incessant torment to him; yet in spite of it all he loves her. Mimi, who has been listening to all this, comes closer, under the cover of the trees.

In an expressive monologue:

(16)

Mi - mi's so sick-ly, so ail - ing,
Mi - mi è tan-to ma - la - ta!

Ev - 'ry day she grows wea - ker,
O - gni di più de - cli - na

Rudolph tells his friend that Mimi is ailing; every day she grows weaker, and he fears she is dying. Marcel, afraid that Mimi may overhear, tries to keep Rudolph further off, but the poet continues his melancholy tale to the accompaniment of heavy, slow-moving chords:

Mimi's incessant coughing, that shakes her fragile frame, and her pallid cheeks, tell their own sad tale, he says; and the weeping Mimi, behind the tree, wails out, " Woe is me! I am dying! " And Rudolph can do nothing for her; he is poor, his room is squalid and cold, and in spite of her attempts to smile he feels that it is he who is answerable for her misfortunes.

The three voices, over the sombre chords shown in No. 16, unite for a moment, Mimi sobbing " Mimi must die! Mimi must die! " At last her weeping and coughing reach the ears of Marcel, who rushes to her, takes her in his arms, and tries to lead her into the tavern. But at that moment a brazen laugh from Musetta peals out inside the cabaret, and Marcel, realising that Musetta is flirting once more, gives a jealous cry and rushes indoors to deal with the hussy.

Left alone with Rudolph, Mimi tells him that she must leave him, for her lover has failed her and she must die. He is to collect the few little things she has left behind her — a bracelet, prayer-book, etc. — and wrap them up in her apron, and she will send round for them. Under the pillow he will find her little bonnet; perhaps he would like to keep that in memory of their love. She sings a sad farewell to him, dwelling on a last remembrance of their kisses.

Just then a clatter of breaking plates and glasses is heard in the tavern, and the voices of Marcel and Musetta in hot recrimination. The quarrel continues after they have emerged into the open; and the four voices unite in a quartet, Marcel angrily reproaching Musetta with her incessant flirting. Musetta defiantly declaring that she will be answerable to no one but herself, and Mimi and Rudolph, who have softened to each other at the thought of parting, singing poetically of the happiness that may be theirs when the winter is over and spring and sunlight have come again.

Hurling a few final insults at each other, Musetta and Marcel

separate, the former rushing out into the street, the latter returning to the tavern. The scene is thus left to Mimi and Rudolph,
who, embracing each other, move slowly off as the curtain falls.

In the interval between the third and the fourth acts the affairs
of the lovers have apparently been going from bad to worse. Marcel has not seen Musetta for months, Mimi has abandoned Rudolph once more; and the poet and the painter, each with his
heart heavy with memories, try to forget their sorrows in work.

When the curtain rises, showing the same scene as in the first
act, Rudolph and Marcel are making a brave attempt to appear
indifferent to the blows of fate. The orchestra having given out
the merry phrase to which the Bohemians were introduced to us
in Act. I (No. 1), we see Marcel standing in front of his easel
and Rudolph sitting at his table, each trying to persuade himself
and the other that he is working.

The rising of the curtain has evidently interrupted a conversation between them. Rudolph has been describing how he has seen
Musetta in a carriage and pair and has asked her how things were
going with her heart; she had replied that if it was still beating
she could not feel it, thanks to the fine velvet dress she was wearing; and we hear in the orchestra the rhythm expressive of
Musetta's superficial gaiety (No. 13). Marcel, greatly chagrined,
tries to pass it off with an assurance that he is glad, very glad!
But his assumed stoicism does not deceive Rudolph, who mutters
aside, " You humbug! You're fuming about it! "

The pair resume their work for a moment, and then it is Marcel's turn. He has seen Mimi — an announcement that causes
Rudolph to stop his writing at once. Like Musetta, Marcel continues, Mimi appears to have risen in the world; she was finely
dressed, and riding in a carriage just like a duchess. " Delightful!
I'm glad to hear it! " says the mortified Rudolph, trying to put
the best face on the matter! and Marcel says to himself, " You
liar! You're pining with love! " Once more the two stricken souls
try to compose themselves to work.

But after a minute or two it becomes impossible to keep up this
pretence. Rudolph throws away his pen with a curse, while

Marcel, equally dissatisfied with his brush, flings it away in a pet. He stares at his canvas for a moment, and then furtively takes from his pocket a bunch of ribbon and kisses it.

A little later Rudolph takes Mimi's tiny bonnet out of the table drawer, and the couple, now thoroughly sorry for themselves, pour out their woes in a moving duet, in which each tells how, through all his attempts at work, he is haunted by the eyes and the hair of his fickle love:

Ah   Mi - mi! false, fickle - heart-ed!
O   Mi - mi tu più non tor - ni.

Ah, beauteous days de - par - ted!
O gior - ni - bel - li,

Marcel puts away the ribbon; Rudolph presses the bonnet to his heart; then, trying to hide his emotion from his friend, he turns to him and carelessly asks him the time. Marcel starts from his dream and, the old Bohemian spirit asserting itself again, answers cheerily, "Time for our yesterday's dinner!"

Schaunard and Colline now enter, and we are soon back again in the gay Bohemian atmosphere of the first act. Schaunard has brought with him four rolls, which he places on the table; while Colline draws from a paper bag a herring, which he lays by the rolls. The four friends seat themselves at the table and gravely compliment themselves on the royal quality of the meal, which is carried through in style.

Placing Colline's hat on the table and putting the water-bottle into it, Schaunard declares that the champagne has gone into the ice. Rudolph, addressing Marcel as "Marquis," offers him the bread and asks him which he will have, salmon or turbot; then, turning to Schaunard with another crust, he ceremoniously invites him to try the excellent vol-au-vent with mushrooms. Schaunard declines most politely on the ground that he dare not, as he is dancing that evening. Colline, after hungrily eating his roll, rises from his chair, and with an air of great importance informs them that he must be going, as the King is waiting for him, and after that he has to see Guizot.

The banter goes on for some time in the same mock-serious key, and at last Schaunard suggests a choregraphic exhibition. The proposition is greeted with great applause; chairs and tables are moved out of the way, and after each of them in turn has suggested a gavotte, a minuet, a pavanella, and a fandango, they decide that it shall be quadrilles. Schaunard hums an appropriate tune and beats time, while Rudolph, approaching Marcel and bowing gallantly, offers his homage to the lady; Marcel, putting on a woman's voice and pretending to be very bashful, implores the gentleman to respect her modesty.

Rudolph and Marcel dance, while Schaunard picks a quarrel with Colline, who, resenting the insult, bids his adversary draw. He rushes to the fireplace and seizes the tongs, while Schaunard takes the poker. Rudolph and Marcel stop their dancing to watch the ferocious combat. It is to be to the death; Schaunard tells them to get a stretcher ready, while Colline orders a graveyard for his unfortunate opponent.

The duel is fought out with great spirit, Rudolph and Marcel meanwhile continuing their dancing. Just when one of the combatants has his opponent at his mercy the door opens and Musetta enters agitatedly. Hurriedly and hoarsely she tells the now sobered Bohemians that Mimi is with her, but that her strength has been exhausted by climbing the staircase. Through the open door Rudolph sees Mimi seated on the top stair; he and Marcel rush to her, while Schaunard and Colline drag the miserable bed forward, and on this she is gently laid by Marcel and Rudolph. At this point we hear in the orchestra a reminiscence of the Mimi motive (No. 5), but with an expressive subtilisation of the former simple harmonies. It is evident at the outset that tragedy is in the air.

While the lovers are passionately embracing each other, Musetta, taking the others aside, tells them that having heard that Mimi had left the old Viscount with whom she had been living, she had sought her out and had just found her, almost dying of privation and exhaustion; Mimi had just strength sufficient to say that she wanted to die near Rudolph. Mimi meanwhile is happy in the arms of Rudolph, but the others see that her condition is serious. Musetta looks round for something to restore her; but the Bohemians have to confess that their larder is empty. Mimi's hands are cold; if only she had her muff! she says softly. Rudolph takes her hands in his and chafes them; she greets the others affectionately, and they exhort her not to talk.

All, except perhaps Mimi herself, are conscious of the coming end. Schaunard, in despair, seats himself on the table and buries his face in his hands, while Colline stands aside, sunk in gloomy thoughts. Marcel has been standing by the bedside; Musetta now draws him away, and taking off her earrings, tells him in a whisper to take them and sell them, get some medicine and bring a doctor; she herself will go for the muff. They leave together. Mimi has become drowsy, and Rudolph, drawing up a chair, sits down beside the bed.

It is now that Colline makes his supreme sacrifice. Taking off the old coat that has been his inseparable companion for so many years, he addresses a strangely moving farewell to it:

(19)

Gar - ment an-tique and   rus - ty!
Vec - chia   zi - mar — ra,   sen - ti,

A last good - bye, fare - well!
lo   res - to al pian, tu a-scen-(dere)

folds it up, puts it under his arm, and is just about to leave when he sees Schaunard. He pauses for a word with him: there is not much that either of them can do, but what they can do they must, each in his own way; " this," he says, pointing to the coat under his arm, " is mine; and yours is to leave them alone together."

Colline goes out, and Schaunard, having looked round for some plausible pretext for making his exit, finally takes up the water-bottle and follows Colline, closing the door softly behind him.

The orchestra gives out softly a theme from the duet in the first act (No. 9), and Mimi opening her eyes and seeing that all the others have gone, holds out her hand to Rudolph, who kisses it gently. She has been feigning sleep to be alone with him, for there are so many things she has to tell him — among them that he is her only love. Does he still think her pretty? she asks him anxiously; but when he replies that she is as " fair as spring " she corrects him — " No, as fair as the sunset! " and the orchestra gives a sinister turn to her words by softly intoning the gloomy chords in No. 16.

Mimi's rapidly tiring brain runs wistfully and pathetically over the past, and especially over her first meeting with Rudolph, when the key was lost and they groped together in the dark and found love. The distracted Rudolph can hardly speak; in a desperate attempt to console her he takes out the little bonnet and gives it to her; she is overjoyed that he should have treasured it. As she 's faintly repeating Rudolph's words at their first meeting, " Your tiny hand is frozen! Let me warm it into life! " a spasm seizes her, and she sinks back on the bed in a swoon, half suffocating.

Rudolph gives an exclamation of alarm, which is heard by Schaunard, who has returned at that moment. He hurries to the bedside. Mimi opens her eyes and, with a smile, tries to reassure them, declaring that she is better. They lower her gently on to the pillows, and the orchestra gives out very softly an expressive version of the typical Mimi motive (No. 5).

No. 13 is heard in the orchestra once more, announcing the return of Musetta, with whom is Marcel. Musetta brings with her the muff, while Marcel has a bottle of medicine; this he shows to Rudolph, telling him that the doctor is coming presently. He lights a spirit-lamp and places it on the table, while Musetta hands the muff to Mimi, who seizes upon it with childish delight and buries her fingers in it, to an infinitely soft accompaniment of No. 8 in the orchestra. Grateful for this new warmth, she stammers out a few faint expressions of love and consolation to Rudolph, and says that now she is warmer she will settle herself to sleep. Her head falls back, and an air of contentment steals over her face. Musetta, who is heating the medicine over the spirit-lamp, intones a prayer to the Virgin, and then bids Marcel place a book in front of the flame, so that the flicker shall not worry Mimi's eyes. One or two of the others talk in whispers to each other, while every now and then Rudolph goes on tip-toe to the bed, looks anxiously at the sleeping Mimi, and then returns as quietly to his companions.

At last Schaunard, who has crept softly to the bedside, returns to Marcel, and in a hoarse voice and with a sorrowful gesture says to him, " She is dead! " Marcel goes to the bed, gives a look at Mimi, and retreats in alarm.

A ray of sunshine comes through the window and falls on Mimi's face. Afraid that it will disturb her, Rudolph, obeying a gesture from Musetta, gratefully takes her cloak and screens the window with it. Turning round, he is about to take Mimi the medicine, which Musetta signifies is now ready, when suddenly he becomes conscious of the strangeness of the demeanour of Marcel and Schaunard. Huskily and almost incoherently he asks them what it all means, and Marcel, unable to bear it any longer, embraces him and stammers some words of sympathy.

The orchestra, which all through this scene has been toned down almost to its faintest, now comes out in a great fortissimo outburst. Rudolph flings himself on Mimi's bed, lifts her up, takes her hands, gives a wild cry of " Mimi! " and falls sobbing upon her body. Musetta, with a piercing cry, rushes to the bed and kneels sobbing at the foot of it. Schaunard and Colline seem dazed at the tragedy; while Marcel turns his back to the audience and sobs silently. The curtain falls slowly to the accompaniment of a moving strain in the orchestra that, after another burst of fortissimo, dies away in the solemn silence. The melody is that to which, a few minutes before, Mimi had told Rudolph that she was only feigning sleep to be alone with him.

TOSCA

*T*OSCA was produced at the Costanzi Theatre, Rome, on the 14th January, 1900.

It appeared on the 12th July of the same year at Covent Garden, when Scotti, who is still singing the part, was the Scarpia, and the great Croatian soprano, Milka Ternina, the Tosca. The opera has always been one of the most popular in the repertory, and we have had a succession of great Toscas, Scarpias, and Cavaradossis. Each of these parts lends itself to fine acting as well as effective Italian singing.

The story is founded on a play of the same name by Victorien Sardou, the prolific French playwright who had such a genius for the invention of absorbing plots and the contriving of telling stage situations.

In spite of the world-wide popularity of the opera, there is an astonishingly large number of people who, one finds, do not quite understand all the details of the action. This is probably because some of the most important of these details are revealed not in the great lyrical moments but in the more conversational episodes, the words of which do not always come over clearly to the audience.

The action takes place in Rome, in June 1800. The curtain rises on the church of St. Andrea della Valle. On the right of the spectator is the chapel of the Attavanti family. On the left is a dais, on which is an easel with a picture that is at first covered by a curtain. Sundry artist's implements lie about; and by the dais is a basket containing refreshments for the painter. There is no overture. The opera commences with three striking chords, given out with the full power of the orchestra; they constitute the motive typical of Scarpia, the dreaded chief of the Roman police:

These three bars are succeeded, as the curtain rises, by a hurriedly descending syncopated theme:

designed to introduce to us Angelotti.

Angelotti is a prisoner who has escaped from the castle of Sant' Angelo. He enters through a door in the background, on the right; he is in his prisoner's clothes, which are badly torn, he is panting, trembling with terror, and obviously almost completely exhausted. He gives a rapid glance around him. " At last! " he says. " In my foolish fright I took every face I saw for that of a police agent! " For a moment terror assails him again, and we hear in the orchestra the frenzied motive of his flight; then, mastering himself, he looks round him more calmly, and with a sigh of relief sees a pillar surmounted by a statue of the Madonna, under which is a font of holy water.

It seems that his sister has written to him saying that she has concealed the key of the Attavanti chapel at the feet of this Madonna. He searches for the key, fails at first to find it, becomes greatly agitated — his discouragement being graphically suggested by a few chords in the orchestra — searches again, and at last, with a choking cry of joy, comes upon the key. With the greatest caution he approaches the Attavanti Chapel, inserts the key, opens the grille, and disappears into the chapel, carefully closing the door behind him. The stage is left empty for a moment, and a few expressive bars in the orchestra awaken afresh our sympathies for the fugitive.

Then the tempo quickens, and we hear a light-hearted theme.

(3)   Allegretto grazioso

that is the characteristic motive of the Sacristan, who now enters from the background carrying in his hand a number of artist's brushes. He bustles about the stage, fussily attending to his duties in connection with the church. He is not precisely a comic character, but a character with certain touches of the ridiculous about it. He is given to nervous movements of the head and shoulders, and to pious bourgeois comments upon the world. The music that Puccini has written for him is very much in the vein of the lighter movements of *La Bohème:*

(4)

The Sacristan begins grumbling about the work given him by the artist who, we are to assume, is engaged on the picture on the easel; he is always having to wash the dirty brushes, and they are " dirtier than the collar of a little choirboy." Looking round, he is surprised to find there is no one on the dais, for the Cavalier Cavaradossi had said he would be returning. Putting the brushes down, he has a peep into the basket, and finding the food in it untouched, he realises that the painter is coming back. The angelus sounds, and the Sacristan kneels down and mutters a prayer.

While he is doing this the painter Mario Cavaradossi enters. Ascending the dais he throws aside the curtain that covers the canvas, and we see a Mary Magdalen with blue eyes and a wealth of golden hair. Cavaradossi stands before it and contemplates it silently, while the orchestra gives out a theme that had better be quoted in the extended form it will assume later (see No. 8). This theme is associated with Tosca, and especially with the curious mixture of love and jealousy that is characteristic of her. (The reason for her jealousy of the portrait will appear later.)

The Sacristan is astonished to find that the features are those of a mysterious lady who has lately been very assiduous in her devotions in the church, especially in front of the Madonna to whose statue the Sacristan points. Cavaradossi tells him that he had noticed the kneeling lady and painted her, but he has incorporated in the portrait some of the features of his own love, Floria Tosca, the celebrated singer; and he rather scandalises the good Sacristan by drawing a miniature of Tosca from his pocket and comparing it with the portrait. The painter pours out a little song of wonder at the recondite harmony of nature in her creations:

There are all types of beauty, he says; his own ardent Floria is a brunette, while the beautiful unknown whom he is painting is a superb blonde; her eyes are blue, and Tosca's black. He finishes up the song with a cry that the sole possessor of his heart is Tosca.

All this while the Sacristan has been busy cleaning the brushes in a little basin by the side of the dais, and muttering his doubts about this impious artist who thus mixes up sacred matters with profane. With these dogs of Voltairians, the Sacristan thinks, it is as well to have nothing to do; and he makes the sign of the cross. He tells Cavaradossi that he is going; but before doing so he points to the basket of provisions, remarks that they are untouched, and asks if the artist is fasting. " I am not hungry," replies Cavaradossi. " Oh, I am very sorry," says the Sacristan ironically, and as he goes out he cannot refrain from rubbing his hands with joy and throwing a greedy look at the basket.

Angelotti, who thinks the church is empty, is now seen inserting the key in the grille of the chapel. Cavaradossi's back is towards the chapel, but he hears the clicking of the key in the lock, and he turns round. Simultaneously Angelotti catches sight of him, and a frenzied outburst of the agitated No. 2 in the orchestra paints the terror that seizes upon him once more.

He pauses for a moment as if petrified, then gives a cry of joy, which he quickly stifles; he has recognised Cavaradossi, and thanks God for having sent him to him. But Cavaradossi remains on the dais in his first attitude of astonishment; Angelotti has been so changed by his imprisonment that his friend does not recognise him at first. When he does so he quickly puts down his brushes and palette and runs towards him, at the same time looking round him cautiously. He gives a cry of " Angelotti! The Consul of the destroyed Roman Republic! "

The agitated motive of Angelotti's danger (No. 2) is heard again as Cavaradossi runs to close the door at the side. Angelotti has only had time to say that he has escaped from Sant' Angelo, and Cavaradossi to say " Dispose of me," when, to a hint in the orchestra of the Tosca theme (the first bar of No. 8), the voice of Tosca is heard outside calling " Mario! " Hearing this, Cavaradossi makes a rapid sign to Angelotti to be silent. " Conceal yourself! " he says; " it is a jealous woman; I will get rid of her in a moment." Tosca calls "Mario! " again, and Cavaradossi answers, " I am here! "

The strain is too great for Angelotti; his mind and body weak, he supports himself against the scaffolding on the dais and says mournfully, " I am at the end of my strength; I can keep up no longer." Cavaradossi seizes the basket and hands it to Angelotti, telling him it contains food and wine, and hurries him into the chapel again. Tosca, now thoroughly anxious and suspicious at the delay in opening the door, calls out petulantly, " Mario! Mario! Mario! " and, Angelotti being safely out of the way, the painter composes himself and opens the door.

Tosca is a woman of quick temper, and, being a prima donna by profession, we can readily understand that she is something of a spoiled child. She enters in a furious rage, looking round her suspiciously, while the orchestra gives out the theme that is mainly associated with her:

Cavaradossi makes as if to embrace her, but she repulses him roughly, and asks why the door was closed. Assuming an air of indifference the artist tries to persuade her that this was due to the Sacristan, but she tells him she has heard whispering, and asks him to whom it was that he was talking. " Where is she, this woman? I heard quick footsteps and the rustle of a gown. Can you deny it? "

Cavaradossi not only denies it but passionately assures her that he loves her. He tries to kiss her, but she repulses him with quiet irony: " Not before the Madonna! " she says. Turning to the statue, she arranges about it the flowers she has brought with her, and then kneels before it in prayer. Having crossed herself, she rises and tells Cavaradossi, who meanwhile has recommenced work on the painting, that she is singing that evening in the theatre, but the performance will be a short one, and he is to meet her as she comes out and they will go to his villa, where they will be alone together.

There is a significant hint of No. 2 in the orchestra, letting us know that Cavaradossi's thoughts at the moment are more full of his distressed friend Angelotti than of his mistress. He keeps answering her distractedly, and at last she becomes irritated with him again. Does he not long, she asks him, to be in their little nest again:

where all is love and beauty? An ardent love burns in her, she declares, and, taking up her soaring phrase, Cavaradossi declares with equal ardour that he will come. But now, he says, she must leave him, for his work presses. A trifle piqued, she is on the point of going, when she catches sight of the portrait, and returning to Cavaradossi she excitedly asks him who is this blonde lady. It is the Magdalen, he answers calmly; does it please her?

"She is too beautiful!" says the jealous Tosca; and when he smiles at her and takes the compliment as applicable to his art, she becomes more and more suspicious; surely she has seen those blue eyes somewhere? "There are plenty like them in the world," says Cavaradossi indifferently; but after a moment's reflection

Tosca bursts out triumphantly, " It is the Attavanti! " She understands everything now — the locked door, the hurrying, the whispering; he is in love with this beautiful blonde. He assures her gravely that he saw her by a mere chance yesterday; she was praying at the statue of the Madonna, and unseen by her he sketched her.

The jealous Tosca swears that the abandoned woman is looking at her and laughing at her; the blue eyes are a particular offence. He takes her in his arms and assures her that there are no eyes on earth like hers, and that she has no occasion to be jealous. She professes herself convinced, but " all the same, let her eyes be black ones! "

Her jealousy and her temper vanish as quickly as they came; all she wants is to be assured that he loves her and no one else. She knows that she is tormenting him with her jealousy without any reason:

He gives her his promise that no other beauty shall be admitted to the chapel while he is at work, and having put in order her somewhat ruffled hair she falls into his arms and implores him to forgive her. She offers him her cheek to kiss, and he playfully repeats her own words: " What! before the Madonna? " " The Madonna is very good! " she says, saluting the statue; and the lovers kiss. Then she leaves him, stopping at the door, however, to look again at the picture and say once more, " But let her eyes be black ones! "

Cavaradossi looks thoughtful and perturbed. The Angelotti theme is heard again in the orchestra as he runs to the door, looks out, and makes sure that Tosca is no longer in sight. Reassured on this point, he hastens back to the chapel; he lets Angelotti out and they shake hands affectionately. Angelotti has of course heard the dialogue between Cavaradossi and Tosca, and the artist thinks it as well to assure his friend that though his mistress is good at heart, she probably would not be able to conceal anything from her confessor, so that he thought it wise not to tell her anything. What are Angelotti's plans? he asks.

His friend tells him that his sister, the Attavanti, had hidden for him some woman's clothes under the altar; in these he hopes either to remain safely concealed in Rome or to cross the frontier. Cavaradossi now understands the extraordinary intensity of the Attavanti's devotions; previously he had thought these to be merely the cover for some love intrigue. It was indeed love, he sees now, but a sister's love. " Yes," replies Angelotti; " she has risked everything to save me from the abominable Scarpia "; and in the orchestra we hear the Scarpia theme raising itself aloft like a huge, threatening hand. " Scarpia! " ejaculates Cavaradossi. " A bigot, a satyr, who uses piety as a cloak for his lascivious designs; at once confessor and executioner! "

To save his friend from such a man Cavaradossi will risk his own life. To wait in the chapel until nightfall may be dangerous; Angelotti must get away at once. Outside the chapel is a garden, from which a bypath runs across the fields to Cavaradossi's villa. He gives Angelotti the key of the house and tells him he will join him there before nightfall. Angelotti takes up the bundle of garments left for him by his sister, but Cavaradossi thinks there is no need for him to don them now, as the path is deserted. As the fugitive is leaving, the artist gives him a last piece of advice; if the danger should be urgent, he can hide in the well in the garden, halfway down which is a narrow passage leading to a dark cellar in which he can take refuge without fear of discovery.

Just then a cannon shot is heard, and the two friends look at each other anxiously. It is the cannon of the castle, announcing the discovery of the prisoner's escape; Scarpia and his police will soon be on his track. Angelotti bids his friend good-bye; but Cavaradossi comes to the sudden resolution that he will accompany him, and if they are attacked they will fight. They make their exit quickly through the chapel just as the Sacristan, whose characteristic motive has already made its appearance in the orchestra, comes in breathless, exclaiming " Splendid news, your Excellency! " He is both astonished and sorry to find that Cavaradossi has gone, for, as he says, whoever grieves an unbeliever wins an indulgence, and he has some news that he thinks will particularly vex the painter, whose political as well as his anti-religious opinions he cordially dislikes.

Boys rush tumultuously from all quarters, followed by acolytes, choristers, and various other types of people connected with the church. The Sacristan, too much out of breath to sing, manages to stammer out that the scoundrel Bonaparte has been beaten, smashed, pounded to pieces by Beelzebub.

The others are somewhat incredulous, but the Sacristan, to the accompaniment of a joyous melody of the same simple type as himself:

announces that there will be great celebrations that night, a grand torchlight procession, a gala performance at the Farnese Palace, hymns in all the churches, and a new cantata expressly written for the purpose (they were evidently quick workers in those days), to be sung by Floria Tosca. He sends off the choirboys to put on their vestments. All laugh uproariously at him and resist his attempt to drive them into the sacristy. " Hurrah! " they cry. " Double wages! *Te Deum, gloria!* Long live the king! "

They are enjoying themselves hugely to the tune of No. 9, when suddenly the domineering theme of Scarpia comes out in the orchestra, and the dreaded Chief of Police himself is seen standing in the doorway; all stand still as if spellbound. Scarpia is followed by Spoletta and other police agents. He reproaches the people authoritatively for their scandalous behaviour in the church, and cutting short the Sacristan's apologies, bids them all make ready for the "Te Deum." The frightened people creep out, and the Sacristan is about to follow them, when Scarpia orders him to stay. Spoletta, who is the chief tool of Scarpia, is told to search everywhere for the escaped prisoner; he goes out, signing to two other agents to follow him.

Scarpia gives similar orders to the others, and then, turning to the trembling Sacristan, orders him to answer his questions. A prisoner of State has just escaped from the Sant' Angelo castle, and has taken refuge here in the church. Which is the Attavanti chapel? The Sacristan points it out, and, going up to the grille, finds not only that it is unlocked, but the key left in it is not the usual one. He and Scarpia go into the chapel and return at once; Scarpia, who is obviously out of humour at not finding Angelotti as he expected, holds in his hand a closed fan, which he flutters nervously.

It was a grave mistake, he says, to fire that cannon, as it gave the fugitive warning that they were after him; however, he has left a precious piece of booty behind him; who was the accomplice who helped him to escape? He thoughtfully scrutinises the fan, and then, perceiving the crest on it, he cries out, "The Marchesa Attavanti!"

He looks all round the church, and at last his attention centres on the scaffolding. The picture of the Magdalen on the easel, he sees, is that of the Marchesa, whose features are well known to him. In answer to Scarpia's question, the Sacristan tells him that the painter of the picture is the Cavalier Cavaradossi; and just then a police agent comes out of the chapel, carrying in his hand the basket taken there by Angelotti.

Scarpia extracts from the Sacristan the information that he had brought it earlier in the day to Cavaradossi full of food and wine, that it was impossible for the painter to have put the basket in the chapel, as he had no key to this, and that Cavaradossi had assured him that he did not need the provisions, as he was not hungry. Scarpia's busy brain has meanwhile been piecing all the evidence together — Cavaradossi, himself a man whose political and religious opinions are suspect, and the lover of Tosca, on whom Scarpia himself has set his longing eyes; evidently the provisions have been eaten by Angelotti, and Cavaradossi is somehow involved in the prisoner's escape.

At this moment Tosca herself enters, and Scarpia resolves to make use of the incident of the fan to achieve a double purpose — that of encompassing Cavaradossi's ruin and that of getting Tosca into his toils: " to work upon jealousy," he says, " Iago had a handkerchief; I have a fan! " Tosca is in her usual state of impatience, calling loudly, " Mario! Mario! " The Sacristan tells her that the painter is no longer there, and then prudently makes himself scarce.

When the singer entered the church, Scarpia had concealed himself behind the pillar bearing the statue of the Madonna, waiting for her to say something that would disclose the state of her mind. Her ejaculation, " Has he deceived me? No! He could never do that! " shows Scarpia that the seeds of jealousy are already germinating in her mind.

Coming from behind the pillar, he dips his fingers in the font and courteously offers holy water to Tosca, the bells meanwhile ringing to church. Insinuatingly and flatteringly he speaks of her noble qualities and her wonderful influence — she who by the magic of her song revives the faith of men in heavenly things. She thanks him with a distracted air for his courtesy, her thoughts evidently being elsewhere. During the scene that follows the church gradually fills with worshippers.

Pious women, Scarpia continues, are rare; Tosca, though by profession an actress, comes to the church to pray, not like certain wantons who — here he points to the portrait and puts the utmost possible amount of meaning into his words — " look like Magdalens but come here to carry on intrigues with their lovers." The startled and agitated Tosca asks him what he means. " Is this," he replies, showing her the fan, " a painter's tool? " He found it, he assures her, on the dais; no doubt the lovers had been disturbed, and in her hasty flight she left behind her some of her feathers! Tosca, having examined the fan, recognises the crest, and cries " The Attavanti! My suspicion was correct! " while Scarpia, Iago-like, mutters " My end is gained! "

From time to time, during the foregoing scene, the orchestra gives out a motive:

(10)

that symbolises the power placed in Scarpia's hand by the dis-covery of the fan.

Tosca, hardly able to hold back her tears, and forgetful both of the place and of Scarpia, pours out her woes: she came here in sorrow, she says, to tell Mario that she could not meet him that evening as had been arranged, for she would have to take part in the celebrations of the victory over Napoleon. Seeing that his poison is working, Scarpia approaches her and asks who it is that has thus distressed her: he would give his own life to dry her tears. Not heeding him or listening to him, Tosca bewails her sad loss afresh: while she is sorrowing here, he is deriding her in the arms of her rival! But she will cleanse her villa, her beautiful nest, of this mud! The Attavanti shall not possess him that evening, she swears.

Scarpia hypocritically reproves her for this oath in church, but, bursting into tears, Tosca swears that God will forgive her, for she loves. Paying her the gentlest attentions, Scarpia accompanies her to the door, and then, returning to the pillar, makes a sign, whereupon Spoletta suddenly appears. The crowd by this time has grouped itself at the back of the church, where it awaits the Cardinal; some have fallen on their knees and are praying. " Three agents . . . a carriage . . . quickly . . ." Scarpia says hurriedly to Spoletta " Follow her wherever she goes, but do not let her see you. Rejoin me at the Farnese Palace." Spoletta goes out hurriedly, and Scarpia, with a sardonic smile, says, " Go, Tosca! In your heart Scarpia is taking root! "

The Cardinal and his train arrive, and the Swiss Guards make the crowd give way and group itself on either side. The organ peals out softly, and to the accompaniment of religious music and occasional firing of cannon, Scarpia gloats venomously over the cunning achievement of his double purpose — the ruin of Cavaradossi and the capture of Tosca — " One to the halter," he cries savagely, " the other in my arms! "

The Cardinal passes by, blessing the crowd, which turns towards the High Altar. Scarpia stands motionless for a time, staring into space; then, coming to himself as if out of a dream, he cries, " Tosca, for thee I forget God! " and then, in an access of religious enthusiasm, kneels and joins the others in the " Te æternum Patrem omnis terra veneratur! " Three times his characteristic motive (No. 1) raises its hand in the orchestra, and the curtain falls.

With all its occasional banality, this first act of *Tosca* has an unmistakable bigness about it: it was the first certain sign that the Italian succession to Verdi was assured. But in the second act Puccini was to reveal an unsuspected power.

The next scene shows us Scarpia's apartment on an upper floor of the Farnese Palace. The table is laid for supper. It is night. On the left of the room is a large window overlooking the Palace courtyard. We are to understand that in a room on a lower story of the Palace Queen Caroline is giving a fête in honour of General Melas.

Scarpia is seated at the table, supping; every now and then he draws his watch from his pocket and shows nervous signs of anxiety and disquiet; he is feverishly awaiting the hour of his interview with Tosca and his triumph over his enemy. Tosca is a good hawk, he says in his opening soliloquy, and by this time, he is certain, his agents have the two men in their hands; tomorrow at dawn Angelotti and Cavaradossi will both be hanging on the gallows.

He rings a handbell, and the gendarme Sciarrone enters. Is Tosca in the Palace? Scarpia asks. A chamberlain has been sent for her, replies Sciarrone. At Scarpia's bidding he opens the window, and from the story below we hear very faintly the melody of a gavotte:

From this Scarpia gathers that the Queen's guests are dancing while awaiting the coming of Tosca.

He crosses the stage to a desk and hurriedly writes a letter which he hands to Sciarrone, telling him to wait for Tosca at the entrance to the Palace, and to give her the letter and say that he expects her when the cantata is finished. She will come, he says to himself after Sciarrone has left, for love of her Mario! and we hear in the orchestra a suggestion of No. 8, which is succeeded by the Scarpia motive, this time ending in a sinister diminuendo and pianissimo, as he repeats, " For love of her Mario she will yield to me; such is the profound misery of a profound love."

As for himself, he says feverishly, he prefers a violent conquest to a soft consent. He is not expert in sighs and romance by moonlight, nor in touching the guitar, nor in the lore of flowers; he cannot, he says disdainfully, make eyes or coo like a dove. Rising imperiously and standing by the table, he continues: " I strive for what I desire, and when I have won it I throw it away and turn to some new attraction. God created diverse forms of beauty, diverse wines; I would drink deep of these gifts of heaven! "

Announced by Sciarrone, Spoletta enters. He remains standing at the door while Scarpia, mastering his agitation and resuming his supper, puts his questions without looking at him. How has the hunt gone? Coming forward a little and showing signs of great terror, Spoletta tells him that, having followed the track of the lady, they came to a little villa hidden among trees; the lady entered, but came out again at once, alone. The Spoletta climbed the garden wall and entered the house with his companions.

" Well done, good Spoletta! " ejaculates the pleased and expectant Scarpia. But Spoletta, very hesitatingly and timorously, confesses that their search of the house was in vain. Frowning and pale with rage, Scarpia rises and asks for news of Angelotti. When he hears that the fugitive has not been found he bursts out in wild fury against Spoletta, whom he threatens with the gallows. The agent timidly tries to placate him with the news that the painter Cavaradossi was in the villa; from his ironic words and gestures it was evident that he knew where the other was hidden, so Spoletta arrested him. " He is there," he says, pointing towards the anteroom on the right. " That is not so bad," says Scarpia.

He walks about, apparently lost in thought; then he stops suddenly as he hears through the open window the old-world music of the cantata:

(12)

that is being sung by the choir in the Queen's apartments, and from which he knows that Tosca has returned. Meanwhile the orchestra has given out a motive:

(13)

that will figure largely during the following scene of the questioning and torture of Cavaradossi; it is a typical example of the effect Puccini knows how to make by harping incessantly on the same two or three notes.

All the while the cantata is proceeding — it is in five vocal parts, with the voice of Tosca soaring above them — the tragedy is piling itself up in the room below. An idea has struck Scarpia; he orders Spoletta to bring in the prisoner, as well as Roberti (the executioner) and the Judge of the Exchequer.

Spoletta and three police agents bring in Cavaradossi, followed by Roberti, the Judge, and the latter's clerk. Scarpia has seated himself again at the table, and with deadly courtesy he begs the angrily protesting Cavaradossi to be seated. The painter refuses the proffered chair and demands to know the meaning of this outrage. To-day, Scarpia tells him, looking at him searchingly, a prisoner escaped from Sant' Angelo; Cavaradossi is suspected of having met him in the church of Sant' Andrea and provided him with food and clothes, and afterwards guided him to his villa in the suburb.

Cavaradossi energetically denies everything and demands to know who accuses him of all this. " A faithful servant," says Scarpia suavely. " Your agent," replies Cavaradossi ironically, " has searched my villa in vain "; to which Scarpia replies, " A proof that Angelotti was well hidden." The offended Spoletta, whose armour-propre has been hurt by his failure, here interjects, " He laughed at all our searching." " And still laughs! " says Cavaradossi.

The painter's irony and the cantata combined get on Scarpia's nerves. As Tosca and the sopranos of the choir soar to a fortissimo on the high B natural he rises in irritation and closes the window violently, cutting the cantata short, so far as the people in the supper room and we in the theatre are concerned, on an unresolved chord. Then he sets himself to question Cavaradossi again.

The painter obstinately denies all knowledge of Angelotti — denies that he hid him, fed him, or supplied him with garments.

Scarpia suddenly changes his tactics; from being violently angry he becomes deadly suave, and in an almost paternal manner he advises Cavaradossi, in his own interests, to make a full confession. In the orchestra we hear a wailing theme:

that is a foreboding of the scene of torture that is to follow; it is used and expanded later with all the art that Puccini knew how to put into a suggestive phrase of this kind.

At this point Tosca enters in great distress, and seeing Cavaradossi, runs up to him and embraces him. Under his breath he says to her, " Say nothing of what you saw *there,* or you will kill me! " and Tosca gives a sign that she understands. Scarpia solemnly tells Cavaradossi that the judge is waiting to take his depositions, and at a signal from Sciarrone opens the entrance to the torture chamber, while the orchestra thunders out the sinister torture theme (No. 13). To the executioner, Roberti, Scarpia says, " First the usual form; afterwards as I shall order you." The judge goes into the torture chamber, followed by Cavaradossi and the others, while Spoletta withdraws to the door in the background.

Only Tosca and Scarpia remain behind. With elaborate courtesy he signs to her to be seated and invites her gallantly to a little conversation as between two good friends:

(She does not yet know that her lover is to be tortured; she thinks he has been taken into the other room merely to be

questioned.) Scarpia, leaning insinuatingly over the back of the
sofa on which she is seated, tries to reawaken her jealousy over
the incident of the fan; but Tosca, with simulated indifference,
assures him that her jealousy on that occasion was silly. " The
Attavanti, then," he asks, " was not at the villa? " She assures
him that no one was there but Cavaradossi. In answer to another
pointedly malicious question, she insists again that the painter
was alone.

Scarpia twits her on her vehemence, and, turning towards the
door leading to the torture chamber, calls out, " Sciarrone, what
does the Cavalier say? " " Nothing! " replies Sciarrone from the
doorway. " Be more insistent," says Scarpia loudly.

Tosca, still not understanding what is going on behind the
door, laughs at him, but he gravely advises her to wait a little and
see. Not quite realising the situation even yet, she ironically asks
him whether he wishes her to tell him untruths. His answer is,
" No; but the truth might abbreviate his hour of anguish."

While the orchestra insists, in Puccini's most effective manner,
upon No. 14 and other motives of a similar harrowing nature,
Scarpia tells her that in the adjoining room her lover lies bound
hand and foot with a fillet of hooked steel about his temples, that
mercilessly brings the blood spurting out from his head at each
of his denials. In confirmation there comes a deep groan from
Cavaradossi. Scarpia again advises Tosca to speak out and save
him. She implores him to release Cavaradossi for a moment, and
this is done. She is not allowed to enter the torture chamber, but
from the door she calls to Mario within, who, in a voice weak
with pain, adjures her to be brave and keep silence.

Another appeal on her part to Scarpia for mercy is rejected:

and at last, angered by her obstinacy, he orders the door to be thrown open so that she may better hear Mario's groans. Horror on horror is piled up in the orchestra, while Spoletta, in an attitude of prayer, mutters some lines from the Church's ancient prayer for the dead — " Judex ergo cum sedebit, quid-quid latet apparebit, nil inultum remanebit." Cavaradossi keeps urging Tosca to be steadfast, and at last the infuriated Scarpia calls out loudly, " Compel him to be silent! " There is a prolonged cry of agony from Cavaradossi, whereupon Tosca, unable to endure any more, leaps up from the sofa on which she has fallen and in a stifled voice says rapidly to Scarpia, " In the well . . . in the garden."

Scarpia's triumph is signalised by some repetitions of his motive in the orchestra. He stops the torture, and in response to Tosca's plea that she may see Mario, he orders Cavaradossi to be brought in. To the dolorous melody of No. 13 the painter is carried in in a swoon and laid on the sofa. Tosca runs towards him, but is horrified at the blood on his forehead and stands suddenly still, covering her eyes with her hands; then, ashamed of her weakness, she kneels by him, covering him with kisses and tears.

Sciarrone, the judge, the executioner, and the clerk go out; but Spoletta and the three agents remain behind in obedience to a gesture from Scarpia, who has still a fiendish card to play. While Tosca is consoling Cavaradossi, and he is faintly asking her whether in his agony he has said anything, Scarpia calls out loudly to Spoletta, " In the well in the garden! Go! " Spoletta goes out hurriedly. Cavaradossi, with a cry of " Thou hast betrayed me! " tries to rise from the sofa, but falls back in his weakness, repulsing and cursing Tosca.

At this moment Sciarrone rushes in to announce unpleasant news; the royal troops have been defeated by Napoleon at Marengo, and Melas is in flight. The news puts life into Cavaradossi; he rises with an exultant cry of " Vittoria! Vittoria! " and breaks into a vigorous song in praise of freedom and vengeance upon tyrants:

(17)

L'al - ba   vin - di-ce ap-par
Thou spirit of   ven - geance, a - wake!

che   fa   gli em - pi   tre - mar!
Let tyrants and   myr - mi - dons quake!

Li - ber - tà   sor - ge,
Free - dom,   brand - ish thy glaive and

crol - lan   ti -   ran - ni - di! ___
strike down   thy   en - e - mies!___

He pours out his scorn and hatred of the butcher Scarpia, who
contemptuously orders him to be taken away, telling him that
the hangman is awaiting him. Mario is dragged out by the police
agents, Tosca, who has tried to go with him, being brutally thrust
back by them.

Scarpia closes the door and suavely invites the agitated Tosca
to resume his interrupted supper with him. To the melody of No.
15 he asks her whether they cannot hit upon some plan together
of saving Mario. Polishing a wine-glass with his napkin, filling the
glass with " wine of Spain," and looking fixedly at her across the
lights of the candelabra, he politely asks her to drink with him,
for the wine will revive her.

She cuts his polished comedy short. Seating herself opposite him
and looking hard at him, leaning her elbows on the table and
shading her face with her hands, she asks him, in tones of the
profoundest disdain, " How much? " And as the imperturbable
Scarpia pours himself out some wine and mockingly repeats her
words after her, she says, in almost a speaking voice, " Your
price? "

With a laugh Scarpia assures her that, though people call him
venal, he does not sell himself to beautiful women for money. Her

beauty, he says, has maddened him, and her rage, her hatred, and her devotion to her lover have only made him the more resolute that she shall be his.

She makes for the door, the thought having suddenly occurred to her to appeal to the Queen. Scarpia, who has swiftly divined her thought, makes no attempt to restrain her, but tells her ironically that it will be useless to ask the Queen to pardon a dead man. This makes her pause and again he approaches her, inflamed with passion, cynically declaring that, while he knows that she hates him, " the spasms of hatred are not so very remote from those of love." He is just about to seize her, and she is calling frenziedly for help to the melody of No. 16, when the distant sound of drums is heard. Both stand still. It is the escort of the condemned men, Scarpia tells her. Time is passing; there, he says, pointing to the window, his agents are erecting a scaffold; her Mario, by her own will, has only another hour to live.

Completely broken, Tosca falls back on the sofa. Scarpia coldly leans against the edge of the supper table, pours a cup of coffee for himself, and keeps his eyes fixed upon Tosca while she sings the aria " Vissi d'arte " :

(18)   Andante lento appassionato

Vis - si   d'ar - te,   vis - si   d'a-
Love and   mu - sic,   these have I

- mo - re,   non   fe - ci   mai
lived   for,   nor   ev - er have

ma - le ad a - ni - ma   vi - va!
harmed a   liv - ing   be - ing!

in which, mostly to the accompaniment of the typical Tosca motive (No. 6), she tells how she has lived unselfishly for love and her art, never harming any living thing, helping the poor, and fulfilling the duties of religion both in her life and in her song.

The aria finished, she once more pleads with Scarpia for mercy, and he again lays down his terms. She is just repulsing him with scorn, when Spoletta enters hastily with the news that Angelotti swallowed poison when they seized him, and in the orchestra we hear the Angelotti motive (No. 2) for the last time. "Let them hang his corpse on the gibbet!" says Scarpia ferociously.

Spoletta enquires what is to be done with the other prisoner, and Scarpia turns to Tosca with the quiet query, "Well?" She gives a nod of consent, and, weeping with shame, buries her head in the cushions of the sofa.

Then comes Scarpia's crowning piece of duplicity. He tells Tosca that he cannot release Cavaradossi on the instant, as it is necessary that people should believe him dead; the faithful Spoletta, however, can be trusted to see that everything is done properly. Looking fixedly at the cunning agent, who by his expression and gestures indicates that he fully understands Scarpia's real meaning, he tells Spoletta that he has changed his mind: Cavaradossi is to be shot — "a simulated execution, as in the case of Count Palmieri." Having driven his sinister meaning in upon Spoletta he dismisses him, after having directed him to admit Tosca, as she desires, to be the one to tell Cavaradossi of the change in plans; she is to be admitted at four o'clock. "I understand," says Spoletta meaningly as he goes; "just like Palmieri."

Turning passionately to Tosca, Scarpia declares that he has now fulfilled his promise and claims his reward. She demands, however, a safe-conduct enabling her and her lover to quit the country; and having learned from her that she proposes to travel by the shortest route, that of Civita Vecchia, he seats himself at the desk to write the order. At this point a new and expressive theme:

(19)

winds its slow way in and out in the orchestra.

While Scarpia is writing, Tosca goes to the table and, with a trembling hand, takes up the glass of wine he had poured out for her. As she raises it to her lips she notices a sharp-pointed knife on the table. Casting a rapid glance at Scarpia to make sure that his back is still turned to her, she picks up the knife with infinite caution, hides it behind her, and, with her eyes fixed on him, leans on the table trying to collect her strength.

Having finished his writing, Scarpia seals and folds up the safe-conduct, and then, crying, " Tosca, at last thou art mine! " approaches Tosca with his arms open to embrace her. His voluptuous tone changes to a horrible shriek as Tosca stabs him full in the breast. He falls to the ground cursing her, while she hisses at him, " This is Tosca's kiss! " In his agony he writhes towards her and tries to clutch her by the robe, but she recoils from him in horror. In the madness of her hatred she pours out insults on him in his last agony. Is his blood choking him? Killed by a woman! He tortured her enough; now let him look at his Tosca! Scarpia makes a final effort to reach her and falls back; bending over him, Tosca says, " He is dead! Now I forgive him! "

Hardly another word is spoken until the end of the act, but the action, melodramatic as it may be, is as effective in its way as anything in opera. To the accompaniment of No. 19 in the orchestra, Tosca, still keeping her eyes fixed on the corpse, goes to the table, dips a napkin in the water bottle, and washes her fingers; then, going to a looking-glass, she arranges her hair, which had become disordered in the struggle.

Feverishly she looks everywhere on the desk for the safe-conduct, but cannot find it. At last she perceives it in the clenched fingers of Scarpia. With a shudder that is punctuated by a sudden convulsive *forte* in the orchestra she raises his arm, takes the safe-conduct, places it in her bosom, and releases the arm, which falls helplessly. She looks at the body and says in low tones, " And before this man all Rome trembled! "

Before leaving she takes the two candles that are on the desk and lights them at those in the table candelabrum, afterwards extinguishing these. The Scarpia motive is heard in the softest tones

of the orchestra, pale and exhausted, as it were, as she places one
candle at the right of Scarpia's head, the other at the left. Looking round her again she sees a crucifix hanging on the wall. Taking
it down and carrying it with religious reverence, she kneels and
places it on the breast of the corpse. There is a roll of distant
drums as she rises and departs with the greatest caution, closing
the door after her; and the curtain falls on one of the most effective stage situations ever devised, and one that has been made a
thousand times more effective by Puccini's music.

When the curtain rises for the third act we see a platform of the
castle of Sant' Angelo. On the left is a casemate containing a
table, on which stands a lantern, a large register book, and writing materials; near the table are a bench and a stool. On one of
the walls of the casemate is a crucifix, in front of which hangs a
lamp. On the right of the scene is the top of a small flight of steps
leading down from the platform. In the background we see the
Vatican and St. Peter's Church.

It is a serene and starry night, and the orchestral prelude, with
its succession of falling thirds and fifths:

admirably conveys the atmosphere and spirit of the time and
scene.

It is a long while after the curtain rises before anything happens on the stage. In the distance are heard sheep-bells, the sound of which becomes fainter and fainter. A shepherd's voice, very far off, is heard singing a simple ditty to the accompaniment of No. 20. As the grey light dawns, distant church bells are heard ringing for matins; they are answered by bells closer by.

A gaoler bearing a lantern comes up from the staircase, goes to the casemate, and lights first the lamp in front of the crucifix, then the one on the table; then he goes to the background and looks over the platform to see if the condemned man and the firing party have arrived. He meets a sentry who is patrolling the platform, exchanges a few words with him, returns to the casemate, sits down, and waits, half dozing.

An anticipation of another Cavaradossi theme:

is heard in the orchestra as a picket, commanded by a sergeant, ascends to the platform, bringing the painter with them. The picket is halted and the sergeant conducts Cavaradossi to the casemate. The gaoler rises and salutes the sergeant, who hands him a paper, which the gaoler examines; then he opens the register and writes down the answers he receives to the questions he puts to Cavaradossi.

The sergeant having descended the steps, the gaoler tells Cavaradossi that he has another hour to live, and that a priest is at his service. Cavaradossi declines this offer, but asks as a favour if he may write a few words to a dear one whom he is leaving behind him, and in the 'cellos we hear a gentle and touching reminiscence of the Tosca motive (No. 8). With his last remaining possession, a ring, he bribes the gaoler to pledge himself to convey the letter.

Cavaradossi, again to the soft accompaniment of No. 8, sits down and writes for a while; then, laying down his pen, he gives himself up to the old memories that come crowding upon him. It is at this point that he sings his aria " E lucevan le stelle," the salient phrases of which are those shown in No. 21. The burden of the song is the happy hours of Tosca's visits to the villa in the garden, when the stars are shining and the air full of sweet perfumes; now the dream of love is over, and just when life is most precious to him he is about to die. Covering his face with his hands he bursts into tears.

No. 8 is once more heard in the orchestra as Spoletta comes up by way of the staircase, accompanied by Tosca and the sergeant, the latter carrying a lantern. Spoletta indicates to Tosca where she will find Cavaradossi, gives orders to a sentry to keep his eyes on the pair, and then descends the stairs with the gaoler and the sergeant.

As the orchestra rises to a great fortissimo Tosca rushes up to the weeping Cavaradossi, raises his head, and shows him the safe-conduct. They both read it aloud — " Safe-conduct to Floria Tosca and the Cavalier who accompanies her." Perceiving the signature at the foot of the document Cavaradossi looks hard and interrogatively at Tosca. This was Scarpia's first concession, he says meaningly. " And his last," replies Tosca, taking the safe-conduct from him and putting it into her bag. Swiftly and agitatedly she tells him what happened in the supper room; she killed him, she says, and her hands were reeking with his blood. Taking her hands lovingly in his own, Cavaradossi sings a tender song of praise and pity over them.

She tells him that everything is ready; she has collected her jewels and money, and a carriage is waiting. But first — and here she bids him smile with her — there is a little comedy to be played; he must go through the pretence of a merely mimic execution; when they fire he is to fall down as if dead; the soldiers will retire, and then to Civita Vecchia and freedom! In a melodious duet they lose themselves for a while in the ecstasies of the thought of their reunion. They are recalled to the present reality

of the situation by the entry of the firing party and its commanding officer, accompanied by Spoletta, the sergeant, and the gaoler.
Spoletta gives the soldiers the necessary instructions, while, as
the light of the dawn increases, Tosca murmurs to Cavaradossi,
" I will close thine eyes with a thousand kisses and call thee by a
thousand loving names."

The gaoler, approaching Cavaradossi, tells him the hour has
come, points out the officer to him, takes off his cap, picks up the
register, and goes out by way of the staircase as the church clock
strikes the hour of four. Tosca, going up to Cavaradossi, and
speaking in low tones, hardly able to suppress her happy laughter, tells him once more to remember that as soon as they fire
he is to lie down, to fall lightly, give no sign that he understands
he is playing in a comedy, and wait.

Cavaradossi follows the officer and takes up his position with
his back to the wall of the castle, Tosca remaining at the casemate.
The sergeant offers to bandage the painter's eyes, but he smilingly
declines the handkerchief. A new theme:

with its pendant:

accompanies the action at this point; once more we discover how
well Puccini knows how to intensify the horror by the incessant
repetition of the same phrase.

Anxious, but still confident, Tosca keeps commenting upon the
action point by point. The firing party is drawn up, and as the
officer is about to lower his sword as the signal to fire she stops
her ears with her hands, but nods to Cavaradossi as a signal to
remember her instructions. The sword is lowered, the soldiers fire,
and as Cavaradossi falls she praises the naturalness of his acting.

The sergeant inspects the body and is about to give the usual *coup de grâce,* when he is stopped by Spoletta, who leads the whole party down the steps. Tosca's one fear all this time has been that Mario may spoil everything by some indiscretion. Even after the soldiers have gone she exhorts him softly not to move yet, but to lie quietly and be silent. She looks over the parapet and finds the soldiers have disappeared; then, returning to Cavaradossi, she tells him he can now get up. As he does not move she touches him, and breaks out into a desperate cry of " Dead! Dead! "

She throws herself on the body and is moaning in an agony of grief, when voices are heard behind the scene; Sciarrone is telling the others that Scarpia has been found, stabbed to death. " It was Tosca! " replies Spoletta. They come up from the staircase and Spoletta rushes to Tosca to seize her; she thrusts him back violently, springs on the parapet of the terrace, and as No. 21 thunders out in the orchestra she throws herself down from the height. Sciarrone and the soldiers look over the parapet, awestruck, while Spoletta stands paralysed with horror and fear.

THE fashion of the sentimental Japanese love romance was probably set by Pierre Loti in his *Madame Chrysanthème*. A later creation of the same kind was the *Madam Butterfly* of John Luther Long, which was turned into a drama by the American David Belasco.

This play was brought to the Duke of York's Theatre, London, where it was seen by Puccini; apparently he had been taken or sent there by Mr. Frank Neilson, at that time stage manager of the Covent Garden Opera, who seems to have had an intuition that the subject would prove to be one after Puccini's own heart. Puccini saw the drama, and although he understood hardly a word of English he perceived at once the operatic possibilities of it. It obviously appealed to the two cardinal qualities in his make-up as a musical dramatist — his sympathies with a heroine in distress, and his love for a strong theatrical situation.

We can see the former influence at work in his choice of such heroines as Manon Lescaut, Tosca, Mimi, Madam Butterfly, and Suor Angelica, all of them women who have been badly used by the Fates. As an operatic composer Puccini was a strong feminist; his men are rarely drawn with the sympathy, the assurance, and the force that his portraits of women have.

He dearly loved also the telling dramatic moment, and it is probable that in some cases a moment of this kind was his actual starting-point. In *Tosca*, for example, the two vital points of the drama are Tosca's encounter with Scarpia in the second act and the chain of events that leads up to her throwing herself from the castle walls in the third. In *Manon Lescaut* and *La Bohème* the great attraction to him in each case was the possibilities of pathetic expression afforded by the death-scenes.

Sometimes his absorption in the big climactic scene was so complete as to mislead him as to the virtues of the subject as a whole. One has the impression, for example, that when he saw the Belasco play upon which *The Girl of the Golden West* was founded, what took his imagination captive was the opportunity for blood-curdling expression offered him by the scene in which the concealed hero is detected by the slow falling of drops of blood from his wound; and he was so taken up with this one scene that he did not sufficiently reflect upon the thinness of the interest of most of the remainder of the drama.

We may be tolerably certain that when he saw the play of *Madam Butterfly* he realised at once how infinitely more poignant the scene of the death of Butterfly could be made by means of music, and that this was sufficient to determine him to make an opera out of the subject. So fascinated was he with the pathetic possibilities of the character of Butterfly herself that he does not seem to have considered how lacking in definition the other characters are. Suzuki becomes something of a positive personality in the later stages of the opera, but that is because she shares in the intensity of life that overflows from Butterfly.

Pinkerton is throughout more negative than positive; his main function is to provide a background of moral ineffectiveness and unworthiness against which Butterfly's capacity for suffering can show up all the more vividly. The American Consul, Sharpless, and the marriage broker, Goro, are little more than lay figures, though the dramatic weakness of these characters in themselves is skilfully disguised by the variety and piquancy of the orchestral background.

Puccini chose as librettists his usual associates, Illica and Giocosa, and he seems to have begun serious work upon the opera during 1902. He took a great deal of trouble over the local colour, consulting all the Japanese authorities he could, and in some cases having genuine Japanese melodies transcribed for him.

His first plan was to deal with the Butterfly subject in one act, with an orchestral intermezzo between the last two scenes. It is probable that the too continuous tissue of the opera, which was something to which the Italian audiences of that day were not accustomed, was partly accountable for its unfavourable reception at its production at the Scala, Milan, on the 17th February, 1904.

The critics are often blamed for their unsympathetic attitude towards the music of an innovator. In the case of *Madam Butterfly* it was the whole audience that refused to give the new work a fair chance. Some of them no doubt disliked the exotic quality of much of the music, necessitated by the Japanese atmosphere. Perhaps, again, the singers and the performance generally were not as efficient as they might have been. But whatever the reason for the fiasco, of the fact of the fiasco there was no doubt. The audience that night behaved as badly as only an Italian audience can do when it is not being given the fare it expects. Puccini was so angry that after the performance he took the score away with him, thus making a second performance impossible.

On the 28th May of the same year the opera was put on again at Brescia. On this occasion it was given in two acts, while the second part of the second act really ranked as a third act, separated from its predecessor by the intermezzo. The score had been revised somewhat since the first performance, the chief addition to it being a short aria for Pinkerton in the final scene. This time the opera was an instantaneous success. It was given at Covent Garden on the 7th July, 1905, with Caruso as Pinkerton, Scotti as Sharpless, and Emmy Destinn as Butterfly. The following year it was given at the Metropolitan, New York, and in a very little while it became a part of the repertory of every opera-house in the world.

When the curtain rises we see, on the left of the stage, a Japanese house, with a terrace and garden. The house evidently stands on a hill, and below, in the background, are the bay and town of Nagasaki.

There are a number of themes in *Madam Butterfly* that are

repeated so frequently that they have the appearance of leading motives. It is difficult, however, to attach any precise psychological or descriptive significance to some of them; they seem to be used mostly just as an orchestral background for conversation, at the same time playing their part in suggesting the Japanese milieu.

There is no formal overture, its place being taken by a brief introduction consisting of a quasi-fugal working of the following theme:

Variety is given by another phrase that is occasionally used:

When the curtain rises, two characters emerge from the little house. One of them is Goro, who is known to himself and his clients by the delicately flattering title of a marriage broker; the other is a young American naval officer, Lieutenant B. F. Pinkerton.

The young man, it seems, has taken the house on a long lease — nine hundred and ninety-nine years — and along with it a Japanese bride. Goro, who has carried through both transactions for him, is obsequiously pointing out to him the beauties of the house, and explaining those details of Japanese construction with which an Occidental is not likely to be familiar. A good deal of what Goro has to say is said over a frequently reiterated little phrase:

that seems to be illustrative of the bowing and scraping of this oily, servile pimp.

Pinkerton cannot quite make out the structure of the house, and Goro has to show him how rooms can be created or abolished at will by the mere sliding of a partition. Goro claps his hands three times, whereupon two men and a woman enter slowly and kneel humbly before Pinkerton. These are the lady's maid, the cook, and the general servant of the future Mrs. Pinkerton. Goro describes them by their poetic Japanese names — in the English version of the libretto, Gentle Breeze of Morning, Ray of the Golden Sunbeam, and Sweet-scented Pine Tree. The first of them will become better known to us by the name of Suzuki; the others remain innominate.

Pinkerton, who is a matter-of-fact and rather crude young sailorman, makes fun of these poetical appellations: he prefers, he says, to call the three women " Scarecrow First, Scarecrow Second, and Scarecrow Third." Encouraged by his self-complacent smile, Suzuki, growing bolder, raises her head and gives him the benefit of a few Japanese aphorisms: " Thus spake the wise Ocunama; a smile conquers all, and defies every trouble. Pearls may be won by smiling; smiles can open the portals of Paradise," and so on. But the young lieutenant has no appetite for this poetic Japanese imagery, and his attention obviously wanders. Seeing that he is bored, Goro claps his hands thrice, and the three servants, rising to their feet, disappear into the house; whereupon Pinkerton indulges in the profound reflection that when women begin to talk they are all alike.

Meanwhile Goro has gone to the back and is looking down the

hill. He explains to Pinkerton that he is watching for the arrival of the bride; everything, he assures his client, is ready, down to the smallest detail. To the accompaniment of a piquant little orchestral figure of the chopstick order:

he explains that the company will include the Official Registrar, the relations of the bride, the American Consul, and, of course, the bride herself. The relations are fairly numerous — the bride's mother, her grandmother, her cousins, male and female, a few ancestors, and sundry other blood relations; in all a couple of dozen or so.

The most notable of the relations is a Bonze (a Japanese priest); but he is hardly likely to be present, says Goro, as he is certain to disapprove of his niece's adventure into matrimony with an American.

From the subject of ancestors Goro turns, by a natural transition, to that of descendants; but these, as he slyly hints, can be safely left to his Honour Lieutenant Pinkerton and the beautiful Butterfly.

Just as Pinkerton is complimenting this prince of marriage brokers on the efficiency with which he manages his business, the voice of Sharpless is heard in the distance, cursing the steepness of the ascent. The Consul enters out of breath, for the day is hot. Two new orchestral figures make their appearance at this point:

It is over these, with occasional incursions of No. 1, No. 2, and No. 3, that the conversation of the two Americans is carried on. At the bidding of Pinkerton, Goro and the two under-servants bring out wicker chairs, glasses, and bottles, the latter being placed on a small table in the garden. Pinkerton invites his friend to admire the beautiful view, and explains to him that he has taken this house for nine hundred and ninety-nine years, with the option of cancelling the contract any month he likes.

The orchestra gives out a fragment of " The Star-spangled Banner," and Pinkerton breaks out into a song of praise of the Yankee who goes all over the world:

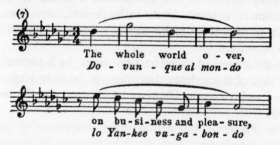

The whole world o - ver,
Do - vun - que al mon - do

on bu - si - ness and plea - sure,
lo Yan-kee va - ga - bon - do

getting the best that is to be had out of each country; he interrupts his recital only to ask Sharpless whether he will have a milk punch or a whisky. " An easy-going gospel," comments Sharpless when Pinkerton has finished the exposition of his philosophy — " a very easy gospel, which makes life very pleasant, but is fatal in the end."

Pinkerton continues his eulogy of the gay, adventurous American; here is he himself " marrying in Japanese fashion, tied for nine hundred and ninety-nine years, though free to annul the

marriage monthly "; and the pair end convivially with " America
for ever! " to the tune of " The Star-spangled Banner " once
more.

Meanwhile Goro has drawn near again, and when Sharpless
asks Pinkerton whether the bride is pretty, it is the officious
broker who gives the answer. She is like a garland of fresh flowers,
he says, like a star in the sky. And what does it cost Lieutenant
Pinkerton? Nothing; a mere hundred yen! If his Honour the
Consul would be good enough also to entrust him with an order,
he has a fine selection. Sharpless waves the offer aside with a
smile, and Pinkerton, turning to Goro, impatiently bids him go
and fetch Butterfly.

When he has left, Sharpless seizes the opportunity to talk
seriously to the young lieutenant. Has he lost his head in this
affair? Sharpless can call it intoxication if he likes, replies Pinkerton; all he knows is that he has been hopelessly fascinated by the
grace and charm and daintiness of the little Japanese girl, who
seems to have stepped straight out of a screen.

But Sharpless still has a misgiving. The other day, he says, she
called at the Consulate; he did not see her, but he heard her
speak, and the mystery of her voice touched his very soul; surely,
he thought, that is how love speaks when it is sincere. It would
be a pity to tear off those dainty wings, and perhaps bring
misery to a trusting heart. The young lieutenant once more
brushes the Consul's middle-aged philosophy aside, mixes him
another whisky-and-soda, and invites him to drink to the day on
which he, Pinkerton, will wed in *real* marriage — this time to a
real wife, an American.

Goro now reappears breathless, with the news that the procession is approaching the summit of the hill, and behind him we
hear the voices of Butterfly's girl-friends. In the orchestra we
hear a theme that henceforth will always be associated with the
love of Butterfly:

and blending with the voices of the girls is that of the still invisible Butterfly, calling them all to witness that she is the happiest girl in Japan — or even in all the world. For she has come in answer to the call of love, and is now nearing the threshold where all the meaning of life and death is awaiting her:

The rapturous theme here quoted is developed in full, and makes a double effect in virtue of the fact that it is the first long stretch of emotional music in the score.

As the melody attains its climax and the singer's voice soars effectively to the high D flat, Butterfly and her friends emerge upon the stage, all carrying brightly-coloured open sunshades. Butterfly sees the three men, recognises Pinkerton, closes her sunshade, and introduces him to her companions, all of whom rise and approach him ceremoniously. Butterfly is full of pretty compliments to her bridegroom, but these are checked by the not unkind but somewhat insensitive young man.

At this point a phrase appears in the orchestra:

of which effective use will be made later.

Sharpless enters into consultation with Butterfly. He learns that she comes from Nagasaki and that her family were once well-to-do, but that it has come down in the world, so that she has had to earn her living as a geisha. Both the men are interested in her artless prattle; and the childlike gravity of the girl's mind is dexterously suggested in the music of Puccini, who can be

an exquisite miniaturist when he chooses. She has no sisters, she
continues, in answer to the Consul's question, but she has a
mother, who, through no fault of her own, is dreadfully poor.

When Sharpless enquires about her father, Goro and the
others all look embarrassed; the subject is evidently an awkward
one. There is a momentary pause, and then Butterfly, by way
of changing the subject, tells Pinkerton of her important uncle
the Bonze, the praises of whose surpassing wisdom and eloquence
are at once sung by her girl-friends. She has another uncle too, she
says — an excellent fellow, but unfortunately rather addicted to
drink.

Pinkerton seizes the occasion to make a rough joke about the
two uncles, one of whom, he says, is a *Bonzo*, while the other is
a *Gonzo* (in the English version, " one thinker and one drinker ").
Sharpless asks Butterfly's age, and is astonished and touched to
hear that she is only fifteen — an age, however, that Butterfly
herself seems to think so closely verging on the venerable as to
call for pity.

Pinkerton orders Goro to summon the three Scarecrows and tell
them to bring sweetmeats and liquors for the refreshment of his
guests. While this is being done, a crowd of Butterfly's relations
come upon the stage. With them are the Imperial Commissioner
and the Official Registrar; these two remain for a time in the
background. Over No. 4 in the orchestra a short ensemble is
built up, the words of which are generally lost in performance.

Pinkerton is amused at the strange spectacle presented by his
Japanese relations, especially his prospective mother-in-law and
the tipsy uncle. Butterfly points to her bridegroom with pride,
while the others comment rather unfavourably upon his appearance, and one of the cousins assures Butterfly that Goro had
already offered Pinkerton to *her* but (presumably) she had refused him. The gratified mother declares that a finer man she
never saw, while the bibulous uncle noses round in search of wine.
The distracting clamour is at last partially stilled by Goro, and
we hear Sharpless congratulating Pinkerton on his luck, and the
latter cordially agreeing with him.

The Consul utters a last word of warning to his young friend not to enter into this contract thoughtlessly, for evidently, while for him it is a mere episode, the girl loves him and puts complete faith in him. With great ceremony Butterfly introduces her relations and friends to Pinkerton, who, beginning to be bored with it all, gets them off his hands by drawing their attention to the refreshments. Goro now brings the Consul, the Commissioner, and the Registrar to the front, where the papers are examined and the contract got ready.

While this is being done, Pinkerton enters into conversation with Butterfly. He wonders why she does not take sweetmeats like the rest, and learns that it is because her sleeves are stuffed full of certain apparatus pertaining to women. She spreads the contents of the sleeves out before him, and goes over them in detail — some handkerchiefs, a pipe, a bit of ribbon, a little buckle, a mirror, a fan, and a little jar of carmine; fearing that he does not approve of this last she throws it away. Then she draws forth a long narrow sheath, which she handles reverently, saying, very gravely, " That I hold most sacred." Pinkerton is curious to know what the sheath contains, but she explains that she cannot show it to him with so many people about. One of the most expressive motives of the opera here makes its appearance in the orchestra:

and while Butterfly is still contemplating the sheath reverently, Goro whispers to Pinkerton that it was a knife sent by the Mikado to her father, who, like an obedient subject, committed suicide with it.

Butterfly continues the tale of her childish possessions, and then tells Pinkerton that yesterday she went to the Mission, for, though none of her friends or relations know it, she means to devote herself to the God of her husband. This resolution of hers is sung to the melody of No. 10. In proof of her sincerity she throws away the little images that represent the souls of her ancestors.

Goro now commands silence. All cease chattering, eating, and drinking, and, coming forward, listen intently to the formal reading by the Commissioner of the marriage contract between Lieutenant B. F. Pinkerton, of the gunboat *Abraham Lincoln,* of the United States Navy, and the spinster known as Butterfly, residing in Omara, Nagasaki. Pinkerton, Butterfly, and the relations all sign; the latter begin to congratulate Butterfly, but make the mistake of addressing her as " Madam Butterfly "; she at once corrects them prettily, with her finger raised — " Nay, Madam B. F. Pinkerton."

The Commissioner and the Registrar add their congratulations, and Sharpless prepares to depart with them. Before he does so, however, he turns to Pinkerton, and in significant tones once more exhorts him to be careful. The gay, thoughtless Pinkerton reassures him with a gesture, and Sharpless, his mind anything but at ease, goes down the path to the town.

Pinkerton is now anxious to get rid of the others. He forces drink upon the receptive and grateful uncle, and then invites them all to toast the newly married couple. While this is being done a cry of " Cho-Cho-San! " is heard in the distance. All show signs of agitation and annoyance; it is, as they know, the bigoted Bonze coming to express his opinion of the company and the proceedings. He has heard of Butterfly's visit to the Mission, and he turns the sentiment of the gathering against her by announcing that she has deserted the religion of her fathers. He curses her zealously, consigning her soul to everlasting torment.

By this time Pinkerton has lost patience. He orders them all out, and the Bonze, thinking better of his temper when the irate young lieutenant threatens physical violence, goes away and summons the others to follow him, which they do with a final cry of " We renounce you! "

Gradually the curses die away in the distance, but Butterfly's childish nerves have snapped under the strain. Childlike, however, she is soon smiling again at Pinkerton's loving and comforting words. From within the house comes the subdued voice of Suzuki murmuring her evening prayer (in Japanese). Evening has been drawing in, and Pinkerton leads Butterfly gently towards the house. The way is now clear for the love-duet, which commences with a calm, caressing phrase:

that is divided between the orchestra and the voices.

This is Butterfly's scene rather than Pinkerton's, for it is she alone who is taking this marriage with absolute seriousness. She is completely absorbed in her American husband, to whom her attitude is that of part bride, part adoring child. Pinkerton's more detached attitude towards the girl he has bought is unconsciously shown by his sitting down and smoking a cigarette while Butterfly exchanges her wedding garment for a piece of pure white night-attire that has been brought her by Suzuki, and arranges her hair. To Pinkerton she is just a pretty plaything, " a little squirrel." Butterfly is at once ardent and shy. Her delicate, romantic mind runs to all kinds of poetic imagery, and even Pinkerton at last catches something of the romance that burns in her. She tells him that when the broker at first came to her with the proposal that she should marry an American — a foreigner, a barbarian — she was revolted at the idea; but now he is all the world to her.

The orchestra thunders out a theme that in the preceding

scene was associated with the Bonze's curse and Butterfly's renunciation by her relatives:

and fancying that she still hears their curses she is seized with a sudden panic and puts her hands to her ears. Then she recovers herself and once more turns trustingly to Pinkerton; he is so strong, so handsome, and she is so happy. As a soft phrase steals out in the orchestra:

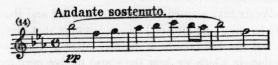

she begs him to love her a little — "Oh, just a very little, as you would love a baby," for she comes of a people grateful for small things in love.

Pinkerton thinks to please her by telling her how appropriate her name of Butterfly is, but his words make her thoughtful and a little apprehensive. She has heard that in his country when a man catches a butterfly he pierces its heart with a needle and then leaves it to perish; and as her voice rises in terror at the thought we hear once more in the orchestra the theme of the curse (No. 13). Pinkerton reassures and consoles her, and the pair pour out their raptures to the now starlit sky.

The final stages of the duet are based on the typical Butterfly love-theme (No. 8). Puccini here finds himself in a slight difficulty. For an effective ending to the act, Butterfly has to soar to a height of passion that is not quite consistent with the conception that has so far been given us of her as just an affectionate child. She now becomes a full-grown woman, and a European —

even an Italian — woman at that. For when he comes to write the music of forthright passion Puccini can no longer keep within the exotic assumed idiom in which so much of the music of this act has been couched. He is not describing Butterfly and her Japanese surroundings now from the outside; he has to speak in his natural voice as a composer, and the result is that Butterfly expresses herself in the same terms as any other Italian opera heroine would do. The music is none the less moving on that account.

Both voices soar up to the high C at the climax of the duet, where the lovers go from the garden into the house. After the voices have ceased there is a passionate little postlude in the orchestra, based on No. 10, and in the final bars, as the curtain is falling, Puccini, by a deft touch, once more restores the quasi-Japanese atmosphere of the scene.

Three years have elapsed between the first act and the second. Butterfly has heard nothing of Pinkerton during that time, and in the interval she has become a mother. After a short orchestral introduction, in which we hear the Curse motive once more, the curtain rises, showing the inside of Butterfly's house. The room is in semi-darkness; Butterfly stands motionless near a screen, while Suzuki prays before an image of Buddah, from time to time ringing the prayer-bell which is supposed to attract the attention of the gods.

Misery and poverty have descended on the little household. Butterfly, to the accompaniment of a theme in the orchestra that dominates this scene (it is obviously related to No. 11):

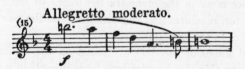

turns from the gods of her fathers to the God of her husband, though He too, she reflects sadly, seems to be oblivious of her trouble. The money of the household has almost disappeared, but Butterfly still preserves her childlike faith that Pinkerton means to return to her; for when he left her did he not say that he would return with the roses, when the robin redbreasts began to nest again?

By skilful insistence on the still essentially childlike quality of Butterfly's mind, Puccini is able to paint a most pathetic picture of her, made up of a large number of tiny musical details. In an aria " One fine day " — that has become a favourite in the concert-room:

she describes to Suzuki (evidently seeing the whole picture in her mind) how one day a thread of smoke will appear far out on the sea, and the ship will glide into the harbour; she will wait on the brow of the hill, and after a while Pinkerton will call " Butterfly! " from the distance, and she will hold herself in and wait, half to tease him, half so as not to die of happiness; and then she will fall into his arms and he will call her by the baby-names of old.

As Butterfly dismisses Suzuki, Goro and Sharpless appear in the garden. Butterfly greets the Consul cordially and does the meagre honours of the house with a kitten-like charm. He has with him a letter from Pinkerton, but in her excitement she chatters so incessantly that he has no opportunity to read it; the one idea in her head is to learn, from this supposed authority on American ornithology, when the robins nest in that country. Goro, it seems, having for his part no illusions about his one-time client, Pinkerton, has been trying to ply his trade once more, and has urged Butterfly to marry a wealthy simpleton of the name of Yamadori, for Pinkerton having deserted her, and her relatives having cast her off, how else can she escape poverty?

At this point Yamadori himself enters with great pomp,

followed by two servants carrying flowers, which Suzuki arranges in vases. Butterfly gaily twits Yamadori on his hopeless passion for her, while Goro calls upon Sharpless to bear out his contention that she is a fool for not accepting this desirable offer. She still thinks, he says pityingly, that she is married! Butterfly corrects him out of the plenitude of her wisdom; desertion may give the right of divorce under Japanese law, but in the great and good United States things are managed more justly. There the judges are honest, and a husband who tries to get rid of the wife of whom he has tired is quickly clapped into prison.

Goro whispers to Sharpless that Pinkerton's ship is already signalled, and to both Goro and Yamadori the Consul confides that that was the very reason why he wished to see her — to try to prepare her for the blow that is about to descend on her. The disappointed Yamadori leaves, after a final appeal to Butterfly, who only laughs at the grotesque figure the unsuccessful suitor cuts.

At last Sharpless induces Butterfly to sit by him. He draws the letter from his pocket, and Butterfly, seizing it, kisses it and presses it to her heart. She asks him to read it to her, which Sharpless does to the accompaniment of a phrase:

that is repeated again and again in the orchestra. The purport of the letter is that the Consul is to see little Butterfly, and with great tact and discretion prepare her for the blow that . . . But Butterfly's excited interruptions, and a pang of pity that he feels for the poor little trusting thing, make it impossible for Sharpless to read the letter to the end.

Gravely he asks her what she would do if Pinkerton were never to return. In a profoundly moving passage, in which a suggestion of impending tragedy is given by the simplest possible musi-

cal means, she declares that there are two things she might do —
become a geisha once more, or else, which would be better, die.

Full of pity, and in utter despair, Sharpless advises her to accept Yamadori's offer. This counsel puzzles Butterfly, who, by
way of showing Sharpless the absurdity of the notion, claps her
hands and bids Suzuki bring in the convincing proof that she is
right — Pinkerton's child. In pride and triumph she shows the
baby to the Consul, drawing his attention to the quite un-Jap-
anese blueness of its eyes and its golden hair. Sharpless must write
Pinkerton and tell him of this incomparable son that has been
born to him, and then, surely, Pinkerton will hasten over land
and over sea to her.

The music of the act rises to its greatest height as she pictures
herself dancing before the people, and the Emperor, passing in
pomp with his warriors, stopping to admire this wonderful child
and make him a prince of his kingdom.

Seeing that it is hopeless to try to bring her to reason, and his
heart sick with pain and pity, Sharpless, after embracing the
child, bows to Butterfly and goes out quickly. Just then a wild cry
is heard outside from Suzuki, who comes in dragging Goro after
her. He has been saying that the child born in these conditions
will be an outcast all his life in America. Butterfly, in a rage,
makes to kill him with her father's dagger that hangs on the wall,
but he is saved by Suzuki, who then seizes the child and carries
him into the inner room, while Butterfly, in disgust, spurns the
terrified Goro with her foot. When he has made his escape, Butterfly remains for a moment as if petrified; then, collecting herself, she restores the dagger to its place, and breaks out into a
passionate promise to the child that soon his and her avenger will
be there, to take them both to his own country.

She is interrupted by the boom of a shot; it is the harbour
cannon announcing the arrival of a man-of-war. Running to the
terrace, Butterfly and Suzuki see the American stars and stripes,
and seizing a telescope Butterfly, trembling with excitement,
manages at last to make out the name of the ship — the *Abraham
Lincoln*. Now she knows that Goro and the rest of them were all

liars! (Throughout this scene there appropriately runs, in the orchestra, the melody of " One fine day "; and as Butterfly declares her faith that the end of all her troubles is at hand with the return of Pinkerton, we hear first of all the accustomed phrase from " The Star-spangled Banner," and then a reminiscence of the rapturous love-duet at the end of the first act.) Butterfly excitedly calls upon Suzuki to help her to shake the white flowers from the cherry tree as a greeting to her lord, and the two women strip the garden of its flowers, with which they decorate the room.

Suzuki brings the baby from the inner room and places it on the floor next to Butterfly, who, with the aid of a small hand-mirror, first of all adds colour to her own faded cheeks and then puts a dab of rouge on the cheeks of the child, so that it too, when Pinkerton comes, may show no trace of the weariness of the long waiting. While the orchestra gives out a reminiscence of No. 12, Butterfly puts on her wedding garment, and Suzuki envelops the baby in the robe that its mother has discarded. Suzuki completes Butterfly's toilet by putting a scarlet poppy in her hair.

Night now falls fast. Suzuki closes the *shosi,* in which Butterfly makes three holes, one high up for herself, a lower one for Suzuki, and a still lower one for the baby, whom she seats on a cushion; lighted lanterns are disposed on the floor in the middle of the room. Butterfly stands erect and rigid, gazing fixedly out, while Suzuki crouches down on the other side of the child. It is now completely dark, the *shosi* being lit up from without by the rays of the moon. No. 17 is heard once more in the orchestra, in the softest tones, accompanied by closed-mouth humming from sopranos and tenors in the far distance. Gradually, as the monotonous and suggestive effect spins itself slowly out, first the baby falls asleep, then Suzuki; but Butterfly is still erect and motionless when the curtain falls.

Between the first and second parts of Act II there is an orchestral interlude, towards the end of which we hear once more a reminiscence of the love-duet in the first act. From far away in the bay there comes the cry — " Oh eh! Oh eh! " — of the sailors, accompanied by the clanking of chains and other sounds from the ships in the harbour. When the curtain rises, to the accompaniment of a new theme in the orchestra:

we see the three figures as we left them at the conclusion of the preceding scene.

The day breaks gradually, the orchestra rising to life with it. At last, when the sunshine fills the room, Butterfly rouses herself, wakens Suzuki, and then takes up the baby tenderly. Seeing how weary Butterfly is, Suzuki implores her to go and rest, promising that she will call her when Pinkerton arrives. Butterfly goes off with the child, singing it a sweet little lullaby that has a curious touch of Grieg about it; after each of the final phrases Suzuki breaks in with a sad " Poor Madam Butterfly! "

To the accompaniment of one of Puccini's typically sombre, slow-treading themes:

Suzuki is opening the *shosi* when a knock is heard at the door. Opening it, she finds Pinkerton, who signals to her to be silent. He enters cautiously on tiptoe, followed by Sharpless. Suzuki tells them of Butterfly's vigil, and how for three years she has examined eagerly the flag and the colours of every ship that has crossed the harbour. Pointing to the flowers, Suzuki shows Pinkerton the preparations that have been made for his return. Hearing a noise in the garden she goes to look out, and is surprised to find a lady there. A fear of coming evil strikes into her heart, and she excitedly implores Pinkerton to tell her who this woman is.

At first he tries to evade the question, simply saying, " She came with me "; but Sharpless thinks it better to tell her the truth at once: it is Pinkerton's American wife. The stupefied Suzuki breaks out into a wild cry of despair and falls to the ground. Sharpless raises her, tries to soothe her, and explains that they have come so early in the morning hoping to find her alone and to be able to count upon her discretion and help. To the strain of No. 19 he tells her that for such a trouble as Butterfly's there is no consolation, but the future of the baby must be their first thought; the lady outside dare not enter, but she will give the child a mother's care. He exhorts Suzuki, however, to go and speak to the lady, and induce her to come in even though Butterfly should see her and learn with her own eyes the bitter truth that none dares tell her.

Meanwhile Suzuki is sobbing out her only half-coherent lamentations, and Pinkerton, seeing his own portrait, is touched by the evidence that he has been in Buterfly's mind all these years. He feels himself unequal to the ordeal of meeting her. Giving Sharpless money for the support of Butterfly, and sobbing out his anguish and remorse, he bids farewell to the house in which he had once known such happiness:

and ends his own difficulties by pusillanimous flight. Sharpless, having shaken him by the hand, bows his head sadly.

Kate Pinkerton and Suzuki enter from the garden, and from their conversation we learn that Suzuki has promised to tell Butterfly everything and give her Mrs. Pinkerton's promise that she will tend the child like a son.

Butterfly's voice is now heard calling " Suzuki! Suzuki! Where are you? " from the room above; and soon she appears at the top of the staircase. She is about to descend the stairs when Suzuki rushes forward to prevent her. But Butterfly will not be withheld. Something has told her that Pinkerton has come, and she paces the room joyously and excitedly in search of him. Seeing only Sharpless, she begins to be alarmed.

After a further search she notices Kate Pinkerton, who is weeping. She asks the strange lady who she is, but receiving no answer, begins to understand everything, and shrinks in upon herself like a frightened child. To Suzuki, as the only one she can trust, she turns with the pitiful question, " Say yes, or no, quite softly; does he live? " Suzuki mutters despairingly " Yes," but at first cannot be induced to answer Butterfly's next question, " They have told you that he will come no more? "

When the truth has been wrung from Suzuki, Butterfly's last illusion is gone: at last she understands. She looks fixedly at Kate, both terrified and fascinated; and Kate can say nothing but " Through no fault of my own I am the cause of your trouble. Forgive me." She would approach Butterfly to console her, but the latter shrinks from her. Calmly she asks, " How long ago was it he married you? " Kate answers, " A year." She blunders on with futile expressions of sympathy and offers to do everything for the child, and Butterfly, seemingly filled with a great calm, the calm of utter despair, congratulates her on her happiness and asks her to take Pinkerton a message that to Butterfly also peace will come. She implores them all to leave her. Kate, still not quite sure of the situation, asks Sharpless, " Can he have his son? " Butterfly, who has overheard this, says gravely, " I will give him his son if he will come to fetch him, in half an hour from now."

When they have gone, Butterfly seems to be on the point of

collapsing, but steadies herself. As the light hurts and offends her, she bids Suzuki close the curtains and the doors, so that the room becomes almost completely dark. Butterfly, after having insisted on the weeping Suzuki leaving her, lights the lamp in front of the Buddah, and stands motionless for a time, sunk in bitter thought. Then, from a convulsive movement of her body, we see that an idea has struck her. She takes the white veil from the shrine, throws it across the screen, takes the sacred dagger from the wall, kisses the blade, and softly reads aloud the words engraved on it — " Death with honour is better than life with dishonour."

She is about to thrust the knife into her throat when the door on the left opens, and Suzuki's arm is seen pushing the child towards his mother. Butterfly drops the dagger, runs to meet the little totterer, clasps him in her arms, and kisses him madly. She bids him an anguished farewell:

telling him that it is for him she is making this last great sacrifice. Then she seats him with his back to the audience, blindfolds him, gives him the American flag and a doll to play with, takes up the dagger again, and, with her eyes always on the child, goes behind the screen.

Sombre and heavily-moving chords in the orchestra intensify the sense of tragic strain and foreboding in the air. There is a moment's silence; then the knife is heard falling to the ground, and the veil is plucked from the screen. Butterfly totters into view, the veil round her neck, groping blindly for the child. She finds him at last, embraces him with her last strength, and falls beside him.

Just then there is a cry of " Butterfly! " behind the scenes; the door to the garden opens violently, and Pinkerton and Sharpless rush in. Butterfly, with a last feeble gesture, points to the child and dies. The horrified Pinkerton falls on his knees in prayer, while Sharpless, sobbing wretchedly, picks up the child and kisses him.

In the last few bars the orchestra, in an expressive unison phrase, once more establishes the Japanese atmosphere of the drama. But it does more than that. The unison motive in the orchestra with which the opera ends is a reminiscence of Butterfly's ecstatic vision of the Emperor pausing on his way to notice her and her child and taking the latter and making a prince of him. This, Puccini seems to be saying at the finish, this was the poor thing's dream, and *this* is the reality. The baby does indeed go to be a " prince " of sorts; but the poor little mother whose whole life he has been is snuffed out like a candle to make his elevation possible.